FREDERICK E. WEBSTER, Jr., Ph.D., Stanford University, is Associate Professor of Business Administration in The Amos Tuck School of Business Administration at Dartmouth College. He has also taught at Stanford University and Columbia University. Dr. Webster has taught in a number of management development programs and is active as a consultant to several companies. He is co-author of *Sales Force Management* and co-editor of *Readings in Sales Force Management*, both published by The Ronald Press Company.

MARKETING
COMMUNICATION

• MODERN PROMOTIONAL STRATEGY

FREDERICK E. WEBSTER, JR.
DARTMOUTH COLLEGE

THE RONALD PRESS COMPANY · NEW YORK

To Mary Alice

Preface

The marketing communication concept is a welcome development on the management scene. It advances the idea that advertising, personal selling, and other elements of promotion are most effective when they are developed to take advantage of their synergistic effects. Following an overall communication approach, management can readily direct each element in the marketing mix toward common, well-defined goals. This approach provides a useful framework for achieving a well-balanced and fully integrated promotional strategy supported by the analytical methods of management science and a sound conceptual knowledge of consumer attitudes and behavior.

Modern industry is rapidly moving toward this view of the communication task, a view reflected in the development of college courses integrating the presentation of not only advertising and personal selling, but also packaging and branding, sales promotion, point-of-purchase displays, reseller effort, public relations and publicity.

This book offers a comprehensive introduction to the behavioral, analytical, and management aspects of marketing communication strategy. In Part I three basic facets of marketing communication are explored: Its role in the broad social context, the role of communication in marketing, and the basic theory of communication. Part II then introduces essential behavioral concepts and market-audience analysis, with chapters on the nature of customer predispositions and the factors—individual, social, cultural, and economic—that influence response.

Part III examines the message as an element of communication strategy, with consideration of the contributions of behavioral science to our understanding of message effectiveness, the nature of the creative process and its management, and the requirements for successful personal selling. The focus throughout is on the central importance of defining the objectives of marketing effort.

Part IV introduces economic and financial criteria, showing how decision making takes into account the problems of budgeting and allocation of selling resources, the development of practical media strategy, and the evaluation of past programs. In these chapters, the analytical rigor of the management science disciplines is brought to bear, and several operations research studies are explored to consider the nature of market response to communication effort.

In Part V specific supplementary communication resources are treated within the framework set up in preceding chapters—e.g., reseller strategies, point-of-purchase displays, and institutional advertising. The text is concluded in Part VI with discussions of techniques for coordinating the elements of marketing communication and establishing feedback for evaluation.

It would not be possible to name the many people—colleagues, students, and other professional associates—who contributed to the development of this text. I do, however, wish especially to thank Dean John W. Hennessey, Jr., of The Amos Tuck School of Business Administration at Dartmouth College, for providing funds and time to support my writing. I owe a special debt to my friend and colleague, Professor Kenneth R. Davis, who picked up some of the teaching load and gave welcome counsel on many of the chapters. I am grateful to Professor Ronald F. Wippern for providing assistance in reviewing the material on economic and financial considerations. Many businessmen also contributed to the development of these materials, including the many who generously cooperated in supplying the illustrations. Mr. H. Lee Smith, Vice President, Ogilvy & Mather, Inc., was especially helpful in responding to a series of requests. Mr. James R. Heekin, Jr., formerly President of Ogilvy & Mather, Inc., provided a keen review of chapter materials as well as permission to reproduce his ideas on creativity. My secretaries, Phyllis Stromberg and Christine Sweeney, were tremendously helpful in managing this flow of correspondence, as well as in preparing manuscript and assisting in the review of proofs.

FREDERICK E. WEBSTER, JR.

Hanover, New Hampshire
January, 1971

Contents

Introduction

The purpose of marketing communication is to convey meanings about products, services, and selling companies to defined market targets. Marketing communication strategy is directed toward the successful pursuit of clearly stated objectives and carefully specified goals. Its effectiveness is measured by the degree of goal attainment; its efficiency is measured by the ratio of outputs (changes in awareness, attitudes, sales) to inputs (promotional resources, manpower, and money). Effective and efficient strategies in marketing communication will be the result of several considerations, including the analytical skill and planning ability of the marketing manager. Of prime importance is his understanding of the social context within which his communication strategy must work, the role of communication in the marketing mix, and the nature of the communication process itself. Each of these subjects is treated, respectively, in the first three chapters of this book.

1

Social Role of Marketing Communication

Marketing communication is concerned with the effective and profitable use of personal and impersonal media by a selling company in its efforts to influence the attitudes and behavior of the markets for its products or services. A related purpose is to create an awareness of the company itself. We who live in the developed nations in this last third of the twentieth century find advertising and personal selling—marketing communication in its most common forms—a pervasive part and fact of life.

The American population is presently exposed to a daily 4.2 *billion* advertising messages in the mass media of radio, television, newspapers, magazines, direct mail, car cards, posters, and billboards. An even larger volume of commercial messages is delivered by sales personnel, point-of-purchase displays, and packaging. If one adds to these the many non-commercial sources of information about products and selling companies —family members, friends, and neighbors, for example—the number of sales messages to which the average consumer is exposed on a typical day probably reaches one thousand or more.

Every commercial message, whether carried by television, salesman, or matchbook, is the result of a decision by the management of a selling firm. This decision is based upon a judgment that a message delivered via this medium to that particular receiver will produce a desired result

3

at a smaller cost then will alternative messages and media. To make this
forecast most effectively, management must understand the characteristics of audiences, messages, and media. An analysis of company objectives and resources, combined with accurate, carefully analyzed information about markets, will then provide the decision basis for the most
efficient investment of promotional dollars and for the most effective
marketing communication strategy.

As marketers seek competitive advantage through communication to
the marketplace, their activities influence the economic society in which
they operate. Marketing communication performs many functions in this
broader social context. It also creates effects which are alleged by some
to be inconsistent with the purposes and values of society. Before turning to the questions of strategic planning in marketing communication,
therefore, it will be helpful to consider issues involving the socioeconomic environment in which marketing communication strategy is made
more or less effective.

DEMAND STIMULATION

In the economist's view, the major purpose of all marketing communication is to stimulate demand for products or services. Certainly this is

*"You know when the magic went out of our marriage, Henry? When
we completed our major consumer-purchase decisions."*

Drawing by D. Reilly; © 1968 The New Yorker Magazine, Inc.

the purpose of company or corporate managements in allocating large portions of current resources to marketing activities. As firms spend to stimulate demand for their own products and services, they can in turn generate demand for goods and services in the aggregate; and by increasing the level of aggregate demand, the rate of economic growth can be increased, thus creating conditions favoring full employment. Promotional activity, then, does have an impact that affects the society in which it operates.

Consumption Stimulates Production

An affluent society is a mass production society, and mass production requires mass consumption. Mass consumption, in turn, requires a high level of demand stimulation. Mass consumption not only provides demand for the results of mass production but, as a prior condition, provides the motivation which makes people want to produce goods and services and thus earn the incomes necessary for consumption. In other words, the desire to consume must precede the desire to produce. Consumer demand fuels the engine of economic growth.

Ernest Dichter, a behavioral scientist and management consultant, has observed that marketing communication has a vital role to play in the economic growth of developing nations. He argues that marketing communication is a form of behavioral engineering and education, and that such education can have either of two objectives: (1) to make people satisfied and content with things as they are, or (2) to create discontent. Assuming that continuous, constructive change is a basic need of man's nature, then creative discontent is a healthy goal for persuasion and education. In this context, the function of marketing communication is to awaken desires and stimulate consumption as a necessary prelude to production and economic growth. Dichter argues that one of the most important tasks of marketing communication is to create an attitude of antifatalism.[1] Although formulated in the context of developing economies, the argument highlights a function performed by marketing communication in any economic system.

"The Affluent Society"

Critics of the use of persuasion as a marketing tool maintain that people are urged to buy things which they really do not "need" and that such expenditures are in some respects undesirable. This point is central to Galbraith's criticism of the affluent society, for example.[2] He

[1]"An Interview with Ernest Dichter," *International Herald Tribune*, June 27, 1967, pp. 11–12.

[2]John Kenneth Galbraith, *The Affluent Society* (Boston: Houghton Mifflin Co., 1958).

argues that there should be more emphasis upon the production of public goods and services, such as highways, conservation, and education, and less upon private goods and services. His example of "the family which takes its mauve and cerise, air-conditioned, power-steered, and power-braked automobile out for a tour [and] passes through cities that are badly paved, made hideous by litter, blighted buildings, billboards, and posts for wires that should long since have been put underground"[3] is a mixture of personal judgment and analysis which makes the point that our public goods and services are often inferior. Galbraith seems torn between two explanations for this state of affairs. One is that people often want the wrong things, as implied by his disagreement with their taste in automobiles and their conduct in public places (littering). The other places the blame upon marketing communication as follows:

> The fact that wants can be synthesized by advertising, catalyzed by salesmanship, and shaped by the discrete manipulations of the persuaders shows that they are not very urgent. A man who is hungry need never be told of his need for food. If he is inspired by his appetite, he is immune to the influence of Messrs. Batten, Barton, Durstine & Osborn. The latter are effective only with those who are so far removed from physical want that they do not already know what they want. In this state alone men are open to persuasion.[4]

Assigning Meanings to Products

Certainly, marketing communication does a good deal to add value and meaning to nonessential products and to make them "desirable." Irving S. White has pointed out, in fact, that the basic function of marketing communication is to assign meanings to products and to guide the consumer toward seeing and feeling a product in a given, predictable way which makes that product desirable for him.[5] It is clearly overstatement, however, to assign to marketing communication sole responsibility for creating consumer wants, regardless of how offensive to one's own value system those wants happen to be. As White pointed out:

> Culturally, then, the function of advertising is to understand, to reflect, and in most instances to accept the value-structure of society before it can go about its creative task of helping to organize in a consistent, gratifying manner the numerous stimulations a product contains for the potential customer. Advertising can help to select and reinforce certain values and needs inherent in the role of the product. It can operate within the limits of culture to create new expectations for the consumer.[6]

[3]*Ibid.*, p. 253.
[4]*Ibid.*, p. 158.
[5]Irving S. White, "The Functions of Advertising in Our Culture," *Journal of Marketing*, 24 (July 1959), pp. 8–14.
[6]*Ibid.*, p. 10.

DEFINING "STANDARD OF LIVING"

White's comments also identify another function of marketing communication, that of defining the meaning of a product or service for the individual and the broader society. Most of the products and services that people value have meanings which go beyond the physical product itself to define what have been loosely called "standards of living" or "life style." An automobile is not just a mode of transportation but a complex constellation of meanings. It serves not only to move its owner about on the surface of the earth but to say a great many things about him to those he passes. He may also regard it as an extension of his own personality and he is likely to find that some brands of automobiles are much more consistent with his self concept than others.

Consumption Communities

Daniel Boorstin, a noted historian, has coined the term "consumption community" to define the shared set of values and meanings people feel for others who consume the same products and services. He argues that consumption communities are peculiarly characteristic of the United States in the twentieth century. Consumption communities could not exist were it not for the three mutually supporting developments of mass production, mass distribution, and mass communication. First, mass production results in millions of identical products—the millions of consumers of Winston cigarettes or Parker pens or Mustang automobiles consume virtually identical products. Second, mass distribution called into being huge merchandising organizations, such as Sears, Roebuck and Company, J. C. Penney, and Macy's, that define large communities of consumers and make it physically possible to distribute the results of mass production. Third, mass communication (advertising) makes it possible to send the same message to thousands or millions of consumers. Advertising is aimed at groups while salesmanship is aimed at individuals. Professor Boorstin sees advertising not as "salesmanship in print," as some have claimed, but as "a form of insurance to the consumer that by buying this commodity, by smoking this brand of cigarette, or driving this make of car he will not find himself alone." He sees advertising as a "conscious effort to create consumption communities."[7]

Materialism and Marketing Communication

Critics of marketing communication point out that the characteristic emphasis on material goods is an undesirable aspect of modern life.

[7]Daniel Boorstin, "Welcome to the Consumption Community," *Fortune*, September 1967, pp. 118, 120, 131–32, 134, 136, 138.

Deeper, more permanent values become blurred with the emphasis on materialism that is stimulated by marketing communication. This is a serious criticism, one worthy of thought, but it cannot be resolved here. We can only point out that there are at least three questions which must be answered in seeking a resolution. First, is there a necessary conflict between materialism and such higher-order values as self-realization or equal opportunity? Second, is the relationship between materialism and marketing communication one of direct causality? Third, to what extent does marketing communication in fact persuade; how powerful are the mass media in particular in defining values?

These are important questions, meriting debate. It is likely that their discussion will reveal that marketing communication has less power to persuade or to implant basic values than the critics seem to assume. It is more likely that marketing communication reflects the basic values of society and that the critics' argument is as much with the basic values themselves as with the practices of marketing communicators in the free enterprise system.

SUPPORT OF MASS MEDIA

Radio, television, newspapers, and magazines play a vital societal role in providing news and entertainment. An informed—and entertained—public depends heavily, then, on the nature of the relationship between the media and the advertisers who support them financially. One likely and frequently debated alternative to this arrangement could be government-supported media. This alternative, however, always poses the threat of control of news content, of "news management," and of the use of mass media as a propaganda weapon for shaping public opinion. A third possibility—direct advertiser control of media editorial content—seems to have been averted, for the most part, by strong, independent managements in the broadcast and print media.

In the United States and other countries where advertising expenditures provide the major source of support for the mass media, marketing communication exists largely on the sufferance of the public. This point and its significance were stressed by Blaine Cook, then Vice President for Marketing Services for United Air Lines, when he said:

> To a degree which is literally astounding, advertising . . . exists only on the tolerance, sufferance, and patience of the American consumer.
> Advertising technique is to find something that the consumer really wants to do—read or be informed, or take a drive in the country—and then to interpose somewhere in the span of the activity an interruption designed to serve our interest. If we are clever enough, the consumer will (hopefully in good humor) tolerate the interruption and be influenced by it.[8]

[8]*Advertising Age*, July 3, 1967, p. 1.

"And when we turned to your generation for guidance, what was your answer? 'Hi ho, hey hey—chew your little troubles away.'"

Drawing by Whitney Darrow, Jr.; © 1968 The New Yorker Magazine, Inc.

The advertiser's recognition of his dependence on the public can be a mixed blessing. On the one hand, he may be tempted to sponsor the media content least likely to offend any segment of the public; and media managers' editorial and production decisions are of course influenced by what advertisers will buy. Directing programs and editorial content to the lowest common denominator of public taste can produce a dreary sameness in media content and a blandness which fails to inform or to challenge but succeeds only in pacifying and dulling the critical faculties of the audience. On the other hand, the marketer's awareness of his dependence on the good will of the public can also produce a sensitivity to the limits of endurance for inane selling messages and other abuses of the mass media and can contribute significantly to a high quality of execution in commercial messages. It has been said that, in many instances, television advertising is better than television programming.

PROMOTION OF PUBLIC OBJECTIVES

Because of their skills in using the tools and media of communication, marketing communicators have been relied upon heavily to support efforts to promote public objectives such as health, conservation, and education. For example, it was estimated that, in 1969, advertising worth a total of over $450 million, if paid for at regular rates, was voluntarily contributed by the media and by advertisers. The causes supported by this expenditure included—

Council for Financial Aid to Education

U.S. Forest Service and the National Association of State Foresters (for their "Smokey" fire prevention campaign)

Keep America Beautiful (for an antilitter campaign)

U.S. Department of Health, Education, and Welfare

Peace Corps

National Safety Council (in its program to encourage use of automobile seat belts)

U.S. Savings Bonds

Radio Free Europe Fund

The Urban Coalition

Religion in American Life, Inc.

and many other campaigns in the public interest.[9]

It is significant that not only does the advertising industry provide support for such programs, but also and more basically, marketing communication supports a system of mass media in our society which makes it possible to inform and influence the public about such central aspects of our way of life as voting for political candidates, activities designed to serve our fellow citizens, and increasing the level of national health. In times of emergency, as when a hurricane ravages the Eastern United States, this communication system is likewise ready to serve the public.

STIMULATING COMPETITION

When marketing communication promotes competition within an industry, the consumer is exposed to a broader range of quality products

[9]The Advertising Council, *Annual Report*, 1969.

and services at reasonable prices. The contribution of marketing communication to the level of competition in an industry occurs in two ways.

Facilitating Innovation

First, marketing communication makes it possible for the firm that develops new products to cultivate new markets with the speed required to obtain the necessary returns on investment. The ability to distribute and to communicate the new product is necessary to successful new-product introductions. Firms with highly refined communication skills are often attracted to new market opportunities by a recognition that their communication abilities provide an effective competitive tool. The product is then developed after the basic communication opportunity has been recognized. The possibility of quick market penetration makes the investment in product development appear more attractive.

Product Differentiation

Second, marketing communication—most notably, packaging and branding activities in combination with mass media advertising—stimulates competition by holding the manufacturer responsible for the quality of his product. When products become differentiated by brands and are removed from the "commodity" classification, customers develop preferences and can express their satisfactions and dissatisfactions through their pattern of repeat purchasing. The manufacturer becomes "responsible," in the eyes of the consuming public, for the quality of his product and for variations in product quality over time.

The economic importance of product differentiation can be seen in the actions taken in some communist countries in the use of brands to identify the products of particular manufacturing plants. These steps were taken in an attempt to control and improve the quality of products coming from the plants in an industry, and to permit the identification of sources of inferior products. Some interesting side effects occurred as well. For one, workers in the plants became motivated by a desire to produce a superior product, once their contribution could be identified. Intense competition developed among the several plants. For another, consumers soon developed preferences for the products of certain plants rather than others.

If marketing communication can stimulate competition by permitting product differentiation and developing perceptual relationships among brand names and symbols and product quality, the result is to increase the opportunity for entry into a given industry and to stimulate competition among firms already in the industry through the introduction of new products.

Stifling Competition

A frequently heard criticism of marketing communication is that, in fact, it does *not* stimulate competition. Rather, it is argued, the large sums of money required to enter a market characterized by intensive promotional competition and oligopolistic market conditions forestall new entries. In the automobile, soap, and tobacco industries, the amount of financial resources required to develop the necessary promotional campaigns for entering the market are virtually prohibitive to new competitors.

Under these market conditions, the critics continue, spending for marketing communication is likely to be considerably in excess of what is required for optimum competitive conditions. Firms are motivated to maximize sales revenues rather than profits or stockholders' equity, and by a desire to stifle potential new competitors. As a result, promotional spending may be well beyond the optimum, and thus wasteful of scarce economic resources. A further result may be exaggerated prices in the industry reflecting both the lack of new competition and the excessive costs of promotion.

A Refutation

One of the most recent studies refuting these charges was undertaken by Jules Backman for the Association of National Advertisers.[10] Among his conclusions were the following: First, there is no observable relationship between the extent of economic concentration in an industry and the intensity of advertising as measured by ratios of advertising to sales. Second, there was no observable relationship between advertising-to-sales ratios and changes in prices during the post-World War II period. Third, the promotional power of large companies has not been a barrier to entry of new competitors in those industries examined. This third conclusion was supported by findings that no one brand dominated a product category for any significant length of time, that there was significant competition from "private labels" (retailer-owned brand names) for most of the products examined, and that the high rate of new-product market failures showed that promotional power was no guarantee of success.[11] Other studies have also failed to find any consistent relationship between the extent of industry concentration (measured by the percentage of sales accounted for by the four largest firms) and the volume of advertising expenditures, or between profitability and advertising.[12]

[10]Jules Backman, *Advertising and Competition* (New York: New York University Press, 1967).

[11]*Ibid.*, pp. 155–60.

[12]L. G. Telser, "Some Aspects of the Economics of Advertising," *Journal of Business* (Chicago), 41 (April 1968), pp. 166–73.

Although marketing communication may not result in competition of the price-dominated kind which the economist's theories explain most adequately, the available evidence does not support the conclusion that a high level of promotional activity leads to a lessening of competition. It seems likely that the level of competition is heightened by marketing communication activity, although competition may emphasize product quality differences of questionable importance. A discussion of the importance of various product attributes takes the argument back to matters of values, as noted above in comments on the relationship between materialism and marketing communication.

CONSUMER ATTITUDES

Toward Advertising

A study of consumer attitudes toward advertising, sponsored by the American Association of Advertising Agencies, found that advertising was ranked tenth on a list of ten topics in terms of the strength of opinions about each topic. Only 7 percent of those responding said that they had strong opinions about advertising, compared with 52 percent for religion and 43 percent for bringing up children. However, 41 percent indicated a favorable attitude toward advertising, compared with 34 percent of "mixed" attitude and 14 percent unfavorable. Another 8 percent were "indifferent"; 3 percent could not be classified as to attitude. Some of the major reasons given for favorable attitudes were:

Advertising is informative (general)	35%
It provides specific information on new products	17
It provides specific information on prices	5
It is enjoyable, entertaining	9
It pays for entertainment	4
Business self-interest	22

Some of the major reasons given for unfavorable attitudes toward advertising were:

False or misleading advertising	21%
Too much advertising	19
It interrupts entertainment	12

In general these findings suggest that the American public is indifferent to advertising, but somewhat critical nonetheless. There is a central tendency for the public to believe that advertising is good for business and results in better products and a higher standard of living. At the same time, advertising is seen by many persons as insulting to the intelligence of the average consumer, and as tending to present untrue pictures of products, to increase prices, and to persuade people to buy things they should not buy.[13]

Toward Salesmen

Similar feelings are evident with respect to personal selling. For a wide variety of reasons, most types of personal selling are not among the highly regarded professions in our society. Surveys of college students consistently show that only a small minority regards selling as a challenging and rewarding career possibility. One analyst came to the conclusion that the absence of formalized education and training requirements and the salesman's lack of authority are major reasons for the low prestige of this occupation. These factors were more than enough to offset the positive attractions of a selling career of relatively high (but variable) income, and the freedom of action inherent in the nature of the work.[14]

Door-to-door salesmen are generally resisted by the consumer even when they represent established and reputable firms offering products of the very highest quality. Their salesmen must continually work against the basic fact that people resist obvious attempts to persuade them to buy.

On the other hand, industrial buyers consistently identify the salesman as the most important source of information available to them in buying decisions. This is generally true for all professional buyers. Surveys of the uses of information sources by physicians, for example, have shown that the detailman, the pharmaceutical company's salesman, is consistently regarded as the doctor's most valuable source of information about new drugs.[15]

That such buyers find the salesman's information useful is evidenced by the very fact that he gets an interview with the prospective customer. For, as is not the case in mass communication, the buyer must explicitly grant the interview, whereas the radio listener or TV viewer may listen or watch a commercial out of sheer indifference, boredom, or laziness or equally well "tune out" the advertising message physically or psychologically. But for the salesman to deliver *his* message specifically requires the granting of a block of time in which the prospect agrees to listen. The salesman's job is not an easy one, but the fact that over two

[13]*The A.A.A.A. Study on Consumer Judgment of Advertising* (New York: American Association of Advertising Agencies, May 1965).

[14]John L. Mason, "The Low Prestige of Personal Selling," *Journal of Marketing,* 29 (October 1965), pp. 7–10.

[15]Raymond A. Bauer and Lawrence H. Wortzel, "Doctor's Choice: The Physician and His Sources of Information About Drugs," *Journal of Marketing Research,* 3 (February 1966), pp. 40–47.

million salesmen call on several prospects daily is evidence of the value
of personal selling to the companies who employ them, to the people
who buy from them, and to our economic system.

SUMMARY

The purpose of this chapter has been to outline the major social functions of marketing communication (and to consider some criticism of
these functions) as a background against which to examine the role of
communication in the marketing strategy of the firm. The effectiveness
of marketing communication will be determined by the social context
within which the marketer must implement his strategic decisions.
Public attitudes and the broader industry impact of a firm's activities
must be considered in defining the role of marketing communication.

2

Communication in
the Marketing Mix

Communication is an influence process. At the minimum, the act of communicating requires a sender who is motivated to achieve some end result through communication and a receiver who perceives the message and whose behavior, attitudes, or opinions are important to the communicator's objective. The study of communication can be described as the investigation of WHO says WHAT to WHOM with what RESULT, that is, as the study of senders, messages, receivers, and effects. A communication is successful from the sender's point of view if the receiver is influenced by the message in a manner consistent with the communicator's objective.

In one sense "communication" is synonymous with the term "interaction." All human relationships involve communication, the sending of messages, both verbal and nonverbal, as one person attempts to influence the thoughts, attitudes, feelings, or behavior of another. When people form organizations to achieve their purposes, then these organizations must communicate with those other persons whose behavior and attitudes and so on, are important to the accomplishment of the organization's purpose. Business firms are dependent upon the attitudes and buying behavior of customers for the achievement of a major organizational purpose—providing a maximum return on the owners' investment.

THE MARKETING CONCEPT

Marketing is that function within the business firm charged by top management with the responsibility for influencing customers to behave, react, and perform in a manner that is favorable to the firm. Marketing managers are responsible for generating the maximum level of profitable sales volume. At one time, "marketing" was thought to be synonymous with "selling." *Selling,* or *promotion,* is the flow of influence from producer to consumer, the firm's attempts to make the market do what is in the firm's interest. As the scope and tempo of competition have increased, especially in the past two decades (due to such factors as corporate diversification, product proliferation, increase in disposable personal income, and a shift from a sellers' to a buyers' market), the buyer has gained increased power and ability to control the relationship with sellers. The buyer can demand more precise satisfaction of his needs and wants because he has more alternatives to choose among and because, in many cases, his needs and wants are less urgent and more postponable than they used to be.

More and more, firms are realizing that the "selling" approach—"You need what I've got"—is going to be successful only if the product and service offering has been carefully tailored to the needs of the market. This tailoring of products to markets requires accurate, up-to-date information about buyers' needs, wants, and buying habits. The modern marketing concept thus throws a new light on the marketing function. Marketing management's new responsibilities include making the firm do what the market wants and gathering such information as is necessary to interpret market wants correctly. Emphasis is thus placed upon the flow of influence *from* consumer to producer.

Selling, or promotion, has not become less important in this view of marketing. Rather, the requirements for effective selling are seen to include a product offering—the product features, level of quality, price, product service, and the like—carefully designed to meet the needs of the market. The selling function can be performed more efficiently under these conditions and organizational purpose will be more completely achieved. Stated differently, the flow of influence from producer to consumer will be more effective if it is being controlled by a flow of influence from consumer to producer. As manufacturing firms, distributing companies, and advertising agencies increasingly rely upon marketing research in their decision making, the buyer gains increased control over the marketing function and obtains more precise satisfaction of his needs. Profit is one good measure of the extent to which the firm is satisfying customer needs.

MARKETING AS A FLOW OF INFLUENCE

A standard definition of marketing has been "the performance of business activities that direct the flow of goods and services from producer to consumer or user."[1] It has been argued above that the purpose of marketing is to influence the consumer to behave in a way that is consistent with the objectives of the business. Marketing activities fall under three categories or "mixes," each of which influences the consumer: the goods and services mix; the distribution mix; and the communication mix.[2] The foregoing definition of marketing is incomplete in that it emphasizes the more obvious physical flow of goods but largely ignores the more subtle two-way flow of information between the marketer and his markets. While this book focuses on the communication mix, it is helpful to review briefly the relationships among these three elements of the total marketing mix. Together, these three functions define the responsibilities of the marketing manager; decisions about one element of the mix should always be made in the light of requirements for coordination among all marketing functions.

The Goods and Services Mix

The product offering is itself a major source of influence determining the attitudes and behavior of the potential buyer. The product offering can be defined as all cues available to the potential consumer which are perceived as relating to the degree of satisfaction to be derived from purchase and consumption of the product. This definition includes all physical attributes of the product and its package, such as size, shape, color, odor, texture, and flavor. It also embraces such features as price, ease of opening, number of servings, ease of repair, breakability, and aesthetic appeal. Equally important but more subtle aspects of the product offering include credit terms, guarantee, delivery, and dealer service after purchase. Some of these features of the product offering are very hard to assess except through the direct experience of owning and using the product. Furthermore, relationships among the elements comprising the goods and services mix are important. For example, price and guarantee and dealer service are all related. Also, a decision to buy one product of a particular manufacturer may be influenced by the fact that the manufacturer makes other products—such as the decision to buy a particular razor blade because one already owns that brand of razor.

[1]Committee on Definitions, American Marketing Association, *Marketing Definitions: A Glossary of Marketing Terms* (Chicago: American Marketing Association, 1960), p. 15.

[2]This classification scheme is not new, but it is difficult to decide on whom to credit as its inventor. Gerald Zaltman has used it in his *Marketing: Contributions from the Behavioral Sciences* (New York: Harcourt, Brace, Jovanovich, Inc., 1965), as have Eugene Kelley and William Lazer in *Managerial Marketing: Perspectives and Viewpoints,* 3rd ed. (Homewood, Ill.: Richard D. Irwin, Inc., 1967).

The Distribution Mix

Most manufacturers rely upon a complex network of resellers to put their product offering in the hands of the ultimate consumer. The resellers are usually profit-motivated business firms (with their own goods and services mixes to consider). Resellers perform one or more of the following functions: assorting (i.e., providing an assortment of merchandise), transportation, storage, and extending credit, as well as contact with customers. Resellers may also provide market information to the manufacturer and may assume certain risks for him, such as those involved in maintaining inventories (obsolescence and deterioration) and in collecting from credit customers. Virtually all of these functions must be performed in moving goods and services from producers to consumers. The decision as to whether they should be performed by the manufacturer, by certain resellers—retailers, wholesalers, jobbers—or by the ultimate customer must be based on considerations of cost and of value to the consumer.

The Communication Mix

The communication mix consists of messages about the goods and services mix and the distribution mix delivered through various media to consumers. The nature of a firm's communication mix reflects a myriad of decisions about such variables as motivating appeals, the timing of expenditures, salesman selection and training, and sales territories. These decisions are obviously related to decisions about the goods and services mix. The nature of the product and the character of the market for that product determine the kind of information required by potential customers. A wide variety of communication tasks may be assigned to resellers. At other times, the marketer may decide to retain responsibility for communication. Each channel arrangement creates its own communication requirements. Use of supermarkets, for example, may dictate particular requirements for several aspects of marketing communication including frequency and type of sales call, package design, point-of-purchase display, and mass media advertising.

The communication mix, the goods and services mix, and the distribution mix together define the "marketing mix," the total reponse by a firm to its market. The three elements of the marketing mix interact in complex ways to determine how customers will respond to the firm's offerings. All parts of the marketing mix are designed to facilitate the process of moving potential customers from unawareness to knowledge and favorable attitudes and, ultimately, to purchase and use (and repurchase) of the product. In other words, all of marketing is an *influence process,* with communication as perhaps the most obvious form of influence. For purposes of analysis we will concentrate our attention on communication, but we must never forget that the ultimate success of the communication program is heavily dependent on the effectiveness of the company's product offering and distribution system and on their careful coordination.

PURPOSE OF MARKETING COMMUNICATION

Marketing communication is designed to promote the sale of the company's products and services—that is, to encourage the potential customer to make a decision to purchase the product. Before such a decision is made, however, the potential customer must pass through a series of mental stages, beginning with lack of awareness.

Stages in the Buying Decision

Different observers have characterized this process in various ways. For example, Lavidge and Steiner describe six stages: (1) awareness, (2) knowledge, (3) liking, (4) preference, (5) conviction, and (6) purchase.[3] Rogers, on the other hand, suggests a five-stage process: (1) awareness, (2) interest, (3) evaluation, (4) trial, and (5) adoption.[4] The exact categories one uses to describe this process are not as important as the basic notion that such a process exists.

The nature of this decision process will vary from person to person and from product to product. It may vary in length of time required, in the importance of particular stages, and even in the sequence of stages. Furthermore, the process may terminate at any point.

We all know people who seem to buy on whim and impulse, even in the case of major expense, and others who seem to take forever to make even a minor purchase. Some people simply seem more willing and able to deal with the uncertainty in purchase decisions. On the other hand, the same person may take much longer to move from awareness to purchase of, say, a color television set than he required for the decision to buy a used car costing the same amount of money. It would, of course, be extremely hard to tell at what point a potential buyer was in his decision process or to estimate the speed with which he was moving

[3]Robert J. Lavidge and Gary A. Steiner, "A Model for Predictive Measurements of Advertising Effectiveness," *Journal of Marketing,* 25, No. 6 (October 1961), pp. 59–62.

[4]Everett M. Rogers, *Diffusion of Innovations* (New York: Free Press of Glencoe, Inc., 1962), pp. 76–120.

through the process. It is hard to say when "liking" becomes "prefer-ence," for example; but fortunately that is not relevant to our analysis.

Risk Reduction

The amount of time required for the decision process is a function of the amount of *perceived risk* in the decision by a particular person to buy a particular product. Several factors influence the amount of per-ceived risk, among them characteristics of the decision maker and of the product. For the decision maker, such factors as self-confidence, previous experience with similar products, and financial situation are significant. Important product characteristics bearing on perceived risk include size of expenditure, relative newness, and complexity, as well as the ability of potential customers to judge difference in product quality.

Communication provides information to the decision maker that helps him to assess the risk involved in purchasing the product and thus per-mits him either to terminate his consideration of the product or to move along to the next stage. Marketing communication has value for a poten-tial customer to the extent that it moves him along the decision process. Different types of information have value for different kinds of buyers at different stages in their decision process. For example, the person of low self-confidence may reject information provided by a salesman (for fear of being tricked) and require, instead, the advice of a close and trusted friend before buying a product about which he is highly uncertain.

Notice how far removed we are from the old cliché that the job of the salesman, or the job of advertising, is "to make the sale." Ultimately, yes— the job of marketing communication is to sell the product. But the objective of a given sales call or advertisement may be much more subtle, because of the complexity of the buying decision process and because of the often long lag between initial communication stimulus and ultimate buying response. Thus, the objective of a particular mar-keting communication activity must consider the nature of the market, the nature of the product, and the stage in the product life cycle, for all of these factors influence the buying decision process for that product.

The sale of an established brand of toothpaste, for example, may require simple "reminders," media advertising, and point-of-purchase dis-play, because most customers have been "convinced." A new brand of toothpaste, however, will have posed different communication require-ments: (1) making potential consumers aware of the unique features of the product; (2) convincing them that these features will satisfy their needs better than competing brands; and (3) making customers aware of the package so they can identify it on the supermarket shelf. These requirements might be met by "news"-type advertising in magazines, free samples of the product with coupons to encourage repeat purchase, and media advertisements featuring the package and tie-in point-of-purchase displays.

Thus, marketing communication may have any of several purposes:

1. To make potential customers aware of the product (or service).
2. To provide information with which potential customers can evaluate the suitability of the product for their needs (and thus to develop favorable attitudes toward it).
3. To encourage actual use of the product on a trial basis.
4. To encourage repeat purchase of the product and to develop the "habit" of purchasing it.
5. To generate the maximum volume of profitable sales.

Each of these will be discussed briefly.

Awareness

For new products, the objective of initial phases of a communication program must be to create awareness of the product. Such communication frequently takes the form of "announcement" advertising, as in Figure 2–1. Because it usually takes several years for a new product to reach a substantial portion of the market, however, the objective of creating awareness among nonusers may continue to be a part of the communication program. Also, a marketing strategy may be redesigned for different segments of the market, with the "awareness" objective appearing several times. For example, a new product may be introduced at an initially high price, distributed through exclusive men's shops, and advertised in *The New Yorker*. Later, its price may be reduced, its distribution broadened, and advertising shifted to magazines with more general appeal. Or, more commonly perhaps, a product may achieve national distribution on a region-by-region basis, with each region requiring separate treatment as a target for communication. Finally, the addition of new product features to an established brand may require that the communication program focus once again on awareness objectives.

Evaluation

Once a potential customer becomes aware of a new product or service, he must evaluate the suitability of that product for his needs. Here, we use the term "evaluation" to refer to the *mental* process of evaluation, prior to actual use of the product. Evaluation typically involves the rather careful comparison of particular product features with specific aspects of the customer's situation. In selling a computer, for example, the salesman might first analyze the customer's needs for computation speed, storage capacity, and remote access and then point out the spe-

Fig. 2–1. An "announcement" advertisement. (Courtesy of Estée Lauder, Inc.; AC&R, Inc.)

cific product or combinations of products whose attributes meet those needs. Media advertising can also fulfill this function, as in Figure 2–2. For complex products, however, the evaluation stage in the buyer's decision may require the detailed technical information that is available only from a well-trained salesman.

Potential customers may depend heavily upon friends and neighbors for information at the evaluation stage, especially where information about how other people will respond to one's use of the product is an important input to the purchase decision. This kind of information, for evaluating the "psychosocial" consequences of one's purchases, is especially important for such conspicuous products as fashions, automobiles, and cosmetics.

Finally, marketer-provided information may be useful in suggesting the criteria by which one should judge the product. Some product attributes (such as vitamin content in cereals, the service one's beneficiaries will receive from a life insurance agent, and the potential trade-in value of a new automobile) cannot be objectively evaluated by the potential customer. Advertising can assist in this evaluation, as in Figure 2–3, especially when "hidden" features are important. In this sense, marketing communications can "assign meaning" to products and services, imbuing them with qualities unique in the competitive market. This aspect of communication is often referred to as "image building." An example of this activity is illustrated in Figure 2–4.

Trial

There is no substitute for actual use of the product as the basis for a decision to adopt the new product or to reject it. Trial requires that the product actually be placed in the hand of the potential customer. This may be accomplished in several ways. The automobile salesman uses the test drive, and the office machine salesman leaves a machine for trial use in the potential customer's office. Product demonstration is often central to the salesman's presentation. The television retailer allows "free trial" in the home, the food products manufacturer has a pretty demonstrator distribute samples in the supermarket, and cigarette manufacturers distribute samples in airports. Toothpaste samples are given to children by dentists and samples of detergent and coffee products have been hung on doorknobs in plastic bags. Coupons to facilitate trial are put in packages of other products, sent to households through the mail, and featured in printed advertisements, as shown in Figure 2–5. Free samples, "no obligation" trials, price-off coupons, and reduced-price label-pack deals all encourage trial by reducing the amount of risk involved in first use of the product. In making such an offer, the marketer is betting that

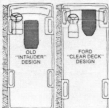

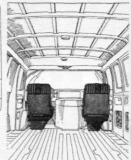

23% more floorspace.
Ford moved the engine forward to give you 23% more unobstructed floor area than any other van can offer. Clear load length measures over 8½ ft. in the Econoline Van . . . over 10 ft in the Supervan.

Outside service center.
Just raise the hood and all these service points are at hand oil, water, battery, windshield washer water, wiper motor, brake master cylinder, voltage regulator. Ford's better van ideas make everything you do easier to do.

"Walk-thru" to rear.
Because the engine is forward out of the way, the driver can step from his seat into the load area. The loadspace is not only bigger, it's easier to reach. Check all the better ideas in the best selling van at your Ford dealer's.

Twin-I-Beam ride.
The independent front suspension made famous by Ford pickups: Twin-I-Beam. Two I-beam axles for strength . . . big coil springs for easy ride. Wide-track design adds new highway stability, even on windy days.

Payloads to 3600 lbs.
Choose from three Econoline series. Payloads to 3600 pounds. As much as 1325 pounds more than in other vans. Power choices include top-performing 302-cu. in. V-8.

Outsells all other vans combined
...because Ford's better ideas make all other vans obsolete!

FORD ECONOLINE VANS *Ford*

Fig. 2–2. An "evaluation" advertisement stressing product features. (Courtesy of Ford Motor Co.; J. Walter Thompson Co.)

Fig. 2–3. An "evaluation" advertisement stressing "hidden" product features. (Courtesy of Best Foods, A Division of CPC International Inc.; Lennen & Newell, Inc.)

Enjoy the unique pleasures of Japan.
All the way round the world.

The cuisine is Continental, but
you many enjoy trying
chopsticks for the Japanese
delicacies served first.

London. Hong Kong. Tokyo. Paris. Singapore. Wherever you're going around the world, we go, too. And we take you there in the nicest way. Come aboard one of our Jet Couriers in New York, San Francisco or Los Angeles and let us introduce you to a way of life you may have missed last time. Your kimono-clad hostess has been trained since childhood in the art of pleasing guests. She greets you with a refreshing *o-shibori* hot towel. A fragile cup of warmed *sake* is offered. And all the while you're relaxing in a brocaded lounge chair—surrounded by the subtle delights of Japan.

Whether you're rushing to a business appointment—or traveling for pleasure, Japan Air Lines brings a special bit of serenity to your trip. Ask your travel agent about us. Why be a passenger on some other airline when you can be our guest?

JAPAN AIR LINES
the worldwide airline of Japan

Fig. 2—4. An example of an "image-building" advertisement designed to assign meanings to a product or service. (Courtesy of Japan Air Lines; Botsford, Constantine & McCarty, Inc.)

Fig. 2–5. An advertisement to induce trial. (Courtesy of American Home Foods; Young & Rubicam, Inc.)

the consumer will be pleased with the performance of the product. If the product does not perform as expected, an increased rate of trial by consumers will simple hasten the demise of the product, when customers try it and find it to be unacceptable.

Repeat Purchase

For many products, habitual purchase patterns are a major determinant of buyer behavior. The marketer of a new product therefore has two tasks: first, to break down existing brand preferences and, second, to establish a new preference, for his brand. Initial trial may accomplish the first task, but repeated purchases are necessary for the second. Repeat purchase is especially necessary for products whose effectiveness can only be determined after repeated use, such as certain skin-care products, dentifrices, floor wax, and laundry detergents. Repeat purchase can be encouraged through use of coupons, price deals, point-of-purchase display, carefully planned sales calls, and advertising appeals such as Budweiser's "Pick a Pair" (of six-packs) promotion. Extra-large packages can also help achieve this objective both by extending the period over which the customer will use the brand and by removing the customer from the market, thus blunting the appeal of competing products.

Maximum Sales

In the belief that achievement of the largest possible market share is the best guarantee of long-term competitive success, some companies devote all possible resources to marketing communication in the short run. Some minimum profit objective may constrain the total level of promotional spending, although it is not uncommon for companies to spend well beyond total revenue for the first several months of a new product's life, in order to establish it firmly in the market. There are conditions under which this strategy is consistent with the objective of long-run profit maximization.

Marketing communication programs designed to achieve the maximum volume of profitable sales typically involve reliance on several modes of communication. For an industrial product, the communications mix would rely on personal selling, supplemented by media advertising, direct mail, trade show exhibits, and publicity. For a consumer product, the major element would probably be either media advertising or some form of sales promotion such as coupons, price-off label packs, or merchandise premiums, supplemented by point-of-purchase displays to be featured by salesmen in their calls on retailers.

In summary, the communicator's objectives can involve any of several stages in the buyer's decision process, from awareness to actual purchase. Frequently, communication objectives involve changing potential customers' attitudes by assigning particular meanings or "images" to products. The nature of the product and its stage in the product life cycle, as well as the nature and extent of competition, are key factors in setting objectives. A different combination of commmunication tools will be required, depending upon the nature of the market and the objectives that have been established for communicating with that market.

TOOLS OF THE COMMUNICATOR

In the previous paragraphs, reference has been made to several modes used by the communicator, including advertising, personal selling, packaging and branding, sales promotion (coupons, deals, etc.) and display, public relations and publicity, and resellers' promotional efforts. These are the major means by which the marketer delivers information (both objective and emotional) about his products and services to potential customers. They are the channels of communication through which promotional messages are delivered. We shall refer to these six channels as "modes" or "methods" of communication, reserving the word "media" for the mass media that provide the channels for advertising and publicity, including magazines, newspapers, outdoor (billboards), radio and television.

The tools of the communicator are the messages (verbal and nonverbal) and the modes he chooses to convey the intended meaning and information about his products. Because substantial parts of this book deal with these two topics, we shall consider each only briefly at this stage.

Messages

The messages of the marketing communicator are the combinations of symbols he selects to transmit intended meaning to receivers. Messages include advertisements, sales presentations, package designs, and other combinations of verbal and graphic materials. Each message consists of all of the symbols used (words, illustrations, facial expressions) and the complex relationships among these symbols. Thus, a message is a symbol system, a set of entities and their relationships. The total impact of a television commercial, for example, is determined by the words used, the objects shown, the sequencing of words and objects, the background music, the particular photographic techniques (zoom shots, close-ups, fade-outs), the use of color, the relationships between music and actions, color, and words. The effectiveness of a salesman's presentation is determined by the words he uses, the tone of his voice, the speed of delivery, the use of printed and other visual aids, his facial expressions, his distance from the prospect, the way he uses his hands, his dress and physical appearance, and the like. Furthermore, the impact of any message is likely to be slightly different in some way for every person reached by that message. Each word, picture, and sound conveys a slightly different meaning to each receiver. The challenge to the communicator is to choose symbol systems that have the highest likelihood of conveying the meaning he intends to the largest number of potential customers and thus the largest probability of obtaining the desired response.

Modes

As previously defined, modes are the channels that carry the messages. Modes can be described in several ways of interest to the marketing communicator, including their cost, the size of their audiences, and technical aspects of their performance. In addition to these characteristics, it is important to recognize that communication channels also *add meaning* to the communication. In the case of the salesman, it is obvious that he determines the qualitative characteristics of the message. Mass media also have qualitative characteristics. *The New Yorker* magazine, the television program "Gunsmoke," the *San Francisco Chronicle*, radio station WABC (in New York)—each of these advertising vehicles assigns certain meanings to products advertised in or on it. These meanings come from the editorial content of the vehicle, the receivers' impressions of the audience of that vehicle, and the technical characteristics of that medium (print, TV, etc.), among other factors.

Thus messages and modes act together to convey meaning in subtle and complex ways. The marketing communicator must carefully analyze the characteristics of messages and communication modes as these affect particular audiences. Such analyses provide the basis for the development of effective marketing communication strategies.

PLANNING COMMUNICATION STRATEGY

The planning of communication strategy must take place within the context of the basic objectives and marketing strategy developed by top management. The central decision in this initial phase of marketing planning is the selection of one or more market segments to be the target for the company's marketing effort. The selection of market segments must be based on a thorough appraisal of the company's strengths and weaknesses, its resources, and its ability to compete.

The choice of market segments should define the best opportunity for the firm to achieve the highest response from the market and to obtain unique competitive advantage with its limited resources. Of all decisions made by top management, none is more critical to the survival and growth of the firm than the selection of market targets. Selection of one or more carefully defined segments, rather than the total market, recognizes the reality that few firms have the resources and ability required to compete with equal effectiveness in all parts of today's heterogeneous, complex markets.

There are, then, three sets of considerations in the selection of a segmentation strategy. First, what are the resource constraints with which the firm must operate during the planning period? A firm's ability to compete is a function of the strengths and weaknesses of its management, financial structure, production facilities, product line, sales force, and distribution structure. Changes in any of these resources are possible in the long run. In the short run, however, each operates as a constraint on managerial action. The task of management is to develop competitive strategies which obtain maximum advantage from the strengths of the organization while minimizing the exposure of the weaknesses.

Second, where in the total market are there needs which are being inadequately served by existing suppliers? Where are the opportunities? The history of the growth of American industry is nothing more nor less than the identification of opportunities to serve needs better with new technologies and new approaches. Often, existing suppliers are too close to the market to see clearly the opportunities to serve it better. Consider the successive growth of the railroad, trucking, and air freight industries, each in turn identifying opportunities. What constitutes an opportunity for a particular firm is a function of how its resources fit with the unfilled needs in particular segments of the market and its ability to capitalize on trends and changes in those segments.

Third and finally, where can the firm obtain unique competitive advantage? In addition to resources and market need, the company also needs a sense of where it can best meet or avoid the actual or potential threat of strong competition. Many small companies compete against industrial giants by concentrating their efforts in regional markets or narrow industrial segments where they have an entrenched position. A company may secure similar competitive advantage by the careful tailoring of unique technological ability to the needs of a carefully defined segment of the market. The skill to make these assessments shrewdly and in a fashion useful for strategic purposes constitutes one of the highest orders of management ability.

Decisions about market segmentation thus define targets for marketing action and, specifically, for marketing communication strategy. The market segment becomes the target audience. This definition of market targets is the key input in the design of communication strategy. The problem of planning market communication strategy can then be phrased as: "What messages, through which modes, have the highest probability of reaching the target audience with the intended meaning and thus producing the highest level of desired response within the limits of our scarce resources?"

Figure 2–6 suggests the major stages of analysis and decision in designing the marketing communication strategy. Most of the elements of Figure 2–6 have already been discussed in this chapter. Here they are organized and presented in a manner reflecting the logic of the planning process. As such, this structure provides a basic framework for the book.

I. Define the Communication Task

A. What are the problems to be solved?
B. What are the opportunities?
C. What are our objectives? What response is desired from what audience?

II. Identify Communication Alternatives

A. What tasks should be assigned to:
1. Advertising
2. Personal selling
3. Packaging and branding
4. Sales promotion and display
5. Public relations and publicity
6. Resellers
B. Appraise the strengths and weaknesses of each of the foregoing

III. Identify Key Uncertainties in Predicting Response

A. Characteristics of potential customers
1. Demographic — age, income, location, etc.
2. Predispositions — awareness, attitudes, habits
B. Influence of informal communications
1. Group influences
2. Cultural influences

C. Influence of formal communications
1. Relative influence of elements in IIA compared with expected strategy of competitors
2. By specific vehicles, especially
   a. Advertising media
   b. Types of salesmen
   c. Types of resellers

IV. Gather Data to Evaluate Alternatives

A. Data about markets (as in IIIA)
B. Data about media
1. Circulation
2. Readership
3. Impact (qualitative)
C. Data about messages
1. Pre-testing
   a. In the laboratory
   b. In the field
2. Post-testing
D. Data to evaluate total programs
1. Market testing

V. Synthesize Campaign Elements

A. Combine markets, messages, and media
B. Continual evaluation and control (Cycle goes back to IA)

Fig. 2–6. Decision stages in developing communication strategy.

SUMMARY

All marketing activities are designed to influence potential customers to behave in a manner consistent with the profit objectives of the firm. The mix of goods and services and the distribution mix provide the basic constraints within which the communication mix must operate in the short run. Advertising, personal selling, sales promotion, resellers' promotional activity, public relations and publicity, and packaging and branding must be carefully integrated to insure maximum market response. Messages must be created to convey the intended meaning about the product offering through these communication channels to the target audience in order to achieve the desired response. The objectives of marketing communication may vary from creating awareness, to evaluation (creating a product image and changing potential customers' attitudes), to stimulating trial and repurchase.

The development of effective marketing communication strategy requires a clear understanding of how the characteristics of messages, modes, and audiences influence response to communication. From an analysis of the communication process, to which we now turn in Chapter 3, it will become clear that most of the power in communication lies on the receiver side of the relationship. This analysis will highlight the need for information about receivers, individually and in the aggregate, as the basis for developing effective and efficient marketing communication strategies.

3

The Communication Process

Communication is the sharing of meaning; it is the process by which an individual transmits stimuli to modify the behavior or predispositions of other individuals.[1] Marketing communication is the sharing of meanings about products and services and the companies that produce them. More exactly, marketing communication is the *conveying* of meaning (information and interpretation) from the marketer to the market, with the objective of creating awareness of, and favorable attitudes toward, the company and its products and services. To understand the requirements for effective marketing communication, we must understand the basic nature of the communication process, the process by which individuals come to share meaning.

All communication involves three basic elements: a source, a message, and a receiver. The source has a certain objective in mind which can be accomplished by changing the knowledge, attitudes, goals, beliefs, or other *predispositions* of the receiver. In other words, the source hopes to accomplish his objective by somehow changing the mental state of the receiver. In order to achieve this objective, he must convey messages, combinations of symbols which transmit the intended meaning to the receiver. Having come this far in defining the basic elements of communication, let us go back and examine more carefully the significant aspects of this process of communication and its various components.

[1]Carl I. Hovland, Irving L. Janis, and Harold H. Kelley, *Communication and Persuasion* (paperback ed.; New Haven: Yale University Press, 1963), p. 12.

THE "ACTIVE" AUDIENCE

The apt point at which to begin analysis of the communication process is the receiver of the message, not the source. The receiver retains
most of the "control" in the interaction, in determining what meaning is
conveyed. No communication occurs until the mental state of the
receiver is altered. The significance of this assertion will become clearer
as this discussion proceeds. For the moment, the basic point is that the
receiver is an active participant in the communication process.[2] We
shall see that the receiver determines which messages he will expose
himself to, those he will pay attention to, those he will remember, and
how they are to be interpreted. He will do this in the context of his
social situation and those decision-making groups and information networks of which he is a part, and he will be influenced in his response by
his personality, economic situation, and physical and emotional needs.

All decisions about marketing communication strategy involve a prediction of buyer behavior—a prediction of how the market (audience)
will respond to particular messages delivered in specific media over a
stated time period. The soundness of any decision is therefore a function
of the decision maker's ability to predict market (audience) response.
To make valid predictions, the decision maker must have some basic
understanding of the characteristics of his audience and some conceptual
knowledge to explain the relationship between those characteristics and
the responses he desires, as specified by his marketing objectives.

Communication theory provides a set of organizing concepts for
understanding how audiences respond to communications. Although
theory can rarely provide *specific* predictions of the kind required by
marketing management, it can often specify the conditions under which
certain events are likely to occur. Most importantly, it can suggest the
kinds of information that are likely to be most useful to the decision
maker. By structuring the problem, communication theory can help to
define data requirements to be fulfilled through market research. For
example, communication theory can suggest those characteristics of the
audience that are most likely to be important determinants of response
and, therefore, the value of information about those characteristics as
the basis for decision making. Likewise, communication theory may suggest particular evidence to be gathered in the process of evaluating
communication effort.

[2]Raymond A. Bauer, "The Role of the Audience in the Communications Process:
Summary," in Stephen Greyser (ed.), *Toward Scientific Marketing* (Chicago: American Marketing Association, 1964), pp. 73–82.

COMMUNICATION THEORY

Communication theory is not one theory but is many theories from the study of individual and group behavior and is concerned with their common problem: How do people share meaning? It is one of the most highly developed areas of behavioral science, due in large part to its free borrowing from a wide variety of disciplines, including psychology, sociology, social psychology, anthropology, political science, and psychiatry. Within the broad area of research on communication it is possible to distinguish three major theoretical threads: learning theory, motivation theory, and the theory of group membership and dynamics.

Learning

Learning theory is concerned with individual response to stimuli such as symbols (words, pictures, objects). The reinforcement of response to repeated stimuli leads to relatively permanent changes in the individual's behavior and mental states. More explicitly, learning theory postulates a relationship among four elements: (1) drive; (2) cue; (3) response; and (4) reinforcement. The individual experiences an internal tension, an unsatisfied need or "drive." An external or internal stimulus or "cue"—a symbol or object perceived by the individual—produces a "response," a change in the individual's physical or psychological state. That response is intended to satisfy the aroused need or drive. If the need is satisfied and the internal tension is reduced, the response (for example, a change in attitude or behavior) is reinforced, that is, the probability that the same stimulus will produce this response is increased. In sum, learning has occurred.

Motivation

Motiviation theory and learning theory are related in that the latter postulates the existence of an aroused drive or need or "motive." Motivation theory enters the study of communication in at least two distinct ways. First, motivation theory helps to analyze the structure and character of individual needs that can be aroused and appealed to in the communication process. Here the concepts of the hierarchy of needs (physiological, safety, love, esteem, and self-actualization) as developed by Maslow[3] are of central importance. In brief, Maslow's theory asserts that needs at one level must be at least partially satisfied before needs at the next level of the hierarchy can emerge and become motivators of behav-

[3]A. H. Maslow, *Motivation and Personality* (New York: Harper & Row, 1954)

ior. Need arousal is the first stage in effective communication. Otherwise, there is no motivation to attend to or respond to the communication.

Second, motivation theory helps us to understand the importance of symbolism. The psychology of Freud stresses the role of symbols in arousing elements of previous experience in the subconscious, thus creating internal tensions. Symbols take on meaning from past experience and influence response to communication in complex ways. In general terms, symbols influence the individual's motive state by creating internal tensions.

Group Theory

Groups influence the communication process in two ways: by providing standards for evaluating one's attitudes and behavior; and by acting as a network for the flow of influence and information. Group influence in a particular situation is very difficult to evaluate, however, and depends upon such factors as the salience of the group for the individual, the cohesiveness of the group, and the consensus of opinion of group members on the issue being considered.

The concept of "reference group" influence is often used in discussions of communication behavior. A "reference group" may be defined as any set of persons, with one or more common characteristics, to which an individual "refers" for standards for his own attitudes and behavior. This definition is broad enough to include the concept of social role ("lawyers" may be a reference group for the law school student) as well as more specific groups such as "neighbors."

Each of these three theories—learning, motivation, and group—makes a significant contribution to our understanding of the communication process.

A definition of communication theory provides a skeletal model of the communication process. As pointed out above, communication theory is concerned with the analysis of WHO says WHAT to WHOM with what RESULT. The basic elements in a model of the communication model are the *source*, the *message*, the *receiver*, and the *response*, as shown in Figure 3–1. Communication is "successful" if the effect obtained is that desired by the source and consistent with his objectives. Effects may range from simple *awareness* through various degrees of *attitude change* to, ultimately, an actual change in *behavior*. In the specific case of marketing communication, the behavior desired is usually an act of purchase

Fig. 3–1. Elements of the communication process.

or consumption. However, the specific objective of the communication may be simply to create awareness or to develop favorable attitudes.

Communication is a *process*—a series of actions leading to a result— and it takes place over time. So let us next consider the *functions* of communication that relate the elements of the model one to the other and yield a dynamic process.

THE FUNCTIONS OF COMMUNICATION

In the communication process, three functions must be performed by the actors: encoding, decoding, and feedback. Messages are developed by encoding. The receiver assigns meaning to the message by decoding. Feedback tells the source whether he has been successful.

Encoding

Communication can be defined as the transmission of information, ideas, and emotions by the use of *symbols* such as words, pictures, and figures.[4] *Encoding* is the development of messages by selecting and combining symbols in a manner intended to best achieve the objectives of the source. Messages are combinations of symbols, and the development of messages is the encoding process.

The source's success depends upon his ability to perform the encoding function, to find the "right" combination of symbols to convey the intended meaning. Symbols convey meaning because we associate them with some aspect of real-world experience—an object, an event, or a feeling. Thus, symbols take their meanings from real-world antecedents. The receiver will assign to a symbol the same meaning as that intended by the source only if both share the same real-world antecedents, only if they associate the symbol with the same objects, events, and feelings. The background against which symbols employed in communication take on meaning can be thought of as "frame of reference" or "culture." Culture can be defined as the mutually shared field of experience that characterizes a society or some part of it. Communication between individuals with different cultural backgrounds is much more difficult because of different fields of experience. For example, the need for communication in several international markets typically poses a significant challenge for the marketing manager.

Decoding

Decoding is the process by which the receiver assigns meaning to the symbols transmitted by the source. As we have noted, the meaning

[4]Bernard Berelson and Gary A. Steiner, *Human Behavior: An Inventory of Scientific Findings* (New York: Harcourt, Brace, Jovanovich, Inc., 1964), p. 527.

assigned to the message by the receiver may not be the meaning intended by the source. The receiver will use his own frame of reference or field of experience in interpreting (i.e., decoding) the message. The mutually shared field defines the opportunity for communication to occur between source and receiver.) These ideas are summarized in Figure 3–2.

Feedback

If the receiver's decoding results in an interpretation somewhat different from that intended, the source may wish to identify this discrepancy and attempt to correct it with a modified message. The receiver's response indicates whether the intended meaning was received. Feedback is communication *from* the receiver *to* the source. The encoding function is now being performed by the receiver and the decoding function is performed by the communicator. The feedback messages may take any of several forms: questions, assertions, answers, grimaces, action. The response of the receiver tells the source whether or not his message has been successful. Personal communication or "interpersonal interaction" is communication in which there is direct feedback from receiver to sender in a face-to-face situation. (Whether a telephone conversation fits this definition is a debatable question.) Direct, immediate feedback permits the sender to instantaneously reinforce or modify his communication to more completely achieve his purpose. Thus, personal communication is much more efficient communication; feedback permits a precise "engineering" of communication.

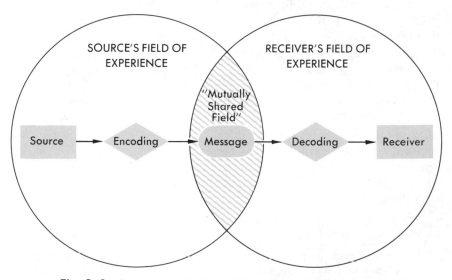

Fig. 3–2. An expanded view of the communication process.

Feedback from mass communication is much more difficult to obtain. Feedback from mass communication in marketing is obtained, for example, by surveying a sample of potential customers or members of media audiences. Sales results provide a very crude form of (contaminated) feedback on the effectiveness of mass marketing communication.

The inclusion of feedback completes the first, simplified model of the communication process (see Figure 3–3). We have identified the three central elements of the communication process—source, message, and receiver—and the three basic functions—encoding, decoding, and feedback. In the next section, we consider more completely how the characteristics of each element operate to determine response to communication.

AN EXPANDED MODEL OF THE COMMUNICATION PROCESS

For an expanded model of the communication process, we consider how the characteristics of the source, the communicator, the message, and the receiver interact to determine the response to communication. Remember that it is the response which is the ultimate objective of the communicator. He must understand, therefore, how response is influenced by the characteristics of each of the elements of the communication process. At several points, the discussion will present evidence that the audience is an active participant in the communication process, not a passive recipient of influence attempts.

Any formal training in communication is likely to begin with a discussion of the importance of understanding the audience. This is the first principle of courses on public speaking, business communication, salesmanship, and advertising, for example. In the following discussion, the audience will be taken as more or less given. The source (or the communicator) cannot significantly change the characteristics of the audience. Having selected his audience, he must adjust his message and his media to take the characteristics of his audience into account.

Source Credibility

Response to communication is significantly influenced by attitudes toward the source of the communication. Sources of communication can

Fig. 3–3. A model of the communication process with feedback.

be individuals, organizations, institutions, media, and so on. In the case of marketing communication, the source of the communication is the company that is selling the product or service being offered. In the mind of the potential customer, there may be some confusion about source. For example, both the manufacturer and the retail dealer are perceived as sources of information on new cars, and attitudes toward both will be a significant determinant of response to the automobile salesman's presentation.

The believability, or credibility, of the source is a characteristic of the source of communication *that is ascribed to him by the receiver*. It is not an objective characteristic of the source; rather, it is the receiver's judgment as to the extent to which the source should be believed. There are two elements to credibility: trustworthiness and expertise. The receiver implicitly asks himself two questions in evaluating sources: (1) Can I trust this source? (2) Does the source know what he is talking about? Answers to the first question are likely to be influenced by perceptions about the motives of the source: whether his intent is to manipulate or simply to inform; how objective he is; and so on. An assessment of expertise depends upon prior knowledge (from other sources of information) about the source.

The concept of source credibility in marketing communication is essentially the same as company reputation, or "image." Many forms of publicity, public relations, and institutional advertising have the aim of developing favorable attitudes toward the company so that specific selling messages will be more effective. Figure 3–4 presents an example of an institutional advertisement. In Chapter 8, we shall explore in some detail the findings from communication research studies of "source effect," and the activities of firms to improve their credibility will be examined.

Communicator-Media Effects

The expanded model includes a distinction between the source and the communicator or medium that actually delivers the message. Characteristics of the communicator or of the media are a significant intervening variable in determining response to communication. If we listen to a salesman's presentation for life insurance, our response is likely to be a function of our attitudes toward the salesman (communicator effect) as much as of our attitudes toward the insurance company (source effect). When we read an advertisement in *Playboy* magazine, our reaction to the advertisement is importantly influenced by the fact that it is in *Playboy* and not *Living for Young Homemakers* (or vice versa). Attitudes toward media and communicators are a significant influence on response to the messages they convey.

Breaking a language barrier

One-tenth of the people in our Jacksonville, Florida plant speak only with their hands and must hear with their eyes. They work at The Finn Industries, a Potlatch subsidiary that produces packages for many famous products, often using materials from other Potlatch plants. To compensate for their silent world, they develop an exceptional acuity of sight and sensitivity of touch that gives them proud proficiency. Communication isn't really a problem because managers and many co-workers have taken the trouble to learn their special language. What are the hands in the picture saying? They're saying, "We can do it better." If you should ever have a problem involving wood, pulp, paper or packaging, bring it to our people. You'll find they speak your language, also. Potlatch Forests, Inc., P.O. Box 3591, San Francisco, California 94119.

Potlatch puts the FOR in FORESTS...for wood products, for paperboard and packaging, for business and printing papers

Lithographed on Northwest Coated Cover, basis 80, another creative product of Potlatch Forests, Inc.

Fig. 3–4. An institutional advertisement. (Courtesy of Potlatch Forests, Inc.; Evans-Williams & Associates, Inc.)

There has been some interesting research on how the characteristics of salesmen and of their presentations influence the prospective customer's reaction. These questions will be examined more carefully in Chapters 11 and 14. In general, it has been found that a good sales presentation can help to overcome the handicap of low credibility or poor company image. It has also been found that salesmen tend to be most effective with prospects who are like themselves in characteristics and attitudes.

The influence of communication media interacts with the influence of the message itself in some very complex ways. The editorial content of magazines is an important influence on our response to advertisements in those magazines, to repeat an earlier example. There is also a host of factors relating to the mechanical and physical characteristics of media, as well as to the characteristic manner in which people use these media, that has a significant influence on the effectiveness of marketing communication in those media. In general, the spoken word is more effective than the written word, personal communication is more effective than mass communication, and a message delivered by television or radio to an individual may produce a greater impact than the same message delivered in print. However, there are significant exceptions to these very crude generalizations. The characteristics of the individual receiver are an important determinant of the effectiveness of the various media.

In developing a marketing communication strategy, therefore, it is vital that we consider the complex interactions among the characteristics of sources, communicators (salesmen and mass media), messages, and receivers (segments of the market).

Message Effects

The development of effective messages in marketing communication is more art than science and demands a high level of creativity. "Outstanding" advertising campaigns are generally believed to be capable of generating double or triple the sales volume of "average" campaigns. Proven talent in the employ of advertising agencies therefore commands a very high price, partly because it is such a scarce resource and partly because we do not know how to apply known principles to "guarantee effective results." Although message effects are very significant, we are a long way from being able to "engineer" effective advertising by the application of proven rules.

Likewise, there are striking differences among salesmen, even in the employ of the same firm, in their ability to produce profitable sales for the company. What is the difference between a "good" and a "bad" sales presentation? If only the causes of those differences were known with precision, it might be possible to train salesmen to deliver sales presentations with exactly the characteristics necessary to produce the desired result. Unfortunately, differences among prospective customers, the unique nature of each sales interaction, and significant shortcomings in our understanding prevent such precision in developing selling messages.

Chapters 11 through 15 will be devoted to consideration of many of the complex issues involved in developing effective selling messages in marketing communications. Chapter 11 will evaluate evidence from communication research on the characteristics of effective messages. Consideration will be given to such areas as the use of one-sided vs. two-sided arguments, the influence of order of presentation, and the use of various kinds of motivating appeals. Once again, it will be necessary to state the conclusions of this research in terms of the characteristics of the audience. For example, it will be seen that one-sided arguments are more effective with persons who are initially in agreement with the opinion being advocated by the communicator and with persons of relatively low intellectual ability.

Audience Predispositions

As has been repeatedly asserted, the audience is an active participant in the communication process. The audience performs the decoding process, as pointed out above, in assigning meaning to the symbols used by the communicator. Another way of looking at the role of the audience in the communication process is to consider the so-called "selective processes": selective attention, selective perception, and selective retention. The receiver in the communication process actively determines which stimuli (among all those he is exposed to) he will pay attention to. He determines the meaning he will assign to those he does pay attention to and, from those he perceives, those he will retain and the manner in which they will be retained. The selective processes function in general to insure that the messages are attended to, perceived, and retained in a manner consistent with the receiver's predispositions.

Predispositions can be thought of as mental states, or as tendencies for the receiver to behave in a particular way toward a particular object in the environment. The general concept of predisposition embraces the more specific concepts of attitude, opinion, belief, value, need, goal, want, feeling, and the like. These are overlapping concepts, however, and since specific distinctions are not necessary at this stage, let us be content with the general concept of "predisposition."

The concept is also broad enough to include such factors as social situation, group membership, information state, and personality traits. Most communication has the objective of changing the predispositions of the audience—creating awareness, changing attitudes, causing a certain action to occur. But the motivation of the individual receiver is usually to maintain some kind of balance—to satisfy needs, to maintain existing attitudes and beliefs, to protect group affiliations. Therefore, most communication designed to change attitudes or to change characteristic behavior patterns is likely to encounter initial resistance. The individual will pay attention to, interpret, and remember communications in a manner consistent with his predispositions. If the "objective" facts presented in the communication are not quite consistent with predispositions, it is likely that the "facts," not the predispositions, will be modified in the individual's perception to bring them into consonance with each other.

Chapter 4 will consider in further detail the manner in which predispositions influence response to communication, for existing predispositions define both the problems facing the marketing communicator and the opportunities available to him.

Response

The response of the receiver to the communication is the payoff to the communicator. It may or may not be consistent with his objective. The problem of specifying the response desired from the market is a central issue in the planning of marketing communication. This problem was alluded to in the previous chapter when we discussed the purposes of marketing communication.

Communication was defined in the beginning of this chapter as the "sharing of meaning" and as "the process by which an individual transmits stimuli to modify the behavior or predispositions of other individuals." The politician's objective is to get his receiver to vote for him; the teacher wants his student to understand the information and arguments being presented; the marketing communicator wants prospective customers to buy and use the product and obtain satisfaction from it.

For many forms of communication activity, it is very helpful to conceive a series of steps leading to the ultimate objective, a hierarchy of the effects of communication. Thus, the marketing communicator may not be concerned with achieving buying action as an immediate objective (it may be impossible for several reasons). He may instead be quite content to achieve a simple awareness of his product offering or to modify attitudes toward his company and its products.

There are several ways of thinking about the sequence of steps leading to the behavior desired by the communicator. Each of them considers a series of mental stages beginning with simple awareness and ending with some kind of overt behavior. For the marketing communicator, the buyer's decision-making process represents the relevant framework for analysis. Two of the most common views of this process were introduced in Chapter 2. These are the "adoption process" model, usually attributed to Rogers,[5] and a six-stage model offered by Lavidge and Steiner:[6]

Rogers (Adoption Process)	Lavidge-Steiner
Attention	Awareness
Interest	Knowledge
Evaluation	Liking
Trial	Preference
Adoption	Conviction
	Purchase

Different messages and media may be required at each stage of the decision process. An understanding of the communication process is required for developing the most efficient combination of messages and media for the specific communication objective. For example, if the objective is simple awareness, mass media advertising that simply highlights the brand name of the product and a few of its essential characteristics and benefits may be the most efficient way of achieving this objective. On the other hand, successful evaluation may require careful detailing of information by a salesman. This is true of the purchase of an expensive encyclopedia, for example, or for the sale of complex industrial equipment.

The appropriate communication objective depends upon the nature of the product or service being sold and the stage in the life cycle and market development of that product or service. For example, the ability of consumers to perceive differences in product quality is a significant consideration in defining the objective of marketing communication. If the product is one, such as beer or cigarettes, where most consumers have limited ability to identify physical differences among brands, the marketing communication objective is often to create a set of attitudes toward the brand that relate to social or psychological need satisfaction. These kinds of objectives are often referred to as "image building" or "product positioning." Marketing communication can define for the consumer the need satisfactions to be derived from the product. The nature of the product is the central consideration in defining such communication opportunities.

[5]Everett M. Rogers, *Diffusion of Innovations* (New York: Free Press of Glencoe, Inc., 1962), pp. 76–120.

[6]Robert Lavidge and Gary Steiner, "A Model for Predictive Measurements of Advertising Effectiveness," *Journal of Marketing*, 25, No. 6 (October 1961), pp. 59–62.

The response desired from a marketing communication program must be stated precisely if the program is to be carefully planned and subsequently evaluated. An objective of creating awareness will result in quite a different set of messages and modes than will an objective of stimulating product trial. The measurements required to judge success in each case will also be different. Therefore, the work of designing a marketing communication strategy must begin by specifying the response desired. Stated differently, the end result of the communication process is the beginning of the planning process. This statement emphasizes the importance of understanding the elements and functions of the communication process as the basis for developing an effective marketing communication strategy. The argument might be summarized as follows: Planning involves predicting response and accurate prediction depends upon understanding the process that one is attempting to influence.

DESIGNING COMMUNICATION STRATEGY

At the end of Chapter 2, in Figure 2–6, we saw that there were five stages in the design of a communication strategy:

1. Define the communication task.
2. Identify communication alternatives.
3. Identify key uncertainties in predicting response.
4. Gather data to evaluate response.
5. Synthesize campaign elements.

This model is essentially a "planning model" that tells the decision maker the steps to be performed in attaining a desired result. But it does not offer much help in actually completing the task. The preceding discussion of the communication process is a bit more helpful in that it specifies the "key uncertainties" in developing a communication strategy. These uncertainties involve the relationships among the characteristics of sources, communicators and media, messages, and receivers in determining response to marketing communication.

The elements and functions of the communication process define in a different way the task of developing a marketing communication strategy. *By starting at the end of the communication process and working backward*, the following steps are seen to be involved in designing a communication strategy:

1. *Set objectives*—define desired *responses*.
2. *Define targets*—select a market segment of intended *receivers*.
3. *Analyze predispositions*—gather such data as required to understand how alternative messages will be *decoded* and responded to.

4. *Create messages*—develop appeals and other *message* elements that are likely to have the greatest success in influencing predispositions to elicit the desired response.
5. *Select media*—define a combination of *vehicles* that can most efficiently and effectively deliver the intended messages to the target market segment.
6. *Build image*—create a reputation, a set of attitudes toward the company as a *source* of communication on products and services.
7. *Provide for feedback*—specifically, plan for gathering direct and inferential *feedback* of response to communication, as an aid in designing subsequent strategies.

Each of these steps will require several chapters of elaboration, but their importance can be briefly suggested here.

The objectives of a marketing communication program are derived from the basic marketing strategy directing corporate effort. But those marketing objectives must be translated into specific communication objectives—awareness, trial, etc. Likewise, the target audience for communication is derived from the basic strategic decision on market segmentation. But these segments must be redefined according to parameters relevant for the message creation and media selection decisions that are required.

The key data required in developing marketing communication strategies are data on audience predispositions—levels of awareness and attitudes concerning the company and its products and services. These data define the problems and opportunities facing the firm. In Chapter 4, we shall consider concepts and techniques relating to the analysis of predispositions as the basis for planning.

SUMMARY

Our overview of the communication process has suggested that the influence of messages and media depends upon audience predispositions. An understanding of predispositions must therefore precede the creation of messages and the selection of media. Competitive and economic considerations must also come into play in developing message and media strategy. Selection of resellers and a definition of their role in communication strategy is an important consideration in determining the most efficient way to deliver messages to prospective customers.

Knowing the importance of attitudes toward the source in determining response, it is essential to know how the company is regarded and to define opportunities for strengthening its image. These are long-term considerations, with changes in image requiring a long time and consist-

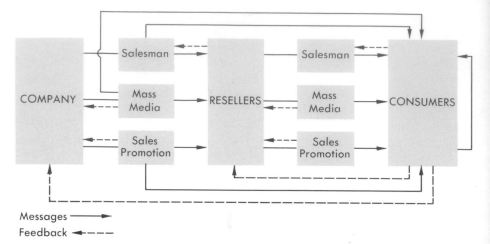

Fig. 3–5. The marketing communication process.

ent effort. Periodic appraisal of corporate image is a vital part of an effective marketing communication program.

Feedback is the key to intelligent evaluation and control of marketing communication effort. The salesman gets feedback on every sales call. He needs to know how to interpret and react to it and how to summarize it and convey it back to company management as an aid in appraising selling strategy. Feedback on mass communication effort and on the communication effort of resellers requires a careful planning of steps to collect the required information.

These flows of communication to and from consumers are summarized in Figure 3–5. Although this model is very simple, it does suggest the complexity of the market communication process and the many combinations of messages and media that must be considered in designing a marketing communication strategy.

Appraising Communication Opportunity

The planning of effective marketing communication begins with the identification of those communication opportunities available to the firm for achievement of its objectives. Opportunities are really the same as problems; they are a difference between what is possible and desired and what is presently being achieved. Since the purpose of marketing communication is generally to change existing levels of awareness, attitudes, or behavior, these are the variables which must be measured in appraising communication opportunity.

Two kinds of information are necessary as the basis for planning marketing communication strategy. In Part I, emphasis was placed on the use of concepts from behavioral science, especially communication theory, for identifying the factors that must be considered by the market analyst. Behavioral analysis can suggest where our understanding of the underlying market processes is inadequate and where additional information is needed. It can tell us what relationships are likely to be most significant in determining response to changes in the stimulus variables, such as the level of selling effort or the appeals used in advertising. Qualitative information about the market—mental and behavioral processes followed in deciding to buy the product, for example—is vital to developing effective marketing communication.

Of equal importance is quantitative information about the nature and scope of those market segments toward which the communication program is to be directed. Estimates of the size of the potential market, number of buying units and rate of purchase, brand switching rates, and so on, are especially significant when the level of communication effort must be established and allocation made to various segments of the total market.

In Part II major attention is devoted to conceptual knowledge useful in defining the need for, and organizing, qualitative information about the market. The entire discussion of qualitative information, the development of "behavioral models," will suggest the need for measurement and quantification as the basis for planning communication effort. Where appropriate, relevant measurement concepts and techniques will be discussed. Finally, Chapter 10 will develop the specific problems of market measurement, especially estimating market potential and forecasting sales, as necessary for planning the marketing communication programs.

4

Audience Predispositions

The message intended by the source and the influence of the message upon the receiver often differ. As discussed in the previous chapter, the audience is an active participant in the communication process—in the selection, interpretation, and retention of some messages and the active rejection of others. It is a well-known fact from psychology that individuals respond to a coherent picture of the world that is far different from the "objective" information provided by their physical senses.[1] Rather, the world they respond to is a "subjective" world, a combination of sensory experience and the meanings assigned to that experience by the individual, based upon his psychological makeup and past experience.

For an individual to be influenced by a communication, at least three events must occur. First, he must be exposed to it (a fact over which he may have relatively little control), he must pay attention to the message, and he must become aware of it. Second, he must perceive the message. That is, he must admit it into his consciousness and assign meaning to it. He must go beyond simple awareness to the more complex act of interpreting the message. Finally, he must remember or retain the message until such time as he has the opportunity to act upon it. For many marketing communications, it is impossible for the receiver to act upon the message when it is received. Having perceived a message, that message (or some modified parts of it) will become part of the "past experience" of the receiver and will therefore influence the way in which he responds to future communications. However, what is retained changes over time as forgetting and related psychological processes come into play.

[1]Bernard Berelson and Gary A. Steiner, *Human Behavior: An Inventory of Scientific Findings* (New York: Harcourt, Brace, Jovanovich, Inc., 1964), p. 99.

Individuals expose themselves to, perceive, and remember communication in a selective fashion. Out of all of the messages in the environment, they actively choose those that will be attended to. Out of all those messages attended to, they selectively perceive the content of those messages, and they select those meanings that will be retained in memory. Obviously, these selective processes are not strictly "rational," the result of a careful thinking-through of what will be attended to, perceived, and remembered. Rather, these processes are the result of conscious, semiconscious, and unconscious motivations and behavior.

These three processes are referred to as selective exposure, selective perception, and selective retention. Together, they are referred to as the selective processes. It is through the *selective* nature of these basic processes that the audience is actively involved in determining the content of marketing communication.

Generally speaking, the selective processes result in behavior which is consistent with existing predispositions. The individual is motivated to achieve a kind of balance between the present communication and his experience, attitudes, and beliefs. He strives for balance and consistency. In addition, he tends to expose himself to, perceive, and retain messages that are pleasurable and not painful. In a nutshell, he prefers messages that are favorable to his existing predispositions.

PREDISPOSITIONS

A more precise definition of the term "predispositions" is necessary. Predispositions provide what is commonly called a "frame of reference." It is impossible to separate the content of predispositions and their influence, because predispositions are "hypothetical constructs." That is, their existence is inferred from observation of their influence, the result which they have on behavior.

We begin with a definition:

Predispositions: The social or psychological state of the audience, or of a member of the audience, at the beginning of the communication: their information, interests, attitudes, group memberships, personality traits. This includes anything that characterizes the audience insofar as the communication is concerned or that may reasonably be involved in the audience's attention, interpretation, or effect. Some predispositions, e.g., class-related attitudes, may be present at the start of the communication but are not conscious or manifest then; in such cases the communication might "bring them out," i.e., make them visible, felt, and operative.[2]

Implicit in this definition is the concept of action, the notion that the individual has a tendency to react to a particular cue in a particular

[2]*Ibid.,* p. 528.

way. The investigator interested in identifying and measuring predispositions would have to proceed by first exposing the individual to a stimulus and then noting the response. He would infer the existence of the predisposition from the response, in speech or action, by the individual to the specific stimulus. Thus, an "opinion" is a verbal response to a question posed by an investigator. We define attitudes in terms of the objects toward which they refer. We talk about "attitudes *toward*" specific objects in the environment.

We may think of the individual, the receiver, as a "black box" which receives and processes information. The black box receives stimuli and produces responses (Figure 4–1). Each black box is slightly different: the same stimulus elicits a slightly different response from each black box. Thus, there must be something different about the contents of each black box, some differences in the internal mechanisms that generate responses to stimuli. It is those internal mechanisms that we have labeled "predispositions."

The remainder of this chapter will consider the influence of market predispositions upon marketing communication strategy and will examine in considerable detail the ways in which predispositions influence response. Among other things, we consider sources of predispositions, some fundamentals of perception, the selective processes, and problems of measuring predispositions.

THE SIGNIFICANCE OF PREDISPOSITIONS FOR STRATEGY

No marketing communication strategy, even for a new product, starts with a clean slate. Even if people have no knowledge at all concerning the existence of the product, they have certain predispositions which will influence their response to that product. Most basically, they have certain needs which the product may satisfy. They have a host of attitudes toward substitute products, toward the company, and toward the various resellers who may handle the product. If the product is to be sold direct to consumers by salesmen, attitudes toward salesmen in general and toward this company's salesmen in particular become an important factor to consider. If the product is to be advertised in mass media, the strategist must evaluate consumers' predispositions toward those media.

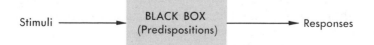

Fig. 4–1. The receiver as a "black box."

For established products, the problem is more complex. Previous communication will have established a wide variety of predispositions toward the company, its products, its dealers, its advertising, and its salesmen. Some of these predispositions will be favorable to the company's objectives, whereas others are not. These existing predispositions provide the base from which the new marketing communication strategy must build; they define both the communication problems facing the firm and the opportunity to use communication to help the firm achieve its objectives.

Predispositions as Targets for Communication

The ultimate objective of all marketing effort is to create a satisfied customer. A satisfied customer is a necessary condition for long-run profit maximization. The probability is high that the satisfied customer will not only repurchase the product ("loyalty") but will also generate favorable messages about the product.

Whether the customer initially buys the product and is satisfied with its performance is a function of many variables including the quality of the product itself, the price, the channels of distribution for that product, and competitors' activities, as well as marketing communication effort. It is usually unreasonable, therefore, to judge the effectiveness of a marketing communication program against the sole criterion of sales volume, for many other variables influence sales volume. Also, as already indicated, the customer's buying decision process may be complex, and there may be significant time lags between the receipt of a marketing message and the end result of a purchase decision. For a given planning period, the objective of marketing communication may be more effectively stated in terms of changing existing levels of predisposition rather than to change behavior or to influence sales volume directly. For example, the simple communication objective of creating awareness among potential customers may be the more reasonable criterion against which to evaluate advertising, since so many other factors will ultimately determine sales volume.

Problems and Opportunities

A "problem" is defined by a difference between what is desired and what is being achieved. That is, a problem is a failure to achieve a stated objective. The diagnostic task of the marketing manager is to identify those areas where the company's marketing achievements are less than what was stated as an objective. For this purpose, he may use such evidence as sales volume compared to quota and forecast, market share, or sales as a percentage of potential. From a communication viewpoint, a problem is defined by a discrepancy between existing predispositions and what is desired. For example, a company has a communication problem when its objective is to have 80 percent of the potential market aware of a product and its specific features and only fifty percent is aware. Or the implicit objective may be to have people completely understand certain essential features of the product offering, but a survey may reveal significant misunderstanding of the product.

To define communication problems, the manager needs data on existing predispositions. He may obtain this information from a wide variety of formal and informal sources, including market surveys, salesmen's reports, advertising agency research, or his own personal interviews with dealers. He also needs some clear statement of communication objectives—of the levels of predispositions to be achieved and the meanings to be conveyed to specific segments of the market. Without a good statement of objectives and a reasonable estimate of existing predispositions, it is hard to be articulate about the specific nature of the communication problem.

People's attitudes toward the company and its products are a complex interaction between reaction to marketing communication and actual experience with the product. Seldom can problems be traced exclusively to either the company's marketing communication activity, or to inadequacy in its product offering (including product quality, price, and distribution). It is attitudes toward the company and its products that determine the communication problem facing management. For example, Eastern Airlines conducted a consumer survey in mid-1963 which defined a serious communication problem, as well as the need for significant improvement in its service. This survey revealed that "frequent travelers rated Eastern the worst in on-time performance by 5 to 1; worst in all-around service by 3 to 1; worst in friendliness by almost 5 to 1; worst in safety by almost 3 to 1."[3] While the first objective had to be improvement in the quality of the service being offered by the airline, a need clearly recognized by new management, it was also necessary to make the potential market aware of the basic changes that were occurring in the quality of the service. Thus, while the marketing problem was to improve service and increase sales volume and share of market, the communication problem was to bring about a fundamental change in people's predispositions toward Eastern Airlines.

An "opportunity" is defined by a difference between what is possible and what is being realized. Thus, untapped market potential represents an opportunity, as does a significant segment of the market that is unaware of the company and its products. An unsatisfied customer represents an opportunity and, to the imaginative and aggressive marketing

[3]George S. Gordon, "Building the New Image at Eastern," in Frederick E. Webster, Jr. (ed.), *New Directions in Marketing* (Chicago: American Marketing Association, Inc., 1965), pp. 151–58, at p. 152.

manager, negative predispositions toward the company and its products represent an opportunity. The saying that "in adversity lies opportunity" applies in marketing as well as in other endeavors.

Definition of opportunities involves definition of what is possible. Here, the requirement is for imagination and creativity as much as for specific information about existing predispositions. It is the ability to define what is possible, to sense new opportunities, that often distinguishes the successful manager from the unsuccessful. At about the time Eastern Airlines was struggling to regain customers, American Airlines and its advertising agency, Doyle, Dane, Bernbach, came upon the results of a consumer survey which showed that American was the preferred airline among frequent travelers. From this finding, American and its agency saw an opportunity for an advertising campaign. By telling people that American was the airline preferred by the frequent traveler, it was possible to convey several messages relating to the quality of American's service, including in-flight service, maintenance, safety, and related factors. From this realization, the "Professional Traveler" advertising campaign was developed. Here again is an illustration of the use of data on predispositions in planning marketing communication strategy.

To summarize: Problems are differences between what is *desired* and what is realized; opportunities are differences between the *possible* and actual. To the extent that the desirable and the possible are both perceived and related to one another, management can establish a set of objectives which represents the best opportunities available for the firm.

In addition to what is possible in the market, the management must also consider how the company's resources—its strengths and weaknesses and past experiences—constrain what is possible for the firm. What is possible is defined not only by market opportunity but by the ability of the firm to capitalize upon market opportunity. Of course, over the long run, new resources can be developed to remove constraints placed upon opportunities by the firm's present resource base. Thus, what is possible is also a function of the time horizon being considered in planning.

Communication problems are defined by differences between existing predispositions (especially levels of awareness and attitudes) and company objectives; opportunities are defined by what is possible compared to existing predispositions. Communication objectives are usually stated in terms of changing predispositions; information about predispositions as well as a clear statement of objectives are both necessary inputs to the planning of marketing communication programs.

MARKETING COMMUNICATION OBJECTIVES

The relevant objectives for a given company's marketing communication program are a function of such factors as company size, stage in product life cycle, nature of distribution arrangements, existing sales force competence, budget constraints, and so on. A "good" set of objectives, one that recognizes the problems, opportunities, and constraints facing the firm, is going to be different from one firm to the next. As a general guideline, however, it is possible to suggest several categories of objectives of general applicability to most firms. This general guideline is provided by the "marketing communication planning matrix" of Figure 4–2.

Communication objectives may be stated in terms of level of awareness, changes in attitudes, or specific buying action desired. Similarly, there are three classes of "objects" toward which the relevant changes in predisposition are to be directed: the company, its products, and its resellers (including both salesmen and distributors). The following is a list of illustrative examples for each behavior/object combination:

Awareness/Company: For many companies, advertising is used simply to inform potential customers or other relevant audiences that the company exists.

Awareness/Products: The first stage in introducing a new product is to create awareness; for example, Boeing has used consumer media to announce the delivery of its 737 model to airlines.

Awareness/Resellers: National advertisers often run ads in consumer media listing their local distributors by state and city.

Attitudes/Company: Advertising is often used to create an "image," a set of particular attitudes toward a company; for example, companies run advertisements promoting their research activities or community service.

Attitudes/Products: Both personal selling and advertising, as well as direct mail, often have the purpose of conveying certain meanings of "images" about products; for example, an ad for a bank may stress the completeness of the services it offers.

Attitudes/Resellers: Advertising is often used to promote the competence of the company's salesmen, or to support the dealer organization.

Action/Company: When a company is selling a generalized competence and problem solving ability, as in the case of defense-oriented R&D firms, or specialized engineering firms, the purpose of marketing communication may be to generate contacts with the

	Company	Products	Resellers
Awareness			
Attitudes			
Action			

Fig. 4–2. The marketing communication planning matrix.

firm by potential users of its services. Another category of action/company objectives is in the area of investor relations and public relations where the desired action might be purchase of the company's stock or writing to a Congressman about the company, etc.

Action/Products: Of course, much communication (especially consumer promotions and deals) is designed to solicit purchase behavior. Any ad where the message is "buy our product" fits this category, as does any sales call on which the salesman asks for the order.

Action/Resellers: Advertising activity may be designed to generate traffic and contacts for resellers. For example, insurance companies often place coupons in their advertising; persons requesting information are referred to the local agent or broker.

The optimum set of objectives for a firm's marketing communication strategy is a function of its total marketing mix and the role of communication within the overall marketing strategy. The foregoing examples are illustrative of the kinds of objectives that are possible, and Figure 4–2 simply suggests a way of thinking about the need for communication activity. Predispositions toward the company, its products and services, and its resellers may all be important objectives for the marketing communication program.

The preceding paragraphs have concentrated upon the planning implications of predispositions and the need for information about predispositions as the basis for developing communication strategy. The next task is to develop in greater detail our understanding of the sources of predispositions and their influence on response to marketing communication. It will be necessary to explore in some depth the basic psychological process of perception, the assigning of meaning to symbols relating to objects in the environment. The discussion will thus move away from planning considerations and toward a consideration of the behavioral processes which the manager is trying to influence and respond to.

SOURCES OF PREDISPOSITIONS

There are three general sources of predispositions: the culture of which the individual is part; social groups with which he is affiliated and with which he identifies; and demographic, socioeconomic, and personality characteristics of the individual himself. These sources are not mutually exclusive but may all operate to determine a particular set of attitudes. An individual's preference for a size and style of house, for example, will be a function of all three sets of variables.

Culture

The first and most general source of predispositions is culture. Of all the influences on predispositions, culture is the most pervasive, the slowest to change, the broadest, and the source that is least likely to come to our conscious attention. The concept of culture is very complex. One study identified 164 definitions of culture.[4] One of the earliest definitions of culture, and one that is still used, is "that complex whole which includes knowledge, belief, art, morals, law, custom, and any other capabilities and habits acquired by man as a member of society."[5] A recent book on consumer behavior defines culture as "the complex of values, ideas, attitudes, and other meaningful symbols created by man to shape human behavior and the artifacts of that behavior as they are transmitted from one generation to the next."[6] This definition incorporates the notion of culture as something that is passed on from one generation to the next, a notion that is central to most concepts of culture.

For the study of communication, it is probably best to think of culture as the link between individuals,[7] the mutually shared field of experience and meanings that provides the basis for all communication. Culture influences both the individual's behavior and his interpretation of the behavior of others. Culture provides answers to the question "What does that mean?" where "that" may be a statement, an action, a gesture, or a unit from any of several "message systems."

A "message system" is any system used by people to share meaning. The most common message system is language, combinations of words. Language, according to one view, is a *sub*system, part of a larger "primary" message system of interaction, with writing and speaking as the most highly developed modes of interaction. Edward Hall has defined ten primary message systems:

Interaction: Words are spoken and written in interaction. Language is one distinguishing characteristic of a culture.

Association: Individuals share meaning by forming groups and affiliations. The kinds of groups and the functions they perform vary from culture to culture.

[4]Alfred L. Kroeber and Clyde Kluckhohn, "Culture: A Critical Review of Concepts and Definitions," *Papers of the Peabody Museum,* 47, No. 1a (1952).

[5]Edward B. Tylor, *Primitive Culture,* third English edition, Murray, 1891, p. 1, cited in Berelson and Steiner, *op. cit.,* p. 646.

[6]James Engel, David T. Kollat, and Roger D. Blackwell, *Consumer Behavior* (New York: Holt, Rinehart & Winston, Inc., 1968), p. 232, attributed to Alfred L. Kroeber and Talcott Parsons, "The Concepts of Culture and of Social System," *American Sociological Review,* 23 (October 1958), p. 583.

[7]Gerald Zaltman, *Marketing: Contributions from the Behavioral Sciences* (New York: Harcourt, Brace, Jovanovich, Inc., 1965), p. 8.

Subsistence: The way in which individuals and groups provide for their livelihood is a source of meaning, a part of culture.

Bisexuality: What is considered appropriate masculine and feminine behavior is defined by the culture.

Territoriality: Attitudes toward physical space, areas, and boundaries are determined by culture and are a part of it. The whole notion of ownership of land, for example, of having one's "turf," is a cultural phenomenon.

Temporality: Attitudes toward time differ significantly from culture to culture. In some cultures, for example, it is rude to be on time for an appointment. Life cycles vary among cultures.

Learning: There are marked differences among cultures in the way people learn, both the process and the content of learning.

Play: Kinds of recreation, and the role of recreation in life style, constitute a fundamental aspect of culture.

Defense: Every culture develops unique and complex methods for defending itself against other cultures, for its members to defend themselves against each other, for defense against microorganisms, and so on.

Exploitation: Man is the only creature to significantly modify his environment in a manner to serve his own ends and correct for his own deficiencies and weaknesses. Cultures are defined by the artifacts, the "things," used by men to achieve their purposes. Man exploits his environment by creating material goods and by developing services to meet his physical and social needs. The accepted ways of doing this are defined by culture.[8]

Marketing communications, including packages, display, outdoor billboards, mass media, and so on, are all aspects of our culture. But to be acceptable they must be integrated and consistent with other aspects of the culture. Values and attitudes toward particular products and behaviors must be considered carefully in developing marketing communication strategies.

One of the many reasons for segmented marketing strategies is a recognition that subcultures are an important cause of the lack of homogeneity in today's markets. Race, religion, national origin, and place of residence can all be significant determinants of values and attitudes, and define subcultures within the total market. For example, we think in terms of the Afro-American market, the Jewish market, the Puerto Rican market, and the New England market. Each of these subcultures may have unique attitudes toward the company's products, may find particular need satisfactions in their use, and will respond to adver-

[8]Edward T. Hall, *The Silent Language,* paperback ed. (New York: Fawcett Publications, Inc., 1961), pp. 42–62.

tising and selling messages in different ways. Tastes and preferences, habits and attitudes, are predispositions importantly influenced by our cultural relationships.

There are certain cultural traits which are generally recognized to be pervasive in America. One summary of the American culture defined its characteristics as: religiosity, achievement, security, other-directedness— the sociable life, the leisure life, youthfulness, and urbanization.[9] Any marketing communication strategy must be sensitive to these basic values and, in addition, should be based upon information about the particular aspects of culture or subculture relevant to this product category. This cultural analysis becomes especially important when marketing activity is planned for new and relatively unfamiliar cultures, as in entering international markets.

Social Groups

Groups are probably the most familiar source of predispositions. An individual's behavior is often explained in terms of "social pressure" from the influence of norms, values, and sanctions of groups with which he identifies. Groups function not only as a source of influence, but also as a source of information. That is, groups are networks of communication.

The groups which influence an individual can be categorized in several ways. If we use the criterion of intimacy in our ranking, the most basic group is the family. The most specific definition of a family is a husband and wife and their children living within the same household. This family unit is perhaps the most important for purposes of marketing strategy. It is a target for many marketing communications, it is often the decision-making unit of relevance for purchase of the product, and it is the consuming unit. A more general definition of family includes all persons related by birth or marriage, whether sharing a residence or not. This definition has less relevance for marketing analysis.

Moving along the continuum toward lesser intimacy, one encounters such groups as neighbors, face-to-face groups (church clubs, work groups, recreational groups), and organizations like political parties and professional associations. The most general concept of group is that of reference group, any collection of persons to which an individual "refers" for standards for his own behavior.

The importance of social groups as sources of predispositions is underscored by the earlier analysis of cultural influences, where the point was made that "other-directedness," the sociable life, is valued in American culture. Related to this observation are such concepts as conformity, "the organization man," and "togetherness," all used frequently

[9]Engel, Kollat, and Blackwell, *op. cit.*, pp. 240–50.

to characterize central tendencies in modern American culture. In fact, these concepts have become rather trivial from overuse.

The ways in which groups provide predispositions and influence the individual's response to marketing communications are so complex that we will spend two chapters in developing this analysis. In Chapter 5, we will consider groups as sources of norms and values, that is, as a source of influence. In Chapter 6, we will examine groups as networks of communication, that is, as a source of information. Because these chapters are planned, we will leave for the moment our discussion of the influence of groups on predispositions.

Individual Characteristics

Because the individual is the product of many influences, including social and cultural influences as discussed above, it is very difficult to talk about "individual characteristics" that are devoid of the influence of other people. Nonetheless, there are certain aspects of the physical, economic, and psychological reality facing an individual that do not depend significantly upon other people. Some aspects of an individual's basic personality characteristics, for example, can be viewed as a mostly determined by heredity; such qualities as aggressiveness, friendliness, and need for achievement have components that are not well explained by reference to the influence of groups and other individuals.

Demographic and Socioeconomic. Basic to the set of facts describing an individual from the standpoint of marketing communication are his demographic and socioeconomic characteristics: income, age, size of family, education, place of residence, and similar data. It is perhaps obvious, but important enough to deserve emphasis, that a major set of relevant predispositions are the needs of the individual for the product or service being offered, his previous experience with it, his ability to pay for that product or service, and its relationship to his life style. Important inferences about each of these can be based upon data relating to demographic and socioeconomic characteristics.

Most consumer goods marketing communication strategies start with a definition of the "consumer profile" for the product. For example, the consumer profile for a manufacturer of station wagons might be "heads of households, aged 25 to 45, with two or more children, with income over $7,500 per year." Each of these variables—marital status, age, number of children, income—not only influences the individual's need for the product, but also the kinds of media he is exposed to, the appeals that will be most interesting to him, his ability to pay, and so on.

Life Cycle Stages. The concept of "life cycle" is a variable which summarizes many demographic and socioeconomic variables. The family is the unit of analysis for the life cycle concept. The stages in the family life cycle begin when the young adult leaves the home of his parents and sets up his own "household." Next he marries. The couple then has children and the life cycle concept divides households into categories depending upon whether the youngest child in the family is under six years old or older. Next, the children leave home (to begin their own life cycle), and the family assumes the status of "older couple without children at home." At this stage, the important purchases of the family have probably been completed, except for replacement or such items as automobiles and major appliances. Clearly, the family life cycle is an important determinant of the need for certain products and services, and of the ability of the family to pay for those products. At each stage, the need for certain products and services emerges (especially consumer durables such as major appliances, furniture, and baby accessories).

Social Class. Another "summary" concept, like life cycle, from the behavioral sciences is the concept of social class. Social class is a way of describing an individual (not groups, as the name might imply) by combining several characteristics including occupation, education, income, and residence. Table 4-1 presents two different views of social classes, one by Warner and one by Hollingshead.

Socioeconomic and demographic variables, whether considered individually or combined into more complex variables such as life cycle or social class, are significant determinants of predispositions. Product ownership is often correlated with several of these variables, although there is likely to be little correlation between a single demographic variable and predispositions. For example, Coleman reports a study of market segmentation in which income alone proved to be a poor predictor of automobile ownership. Likewise, social class analysis did not reveal any clear relationship between social class and automobile ownership (make, model, value). When income was combined with social class, however, significant relationships began to emerge. It was found that within each social class, if one segmented the population further on the basis of income, automobile ownership then began to fit a pattern. Within each social class, there were certain individuals whose income was below average for that class while others were, obviously, above average. These can be called the "underprivileged" and the "overprivileged," respectively. Recognizing that these characterizations refer only to a comparison with other people in that social class, they provide a significant basis for thinking about attitudes toward certain products.[10]

Occupation. Occupation is a variable which tends to be a surrogate or "proxy" variable for several others, including income, education, resi-

[10]Richard P. Coleman, "The Significance of Social Stratification in Selling," in Martin L. Bell (ed.), *Marketing: A Maturing Discipline* (Chicago: American Marketing Association, 1961), pp. 171–84.

Table 4–1. Two Views of the Social Class Hierarchy

Class	Definition	Percentage
	A. Warner's Classifications	
Upper-upper	Aristocracy, "old family," inherited wealth	1.4
Lower-upper	Similar to upper-upper in income, occupation, and costly homes, but newer, lacking distinguished ancestry	1.6
Upper-middle	Professionals and substantial businessmen, civic leaders but not "society"	10.2
Lower-middle	Small businessmen, white collar workers, smaller homes, "good common people"	28.1
Upper-lower	Semiskilled workers, lower incomes, less desirable homes, "poor but hardworking people"	32.6
Lower-lower	Semiskilled and unskilled, worst homes, often on relief, low incomes, "level below the common man"	25.2
Unclassified		0.9
	Total	100.0
	B. Hollingshead's Classifications	
I	"Old families," top business management and professional occupations, high incomes, highly educated, expensive homes, the social elite	3.4
II	Business managers (but not policy formulators), lesser professionals, (engineers, etc.), often college graduates, socially sensitive, "on the way up"	9.0
III	Employees in various salaried administrative pursuits, small business owners, average incomes, high school graduates, most homes in "good" areas	21.4
IV	Semiskilled and skilled manual employees, below average incomes, many are homeowners but live in multiple units, many had some high school but did not graduate, often members of minority ethnic group (Italian, Irish, etc.)	48.5
V	Unskilled and semiskilled, low incomes, no savings, live in old tenement areas, most did not finish grade school, "live today, let tomorrow take care of itself."	17.7
	Total	100.0

Source: James H. Myers and William H. Reynolds, *Consumer Behavior and Marketing Management* (Boston: Houghton Mifflin Co., 1967, pp. 210–211). The original sources are: (1) W. L. Warner and P. S. Lunt, *The Social Life of a Modern Community* (New Haven: Yale University Press), *1941* and (2) A. B. Hollingshead and F. C. Reglich, *Social Class and Mental Illness* (New York: John Wiley & Sons), *1958.*

dence, and life style, all of which are closely correlated with occupation. In other words, occupation as a predicting variable serves the same purposes as segmentation within social class according to income. For example, notice that most of Warner's classes (Table 4–1) are defined by occupation. Think of the difference between the life styles and product preferences of a college professor, on the one hand, and a professional truck driver, on the other. Their incomes are likely to be similar. The professor is likely to have a relatively larger investment in his house, will spend relatively more on services, and will be more likely to drive a compact car. The truck driver, by contrast, is more likely to own an expensive automobile, to spend more on major appliances, and to spend more time and money watching spectator sports. It was found, for example, that skilled workers were frequent purchasers of the first color television sets. Their life style made the color television set relatively more important to them than it was to, say, doctors and lawyers with higher incomes (ability to buy), but with less interest in the product itself.

Personality. So far, the discussion has concentrated on socioeconomic factors related to predispositions toward products, services, media, and messages. Another set of factors of significance as a source of predispositions is personality characteristics. It is often asserted that there are certain personality characteristics that make persons more or less susceptible to persuasion. The validity of this assertion will be examined in detail in Chapter 7, where the discussion considers such factors as intelligence, aggressiveness, self-confidence, and psychoneurotic tendencies as they influence response. There the emphasis will be upon predispositions toward persuasive communication in general. Here, let us briefly consider the ways in which personality characteristics may influence predispositions toward products and services.

While attempts to segment the market on the basis of personality type have not always been successful, there are certain areas where the marketing strategy can be fruitfully directed toward individuals with certain personality characteristics. Tucker and Painter report finding a significant relationship between the use of headache remedies and the personality traits of submissiveness and emotional instability. They also found a positive relationship between acceptance of new fashions and the traits of sociability and ascendancy.[11]

Evans analyzed personality data (obtained by administering the Edwards Personal Preference Schedule) for Ford and Chevrolet owners. He noted that there were popular stereotypes which saw Ford owners as "independent, impulsive, masculine, alert to change, and self-confident,

---

[11]W. T. Tucker and John H. Painter, "Personality and Product Use," *Journal of Applied Psychology,* 45 (October 1961), pp. 325–29.

while Chevrolet owners are conservative, thrifty, prestige-conscious, less masculine, and seeking to avoid extremes."[12] His analysis found only one factor, dominance (with Ford owners showing the greater need for dominance), that differed to a significant extent for these two groups, and he concluded that personality was not a significant determinant of brand choice. Other analysts have disputed Evans' findings on the basis of certain technical weakness in the data. They argue that certain brands do in fact appeal to particular personality types. Claycamp found certain personality dimensions which had a weak but significant ability to discriminate between customers of commercial banks and those of savings and loan associations.[13]

This discussion of personality factors as sources of predispositions may be concluded with the observation that there is not significant support for the notion that personality factors account for differences in individuals' choices of brands and products, although there is some weak evidence in that direction and the notion does have some intuitive appeal. For most purchases, personality characteristics are probably not as important as socioeconomic and demographic characteristics in determining predispositions. A discussion of the influence of personality factors on persuasibility and response to influence attempts, that is, on predispositions toward persuasive communications in general, is postponed until Chapter 7.

Our discussion of sources of predispositions has shown us that cultural, social, and personal characteristics all provide sources of predispositions. The influence of each set of factors must be carefully analyzed in developing marketing communication strategies. We shall next consider how predispositions operate to influence exposure, perception, and retention.

THE SELECTIVE PROCESSES

With some understanding of the nature and sources of predispositions, we can now develop an analysis of their influence upon response to persuasive communication. Our earlier analogy of predispositions as the "mechanisms" within the "black box" that generate responses to stimuli (messages) is again called upon. We now consider how those mechanisms operate to influence response to communication.

---

[12]Franklin B. Evans, Psychological and Objective Factors in the Prediction of Brand Choice: Ford Versus Chevrolet," *Journal of Business*, 32 (October 1959), pp. 340–69.

[13]Henry J. Claycamp, "Characteristics of Owners of Thrift Deposits in Commercial Banks and Savings and Loan Associations," *Journal of Marketing Research*, 2 (May 1965), pp. 163–70.

Selective Exposure

The number of marketing messages potentially available to any individual during typical day or week is virtually limitless. Just think of all the advertising in newspapers, magazines, television programs, radio stations, and other media that it would be possible for you to expose yourself to in a typical day. Certainly, you would run out of time long before you ran out of messages! If you were an industrial purchasing agent, there would be no end to the number of salesmen that would visit you if you wished to spend all of your time talking with salesmen. And marketing communication constitutes only one form of communication. There are political messages, public service messages, educational messages, entertainment messages, and many other kinds. There are family members, neighbors, friends, casual acquaintances, and a huge variety of other sources to be contended with. It is virtually impossible for the individual to admit and respond to all of the stimuli available in the environment. In the interest of rationality and cognitive economy, he must shut out certain messages, in order to attend to the rest.

It is a well-documented fact that people actively select those messages they will expose themselves to and pay attention to. Exposure and attention are really separate events, although we will treat them together here. The potential customer selects the advertising media to which he will be exposed. He subscribes to magazines and newspapers, or buys them at a newsstand. He turns on the television set to watch certain programs. In this sense, he "selectively exposes" himself to marketing communication. Furthermore, having purchased an issue of a magazine, or tuned to a television program, he may not see (admit to his consciousness) a particular commercial message. He is more likely to see an advertisement if he is interested in the product, or if the method by which the message is presented is appealing to him in some way. With personal selling, the opportunity to "tune out" the message is greater in that the prospective customer can refuse an interview. But once the presentation begins, it is much harder for the prospect to "tune out."

Some findings from communication research are of interest here. In general, the research shows a preference for information which supports and is consistent with existing predispositions. For example, people are more likely to pay attention to political speeches by those whom they support and agree with. Of particular interest for marketing strategy is the finding that persons who had recently bought a new automobile were significantly more likely to expose themselves to advertising for the brand *after* the purchase.[14] Over time, people tend to organize their

---

[14]D. Ehrlich, I. Guttman, P. Schonbach, and J. Mills, "Post-Decision Exposure to Relevant Information," *Journal of Abnormal and Social Psychology*, 54 (January 1957), pp. 98–102.

environment in a way that insures *de facto* selectivity. Whether they consciously will it or not, people do form associations and establish certain patterns of behavior that result in selective exposure.[15] They tend to expose themselves to information that is useful to them. What information is required, useful, or of interest is determined by such factors as education, social class, and past history of exposure on the issue. For all of these reasons, predispositions are an active influence on exposure to marketing communication.

Selective Perception

Assuming that the individual is exposed, and pays attention, to the message, the next step in the communication process involves the influence of predispositions upon perception and interpretation of the message. One source defines perception as "the way things look to us, or the way they sound, feel, taste, or smell. . . . perception also involves, to some degree, an understanding awareness, a 'meaning' or a 'recognition' of these objects."[16] Another defines perception as the "process by which people select, organize and interpret sensory stimulation into a meaningful and coherent picture of the world."[17] In other words, perception is what goes on inside the black box, the interpretation of stimuli to select responses. Perception goes beyond sensation and the "objective" data presented by the senses, to provide meaning to those data. Perhaps the definition of perception which best captures this idea is to see perception as the comparison of a sensation with categories of meaning stored in the individual's "central control unit," a definition suggested by Engel, Kollat, and Blackwell.[18]

The notion of a comparison process is helpful in understanding selective perception. The individual selects from the messages he receives those meanings which are most consistent with predispositions. He does this through adding and subtracting meanings, by interpreting and distorting the message to fit existing categories of meaning provided by culture, social influences, and individual characteristics.

Attitude Change and Believability. Maloney has examined several forms of selective perception and considered their influence on response to advertising. He contends that in the decoding process messages interact with predispositions to produce one of two categories of response: belief or disbelief. According to his view, any message which conflicts

[15]David O. Sears and Jonathan L. Freedman, "Selective Exposure to Information: A Critical Review," *Public Opinion Quarterly*, 31 (Summer 1967), pp. 194–213.
[16]Floyd H. Allport, *Theories of Perception and the Concept of Structure* (New York: John Wiley & Sons, Inc., 1955), p. 14.
[17]Berelson and Steiner, *op. cit.*, p. 88.
[18]*Op. cit.*, p. 79.

with existing predispositions, any message with the intent of changing attitudes, is not believable. For example, if an individual prefers brand A, an advertisement claiming that brand B is superior will not be believed. The person will not change his attitudes toward the brands. The ad may, however, challenge him to try brand B, and it may offer some incentive for doing so. Thus, the customer may buy brand B on a trial basis. As a result of his experience with the product, the individual may shift his preference to brand B. In this case, behavior change would have preceded attitude change. This argument therefore holds that persuasion, by definition, involves communication of messages that will not be believed because they conflict with existing predispositions.[19]

While this argument has merit, it probably overstates the strength and permanence of predispositions. Certainly, an individual can be persuaded to change his attitudes as the result of communication. For example, a persuasive marketing message may point out certain product features that will enhance it in the potential buyer's mind. It may make the product seem more appealing. But the basic point of Maloney's article is valid: advertising does not have to be "believable" to be effective. It may simply challenge the receiver to try something new, to give consideration to other alternatives. The article by Maloney also raises a fundamental question, still unresolved in social psychology: whether attitude change must precede behavior change. This argument will be considered more thoroughly when we consider the setting of communication objectives, in Chapter 12.

Misperception. In order to bring a message into consonance with predispositions, the receiver may modify the message in two ways. He may *misindex* the message, or he may *distort* it. Misindexing occurs when the receiver's comparison process places the message in the wrong category, or concentrates on the "wrong" components of the message, from the source's viewpoint. For example, the receiver of a marketing communication may get "hung up" on the attention devices used in the ad—as when attractive women are used to advertise after-shave lotion. Or, advertising which imitates competitors may be categorized as, in fact, an advertisement for the competitor's product. Or, attempts to apply a "blanket brand" across several distinct product categories may cause confusion. For example, it is reported that advertising for RCA Communications, Inc., the international communications subsidiary of the Radio Corporation of America, was misindexed in two ways. When people saw advertising for "RCA" they thought of the company as a manufacturer of television receivers, and when they saw a message about international

[19]John C. Maloney, "Is Advertising Believability Really Important?," *Journal of Marketing*, 27 (October 1963), pp. 1–8.

telegrams, they thought about Western Union, RCA Communications' major competitor.[20]

Message distortion involves modifying the message to make it consistent with predispositions. This is done in two ways: leveling and sharpening. Leveling involves overlooking certain features of the message that conflict with predispositions, while heightening the importance of these elements of the message that are consistent with predispositions. Sharpening involves adding elements to the message in order to make it fit predispositions, resulting in a meaning different from that intended by the source. Whether these processes occur in the "perception" stage or in the "retention" stage is a moot point. Certainly, the same kind of modifications can be expected to occur in both stages. This problem simply highlights the fact that we are talking about a process continuous from exposure to attention to perception to retention. To recognize that leveling and sharpening occur is more important than to resolve any minor controversy about whether they occur during perception or retention. The net effect on response to communication will be the same, and that is the whole point of this analysis.

Reminder advertising can be effective because of the operation of sharpening. A simple cue, such as a brand name, may be all that is required to have the receiver recall certain related product cues. The leveling process can often be countered by using effective presentation devices and by emphasizing those elements of the message that are likely to be leveled. Sales presentations often concentrate upon particular features of the product being offered that are likely to be overlooked or misperceived by the prospect.

Further selection occurs once the message has been "stored" in the receiver's memory. Having already passed through several filters, the message will now begin to erode and will continue to be modified. These further modifications will continue to tend toward a balance with existing predispositions. Pleasurable elements will be remembered while painful and unpleasant elements will be forgotten.

Selective Retention

One can think of memory as a file with limited capacity. Some criteria have to be set for determining what information is stored and what is tossed out. The basic criterion is the value of the information to the user. If the potential buyer is actively seeking information about a class of product, prior to making a purchase, he will be much more likely to

[20]Reported in the *RCA Communications, Inc.*, case prepared at the Harvard Business School by Derek Newton, Research Assistant, under the direction of Professor Martin V. Marshall. This case is identified by number 10M48 in the Intercollegiate Case Clearing House bibliography.

remember information about this product once he has been exposed to it. If certain products or services are of importance to him, if they represent a hobby or a leisure time interest, he is much more likely to retain large amounts of detailed information. The baseball fan can remember hundreds of players' names, their club affiliations, the scores of significant games back through history, famous plays and so on. The car buff knows the details of all of the models available, engine specifications, competition records, and such.

The amount and quality of retention is an important consideration for the marketing communication strategist, since purchasing decisions often lag behind exposure to marketing communication. The consumer will have to recall what he has heard about the product to be purchased, and this recall depends upon what was retained.

Cognitive Dissonance

The theory of cognitive dissonance illustrates the operation of each of the selective processes.[21] This theory has received widespread attention in marketing circles in recent years. Another name for cognitive dissonance is "postdecision doubt." In the marketing case, it applies after the customer has purchased a product. Forced to choose one among several attractive alternatives, each of which has certain positive features and certain negative features, the individual must choose the "best" alternative, the one with the most positive features and the least negative features.

Think about the problem of buying an automobile. Each make and model has certain attractive features and certain disadvantages. Once the choice is made, the decision maker is likely to experience doubts about his purchase. He will think about the positive features of the alternatives *not* chosen and he will become increasingly aware of the negative features of the alternative that was chosen. These are "dissonant cognitions."[22] Another relevant cognition in this process is the concept of self; having made a decision with negative consequences may be "dissonant" with one's self concept.

Dissonance Reduction. To reduce the dissonance resulting from a choice among alternatives, the individual may take several steps. First, he may seek additional information that is consistent with his decision. This fact explains the finding by Ehrlich and others, cited above, that

[21]Leon A. Festinger, A *Theory of Cognitive Dissonance* (New York: Harper & Row, 1957). A good brief summary of the theory is Festinger's "The Theory of Cognitive Dissonance," in Wilbur Schramm, *The Science of Human Communication* (New York: Basic Books, Inc., 1963), pp. 17–27.

[22]A "cognition" is an attitude toward, perception of, or belief about one's environment.

new car purchasers are much more likely to be exposed to advertising for the brand of automobile purchased. At the same time, he may actively avoid, and if exposed attempt to refute, information favorable to alternatives not chosen. Or, he may seek the opinions of the other people that will be consistent with his action. Thus, the car buyer is likely to "show off" his new car to friends and neighbors, because their comments are expected to be supportive and even envious, reinforcing the purchaser's self concept. They will, perhaps only through politeness and friendliness and not because of expert knowledge, generate favorable messages.

Another way of reducing dissonance is for the person experiencing dissonance to generate opinions and messages favorable to his choice and then to seek active agreement with them. Thus, the new car buyer may make positive statements about his purchase to friends and neighbors, and ask them to agree with him. There is some evidence that this does in fact occur, and such evidence had led to the suggestion that automobile manufacturers and dealers should consider developing small brochures to give the new car buyers who in turn can give them to their friends, thus helping the seller perform the selling function.[23]

In the process of trying to reconcile these dissonant cognitions, the receiver engages in the three selective processes, exposure, perception, and retention. He becomes a very active seeker and transmitter of information as he tries to modify his predispositions to make them consistent with this action that he has taken. (Note that the action itself cannot be reversed, except at great cost.) He will interpret and retain what he hears to support his decision. Cognitive dissonance can be a significant factor to consider in developing the marketing communication strategy. The information needs of those who have bought the product, and the desirability of having them generate favorable word-of-mouth communication, may suggest the value of aiming communications at those who have recently purchased the product as well as at potential purchasers.

The point of this analysis has been that the marketing communication strategist must have a sound understanding of the predispositions of the market toward his company, its products, and its resellers. These predispositions include needs for the product, attitudes toward the company and the brand, and levels of awareness and information about the product offering. Receivers will respond to marketing communication in terms of the meanings they assign to these messages, and the messages will be attended to, perceived, and retained to the extent that they are consistent with existing predispositions.

[23]Gerald D. Bell, "The Automobile Buyer After the Purchase," *Journal of Marketing*, 31 (July 1967), pp. 12–16.

In order to implement his concern for predispositions, the marketing manager must obtain specific information about them as the basis for his planning activity. We turn briefly to a consideration of the measurement problem and then conclude this chapter with some final suggestions for using predispositions as the basis for marketing communication strategy.

MEASURING PREDISPOSITIONS

It was noted earlier that predispositions are inferred from the observation of responses to stimuli—they cannot be measured directly. In making inferential measurements of predispositions, two kinds of responses are available—overt behavior and verbal behavior, or opinions. Opinions may be defined simply as responses to questions whereas attitudes are action tendencies toward some person, object, or other entity.

As these definitions imply, an opinion expressed in response to a question may differ from the attitude held by the individual, for at least two reasons. First, the attitude may not be socially acceptable; second, the individual may not be completely aware of his own predispositions. That is, they may be held at a semiconscious or subconscious level.

Ultimately, the marketer is interested in attitudes, predispositions to act in the form of purchase of his product, but the attitude cannot be measured directly. The field of study concerned with measuring predispositions is usually called "attitude measurement," a title which is inappropriate, as explained above. The classic report of research on communication, however, carries the subtitle "Psychological Studies of Opinion Change," and the authors point out in their introduction that they have been able to measure only opinions.[24]

The problems of measuring predispositions involve several technical issues that are beyond the scope of this text. Our objective at this stage is simply to suggest the nature of those problems and the factors that must be considered in developing effective measurements.

Surveys. The most common method of measuring predispositions is to conduct a survey among the relevant population. Before the researcher can select his sample, he needs from the marketing manager a good statement of the relevant market segment and research objectives that are consistent with the marketing problems to be solved. Careful attention must be devoted to sample size and the method of sample selection. The value of the information to be collected is a function of how it is to be used; this "value in use" provides a guideline for how much to spend

[24]Carl I. Hovland, Irving L. Janis, and Harold H. Kelley, *Communication and Persuasion: Psychological Studies of Opinion Change* (New Haven: Yale University Press, 1953), pp. 1–18.

for the research and this, in turn, places limits on the size of the sample to be used.[25]

Considerations of cost and kind of information required will lead to choices among several methods of gathering information, including mailed questionnaires, personal interviews (with or without questionnaires or interview guides), telephone, and so on. These are very important questions, especially when there is some possibility that other people (such as a spouse, a child, or a colleague) will influence the response to the question if they are present. Related problems here include the very careful training of interviewers, if they are used, to minimize biases which they may introduce.

Questionnaire Design. Questionnaire design involves several complex issues, but several guidelines can be offered. The questions asked will to a large extent determine the quality of the information received. They should not suggest an answer desired by the questioner. It should be possible for the respondent to answer the question without undue reliance on memory of obscure events or digging deeply into the subconscious. An example of the latter is a question such as "Why do you feel as you do about mouth-care products?" Response categories, when provided, should be mutually exclusive and collectively exhaustive of all possible responses. Sensitive information, as in questions about income, should be placed last in the question sequence.

Small-Group Interviews. Small-group discussions have become quite popular in recent years as the basis for identifying important attitudes toward products and toward advertising. The free give-and-take, with minimum guidance by a trained discussion leader, can develop significant insights into predispositions and the meanings assigned to products and symbols. Group sessions provide good qualitative information but are unreliable sources of quantitative data.

Respondent Ability. It is easy to overestimate the ability of the respondent to answer certain questions. In a desire to be helpful, respondents may fabricate and guess at answers when the questions are difficult to answer accurately. Rationalization may result which significantly obscures their true predispositions. For example, most people would find it very difficult to provide an accurate answer to the apparently simple question, "Why did you buy your last automobile?" "Because we needed a new one and the old one was worn out" represents a rationalized answer that significantly avoids the basic question, "Why *that* car?" The investigator wishing to measure predispositions

[25]For a good discussion of problems of sample selection, see A. W. Frey, *Marketing Handbook*, 2nd ed. (New York: Ronald Press Company, 1965), Section 24, pp. 33–42, a section written by Professor Charles S. Mayer.

must be very humble about his ability to accurately measure these eva-sive characteristics. People are often unaware of their basic predisposi-tions or unwilling to admit their existence.

Attitude Scaling. The most common approaches to measurement of predispositions involve various attitude-scaling devices. There are many technical problems in the design and interpretation of these scales, but they can be a very useful source of information on predispositions. The most common approach to attitude measurement is to present the respondents with a series of dichotomies on interval scales, and to ask them to state their attitudes toward a particular object by placing a mark on the scale. An example of an attitude scale is presented in Figure 4–3. Several alternative scaling procedures are available, includ-

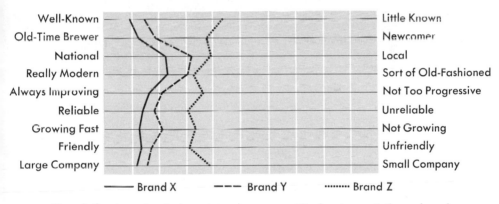

───── Brand X   ─ ─ ─ Brand Y   ·········· Brand Z

Fig. 4–3. A scale designed to measure attitudes toward three brewing companies. Each curve profiles the attitude toward a particular brewer. (Source: W. A. Mindak, *op. cit.*, p. 31. Courtesy of *Journal Marketing*, official quarterly publication of the American Marketing Association.)

ing the equal-appearing-intervals method developed by Thurstone,[26] the method of summated ratings developed by Likert,[27] the semantic differ-ential,[28] and Guttman's scaling techniques.[29]

Projective Techniques. Another common approach to attitude meas-urement is the use of so-called "projective" techniques involving the presentation of an ambiguous stimulus. Among the best known of these

[26]L. I. Thurstone, *The Measurement of Social Attitudes* (Chicago: University of Chicago Press, 1929).

[27]R. A. Likert, "A Technique for the Measurement of Attitudes," *Archives of Psy-chology,* No. 140 (1937), pp. 1–55.

[28]C. E. Osgood, G. J. Suci, and P. H. Tannenbaum, *The Measurement of Mean-ing,* (Urbana: University of Illinois Press, 1957).

[29]E. A. Suchman and Louis Guttman, "A Solution to the Problem of Question Bias," *Public Opinion Quarterly,* 11 (Fall 1947), pp. 445–55.

techniques is the Thematic Apperception Test, involving the presentation of pictures and then asking the respondent to write a story about what is going on in the picture. Word association tests are common, as are sentence completion tests. Attitudes toward companies, or the "corporate image," are frequently measured by asking people to develop a list of adjectives to describe the company.

One of the most famous studies using projective techniques was Haire's "shopping list" study of attitudes toward convenience foods. In this study, fifty women were presented with shopping list I (see Figure 4–4), while fifty women were presented with shopping list II. As you

LIST I	LIST II
Pound and a half of hamburger	Pound and a half of hamburger
2 loaves Wonder Bread	2 loaves Wonder Bread
bunch carrots	bunch carrots
1 can Rumford's Baking Powder	1 can Rumford's Baking Powder
Nescafé Instant Coffee	1 lb. Maxwell House coffee (drip grind)
2 cans Del Monte Peaches	2 cans Del Monte Peaches
5 lbs. potatoes	5 lbs. potatoes

Fig. 4–4. Research instruments used in the Shopping List Study.

see, the two lists are identical except for the coffee items. Respondents were asked to describe the hypothetical woman who went shopping with each list. The findings were interesting:

Forty-eight percent of the people described the woman who bought Nescafé (instant) as lazy; 4 percent described the woman who bought Maxwell House (Regular) as lazy . . .; 48 percent of the people described the woman who bought Nescafé as failing to plan household purchases and schedules well; 12 percent described the woman who bought Maxwell House this way.[30]

The differences between the two kinds of coffee (regular and instant) were strong enough to produce significantly different responses. Respondents were willing to draw inferences from this small distinction and to generalize several other characteristics of the purchaser. By using this projective technique, Haire was able to uncover some strong attitudes toward instant, convenience foods.

Note that this study was conducted quite some time ago. A more recent study found that these differences between attitudes toward the two shoppers had disappeared.[31]

The foregoing comments have been intended only to suggest broadly the major considerations in the measurement of attitudes. Because

[30]Mason Haire, "Projective Techniques in Marketing Research," *Journal of Marketing,* 14 (April 1950), pp. 649–52 at p. 650.

[31]Frederick E. Webster, Jr., and Frederick von Pechmann, "A Replication of the 'Shopping List' Study," *Jou ~al of Marketing,* 34 (July 1970), pp. 61–63.

respondents will tend to give opinions which they regard as being socially acceptable and desired by the interviewer, it is often necessary to develop complex techniques for inferring true attitudes more accurately. In the process of developing these techniques, there is the risk that the researcher will outsmart himself as well and develop questioning techniques that are so complex that he does not know what he has measured when he is finished.

It should be noted in conclusion that prior measures of predispositions are necessary in order to evaluate marketing communication programs which have the objective of changing awareness and attitudes. If the objectives of the program are stated as communication objectives, that is, changes in predispositions, rather than changes in sales, then both "before" and "after" measures of attitudes are necessary in order to evaluate the relative success of the campaign. When he is using data on predispositions as the basis for his planning and evaluation, the marketing manager should recognize that this is a complex measurement problem and he should seek out the best technical help available to him.[32]

Summary

The key importance of market predispositions as the basis for effective marketing communication strategy has been repeatedly stressed in this chapter. We have considered how predispositions define both the problems and the opportunities facing the firm as it plans communication programs. The sources of predispositions were defined, and their influences on the processes of selective exposure and attention, selective perception, and selective retention were illustrated. Problems of measuring predispositions were seen to center around the fact that opinions must often be measured in order to infer attitudes.

Several guidelines for developing effective marketing communication strategy emerge from this analysis. First, it supports the concept of the active audience and makes it increasingly evident that the marketer's ability to manipulate the audience to his ends through persuasive communication is quite limited. This view suggests that it is more appropriate to consider modifying strategy to fit the audience than to think about using strategy to change the audience. Second, there is increased confirmation for the basic notion of the marketing concept that the marketing strategy must be responsive to customer needs. It follows from this recognition that marketing communication will be more effective if

[32]Additional and more detailed information about attitude measurement is available from several sources. The following are suggested: Lee Adler and Irving Crespi (eds.), *Attitude Research at Sea* (Chicago: American Marketing Association, 1966); Osgood, Suci, and Tannenbaum, *op. cit.;* (New York: Basic Books, Inc., 1966).

it first arouses in the prospective customer awareness of such needs, so that he is subsequently more interested in and more responsive to (that is, more favorably predisposed toward) the message. Third, the need for carefully collected and analyzed information about predispositions has been stressed.

Knowing that culture, social influences, and personal factors all provide sources of predispositions, the marketing communication strategist must consider the nature of his particular product and the ways in which each of these sources of predispositions is likely to influence his communication. From this consideration, he can begin to define the stages in the buying decision process for his product and the ways in which various kinds and sources of information are likely to be useful to the buyer at each stage.

5

Groups as Sources of Predispositions

There are very few aspects of buyer behavior that are not influenced directly or indirectly by other people. In Chapter 4, it was said that social influences, along with culture and individual characteristics, provide a major source of predispositions. In this chapter, the ways in which groups influence response to communication will be made much more explicit. Group processes will be explored and implications for the development of marketing strategy will be suggested.

The distinction made here between groups as sources of predispositions and groups as networks is a rather artificial distinction that needs some explanation. Groups can exert their influence upon members in at least two distinct ways: through the *normative* function of providing standards of behavior and through the *informative* function of providing networks for the transmission of information. The processes involved in these two functions are quite distinct, and their influences on response to marketing communication also differ. The normative function of groups is explored in this chapter, while the informative function is reserved for the next chapter. The reader should be aware that this distinction between group functions is made to help our analysis and to permit the development of certain concepts. In actual practice, both functions are performed simultaneously by the same groups and the net impact on the behavior of members is the result of both these processes. Furthermore, this is not the only distinction one can make among group processes. Another distinction one often hears, for example, is a distinction between "task" functions (problem solving) and "process" functions, those relating to the maintenance of the group itself.

KINDS OF GROUPS

A "group" can be defined in several ways. In the last chapter, we used a continuum of "intimacy" for ranking groups from the most intimate, the family, to the least intimate, the reference group. At this point, let us recognize that there are three distinct kinds of groups, and proceed to examine them in greater detail.

Primary Groups

The essential elements of the primary group are contained in the definition by Homans:

. . . a number of persons who communicate with one another often over a span of time, and who are few enough so that each person is able to communicate with all the others, not at secondhand, through other people, but face-to-face.[1]

Each element of this definition is important but the face-to-face character of the primary group and its small size should be stressed. Within this definition fall such identifiable groups as neighborhoods, families, work groups, small communities, gangs, and social clubs. Primary groups can be analyzed in terms of the persons who comprise them and their behavior, which has three elements: activities, interaction, and sentiment.[2] The relevant behavior is "social behavior," behavior characterized by the fact that it is rewarded or punished by another person.[3]

Given all these definitional conditions, it follows that primary groups exert influence on their members. Still unresolved, however, is the *extent* to which these groups influence the opinions, attitudes, and actions of their members, and the processes by which this influence is exerted.

Group Functions. The ability of primary groups to influence their members derives from the fact that these groups provide benefits, instrumental values, to their members. Primary groups can fulfill basic needs for love and affection, for companionship and self-esteem, for knowledge and resources to cope with problems of living. These are the benefits of

---

[1]George C. Homans, *The Human Group* (New York: Harcourt, Brace, Jovanovich, Inc., 1950), p. 1.

[2]*Ibid.*, p. 43.

[3]George C. Homans, *Social Behavior: Its Elementary Forms* (New York: Harcourt, Brace, Jovanovich, Inc., 1961), pp. 2–3.

conformity.[4] Primary groups can also provide a social reality for their members, meanings for situations that do not explain themselves.[5] This function takes us back to our discussion of selective perception, where the point was made that objective reality takes on meaning only when it is filtered through predispositions and established categories of meaning. An example of the function of providing social reality would be the influence of battle veterans upon the attitudes toward combat of soldiers who have recently joined a front-line fighting unit. The group helps the individual interpret his new experience, by providing categories of meaning where they did not exist before because of the newness of the experience for the individual.

From these two functions, problem solving and providing social reality, several relevant concepts for analysis of primary groups can be developed. People are brought together in groups by common interests, needs, and problems. When people begin to develop a collective approach to solving common problems and begin to "see" things in the same way, they create a "shared way of looking at things or of doing them."[6] These shared ways of looking at things or of doing them are called *norms*.

Maintenance and Norms. In order to perform well its two basic functions of solving common problems and providing common meanings for ambiguous experience, the group must maintain itself. Thus, group maintenance becomes a third function of the group and an end in itself. Group maintenance is achieved by enforcing the norms (standards or values) of the group. A norm is an idea about expected behavior under specified circumstances.[7] Norms develop to guide behavior in several areas, and apply to physical action and verbal behavior. These norms become strongly held predispositions for individual members of the group to the extent that the individual values his membership in the group and finds it satisfying. The greater the benefits of conformity, as perceived by the individual, the more he will tend to adopt and defend the opinions and attitudes of the group as his own.

Individuals may be forced by the environment to come into frequent, close, face-to-face contact with one another. This is true of work groups, for example, where the job brings these people into face-to-face contact, although this affiliation is not the basic purpose for the formation of the primary group. It has been found that persons forced to interact in close proximity will tend to develop norms. In other cases, it may be the shar-

[4]Elihu Katz and Paul F. Lazarsfeld, *Personal Influence* (New York: Free Press of Glencoe, 1955), p. 50.

[5]*Ibid.*, pp. 53–56.

[6]*Ibid.*, p. 57.

[7]Homans, *The Human Group*, pp. 121–25.

ing of values and norms that brings the group together in the first place, as in the case of religious groups. Thus, norms may proceed or follow interaction.

The primary group rewards or punishes members' behavior according to whether it is consistent with the norms. Punishment may take the form of sanctions such as the removal of certain privileges, demotion in status within the group, the withholding of affection, or even physical punishment. Punishment may also take the form of rejection from the group, on a temporary or permanent basis.

Status and Role. To facilitate the performance of the basic functions of goal attainment or problem solving, group maintenance, and providing social reality, the group assigns *statuses* and *roles* to members. A status is a position within the structure of the group with certain specified duties and privileges. A *role* is the performance of those duties and privileges by an individual who is assigned the status. A status takes on meaning in relation to other statuses, while a role takes on meaning through its performance. The concepts of status and role are inseparable.[8] In the following discussion, the term "role" will be used to include both role and status. Thus, we can define a role as the social position occupied by an individual, including the goals of that position and the behavioral repertoire appropriate to that position and to the attainment of those goals.

Social positions have associated with them a set of *role expectations*. "Role expectations are bi-dimensional: for every role expectation of other there is a reciprocal role expectation of self. The organized actions of the person, directed toward fulfilling these role expectations, comprise the role."[9]

In the process of introducing our first kind of group, the primary group, we have found it necessary to introduce several concepts relating to group structure and dynamics. These are the elements and processes that define a primary group. Having defined these elements, the importance of primary groups in determining members' responses to marketing communication, by providing predispositions, is almost self-evident. Primary groups define the behavior that is appropriate in the social situation of the individual. Thus, the communication, if it is to be successful, must recommend attitudes or behavior which are consistent with primary group norms and attitudes. It must be consistent with the role of the individual.

[8]*Ibid.*, p. 11.
[9]Theodore R. Sarbin, "Role Theory," in Gardner Lindzey (ed.), *Handbook of Social Psychology* (Reading, Mass.: Addison-Wesley, Inc., 1954), 1, pp. 223–58, at p. 255.

To take an example which shows the negative influence of primary group affiliations, imagine a family (primary group) in which husband and wife (roles) commonly share responsibility for major financial decisions (norm). An insurance salesman trying to get a commitment from the husband in the absence of the wife would be violating a norm. Or, to show a positive influence, there are many direct selling strategies for housewares, beauty aids, and so on that use the "home party" approach. A hostess is given a small gift by the salesman (or, more likely, saleswoman) for bringing her friends together in the relaxed atmosphere of her home where the salesman demonstrates his wares and distributes order forms. It is announced to the group that the hostess will receive additional gifts of merchandise in proportion to the amount of purchases made by the group. A norm of wanting to help one's friends or not wanting to appear "cheap" could create pressure for purchase. On the other hand, some members of the group might feel that this approach violates an implicit group norm against exploitation of the group affiliation by other group members, thus causing a negative reaction to the salesman.

Formal Organizations

Formal organizations can be distinguished from primary groups on the basis of complexity and size. In the formal organization, it may be impossible for all members to have frequent, face-to-face interaction. Examples of formal organizations include business firms, especially large corporations; hospitals, universities, and similar institutions; churches; and governments. Another distinguishing characteristic of a formal organization is its "formality"; it is likely to have an explicitly stated set of goals, policies, rules, and regulations that define appropriate behavior (roles) for its members. Also, it will probably have a hierarchy, a pyramidal arrangement of power and authority relationships. Finally, formal organizations are distinct from primary groups in that the survival of the formal organization is usually not dependent upon the identity of its members. Its permanence is not a function of particular leaders or members (although there are some notable exceptions to this statement.)[10]

Role Relationships. Formal organizations are often referred to as "complex" organizations, and it is this complexity which distinguishes the formal organization. Several roles may be involved in a decision. Buying decisions, for example, can become very complex with several different people (each with a different perspective), a different set of needs, and a different set of evaluation criteria being involved in the

[10]Bernard Berelson and Gary A. Steiner, *Human Behavior: An Inventory of Scientific Findings* (New York: Harcourt, Brace, Jovanovich, Inc., 1964), p. 364.

decision. As targets for marketing communication, formal organizations require very careful analysis.

There is a strong possibility of role conflict in formal organizations, especially when the problems being dealt with have some unique characteristics, thus making existing policies and procedures somewhat insufficient for the task. Role conflict among members of the organization can create severe difficulties for the communicator trying to get agreement to a course of action. The communicator must also be very sensitive to procedures relating to the conduct of organizational affairs, especially for the transmission and processing of information.

As Sources of Goals. As sources of predispositions, formal organizations define the problems and the goals that are to be achieved by the individual decision maker. Thus, the person occupying a position in the organizational hierarchy is trying to achieve the goals of that position and to follow the procedures assigned to it. Along with this set of requirements, however, he is simultaneously trying to find satisfactions for his own needs. He is seeking ways in which he can accomplish organizational purpose while satisfying his own desires. Any buyer in a formal organization is motivated by both his own needs and the needs of the organization.

An individual occupying a particular position in the organization will have a particular set of role expectations both for his own behavior and for how other people should behave toward him. These role expectations can come from several sources, including his superior, a formal organization manual, his observation of earlier incumbents' behavior in that position, his self concept, and a stereotype of how people who hold that position should behave. (A "stereotype" is simply a role consensus shared by a group.) For example, a purchasing agent may behave according to his perception of how professional purchasing agents are expected to behave.

Reference Groups

The most general concept of "group" is that of the reference group. There is considerable disagreement about the scope of this concept and its appropriate usage. Some define the concept quite narrowly while others define it in very general terms. According to one source, a reference group is "any interacting aggregation of people that influences an individual's attitudes or behavior."[11] Another defines it as the groups in

[11]James F. Engel, David T. Kollat, and Roger D. Blackwell, *Consumer Behavior* (New York: Holt, Rinehart and Winston, Inc., 1968), p. 309.

[12]Alberta Engvall Siegel and Sidney Siegel, "Reference Groups, Membership Groups and Attitude Change," in Dorwin Cartwright and Alvin Zander, *Group Dynamics: Research and Theory,* second ed. (New York: Harper & Row, 1960), pp. 232–40, at p. 232.

which an individual aspires to attain or to maintain membership.[12] Both of these definitions are unnecessarily restrictive since the former requires interaction and the latter requires membership aspirations. If these are required conditions, then the concept of primary group or formal organization probably fits.

Types. It is more productive to consider a reference group (if we are to make it a concept distinct from other group concepts) as any group to which the individual refers for standards of behavior (either positive or negative), a collection of people against which an individual evaluates his own status and behavior.[13] Within this definition, one can identify four distinct kinds of reference groups:

1. *Membership groups,* including—
    a. primary groups, as defined above.
    b. groups in which face-to face interaction is absent, but in which membership is held—e.g., a political party or a professional association where membership does not require attending the meetings.
2. *Social roles*—groups or categories of people who share something in common (sex, education, marital status, occupation). This includes the concept of subculture.
3. *Anticipatory groups*—groups in which one aspires to membership, as in the case of the law school student who identifies with lawyers or as in the case of social class.
4. *Negative, dissociative groups*—groups which have negative valence for the individual, groups with which he wishes not to be identified.

Kinds of Reference Group Influence. Reference groups influence behavior by providing *aspiration levels.* They help the individual set goals and measure the extent to which he has attained those goals. Thus they provide a source of both satisfaction and frustration. Second, they provide standards for the *kinds of behavior* that are appropriate for goal attainment. This is the normative function, completely analogous to the function of norms as discussed above in the case of primary groups.[14] Thus reference groups provide two kinds of predispositions, goals and norms. Notice that the concept of reference group has been defined broadly enough to include both primary groups and formal organizations—as long as they are used by the individual to evaluate his own behavior.

Obviously, the individual may have several reference groups at a given point in time. For example, he may be occupying several social

[13]Francis S. Bourne, "Group Influences in Marketing," in Ralph L. Day, *Marketing Models: Quantitative and Behavioral* (Scranton, Pa.: International Textbook Co., 1964), pp. 63–79, at p. 63.

[14]*Ibid.,* pp. 63–64.

roles (each can be thought of as a reference group) simultaneously, such as father, student, liberal, Democrat, and salesman. Each may be exerting some influence on his behavior by providing predispositions. It is not unreasonable to expect some of these roles, and their expectations, to be in conflict. It is not always easy to define which reference groups are most likely to be operative and relevant for an individual in a specific situation. The usefulness of the reference group concept in marketing communication is further limited by the fact that reference groups are very hard to identify for specific individuals or market segments. Finally, there is always the question of how "operational" a given reference group identification may be. For example, media may be lacking to efficiently reach the relevant reference group.

There are many interesting uses of reference group influence in marketing communication, however. For example, the use of well-known athletes has been for a long time an effective appeal to young male consumers. This may take the form of a specific person such as Willie Mays, or it may be a team such as the United States Olympic team or the San Francisco Giants, or it may be a general concept such as "champions." Testimony of successful application of a new product by industry leaders is an often-used appeal in industrial advertising.

Bourne has suggested that reference group influence is likely to be more important as a source of predispositions when the following conditions are found. First, the product must be "conspicuous"; ownership and use must be noticeable to others. Second, when there is relatively little information about the product, reference group influence is likely to be more potent.

The more accurate the communicator's estimates of the reference groups likely to be considered by the individual, the more likely it is that the communicator can successfully identify those norms and goals that will be influential in determining the individual's response. To the extent that a reference group provides values, attitudes, and other predispositions relating to the purchase and use of the product or service being sold, the influence of the group is a significant factor to consider in developing the appeal to be used in the communication.

ROLES IN BUYING GROUPS

The importance of each of the foregoing groups will be illustrated with specific examples. Before moving to those illustrations, however, it is necessary to identify the various roles in a buying group as these relate to the determination of the need for a purchased product or service, the acquisition and processing of information to help make the buying decision, the actual purchase behavior, and the consumption of the product or service. Having said that, we have defined the four roles in a buying group: influencers, deciders, purchasers, and users.

These roles can be found, by definition, only in primary groups and formal organizations. Reference groups are *not* decision-making groups. This is an important distinction. A group is a relevant unit of analysis for the receiving and processing of information (as provided by communication) only if it is a decision-making group. Thus, we can talk about primary groups and formal organizations as *targets* for marketing communications. We cannot talk about reference groups as targets for communication, since their function is limited to providing standards for evaluation of information by the individuals and is not to make decisions.

Influencers

Influencers are persons in the buying group who inform, persuade, or establish certain requirements to be met in the buying decision. There is considerable evidence that teenage children exert significant influence on the family decision to buy a new automobile, for example. Influencers may provide information relating to the purchase, including the identification of alternative courses of action. They may also exert their influence by setting up certain criteria that have to be met by the purchase decision. In industrial buying organizations, the chief financial executive may influence the decision by establishing upper limits on the amount of money to be spent. Similarly, the office manager may set down certain criteria for product performance.

Identification of key decision influencers is a major step in identifying targets for promotional activity, and in defining the kind of information required for a favorable buying decision. For many purchases, especially where there is a trial stage, the potential customer may actively seek out the opinions and advice of other people. In order to achieve the sale in these situations, the marketer must frequently communicate with these decision influencers. In buying baby care products, for example, a mother might solicit the advice of her physician or her pharmacist. The seller of baby care products must therefore identify the role played by the decision influencer although, in this case, he actually lies outside of the decision-making group.

Deciders

Final responsibility and authority for buying decisions often reside with a single individual in the buying group. For example, in the family automobile purchase, the final decision may rest with the wife who, although influenced by the opinions of her children and husband, has the strongest opinions about desirable automobile features and whose opinions are somehow regarded as more "legitimate" than those of the others. In the industrial buying group, it may be the production manager who has the final say on the purchase of raw materials and equipment.

In the purchase of prescription drugs, the physician is the decider. He makes the decision on the basis of his diagnosis and his knowledge, and renders it as an expert, persuading by the authority of his knowledge. Recognizing the importance of the physician in this decision, pharmaceutical manufacturers have extensive forces of detailmen to keep the medical profession informed of new pharmaceuticals. Notice that the analysis of group influences on the purchase of pharmaceuticals requires a special definition of the buying group: the patient, the physician, the pharmacist. Each of these persons has a role to play in the purchase, and needs to be accounted for in planning the marketing communication strategy. Notice that it is a primary group in that they have face-to-face communication and their relationship tends to be a recurring one.

Purchasers

Responsibility for actual purchase usually resides in a single individual. In formal organizations, responsibility for buying action is usually assigned to the position of buyer or purchasing agent. This person may have virtually no influence on the decision and may not be responsible for the decision himself. Rather, he simply attends to the administrative problems involved in executing the purchase order. While this may not be a fair description of the activities of the professional purchasing manager in many firms, it is true that, in most buying organizations, ultimate responsibility for the purchase decision does not reside with the purchasing agent.

In the family buying group, the wife and mother is most often the "purchasing agent." She makes more-or-less routine trips to a shopping area according to a shopping schedule. Because of the repetitive nature of this task, she tends to develop shopping habits and preferences for certain stores and vendors, so she does not have to decide each time where to shop. On the other hand, she tries to get current information about the "state of the market," where the special sales are going on, what the current prices of frequently purchased items are, and where new products may be for sale. Although somebody else may have decided what to buy, she still can decide where to buy and how much to pay. Similar responsibility is often placed on the industrial purchasing agent. The influencers and deciders establish specifications which the purchase must meet, but leave it up to the purchaser to pick a source and negotiate the actual purchase. The children may ask for Sugar Frosted Flakes but mother decides to buy it at the A & P. The production manager may decide to use a particular grade of cutting oil, but the purchasing agent decides which vendor to buy it from.

Users

Finally, the person who actually uses and consumes the product may or may not have had anything to do with the purchase decision or the actual purchase. In the purchase of paint for industrial uses, for example, the person who applies the paint to the product in the manufacturing process probably has relatively little to do with the purchase decision. He may establish certain minimum requirements, such that the paint not have objectionable or toxic odors (he may state this requirement through his local union officials). But the important buying influencers are likely to be a production foreman, or perhaps a customer relations manager who exerts pressure on the purchasing agent to buy paint from one of the company's customers who also happens to be in the paint business.

An interesting case where the user is not involved in any aspects of the buying decision itself is the case of the purchase of pet foods. Here the user exerts a major influence on the repurchase decision. When the cat won't eat the cat food, another brand is tried next time. In general, users exert their major influence on the decision process by evaluating the product after it has been purchased, or during a trial period, and reporting the results of that evaluation back to the purchaser or the decider. A secretary may evaluate a typewriter, for example, and report her opinions to the office manager, who makes a decision which he passes on to the purchasing agent. A mother may ask her children if they like the new soup she served them.

In order to attain the ultimate purpose of marketing communication— a satisfied customer—the strategist must identify each of the persons involved in the buying decision process, the role they play, the information they require, and the best way to reach them with this information. For some (such as buyers), simple awareness may be a sufficient communication objective (so that the purchasing agent knows where to buy the product decided upon by the laboratory manager). For others, communication must go beyond awareness to the development of favorable attitudes, as in advertising automobiles to young men in the family who will exert major pressures on their fathers' next automobile purchase. In other cases, the communication objective must be to get actual buying action, as in retail store advertising designed to generate store traffic. Finally, marketing communication may have the objective of providing the user with information that will help him evaluate the product in a favorable way. An automobile salesman will point out positive features of an automobile's performance during a test ride, for example.

The point of this discussion is that there are multiple buying influences, with each role applying different criteria (predispositions and norms) and requiring different information. Whenever the buying decision is made in a group context, we have a very complex target for marketing communication effort.

GROUPS AS TARGETS FOR COMMUNICATION

Having identified the several roles, often occupied by different persons, within the buying group, we can now examine the operation of three major groups that serve as targets for communication effort: the family, industrial buying organizations, and subcultures or "ethnic" markets. There are, of course, many other kinds of groups one could identify as targets for communication effort including friends and neighbors, industries, communities, and so on. Each of these three groups will be examined in a way which highlights the influence of predispositions and the importance of considering group variables in designing the communication strategy.

The Family

The family exerts a major influence on the response to marketing communication because it is a consuming unit. The development of the family creates the need for certain products and services, and these needs are a major category of predispositions defining opportunities for the communicator. Characteristics of the family that provide good measures of its potential responsiveness to messages for specific products include the age and occupation of the head of household, number of children, family income, and so on. The family life cycle is a useful way of analyzing the development of the family, as explained in the previous chapter.

In addition, the family is a major source of values for each individual member of the family. Attitudes toward certain products take shape within the context of the family and the parents become a significant influence (positive or negative) upon the development of the attitudes of the children. Communication strategists must be extremely sensitive to the influence of family values when communicating with individual members of the family. Advertising messages aimed at young children and teenagers must be acceptable to the parents or else the parents may interfere with the transmission of the message.

Many products are sold to and consumed by families and not individuals. Automobiles and major appliances are often, but not always, used by the entire family, as opposed to each individual having his own. Certain foods and health and beauty aids are used by the family. The Gillette Company introduced "Right Guard" deodorant several years ago as a product for men. It was soon discovered, however, that all members of the family were using the product because the aerosol can permitted sanitary use by several people. As a result, the advertising strategy shifted away from the use of male-oriented appeals in male-oriented media and toward such general appeals as "Hey! Who's got my 'Right Guard?'" and "Don't leave your family defenseless!" in general-appeal media such as situation comedies on television.

The family serves as a mediating influence between the larger cultural pressures upon the individual and the individual himself. The family interprets society's values to the individual and may significantly alter the manner in which the larger social system influences the consumption habits and attitudes of the individual.[15] Most often this mediating function involves the parents' interpreting (and enforcing) society's values for the children, although the children may also take some responsibility for interpreting current values for the parents. It should be stressed also that the role of the family and the extent of its influence varies significantly from one subculture to another.

Many family buying decisions represent a compromise among divergent attitudes of the individual family members. The problem of preparing a menu suitable to all family members while preserving a little bit of creativity and convenience represents a complex purchasing problem for the mother. An advertisement which promises her a product that will permit application of her skills as a cook, convenience of preparation, and praises from her family will find a responsive listener in the kitchen.

In summary, family influence is likely to be very significant for products which are consumed by the family as a unit, and for products that represent a significant commitment of the family's scarce economic resources. Individual purchases are likely to be influenced by other members of the family where one member of the family feels or assumes a responsibility for interpreting society's values for the other members. For example, parents may protest their children's clothing and hair style preferences as being in bad taste, while the children try to explain to their parents that their preferences are a little out of date, or "square."

When the family is the relevant unit of analysis in planning communication strategy, care must be taken to identify which family members are most likely to exert the dominant influence in the purchase decision. Marketing communication may concentrate on the dominant individual, or may aim at several different individuals (mother, father, and children), each with a slightly different message. Insurance selling requires a careful analysis of the relative influence of husband and wife, for example, and the insurance agent must be able to tailor his presentation

[15]Engel, Kollat, and Blackwell, *op. cit.*, p. 327.

to fit the specific situation of needs and influence patterns within that family.

Industrial Buying Organizations

As targets for communication, industrial buying organizations represent a complex object for analysis. Industrial purchasing involves multiple decision influences. Seldom will one individual perform all of the roles involved in the buying group. Our definition of formal organizations emphasized the fact that these groups have procedures, hierarchies, goals, rules, and policies that define and constrain the responsibility and authority for action of individuals within the group.

Developing effective communication strategies for industrial markets usually requires analysis of the characteristic patterns of decision making in the firms that comprise the potential markets. Several characteristic patterns may exist within the segments that comprise the total market. For example, it may be necessary to classify and analyze potential industrial customers according to their industry affiliation, their size (in terms of number of employees or total sales), or location. In a heterogeneous industrial market, firms are likely to exhibit wide differences in predispositions toward certain product features. For example, the market for protective coatings consists of some firms that buy on the basis of lowest applied cost while others are looking for such product features as durability, gloss, fireproofness, or coloration.

Reciprocal Buying. A major problem in determining communication strategy in industrial markets is to understand the nature and extent of reciprocal buying arrangements. In some industries, it is standard operating practice to buy only from firms that are also customers. This practice is most likely to be found in industries where there are relatively small differences in product quality among competing firms and where the products or services being sold are used by a wide variety of customers. Such industries include petroleum, rubber, chemicals, and transportation.[16] Predispositions toward reciprocity are a major factor to consider in approaching an industrial buying organization.

Reciprocity illustrates one kind of predisposition of importance in analyzing industrial buying organizations, that is attitudes toward the conduct of the buyer-seller relationship itself. In addition to reciprocity, several other factors must be considered, including expectations about the amount of technical knowledge possessed by sales representatives, the amount of entertaining (there are likely to be norms for both the minimum and the maximum amount), and characteristic methods of

---

[16]For an evaluation of these practices, see Dean S. Ammer, "Realistic Reciprocity," *Harvard Business Review,* 40 (January–February 1962), pp. 116–24.

negotiating and bidding. These provide a set of norms, a set of expectations about how the buyer and the seller are to perform their roles and behave toward one another.

Needs and Goals. The other category of predispositions to be considered in analyzing buying organizations is the set of needs and goals relating to purchase of the product itself. What things does this company value? What problems does it try to solve through purchasing products and services? These needs and goals define a set of criteria that will be used in evaluating alternative product offerings from potential vendors. The criteria in turn specify the kind of information which the marketing communication strategy of the seller must provide. For example, dairy firms evaluate equipment used in the pasteurization and packaging of milk in terms of the ease of cleaning that equipment when the day's work has been completed. The equipment salesman must provide convincing evidence that the equipment can be cleaned thoroughly and easily. In general, needs and goals can be translated into requirements for product quality and performance, service, delivery, and price in the offering of the vendor. The goals of the firm will define its needs for these various elements of the product offering. Therefore, in approaching an industrial customer, the marketing communicator must make it the first order of business to identify the specific goals and needs that will motivate the customer's interest in the product and define his attitudes toward it.

As in the case of primary groups, formal organizations have needs and goals, norms, and values, that must be defined and analyzed if one is to make accurate predictions about organizational response to communication.[17]

Subcultures: The Afro-American Market

A subculture is one kind of reference group. It provides a point of view, a set of standards, for evaluating one's own behavior and attitudes. As earlier noted, reference groups can perform the functions of creating aspiration levels and providing standards of behavior. The rapidly growing Afro-American market is probably the most significant subculture for consideration by many marketing communication strategists in analyzing their markets. The fundamental question is whether to treat the Afro-American market as a separate market.

Population and Income. A few facts about the Afro-American market are in order. There are an estimated 21.6 million black people in the United States and they are believed to spend approximately $30 billion

[17]Frederick E. Webster, Jr., "Modeling the Industrial Buying Process," *Journal of Marketing Research*, 2 (November 1965), pp. 370–76.

annually. In 1965, median income for nonwhite families was $3,396, compared to $6,299 for whites. While 23 percent of white families had incomes of over $10,000, the same was true for only 7.4 percent of non-white families. At the other end of the scale, 44.7 percent of nonwhite families had incomes of less than $3,000 compared with only 23 percent of white families. The black population is growing at a much faster rate than the white population, with a birth rate of 26.5 per thousand compared to 17.5 for whites. Between 1960 and 1966, the black population increased 14.2 percent compared to 8.6 percent for the whites. In the same time period, the number of black youths aged 14 to 17 increased 40 percent compared with 26 percent for their white counterparts.[18] Finally, it should be noted that the black population tends to concentrate in metropolitan areas and, still further, within the center city. The Afro-American market can thus be described as urban, young, with below-average income, and large and growing. But is it truly a distinct market?

A Distinct Market? The unequal status of the black man in American society is a fact that it has become increasingly difficult to deny, especially because that status is changing, albeit slowly. One of the principal areas of inequality has been housing. It is discrimination in housing that forces the black man into the ghettos of center city and, at the same time, brings him into closer contact with the black subculture. Forced housing concentration is only one of many ways in which the choices available to the Afro-American consumer are constrained. The result is that he spends more on the things that he *can* buy, and in those areas where he has more freedom of choice.

The mass media have played an important part in communicating to the Afro-American an awareness of, and a desire for, a better standard of living. This has been called "the revolution of rising expectations"; its effect has been increased desire for identity and recognition, increased desire for self-respect and for the respect of others, for self-improvement and for bettering the conditions within which one's family lives. This newly aroused set of expectations has been expressed constructively in the rise of "black capitalism" and the development of job training programs, for example, and it has been expressed destructively in the violence of the ghetto riots in New York, Detroit, and other cities.

In purchasing behavior, these predispositions express themselves in the purchase of products which permit self-expression and identity, which help the individual satisfy his desires for status and recognition. Thus, it has been found that Afro-Americans account for 25 percent of all the Scotch whiskey consumed in the United States, and that they

[18]"Why the Negro Market Counts," *Business Week*, September 2, 1967, p. 64.

regard Scotch as a high-status drink.[19] It has also been found that Afro-Americans are significantly more interested in fashion and tend to be style leaders. Several studies have revealed that the Afro-American is more brand conscious and brand loyal. A study by *Ebony* magazine has found that blacks "consistently will buy the brands that are nationally advertised, the ones that have the prestige connotation and the brands about which they can feel pretty sure."[20]

The existence of brand loyalty for products with status connotations is consistent with an earlier observation about reference group influence, viz., that reference group influence is likely to be strongest where the product is "conspicuous." For the Afro-American market, which does more entertaining in the home and tends to spend a larger portion of its income on food, liquor, home furnishings, and personal care items, more products are likely to be consumed "conspicuously" than in the case of the white family that does less entertaining in the home.

This suggests that the answer to the question "Is there a distinct Afro-American market?" is "It depends upon the nature of the product." For products that have status connotations and that are consumed in a manner noticeable to other people, the answer is probably "yes." If the product permits self-expression, if it can help achieve self-identity, if it says something about the person using the product, then the attitudes of other relevant persons (i.e., members of the reference group) are likely to be a significant consideration.

Reference Groups for Blacks. Analyses of Afro-American markets published several years ago suggested that, for most blacks, upper-middle-class whites provided a significant reference group. It was suggested, in fact, that the black man who aspired to move up the ladder of social mobility would have negative attitudes toward black media and black-oriented advertising messages. It seemed that the Afro-American was trying to throw off his black identity; he didn't want to be like white people, he just wanted to be able to live like whites do.[21] Still later, it was suggested that the Afro-American market could be segmented according to whether middle-class whites or upper-class blacks represented the relevant reference group, although the evidence on this point is not complete.[22]

[19]Raymond A. Bauer, Scott M. Cunningham, and Lawrence H. Wortzel, "The Marketing Dilemma of Negroes," *Journal of Marketing,* 29 (July 1965), pp. 1–6.

[20]"The Negro Market," *Marketing Insights,* 2 (January 29, 1968), pp. 9–12, at p. 11.

[21]Henry Allen Bullock, "Consumer Motivations in Black and White—II," *Harvard Business Review,* 39 (July–August 1961), pp. 110–24.

[22]Raymond A. Bauer, "Negro Consumer Behavior," in Joseph W. Newman (ed.), *On Knowing the Consumer* (New York: John Wiley & Sons, Inc. 1966), pp. 161–65.

Most recent evidence suggests that the Afro-American market is increasingly a distinct market segment, with its own values and norms, although this is by no means true for all products. In general, the product distinctions made earlier still apply, with reference group influence being more or less important, depending upon the nature of the product. There does seem to be an increasing amount of solidarity within the Afro-American community. This is seen in the acceptance of the more moderate forms of "Black Power" as a political force, in the acceptance of the "black is beautiful" notion, and in the almost faddish acceptance of the "Afro" look in clothing and hair styles.[23] Increased awareness of race takes a wide variety of forms, including a major increase in interest in black media. Radio stations with distinct appeal to the black community have increased significantly in the 1960's, and several new magazine and newspaper ventures have been launched.[24]

Attitudes Toward Companies. There is also evidence that, in their buying decisions, Afro-Americans are increasingly sensitive to whether or not companies are doing something to improve the conditions facing black people. They expect large corporations to advertise in black-oriented media and to use black models in their advertising.[25]

All in all, it does appear that the Afro-American subculture is becoming more important as a reference group for the Afro-American market. These predispositions must be considered very carefully in developing a strategy for reaching the Afro-American market. Fortunately, this increased black self-consciousness has been accompanied by an increase in the availability of black media, making it possible to reach the Afro-American market more efficiently and more effectively. At the same time, one cannot simply assume that it makes sense for every firm to approach the Afro-American market as a separate market. Only if the product has status connotations or specific and distinct meanings for the Afro-American market should it be considered as a separate segment.

In the foregoing paragraphs, we have suggested how the concept of groups as sources of predispositions could be related to the planning of marketing communication strategies. We have considered the family as a primary group, the industrial firm as a formal organization, and the Afro-American market as a subculture, and, thus, a reference group. Other examples could have been used, such as neighborhood groups, hospitals, and the Jewish market. The purpose of this analysis has been to suggest the many ways in which groups can provide norms and values that influence response to communication.

[23]"Is There Really a Negro Market?," *Marketing Insights,* 2 (January 29, 1968), pp. 14–17.
[24]"Why the Negro Market Counts."
[25]"Is There Really a Negro Market?"

Before our discussion of groups as sources of predispositions is complete, we must finally consider the processes by which group norms influence response to communication. So far, the argument has been that when norms exist they do exert an influence. It remains to be shown *how* that influence is exerted.

GROUP NORMS AND RESISTANCE TO INFLUENCE

The importance of group norms as a mediating influence upon an individual's response to persuasive communication will be related here to several factors. These factors include the extent to which the individual values membership in the group, the "salience" or importance of that group for the individual in that situation, his social status within the group, and whether the communication itself highlights the group.

Many marketing communications, especially promotion for new products, advocate a change in the receiver's attitudes and behavior. Often these changes will be "evaluated" by one's friends and involve a change in a definition of acceptable behavior by one or more groups of importance for the individual. Something as simple as a change in one's brand of beer or cigarettes, or the purchase of the latest style in a sports jacket or trousers, may be the cause for much comment by one's friends. The sensitive individual will try to anticipate the reactions of his family, friends, and neighbors in deciding whether to purchase something new. Under what circumstances will group norms be an important influence upon the response of the individual?

Value of Group Membership

The extent to which an individual values his membership in a group is directly related to the degree of conformity to its norms that he exhibits. Thus, conformity is a measure of the individual's valuation of group membership. Research evidence suggests that persons who place the most value upon their membership within the group are least likely to be influenced by communication which they perceive to be in conflict with the norms of the group. The amount of opinion change produced by a "counter-norm" communication will be inversely proportional to the extent to which the individual values his membership in the group.[26]

Status

Next, let us consider the influence of status upon response to communication. One could argue that the person who has high status in a

---

[26]Carl I. Hovland, Irving L. Janis, and Harold H. Kelley, *Communication and Persuasion: Psychological Studies of Opinion Change* (New Haven: Yale University Press, 1953), pp. 139–44.

group has that position because other members of the group place high value upon that individual's belonging to the group. It would then seem logical to conclude that the person of high status would be freest to deviate from the group's norms without having sanctions imposed upon him. Research results fail to confirm this guess, however. On the contrary, it has been found that the most popular members of a group show the strongest conformity to group norms and the least amount of change in response to counter-norm communications.[27] It seems that individuals of high status behave as if their status depended upon their conformity, and not upon their contribution to the group. This finding suggests that a strategy of seeking out community leaders as targets for communications may be ineffective if the action being sought conflicts with group norms.

Salience

In a specific communication situation, the influence of group norms will depend upon the extent to which those norms are made explicit. Stated differently, conformity depends upon the existence of situational cues which evoke the relevant motives and norms. The extent to which an individual is aware of the group in a given situation can be referred to as the "salience" of the group. Logic suggests that the higher the degree of salience, the less effective will be communication that is contrary to group norms while, conversely, communication favorable to these predispositions will be more effective. This expected relationship has been confirmed by experimental findings.[28] For the planning of communication strategy, these findings seem to suggest that the communicator should attempt to give cues which heighten group salience when his communications are consistent with predispositions of the group and should avoid reference to group norms when they are contrary to the purpose of the communication. Furthermore, if the communication advocates a particular kind of behavior, that behavior should be appropriate to the individual's situation, as that situation is influenced by group memberships.

Cohesiveness

One other factor which seems to determine the effect of group norms upon the individual's response to communication is the degree of cohesiveness demonstrated by the group. Cohesiveness is a summary measure of the group's attraction for its members. Research evidence strongly supports the argument that the attractiveness of a group for its members is related to the amount of influence which the group exerts on their

[27]*Ibid.*, pp. 149–54.
[28]*Ibid.*, pp. 157–59.

behavior. Greater conformity in attitudes and behavior is found in more cohesive groups.[29]

The validity of this finding for consumer behavior has been confirmed in a study by Stafford. He found that cohesiveness *by itself* did not have a noticeable influence upon the brand loyalty of individual members. However, Stafford found that the leader of the (informal) group does exert an influence on brand choice and that the amount of that influence is a function of cohesiveness. He concluded that "in more cohesive groups, the probability was much higher that the members would prefer the same brand as the group leader. Thus cohesiveness appeared to have its most important function in providing an agreeable environment in which informal leaders could effectively operate."[30] The greater the degree of loyalty to a given brand evidenced by the leader, the higher was the percentage of the group also becoming brand loyal and the higher was the probability that group members would prefer the same brand.

SUMMARY

The purpose of this chapter has been to examine the ways in which various kinds of groups influence their members' response to marketing communication. It has been suggested that the marketing communication strategist must carefully consider the structure of roles within the group, group norms, and the likelihood that group influences will be important in the purchase of his product or service. It was seen that the influence of the group depends upon the particular product or service being sold as well as the salience of the group for the individual in the specific situation.

It should be emphasized that this is only a modest beginning on showing the relevance of group theory for marketing communication strategy. There are hundreds of research findings on the functioning of small groups, formal organizations, and reference groups with potential relevance for understanding the processes by which marketing communications exert their influence. The purpose of this chapter has not been to provide a complete review, but rather to suggest the relevance of this body of knowledge for marketing communication strategy.

This chapter has emphasized the "normative" function of groups—that of providing aspiration levels and standards of behavior. Now, we turn to the other major function which groups perform for their members—the *informative* function.

[29]Leon Festinger, Stanley Schachter, and Kurt Back, *Social Pressures in Informal Groups* (Stanford, Calif.: Stanford University Press, 1950).

[30]James E. Stafford, "Effects of Group Influences on Consumer Brand Preferences," *Journal of Marketing Research*, 3 (February 1966), pp. 68–75, at p. 74.

6

Groups as Networks

In addition to their function of providing standards of behavior, groups also provide channels of communication, which carry information to their members. In the marketing context, people hear about products and services not only from the sellers but also from friends, neighbors, family members, fellow workers, and so on. How a person responds to a marketing communication will depend significantly upon what other people have told him about the product or service. These product-related conversations are usually referred to as "word-of-mouth advertising." We prefer not to call it "advertising," since this is a misnomer. Rather, we shall refer to it as "word-of-mouth communication."

The marketing communication strategist must be aware that these patterns of influence already exist within the public he is trying to persuade. He must identify and understand these processes. If he can clearly identify them, there is always the possibility of using them to his advantage, although there are significant difficulties in this strategy. On the other hand, if he ignores them or tries to get around them in some way, chances are the result will be a decrease in the effectiveness of his strategy, and even outright failure.

This chapter is devoted to developing an understanding of how word-of-mouth processes operate. We shall examine the elements of those processes, the nature of interpersonal communication, factors which contribute to the level of word-of-mouth activity, the concept of opinion leadership, and the use of word-of-mouth networks in strategy. We shall see that the nature of the product or service being sold and the stage in the product life cycle are significant determinants of the level and quality of word-of-mouth. We shall examine research findings on word-of-mouth pertaining to marketing, and assess its power in influencing response to marketing communication.

THE DYAD—PAIRS IN THE NETWORK

At the simplest level, communication requires at least one communicator (source) and one receiver. This is the simplest of all social units— the "dyad." A dyad is simply two people in interaction, and it is the two interacting parties taken together as a unit of analysis, not individually. Within the larger group, communication flows through the process of dyadic interaction; A talks to B, B talks to C, and so on. So, before we can discuss groups as networks, it is first necessary to have some understanding of dyadic interaction.

Much of the groundwork for developing an understanding of interpersonal interaction was laid in Chapter 4 in the discussion of the selective processes. The processes of selective attention, selective perception, and selective retention apply with equal validity when we are considering how people react to other people, as well as to information and communication. Persons tend to form associations with other persons whose interests, values, attitudes, and other predispositions are similar to their own. They tend to attribute to these friends predispositions similar to their own as well. That is, perceived similarity of predispositions is apt to be even greater than objective similarity.

Person Perception

The ways in which people perceive other people in their environment are very interesting to consider, for we do not regard other people with the same cold, hard-headed objective view that we use with inanimate objects. In particular, "person perception" is different from the perception of other objects in the environment because "the perceiver regards the (other person) as having the potential of representation and intentionality."[1] Both "representation" and "intentionality" in this quotation need some explanation, for they are at the heart of the unique nature of person perception.

We draw inferences about people from observation of their behavior. We do not describe their physical actions, but we describe behavior by inferring the reasons for their actions and the consequences of those actions. We assign meaning to behavior based upon the inferences that we make about the intentions of that other person, especially his inten-

[1]Renato Tagiuri and Luigi Petrullo (eds.), *Person Perception and Interpersonal Behavior* (Stanford, Calif.: Stanford University Press, 1958), p. x.

tions toward us. The natural tendency is to internalize and to personalize the behavior of other people in our environment. "Each observes that the other directs himself toward him; each can make known to the other that he is sensitive to the other's direction toward himself. These operations provide the 'mutually shared' field in interaction—the prerequisite for all true social processes."[2]

Likewise, we see other people's behavior as being caused by certain "representations" which they have, certain ways of viewing the world. The concept of *representation* is similar to the concept of *predisposition*. A "representation" is a way of perceiving the environment which we ascribe to the other people with whom we interact. We endow them with certain frames of reference or predispositions, and interpret their behavior in that light. In marketing, the notion of "assigning representations to the other person" is perhaps best seen in the salesman's "sizing up" of his prospect. Based upon what the salesman knows about the prospect, he makes certain inferences about how that prospect will respond to his presentation.

To appreciate the true complexity of dyadic interaction, it is necessary to realize that both members of the dyad perform both sender and receiver roles. Both engage in encoding and decoding. Both assign representations to the other and attribute to them certain intentions. A message directed toward one becomes feedback for the other. These concepts become particularly significant in analyzing personal selling, and the interaction between the salesman and his prospects. That analysis is postponed until Chapter 9, when we discuss the relative effectiveness of mass and personal communication. Here, our attention is directed to interaction between potential customers, targets for marketing communication.

Determinants of Interaction

As a general rule, people are most likely to engage in dyadic interaction, or word-of-mouth, with people who are like themselves. They are more likely to initiate conservations with, or to seek the opinions of, persons who are in situations similar enough to their own to make their experience relevant for the seeker's problem. For example, Feldman and Spencer report finding that new persons in a community seek advice about selection of a family physician from persons who have at least as many children as they do and from persons in the same general socioeconomic class.[3] This study and others have also found that physical prox-

[2]*Ibid.*, p. xi.
[3]Sidney P. Feldman and Merlin C. Spencer, "The Effect of Personal Influence in the Selection of Consumer Services," in Peter D. Bennett (ed.), *Marketing and Economic Development* (Chicago: American Marketing Association, 1965), pp. 440–52.

imity is important; people tend to seek advice from those who are nearby.

It has been found that the flows of information through a social network also tend to follow closely patterns of physical traffic flow and interaction. For example, the shape and physical dimensions of a residential area or an apartment building dictate the flow of people. These physical factors determine the pattern of "passive" (or unintentional) contacts among the residents. The passive contacts lead, however, to the development of friendships and frequent interaction. Persons in more accessible locations will be named more frequently as friends and conversation partners.[4] In a study of airconditioner ownership in Philadelphia row houses, Whyte found that ownership was significantly clustered. He explained this on the basis of such patterns of traffic and interaction.[5] Several studies have also confirmed that the family plays a major role in the flow of interpersonal communication.[6] Finally, information seekers tend to seek out persons who are perceived as being more qualified than themselves on the topic.[7]

In conclusion, the interaction dyad is likely to involve persons of similar age and social status, and it is also likely to involve family members (including those not living in the same household). Both physical and social proximity are important because they facilitate the flows necessary for interaction.

THE "GATEKEEPER" FUNCTION

If we consider a group as a network of linked dyads, pairs of receivers and senders linked to other pairs by one of the members of the dyad, we have identified the basic elements of the word-of-mouth processes. This view begs the question, however, "How does information come into the group?" The answer is obvious, but not so simple as one might think at first glance. Information comes into the group through particular group members. Often, the information comes through the network of another group. That is, a member of Group X may also be a member of Group Y and bring information to members of X from mem-

---

[4]Leon Festinger, Stanley Schachter, and Kurt Back, *Social Pressures in Informal Groups* (New York: Harper & Row, 1950) especially ch. 3, "The Spatial Ecology of Group Formation," pp. 33–59.

[5]William H. Whyte, Jr., "The Web of Word-of-Mouth," *Fortune,* 50 (November 1954), pp. 140 ff.

[6]Charles W. King and John O. Summers, "Dynamics of Interpersonal Communication: The Interaction Dyad," in Donald F. Cox (ed.), *Risk-Taking and Information Handling in Consumer Behavior* (Boston: Division of Research Graduate School of Business Administration, Harvard University, 1967), pp. 240–64.

[7]*Ibid.,* p. 261.

bers of Y. Certain individuals within each group seem to perform the unique function of being "gatekeepers" for the admission of information into the group. They perform the function of linking the group with the outside world.[8] They control the flow of information (and, sometimes, of people and material) into the group and have the power to determine which items will get to the group.

One of the best examples of a gatekeeper comes from the marketing area. The purchasing agent in the formal buying organization is a gatekeeper. He provides a close control over the flow of information, salesmen, and some materials into the organization. In many buying organizations, he has the authority to exercise rather complete control over the interaction of salesmen with people in the organization. If a salesman wishes to talk with a design engineer, for example, he will first have to get the formal permission of the purchasing agent.

In the family buying unit, the role of gatekeeper may be performed by any of the family members. Young children may provide the family with information about breakfast cereals, for example, because of their exposure to advertising on children's television programs.

In the case of professional groups, certain members may keep the group informed about important developments related to professional activities. A group of community doctors, for example, may rely upon those few colleagues who regularly attend national and regional medical association meetings and who have important professional contacts outside of the local community. These doctors would provide the gatekeeper function of bringing new information from outside into the group. Because of their position, these gatekeepers have the power to determine whether or not the information will reach other members of the group.

The concept of the gatekeeper is in many respects related to the concept of "opinion leader" to be discussed below. However, the gatekeeper function is a much more limited one of simply passing on information, whereas the opinion leader also exerts influence because of his status and because of "who he is" as well as the information he has at his disposal.

OPINION LEADERS AND THE "TWO-STEP FLOW"

In virtually any social system or community there are certain individuals who are looked up to and respected by others and whose opinions are sought out by and influential upon other persons in the community.

---

[8]Kurt Lewin, "Group Decision and Social Change," in Eleanor E. Maccoby, Theodore M. Newcomb, and Eugene L. Hartley (eds.), *Readings in Social Psychology*, 3rd ed. (New York: Holt, Rinehart & Winston, 1958), pp. 197–211.

These influence relationships can be found in such diverse areas as politics, fashions, reading habits, movie attendance, the patronage of restaurants, and the use of particular products. This commonsense notion finally entered into research on communication in a study of the 1940 Presidential campaign, but it entered in a way that was not quite so obvious. Since that time, the concept of the "opinion leader" has played a very important part in research on mass communication and in understanding flows of influence within social systems of various kinds. The results of this research have special significance for the marketing communication strategist.

Who Are the Opinion Leaders?

In this study of the 1940 Presidential election campaigns in the United States, Lazarsfeld, Berelson, and Gaudet found that the mass media exerted their primary influence upon "opinion leaders" who in turn influenced others by passing on what they had read and heard in the mass media. This hypothesis, which was more suggested than confirmed by the data from the study, was called "the two-step flow of communication."[9] Several subsequent studies attempted to confirm the existence of opinion leaders and the two-step flow. One of these, the so-called "Decatur study" (because it was conducted in Decatur, Illinois) has special significance for marketing because it studied the purchase of fashions, movie-going, and shopping for grocery products as well as public affairs issues.[10]

Methods of Identification. The question "Who are the opinion leaders?" cannot be answered without also noting how they were identified in the research studies. In the 1940 "People's Choice" study, opinion leaders were self-designated by their answers to two questions: "Have you recently tried to convince anyone of your political ideas?" and "Has anyone recently asked you for your advice on a political question?." Twenty-one percent of the sample answered "yes" to at least one of these questions, and were designated as opinion leaders.

The analysis revealed that the self-designated opinion leaders were more interested in the election, were fairly evenly distributed throughout social classes and occupations, and were very much like the people they influenced. It is significant that opinion leaders were not necessarily the most socially prominent or richest people in the community. Further-

[9]Paul F. Lazarsfeld, Bernard Berelson, and Hazel Gaudet, *The People's Choice,* 2nd ed. (New York: Columbia University Press, 1948), p. 151.

[10]Elihu Katz and Paul F. Lazarsfeld, *Personal Influence: The Part Played by People in the Flow of Mass Communications* (New York: Free Press of Glencoe, 1955).

more, these opinion leaders were found to be significantly more exposed to the mass media than were the followers.[11] The validity and reliability of these conclusions is subject to question, however, because of the "self-designating" feature of the research.

The Decatur study examined both the advisor and the advisee in the "opinion leadership" dyad. "Influentials," as opinion leaders were called in this study, were identified by asking a direct question: "Do you know anyone around here who keeps up with the news and whom you can trust to let you know what is really going on?" This question was followed by others designed to identify specific reasons for changing opinions over time. The direct question identified what were called "general influentials" (who had to have direct face-to-face contact with those who designated them in order to qualify). The other procedure identified "specific influentials." Finally, respondents were asked to identify their "everyday contacts" with the question: "When you hear something on the radio or read something in the newspapers, are you inclined to talk it over with someone before you make up your mind? If so, whom?" Analysis of the data was limited to respondents who provided an affirmative answer to all three sets of questions (136 out of 800, or 17 percent). This analysis revealed that general influentials were most likely to be outside of the family (51 percent); the specific influentials were intermediate (34 percent); and the everyday contacts were least likely to be outside of the family (15 percent).[12]

A self-designating procedure was also used to identify opinion leaders in the Decatur study. Precaution was taken, however, to confirm that women who designated themselves as opinion leaders had actually engaged in influence attempts. Among the procedures followed was to ask the self-designated opinion leader to identify the person she had attempted to influence. These people were then sought out and asked to confirm the influence attempt.[13]

Characteristics. It was found that opinion leaders come from all strata of the social hierarchy, that they tend to influence people who are pretty much like themselves, that they specialize in a particular area—such as fashions, or "marketing" (i.e., shopping), or movie-going—rather than being looked to for their opinions on a wide variety of matters. Furthermore, there is usually some objective basis for their position of opinion leadership. For example, the mother of a large family is more likely to be respected for her opinions about marketing. In another study of patterns of influence among doctors in a medical community, it was similarly found that the opinion leaders in pharmaceutical adoption were

[11]Lazarsfeld, Berelson, and Gaudet, *op. cit.*, pp. 50–51.
[12]Katz and Lazarsfeld, *op. cit.*, pp. 140–144.
[13]*Ibid.*, pp. 149–61.

better informed about new drugs and therefore better able to give advice. The fact that this information resulted from a significantly higher level of exposure to the mass media also confirmed the two-step flow hypothesis.[14]

Finally, both the Decatur study and an earlier study (referred to as the Rovere study[15]) found that opinion leaders could be classified as "cosmopolitan" or "local" in their influence. The "cosmopolitan" influentials were more concerned with the news outside of their community, had more exposure to nonlocal media, and had social contacts with other opinion leaders beyond the local community. The locals were the experts on local affairs, and had "local" communication habits, greater exposure to local media. In the Decatur study, the cosmopolitans were more influential in the areas of public affairs and fashion, while the locals were more influential in marketing and movie-going.[16] It should be noted that there is a close similarity between the notion of a gatekeeper and that of a cosmopolitan opinion leader who has contacts outside the local community and more exposure to nonlocal information sources, and brings this information into the local community.

Motives of the Communicator

For purposes of discussion, let us focus our attention upon the opinion leader as an initiator of the dyadic interaction. In other words, we shall assume that he volunteers his opinions as opposed to having the receiver solicit them. (In Chapter 7, we will consider information-seeking on the part of the receiver and will examine in detail factors associated with the level of information-seeking.) Various studies have examined the reasons why opinion leaders offer their advice. Arndt has summarized these studies and identified six classes of motives: (1) altruism; (2) instrumental; (3) ego-defense; (4) interest; (5) establishing cognitive clarity; and (6) reducing cognitive dissonance.[17]

The communicator may have the altruistic desire to share some information or special knowledge or point of view with his receiver on the assumption that the communication has some value for the receiver. Dichter presented evidence that 20 percent of the interactions he studied were motivated by a desire to help others.[18] In other cases, the

[14]Herbert Menzel and Elihu Katz, "Social Relations and Innovation in the Medical Profession," *Public Opinion Quarterly*, 19 (1955), pp. 337–52.

[15]Robert K. Merton, *Social Theory and Social Structure* (rev. ed.; New York: Free Press of Glencoe, Inc., 1957), pp. 392–95.

[16]Katz and Lazarsfeld, *op. cit.*, pp. 313–15.

[17]Johan Arndt, *Word of Mouth Advertising* (New York: Advertising Research Foundation, Inc., 1967), especially pp. 49–57.

[18]Ernest Dichter, "How Word-of-Mouth Advertising Works," *Harvard Business Review*, 44 (November–December 1966), pp. 147–66.

communicator will have some end objective in mind that motivates his activity, and the communication will be instrumental to that goal. The Rovere study, for example, found that local influentials developed networks of interpersonal relations because they needed support for business and political activities.[19]

Ego-defense and projection are a third set of motives for the opinion leader. Bad experience with a product may cause him to generate negative word-of-mouth about that product, to absolve himself from responsibility for the failure. Ego-involvement and interest provide a fourth set of possible motivations. Interest in a topic may provide sufficient reason to initiate conversations about it. This finding has been confirmed in the study of the 1940 Presidential campaigns, in the Decatur study, and in the Dichter study—where it was found that 33 percent of product-related conversations were motivated mainly by interest in the product.

Communicators may also be motivated by a desire to establish "cognitive clarity," to establish in their own minds the validity of a particular attitude or the reasons for a particular event. Talking these things through is often helpful in firming up one's own understanding. A related set of motivations is the reduction of cognitive dissonance. As reviewed in Chapter 4, one way of reducing cognitive dissonance is to obtain information favorable to one's actions and attitudes, even if one has to generate it himself. This information-seeking is especially likely to occur after a major purchase decision.

Determinants of Opinion Leaders' Effectiveness

Compared to commercial nonpersonal sources of communication (especially mass media), opinion leaders have been found to be much more effective in producing opinion change, although the mass media may be more effective in creating initial awareness. In comparison with the mass media, personal influence seems to be more effective: it is more credible; it is more flexible in countering resistance; it is often accompanied by some form of social control; and it can provide information of an evaluative nature.

Credibility. Opinion leaders are respected members of the community and are perceived as being trustworthy. While the mass media are often seen as being biased and having the specific intent of persuasion, opinion leaders are perceived as more objective and fair.

Flexibility. Flexibility is a common characteristic of all personal communication, in that the communicator gets immediate feedback and can alter his message to take into account specific attitudes and reactions of

[19]Merton, *op. cit.*

the receiver. Personal interaction permits the communicator to identify and counter the resistance and questions of the receiver.

Ability To Provide Negative and Psychosocial Information. Opinion leaders also have the advantage of being able to provide negative information, whereas the mass media are seen as presenting only the positive side of an argument—the side favorable to the communicator's objective. In the case of advertising, possible negative consequences of using the product are seldom presented, nor is there an opportunity to compare the positive and negative features of several brands of a product using only information from the mass advertising media. Because it is capable of supplying negative information, personal influence is likely to be more effective. In a related manner, personal information sources may also provide "psychosocial" information with which to evaluate the social and psychological consequences of using a product, such as the possible reaction of one's close friends. This kind of information cannot be provided by the mass media in any reliable way, but it may be a vital part of the purchase decision. These considerations are developed more fully in the next chapter.

Social Sanctions. Finally, opinion leaders have various forms of social control at their disposal which increase the probability that their opinions will be accepted by others. It was noted earlier that the distinction which has been made in Chapters 5 and 6 between groups as sources of norms and groups as networks was an artificial distinction for purposes of analysis. Because of their status and perhaps position of authority within the group or community, opinion leaders are able to give rewards and punishments for compliance with their viewpoints. These sanctions can range from affection and friendship to rejection from the group. Social pressure accompanies the transmission of information and leads to opinion change.

To conclude, opinion leaders are likely to have approximately the same socioeconomic characteristics as those they influence, although they are likely to be slightly better educated and better informed on the specific topics on which they are opinion leaders. They tend to specialize in their influence. The mass media exert their influence through the opinion leaders, who are much more exposed to the mass media and who tend to pass on what they read and hear to the followers. Information flows through the network by means of individual exchanges within dyads, with the receiver in one becoming the communicator in the next. Communicators are motivated by any of several factors, especially interest in the topic (or product), and tend to be more effective than mass media in producing opinion change.

Now the discussion will be expanded beyond the leader-follower dyad to consider the broader word-of-mouth process which spreads ideas throughout the social system.

THE WORD-OF-MOUTH PROCESS

Word-of-mouth is the process by which opinion leaders exert their influence. Many opinion leaders may be involved in the network as an idea spreads. It has been found that, although opinion leaders have significantly greater exposure to the mass media than do followers, personal sources of information are still most important for the opinion leaders themselves. That is, opinion leaders are the major source of information for other opinion leaders. This observation suggests that there is a hierarchy of opinion leaders, and there is much evidence that this is the case.[20]

Time is also a significant factor in the word-of-mouth process. The characteristics of opinion leaders and the functions which they perform change over time as the product (or, more generally, the idea that is being transmitted) becomes more fully accepted. Chapters 2 and 3 introduced the concept of the adoption process, a five-stage decision process consisting of awareness, interest, evaluation, trial, and adoption. It is helpful to look at the influence of word-of-mouth as the decision maker passes through each of these stages, over time. Also, it is enlightening to distinguish among individuals in terms of the relative earliness or lateness with which they come to accept a new idea or product. The diffusion of an innovation through a social system over time is the result of a series of individual decisions. Some individuals move from awareness through to adoption much more quickly than others; as more and more people complete this decision process, the innovation gains increased acceptance.

Diffusion

Diffusion is the process by which a new idea (or product) spreads through a social system (or market) over time. Adopters of a new product can be categorized according to the time at which they adopt the product.

Adopter Categories. A widely accepted set of categories has been presented by Rogers:

> *Innovators*—the first 2½ per cent to adopt a new product. The innovators are venturesome and eager to try new ideas. They tend to be oriented outside of the local community and cosmopolitan in their relationships.

[20]Arndt, *op. cit.*, pp. 33–36.

Early adopters—the next 13½ percent to adopt the product. They are respected, well-integrated into the local community, and much more likely to hold positions of responsibility in local organizations. They tend to be "solid" both financially and socially.

Early majority—the next 34 percent to adopt, bringing to fifty percent the adoption rate in the population. The early majority are deliberate and need evidence of successful adoption by others before they commit their own resources. Like the early adopters, the early majority are active and well-integrated in the local community, but they are not as likely to hold leadership positions.

Late majority—the next 34 percent to adopt. They tend to be skeptical about new things and need a long time before economic necessity and social pressure combine to force them to adopt. When public opinion clearly favors the innovation, they finally succumb. Financially, socially, and perhaps psychologically, the late majority cannot afford to take the risk of being innovative.

Laggards—the last 16 percent to adopt an innovation. The laggards are described as traditional in their orientation, suspicious of anything new, and actively resisting change. They tend to be family-oriented, withdrawn from the local community, lower-income, less educated, and older.

These generalizations summarize a very large number of research studies in rural sociology and related fields, and have been confirmed with several different populations including farmers, doctors, housewives, and business managers.[21] These definitions of adopter categories are based upon standard deviations around the mean adoption time as indicated in Figure 6-1.

Earlier adopters (innovators and early adopters) tend to be younger and better educated than later adopters (early majority, late majority, and laggards). In the case of farmers, they tend to have larger farms and more specialized operations. Earlier adopters have also been found to have higher incomes and to be more mobile, both physically (moving from place to place frequently) and socially and economically (career advancement).[22] Finally, earlier adopters tend to have slightly higher social status than later adopters.

Influence Processes. Each of the adopter categories influences the decision of the next, but in a slightly different manner. The innovators influence the early adopters by providing a demonstration of the innovation. The innovators tend to be social isolates, however, more oriented

[21]Everett M. Rogers, *Diffusion of Innovations* (New York: Free Press of Glencoe, Inc., 1962) pp. 148–92.

[22]*America's Tastemakers* (Princeton, N.J.: Opinion Research Corporation), Research Report No. 1 (April 1959) and No. 2 (July 1959).

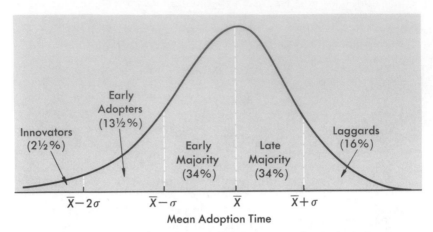

Fig. 6–1. Adopter categories defined by standard deviations around mean adoption time.

outside of the community than toward the local community. The innovators are watched, but at a distance.

The early adopters are most likely to be opinion leaders. They are respected and well integrated into the community, and have a maximum opportunity to exert influence through the social system. The early adopters thus make the innovation legitimate or socially acceptable, a function that could not be performed by the innovators because the latter are regarded as deviants. The early adopters thus add the dimension of social pressure to the diffusion process.

Once the early adopters come into the process, diffusion gains momentum quickly as all of the aspects of group functioning come into play—transfer of information, exertion of social pressures to conform, and the giving of social support for decisions once made. When the early majority adopt, reference group influence of neighbors and friends becomes strongly influential.

The ways in which the social network influences the rate of adoption have been well stated in the report of a study of the diffusion of a new pharmaceutical, given the fictional name of *gammanym* in this study:

At first the influence of these social networks operated only among the doctors who were integrated into the community of their colleagues through ties of a professional nature—as advisors or as discussion partners. Then it spread through the friendship network to doctors who were closely tied to the medical community through their friendship relations. By this time, social influence had also become operative in the more "open" parts of the social structure—i.e., among the relatively isolated doctors. Finally, there came a phase during which most of the remaining doctors introduced gammanym but did so in complete independence of the time at which their associates had introduced it: the network showed no effect.[23]

Because the late majority and the laggards are less well integrated into the social system, word-of-mouth is likely to be less important for them, although by this time the adopters outnumber the nonadopters and the probability of exposure to the innovation is much greater.

Word-of-mouth, or personal influence, takes on different functions for each of these adopter categories, and its importance is also a function of the stage of the adoption decision process. While the notion of the diffusion process is of general interest in developing marketing strategies, it is especially significant in the area of communication and can assist in the planning of advertising and personal selling strategies for introducing new products. In Chapter 9, these considerations will be related to the specific problem of allocating communication effort between advertising and personal selling.

Importance of Word-of-Mouth

The foregoing paragraphs have suggested several factors influencing the frequency and impact of word-of-mouth. These include the nature of the product, the adopter's decision stage, the adopter category, and the individual's position in the opinion leader–follower dyad.

Nature of Product. Some products are inherently more conducive to word-of-mouth than others. The products must have some "news value" and involvement for the individual. Automobiles, for example, seem to generate a large amount of word-of-mouth among young men. Women are more likely to talk about fashion. It is misleading to talk about the product by itself, however. Rather, it is the individual's interest in that product that is relevant. It is also difficult to generalize about those features of new products that are likely to generate interest and to be conducive to word-of-mouth. Perhaps uniqueness will stimulate word-of-mouth, as in the case of freeze-dried coffee, which was a sufficiently new concept to generate a large amount of interest. In the case of Maxim, General Foods' freeze-dried coffee it was found that word-of-mouth generated high levels of new product awareness in given areas even before the promotional program started in that area.

Individuals are more likely to seek out the opinions of others prior to purchasing a product when they see high risk in purchase of the product. Risk may be of two kinds—social risk, and the risk of poor product performance. Where there is high perceived social risk, that is, where the opinions of others are important in the purchase decision, word-of-

[23]James Coleman, Elihu Katz, and Herbert Menzel, "The Diffusion of an Innovation Among Physicians," *Sociometry*, 20 (December 1957). pp. 253–70, at p. 268.

mouth is likely to be more prevalent. Perceived risk is also a function of the self-confidence of the decision maker, however. The complex relationships among product characteristics, personality factors, and information handling are the subject for the next chapter.

Stage in the Adoption Process. The adopter's decision stage is a significant determinant of the use and effectiveness of word-of-mouth. Several studies have found that commercial sources and the mass media are the most frequent source of awareness of new products. As the individual moves closer to a decision, however, personal influence becomes increasingly important. Word-of mouth is likely to be most important at the evaluation stage of the decision process. It is more important than any other source of information at the evaluation stage, and it is more important at the evaluation stage than at any other stage.

The reasons for the greater effectiveness of word-of-mouth at the evaluation stage were suggested earlier. Word-of-mouth has the advantage of being able to provide negative information and information with which to evaluate the psychosocial consequences of a purchase decision. Personal sources, especially close and trusted friends who are like oneself and have recent experience with the product, are likely to be perceived as most qualified to help one evaluate the suitability of a product.

By Adopter Category. Word-of-mouth is likely to be more important for later adopter categories than is information from mass media. Earlier adopters are more exposed to the mass media and to technically more accurate sources of information as well as to other earlier adopters. Word-of-mouth is more likely to be a source of awareness information to later adopters, who are less exposed to the mass media.[24]

The drug study presents an interesting exception to this set of general findings, however. In the diffusion of gammanym it was found that the later adopters were less likely to be strongly influenced by word-of-mouth. The explanation offered was the doctors who adopted later tended to be less integrated into the local community and to adopt the innovation on a more individualistic basis. Although personal influence was still important for the less-integrated doctors, it was slower and weaker for them.[25]

Opinion leaders have more frequent and more numerous word-of-mouth interactions than do followers. Opinion leaders are more likely to receive as well as to send word-of-mouth messages. Several studies have found that opinion leaders are likely to seek advice from other opinion

[24]Arndt, *op. cit.*, pp. 40–41.

[25]James S. Coleman, Elihu Katz, and Herbert Menzel, *Medical Innovation: A Diffusion Study* (Indianapolis: Bobbs-Merrill Co., Inc., 1966), pp. 95–132.

leaders and this leads to the notion of a multistep flow, rather than a two-step flow, as indicated earlier.[26]

To summarize, word-of-mouth is likely to be most important for earlier adopters, especially at the evaluation stage. It is facilitated by the amount of interest generated by the product itself, and opinion leaders are much more active both as receivers and as senders of word-of-mouth messages.

Industrial Markets: A Special Case

None of the studies we have referred to dealt with the special case of industrial markets, where the customers are business firms. A little reflection suggests that word-of-mouth is likely to play a very minor role in industrial markets when compared with consumer goods markets. Several features of industrial markets would seem to create less need and opportunity for word-of-mouth and even some barriers.

Motivation for Word-of-Mouth. First, industrial marketers often provide more complete information about product performance to their customers than do consumer goods marketers. The greater reliance upon personal selling in industrial markets is one major reason for this. Manufacturers' salesmen are usually well trained and possess a high degree of product knowledge. Often the salesman alone is the expert on the product. Other users would simply not have the knowledge necessary to help a potential buyer evaluate the suitability of the product for his application. Thus, there would seem to be less need for word-of-mouth in industrial markets.

Second, economic and rational buying motives are likely to be more important than emotional or psychosocial buying motives in industrial markets. The unique ability of word-of-mouth to supply information with which to evaluate psychosocial consequences of purchases would seem to have less significance in industrial markets than in consumer markets.

Third, it can be argued that the long-term nature of most buyer-seller relationships in industrial markets places a special premium on the successful application of the seller's products by the buyer. In other words, industrial marketers probably show more concern than consumer goods marketers about the careful and proper application of their products. In order to avoid the negative consequences of misapplication, industrial salesmen may be careful to point out potential negative consequences of using their products, and the conditions under which use is inadvisable. There is some evidence that industrial salesmen are regarded both as more competent and as more trustworthy than other sources of informa-

[26]Arndt, *op. cit.*, pp. 33–36.

tion by industrial buyers. Again, these considerations suggest that there is less need for word-of-mouth in industrial than in consumer markets in the sense that word-of-mouth is often intended to supplement the information provided by marketers.

Fourth, there are many situations in which industrial buyers do not want to share information with other firms, especially actual or potential competitors. Often, the only relevant source of word-of-mouth in industrial markets would be other firms in the same industry—competitors. To the extent that a purchased product does give the firm some relative advantage, the buyer may not be anxious to share information about that product with other firms.

Carrying these ideas one step further, it is hard to imagine many situations in which a satisfied user would be motivated to initiate conversations about his purchases. In other words, initiative would seem to be overwhelmingly on the side of the receiver. Earlier, it was suggested that there were six classes of motives for communicators in the word-of-mouth dyad. Most of these would seem to have little applicability to the industrial buyer—altruism, establishment of cognitive clarity, reduction of dissonance, etc.[27]

Word-of-Mouth Less Important. An interview study of fifty industrial buyers (including purchasing agents, top management, engineers, and others) supported the foregoing arguments. It was found that discussion of new purchased products between buying decision makers in different companies is an infrequent occurrence. Over half of the respondents felt that the manufacturer's salesman was their most trusted source of information, as well as the most competent, on new products. (This finding is an interesting contradiction of the stereotype of the salesman as biased and pushy.) Information about the successful application of new products by other companies was of interest to the industrial buyer, but he relied upon the manufacturer's salesman to provide that information for him. In other words, if there is word-of-mouth in industrial markets, it flows through the manufacturer's salesman. He is a party to both dyads (satisfied user to salesman and salesman to potential customers) and arranges any direct interaction between the past and potential customers. This underscores the importance of the salesman in industrial marketing and suggests that excessive reliance upon word-of-mouth (unless stimulated by the salesman) would be wishful thinking.

By Adoption Stage. This study also found that trade journals were the most important source of information at the awareness stage, followed closely by manufacturers' salesmen and trade shows. At the inter-

[27]Frederick E. Webster, Jr., *Word-of-Mouth Communication and Opinion Leadership in Industrial Markets,* paper presented at the Educators' Conference of the American Marketing Association, Denver, August, 1968.

est stage, the salesman was by far the most important, as he was also at the trial stage. At the evaluation stage, engineers and buyers in other companies became an important source—confirming the general finding that personal sources are most important at the evaluation stage—but, in this case, they were less important than the manufacturers' salesmen. In summary, manufacturers' salesmen were the most important source at all stages except awareness, but engineers and buyers in other companies became important at the evaluation stage.

Are Some Firms Opinion Leaders? Finally, this study also attempted to identify opinion leaders in industrial markets. The general questions were "Are there opinion leaders in industrial markets?" and "If so, what are their characteristics?" Only in a couple of isolated cases was it possible to identify opinion leaders—firms in a given geographic area or industry that more or less consistently were among the first to adopt new products and who were watched by other firms. The major reasons for this finding seem to be the uniqueness of each company's buying situation and problems and the fact that a major "innovative" purchase (especially of new equipment) is likely to take the firm out of the market for several years, thus preventing its continued influence as an opinion leader on that class of product. In the isolated instances, however, there was enough uniformity in respondents' description of opinion leaders to be of interest, especially since these descriptions are consistent with the characteristics of earlier adopters cited earlier. Where opinion leader firms were thought to exist, they had the following characteristics: large size, within the same industry as followers, committed to new product development, growth company, financially successful, and progressive top management.[28]

USING WORD-OF-MOUTH IN STRATEGY

Even when one realizes the potential power of informal networks and word-of-mouth for generating acceptance of new products, it is not obvious how to proceed to use these networks as vehicles for accomplishing the communicator's objectives. There is an interesting flow of word-of-mouth among advertising people about the supposedly successful use of word-of-mouth in marketing campaigns, but little hard evidence is available to confirm or deny these instances. It is reported, for example, that a certain brand of scotch whiskey was successfully introduced by having very attractive young ladies visit cocktail lounges and ask for that brand in a manner designed to attract the attention of the patrons and the bartender.

[28]Frederick E. Webster, Jr., "Informal Communication in Industrial Markets," *Journal of Marketing Research,* 7 (May 1970), pp. 186–89.

Arndt reports several instances in which word-of-mouth supposedly influenced sales of automobiles, cigarettes, razor blades, and books.[29] When the Gillette Company introduced the new *Super* Blue Blade in 1960, promotional strategy was designed to generate favorable word-of-mouth by supplying opinion leaders with free samples of the blade and by careful use of advertising copy and media to generate news interest in the product.[30]

Problems of Implementation

The problems in developing favorable word-of-mouth can be placed in three categories. First, there is the problem of identifying the opinion leaders. Whereas the research we have cited offers some rather firm evidence of the characteristics of opinion leaders in general, it is not clear that these characteristics have much relevance for a specific product or service. For example, who would be the opinion leaders on coffee? It is often hard to eliminate anybody from consideration as a potential opinion leader and a target for promotional effort.

Second, the relationship between stimulus and response is not clear. The word-of-mouth process does not appear to be so "neat" and precise as to permit the marketer to specify exactly what kind of information is required by the opinion leaders in order to stimulate them to generate the desired messages. If we think of the opinion leader, or the whole informal communication network, as a mechanism that generates output in response to certain inputs, the relationship between outputs and inputs is not understood well enough to permit efficient use of the mechanism.

A third problem is that of measurement. Systematic, planned use of word-of-mouth would require the marketer to specify certain objectives and then to subsequently measure his success in attaining those objectives so that future use of word-of-mouth could be more efficient and effective. It would seem to be almost impossible to subsequently measure the extent to which an advertising campaign, for example, had been successful in stimulating opinion leaders to generate word-of-mouth that was favorable to the communicator's objectives. Even if a successful technique for determining causal relationships between the promotional campaign and any changes in awareness and attitudes attributable to word-of-mouth could be designed, the research methodology would probably be so complex as to be prohibitively expensive.

[29]Arndt, *op. cit.*, pp. 3–5.

[30]"Gillette Company" case study in Kenneth R. Davis, *Marketing Management,* (New York: Ronald Press Company, 1961), pp. 646–53.

Reasons for Trying

Despite these difficulties, the general notion of using word-of-mouth as a planned part of marketing communication strategy retains some inherent appeal. The greater credibility and effectiveness of personal sources is hard to overlook. Furthermore, word-of-mouth will be generated on many products whether or not the marketer does anything about it. It is to his advantage to at least consider ways in which word-of-mouth can be made effective and consistent with his objectives. Several specific suggestions can be made, although they add up to less than a complete program for planned use of word-of-mouth.

Some Guidelines

The general characteristics of opinion leaders should be kept in mind in any marketing communication program and as much specific definition as possible should be attempted. Media selection for advertising campaigns, and the selection of specific prospects for personal selling, should attempt to consider what the characteristics of opinion leaders are likely to be in that market. It should be remembered, however, that there are likely to be several layers of opinion leaders, especially within each social class and each adopter category.

Certain gimmicks for stimulating word-of-mouth may have some merit. For example, taxicab drivers have been told that there are certain "mystery riders" who will be taking cab rides on a random basis. If the driver asks the mystery rider the right question (such as "Have you tried new ——?"), then he wins a prize, usually a small amount of cash. Similar campaigns have been conducted with housewives where the game involves answering the telephone in a specified way.

Sampling the product to selected individuals may help to generate word-of-mouth. In the case of the Gillette *Super* Blue Blade mentioned earlier, it was assumed that such professional people as lawyers, doctors, etc., would be believed if they talked about the superior shaving properties of the blade, and they were sent two free blades. (Mailing lists for specific populations are easily obtained.) Furthermore, management had confidence in the superior quality of the blade and believed that the shave would be so remarkably better than with previous blades that the opinion leaders would be motivated to talk about it, and that word-of-mouth would be favorable. (Word-of-mouth can hurt sales of a poor product just as easily as it stimulates sales of good products.)

Another strategic approach is to create advertising that is interesting and distinctive enough to generate word-of-mouth. In casual conversation, a person might ask, "Have you seen the ads for ——?" Television commercials using humor may be particularly effective in this way although there is always the moot question whether the humor obscures the selling message. "Teaser" campaigns are a special case of advertising designed to stimulate interest and word-of-mouth concerning a product about to be introduced.

Finally, it is important to consider ways in which formal channels and mass media might be used to provide opinion leaders with information that will help them perform their function. An example used earlier was to provide automobile purchasers with several copies of literature about their new car which they could pass on to friends. Advertising copy might be designed to make potential word-of-mouth communications interesting, providing the communicator with memorable comments about the product.

While there are several ways in which advertising media, advertising and sales messages, and targets for selling effort might be selected to stimulate word-of-mouth, it is not possible to state a specific procedure that will guarantee success. Constant awareness that there are opinion leaders and networks of influence can, however, provide appropriate caution for the marketing communication strategist. Most importantly, he should take whatever steps feasible to assure that, since word-of-mouth is going to occur regardless of what he does, the word-of-mouth will be favorable. The basic building block for an effective strategy using word-of-mouth is an excellent product that delivers above average value and creates a satisfied customer.

SUMMARY

Networks of interpersonal communication are an important part of the fabric of any social system and carry messages that supplement and extend communications from the mass media. Opinion leaders transmit information from the mass media, to which they have much greater exposure, to others. Personal influence is more effective than impersonal communication because of its greater flexibility, credibility, and opportunity to exert social pressure.

The role of the informal network changes over time as the new product gains acceptance. Later adopters are more reliant upon personal influence but, because they tend to be less integrated into the social system than earlier adopters, the effectiveness of word-of-mouth may be slower and have less impact for them. The early adopters (not innovators, who tend to be social isolates and deviants) are most likely to be the opinion leaders. It is important to recognize that there may be several opinion leaders and that opinion leaders tend to be like those they influence with respect to such variables as social class, although they may be slightly better educated and, perhaps, a little older.

While word-of-mouth can be a powerful influence mediating the effectiveness of a marketing communication program, it is hard to suggest a specific set of principles that will lead to the most efficient use of informal networks. In industrial markets, evidence suggests, networks are very weak and the salesman plays a major role in bringing together a communicator with successful experience with the product and a potential customer who wants to know about that experience.

An understanding of the significance of word-of-mouth and of the conditions under which it is likely to be most prevalent and effective can suggest opportunities for stimulating favorable word-of-mouth. The marketing communication strategist should recognize, at the minimum, that his use of advertising, public relations, and personal selling will have an effect that results from the interaction of these formal communications with informal communication along the network of social influence.

7

Individual Determinants of Persuasibility

Previous chapters have stressed the influence of other people upon the receiver's response to communication. Only in a general discussion of the sources of predispositions did we recognize that the physical, economic, and psychological reality facing the individual was an important influence on his behavior. Demographic, socioeconomic, and psychological variables describing the potential, market audience may provide significant clues about the ways in which that audience will respond to marketing communication. So, having examined the impact of culture, reference groups, primary groups, and the dyad, the discussion now comes back to the individual himself.

Persuasibility means susceptibility to persuasion (as measured by amount of opinion change); it may be thought of either as a general characteristic of the individual or as specific to certain topics or kinds of messages. The following discussion begins by looking at general or "topic-free" persuasibility. Later, the influence of the product, the "topic" in a marketing communication, will be analyzed. For the moment, however, the question becomes "Are there certain characteristics of individuals which make them more or less susceptible to persuasion in general?" Communication research suggests an affirmative but highly qualified and hedged answer.

PERSONALITY AND PERSUASIBILITY

Early in their work, communication researchers turned their attention to the search for personality characteristics that were correlated with persuasibility. This research direction was a logical result of the simple communication model incorporating source, message, and receiver. (Characteristics of sources and of messages have also been systematically examined in communication research, and these results will be reviewed in Chapters 8 and 11.) Individuals exposed to the same messages from the same source, and subject to the same social pressures, responded differently. Thus, the search began for personality characteristics associated with susceptibility to persuasion. Factors that were found to be related to persuasibility included both ability factors and motive factors.

Ability Factors

The general intellectual ability of an individual, as measured by intelligence, education, and related variables, would be expected to influence persuasibility in three ways. First, these factors would influence the individual's *ability to learn,* to learn and remember more from a given experience. Second, they would influence his *critical ability,* his ability to consider the soundness and logic of arguments to which he is exposed and the basic reasonableness of the communicator's assertions. Third, *ability to draw inferences* would be related to basic intellectual ability and would be expected to influence the individual's ability to generalize and draw meaning from a communication.[1]

Studies of the effects of U.S. Army documentary films during World War II suggested that better educated men were more likely to be persuaded, but there were important exceptions to this finding. In some cases, there was a negative correlation between intelligence and amount of opinion change.[2] Review of these apparently contradictory findings led to the formulation of two explanations for the influence of intellectual ability upon persuasibility:

1. There will be a positive relationship between intellectual ability and amount of opinion change when the messages employed rely upon logical argumentation.
2. There will be a negative relationship between intellectual ability and persuasibility when the communications rely upon arguments that are false, irrational, irrelevant, or based upon faulty generalizations.

[1]Carl I. Hovland, Irving L. Janis, and Harold H. Kelley, *Communication and Persuasion* (paperback ed.; New Haven: Yale University Press, 1963), p. 182.

[2]Carl I. Hovland, Arthur A. Lumsdaine, Fred D. Sheffield, *Experiments on Mass Communication* (Princeton, N.J.: Princeton University Press, 1949), pp. 147–75.

In the former case, ability to draw inferences is significant; in the latter, it is critical ability that makes the difference.[3]

The relationship between intellectual ability and persuasibility is thus a function of the kind of messages used in the communication. Messages and the intellectual ability of the receiver interact in a complex manner, and different kinds of messages require different kinds of intellectual abilities.

Motive Factors

Changing one's opinions in the direction advocated by a communicator can be the result of two kinds of reactions. In one type of reaction, the argument being advanced is sufficiently sound and logical that the wisdom of the communicator's position becomes clear as the receiver comes to accept the premises and reasoning advanced by the communicator. In this kind of response, the communicator influences by what he says. In the other case, the communicator may influence more by who he is. The receiver may be motivated by a desire to win the approval and affection of the communicator. Both kinds of responses are likely to be mixed in a single situation, but one may be dominant.

The search for social approval has been implicitly considered as a significant motive in much of the discussion of the last two chapters. In this chapter, the focus shifts slightly to a consideration of those personality factors which are likely to be related to the need for social approval.

Need for Social Approval. Several research studies have examined the relationship of persuasibility and variables related to the need for social approval. These variables include self-esteem, hostility and aggressiveness, and psychoneurotic tendencies. Logic would suggest the following relationships. First, a person with high self-esteem would be more confident and self-reliant, less likely to need the approval of others, and therefore less persuasible. Second, people who tend to be hostile and aggressive would likewise seem to have a low need for the approval of others and would therefore be expected to be less persuasible. Finally, psychoneurotic tendencies would seem on balance to be related to a lesser felt need for social approval and would therefore lead to low persuasibility.

In general, research findings supported the foregoing line of reasoning. It was found that low self-esteem, feelings of social inadequacy, inhibition of aggression (i.e., compliance), and the presence of depressive affect ("the blues," an indicator of low self-esteem) were correlated with high persuasibility. On the other hand, low persuasibility was found in persons who tended to resist social influence because of a persistent

[3]Hovland, Janis, and Kelley, *op. cit.*, p. 183.

aggressiveness toward others, social withdrawal tendencies, or acute psychoneurotic complaints.[4] The results of these early studies provided evidence that was quite consistent with the general notion that being motivated, for one reason or another, to earn the approval and affection of the communicator was a contributor to persuasability. It should be noted that aggressiveness is often based upon a distrust of others. Some of the research suggested that it was this basic distrust of others that led to hostility and aggressiveness and explained the resistance to social influence.

These relationships were not consistently found, however, for example, a subsequent study failed to confirm the relationship between persuasability and aggressiveness.[5] Subsequent research also examined the influence of a characteristic called "richness of fantasy." It was found that the ability to imagine anticipated favorable results from changing one's attitudes or behavior in the direction advocated by the communicator was related to persuasability. To the extent that psychoneurotic tendencies hinder one's ability to trace through the consequences of a particular course of action, this finding also supports the notion that such tendencies lead to low persuasability. Interestingly, this relationship between richness of fantasy and persuasability was found for male subjects but not for females.[6] This raised anew the question of potential differences between males and females in persuasability.

Are Women More Persuasible? The evidence suggests that women are more easily persuaded than men. While the differences are not great, they tend to be rather consistent and have been duplicated in several studies. It is also interesting that persuasability scores for men show a larger standard deviation than in the case of women. In reviewing these studies, Hovland and Janis suggested that these differences are explained by the fact that our culture seems to demand greater acquiescence from females, especially in regard to prestigeful sources.[7] Then general tendency toward acquiescence may in fact be strong enough to "swamp" any relationship between persuasability and self-esteem in women.

Relationship to Self-Confidence. One of the most recent studies of the relationship between personality and persuasibility was reported by Cox and Bauer. Following the line of inquiry described above concerning the relationship between self-esteem and persuasability (especially in

[4]*Ibid.*, pp. 187–199.

[5]Irving L. Janis and Carl I. Hovland (eds.), *Personality and Persuasibility* (New Haven: Yale University Press, 1959), p. 232.

[6]Irving L. Janis and Peter B. Field, "Sex Differences and Personality Factors Related to Persuasibility," in Janis and Hovland, *op. cit.*, pp. 55–68.

[7]Carl I. Hovland and Irving L. Janis, "Summary and Implications for Future Research," in Janis and Hovland, *op. cit.*, pp. 225–54, at p. 238.

women, as noted), these investigators found evidence of a curvilinear relationship between these two variables. They found that women of *medium* generalized self-confidence were most likely to be persuaded by a salesgirl's presentation on nylon hosiery, while women who scored either high or low were less persuasible. Cox and Bauer suggested that these findings could be explained as follows. Women of low self-confidence were acting in an ego-defensive manner, rejecting the salesgirl's advice as a means of defending their own fragile self-concept. Women of high self-confidence, on the other hand, were not easily persuaded because they were comfortable with their judgment and did not feel the need to comply with the communicator.[8]

These findings about the relationship between consumer self-confidence and persuasibility seem to be contingent upon several factors, however. There is an important distinction to be made between the receiver's general self-confidence and his specific self-confidence to make the judgments required in a particular situation. We shall come back to this distinction shortly.

Relationship to Other Communication Variables

Each of the individual characteristics mentioned above has what can be called an "external analog," a related set of variables in the communication process but beyond the individual himself. A useful way to summarize the foregoing discussion is to suggest the nature of these relationships. It is also worth noting once again that this is a partial analysis. We have looked at characteristics of the receiver and have tried to avoid prolonged discussion of relationships to characteristics of messages and of sources. It must be remembered that the effect of a communication is the result of the interaction of these three sets of variables.

It will be recalled that the following factors are related to persuasibility: (1) intellectual ability, (2) self-esteem, (3) aggressiveness and hostility, (4) social withdrawal tendencies, and (5) psychoneurotic symptoms. The effects produced by changes in each of these variables could also be produced by the manipulation of one or more variables external to the receiver. For example, the influence of intellectual ability can lead to the same consequences as changes in the organization of persuasive argument. It was noted that rational, logical argumentation is more effective with persons of higher intellectual ability.

Likewise, it would be possible to achieve the same consequences attributable to differences in self-esteem by varying the amount of group approval or by using "bandwagon appeals" which stress the importance

[8]Donald F. Cox and Raymond A. Bauer. "Self-Confidence and Persuasibility in Women," *Public Opinion Quarterly,* 28 (Fall 1964), pp. 453–66.

of conforming to generally accepted patterns. The influence of tendencies toward aggressiveness and hostility, especially to the extent that they are motivated by a basic distrust of others, could be duplicated by varying the amount of source credibility (competence and trustworthiness). Social withdrawal tendencies have the same influence upon the receiver as would the exertion of group pressure and appeals to group norms. Finally, use of emotional (as opposed to rational) appeals, especially fear-arousal appeals, influences the level of anxiety experienced in response to a communication and thus is analogous to the effects of psychoneurotic symptoms upon response.

In Chapter 8, the influence of the source is examined in detail. In Chapter 11, the influence of different kinds of appeals and of different organizations of arguments is considered. The ways in which message effects are contingent upon the characteristics of receivers will be developed more completely at that time.

Strategic Implications

Once again, the opportunities for the marketing communication strategist to use these tentative research findings as the basis for planning a promotional program are limited. While these studies have suggested some of the factors associated with individual differences in persuasibility, they do not permit any specific predictions about response to alternative marketing communication approaches. Furthermore, many of the concepts are not operational because the information necessary to identify the distribution of these characteristics within the potential market audience is often not available. It may be possible to make some reasonable guesses about the level of intellectual ability within the market—as when the product is high-priced relative to alternatives, suggesting appeal to a high-income and, hence, better-educated segment (to the extent that education and income are correlated)—but such guesses will be relatively weak.

The literature on the influence of specific personality and demographic or socioeconomic characteristics on consumer behavior is in general rather discouraging. Differences in shopping behavior, brand preference, degree of loyalty, or other measures of buying behavior, have been found to be relatively uninfluenced by differences in individual characteristics. There seems to be little opportunity for the marketing communication strategist to identify specific individual characteristics that are closely correlated with identifiable differences in consumer behavior.

Attitudes Mediate Influence of Personal Attributes. One of the more extensive studies of the influence of individual characteristics upon purchasing behavior involved the specific case of coffee, tea, and beer. (It should be carefully noted that results attained from the study of frequently purchased, low-dollar-value packaged goods may not be generalizable to other products such as fashions, durables, or intangibles.) This study attempted to measure the influence of personal attributes upon such aspects of consumer behavior as frequency of shopping, store loyalty, brand loyalty, and amount purchased. Socioeconomic variables were found to explain less than 5 percent of the variation in purchasing behavior for these products. Furthermore, adding personality variables as predictors increased the accuracy of the prediction in only one out of four cases. The authors of this study therefore concluded that there was no direct or obvious relationship between personality, demographic and socioeconomic characteristics, and purchasing behavior and suggested that it was necessary to consider attitudes toward the products and brands themselves, and other stimuli, before meaningful relationships could be identified.[9] Attitudes are clearly an important mediating influence between individual characteristics and buying behavior.

Similar caution in the use of personality variables was advocated by Carey, who based his argument on three observations. First, the findings on the relationship between personality factors and persuasibility are, as we have seen, incomplete and in some cases contradictory. Second, these findings are not operational. People don't wear signs identifying their position in the persuasibility spectrum; those persons low in self-esteem are not known to have particular product preferences or to be homogeneous in any other way; people do not accumulate in media in any way identifiably related to persuasibility. Third, all behavior of interest to marketing strategists is individual behavior in a social setting and it is relatively fruitless to look at individual characteristics out of the social context.[10]

While there is a great deal of wisdom in these observations, to say that knowledge of the influence of individual characteristics, as mediated by other social variables, is of no use to the strategist is to go too far. Although these individual characteristics by themselves may explain little of the variability in response to persuasive communications, the fact remains that individual differences are important. They are part of the puzzle and we must have all of the pieces before we can complete the picture. The material we have been reviewing here does help to increase our understanding of the processes by which individuals

---

[9]William F. Massy, Ronald E. Frank, and Thomas Lodahl, *Purchasing Behavior and Personal Attributes* (Philadelphia: University of Pennsylvania Press, 1968), especially p. 113 and pp. 123–26.

[10]James William Carey, "Personality Correlates of Persuasibility," in Stephen A. Greyser (ed.), *Toward Scientific Marketing* (Chicago: American Marketing Association, 1964), pp. 30–43.

respond to marketing communication and it is that understanding and sophistication, rather than specific predictions of response, that is our objective in reviewing the literature of communication theory and research.

There is another and, to our way of thinking, more valid criticism to be made of the traditional research on personality and persuasibility, however. That is a criticism of the basic emphasis or viewpoint of the research approach itself.

PROBLEM SOLVING AND THE "PSYCHOSOCIAL GAME"

The traditional research on personality and persuasibility emphasizes a set of motives which can be called "psychosocial," a concern with defending one's ego and winning the respect and affection of one's peers. This viewpoint is reflected in concern for self-esteem, need for social approval, and similar variables. While psychosocial variables certainly are significant determinants of many kinds of behavior, there are many other explanations for the ways in which people respond to communication. A relatively straightforward way is to think of consumer behavior as problem solving. Consumers are motivated to achieve certain goals and to fulfill certain basic physiological and psychological needs through their purchases of goods and services. Economic and physical reality may be as important as complex psychological motivations in determining the way an individual responds to marketing communication. A look at the problem-solving or rational aspects of individual behavior provides a necessary balance to the view of consumer behavior as the search for a psychosocial equilibrium. No one has expressed this better than Raymond Bauer, who has called this "the psychosocial game":

If someone rushed up to you in the hall and asked you anxiously where the men's or ladies' room—whichever was relevant—was, and you told him or her as the case may be, and he or she, as the case may be hurried off in the direction you indicated, would you call that person "persuasible," "suggestible," "subject to social influence," or something of that sort? Probably not! But I am going to suggest that communication researchers have been saying things like that on a regular basis, publishing articles, writing books and giving lectures in which they say this, and they get applauded, promoted, and—worse —paid for it.[11]

Bauer and his students, especially Donald F. Cox, have been the major contributors to a different view of consumer response to communication which considers consumer behavior as a form of risk taking in

[11]Raymond A. Bauer, "Games People and Audiences Play," Paper presented at Seminar on Communication in Contemporary Society, University of Texas, March 17, 1967.

which risk is reduced by information acquisition, processing, and transmission. It looks at consumer behavior as a decision-making process and considers response to communication in the context of that process. This analysis sheds further light on the circumstances under which differences in individual personality characteristics are likely to be significant determinants of response. It also suggests those characteristics that are of greater significance in influencing response to communication.

CONSUMER BEHAVIOR AS RISK TAKING

Risk is a product of two variables: uncertainty about the consequences of alternative courses of action and the value of those consequences when they occur. If the consequences are of no value or significance to the decision maker, then there is no risk. Likewise, if there is certainty as to the consequences of action, then there is no risk either. For example, a decision to change your brand of toothpaste may involve some risk because (1) you see some positive probability that the new toothpaste won't be as effective in preventing cavities as your old brand (uncertainty) and (2) cavities are painful and expensive to have filled (consequences). The possible gain (e.g., better flavor) may not be worth the risk (uncertainty times consequences).

Risk Is Subjective

Risk is a personal, subjective variable. It is a function of the interaction of a specific set of facts about the environment (brands, prices, information, etc.) with the situation of the individual decision maker. Consequences of major significance for one individual may be of little or no significance for another. For example, the consequences of a decision to buy a major appliance probably become less significant in the judgment of the decision maker as income increases, other things being equal. The fashion-conscious person may take the consequences of purchasing a new suit or dress much more seriously, and therefore the purchase decision has more risk for him or her.

The relevant concept here is *perceived* risk, the decision maker's subjective assessment of the uncertainty and consequences of a course of action. The individual's subjective assessment of the risk involved is the basis for his behavior and for his interpretation of communications relating to the decision.

Elements of Perceived Risk

The amount of risk which the individual perceives in a given decision-making situation is a function of uncertainty and consequences, as noted above. Uncertainty results from the fact that the individual has imperfect information. Uncertainty has three components: (1) uncertainty about one's buying goals, (2) uncertainty as to which purchase decision will best achieve these goals; and (3) the perceived possibility of adverse consequences and failure to achieve goals.

There are two kinds of consequences for purchase actions which must be considered. There are performance consequences, outcomes associated with the physical attributes and performance of the product itself. And there are psychosocial consequences associated with the satisfactions one derives from the use of the product and from the reactions of other people to one's purchase and use of the product.

The significance of the consequences of a purchase action for the individual will also be a function of two sets of variables. First is importance of the goals or needs which the individual is pursuing in the purchase of that product or service. Second is the amount of investment of dollars, effort, time, and "self" (psychological commitment or investment) required for the purchase. Clearly, the purchase of an automobile involves more important (dollar) consequences than the purchase of a lawn mower. For the fashion-conscious woman, the purchase of a new hat may involve more significant (psychological) consequences than the purchase of a more expensive kitchen appliance.

To summarize, these are the major components of perceived risk: type of uncertainty (performance and psychosocial); importance of buying goals and amount of investment, as determinants of the significance of consequences; and the amount of perceived risk (high, medium, or low) as defined by the interaction of uncertainty and consequences.[12] These relationships are analyzed in Figure 7–1.

Communication Reduces Perceived Risk

Having laid out this framework of the concept of perceived risk, we have a way of viewing response to communication quite different from that offered by the traditional "personality and persuasibility" framework. Information provided by marketing communication can be thought of as permitting the consumer to reduce the amount of perceived risk in a purchase. It should be noted, however, that marketing communication may *not* help to reduce the amount of perceived risk unless the information is of relevance to the consumer's needs and goals (that is, it is useful for predicting outcomes that are of relevance to the decision maker) and unless the information source (the company, its

[12]Donald F. Cox (ed.), *Risk Taking and Information Handling in Consumer Behavior* (Boston: Division of Research, Graduate School of Business Administration, Harvard University, 1967); this summary is based on his Introduction to the volume (pp. 1–19).

Uncertainty[a]		Consequences			Perceived Risk[c]	
		Type of Consequences				
Type of Uncertainty	Amount of Uncertainty[a]	Importance of Buying Goals	Amount of Investment (time, effort, dollar investment, psychosocial investment)	Seriousness of Consequences[b]	Type	Amount of Perceived Risk
Performance	H	Performance (importance of)	(Investment to try to achieve performance goals)	H	Performance	H
	M			M		M
	L			L		L
Psychosocial	H	Psychosocial (importance of)	(Investment to try to achieve psychosocial goals)	H	Psychosocial	H
	M			M		M
	L			L		L

[a]This can refer to goal *identification* uncertainty, goal purchase matching uncertainty, or both.
[b]Seriousness of consequences is a function of importance of buying goals and amount of investment.
[c]Perceived risk can involve goal *identification* risk, goal-purchase *matching* risk, or both.

Fig. 7–1. Components of perceived risk. (Source: Cox, *op. cit.*, p. 8. Courtesy of Division of Research, Graduate School of Business Administration, Harvard University.)

salesmen, its advertising media, or its resellers) is perceived as trustworthy and competent. These dimensions will be referred to as the "predictive value" and the "confidence value" of the information as we go along.[13]

The concept of perceived risk has some dynamic qualities to it that must be more carefully explored. Risk must be reduced to some reasonable level before the consumer is willing to make a decision or commit to a course of action. This suggests that individuals develop certain strategies for reducing the amount of perceived risk. Remembering that risk is a function of both uncertainty and consequences, it can be inferred that risk will be reduced either by increasing the level of information (or certainty) or by reducing the amount and significance of the consequences. Furthermore, one would hope to be able to identify certain individual characteristics which influence the amount of risk that the person perceives in a given purchase and which lead to more or less characteristic strategies for reducing the amount of risk.[14] This line of reasoning spells out the main parts of the remainder of this chapter.

[13]Donald F. Cox, "The Sorting Rule Model of the Consumer Product Evaluation Process," *ibid.*, pp. 324–69.

[14]Donald F. Cox, "Risk Handling in Consumer Behavior—An Intensive Study of Two Cases," *ibid.*, pp. 34–81, at pp. 80–81.

Strategies for Reducing Risk

Buyers develop strategies for coping with perceived risk and these strategies become more or less characteristic of them. Strategies may be designed either to reduce the uncertainty or the amount at stake. Cox reported from an intensive study of the strategies used by two women that it was much more common to try to reduce uncertainty. "Only when they could not become certain in their own minds that they would achieve their buying goals, would they fall back on the other strategy: reducing the amount at stake."[15] Several strategies for reducing risk will be identified and discussed briefly.

Avoidance. One way of reducing the amount of risk is to avoid situations calling for a decision. The consumer maintains goals and aspirations at the status quo and simply does not think about opportunities for achievement of a higher level of need satisfaction. The late majority and laggards in the diffusion process have avoidance as a characteristic strategy for reducing risk. Their behavior is different from that of the typical person because it is not characterized by an increase in aspiration level as the result of successful goal attainment. They have stopped growing and defining new challenges for themselves. They are happy to maintain their goals at a level which is quite acceptable to them.

For the more "average" consumer, avoidance may be adopted as a strategy if initial search for acceptable level alternatives fails to turn up a satisfactory course of action. The woman shopping for a new dress may decide to "make do" with her old one if she does not find what she wants in a reasonable length of time. An adjustment of goals back downward avoids the necessity of having to choose among courses of action that are not attractive. A strategy of avoidance reduces the amount at stake, the consequences of the decision.

Loyalty. Some individuals show much more habitual behavior in their shopping and brand choices than do others. Brand loyalty and store loyalty are strategies for reducing the amount of perceived risk by both increasing certainty and reducing the consequences at stake. If an individual has used a brand of a product before, she is reasonably certain about the kind of performance to expect from that brand along whatever dimensions of product performance and quality are significant for her. On the other hand, she gives up any possibility of improving her level of goal attainment; she reduces the possibility of any improvement in consequences.

Similar comments apply to the concept of store loyalty. A woman may shop at the same grocery store week after week because she finds

[15]*Ibid.*, p. 72.

the quality, assortment, prices, and services offered by the store acceptable according to her set goal. On the other hand, she relinquishes any
possibility of improving the value or convenience she obtains from shopping. She avoids the potential negative consequences of changing stores.

People remain loyal to brands and stores so long as the perceived risk
of changing (especially the possibility of negative consequences) is not
offset by the promise of a significantly better level of goal attainment.
Viewed in this light, one of the major functions of marketing communication designed to stimulate trial of a new product is to reduce the
amount of perceived risk by either increasing the consumer's expectations of significantly better goal attainment or reducing his perceptions of
possible negative consequences. Like all habitual behavior, loyalty minimizes the investment of time and effort required to reach an acceptable
level of goal attainment.

Information Acquisition. The possibility of a higher level of goal
attainment may stimulate the potential consumer to engage in activities
designed to identify and evaluate alternative courses of action. The consumer may rely upon formal or informal, commercial or noncommercial
sources to provide this information. She may go shopping, read advertisements in magazines, peruse mail-order catalogs, talk with friends, call
stores on the telephone, or rely upon whatever other methods of information acquisition have worked well for her in the past. As in other
realms of behavior, information acquisition tends to follow habitual patterns, with the search for alternatives proceeding along lines that have
worked in the past. The search for additional information will continue
until an acceptable alternative is identified or goals are reduced to the
level where there are acceptable alternatives. Search will be stopped
when the decision maker judges that the amount of time and effort
required to generate additional information is not justified by the possibility of finding alternatives that have more positive consequences or
when circumstances require a decision without further delay.

Information Processing. People differ in the manner in which they
evaluate and respond to information about products and services. Previous chapters examined in detail the influence of predispositions upon
the perception and retention of messages. A reasonable generalization is
that an individual is more likely to pay attention to and remember a
message if it has predictive value for him—if it helps to evaluate alternative courses of action for achieving goals that are important to him.
Because level of goal attainment changes over time, information processing with respect to particular kinds of messages is also likely to change.
A man contemplating the purchase of a new automobile is likely to be
much more systematic and explicit in his processing of information
about new automobiles than is the man with only a general interest in

automobiles. His habits for processing information will change after the purchase.

Information Transmission. In Chapter 6 the generation of word-of-mouth communication was analyzed in considerable detail. Here we need only add that perceived risk may be a significant determinant of information transmission behavior. The greater the amount of perceived risk, the more likely that the consumer will generate word-of-mouth either to reduce postpurchase doubt, or to help one's friends to avoid the potential negative consequences of a wrong decision. For product categories with high perceived risk there is also going to be more information seeking; the opinions of those who have recently bought the product will more likely be actively sought.

Within each of these strategies for reducing risk there are several variations or "substrategies." For example, information acquisition may take several forms, including heavy reliance upon magazines, use of sources such as *Consumer Reports*, asking the advice of others, and so on. These tendencies represent a characteristic method developed by the individual of coping with the risk of purchase behavior. Assuming that the individual is not satisfied with the status quo (that is, does not adopt the strategies of avoidance or loyalty), then some form of information acquisition and processing will take place. The amount of information acquisition and processing will be positively related to the amount of perceived risk.

Self-Confidence and Perceived Risk

It was stressed earlier that perceived risk is the result of a subjective assessment of uncertainty and consequences. The amount of risk perceived in a set of alternative actions will differ from one individual to another as a function of the self-confidence of the decision maker. Once again we must distinguish between generalized self-confidence and specific self-confidence, the latter being the individual's perception of his ability to make the judgments required in a specific set of circumstances. Generalized self-confidence relates to the more pervasive personal qualities of feelings of self esteem, personal adequacy, independence, and self-reliance.

Other things being equal, it seems reasonable to expect that persons low in self-confidence will be more uncertain in a given decision situation. If they are more uncertain, they will perceive more risk and higher perceived risk will lead to a greater tendency to rely upon whatever strategy characterizes that person's reponse to risk. That is, persons of low self-confidence would be expected either to avoid decision situations or to show more loyalty or to engage in more information acquisition. These assertions will be evaluated shortly.

Influence of the Product

The nature of the product influences amount of perceived risk because it determines the importance of the consequences of the purchase decision. Both product performance consequences and psychosocial consequences are a function of the nature of the product as perceived by the decision maker. People differ significantly in the extent to which they take products seriously. For example, one man may consider an automobile to be strictly a method of transportation while to another an automobile is an important extension of his ego and an expression of his self concept. The former is concerned with performance consequences more or less exclusively while the latter stresses psychosocial consequences.

Amount of specific self-confidence is also a function of the nature of the product. Some people are more comfortable evaluating a given product than others. You may consider yourself to be somewhat of an expert on hi-fi equipment and thus would not hesitate to make judgments about the consequences of purchasing various brands while having much less confidence in your ability to judge photographic equipment. In the latter case, you might find yourself relying much more heavily upon friends whom you regard as being better judges of photographic equipment, or upon the retail sales clerk.

The previous paragraphs have outlined the several factors that must be considered in assessing the likelihood that an individual will be persuaded by marketing communication. These factors include perceived risk, specific self-confidence, generalized self-confidence, and the nature of the product. Consideration must be given also to the characteristic manner in which the person responds to risky situations. These factors when taken together constitute an alternative theoretical framework to the more simple view of persuasibility as a function of personality traits.

THE INFLUENCES OF INDIVIDUAL DIFFERENCES

The application of these ideas to the analysis of the effects of communication can be illustrated by summarizing briefly several studies developed to test these various concepts. In general, these studies support the conclusion that the amount and nature of perceived risk determine the consumer's information needs and that consumers seek out the amount, types, and sources of information that are most likely to satisfy their particular information needs.[16] Formal communications provided by the marketer are likely to have little confidence value for the consumer in those cases where psychosocial consequences are important or where the

[16]*Ibid.,* p. 604.

possibility of negative consequences is perceived. Word-of-mouth can be expected to be more significant in such situations.

Cunningham[17] and Arndt[18] both report studies in which a positive relationship was found between amount of perceived risk and amount of brand loyalty. Cunningham also found that word-of-mouth was greatest in product categories which consumers regarded as most risky, such as headache remedies and fabric softeners, compared to low-risk products such as dry spaghetti.[19] This study also suggested that persons high in generalized self-confidence who were also high in perceived risk were most likely to engage in word-of-mouth. Conversely, those low in generalized self-confidence and low in perceived risk were least likely to do so.

As noted earlier in the chapter, Cox and Bauer found a curvilinear relationship between self-confidence and persuasibility with women of medium self-confidence showing the greatest tendency to be persuasible. This study also found that generalized self-confidence was of virtually no influence when specific self-confidence was high. In other words, confidence in one's judgments about the specific topic is of much greater importance than generalized self-confidence when the former is strong. Generalized self-confidence comes into play only when specific self-confidence is weak.[20]

In a similar study, Brody and Cunningham attempted to determine the conditions under which personality variables are most likely to influence consumer decisions. They found that the influence of personality variables was contingent upon perceived performance risk, perceived social risk, and specific self-confidence. Personality variables helped to predict brand loyalty when there was high perceived performance risk, high specific self-confidence, and low perceived social risk. (In the case of high perceived social risk, the influence of social system variables complicates the influence of personality variables.)[21]

SUMMARY

The perceived risk model suggests how differences in individual characteristics, especially self-confidence and strategies for reducing risk, interact with other factors in the decision situation to determine

---

[17]Scott M. Cunningham, "Perceived Risk and Brand Loyalty," *ibid.*, pp. 507–23.

[18]Johan Arndt, "Perceived Risk, Sociometric Integration, and Word-of-Mouth in the Adoption of a New Food Product," *ibid.*, pp. 289–316.

[19]Scott M. Cunningham, "Perceived Risk as a Factor in Informal Consumer Communications," *ibid.*, pp. 265–88.

[20]Cox and Bauer, *op. cit.*

[21]Robert P. Brody and Scott M. Cunningham, "Personality Variables and the Consumer Decision Process," *Journal of Marketing Research*, 5 (February 1968), pp. 50–57.

response to both formal and informal communications. It suggests a set of factors (high perceived risk, medium self-confidence, product important to the consumer) which tends to produce the highest amount of responsiveness to a marketing communication. The result of this model is a more complete understanding of the consumer decision process than that offered by the simple "personality correlates of persuasibility" model which explains only a small amount of the variability in consumer behavior. The personality correlates model implicitly assumes that the receiver is primarily motivated by a need for social approval and considers personality determinants of that need.

The distinction between problem solving and the "psychosocial game" offered in this chapter is instructive because it highlights the two ways in which a communicator exerts his influence—by what he says and by who he is. The perceived risk framework considers both the predictive value of the information (what) and the confidence value (who). These dimensions are related to the two components of source credibility—competence and trustworthiness. In the next chapter, the influence of attitude toward sources and communicators is analyzed in detail.

8

Attitudes Toward Communicators

Characteristics of the communicator or source, especially reputation or credibility, are known to have a significant influence on response to communication. Evidence from communication research suggesting how source credibility influences response will be reviewed in this chapter, and the implications for effective marketing communication strategy will be developed.

Previous chapters have shown how social influences have an impact on the receiver. To the extent that both communicator and receiver are part of the same social system, the communicator may also influence receivers through social pressure. Likewise, it was seen that a desire for social approval by the receiver may motivate him to accept the communicator's message. Thus, attitudes toward the communicator may be derived from the receiver's feelings of admiration and affection, from a desire to emulate the communicator, or from perceptions of the communicator's ability to reward or punish. In addition, attitudes toward the communicator may be derived from feelings of trust and confidence, from beliefs about his knowledge, intelligence, honesty, and sincerity.[1] It is this last set of attitudes, which can be summarized by the concept of "credibility," that provides the predispositions to be analyzed in this chapter.

Attitudes toward the communicator are an important class of predisposition held by the receiver. It is important to note that "source credibil-

[1]Carl I. Hovland, Irving L. Janis, and Harold H. Kelley, *Communication and Persuasion* (New Haven: Yale University Press, 1953), pp. 19–21.

141

ity" is not an objective characteristic of the source, something that some communicators have and others do not. Rather, it is a set of attitudes toward the source held by the receiver. It is the receiver's subjective assessment of the communicator.

An example which helps to stress the subjective nature of credibility is provided by a phrase that became popular during Lyndon Johnson's term of office as President of the United States, "credibility gap," which was said to describe the state of affairs between the President and his administration and the public. The credibility gap was not an objective fact of the Johnson administration (although it may have had some objective basis) but a set of attitudes held by the press and the public toward that administration. The result was a lessened willingness to believe and to be motivated by statements and appeals that were issued by President Johnson and his staff. As a consequence, his ability to win support for programs he regarded as important was reduced, especially in the later stages of his administration.

Credibility is a subjective assessment of the trustworthiness and the competence of the perceived source of the communication, the receiver's predispositions toward that source. As noted in Chapter 4, predispositions define both the problems and the opportunities facing the marketing manager as he develops a marketing communication strategy. Attitudes toward the company and its salesmen and resellers are as important as attitudes toward products and services in defining the tasks which must be performed by communication and the opportunities for it to accomplish stated objectives in a given planning period. Such predispositions change slowly, and a poor reputation (or low credibility) cannot be corrected overnight. But attitudes toward the company and its spokesmen as communicators must be carefully appraised as part of the planning process, for they define the limits within which communication can be effective.

SOURCES OF MARKETING COMMUNICATION

In marketing activity, there are at least five kinds of sources of communication: the company; salesmen; resellers (especially retailers; other resellers may be less actively involved in promotion); mass media; and hired spokesmen. The receiver may be uncertain as to which source is most significant in a given communication, and his attitudes toward one may be quite different from those toward another source. These sets of attitudes interact in important ways in determining the amount of influence exerted by a channel of communication. Each element must be supportive of the others if the marketing communication program is to have maximum effectiveness.

Most marketing communication has more than one source and intelligent observers may disagree as to the most important communicator in a given situation. When a retail clerk makes a sales presentation about a nationally advertised brand of clothing, who is the communicator—the retail clerk, the retail store, or the manufacturing company? When a salesman for a steel warehouse suggests to the customer that he should buy United States Steel's stainless steel sheets, who is the communicator—the salesman, the warehousing company, or the United States Steel Corporation? When a housewife reads an advertisement for cosmetics in a fashion magazine and a famous movie star is featured in the ad, who is the communicator—the company, the magazine, or the movie star? It is not important to assign sole responsibility to one of these communicators in each case; in fact, it would be wrong to do so. Each of these communicators may have some impact on the receiver's acceptance of the message and thus on his final response.

More on the basis of convenience than as the result of empirically verified conclusions, let us accept the use of the word "source" in marketing communication to mean the selling company as perceived by the potential customers, a usage foreshadowed in Chapter 3 ("Communicator-Media Effects"). This will permit a distinction between the company as a *source* of communication and its salesmen and other representatives as *communicators*. The latter can be thought of as channels of communication, but not the original source. For a given marketing communication, there may be several communicators or channels but only one source. This is an important distinction and will help to clarify some of the material to follow, but it should be recognized that it is not firmly based on experimental evidence. In many of the experimental studies to be referred to, no distinction was made between the source and the communicator. In the case of a newspaper, for example, they are one and the same.

DETERMINANTS OF CREDIBILITY

Early research revealed that the attitude of the receiver toward the source was a significant determinant of the influence of the communication. Logic suggests several reasons why this may be so.

Expertise

Perhaps most obvious is the notion that some sources are more qualified to talk on a given subject than others, because of particular knowledge, background, experience, or basic intelligence. Most of us ask, when exposed to a source, "Does he know what he is talking about?" Evidence to help us answer that question may have been provided when the source was introduced to us and we were given certain facts about him, as when an instructor introduces a guest speaker and gives educational background and other relevant facts concerning the speaker's qualifications for talking on the assigned subject. The basic question we are asking is how well informed the source is—whether he has sufficient expertise that we should seriously consider what he says.

In the absence of specific information, receivers rely upon less-direct data to make inferences about the expertise of the source. Mode of dress, mannerisms, habits of speech, gestures, or other characteristics of the source may provide the basis for such inferences. Any cues relating to the ability and knowledge possessed by the source are likely to be used in the absence of more specific evidence.

Trustworthiness and Intent To Persuade

In addition to the source's expertise, his honesty and trustworthiness may be assessed. Of particular importance as a determinant of trustworthiness is the *perception of manipulative intent*. If the receiver judges that the source's objective is to persuade him to change his opinions or behavior, his defenses are sharpened. The receiver is likely to attribute to the source such bias (and therefore tendency to misinform) as appropriate and instrumental to the accomplishment of that objective. A perception of manipulative intent results in a decrease in the effectiveness of the communication. When the source is suspected of having the objective of personal gain, he is also seen as less worthy of trust.[2]

Social roles provide some significant cues from which inferences can be drawn about both the expertise and the trustworthiness of the source. Persons occupying such roles as salesman, radio announcer, and politician are generally regarded as having some intent to persuade as a result of their occupations. People who carry such titles as engineer, professor, lawyer, accountant, or doctor are assumed to have expertise and knowledge in a particular area and exert their influence primarily because of this knowledge.

As we noted in Chapter 6, opinion leaders exert their influence in part because of their credibility. They are respected members of the local community and are perceived as being trustworthy. Compared to commercial sources, opinion leaders are not perceived as having the intent to manipulate. It is for similar reasons that conversations that are "overheard" may often have a greater influence. This was part of the reasoning supposedly behind the apocryphal case of the attractive young ladies who were hired to promote a new brand of scotch whiskey by drawing

[2]Hovland, Janis, and Kelley, *op. cit.*, p. 23.

attention to themselves as they ordered the brand in cocktail lounges. The greater effectiveness of "accidentally overheard" conversations has also been confirmed under controlled experimental conditions.[3]

RESEARCH ON SOURCE EFFECT

The classic research study most often cited as evidence of the influence of source credibility was conducted by Hovland and Weiss.[4] Similar messages on each of four different topics were presented to experimental subjects. In some cases, the communication was attributed to a high-credibility source and in others to a low-credibility source. For example, on the topic "Can a practicable atomic-powered submarine be built at the present time?" the high-credibility source was the famed American scientist J. Robert Oppenheimer while the low-credibility source was the official Russian newspaper *Pravda*. (This research was conducted at a time when the Korean War and other factors had substantially increased anti-Russian sentiment in the United States.) Or, on the issue "As a result of TV, will there be a decrease in the number of movie theatres in operation in 1955?" the high-credibility source was *Fortune* magazine while the low-credibility source was a well-known woman movie-gossip columnist.

In each of the four cases, responses to the high credibility source were significantly more favorable than those to the low-credibility source. In each case, the high credibility source was considered more "fair" in its presentation. Likewise, respondents considered the high-credibility source to be more justified in drawing its conclusions from the facts cited. It is worth repeating that in each case the message was identical, only the attributed source was different.

Of greater significance than the differences in judgments of "fairness" and "justifiability" is the fact that opinion change in the direction advocated by the communication was significantly greater for three of the four topics in the case of the high-credibility source. Thus, this experiment provided evidence of a source effect attributable to differences in the credibility of the source.

These results were supported by another study by Kelman and Hovland.[5] Another interesting finding of this study was that the amount

[3]Elaine Walster and Leon Festinger, "The Effectiveness of 'Overheard' Persuasive Communications," *Journal of Abnormal and Social Psychology*, 65 (December 1962), pp. 395–402.

[4]Carl I. Hovland and Walter Weiss, "The Influence of Source Credibility on Communication Effectiveness," *Public Opinion Quarterly*, 15 (Winter 1951–52), pp. 635–50.

[5]H. C. Kelman and C. I. Hovland, "'Reinstatement' of the Communicator in Delayed Measurement of Opinion Change," *Journal of Abnormal and Social Psychology*, 48 (July 1953), pp. 327–35.

of opinion change was unrelated to the amount of learning or information retention by the receiver.

Several subsequent studies have examined the conditions under which the credibility of the communicator is likely to be especially significant in determining response to communication. Two of the most interesting and important findings for marketing communication relate to the dimensions of intent and the amount of change advocated. These later studies have found that fairness is a more important dimension of trustworthiness than is "propagandistic" intent. To a certain extent, all communicators seem to be perceived as having some persuasive intent, but this is more or less accepted. It is perceptions of fairness that seem to have the greater significance. Similarly, amount of change advocated is significant. The more change advocated, the less is the amount of opinion change and the less the influence of the communicator.[6]

For the marketing communication strategist, there are two important implications here. First, commercial sources may still be persuasive and effective as long as they are perceived as being fair (and competent). Second, radically new concepts will take longer to gain market acceptance than those innovations which represent only slight change from existing practice and attitudes. This latter conclusion is also consistent with the finding (cited in Chapter 7) that those who perceive high risk in a decision situation need more information before making a decision compared with those who perceive low risk.

The evidence is rather clear, then, that high-credibility sources bring about more opinion change than low-credibility sources. There still remains the question whether such differences persist over time.

Sleeper Effect

All of the evidence cited so far relates to the amount of opinion change measured immediately after exposure to the communication. Interestingly, in the classic Hovland and Weiss study, these differences had disappeared when respondents were asked to fill out similar questionnaires four weeks after the experiment. The results from these two questionnaires are illustrated in Figure 8–1. Not only had the differences originally attributable to source effect disappeared, but even more interesting was the observation that the amount of opinion change among those exposed to the low-credibility source was slightly greater. Although this difference was not statistically significant, it was no less intriguing. The tendency for differences attributable to source effect to

---

[6]Arthur R. Cohen, *Attitude Change and Social Influence* (New York: Basic Books, Inc., 1964), pp. 28–32.

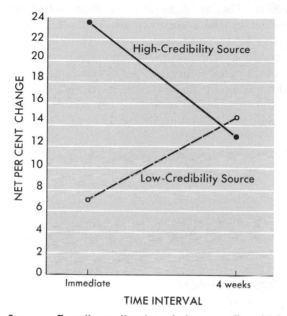

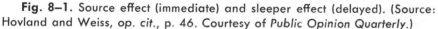

TIME INTERVAL

Fig. 8–1. Source effect (immediate) and sleeper effect (delayed). (Source: Hovland and Weiss, *op. cit.*, p. 46. Courtesy of *Public Opinion Quarterly*.)

disappear and for low-credibility sources to have a slightly greater effect over time was called the "sleeper effect." This name had originally been given by Hovland, Lumsdaine, and Sheffield in their Army film studies to explain the facts that opinion change on certain items increased over time after exposure to the films.[7] They suggested that the sleeper effect resulted from the interaction of two kinds of responses to the communication—a response to the information conveyed by the communication and reactions of skepticism about and resistance to the source as a result of the perceived attempt to influence. They reasoned that the latter reaction might "wear off" more quickly, allowing the information content to have a greater influence over time.

Hovland and Weiss offered a similar explanation. They reasoned that, over time, the receiver tended to dissociate the message and the source. As a result, differences attributable to source effect would "wash out."

Still to be explained is the slightly greater influence of the low-credibility source four weeks later, as shown in Figure 8–1. This difference could result from the fact that low-credibility sources cause the receiver to pay more attention to the communication because they are perceived

[7]Carl I. Hovland, Arthur A. Lumsdaine, and Fred D. Sheffield, *Experiments on Mass Communication* (Princeton, N.J.: Princeton University Press, 1949), pp. 188–89.

as less trustworthy. That is, there may be more active participation in the communication by the receiver when exposed to a low-credibility source. While this latter point could not be empirically verified, it was found that respondents who had been exposed to low-credibility sources found it significantly more difficult to recall the name of those sources as compared to those respondents who had been exposed to high-credibility sources. Thus, the explanation of sleeper effect as resulting from dissociation of message and communicator over time was supported by the analysis.

This result was also supported by the subsequent study by Kelman and Hovland. They found that the original differences attributable to differences in source credibility *reappeared* when subjects were reminded of the source. This confirms the explanation of sleeper effect offered by Hovland and Weiss and it has some implications for marketing communication strategy. It is hard to imagine many marketing situations in which there is a dissociation of message and source. The company is almost always identified in a marketing communication. It may be wishful thinking therefore to expect the handicap of a poor company image to disappear over time unless the company takes specific steps to strengthen and modify that image. However, research to be discussed below indicates that the initially favorable influence of a good company reputation may wear off over time.

These theoretical results suggest the importance of the trustworthiness and competence of the company and its representatives in determining the effectiveness of a marketing communication program. But because none of the studies reported here have been conducted in the context of a marketing situation, caution is appropriate in drawing implications for marketing strategy from this research. Fortunately, Theodore Levitt has tested the specific applicability of these findings to the marketing situation.

Source and Communicator Effects and Perceived Risk

Levitt designed an experiment to measure the influence of four sets of factors upon buyers' responses to communication: company reputation, salesman presentation, audience characteristics, and amount of perceived purchasing risk.[8] A review of his research study will help to relate the influence of source and sleeper effects and the quality of the salesman's presentation to the influence of perceived risk as analyzed in the previous chapter. In Levitt's study, there were three companies, two sales

---

[8]Theodore Levitt, *Industrial Purchasing Behavior: A Study of Communications Effects* (Boston: Division of Research, Graduate School of Business Administration, Harvard University, 1965).

representatives, two audiences, and two levels of risk. These were as follows:

Sources
  Monsanto Chemical Company—high-credibility source
  Denver Chemical Company— medium-to-low-credibility source
  "Anonymous" Chemical Company—low-credibility source

Communicators
  "Good" sales presentation
  "Bad" sales presentation

Audiences
  Industrial purchasing agents
  Industrial chemists

Risk
  High—a decision to purchase
  Low—a decision to recommend that the product be given further hearing elsewhere within the buying company

There were therefore twenty-four possible combinations of the experimental variables ($3 \times 2 \times 2 \times 2$), although all respondents were asked to make both decisions—resulting in only twelve experimental treatments. The product involved was a chemical ingredient used in the manufacture of paint. Experimental subjects were adult males occupied in jobs that legitimately fitted the two occupational categories cited above.

Analysis of results revealed that source effects occurred. Company reputation had a significant influence. Salesmen for the Monsanto Chemical Company received a more favorable response. Furthermore, the influence of reputation was greatest for the low-risk (recommend further hearing) decision, although it was still favorable even in the high-risk case. Source credibility (company reputation) is an important influence on buyers' responses to a sales presentation.

In addition, the quality of the salesman's presentation also had a definite effect. The good sales presentation (roughly analogous to "communicator credibility" and perceptions of expertise) always received a more favorable response than a poor presentation. There appeared to be a "communicator effect" as well as a "source effect" for industrial salesmen. The differences attributable to communicator effects were greater in the case of a high-risk decision (to buy).

For low-risk decisions, a poor presentation by a salesman for the well-known company was about as effective as a good presentation from the low-credibility source. In high-risk buying decisions it appeared that communicator effects were greater than source effects: a good presentation by an anonymous company was found to be much more effective than a poor presentation by a well-known company. The clear implication here is that a well-trained salesman for an unknown company can overcome the advantage of the better-known company's general reputation, especially if the latter's salesmen don't live up to the expectations created by that image. Another interpretation of these findings is that source effect becomes less significant as the amount of change advocated (high-risk vs. low-risk decisions) increases.

The presence of sleeper effect was also confirmed by Levitt's experiment. Differences originally attributable to company reputations were found to disappear with the passage of time. The stronger an original positive reaction to the presentation, the less the amount of attrition in source effect when measured five weeks later. This result was *not* found when the original reaction was negative. If the respondent had strongly rejected the presentation at first, he was much more inclined to give it another hearing five weeks later. This can be explained as an attempt to reduce cognitive dissonance, some doubt about the wisdom of the initial rejection (which doubt might reasonably be expected to be the greater, the stronger the original rejection).[9] These are among the more important conclusions from Levitt's research although there were many others as well. The important point is that the presence of source and sleeper effect was confirmed in a marketing context. Furthermore, effects attributable to source (company) and communicator (salesman) were found to be different in several important respects.

IMPROVING CREDIBILITY

Every seller must be concerned with credibility. Whether or not he takes any explicit action to improve it, the fact of the matter is that potential customers are going to make judgments about the competence and trustworthiness of the company and its representatives. It will be helpful here to consider some of those factors that operate to improve credibility in the interaction of seller and buyer.

Company Reputation and Capability

Companies have reputations or images that affect their credibility as sources of marketing communication. The concept of "image" is a muddy one but can generally be thought of as a constellation of values ascribed to a company, its "personality," or the things it stands for. This would include impressions of the kind of company it is to work for, its responsibility as a citizen of the community or the country, the attitudes and actions of its top management, its product quality, and its research capability, to suggest some of the components of "image."

As with other communicators, companies will be evaluated on two dimensions—expertise and trustworthiness. Claims for product quality,

[9] *Ibid.*, pp. 161–79.

for example, would seem to be evaluated in part upon the basis of the receiver's perceptions of the ability of the company to support that claim. Thus, a large oil company stressed the extensive research which it did through a large-scale consumer advertising program. The objectives of the campaign were to provide a background for the successful introduction of new products (such as extra-high octane gasoline) and to encourage consumers to try the brand of gasoline and become loyal to it. A rather classic case of the influence of perceived expertise on consumer behavior is provided by the attempt of the General Mills Company, twenty years or so ago, to market a line of Betty Crocker small appliances such as irons and toasters. The product line failed; one reason was that consumers could not accept "Betty Crocker" as an expert on electrical appliances, despite a very high level of perceived expertise on matters relating to recipes and cooking.

In industrial markets especially, company reputation may be a critical dimension of acceptance. There are many industrial marketing situations in which a generalized capability is being sold, rather than specific products or services. For example, an industrial construction firm does not have a "product line" in any formal sense. It has, rather, a capability to construct a facility that will meet the needs and specifications established by the customer. Here, both trustworthiness and competence are significant determinants of the response to its selling efforts. Other examples of marketing where "promises" are sold rather than products include contract research, the development of sophisticated systems for space exploration and defense, commercial aircraft, and large-scale electronic data processing installations. In each of these cases, the customer buys a promise of solutions to his problems, and the importance of company reputation in this kind of selling is especially obvious.

Companies may use several tactics and strategies to build an image and a reputation for competence and trustworthiness. Public relations, publicity, and corporate advertising campaigns often have the objective of building a generalized reputation for excellence. These campaigns frequently stress the company's research activities. (See Figure 8–2.) Another strategy is to stress the successful use of the company's products or services by customers who themselves have high credibility and prestige. An example of this kind of advertising is shown in Figure 8–3. This kind of testimonial can be especially convincing because it is assumed that the customers would not allow their names to be used unless they were completely satisfied with the product. (More about this when we consider spokesmen as communicators.)

One major objective of corporate advertising is often to create a heightened level of acceptance for the company's salesmen or for its resellers. It is hoped that the advertising will gain a higher level of ini-

Fig. 8–2. A corporate advertisement to build reputation. (Court

What's 11 feet tall, walks on 4 legs and drinks gasoline?

one of several machines being developed by General Electric to do things no machine...or no man...has ever done before.

It looks like something out of science fiction. But it's something out of science. The science of Cybernetic Anthropomorphous Machine Systems. CAMS, for short.

CAMS, quite simply, are machines that copy and magnify man's own movements. The man in this machine, for instance, can actually "feel" where it's walking. He's even able to make it flick aside heavy obstacles... lift hundreds of pounds out of the way without losing its balance. Soon he'll be taking it over fallen trees, across rough terrain. This walking machine is being developed for the U. S. Army by General Electric. GE has already applied CAMS principles to build machines that are at work on production lines. And is planning others to work at construction sites and even in space. Machines that will enable man to do things he's never done before. General Electric is easing man's work in many ways. Process computers are running steel mills. Industrial x-rays are measuring ingredients inside packages. Electric motors are freezing food, opening cans, washing dishes and doing dozens of other household chores. It's a nice way to make progress—letting machines do the work for you.

Progress is our most important product

GENERAL ELECTRIC

General Electric Co.; Batten, Barton, Durstine & Osborn, Inc.)

Fig. 8–3. An advertisement stressing prestige of users. (Courtesy of Remington Rand, Inc.; Young & Rubicam, Inc.)

tial acceptance for the salesman on cold calls and make his presentation more believable. (See Figure 8–4 for a classic advertisement stressing the role of business-paper advertising in gaining acceptance for the salesman.) Finally, the advertising may also serve the purpose of increasing the loyalty and enthusiasm of the salesman or resellers. If it is intended that resellers should be the primary benefactors of the advertising, it may be possible to list the names of the company's resellers in the body of the advertisement.

Chapter 24 is devoted to a further consideration of corporate advertising, public relations, and publicity, major tools in the marketing communicator's kit for developing a favorable image for his company. Corporate advertising, as indicated above, may also have this purpose. Any communications that say something about the company itself, whether paid for or free (as in the case of publicity) and whether the result of careful planning or random occurrences, will have a substantial impact on the acceptance of communication delivered by the company's salesmen and resellers. It makes sense, therefore, to develop specific programs to make sure that these communications are favorable to the company and provide the necessary support for other marketing communication effort. Company reputation is a major determinant of the success of the marketing communication activities of the firm.

The Salesman as Communicator

There are certain attributes of salesmen which, independent of the company's reputation, influence the response of prospective customers to the salesman's presentation. These fall into two categories: individual characteristics of the salesman himself, including personality, appearance, and knowledge; and attitudes of the receiver toward persons occupying the role "salesman."

Individual Characteristics. One set of attitudes toward the salesman possessed by the prospect will be a function of that individual's response to the salesman as an individual. In general, there is evidence to support the assertion that prospects will respond most favorably to salesmen who are similar to themselves. This assertion has been found to be true for such characteristics as age, sex, religious beliefs, political preference, smoking habits, attitudes toward the product being sold (insurance in the research being cited), and income.[10] It stands to reason that a person is more likely to trust another who is like himself because he will be perceived as having more similar interest and viewpoints. The result is that the salesman who is like his prospect is more likely to have high

[10]Franklin B. Evans, "Selling as a Dyadic Relationship—A New Approach," *American Behavioral Scientist*, 6 (May 1963), pp. 76–79.

"I don't know who you are.

I don't know your company.

I don't know your company's product.

I don't know what your company stands for.

I don't know your company's customers.

I don't know your company's record.

I don't know your company's reputation.

Now—what was it you wanted to sell me?"

MORAL: Sales start **before** your salesman calls—with business publication advertising.

McGRAW-HILL
market-directed *
PUBLICATIONS

Fig. 8—4. An advertisement stressing the value of advertising to support the salesman. (Courtesy of McGraw-Hill Publications, a division of McGraw-Hill, Inc.; Ketchum, McLeod & Grove, Inc.)

credibility—because he tends to be more trusted, not because he necessarily is perceived as being more expert.

On a more straightforward level, there are certain characteristics of salesmen that will determine the prospect's reaction. Does he present a good appearance? Is he well spoken and does he have an apparent self-confidence about him? Is he polite and respectful and does he meet our standards of good behavior? Is he prompt for the appointment and does he seem business-like or is he wasting my time? All of these aspects of the salesman's behavior will be significant determinants of the prospect's response to him.

Perhaps most obvious as a determinant of his credibility is the salesman's competence. His competence is largely a function of his background and training for the job, as well as the quality of the supervision which he receives from his management. The importance of the salesman's product knowledge, his ability to understand and find solutions to customers' problems, and his knowledge of the skill of persuasive salesmanship cannot be stated too strongly. The receiver will be quick to form judgments about how qualified the salesman is to solve his problems.

The Occupational Stereotype. The salesman's appearance and his knowledge are objective characteristics, although they become significant only to the extent that they produce a certain (subjective) response from the prospect. In addition to the salesman as an individual, the prospect will also be responding to the salesman as a salesman, as one who occupies the role "salesman," and to the stereotype of salesman. A stereotype is a consensus of role expectations shared by a significant segment of the population with respect to some role. There are stereotypes of most occupations (truckdriver, undertaker, teacher) that define how a person who occupies that role should behave. This consensus of role expectations will guide the behavior of persons who occupy that role as well as those who interact with them. Stereotypes may have a basis in objective reality, although they seem to change more slowly than the reality that produces them. A major source of stereotyping is repeated interaction with persons occupying that role.

There is definitely a stereotype of the salesman. It attributes to him such characteristics as "talkative," "excitable," "optimistic," "competitive," "easy-going," and "enthusiastic." Both salesmen themselves and buyers describe them in these terms.[11] During the first stages of interaction with a salesman, the prospect is likely to be reacting to the stereotype of the salesman rather than to the salesman as an individual.

[11] Wayne Kirchner and Marvin Dunnette, "How Salesmen and Technical Men Differ in Describing Themselves," *Personnel Journal,* 37 (April 1959), pp. 418–19.

The fact that the salesman is trying to persuade the prospect has an influence upon the receiver's perception of his trustworthiness. Part of the stereotype is that the salesman will be boastful about his product's quality and performance. A certain amount of puffery is expected, and this leads to a reduction in his credibility. As suggested earlier, the general "intent to persuade" attributed to the salesman will not be as significant as perceptions of his fairness.

It is also appropriate to note here the fact that, in general, many salesmen have little occupational prestige. Lack of prestige may be due to the absence of formalized educational and training requirements for many of those who fill the salesman role, and the lack of authority of the salesman in the buyer-salesman relationship. The receiver's perception of the salesman's lack of authority may lead to the expectation that he will use misleading information or withhold information in an attempt to control the behavior of potential customers. This may be one source of the perception of low trustworthiness attributed to the stereotype.[12]

A New Image. In the past several years, the pressures of increased competition and the advent of the marketing concept have resulted in a significant improvement in the quality of the selling effort being fielded by most manufacturing companies. It is generally agreed by informed observers of the business scene that the old-time drummer whose major tactics were of the wining and dining variety, who relied upon his personal charm and a well-timed hard-sell, has disappeared. He has given way to a well-informed, service-oriented company representative whose objective is to build a long-term relationship with his customers by providing the best solutions to their problems.[13] The company that devotes less than its best efforts to the development of an effective field sales organization will suffer because of the importance which today's customers attach to the trustworthiness and competence of their vendors' salesmen.

Resellers as Communicators

Most resellers can be thought of as "companies" in themselves, and many of the comments made earlier about reputation apply with equal validity to the special case of the retailer, wholesaler, or other type of reseller who acts, in effect, as an agent of the selling company. The point is that potential customers will have set attitudes toward the middlemen and resellers used by the company, and these attitudes represent an important variable in marketing communication strategy.

[12]John L. Mason, "The Low Prestige of Personal Selling," *Journal of Marketing*, 29 (October 1965), pp. 7–10.
[13]Carl Rieser, "The Salesman Isn't Dead—He's Different," *Fortune*, 66 (November 1962), pp. 124 ff.

The image and reputation of the reseller may be an asset for the manufacturer and significantly improve his credibility. For example, a little known brand of clothing may achieve a high level of market acceptance if actively promoted by the more prestigious retailers. Many large retailers attempt to build upon this asset of a reputation for quality and value by offering their own brand names, or "private labels." Retailer-controlled brands are often sold at slightly reduced prices for quality equal to national brands because the expense of national advertising to maintain the prestige of the national brand is avoided to some extent.

For many product lines it is necessary to achieve extensive distribution through thousands of retailers (and perhaps as many as a hundred or more wholesalers) throughout the country. Major appliances such as television sets provide a good example. Retailers will vary widely in their reputation within the communities they serve and the share of market which the brand achieves at the local level will reflect the retailers' reputation. Other things being equal, the company becomes more dependent upon its local retailers as the amount spent on creating a national reputation decreases. As the brand name becomes more important, retailer reputation becomes less important.

Money and effort spent by the manufacturer to strengthen the retailers and to improve their standing in the local community may return handsome dividends to the manufacturer. Determining the role of the reseller is a critical step in planning the marketing communication program. It can be especially important that retail sales clerks have sufficient knowledge to thoroughly and convincingly explain the product's features to prospective customers. If there is evidence that manufacturers' salesmen today are cut from different cloth than their predecessors, as noted earlier, there is evidence almost as strong that the quality of retail selling (and of industrial distributors' selling) has deteriorated during the same time.

It is a shame that the potential payoffs from a well-executed marketing communication program at the national level may disappear at the critical stage when the potential consumer has to cope with a poorly informed and poorly motivated retail clerk. Such is too often the case.

Credibility of the Mass Media

The mass media have their own credibility; this is another significant variable to consider in developing the marketing communication strategy. Media vehicles may influence the credibility of the messages they carry in three ways. First, they may be influential because of their perceived expertise and unique competence on relevant issues. Second, they may be regarded as of exceptional honesty, not afraid to report the truth and not willing to accept advertising unless there is evidence of product performance in support of the claims made in the advertising. Third, they may have a unique influence on their audience because of individuals' perceptions of the characteristics of the audience. In other words, persons who read magazine X may regard it highly because they believe the audience of magazine X to be intelligent, articulate, high status, or whatever. This is the same as saying that the audience of magazine X provides a reference group for the receiver.

Products take on certain meaning from the media in which they are advertised. Magazines such as New Yorker and National Geographic are generally regarded as lending their prestige to the products advertised in them. The feeling is that the image of the product is enhanced by this affiliation and the claims made for the product perhaps become more believable. One study found that the prestige of the magazine and the selling company were both influential on attitudes toward new products.

An explicit case of the influence of advertising media upon credibility is the practice of some magazines of awarding a "seal of approval" to certain products advertised in their pages. Usually, this approval has significance because the products must be carefully tested before the approval is granted. Once tests have been completed, the advertiser can use the fact of this approval in his advertising copy and to identify his product with this seal of approval. In this case, the claims made by the advertiser are supported by the advertising medium. The testing procedure increases credibility by adding both dimensions of expertise and trust to the message.

Spokesmen and Credibility

Hired, professional communicators may enhance the credibility of the message. There are three different kinds of spokesmen: persons who have won fame in some profession or endeavor unrelated to the product or company being advertised; professional announcers who earn favor in the public's eye because of frequent exposure and their method of presentation; and persons who become familiar as long-standing spokesmen for a given company's products. The first type is illustrated by the famous actor or sports figure who delivers advertising messages or "testimonials" for products unrelated to his accomplishments. A recent example is the French skier, Jean Claude Killy, who won fame in the 1968 Olympics and who is now seen in advertising both related and unrelated to skiing. The second type is exemplified by Ed McMahon, who has appeared for many years on the "Tonight" television show and earned public recognition and acceptance as a spokesman for many products.

---

[14]Douglas A. Fuchs, "Two Source Effects in Magazine Advertising," *Journal of Marketing Research,* 1 (August 1964), pp. 59–62.

He has become a spokesman for Budweiser Beer, both on the "Tonight" show and in other advertising vehicles. An example of the third type of spokesman is Ed Reimers, who became especially noted as the spokesman for Allstate Insurance, although he had represented many other products and services as well.

Such spokesmen become recognized by the American public and come to gain acceptance and credibility. They thus deliver above-average value for the advertiser's message. Typically, the fees for their services reflect this greater value. Such spokesmen can provide recognition and identity for the company's products as well as improve the competence and trust which the receiver attributes to the message.

It appears that a major dimension of the spokesman's effectiveness is the sincerity which the receiver ascribes to him, one aspect of trustworthiness. In a classic study of a war bond drive during World War II, in which the vehicle was an eighteen-hour radio marathon appeal featuring the famous singer Kate Smith, the influence of the spokesman's sincerity was clearly identified. This drive was highly successful, and researchers attributed this success to Miss Smith's perceived sincerity in the minds of the audience. Such comments as " . . . she *really means* anything she ever says" were reported as typical. It was felt that the stress and strain of her eighteen-hour series of broadcasts served to validate her sincerity and selflessness.[15]

SUMMARY

The way in which various elements of the marketing communication strategy take on credibility have been suggested here. Five possible "communicators" were identified: the company, the salesmen, resellers, media, and spokesmen. Each of these communicators will be evaluated on the basis of perceived competence and trust, and this evaluation will be a significant filter for the meaning ascribed to the communication by the receiver. Credibility is a set of attitudes, or predispositions, toward each of these communicators held by members of the audience. The dimensions of credibility must be analyzed and appropriate strategies for their development planned as part of the marketing communication task.

[15]Robert K. Merton, *The Social Psychology of a War Bond Drive* (New York: Harper & Row, 1946), pp. 83, 90.

9

Effectiveness of Mass vs. Personal Communication

One of the most basic strategic decisions required of the marketing manager concerns the relative importance of mass and personal communication in the promotional mix. The major dimensions of this decision are the amount of investment in personal selling and advertising, and the communication tasks to be assigned to these two major activities. These strategic decisions will influence the structure of the marketing organization and the marketing channel and will also shape the company's policies in both product and pricing matters.

Because this text combines consideration of all communication variables, it is possible to analyze this basic allocation problem rather than to assume that a certain role has been prescribed for advertising or personal selling or other communication tools. While there is no well-defined and generally accepted conceptual framework within which to make this analysis, there are several ways in which the problem can be rigorously attacked. This chapter develops some of the major factors to be considered in determining the relative importance of personal and nonpersonal communications in the marketing communication strategy.

Previous chapters have laid important groundwork for this one. Some reasons for the relative effectiveness of personal and nonpersonal communications were discussed in Chapter 6. Chapter 6 also suggested that different sources of information change in importance as innovations

162

spread throughout the market. Analysis of the communication process has suggested the importance of feedback and the greater "efficiency" of personal communication. Interactions between source effects and communicator effects were developed in the last chapter.

There are also several other variables to be considered that tend to involve economic and strategic factors that go beyond communication per se. Company resources and the nature of competition may place significant constraints upon the firm's alternatives for communicating with its markets. These are also explored in this chapter.

KINDS OF COMMUNICATION

There are several ways in which to distinguish among the various kinds of communication available to the marketing communicator. Unfortunately, the distinctions that have been made in communication research are not quite appropriate to the marketing situation. Communication research has tended to distinguish between "personal" and "impersonal" sources *without* distinguishing between commercial and noncommercial sources. In the last chapter, it was seen that the commercial vs. noncommercial distinction is important because commercial sources may be perceived as having manipulative intent, thus reducing credibility.

Communication research has combined both commercial and noncommercial sources in analyses of the relative influence of personal and impersonal sources. Thus, relatives, friends, neighbors, landlords, former employers, veterinarians, salesmen, agricultural agents, and farmers were all called "personal sources" in a study of the diffusion of agricultural innovations. In this same study, "impersonal sources" were defined to include newspapers, magazines, television, printed directions on sacks or containers, commercial circulars, and agricultural college publications.[1] This tendency to combine both commercial and noncommercial sources hinders any attempt to trace the implications of this research for marketing communication strategy. Further refinements in definitions seem warranted.

For the following discussion, two distinctions among information sources will be sufficient. We shall distinguish between commercial and noncommercial sources, and between mass and personal communications. Commercial sources will be defined as those motivated by a desire for economic gains and will refer primarily to selling companies. Noncommercial sources include the many social influences discussed in ear-

---

[1]Everett M. Rogers and George M. Beal, "The Importance of Personal Influence in the Adoption of Technological Changes," *Social Forces*, 36 (May 1958), pp. 329–35.

lier chapters, as well as educational institutions, the editorial content of mass media, and so on. Mass communications are those directed to a large (impersonal) audience, while personal communications involve interpersonal interaction. Examples of each of these kinds of information sources are shown in Figure 9–1.

It may be helpful to think of personal/noncommercial sources as "informal" because the communication is likely to be relatively spontaneous and specific to the situation and not based upon some guiding strategy or plan. Referring to Figure 9–1, it can be seen that all other sources are more "formal" in the sense that their activities are planned and are aimed at multiple audiences on a more or less repetitive basis. The lower right-hand corner of that illustration contains "informal" sources characterized by spontaneity of response to the individual's needs and high credibility relative to other sources.

These distinctions provide the definitions and bases for the following discussion.

PERSONAL COMMUNICATION: MORE EFFICIENT

As communication, personal sources are more "efficient" than mass communication. (This comment has nothing to do with economic efficiency, to be discussed toward the end of this chapter.) Personal communication is more efficient because there is *immediate and direct feedback* to tell the communicator whether he has been successful in conveying the intended meaning. As a result, there can be a precise tailoring of the message to respond to the receiver. There is flexibility when countering the receiver's natural resistance to change. There is more information available to the communicator concerning his receiver and therefore the communication can be more specific.

	COMMERCIAL	NONCOMMERCIAL
MASS	Advertising in Broadcast and Print Media Direct Mail Trade Shows and Displays Outdoor Advertising Car Cards	Editorial Content in Broadcast and Print Media Scientific Exhibits Academic Papers Professional Association Communications and Conferences
PERSONAL	Salesmen Retail Dealers Applications and Service Engineers Demonstrators	Friends and Neighbors County Agents Professionals (doctors, dentists, architects, etc.) Family Members

Fig. 9–1. Categories of information sources.

By way of contrast, mass communication must be directed at some kind of "average" or typical receiver. In an advertising campaign, the message has to be developed to appeal to the maximum number of potential receivers-customers. As a result, it may be "ideal" for only a small part of the total audience. Because there is no possibility of immediate and direct feedback to the communicator, it is not possible to detect the need for message refinements and changes without substantial delays. The advertiser must rely upon such devices as opinion surveys, store audits, or customer orders as indirect measures of communication effectiveness. Each of these potential sources of feedback has "noise," that is, erroneous, irrelevant, or meaningless information, which makes it difficult to attribute changes in opinions or sales to the specific advertising campaign being evaluated.

Personal communication is also more efficient in conveying meaning because it allows for use of multiple "symbol systems," a richer variety of methods for conveying meaning to intended receivers. In addition to the obvious use of language (words), the communicator also conveys meaning by the qualities of his voice—tone, inflection, accents, loudness, and so forth. Other symbol systems are used as well—facial expressions, hand gestures, body motions, distance between communicator and receiver, mode of dress—and these also convey meaning as defined by the cultural context within which the dyad is operating.

In the case of personal selling, the communicator also has the opportunity to demonstrate the product and use other sales aids to deliver his message. In addition to the spoken word, pictures, models, or the product itself may be used along with the verbal presentation. Such devices substantially increase the opportunity for the receiver to understand the product and its use and to evaluate its suitability for him. All of these factors lead to a more efficient and precise communication, in the sense that the output from the communication process, the response desired by the communicator, is more likely to occur. Messages (inputs) can be precisely developed (encoded) to account for the needs and attitudes (predispositions) of the potential customer (receiver) to obtain the desired changes in awareness, attitudes, or behavior (response)

INFORMAL COMMUNICATION: MORE EFFECTIVE

Many times in the previous chapters it has been stated that noncommercial and personal sources of information result in more opinion change. Evidence was cited to support the assertion that credibility is highest when there is no perception of persuasive intent. Furthermore, persuasive intent is likely to be perceived to some extent in any commercial or professional communicator, including the mass media.

Informal communication combines the advantages of both personal and noncommercial communications. It has the opportunities for precision that are found in all personal communication, and it has the credibility of noncommercial sources. Analysis of word-of-mouth communication (in Chapter 6) emphasized the fact that informal communication sources may also have the opportunity, because of positions of status within the group, to exert some form of social pressure along with the information exchanged in the communication. It was also noted that informal sources, because they are in the "noncommercial" category, are more likely to be relied upon for information of an evaluative nature. This is especially the case where the consequences of purchase being evaluated are psychosocial in nature.

These comments suggest that the marketing communicator should make maximum use of informal sources because they are more effective. In Chapter 6, however, it was shown that there are major difficulties involved in the planned use of word-of-mouth as part of the communication strategy. While it may be more "effective" because it is more credible, more flexible, and more capable of exerting social control on the receiver, it also is least controllable and can have significant negative, as well as positive, consequences.

The assignment facing the marketing communication strategist is to find the right combination of those modes of communication that he *can* control so that the probabilities of using informal communication to best advantage are highest. He must carefully blend advertising, personal selling, public relations, publicity, sales promotion, point-of-purchase display, and packaging in such a manner that word-of-mouth and opinion leadership processes come into play to help accomplish his objectives.

INFORMATION AND ADOPTION DECISIONS

The effectiveness of the various forms of communication will depend upon the stage in the buyer's decision process. To view the consumer buying process as essentially a decision-making (or rational as opposed to emotional) process highlights the need for information with particular characteristics at each stage of the decision.

The following comments assume that the consumer has not previously bought whatever it is that is being sold by the marketing communicator. (Communication to encourage repeat usage is no less important, and will be treated separately.) That is, the communication must bring about a change in behavior (or in attitudes, or both) and the potential customer must decide whether to change or to maintain the status quo, that is to minimize the risk involved in change.

One way to analyze the use of information by potential new product adopters is within the structure of the five-stage adoption decision process: awareness, interest, evaluation, trial, and adoption. This is the framework within which most of the research to be cited has been conducted. It is doubtful whether the interest stage is a distinct mental stage of sufficient importance to the marketing strategist. In Chapter 2, a shortened structure was presented in which interest and evaluation were combined in a single "evaluation" stage representing all of the "information processing" activities of the adopter between initial awareness and actual trial of the product. In the following paragraphs, somewhat refined versions of the five-step adoption process will be used as dictated by the evidence we are examining. The reader should not forget, however, that we are talking about the same decision process—a potential customer moving from initial unawareness of a product to awareness, then to active interest and evaluation of the suitability of the product for his needs, to actual trial use of the product, and finally to full-scale adoption of the product.

Information Use and Decision Stage

Our discussion will organize and relate the several research studies that have dealt with the question of the importance of different information sources in the several stages of the decision process. Conclusions that are generally supported by the research will first be stated, and the relevant studies then cited.

1. *Commercial sources of information are most important at the awareness stage.* Awareness is frequently an accidental phenomenon. The receiver is exposed to information concerning a new product without having been consciously seeking that information. Furthermore, the level of promotional activity reflects the manufacturer's spending plans, which may have the objective of exposing the average consumer to the message several times within a relatively short time period. It should therefore not be surprising that communication research has offered evidence which supports the conclusion that commercial sources of information are most important at the awareness stage. It is one of the major objectives of virtually every advertising or selling campaign, especially and obviously for new products, to create awareness of the product and its features among potential customers.

When the objective is not evaluation or action but simply to inform potential customers that the product exists and where it is available, credibility is hardly an issue. It is only at the evaluation and action stages where the subtleties of credibility become more important.

Both mass and personal sources of "commercial" information have been found to be important at this stage. Ferber and Wales reported finding that detailmen were most frequently mentioned by doctors as the source of information most likely to bring a new pharmaceutical to their attention.[2] In reviewing this study and several others, Bauer and Wortzel concluded that ". . . commercial sources of information form a major, and probably a predominant, part of the physician's means of keeping informed about new drugs."[3] They cited one study as representative of the findings relating to pharmaceuticals. This study found that doctors preferred information sources in the following order:

1. Detailmen
2. Medical journal papers and articles
3. Medical journal advertising
4. Direct mail
5. Conversations with other doctors
6. Drug samples
7. Staff meetings

An earlier study by Bauer, summarized briefly in the Bauer and Wortzel article, found that the reputation of the selling company became a more important influence than the doctor's relationship with the salesman as the amount of risk involved in using the new drug increased.[4] To apply the concepts and terminology developed in the previous two chapters, source effect becomes more important than communicator effect as the amount of perceived risk increases. This finding is contrary to that of Levitt reported in the previous chapter.

In an earlier study of the diffusion of a new hybrid seed corn among farmers in Iowa, it was found that over half of the farmers reported first learning about the seed from a salesman.[5]

A study of industrial purchasing agents revealed that, in the purchase of a product such as office equipment, these professional buyers would most likely learn about the availability of a new product from the equipment company's salesman, from an advertisement, or from a direct mail circular, in that order. They would have *preferred* to learn about it from the equipment company's salesman (68 percent), next from direct mail

[2]Robert Ferber and Hugh G. Wales, *The Effectiveness of Pharmaceutical Promotion* (Urbana: Bureau of Economic and Business Research, University of Illinois, 1958), p. 21.

[3]Raymond A. Bauer and Lawrence H. Wortzel, "Doctor's Choice: The Physician and His Sources of Information about Drugs," *Journal of Marketing Research*, 3 (February 1966), pp. 40–47.

[4]Raymond A. Bauer, "Risk Handling in Drug Adoption: Role of Company Preferences," *Public Opinion Quarterly*, 25 (Winter 1961), pp. 546–59.

[5]Bryce Ryan and Neal C. Gross, "The Diffusion of Hybrid Seed Corn in Two Iowa Communities," *Rural Sociology*, 8 (May 1943), pp. 15–24.

(15 percent) or from a mazagine advertisement. Less than 5 percent of the respondents indicated any preference for a noncommercial source at the awareness stage. Those who preferred impersonal sources rather than salesmen cited the greater time commitment required to talk to a salesman compared to the relative efficiency of reading an advertisement or a direct mail piece.[6]

A later study of industrial markets suggested that buyers found trade journals and manufacturers' salesmen to be of about equal importance, with a slight edge for journals (90 percent compared to 84 percent). In addition, trade shows were an important source of awareness information for over three-quarters of the respondents, with trade associations important only to a minority. Noncommercial sources such as buyers and engineers in other companies were important at the awareness stage for only one in four respondents.[7]

2. For evaluation, noncommercial sources become important. Earlier analysis of word-of-mouth, of credibility, and of the perceived risk concept have all suggested reasons why this generalization is valid. When the potential buyer begins to ask the evaluation question, "Is this product the right one for me?" he may want two kinds of information that he does not expect commercial sources to be able to provide. First, evidence about negative product performance characteristics could not be found in commercial sources. Second, commercial sources cannot provide much relevant help in assessing the psychosocial consequences of purchase (although advertising appeals may suggest psychosocial consequences).

We can think of two kinds of noncommercial sources that will be of significance, depending upon the nature of the product. Mass media of various types may be significant noncommercial sources of information with which to evaluate new products. In such fields as medicine and engineering, there are professional and academic journals which report the results of careful evaluations of new technologies and devices. In the consumer field, there are such magazines as *Consumer Reports*, which claim to objectively evaluate products in a given category against a set of standards of importance to a majority of customers and to follow careful scientific procedures in conducting these evaluations.

Most often, however, research evidence has shown the importance of informal (i.e., personal, noncommercial) sources at this stage. Only informal sources can help evaluate psychosocial consequences. Further-

[6]Frederick E. Webster, Jr., and Douglas D. MacDonald, *Industrial Buyers' Preferences for Information Sources,* unpublished paper, Amos Tuck School of Business Administration, Dartmouth College, 1966.

[7]Frederick E. Webster, Jr., "Informal Communication in Industrial Markets," *Journal of Marketing Research,* 7 (May 1970), pp. 186–89.

more, credibility is likely to be highest for informal sources, since all other sources, whether mass media or commercial personal sources, may be perceived as having some persuasive intent.

These findings have been supported by research in each of the fields cited earlier—pharmaceuticals, agricultural innovations, and the industrial market. Wilkening has reported a study showing that "other farmers" were the most important source of information for farmers at the "decision-making" stage, which includes evaluation as defined here.[8] Ferber and Wales in their study of the use of information sources by physicians concluded that ". . . colleagues are more important as a convincing source than as a source of notice, which suggests that doctors are more likely to discuss new pharmaceuticals with colleagues only after hearing of the product from other sources."[9] The study of industrial buyers also found that buyers and engineers in other companies were more important at the evaluation stage than at any other stage *but* they still were not as important as the manufacturer's (i.e., seller's) salesman even at this stage.[10]

These generalizations must be qualified by the observation that different adopter categories do not show the same information source preferences at each stage. The nature of those qualifications will be suggested in a moment.

3. *For trial and buying action, personal, commercial sources become important.* Most purchasing behavior, even if it is only a one-shot trial, requires some interaction with a sales representative. For most products other than consumer packaged goods, product demonstrations become important and these almost always require the attention of a salesman. In the industrial market especially, the failure of a salesman to carefully supervise the trial stage in the testing of a new product by a potential customer has often resulted in a lost sale. If the product is complex or involves features with which the potential customer is not familiar, the importance of the salesman is obvious. Test-driving a new automobile, for example, requires at the minimum some instruction about the important features of the car such as the location of the starter, the operation of the gearshift, and such functions as steering and braking (especially if these are power-assisted).

Any product or service requiring instruction in operation or other technical matters requires two-way communication to be effective. Feedback tells the communicator whether or not the receiver understands well enough to proceed to the next stage. Being able to see or hear or

[8]Eugene A. Wilkening, "Roles of Communicating Agents in Technological Change in Agriculture," *Social Forces*, 34 (May 1956), pp. 361–67.

[9]Ferber and Wales, *op. cit.*, pp. 24–25.

[10]Webster, *op. cit.*

observe the operation of actual materials and equipment is often necessary before the basic product concept and qualities can be grasped. In selling street-sweeping equipment to municipalities, as an illustration, the most important information required by the prospective buyer is how the machine operates (driver safety, driving speeds, maintenance requirements) and how cleanly it sweeps the pavement. The only way that information can be provided is by a product demonstration—actually sweeping the street—and a well-trained salesman who carefully points out the relevant product features to meet the criteria established by the buyer.

Rogers reports a summary evaluation of several studies to the effect that "commercial change agents are more important at the trial stage than at any other stage in the adoption process."[11] This statement obviously applies to personal sources because impersonal (mass) communications could not be of much assistance in this matter. On the other hand, the statement of Bauer mentioned above, that source effect becomes greater than communicator effect in conditions of high risk, should be recalled. Likewise, the study of industrial buyers showed that salesmen became more important at the trial stage, while buyers and engineers in other companies once again declined in relative importance.[12]

The preceding generalizations provide some very important guidelines for determining the relative importance of mass and personal communications in the marketing communication mix. They suggest the conditions under which each kind of information is going to be most relied upon by the consumer as he passes through the stages of the adoption decision process. There are important differences among potential customers, however, in the way in which they proceed through this decision process. The notion of the diffusion process, and of adopter categories, introduced in Chapter 6, provides a framework for analyzing some of these important differences.

Information Use and Adopter Category

Not only are earlier adopters different from later adopters, but the kinds of information available to them are different. The innovators almost "by definition" have to rely upon more commercial and less informal sources of information because there are not many other adopters around from whom they can get information. However, it should be recalled that the opinion leaders (who tend to be early adopters) have

---

[11]Everett M. Rogers, *Diffusion of Innovations* (New York: Free Press of Glencoe, 1962), p. 263.

[12]Webster, *op. cit.*

been found to rely upon still other opinion leaders but of a more cosmopolitan and less local orientation. Thus, innovators may be influenced by innovators in other communities. To consider differences among adopter categories, the following comments will, as before, state a generalization supported by available research evidence and then review the major reasons and findings relating to that generalization.

1. *Earlier adopters tend to rely more heavily upon mass media and commercial sources.* This generalization refers to both innovators and early adopters who have been grouped together here in the category "earlier adopters." Copp and others argued that ". . . . the early adopters of necessity must rely on the mass media and professionals because local farmers will not have heard of or tried out the new practice."[13] Likewise, Rogers reports that earlier adopters tend to report that commercial change agents (such as salesmen and dealers) are more likely than peers to be a source of influence.[14]

These findings are consistent with evidence offered earlier in connection with the discussion of the importance of word-of-mouth. It was found that opinion leaders tend to rely more heavily upon the mass media and to report more exposure to all sources of information, both personal and nonpersonal. This finding was the basis for two-step flow hypothesis that influence flows from the mass media to the opinion leaders and from them to the rest of the population. When we combine this set of observations with the further evidence that early adopters tend to be the opinion leaders, we have the logical basis for the conclusion that early adopters tend to rely more heavily upon the mass media and commercial sources.

This generalization also applies to industrial firms. Innovative industrial firms subscribe to more high-quality journals, have more contacts with people at high levels in universities and research laboratories, have executives who travel more extensively, and have an active program for searching out new ideas.[15] Likewise, innovative doctors were found to subscribe to more medical journals and to have more contacts with medical institutions outside the local community.[16]

Viewing diffusion as a kind of "contagion process" suggests some reasons for this finding. The argument is very simply that, the greater the number of people who have adopted the product, the higher is the prob-

[13]James H. Copp, Maurice L. Sill, and Emory J. Brown, "The Function of Information Sources in the Farm Practice Adoption Process," *Rural Sociology*, 23 (June 1958), pp. 146–57, at p. 154.

[14]Rogers, *op. cit.*, pp. 220–21.

[15]C. F. Carter and B. R. Williams, "The Characteristics of Technically Progressive Firms," *Journal of Industrial Economics*, 7 (March 1959), pp. 87–104.

[16]James Coleman, Elihu Katz, and Herbert Menzel, "The Diffusion of an Innovation Among Physicians," *Sociometry*, 20 (December 1957), pp. 253–70.

ability on a strictly statistical basis that the remaining elements of the population will be exposed to information about the product. While there is some evidence in support of this argument, it tends to be true only up to a certain point in the adoption process—the transition point from early majority to late majority. Later adopters (late majority and laggards) tend to show quite different information acquisition and processing behavior than do earlier adopters and these differences invalidate the argument offered on purely statistical grounds.

    2. *Later adopters tend to rely more heavily upon personal and noncommercial sources.* While this observation is simply the converse of the one above, it has its own significance and evidence. Later adopters are less involved in the affairs of the local community, but they are "local" as opposed to "cosmopolitan" in their orientations. They do not hold positions of leadership or influence within the local community but they do tend to rely upon local sources of information. As followers rather than leaders, they tend to rely upon personal sources of information (opinion leaders) for their information. Copp and others found, for example, that ". . . farm operators relying upon friends and neighbors for information in the early stages of the adoption process tend to have lower progress scores than farmers who do not cite peer influences."[17] Rogers and Beal found that personal sources were more frequently mentioned than impersonal sources by the laggards.[18] In conclusion, informal sources tend to be more important for later adopters because they have less exposure to mass media, are more oriented toward local information sources, and tend to rely heavily upon the judgment of others as the basis for their decisions. Because of their semi-isolated position, the later adopters tend to rely more heavily upon family, relatives, and friends.[19]

    The review of evidence concerning the relative importance of mass and personal communications, and commercial and noncommercial sources, provides a useful framework for thinking about the development of a basic marketing communication strategy. It has suggested at least that the importance of a particular type of information is a function of the stage in the buyer's decision process and the relative "innovativeness" of that buyer. These findings indicate that advertising and the mass media are of major importance as sources of awareness information, especially for earlier adopters. Informal sources become more important at the evaluation stage of the decision process and for later adopters. Personal selling is likely to be more important at the trial stage (and perhaps at the awareness stage in the industrial market) as well as

[17]Copp *et al.*, *op. cit.*, p. 153.
[18]Rogers and Beal, *op. cit.*, p. 335.
[19]Rogers, *op. cit.*, p. 185.

for later adopters. These are not hard and fast conclusions that apply in all situations. Rather they are indications of general tendencies, guidelines for thinking about the ways in which communication effectiveness depends upon the kinds of people who constitute the potential market at a particular stage and the kinds of information that will help them progress toward a favorable decision.

But there are many other factors to consider before the planner has a sound basis for developing strategy. While communication considerations are of major importance, there are also economic and competitive factors to consider.

Relationship to Product Life Cycle

A moment's reflection will suggest a very direct relationship between these concepts of adoption and diffusion and the concept of the product life cycle. The stages in the product life cycle have been described as introduction, growth, maturity, saturation, and decline.[20] The product life cycle and the diffusion process describe the same phenomenon from different viewpoints; the former concentrates upon the sales and profit implications for the firm, while the latter considers changes that occur in the market.

The findings from communication research suggest, without being very specific, that the relative importance of mass and personal communications should change over the product life cycle. While the product is in its introductory and growth stages, the evidence suggests relatively greater emphasis upon mass communications and attempts to identify and influence the opinion leaders. At later stages, it suggests that advertising expenditures might be cut back (because later adopters are relatively uninfluenced by the mass media). Because later adopters are more difficult to persuade, it might be argued that they can be more effectively reached and influenced by personal selling. Given their reluctance to change, however, the expense of personal selling might not be justified. There is some basis for an argument that one must let "nature take its course," and wait for peer influence to finally convince the later adopters. Such a passive attitude probably goes a little too far but it may be a useful balance against the overly optimistic point of view that more advertising or more personal selling is all that is required to saturate the market.

PUSH AND PULL STRATEGIES

A frequently used dichotomy in marketing management discussions is that between "push" and "pull" strategies. A major dimension on which

[20]Arch F. Patton, "Top Management's Stake in the Product Life Cycle, *Management Review*, 48 (June 1959), pp. 9 ff.

this distinction is made is the relative emphasis upon mass vs. personal communication in the marketing mix. This push-pull distinction provides a concise way of showing the relationship between this mass vs. personal communications decision and other economic, company, and market considerations in designing the marketing mix. These two strategies are distinguished on the basis of the predominant flow of influence, as shown in Figure 9–2.

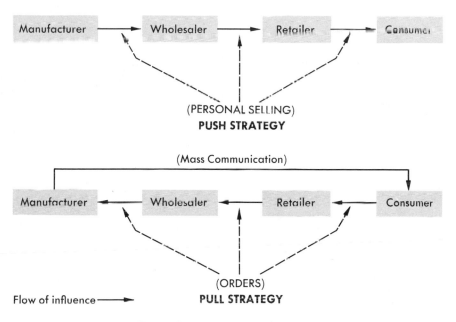

Fig. 9–2. Push and pull strategies.

Push Strategies

Push strategies are characterized by a heavy reliance upon personal communication as the basic method of delivering messages to prospective customers. This emphasis occurs at all stages of the marketing channel. The manufacturer's salesmen *push* the product to the wholesalers. That is, they aggressively explain the value of stocking the product and actively solicit orders. Likewise, the wholesaler *pushes* the product to retailers who, in turn, *push* it to consumers. At all stages, the emphasis is upon personal selling—salesmen explaining the product benefits and aggressively seeking the customer's favorable decision.

In order to make the push strategy work, the manufacturer must provide sufficient economic incentive so that each of the resellers finds it worthwhile to take the time required to actively sell the product. Thus, one characteristic of a push strategy is relatively high margins for the trade. Why should the retail clerk take the time to explain a particular product to the consumer unless it promises a greater return to him than if the consumer chooses some other product? For this reason, some manufacturers have followed the practice of giving so-called "push money" to retail clerks to encourage them to put effort against this product.

Another requirement for an effective push strategy is a high-quality product with unique product features and "talking points" for salesmen. The emphasis upon personal selling requires that the salesman have something significant to say, some product features that are not obvious but are significant to the customer. A run-of-the-mill product provides a weak basis for a push strategy because resellers' salesmen will soon respond to the customers' feedback of an indifferent reaction, and give up trying to sell the product.

The push strategy also tends to require a relatively high-priced product, for several reasons. First, the dollar margin to the reseller (percentage margin times retail selling price) must be sufficiently large to justify the efforts required. Second, product quality requirements lead to relatively higher prices. Third, sales calls tend to be expensive in themselves and thus require either a high-priced product or a broad line of medium-to-low-priced products so that the expected value of the order is sufficient to justify the cost of the sales call. These are the characteristics of such classic push strategies as Fuller Brush and Electrolux.

Thus, the distinguishing characteristics of a push strategy are high prices, high trade margins, product quality, and a reliance upon personal selling as the major promotional variable. Notice that the combination of high margins and heavy expenditures for personal selling leaves little to spend on advertising. Mass media may be used sparingly as required to create some national recognition of the brand name and awareness of the product, and perhaps to presell the salesman and to support the reseller's promotional efforts. But advertising will play a relatively minor role in a push strategy, primarily because there are not sufficient funds to support it and make it profitable to the company.

Pull Strategies

A pull strategy is the opposite of a push strategy. Pull strategies are characterized by relatively low trade margins, less emphasis upon personal selling at all stages of the marketing channels, an order-taking role for the salesmen as opposed to an order-generating role, relatively lower retail prices, and smaller dollar volumes per transaction. The major element of a pull strategy is extensive advertising in mass media. The purpose of this advertising is to generate consumer demand that will create a "vacuum" at the end of the marketing channel. This vacuum of consumer demand has the effect of pulling the product through the channel from the producer to the consumer. The retailer *has* to stock the product because consumers demand that he do so. While his margins are less than for products supported by push strategies, the retailer is happy to stock the "pull" product because there is established demand for the product, he has to invest little time or effort to sell it, and there is high turnover resulting in above-average dollar volume per unit of sales area or shelf space.

Consumer advertising requires major investment in mass media, and pull strategies are characterized by a much higher ratio of advertising expenditures to sales revenues. Advertising appeals may tend to be rather emotional and to emphasize hidden benefits as opposed to hidden features that can be brought out by an effective personal sales presentation as is the case with a push strategy. To illustrate this distinction between benefits and features, it is possible to imagine a salesman giving a presentation for a vacuum cleaner involving the stressing of a hidden feature such as "look here at how much more dirt the new Ajax power nozzle picked up than your old machine." It is harder to imagine a salesman stressing a hidden benefit such as "using this new deodorant will make you happier and more socially secure," although such appeals are common in advertising. While this distinction between hidden features and hidden benefits is more a distinction of degree than of kind, it is a relevant distinction for thinking about the opportunities to use mass and personal communication in the marketing mix.

Pull strategies are characteristic of the marketing programs of most consumer package goods including foods, cigarettes, health and beauty aids, beverages (except fresh milk), and some low-priced consumer durables. Extensive national advertising creates strong consumer brand preferences and loyalties. There are important exceptions, however. One notable exception in the health and beauty aid category is Avon Products, which has very successfully used a push strategy in this field characterized by almost pure forms of the pull strategy.[21] Push strategies are used heavily in industrial markets, as well as for consumer products that require careful demonstration and, therefore, an emphasis upon personal selling. For example, life insurance is a very complex intangible product that requires an effective sales presentation before the potential customer can grasp the significance of product features and benefits and apply them to his own situation.

[21]Seymour Freedgood, "Avon: The Sweet Smell of Success," *Fortune,* 68 (December 1964), pp. 108 ff.

It is hard for a small company to launch a successful pull strategy because of the requirement of extensive and skillful investment in mass media advertising and related promotions. For many small companies in markets requiring pull strategies because of the way customers are accustomed to buying, a compromise may lie in competing on a regional basis. This strategy has become more feasible in recent years because of the increased availability of regional media—especially magazines.

These comments on push and pull strategies have been intended primarily to suggest the relationship between the promotional mix (and the question of the relative importance of mass and personal communication, in particular) and other marketing elements: product variables, price and margin variables, and the marketing channel. The importance of a careful blending of these marketing program elements to achieve the right balance in the marketing strategy should be clear.

Let us now consider more carefully how the nature of the market, the nature of the product, and the nature of the market being served influence the decision on push vs. pull strategies.

FACTORS TO EVALUATE AS THE BASIS FOR STRATEGY

The fundamental choice between a push strategy and a pull strategy, relative importance of mass and personal communication, and the communication tasks assigned to advertising, personal selling, and the other communication modes must be based upon careful evaluation of several critical factors. These factors can be combined into three categories: market and customer variables, company variables, and product variables. There are three key questions which must be answered as the very first step in developing marketing communication strategy:

1. Who do we want to reach?
2. What are our strengths and weaknesses as a company?
3. What are we selling?

There are significant interrelationships among these questions that must not be ignored. For example, what we are selling is defined by customer benefits, not by physical product features, and these benefits are specific to whatever market target is defined in answer to the first question above. However, orderly analysis requires that we break the problem into manageable parts, and the three sets of factors identified provide a reasonable basis for proceeding.

Market and Customer Variables

The definition of a market target is perhaps the most basic decision made by the management of any firm because it creates a set of requirements and criteria of effectiveness that must be met by virtually all aspects of the company's operations. Markets can be defined in many ways. Some of the most common bases are these: geographic location; socioeconomic and demographic variables; industry affiliation, in the case of industrial markets; and attitude toward, and patterns of use for, particular products and services.

Defining Market Segments. The careful definition of market targets requires a high degree of creativity and insight into the nature of the market as well as hard-nosed analysis of available data to determine where the opportunities are and where the product being offered and the available resources for marketing effort are likely to generate the most favorable response. In evaluating the attractiveness of alternative market segments as targets for promotional effort, it is helpful to ask several questions. How many customers are there and what is their ability to spend? Why would these people buy our products? What needs are most likely to be effective motivators of their buying behavior? What are the characteristic patterns of buying? What is the nature of the buying decision? Who is involved in that decision and on what basis will they decide?

Other questions to ask relate to the nature of the market in terms of variables other than the customers. For example, it is important to determine if there are communication media available at a reasonable cost with which to reach the segment as defined. It would make little sense, for example, to define the market target for a product in terms of personality variables because that definition would probably not be operational as the basis for media strategy. Compulsive eaters do not congregate in certain advertising media nor do they live in concentrated neighborhoods where they could be efficiently reached by salesmen.

Competitive Practices. Competitive practices must also be considered from two viewpoints. First, competitive practice may be firmly enough established to have created a set of buying habits that a single marketer cannot successfully challenge. For example, a manufacturer of high-fashion sweaters for men faces a very limited number of marketing channel and promotional alternatives. These include some carefully chosen set of men's clothing stores and a limited number of advertising media, principally magazines that feature men's fashions such as *Esquire* and *Playboy*. Customer buying habits preclude many alternatives that might be justified on other grounds.

On the other hand, present competitive practice may define a major opportunity for innovation in the market. There may be significant gaps in present competitive approaches defining opportunities for reaching a segment of the market in new ways. If potential customers are rather hard to define, a limited advertising campaign relying upon general advertising media, and a careful noting of those segments of the market which show the greatest responsiveness, may be wise. In other cases, especially where the product is complex enough to require personal selling and expensive enough to support it, personal selling may be the best way to dig out potential customers. A manufacturer of industrial welding equipment followed the first kind of strategy for long enough to define the specific industries that had the greatest need for the kind of specialized equipment he was selling and then shifted his advertising budget into business papers aimed specifically at those industries. In another case, a major airline decided to use personal selling to call upon small business firms and professional offices in certain metropolitan areas in an attempt to identify specific individuals with needs to travel frequently but who were not big enough to receive routine selling effort.

Definition of market targets is a major step that should be taken very explicitly and with the best information available because it shapes all other elements of the marketing communication strategy.

Company Variables

In the choice of communication strategies, it is important to assess the ability of the company to support and execute the contemplated strategy. The ability to sustain the required financial commitments is especially significant. For example, a pull strategy on a new product may require the commitment of several million dollars for advertising expense (which, although it is an investment in the future, must be treated as a current expense for accounting purposes) over the first few years in order to establish the product firmly in the market against strong competition. Can the company afford the drain upon current assets that this commitment represents? A subsequent realization that the funds are not available to continue spending at the planned rate could mean that returns to the initial investment will be only a fraction of what was planned and the investment will have been largely wasted.

Management Resources. In addition to financial resources, manpower resources should be carefully appraised. More than one small regional company has found itself in major trouble as the result of trying to challenge one of the national packaged goods manufacturers. As often as not, the deciding factor is not the financial muscle of the national firm but the higher level of management ability and marketing skill it exerts on the market. Many small companies simply do not know enough to be able to compete effectively in an expanded market. The relevant knowledge here includes both access to particular kinds of market information and the analytical ability to use that information creatively and wisely.

It includes the ability to purchase time and space in advertising media in the most efficient manner and to skillfully deploy a sales force. Management and financial resources are the major elements to consider in any assessment of the company's strengths and weaknesses as the basis for selling strategy.

Sales Force Capability. The development of an effective sales organization requires a particular set of resources that should be examined as honestly as possible before the company embarks upon a program that depends significantly upon the size and quality of the sales organization. Can the company attract the necessary manpower? Does it have the right job definition, compensation plan, training program, and field supervision to attract and to hold the best men available and required by the competitive situation? Will financial needs permit the company to carry salesmen at a living wage even when sales volume drops significantly due to economic cycles and similar demand patterns?

The company may also face a particular need for information from the market that will require the use of personal selling rather than mass communication or hired agents. A company in the fashion clothing business may decide to deploy its own sales force because of the need to obtain a controlled flow of information back from the market about style trends and inventory levels. A manufacturer of electronic instrumentation may require a carefully trained sales force to identify major bidding opportunities as soon as possible so that the company can be in a position to submit a detailed and responsive proposal when they are finally requested by the buyer. Management ability, market knowledge, sales force capability, and the quality of information available may be more important than financial and production resources in defining the ability of a firm to compete for a share of specific market segments.

Product Variables

The product itself will create many requirements for the balance between mass and personal communication. Complex products are more likely to require personal selling, as are those requiring applications assistance. The amount of perceived risk involved in the purchase of a product will influence both the quality and the quantity of information required by the market. Frequency of purchase is positively related to the relative importance of mass communication in the marketing strategy.

As indicated earlier, the ability of the customer to determine the specific benefits that the product offers him is a significant factor. The sale of an encyclopedia, for example, usually requires an effective salesman to help the customer understand his need for the product and the ways in which the product will render its service. (In this case, it is the "educational" service offered by the encyclopedia that the customer is buying, not the physical product represented by the bound volumes.) As the discussion of push strategy revealed, it is necessary to look at such product features as retail price and margins, breadth of the product line, and the need for demonstration as major determinants of the opportunity to effectively use personal selling.

The importance of a careful assessment of these variables might be brought home by citing the fact that, as a grand average for all United States industry, a sales call cost $42.92 in 1967, compared with $35.55 in 1965 and $17.29 in 1955. The wide range in sales call costs is suggested by the fact that a steel tubing company reported a cost of $3.75 per call compared to $450 for a pyrotechnics company salesman, according to a study reported by McGraw-Hill Publications.[22] These costs include salesman salary, travel expense, and an allocation of supervisory and organizational overhead. Earlier in this chapter, the point was made that personal communication is the most efficient form of communication. Clearly, it is much less efficient in an economic sense.

By way of contrast for the figures on the cost of a sales call, the cost of advertising space in a business publication may be on the order of $15 per thousand readers. That is the cost for delivering a single exposure, a one-way communication, to a mass audience. While these comparisons are not quite valid (we are comparing apples and oranges, as the saying goes), they do suggest why, for example, personal selling is too expensive as a source of awareness information if awareness is the communicator's sole objective.

In conclusion, it has been stressed that market, company, and product factors significantly influence and constrain the range of alternatives available to the marketing communication strategist in planning the relative importance of mass and personal communications in his promotional mix. The ways in which these variables influence the final decision have only been suggested by the foregoing discussion and examples since the problem is too complex to permit any precise rules. A high degree of creativity is required of the marketing communication strategist as he analyzes each set of factors and begins to formulate the major dimensions of the strategy.

SUMMARY

In this chapter we have looked at the implications of findings from communication research on the relative effectiveness of mass and per-

[22]"McGraw-Hill Survey Shows Sales Call Costs Average $42," *Advertising Age* (May 6, 1968), p. 114.

sonal communications as the basis for marketing communication strategy. Several generalizations about the importance of mass and personal, commercial and noncommercial sources in various stages of the adoption and diffusion processes were offered. These generalizations were then related to other elements of the marketing mix (product, price, and channels) as the basis for a distinction between push and pull strategies. Finally, the significance of market, company, and product variables as the factors that must be evaluated in making these strategic choices was stressed.

It bears repeating that potential customers' needs for and uses of information provide the only sound basis for marketing communication strategy. The strategist can usefully question whether he knows enough about his market in this respect to be able to make an intelligent choice among alternatives. It is hard to imagine an area of marketing management where similar amounts of information would have more value and provide more opportunity for the effective allocation of scarce resources.

The past six chapters have examined a host of qualitative factors and concepts useful in appraising the opportunity of communication. These chapters have stressed the key role played by predispositions as filters of messages, the central importance of group influences, and related findings on buyer behavior as the basis for strategy. Equally important in appraising opportunity to communicate are quantitative measures of the market—estimates of market potential and sales forecasts that provide the basis for all financial aspects of the strategic decisions.

These quantitative measures and their uses provide the focus for the next chapter.

10

Market Measurement and Forecasting

Measurement is one of the most important tasks of management. It is the quantification of significant variables and relationships as the basis for the analysis, planning, and control of management action and decisions. It provides the necessary data for most forms of evaluation and for the allocation and budgetary control of financial resources. Measurement is one of the hallmarks of the "scientific" approach to marketing management, for it permits the application of rigorous analysis to objective data concerning the key variables in the system that the manager is trying to design, influence, or control. "When description gives way to measurement, calculation replaces debate."[1]

In this chapter, major concern is for the use of measurement and forecasting (or prediction of parameter values in the future) as the basis for appraising market opportunities and as inputs for the planning of marketing communication strategy. To put the measurement problem into focus as part of the problem of planning marketing communication strategy, it is useful to recall that our ultimate concern is with market *response* to marketing communication. In the process of planning, the strategist must evaluate alternative courses of action including both unique approaches and various levels of effort for each of these approaches. He must consider which of several message strategies to use, which of several media to use, and the amount of money to spend

[1]Abraham Kaplan, *The Conduct of Inquiry* (San Francisco: Chandler Publishing Co., 1964), p. 172.

for each. To make these decisions, the strategist must make a prediction of market response.

The communicator's objective is to obtain the maximum response from the market (in terms of how he has stated his objectives—awareness, attitudes, sales volume, etc.) with the resources he has available to commit to the task. For a sound decision, he needs sufficient information to predict market response to each of the alternative courses of action being evaluated. The soundness of his predictions will be influenced by the quality of the information he has available and his grasp of the concepts required to organize and draw inferences from that information. Skill and accuracy in measurement combine with conceptual analysis of the behavioral and economic characteristics of the market to determine the manager's knowledge base for prediction and planning.

RESPONSE FUNCTIONS

Implicit in the foregoing comments is the notion of a response function—a relationship between some input variable (stimulus) and some outcome (response), with the further implication that there is a causal relationship between the stimulus and the response. The last several chapters of this book have explored various ways of thinking about how the consumer responds to the stimuli of communication. Figure 10–1 suggests how three different measures of response might change as a function of the level of advertising or sales effort. Each of these is an example of a response function. Notice that, in most cases, response is nonlinear over a significant range of values for the independent variable. For example, preference increases as a function of advertising dollars (d) and it increases at an increasing rate until expenditures reach around $140,000; then it continues to increase but at a decreasing rate. When spending exceeds about $200,000 in this example, the percentage of the market preferring this product actually begins to decrease, reflecting some antagonism perhaps toward this level of advertising effort, although sales volume (f) does not respond in the same manner.

This chapter will emphasize the use of market measurement in analysis and planning and will assume that communication and sales volume objectives have not been firmly defined. Measurement for purposes of evaluation and control, after strategy implementation, is the subject of later chapters. For the present, however, it will be assumed that the marketing communication strategist is attempting to appraise market opportunity and to forecast future market conditions. The measurement problem is examined from the preplanning perspective. Remembering

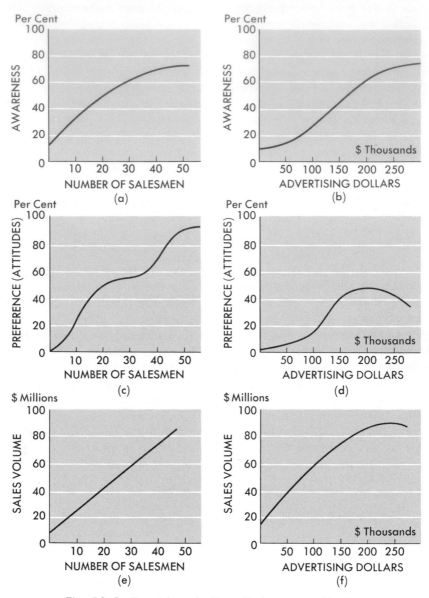

Fig. 10–1. Examples of alternative response functions.

that the objective of measurement is to predict market response, the first step in market measurement and forecasting is, therefore, to define what market characteristics are most likely to influence market response.

Previous chapters have suggested many variables that should be considered in that assessment, including demographic and socioeconomic factors as well as personality characteristics and social affiliations in certain instances. In those previous discussions, the concern was with individual response to market communication rather than receivers in the aggregate. When we consider requirements for market measurement, however, focus shifts to the aggregate level. The problem is to estimate the distribution of the important variables such as income, age, and predispositions within the population that constitutes the potential market and audience. Behavioral analysis of individual response has suggested several classes of factors that are important descriptors of the receiver. Market measurement estimates the distribution of those factors and the extent to which they are likely to influence attitudes and sales response.

MARKET DEFINITION

The first step in market measurement is to define the market, the population of individuals, families, institutions, or firms to which communication and other marketing effort is to be directed. Stated differently, the population of potential consuming units must be defined and then the important characteristics of that population (for purposes of predicting response) can be specified.

Market definition is the result of the firm's basic segmentation strategy, as discussed at the end of Chapter 2. It was said that this is perhaps the most critical decision made by management as the basis for future growth and survival. Market segmentation strategy should be based on an appraisal of where the firm can obtain the best response from its total marketing effort, given its resource constraints and unique competitive advantages and disadvantages.

While this is not the proper place for a lengthy debate on the planning process, it is helpful to point out that the process does not proceed neatly and in linear fashion from one step to the next. It is this mistaken assumption of a linear process that leads to such questions as: "Should forecasting precede planning or should the plan be developed first and serve as an input to the forecast?" and "Should market measurement come before or after definition of market objectives?" Planning should be thought of as an "iterative" process in which a series of steps may be repeated several times, each adding a degree of refinement until there is sufficient definition and specification. For example, a very general qualitative definition of the market (e.g., women over age 40) may be sufficient for market measurement which may, in turn, permit a more precise market definition.

For purposes of market measurement, at least two dimensions of the target market must be defined: its geographic boundaries and the major identifying characteristics of the consuming unit. The need for a geographic definition is obvious and is usually related in the short run to such considerations as distribution arrangements, sales force size, and plant capacity. Over the long run each of these constraints becomes variable and can be altered by management decision. Consuming units may be individuals, households, institutions (hospitals, schools, etc.), or business firms or some subset of these. Subsets of consuming units are defined by categories according to an additional variable such as size, income, age, or sales volume. For example, the market may be defined as "hospitals," or "hospitals with over 50 beds," or "psychiatric hospitals with over 50 beds," depending on the product or service being sold and the basic segmentation strategy.

POTENTIAL AND FORECAST

There are several different concepts of market measurement, and it will avoid confusion if we make some attempt at defining these concepts before proceeding. The concepts to be defined are market potential, sales potential, and sales forecast.

Market potential may be defined as the capacity of a market to absorb a product during a specified time period. It is a measure of demand for a class of product or service and for all sellers of that product. In other words, market potential is an industry statistic, a measure of demand for the output of a specified industry. Measures of market potential are stated for a given geographic market definition, for specified consuming units, and for a limited time period. The potential market for farm tractors in the United States in 1975 is an example of a market potential estimate. Our particular definition of market potential is consistent with that adopted by the American Marketing Association: "A calculation of maximum possible sales opportunities for all sellers of a good or service during a stated period."[2] The basic determinants of market potential are population and income, and these variables will be discussed more completely in the following section.

Sales potential is the level of potential demand for the goods or services of a specified seller. Once again, sales potential must be stated for a specific time period, geographic area, and consuming unit definition. Another way of defining sales potential is

Sales potential = (Market potential) × (Market share)

A seller's share of a potential market is a function of buyer preferences, marketing effort, and the product offering. Sales potential is a measure

[2]*Report of the Definitions Committee* (Chicago: American Marketing Association, 1961).

of company demand while market potential is a measure of industry demand.

The *sales forecast* is a prediction of the level of sales revenue to be obtained by the seller from a specified market in a specified time period. The sales forecast is in most instances the single most important planning statistic used by the firm, not only in marketing, but in financial and personnel planning as well as in production, inventory, and distribution planning. The forecast may be less than the sales potential because the sales potential is based upon an assumption of maximum effort being devoted to demand creation in that market. Remember that potential defines an upper limit to what the market can produce for all sellers and for a given seller. The cost of generating demand will probably increase as market share increases beyond some point, with the result that it will become unprofitable for the seller to continue to spend beyond a certain point. The sales forecast is therefore below sales potential in most instances. These arguments are summarized in Figure 10-2.

Market potential, sales potential, and sales forecast are three distinct measurement concepts and should be so treated. They should not be used as synonyms; each measurement concept is important for certain uses. Measures of potential define what is possible. The forecast is a prediction of what is likely to happen given the planned marketing effort and some assumptions about the response function.

BASIC DEMAND DETERMINANTS

Given a definition of consuming units and geographic boundaries (e.g., restaurants in Oklahoma, all United States households, high-school girls in the Middle Atlantic States, or whatever), the first job of market measurement is to estimate their number (population) and ability to spend (income or a related measure). Population and income are the two basic determinants of demand and market potential.

Number of Consuming Units

Population is measured by some form of census data. The U S. *Census of Population* is issued every ten years and provides information about individuals and households, their numbers and characteristics. In addition, the Bureau of the Census uses these data as the basis for projections of population growth under four different assumptions of growth rate. *Census of Population* data provide the basic input for most measures of consumer markets.

For industrial markets, similar data are provided by the *U.S. Census of Manufacturers.* These data are published approximately every five

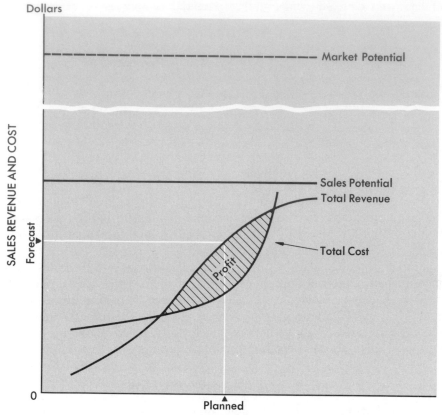

Fig. 10–2. Relationships among three market measures and planning.

years and report the number of manufacturing firms in each Standard Industrial Classification (SIC) industry by geographic location, number of employees, value of shipments, and other details. The *Annual Survey of Manufacturers* provides supplementary data of a less detailed but more current nature. Other censuses of interest to marketers include the *U.S. Census of Business,* which is conducted every five years and includes data on wholesale, retail, and selected service trades, and the *U.S. Census of Housing,* which has been conducted every ten years and provides data on the number, size, and type of dwelling units, including equipment and facilities. There are also censuses of transportation and agriculture. *The Statistical Abstract of the United States* is published annually and is probably the best current single source of data on basic demand determinants.

Advertising media can often provide current and reasonably complete data on the consuming units to which they are directed. Industry trade associations, professional associations, and similar groups typically collect accurate statistics on special populations of interest to the marketer. The value of these data depends upon the degree to which the media audience or association membership matches the market definition adopted by the marketer. Media data are designed to sell the value of the audience delivered to the marketer by that advertising vehicle. This bias should be kept in mind by the data user.

Ability to Spend

Ability to spend is determined by such factors as the income and size of the consuming unit. A family's ability to spend is related to income (which is a function of occupation and education), wealth (especially savings), credit availability, and family size in relation to income. The ability of a business firm to spend is related to its level of activity and its size as measured by such variables as sales volume, number of employees, total assets, and plant size. Liquidity—the availability of cash or credit—is an important demand determinant for consuming units regardless of definition.

On a national level, ability to spend is reflected in such measures of aggregate economic activity as gross national product and disposable personal income. The level of economic activity as measured by such indicators may not be as important a demand determinant as the rate of change in them. Rate of change tends to influence customer expectations, which have significant impact on plans for spending and saving. Historical data on several of the factors we have been discussing are provided in Tables 10–1, 10–2, and 10–3. Close examination of these tables suggests some of the basic features of the American economy in the late 1960's, including growth, mobility, and regional differences.

Survey of Buying Power

In consumer market measurement, one of the most common sources of market information is the annual *Survey of Buying Power* issue of *Sales Management* magazine. This source provides information on population, income, and retail sales by metropolitan area and county for the entire United States. Retail sales data are given for nine different classes of outlets. In addition, the "Buying Power Index" is given for each area. This measure is a weighted average of the three basic factors: (population $\times$ .2) + (income $\times$ .5) + (retail sales $\times$ .3). Each of the three variables is stated in terms of "% of U.S.A." as is the Buying Power Index itself. For example, a Buying Power Index of .0996 for Worcester, Massachusetts, means that the population of this area has about one tenth of 1 percent of total United States retail buying power. The Index is intended primarily for estimating the market potential for rela-

Table 10–1. Examples of Measures of Basic Demand Determinants: Population

Year	Total Population (millions)[a]	Total Households (millions)	Median Age of Population	65 Years and Older	Under 5 Years	Births	Non-White Population
					(000 omitted)		
1960	180.7	52.8	29.5	16,560	20,364	4,307	20,491
1961	183.8	—	29.1	17,011	20,609	4,317	21,254
1962	186.7	54.7	28.8	17,308	20,746	4,213	21,660
1963	189.4	55.2	28.6	17,567	20,722	4,142	22,078
1964	192.1	56.0	28.3	17,861	20,658	4,070	22,580
1965	194.6	57.3	28.0	18,156	20,434	3,801	23,141
1966	196.9	58.1	27.8	18,457	19,851	3,661	23,493
1967	199.1	58.8	27.8	18,796	19,191	3,555	24,062
1968	200.8[b]	—	—	—	—	—	—

[a] Includes Armed Forces abroad.
[b] Estimated.
Source: U.S. Department of Commerce, Statistical Abstract of the United States, 1968, and other selected years.

Table 10–2. Examples of Measures of Basic Demand Determinants: Income (Current Dollars)

Year	Gross National Product ($ billions)	Total Disposable Personal Income ($ billions)	Per Capita Disposable Personal Income (dollars)	Personal Savings ($ billions)	Percentage of Total U.S. Income Received by Top 5% of Population	Median Family Income (dollars)	Percentage of Families with Incomes less than $3,000	Percentage of Families with Incomes $15,000 and Over
1955	398.0	275.3	1,666	15.8	21.7%	5,377	22.8%	2.9%
1960	503.7	350.0	1,937	17.0	20.0	6,174	19.5	5.3
1963	590.5	404.6	—	—	21.2	—	—	—
1964	632.4	438.1	2,280	20.2	22.6	6,371	16.4	7.4
1965	683.9	472.2	2,427	27.2	20.2	7,154	15.5	8.4
1966	743.3	508.8	2,584	25.8	21.8	7,436	14.3	9.2
1967 [a]	785.0	544.7	2,736	36.7	—	—	—	—

[a] Estimated.

Source: U.S. Department of Commerce, Statistical Abstract of the United States, 1968.

Table 10–3. Examples of Regional Differences in Basic Demand Determinants, Selected Years

Region	Total Resident Population (millions)		Population per Square Mile of Land Area		Per Capita Income (dollars)		Percentage of Negroes
	1957	1967	1950	1967	1956	1967	1960
New England	9.9	11.3	147.5	179.7	2,202	3,436	2.3
Middle Atlantic	32.6	37.0	300.1	368.1	2,273	3,525	8.2
East North Central	35.0	39.1	124.1	160.1	2,159	3,392	8.0
West North Central	15.3	16.0	27.5	31.4	1,699	2,995	3.6
South Atlantic	24.7	29.5	79.0	110.3	1,594	2,734	22.5
East South Central	11.8	13.0	63.8	72.3	1,232	2,232	22.4
West South Central	16.3	19.0	33.8	44.2	1,555	2,580	16.3
Mountain	6.4	7.8	5.9	9.1	1,753	2,814	1.8
Pacific [a]	18.4	25.2	45.3	28.3	2,311	3,580	4.5
Total United States	170.3	197.9	50.7	55.9	1,940	3,137	10.5

[a] Including Alaska and Hawaii for 1967 but not for 1950.

Source: U.S. Department of Commerce, Statistical Abstract of the United States, 1958 and 1968.

tively inexpensive and frequently purchased consumer goods. Figure 10–3 illustrates data available from the *Survey of Buying Power.*

A major advantage of these data is that they can also be purchased on punched cards suitable for computer analysis. The data user is certainly not limited to the Buying Power Index but can use statistical analysis to determine the unique relationship of his sales volume to these factors. Once these relationships have been identified (using regression analysis, for example) the marketer has a basis for forecasting sales, given estimates of future values for the three independent variables.

There are, of course, many other sources of data on the two basic determinants of demand, population and income. The purpose of the foregoing comments has not been to suggest all possible sources of data but to indicate that such data are available in secondary (i.e., published) sources and that such measures provide the basis for any appraisal of market opportunity. Measurement of basic demand determinants gives a basis for estimating market potential. Additional information is needed as the basis for estimating sales potential and for sales forecasting.

Sales potential depends upon the company's product offering and buyer preferences. It reflects the company's segmentation strategy and the way in which its product offering is positioned within the total market. To estimate sales potential, it is necessary to obtain measurements beyond those of population and income. These measurements usually involve collection of primary (unpublished, special-purpose) data on predispositions, including needs, levels of awareness, attitudes, and existing product preferences. Notice that measures of sales potential are independent of an assessment of market response to various levels of effort. Rather, sales potential is based upon an assessment of basic preferences and buying habits, as well as attitudes toward the company and its products.

MEASURING PREDISPOSITIONS AND INFLUENCE

As a basis for planning market communication strategy, it is necessary to have some minimum amount of data on market predispositions and social influences on the buying decision. In Chapter 4, problems of measuring predispositions were discussed because they helped to clarify the nature of predispositions. Attention there was concentrated on the various techniques of attitude measurement, including scaling and projective techniques. Here, the discussion will be concerned with the kinds of data required as the basis for planning communication and with various data sources and collection procedures. Technical aspects of atti-

MASSACHUSETTS

COUNTIES CITIES	Met. Area Code	POPULATION ESTIMATES, 12/31/69			EFFECTIVE BUYING INCOME ESTIMATES, 1969			% Hslds. by Cash Income Groups: (A) $0-2,999; (B) $3,000-4,999; (C) $5,000-7,999; (D) $8,000-9,999; (E) $10,000 and Over					RETAIL SALES — SM ESTIMATES, 1969							Buying Power Index
		Total (thousands)	% of U.S.A.	Households (thousands)	Net Dollars (000)	% of U.S.A.	Per Hsld.	A	B	C	D	E	Total Retail Sales (000)	% of U.S.A.	Food ($000)	General Mdse. ($000)	Furn.-House.-Appl. ($000)	Automotive ($000)	Drug ($000)	
Barnstable		84.1	.0413	27.5	255,461	.0408	9,289	22.4	12.7	23.0	14.4	27.5	259,143	.0745	61,334	27,156	9,063	30,205	9,001	.0510
Barnstable		17.2	.0085	5.7	55,868	.0089	9,801	19.9	11.2	23.3	16.1	29.5	82,043	.0236	14,945	15,381	4,126	14,277	2,180	.0132
Falmouth		17.0	.0084	5.8	59,959	.0096	10,338	18.1	11.3	18.9	15.4	36.3	45,781	.0132	10,556	4,512	1,359	8,471	1,736	.0104
Berkshire	208	148.7	.0731	47.4	457,575	.0731	9,653	17.0	11.4	24.9	17.1	29.6	269,961	.0777	67,633	41,117	13,021	42,293	7,633	.0745
▲North Adams		19.6	.0096	6.6	54,658	.0087	8,282	19.4	13.5	26.5	17.3	23.3	39,677	.0114	10,955	3,283	3,161	8,147	453	.0097
▲Pittsfield		56.2	.0276	17.9	184,739	.0295	10,321	16.9	10.3	22.3	17.0	33.5	144,196	.0415	34,422	28,907	7,188	21,686	4,013	.0327
Bristol	180	425.6	.2091	137.7	1,303,727	.2082	9,468	9.0	13.6	33.1	19.2	25.1	678,082	.1949	176,268	92,794	40,917	105,797	21,782	.2044
Attleboro		30.2	.0148	9.6	103,497	.0165	10,781	5.9	10.3	30.6	19.5	33.7	57,009	.0164	14,504	4,251	2,111	14,678	1,377	.0161
▲Fall River		96.4	.0474	32.7	285,502	.0456	8,731	9.9	16.2	36.0	17.9	20.0	168,097	.0483	35,831	34,159	17,155	23,042	5,922	.0468
▲New Bedford		103.3	.0508	36.4	317,539	.0507	8,724	11.8	15.6	32.6	18.5	21.5	174,900	.0503	39,045	29,827	11,734	22,497	6,430	.0506
▲Taunton		43.3	.0213	12.9	132,107	.0211	10,241	8.3	12.2	33.4	19.6	26.5	59,704	.0172	15,922	2,582	4,048	9,632	1,864	.0200
Dukes		6.0	.0030	2.0	16,053	.0025	8,027	25.6	12.4	27.2	14.6	20.2	18,577	.0054	5,188	2,188	523	2,603	622	.0035
Essex	40	632.6	.3109	200.8	2,329,828	.3721	11,603	7.1	9.4	25.5	19.3	38.7	1,136,819	.3268	253,673	230,121	47,416	169,547	36,327	.3462
Beverly		40.4	.0199	12.2	145,321	.0232	11,912	6.5	8.0	23.7	20.1	41.7	75,956	.0218	21,208	10,415	3,075	18,602	2,135	.0221
Danvers		27.6	.0136	7.2	93,709	.0150	13,015	4.6	7.3	21.7	21.6	44.8	42,943	.0123	12,693	4,334	1,907	5,404	873	.0139
Gloucester		27.4	.0135	8.7	84,135	.0134	9,671	8.9	13.3	32.6	17.9	27.3	50,584	.0145	13,294	8,076	821	7,396	1,626	.0138

*Waltham	59.7	.0293	16.6	211,853	.0338	12,752	4.9	7.2	24.4	20.7	42.8	146,993	.0423	32,680	33,412	6,144	17,558	9,954	.0355
Watertown	41.1	.0202	12.5	154,400	.0247	12,352	4.5	7.1	23.3	19.6	45.5	52,558	.0151	9,497	2,714	1,326	14,189	1,788	.0209
Woburn	39.3	.0193	10.8	122,220	.0195	11,317	4.6	7.0	25.5	23.1	39.8	72,072	.0207	23,240	17,141	1,693	11,401	1,253	.0198
Chelmsford	29.3	.0144	8.5	105,975	.0169	12,468	4.8	6.6	19.9	22.7	46.0	46,476	.0154	18,092	12,704	234	1,770	1,470	.0154
Nantucket	3.9	.0019	1.3	12,095	.0019	9,304	20.1	12.2	24.7	14.5	28.5	13,383	.0038	3,047	763	256	1,871	416	.0024
Norfolk............40	606.5	.2981	176.1	2,482,356	.3964	14,096	4.4	6.2	21.5	19.0	48.9	1,067,864	.3070	245,429	179,366	76,399	192,585	30,977	.3500
Braintree	37.1	.0182	10.3	134,398	.0215	13,048	4.2	5.4	19.8	20.1	50.5	121,079	.0348	17,090	57,489	3,447	11,699	1,345	.0248
Brookline	53.3	.0262	19.5	337,234	.0539	17,254	5.2	7.5	19.1	14.6	53.9	68,549	.0197	16,618	5,344	4,214	10,118	3,039	.0381
Dedham	29.2	.0144	8.3	107,267	.0172	13,008	3.6	5.7	22.9	20.4	47.4	104,569	.0301	13,945	16,566	38,585	13,237	1,802	.0205
Needham	32.6	.0160	9.5	166,022	.0265	17,476	3.1	3.8	13.1	14.3	65.7	57,443	.0165	15,482	2,372	1,379	13,749	1,664	.0214
Norwood	33.0	.0162	9.3	118,497	.0189	12,752	4.5	6.2	20.1	20.8	48.4	93,793	.0270	18,371	16,680	1,740	31,104	2,297	.0208
*Quincy	88.1	.0433	27.7	329,506	.0526	11,895	5.5	7.4	24.5	19.8	42.8	208,904	.0601	40,450	45,006	16,405	33,141	5,387	.0530
Wellesley	28.4	.0140	7.8	176,255	.0282	22,661	3.5	4.1	12.1	11.0	69.3	67,527	.0194	12,611	2,461	2,514	18,697	2,254	.0227
Weymouth	53.6	.0263	15.1	178,563	.0285	11,812	4.2	5.9	23.0	22.2	44.7	67,056	.0193	22,056	6,416	1,688	12,071	2,687	.0253
Plymouth............44	330.3	.1623	100.5	1,081,584	.1727	10,762	5.6	10.9	33.5	20.2	29.8	533,665	.1535	136,638	92,273	20,555	83,091	15,422	.1648
▲Brockton	92.4	.0454	30.2	310,026	.0495	10,266	5.6	11.4	35.1	20.5	27.4	202,409	.0582	45,187	52,842	10,864	26,846	4,384	.0513
Hingham	18.5	.0091	5.3	78,813	.0126	14,870	3.8	6.2	22.7	17.4	49.9	42,285	.0122	8,956	8,302	512	9,678	1,281	.0118
Plymouth	15.7	.0077	5.4	53,139	.0085	9,835	7.5	13.7	34.9	19.5	24.4	40,819	.0117	9,890	5,534	1,697	7,525	1,389	.0093
Suffolk............40	686.4	.3373	228.2	2,058,772	.3288	9,022	13.7	14.3	26.8	15.0	25.2	1,763,399	.5067	308,800	414,230	72,237	241,669	50,882	.3839
▲Boston	594.4	.2921	199.7	1,759,838	.2810	8,812	20.2	14.8	26.5	14.4	24.1	1,598,721	.4597	263,219	394,843	65,581	210,333	44,977	.3368
Chelsea	26.9	.0 32	8.4	81,187	.0130	9,665	10.2	13.7	31.1	17.9	27.1	56,735	.0163	14,384	6,550	1,915	11,573	2,237	.0140
Revere	44.7	.0220	13.8	142,657	.0228	10,335	7.3	9.3	30.7	19.8	32.9	93,216	.0268	27,272	12,393	4,621	16,715	2,372	.0238
Worcester............296	621.9	.3056	191.9	1,999,862	.3193	10,421	6.2	10.9	32.8	20.6	29.5	1,012,919	.2912	253,818	137,849	49,489	171,181	32,896	.3081
▲Fitchburg	43.4	.0213	14.0	137,864	.0220	9,843	6.8	11.7	33.3	20.4	27.8	78,023	.0224	18,314	9,709	3,298	11,158	2,643	.0220
Gardner	21.2	.0104	6.8	72,118	.0115	10,606	6.5	10.7	35.7	21.1	26.0	31,920	.0092	8,066	4,866	2,202	4,524	1,568	.0106
▲Leominster	32.1	.0158	9.8	102,185	.0163	10,427	5.8	10.5	33.2	19.7	30.8	60,111	.0173	16,252	16,977	3,258	7,220	1,877	.0165
Shrewsbury	19.5	.0096	5.7	68,515	.0109	12,020	3.7	7.5	26.5	21.5	40.4	61,152	.0176	22,353	16,429	2,678	1,524	1,389	.0127
Southbridge	21.7	.0137	7.2	70,472	.0113	9,788	5.9	10.8	34.3	21.4	27.6	28,453	.0082	9,518	4,191	1,580	2,370	1,259	.0103
▲Worcester	181.6	.0892	57.5	609,831	.0974	10,606	7.1	12.1	32.5	19.3	29.0	383,375	.1102	79,553	68,312	21,874	72,577	11,418	.0996
STATE TOTALS	5,518.6	2.7120	1,700.6	18,948,728	3.8259	11,142	9.4	10.4	27.2	18.5	34.5	10,170,519	2.9924	2,317,361	1,831,577	497,837	1,593,343	322,144	2.9326

*Satellite City. See introduction to Section C.

Fig. 10–3. An example of information available from the Survey of Buying Power. (Copyright © 1969, Sales Management Survey of Buying Power; further reproduction is forbidden.)

tude measurement and scaling are beyond the scope of this text, but the frequent use of scaling techniques in marketing communication research means that the strategist should have some familiarity with these technical considerations.[3]

SOCIOECONOMIC AND DEMOGRAPHIC CHARACTERISTICS

Earlier discussions have suggested several interesting ways in which socioeconomic and demographic characteristics may influence response to market communication. Such concepts as social class and life cycle are combinations of simple variables such as occupation, education, income, housing, and number of children. These clusters of characteristics define the physical and economic realities of the buyer's situation and thus provide an important source of predispositions that influence needs, goals, ability to spend, and attitudes toward certain types of products and services. They also suggest the kinds of social influences to which the receiver will be exposed. For example, family and local influence are likely to be more important for older persons with below-average income and education (the laggards).

The measures of population and income discussed earlier may provide adequate data for measuring the relevant socioeconomic and demographic characteristics in particular marketing situations. For example, if the market has been defined as all households with children living at home, data are available from secondary sources to measure the distribution of these families in various geographic areas and to indicate the distribution of parameters such as income, number of children, or education, within this population.

At other times, the measures needed may be more specific and more sophisticated than available from secondary sources. In such cases, it becomes necessary to design a procedure for generating the required information. Data on preferences and usage rates for a particular class of products, and how these are related to demographic and socioeconomic characteristics, usually require some form of primary data collection, such as a survey. Planning questions such as "How often will consuming units in the target market purchase this product?" and "What factors will influence the rate of product usage?" cannot be answered without additional information about buying habits. Special studies may also have to be developed to determine the information sources, formal and informal, used by the potential market or to identify the buying

[3]For an excellent discussion of the use of scaling techniques in marketing, see Paul E. Green and Donald S. Tull, *Research for Marketing Decisions* (Englewood Cliffs, N.J.: Prentice-Hall, Inc. 1966), especially ch. 7, "Measurement and Scaling in Marketing Research," pp. 183–213.

decision influencers in a specific situation. In industrial markets, the persons and organization positions involved in buying a particular class of product often cannot be identified without a field study, although industrial advertising media may have published some data on the relevant market.

When the necessary information has been collected from a sample of the market and analyzed, it may be possible to project the results of this sample survey to the total population. It may also be possible to identify certain demographic characteristics (measurable with data from the study itself or from secondary sources) that are correlated with the behavior and attitudes of interest. This relationship can then be used to develop measures of the relevant parameters in other markets, not yet surveyed, or in the total market. For example, demand for air travel is related to occupation and income. Once the nature of that relationship has been estimated from studies in a limited market area, estimates of demand for air travel in other areas can be developed based upon data on occupation and income for those areas, assuming that the basic relationship does not vary significantly among regions.

Survey Research

Information on predispositions and social influences on the buying process often require the use of sample survey research techniques for collecting the data. Survey research techniques involve some complex technical and management problems that have been covered well in several good texts on marketing research.[4] Surveys are probably the most commonly used method of marketing research. Here we need only take note of the major features of surveys, the potential sources of error, and factors determining the usefulness of survey data for purposes of planning marketing communication strategy.

Sampling. The key question to ask of a survey is whether the sample is representative of the larger population of interest. In order to apply the techniques of statistical inference, the sample must be a true random probability sample, which means that each element in the population must have an equal and known probability of being included in the sample. "Random" does *not* mean "unplanned" or "according to the will of the interviewer"; it means just the opposite—"carefully planned and

[4]In addition to the Green and Tull text cited earlier, survey research procedures are carefully analyzed in R. Ferber, D. F. Blankertz, and S. Hollander, Jr., *Marketing Research* (New York: Ronald Press Company, 1964); H. Barksdale and W. Weilbacher, *Marketing Research: Selected Readings with Analytical Commentaries* (New York: Ronald Press Company, 1966); H. W. Boyd and R. Westfall, *Marketing Research: Text and Cases*, revised edition (Homewood, Ill.: Richard D. Irwin, Inc., 1964).

beyond the will of the interviewer." Stated differently, there must be no bias in sample selection. A true probability sample requires a sampling frame (or list) containing all elements of the population. Drawing names from a telephone book does not give a true random sample of the total population of a community, for example, because not all households have telephone numbers listed in the directory. Random sampling may be simple random sampling or it may be *sequential* random sampling in which the first item is drawn at random between the first and tenth items in the frame and then every nth item is picked, where $1/n$ is the sampling proportion.

In the interest of economic efficiency, or to gain increased statistical efficiency, more sophisticated sampling procedures may be used. *Cluster* sampling involves using a probability sample of some aggregative units of the population, say, several city blocks, and then taking the relevant measurements with all population units within the cluster. *Area* sampling is the most common form of cluster sampling. It should be noted that the basic assumption in cluster sampling is that each cluster is representative of the total population being studied. This is not likely to be the case in area sampling. A particular city block or group of blocks is likely to be relatively homogeneous with respect to such socioeconomic characteristics as ethnic group, income, and education level. To the extent that these are correlated with the variable or variables being estimated, there will be bias in the estimates.

In cluster sampling, the theoretical objective is to maximize the within-cluster variance on the parameter being measured. That is, the objective is to have clusters that are as similar to each other as possible, while each cluster also contains the full range of parameter values found in the total population. In *stratified* sampling, the objective is just the opposite: to minimize within-stratum variance and to maximize the variance among strata. For example, a stratified sample might be based on family size, with separate strata for families with one, two, three, and four or more children comprising four strata within the population of families with children. Typically, this would be a *proportionate* stratified sample, with the number of families in each stratum in the sample being in proportion to their distribution in the population. Stratified sampling permits greater statistical efficiency while cluster sampling, especially area sampling, permits greater economic efficiency, especially in reduced interviewer/travel time.

Quota samples are frequently used for reasons of economy, but it should be stressed that these are not probability samples. In a quota sampling procedure, the interviewer is given a certain quota of respondents with particular characteristics, but he is free to pick those in the manner he desires (subject to certain administrative guidelines). This is not a probability sample because each population unit no longer has an equal probability of being included in the sample. For example, an interviewer of college students may be given a quota of 40 dormitory residents, 30 residents of fraternity and sorority houses, and 30 off-campus residents. These proportions would be defined according to the purpose of the survey and may or may not be equal to the population proportions. The interviewer in this example could then go to one dormitory to get 40 interviews, and he would probably not pick it in a true random fashion. Because residents of other dormitories would not have an equal chance to be included in this sample, it is not a true random sample.

Statistical inference can properly be done only if the sample is a true probability sample. Statistical inference permits the placing of "confidence intervals" around the parameter estimate derived from the sample data. These confidence intervals state the probability that the true population value on the estimated variable lies within a certain range of the estimated value based on the sample data. This calculation recognizes that there is sampling error, introduced by the very fact that the estimate is based on a sample and not on a complete enumeration of the total population. The sample variance provides an estimate of the population variance, which is used to define the confidence intervals.[5]

There is an intrinsic danger in talking about confidence intervals, however, because this concept includes only error attributable to sampling. There are many other potential sources of error in survey data that are not systematically evaluated by statistical procedures, and these can be much more significant sources of error than the sample itself.[6] Many of these problems involve communication processes.

The Research Instrument. The research instrument is often a questionnaire, either mailed to the respondents or used by an interviewer who calls in person or over the telephone. Where the objective of the survey is to measure attitudes, projective techniques and one or more scaling techniques, as discussed in Chapter 4, are likely to be part of the research instrument. Questionnaires may be elaborate series of questions with complex instructions, or they may take the form of an interview guide, unstructured and allowing the interviewer considerable discretion in covering certain broad areas of interest. While there is no exact science of questionnaire design, there are several potential sources of error that can be guarded against. Many of these problems can be identified

[5]For a complete discussion of sampling techniques and estimation procedures, see M. H. Hansen, W. N. Hurwitz, and W. G. Madow, *Sample Survey Methods and Theory*, volumes 1 and 2 (New York: John Wiley & Sons, Inc., 1953).

[6]Rex V. Brown, "Evaluation of Total Survey Error," *Journal of Marketing Research*, 4 (May 1967), pp. 117–27.

and corrected in a pretest of the research instrument. Pretesting is an absolute necessity in any responsible research effort.

Two major sources of error are question wording and the sequence of questions. Ambiguities in questions may lead to serious variability in responses as people interpret the question in various ways. Even the simplest question may have ambiguity: "Where did you buy that dress?" (Does the question ask for store name, or city where purchased, or both?) The meaning assigned to the question by the respondent may be entirely different than that intended by the designer of the questionnaire. The result is a breakdown in communication; there is no sharing of meaning.

The sequence in which questions are asked can also lead to bias, and this may occur in several ways. The question sequence may lead the respondent to believe that certain answers are more appropriate than others; earlier questions may arouse defensive mechanisms in the respondent, as when rather personal questions are asked early in the sequence; or initial questions may suggest something about the purpose of the interview that distorts the respondent's perceptions of the interviewer. All of these problems can be seen as special cases of the many kinds of communication phenomena discussed earlier, including credibility, perception of manipulative intent, and selective perception.

In evaluating the research instrument it is always helpful to ask if the questions used actually get the kind of information that was specified by the research objectives. It is very easy either to miss certain key areas that should have been covered or to ask for information which was not needed to achieve the purpose of the research. The latter can be especially significant because lengthy questionnaires may lead to nonresponse or respondent fatigue and introduce additional error into responses.

A common problem arises in questions which require the respondent to fabricate answers, perhaps unconsciously. Fabrication will occur when the respondent is unwilling or unable to provide the information requested. These problems are most likely to occur in instances where the respondent is asked to recall items from the past and where the questions call for an above-average amount of personal insight. They will also occur when the behavior being described is not socially acceptable according to some standards inferred by the respondent. A question such as "What were the most important sources of information to you in your decision to buy a new car?" is really very complex, and an accurate response is impossible because no respondent could remember and objectively evaluate all of the information sources to which he was exposed. The question "Why do you prefer this brand of cigarettes?" requires an answer based upon significant personal insight and an unreasonable amount of objectivity in talking about some very "slippery" aspects of the image of the brand. The respondent may make up an answer that would satisfy the interviewer, but it may be misleading. Finally, a question such as "What magazines do you read?" may elicit responses that the respondent thinks will be acceptable to the researcher. Some high-status magazines may be added to the list while less-respectable publications may be conveniently forgotten by the respondent. In summary, it is always helpful to ask two basic questions about the research instrument: "Are respondents able to provide the information requested?" and, "Are there reasons why respondents might be motivated to provide inaccurate responses?"

An understanding of the communication process can suggest sources of error in the research instrument. Careful attention to the basics of the selective processes and credibility may suggest potential problems. Simple word choice may turn out to be a very complicated affair when certain aspects of the communication process are considered. For example, changing one simple word may result in two completely different pieces of information. Consider a survey of physicians in which the objective is to evaluate the sources of information used by the doctor. The question "Where did you first *learn* about pharmaceutical XYZ?" may be interpreted by some doctors to mean *awareness* and by others to mean *evaluation*. Changing "learn" to "hear" would increase the probability that it would be interpreted to mean awareness, while changing the question to "What convinced you to use pharmaceutical XYZ?" would get at the later stages of the adoption process. These are not trivial problems because they define the fundamental quality of the information being gathered.

The Interviewer. The interviewer is a communicator and should be trained and evaluated as such. Many of the basics of dyadic interaction can be reviewed to provide insight into the nature of interviewer-respondent interaction.[7] Especially in those surveys where the interviewer does not simply fill in the blanks on a printed questionnaire, but where he probes for additional information and discusses nuances of the answer with the respondent, the interviewer has a major role in determining what information is collected. In these situations, the interviewer needs to be carefully trained as a listener and needs to be very sensitive to how his words and actions influence the respondent.

Many commercial research organizations depend upon part-time interviewers, often housewives who work for a few hours during the week and who are loosely supervised by a woman who lives in the area. There are many potential difficulties in these arrangements, from out-

[7]Floyd J. Fowler, Jr., "Respondent-Interviewer Interaction," in Frederick E. Webster, Jr. (ed.), *New Directions in Marketing* (Chicago: American Marketing Association, 1965), pp. 361–68.

right falsification of responses to the more subtle bias introduced by the way the supervisor selects and supervises her workers. Are they all her friends or members of the same local organizations? Does she carefully instruct them on the details of each study and questionnaire and follow-up with a check on their procedures?

The training of the interviewer is especially significant where the interviewer is asked to make certain key judgements about predispositions held by respondents as part of the survey. For example, if the interviewer is asked to indicate the extent to which the respondent is interested in the product category, or a probability that the respondent would purchase if offered the opportunity to buy, the interviewer needs very well defined guidelines for providing such estimates. An interviewer charged with responsibility for identifying buying influences within an industrial organization needs careful instruction on how to obtain information about several parts of the organization. He needs the skills and perseverance to gain access to persons who might be less than enthusiastic about granting an interview, but whose influence on the buying decision is major.

The foregoing comments have only briefly suggested the many sources of potential error in survey research and the factors that should be evaluated by the user of information provided by such surveys. These comments have stressed those sources of error which are related to the communication aspects of survey research. Attempts to measure predispositions and buying influences usually require keen judgment and careful assessment of many qualitative factors that are not easily measured. This increases the possibility of error and suggests the need for careful evaluation of potential sources of error.[8]

Group Interviews

Recently, small-group interviews have become increasingly popular as a method of gaining information about basic predispositions and social influences on the buying process. While these are typically small-sample studies, often using as few as four or five groups of five or six persons each, they can provide rich insight into the basic behavior of interest to the marketer. It has been found that such groups serve the function of stimulating members to express themselves on the matters brought before the group by the researcher and lead to an in-depth look at some of the basic motivations and attitudes involved. Instead of the limited one-to-one relationship of the interviewer-respondent dyad, discussion

---

[8]For a procedure for evaluating the quality of information provided by contract research firms, see Charles S. Mayer, "Evaluating the Quality of Market Research Contractors," *Journal of Marketing Research,* 4 (May 1967), pp. 134–41.

groups provide each member with many stimuli and lead to a richer insight as a result.

While these interviews are definitely a form of measurement, they cannot be used as the basis for quantitative estimates of population parameters. For example, it would be erroneous to base estimates of total market potential upon interviews with five groups of six women each. These thirty respondents would certainly be an inadequate base upon which to develop estimates of national purchase and usage rates. Chances are that the women would not be a representative sample of the total population and that they would have developed such estimates under the very biased conditions of the group interview.

Group interviews are typically used in two situations. One frequent use is to show people the product and to ask them to talk about it. Such research studies have been reported for such diverse products as automobiles and coffee and a wide variety of food, child care, and home care items. Another frequent use is for pretesting advertising. In the latter case, it is often possible to uncover potential misinterpretations or aspects of response to the advertising which had not been anticipated. These techniques are discussed in further detail in Chapter 15.

In addition to the function of stimulating ideas, the group interview also permits the researcher to observe the basic nature of the group process itself and may thus permit insight into how people will talk to each other about the product. That is, it provides some evidence about the basic nature of informal communication that is likely to occur with this product or service. It permits the appraisal of how people are likely to maintain or modify their attitudes as the result of opinions expressed by others. It permits some judgment about the amount of risk which people perceive in the purchase and use of this product, and the extent to which the psychosocial consequences of purchase are likely to be significant. It can also suggest how these judgments are likely to be influenced by other people. Furthermore, these basic predispositions are likely to be discussed much more freely and openly in a group interview than they would be in a one-to-one interaction with the interviewer.[9]

Panel Data

A panel is any group of respondents that is used on a periodic and repetitive basis. The best-known type of panel is the kind maintained by the Market Research Corporation of America, in which the panel members report regularly on their purchases of certain products. In addition to panels of households, there are other kinds of panels such as those

[9]Alfred E. Goldman, "The Group Depth Interview," *Journal of Marketing*, 26 (July 1962), pp. 61–68.

involving drugstores and grocery warehouses. The following comments apply mainly to consumer panels.

Panels do not typically provide complete data on predispositions and buying influences, but they may provide unique information about certain variables such as personality and household characteristics. The only alternative source of these data may be an expensive market survey. The availability of data permits the testing of relationships between these variables and such aspects of buying behavior as shopping activity, brand loyalty, and brand choice, as also reported by panel members. Panel members may complete a personality profile test upon entering the panel and the data on each household might include race, religious preference, number of children, age of head of household, whether the wife works, head of household's occupation, income, education, and type of dwelling.

Respondents report their purchases of grocery items and indicate whether the items were purchased on a regular basis or on the basis of some kind of deal, for example a coupon or a special price package. Response to deals may be found to be correlated with basic socioeconomic variables. One study using panel data found that deal proneness tended to be positively related to the age of the housewife and to the number of different brands purchased, but negatively related to brand loyalty and total units purchased. No other socioeconomic, demographic, or personality characteristics were found to be related to deal proneness.[10]

One large manufacturing company has created its own consumer panel, which annually studies the purchasing of major consumer durables by a sample of over 20,000 households. One third of the sample is replaced every 6 months, and information is collected on the same cycle. Thus, each family stays in the sample for three reporting periods, a total of 18 months. This panel has the unique ability to trace changes in purchasing behavior and product usage over time, a technique that is referred to as "longitudinal analysis." Supplementary interview data can help trace the buying decisions which lead to changes in the household's inventory of durable goods, and to assess the impact of various formal and informal communications on that process.

The major problem with panel data, especially for panels requiring the weekly or monthly reporting of purchases of groceries and similar items, is that there are likely to be significant nonresponse rates and similar sources of error. If the respondent becomes lax in keeping track of current purchases and begins to fabricate responses, based upon inadequate memory of what was actually purchased, major inaccuracies are

[10]Frederick E. Webster, Jr., "The 'Deal-Prone' Consumer," *Journal of Marketing Research*, 2 (May 1965), pp. 186–89.

likely to result. There is also a difficulty in replacing panel members who drop out of the panel and in maintaining the representative nature of the sample. Persons with above-average incomes and in professional occupations are less likely to participate in panels, because of their life styles and because the financial incentives offered are less likely to be significant for them. Despite these limitations, however, panel data are a unique source of information about the purchasing behavior of households and provide one of the few major sources of aggregate data on actual purchasing behavior.

ESTIMATING MARKET RESPONSE

Data on the basic demand determinants may be helpful in developing estimates of market potential. Information about predispositions and buying influences, collected from surveys, group interviews, panel data, and other sources of information may help to estimate sales potential and market share. But the marketing communication strategist may wish to go beyond measures of potential to estimates of market response. The question he wishes to answer is: "Given market and sales potential, how will the market respond to various kinds and levels of marketing effort?" This question explicitly introduces the marketing stimulus into the measurement problem. Information on socioeconomic and demographic characteristics and on predispositions provides useful insights about the organism in our basic stimulus-organism-response model, but the prediction of response (which, we have said before, is our ultimate objective) requires an explicit consideration of the relationship between stimulus and response.

Each of the research techniques discussed above may be useful in attempting to predict market response. Surveys may be especially helpful in gauging the basic acceptability of a product and a marketing campaign for that product. But surveys have the inherent weakness of reporting only what people say. They do not necessarily permit a good prediction of what people will actually *do* when exposed to the stimuli of the marketing program.

Test Marketing

The greater the amount at stake, the more likely that the company will use one or more test markets to evaluate market response to the product and the marketing effort to be devoted to that product. Test marketing may or may not involve the use of formal experimental designs, to be discussed in the next section. A good test market program is one which exactly duplicates the conditions under which the product will be marketed on a full scale, including the product form, the package, the price, the channels of distribution used, and the marketing communication program, with respect to both quality and level of effort.

The market areas chosen for a test market must meet certain criteria, if the results are to be projected to the national market. First, the population of the area must be a representative cross section of the national market with respect to demographic and socioeconomic characteristics. Second, the area must have competitive circumstances resembling those to be faced on a national basis. Third, it should have representative advertising media available, and there should be no overlap of media from other market areas. Finally, distribution in the area must be possible to control and there should be a minimum leakage of product out of the test market.

There are very few areas of the United States that meet all these criteria, and thus certain market areas have come to have a significantly above-average usage as test markets. These areas include the Albany-Schenectady-Troy market, Columbus, Syracuse, and a few other markets. These markets are so frequently exposed to new products on a test market basis that there is room to question whether they are still truly representative markets. Given the significantly above-average rate of new product introductions into these markets, people may become rather indifferent toward new products in general.

Another problem in using such test markets is that competitors may watch these areas closely for new-product marketing activity. They may then develop a counterstrategy aimed at destroying the test marketer's ability to derive meaningful measurements from the test market. Tactics used for this purpose include substantially increasing advertising effort, special mailings of promotional incentives such as coupons to households in the market, and actually purchasing a large volume of the product being tested in order to generate exaggerated sales volume estimates. The competitor may instruct his salesmen to buy all of the product they can obtain, to remove it from the supermarket shelves and place it back in storerooms, or to do other equally questionable things to destroy the value of the test market.

Even if there is not abnormal retaliation by competitors, there may be major difficulties in interpreting the results of test markets. One major consideration is that those persons who try the product first may behave quite differently than those who adopt later. Our earlier analysis of adopter categories revealed substantial differences. Initial sales results may thus be quite unstable, and certainly provide an inadequate basis for developing estimates of the size of the total market. The test market should therefore last long enough to permit the market to settle down to something reasonably close to normal market performance. Countering this desire for long test markets are competitive considerations. The longer the product is on the market, the higher is the probability that competitors will be able to develop an effective counterstrategy for use when the product is introduced on a full-scale basis. As the General Manager of the Maxwell House Division of General Foods has pointed out, it may be preferable to learn about competition in test market, rather than to race into national distribution with the idea of preempting inevitable competitors.[11]

Despite the major expense involved, test markets may be an efficient way of predicting market response to a new product or a new marketing program involving major dollar expenditures. Test markets permit a test of the basic desirability of the product as an addition to the product line, and provide the final basis for a yes or no decision. They may also permit the testing of several alternative marketing strategies, allowing the selection of the most efficient communication program. Finally, the test market may permit obtaining more precise measurements of market characteristics and response as the basis for planning the national marketing program. These advantages can be gained if the test is allowed to run long enough to permit abnormal factors to "settle out" in the market, and if competitors do not completely destroy the representative nature of the market.

Experimentation

If the objective of the research program is to establish a causal relationship between stimulus and response, then experimentation must be used. For example, an experiment is required to answer the question "Does the number of sales calls influence the volume of sales?" although statistical procedures may establish the tendency of these two variables to move in the same direction.

An experiment involves the systematic variation of certain factors and the careful control of other factors that are thought to influence response. To illustrate, an experiment to test the influence of salesman training on sales volume would require that different levels and kinds of training be tested and that all other variables be controlled, including the characteristics of the salesmen, the quality of their supervision, the mix of customers, and other territory conditions. Such an experiment might be physically impossible. Where physical control of the "other" variables in the experiment is not possible, various statistical procedures may be used to provide such control.

The experimental treatments in an experiment to estimate market response might include alternative advertising media, alternative levels

---

[11]Victor A. Bonomo, "The Do's and Don'ts of Test Marketing a New Product," *The Nielsen Researcher*, 26, No. 3, 1968, pp. 3–13.

of spending for advertising, number of sales calls, types of salesmen, different time sequences of promotional effort, alternative promotional efforts such as coupons, price label packs, and point of purchase displays, or alternative creative approaches to advertising copy and illustration.

Experiments of a more complex nature can be designed to measure the interaction among several variables such as level of communication effort, price, and different retail outlets. There are many forms of experiments of varying degrees of complexity to permit the testing of the influences of several variables, with several degrees of precision. Experiments may be conducted in the field or under laboratory conditions (where there is greater opportunity for control). Split-run, block, and factorial designs each have certain advantages and disadvantages. The quality of an experiment, as with other forms of research, is influenced by the care with which it is designed and executed, the quality of the sample (the selection of experimental and control units), the quality of the research instrument used, and the care with which administrative procedures are executed.

Because of its greater precision and its unique ability to establish causality, experimentation is finding increased use in marketing, despite its expense. Money invested in experimentation may reveal significant opportunities to reduce the level of spending or to spend more efficiently. The basic requirement for effective use of experimentation is a management with the courage to permit systematic variation of the independent variables. For example, an experiment to test the influence of the level of advertising effort on sales volume would require the testing of several alternative levels of spending in several markets. If management's careful analysis and previous experience has suggested that a certain level X is optimal, it then takes a special point of view to permit the spending of $\frac{1}{2}X$ in some markets and $2X$ in other markets, with the probability of sales decreases and competitive losses in the first situation and inefficient expenditure in the other. Of course, such experimentation may also reveal that X is not optimal and that something less than X represents the most efficient level. Here again, it is important that the experiment be conducted for sufficient time to permit the leveling-off of abnormal responses.

Experimentation is usually combined with test marketing procedures, and in such cases it has the same advantages and disadvantages as any form of test marketing, plus a few of its own. Control is vital to successful experimentation, and competitive retaliation may be especially costly to a well-designed experiment. Experimentation also may require the use of several market areas, increasing the difficulty of controlling certain variables and reducing the probability of avoiding competitive notice and "jamming" actions. Furthermore, the planning and execution of experiments requires a high order of technical competence.[12]

Simulation

In many situations, it is impossible or undesirable to conduct experiments. In addition to the problem of tipping the hand to competitors, experimentation may be ruled out by the inability of management to manipulate the variables that must be examined, or the costly nature of such variation. Such would be the case with an experiment to test the impact of alternative sales territory assignments, for example, where it would be unwise to arbitrarily move salesmen and their families or to ask customers to put up with a continuous change of salesmen and sales call frequencies. Lags in response to such changes would further complicate the situation. While these factors would not completely rule out experimentation, they would significantly reduce its desirability.

As an Alternative to Field Experimentation. Simulation provides a method for systematically assessing the impact of several factors while controlling for the influence of other factors. It can be particularly valuable in situations not permitting field experiments, although there are many factors which make simulation a valuable tool for managerial analysis. The use of simulation by management is a relatively recent development and it promises to increase in importance, especially as time-shared computer capability brings the possibility of controlled experimentation into the manager's office.

Model Validity Is Critical. The hallmarks of simulation are a high-speed computer and a descriptive model of the process which management is trying to control or influence. The critical feature in determining the value of the simulation is the basic validity of the underlying model. It must be a reasonably accurate description of all the important variables and their relationships in the process that management is trying to influence. On the other hand, the model must involve some simplification from the real world, otherwise there would be little value in the model. Simplification can permit the identification of important variables and relationships and can usefully sacrifice descriptive detail for sharper focus on essential elements.

A Microanalytic Simulation. The nature of simulation and its usefulness in estimating market response can best be illustrated by an example. The example, one of the most elaborate simulations reported in the

[12]For a thorough and sophisticated discussion of experimentation in marketing, see Seymour Banks, *Experimentation in Marketing* (New York: McGraw-Hill Book Co., Inc., 1965).

literature, is chosen because it deals directly with response to marketing communication. This simulation involves the modeling of the market of a pharmaceutical firm by Claycamp and Amstutz, and is based on an actual marketing situation using real data.[13] The purpose of this simulation was to permit the drug manufacturer to evaluate alternative communication strategies.

Simulations permit the tracing of responses by the system to changes in policy variables over time. The simulation runs for many periods and shows how various measures of market performance (changes in attitudes, sales volume, market share, etc.) are influenced by alternative strategies. In addition to prediction of market response (output), the simulation provides insight into the basic process itself.

The Claycamp-Amstutz simulation is a *microanalytc* simulation in that it simulates the behavior of individual units in the system—doctors. The simulation considers how the doctor responds to salesmen, media, and direct mail promotion. It includes interaction among doctors and the generation of word-of-mouth communication. The system also includes patients, hospitals, wholesalers, pharmacies, and detail men (salesmen), as well as feedback information to the company from panel research, direct mail research, and from detail men. The data inputs into the simulation were based on monthly audits of drugstore invoices, weekly audits of prescriptions written by doctors, audits of the distribution and content of journal advertising, quarterly reports from panels of doctors on patient treatment, direct mail received, and sales calls by detail men, as well as special studies to determine doctor knowledge, experience, attitudes, and treatment procedures. The validity of the simulation, and its ability to predict reasonably well how the market will respond to various marketing actions, reflects the care taken to develop these data inputs.

The Claycamp-Amstutz simulation actually simulates the doctor's decision process concerning patient treatment. Having noted the indications (symptoms), the doctor searches his past experience for information about possible drugs to prescribe. The doctor deletes from consideration those drugs with which he has had negative experience, which is treated as an attitude variable. There is also a file of information on the previous drug treatment received by each patient. If the doctor is in a hospital, there is a check made to determine whether the pharmaceutical is available in the hospital's formulary. The doctor eventually chooses that available drug toward which he has the most favorable attitudes.

    [13]Henry J. Claycamp and Arnold E. Amstutz, "Simulation Techniques in the Analysis of Marketing Strategy," in F. M. Bass, C. W. King, and E. A. Pessemier (eds.), *Applications of the Sciences in Marketing Management* (New York: John Wiley & Sons, Inc., 1968), pp. 113–50.

The simulation provides for a continuous monitoring of the attitude change which results from exposure to various sources of information including both formal and informal communication. The model includes selective exposure, perception, and retention, as well as forgetting and is a sound analogy to the communication process as described in previous chapters. The output of the simulation is the doctors' prescribing behavior and changes in attitudes, as influenced by the firm's marketing communication activities, competitive behavior, and informal communication.

Other Simulations. While no other simulation has shown this much concern with the basic communication behavior of the system being simulated, there have been several other successful developments. So-called business games have been developed at many of the leading business schools. Amstutz has reported an elaborate microanalytic simulation of consumer behavior.[14] A large-scale simulation of an industrial market has been developed at Berkeley.[15] With the necessary technical assistance from market researchers and management scientists, the manager can develop a simulation of his own market for purposes of predicting response to change in communication strategy. It is possible to simulate the way in which a market will change over time as a new product or service is accepted, for example, and this can provide significant clues as to how the messages and media employed should be altered to reflect changes in the market. The creative combination of insight from the behavioral sciences and the analytical rigor of mathematics and simulation provide significant opportunities for increased competitive effectiveness.[16]

Stochastic Models

Stochastic models conceptualize buyer behavior as a probabilistic or random process. The major elements of the model are the probabilities that a consumer will choose a specified brand on a given purchase. These transition probabilities reflect the impact of marketers' efforts, including price, product, and promotion policies. Stochastic models can be used as part of a simulation model, especially where the causal rela-

[14]Arnold E. Amstutz, *Computer Simulation of Competitive Market Response*, (Cambridge: M.I.T. Press, 1967).

[15]F. E. Balderson and A. C. Hoggatt, *Simulation of Market Processes* (Berkeley: Institute of Business and Economic Research, University of California, 1962).

[16]Raymond A. Bauer and Robert D. Buzzell, "Mating Behavioral Science and Simulation," *Harvard Business Review*, 42 (September–October 1964), pp. 116–24; William D. Wells, "Computer Simulation of Consumer Behavior," *Harvard Business Review*, 41 (May–June 1963), pp. 93–98.

tionships between marketing stimuli and consumer behavior are not well established.

Stochastic models have been used to analyze such buying behavior as brand loyalty and switching, shopping habits, and the diffusion of a new product. The usual data source for these models is a consumer panel. Analysis of stochastic models can suggest specific hypotheses to be tested in a program of experimentation or in a survey.

There are three distinct kinds of stochastic models that have been used to study brand loyalty and switching. *Zero-order* models assume that previous brand choices do not influence future brand choice. *Markov* models assume that only the most recent purchase affects the next brand choice. *Learning* models assume that the next brand choice is influenced by all previous history of brand choices. (Strictly speaking, higher-order Markov models are possible, in which the next choice is dependent on more than one previous choice, but these can be reformulated as first-order Markov processes.) The last decade has seen many large-scale studies of consumer behavior using stochastic models, which have been found to be most useful for frequently purchased consumer package goods.[17]

The Switching Matrix. Stochastic models involve a matrix of probabilities for moving from one state to another state. Figure 10–4 illustrates such a matrix. Computer simulation using these models can yield predictions of market share after a stated number of periods, and can also be used to trace the impact of promotional efforts designed to change the probabilities. In the example in Figure 10–4 (which is a Markov process, since brand choice is said to depend on the most recent brand choice), it can be seen that Brand A has the most loyal customers and is also attracting customers from Brands D and C with significant frequency. Brand C has very little loyalty and is not likely to attract

BRAND PURCHASED AT TIME $t + 1$

		A	B	C	D
BRAND PURCHASED AT TIME t	A	.63	.10	.17	.10
	B	.22	.51	.13	.14
	C	.25	.22	.34	.19
	D	.40	.05	.00	.55

Fig. 10–4. A simple Markov model of brand choice.

[17]For an excellent review of much of the significant work in this area, see David B. Montgomery and Glen L. Urban, *Management Science in Marketing* (Englewood Cliffs, N.J.: Prentice-Hall, Inc., 1969), especially ch. 2, "Models of Market Response," pp. 28–93.

many switchers, either. Notice that in such formulations as this one Brands A, B, and C might be true brands, while Brand D could include all other brands.

Use of stochastic models requires a high order of statistical skill and very careful attention to the basic assumptions that must be made in structuring the model. There is still a large amount of controversy among marketing scholars concerning such models and the debate promises to continue at a lively pace for some time because of the complexities involved. Given some information from experiments, surveys, or panel data about the influence of alternative promotional activities on the basic probabilities of brand choice and brand switching, stochastic models provide a useful tool for tracing the impact of such promotions over several periods into the future. They therefore can play an important role in the formulation of marketing communication strategy for the firm willing to make the necessary investment in market information and skilled analysis.

FORECASTING SALES

When all of the available data have been analyzed, there still remains the task of developing a specific estimate of the revenue to be generated in the market during a stated period. This is the sales forecast. Several approaches to the development of a sales forecast will be examined briefly, after considering the basic inputs to a sales forecast.

Inputs

At least three basic inputs are required for any sales forecast: some measure of market potential, an estimate of the amount and quality of marketing effort to be applied against that potential, and an estimate of the kind of environment within which the firm will be operating. Previous sections of this chapter have discussed the estimation of market potential and methods for assessing how the market will respond to marketing effort. Predicting the environmental influences within which the firm will be operating requires a high level of seasoned judgment as well as good current information about a wide variety of subjective factors. Economic, political, and technological trends all need to be carefully assessed by a competent observer. Basic trends in gross national product, national income, government policies on taxation and fiscal and monetary matters, foreign trade policies, developments in the international arena, local political developments—all of these factors may be vitally significant to the firm's success in the coming period.

Technological forecasting is increasingly necessary in an age of rapid and increasing technological change. In industries characterized by a rapid turnover in technology, such as aircraft, electronics, nuclear technology, and computing equipment, competitive developments must be carefully watched and appraised. Company planning may also require some careful estimates of the success likely from research and development activities, with inherent uncertainty in this process. A failure to anticipate the times when new products will be available for market testing and full-scale introduction, or failure to assess the importance of pushing developments to the commercialization stage as quickly as possible, can throw a monkey wrench into any attempt to plan the marketing program.

The problem of forecasting the political and economic environment takes on greater complexity as well as greater importance for the multinational corporation. Published sources of information may be useful here, but there is no substitute for a trained observer of the local scene who knows of such developments long before they are reported in the press.

Executive Judgment

Given an economic and political forecast of some kind, many firms (especially the large number of small, owner-managed firms) rely almost exclusively on the seasoned judgment of one or a few key executives to develop the revenue forecast. The forecast then becomes the key planning statistic for the firm. For many firms, the development of a specific, written sales forecast is the first step toward a more "scientific" management and there are a large number of firms that have not yet reached that level of sophistication!

One variation on the technique of executive judgment involves the use of a "jury of executive opinion" in which several executives are asked to state their expectations about sales in the coming period. These estimates are pooled and there then may be a meeting at which each estimator is allowed to defend his estimate. As the result of these discussions, a final figure is arrived at which represents the best judgment of the group as a whole.

Sales Force Estimates

An alternative approach to the development of a sales forecast involves asking the company's salesmen (or its agents or resellers) to estimate the volume of sales they expect to generate during the coming period. These estimates may or may not be checked and modified by an intermediate level of management, such as district sales managers, before they are submitted to a central authority for summation. Despite the obvious subjective nature of this process, it does have certain advantages. Salesmen should be *the* experts on conditions in the market and with specific customers. They are in daily contact with those persons (customers) whose behavior determines what the sales volume will be. Customers may be more than willing to provide the salesmen with detailed information about their purchase plans, especially if they perceive that this information will result in better planning by the selling company and, therefore, better service for their needs.

Against these positive considerations, one must also evaluate several negative features. Salesmen may be unable to assess the consequences of such factors as economic trends with the same degree of sophistication possible from the point of view of top management surveying the total market. Furthermore, the salesmen may not have adequate information about the future marketing plans of the company (e.g., new products or pricing changes) to permit an accurate prediction of sales volume. Customers may be unwilling to provide the required information or may provide exaggerated estimates in the hope of getting the best possible response from the salesman. More basically, customers may not know what their purchases will be. Finally, the salesman may be motivated to provide conservative estimates, especially if the figure he gives becomes the basis for a quota against which he is to be evaluated and compensated.[18]

Surveys of Customer Intentions

Much of the information discussed above on customer buying intentions can be gathered by some means other than use of the company's salesmen. Hired interviewers may be used for this purpose (either in the employ of the company or on a contract basis from a market research firm) or a mailed questionnaire can be used to solicit the desired information. Many of the positive and negative features of such arrangements were mentioned above, including the ability and willingness of respondents to provide such information. Furthermore, it has all of the potential sources of error inherent in any survey including nonresponse error and interviewer error.

Such surveys have special value in those markets characterized by a relatively small number of large customers. The manufacturer of instruments for use in aircraft, or of automobile equipment, faces this kind of situation. He needs to know whether these customers plan to do business with him and the amount of that business. To have inaccurate information about any one of them could create significant difficulties for him. Because they also are dependent upon him in order to keep

---

[18]Frederick E. Webster, Jr., "The Industrial Salesman as a Source of Market Information," *Business Horizons*, 8 (Spring 1965), pp. 77–82.

their plants running, they may provide the required information very willingly, assuming they know what their purchase plans are.

Projection

Projection is a simple technique for extrapolating a series of historical data into the future. Company sales may be plotted on graph paper and an "eyeball" fit of a straight line to the data made. Or the same series of data may be analyzed arithmetically and an estimate of the next period's sales volume made on the basis of average dollar or percentage increases in sales from one period to the next that has been experienced in the past.

The major assumption made in projection is that the future will be like the past. The same conditions that have led to whatever behavior is observed in the time series are expected to continue into the future. Simple arithmetic and "eyeball' line-fitting techniques may be replaced by more sophisticated statistical techniques. One such technique is the least squares curve-fitting technique, in which the statistical criterion used is to minimize the square of the vertical distances of data points from the line. This is an application of regression analysis, discussed in the next paragraphs. In projection, the independent variable is time, and the dependent variable is sales volume. It should be noted that there is no causal relationship established by such analysis; time does not *cause* anything. The changes in sales volume that occur over time are due to factors which are not explicitly considered in the use of projection. Projection depends upon historical data and looks at the past to determine what will happen in the future. The real challenge in forecasting, on the other hand, is to look at those conditions that will be likely to influence sales in the future.

Regression Analysis

Regression analysis is a technique for estimating the extent of relationship between two or more variables. It measures the tendency of the dependent variable to change as the independent variables change, but there is no basis for showing that there is a casual relationship. Regression analysis produces an equation of the form

$$Y = a + b_1X_1 + b_2X_2 + \cdots + b_nX_n$$

where Y is the dependent variable (sales volume) and the X_i's are independent variables. These independent variables might be measures of market potential (population, income, etc.) or variables reflecting various measures of the company's marketing activity, such as advertising dollars, number of salesmen, number of deals, number of years the product has been on the market, and so on. Various models may be used to test the possibilities of nonlinear relationships including transforming the data into logarithmic, quadratic, exponential, or other functional forms.

An analysis of historical data may reveal relationships between sales and these independent variables. The extent of the relationship is indicated by the size of the b_i's (the regression coefficients), and the significance of that relationship can be stated in terms of a confidence interval on the estimate. These relationships then provide the basis for prediction of the dependent variable, given future values for the independent variables.

The basic requirement for regression analysis is an accurate bank of historical data on the variables to be included in the analysis. The other requirement is for accurate predictions of the values of the independent variables in the forecast period. If population and gross national product and disposable personal income are in the equation, then these variables must be estimated for the planning period before it will be possible to predict sales volume. This is true where there are no lags in the relationship. It may be that some variables are "leading indicators," as when the value of a variable at time t is seen to influence the value of the dependent variable at time $t + n$. Unless the values of the independent variables are more easily predicted than those of the dependent variable, nothing is gained in forecasting ease and accuracy

Time Series Analysis

Time series analysis provides a basis for decomposing a time series, such as historical data on sales volume, into four basic components: (1) trend, (2) seasonal, (3) cyclical, and (4) random elements. The time series model may be either multiplicative or additive. In the former case, the trend would be identified and then the other components would be treated as correction factors. In the latter case, the influence of each component would be added to the others to yield a prediction of sales.

The trend component reflects the basic growth or decline being experienced in demand for the company's product. The seasonal factor adjusts for month-of-year, day-of-week, or other recurring and regular patterns of time influences on demand. Cyclical forces result from such basic elements as the business cycle or other regularities in the variations in demand which occur over time periods extending *beyond* the length of the forecasting period. Finally, the "random" factor includes all variations in demand that are not explained by one of the three preceding factors. This so-called random element could include special promotional efforts by the company or its could include a measure of the effect of competitors' actions, for example.

Both regression and time series analysis can be done much more efficiently with the use of an electronic computer, although simple calculating equipment is also adequate. The technical aspects of these statistical procedures are probably beyond the grasp of many marketing managers, but that need not be a significant hindrance to their use, especially with the availability of time-shared computers where the manager can interact directly with the computer through the use of remote-access teletypes. Time series analysis in particular requires the availability of forecasts of general economic activity and reliable seasonal adjustments, as well as enough regularity in the basic demand pattern to make time series analysis meaningful.[19]

Preparing the Forecast

When the data have been analyzed, using whatever techniques are best suited to the data available and the degree of accuracy required, a final forecast must be prepared and given to management for use in the planning process. There are a few basic administrative considerations that need to be stressed in developing the final forecast. First and foremost, the forecast should be written. The basic assumptions used by the forecaster should be very clearly stated, so that they can be carefully evaluated by the forecast user, and so that the forecast can be assessed from time to time to make sure that the basic assumptions are still valid, especially assumptions about the company's marketing effort. The major sources of information used in preparing the forecast should be cited, and the techniques used should be identified and explained in sufficient detail for the user to assess their reasonableness. Finally, the forecast should be frequently reviewed and checked for accuracy.[20]

SUMMARY

This chapter has taken a broad brush to the problem of market measurement and forecasting as the basis for planning marketing communication strategy. The central argument of this chapter has been that all planning is based upon some prediction of market response. Behavioral science concepts as developed in Chapters 3 through 9 have analyzed the processes of individual communication and response to communication in considerable detail. In this chapter our focus has shifted to the

[19]Robert L. McLaughlin, *Times Series Forecasting* (Chicago: American Marketing Association, 1962).

[20]For a review of company procedures in forecasting sales see National Industrial Conference Board, *Forecasting Sales,* Studies in Business Policy, No. 106 (New York: The Board, 1964).

aggregate level and we have discussed many approaches to the development of quantitative measures of market potential and sales forecasts. Several techniques, such as simulation and stochastic models, were suggested for combining the theory of individual response to communication with the analytical rigor of quantitative techniques.

Methods for data collection and analysis were discussed, including surveys, group interviews, consumer panels, test markets, experimentation, simulation, and stochastic models. The major classes of techniques for forecasting sales volume were reviewed briefly. Throughout this review of technique, stress was laid on the value of sound information and conceptual frameworks as the basis for the exercise of seasoned executive judgment.

III

Developing Effective Messages

In the last seven chapters, concepts and measurement techniques for appraising market opportunity were developed. Some basic concepts of market behavior were combined with an appraisal of other strategic variables, including company resources, to define opportunities for market communication. Predispositions were seen to be a critical consideration in this planning activity. Part II was completed with an overview of some central problems and methods of market measurement and forecasting.

Analysis and definition of market targets and response characteristics are the first important steps in developing marketing communication strategy. Having completed the analysis, the strategist is ready to begin the task of developing messages for obtaining the desired response from the target market. These considerations are developed in Part III.

Chapter 11 reports findings from communication research and especially psychology on the characteristics of effective messages, both verbal and nonverbal. Chapter 12 introduces other considerations in marketing planning relative to developing the message strategy, including objectives for the meanings to be conveyed to potential customers. These objectives are often referred to as "product positioning" and are differentiated from objectives such as sales volume and profit that relate to the level of effort, as opposed to qualitative considerations in message strategy.

In Chapter 13, the creative process is analyzed and is seen to be a major determinant of the quality of the company's communication program, especially its advertising. Chapter 14 presents an overview of some of the central problems in developing an effective sales force, including recruiting, selection, training, and supervisory activities. Concepts and techniques relevant for the measurement of the potential effectiveness of alternative messages, especially advertisements, are discussed in Chapter 15. As in Part II, these next five chapters begin with some basic behavioral concepts and end with a consideration of the measurement problems in communication decision making.

11

Characteristics of
Effective Messages

The marketing communicator attempts to convey meaning to his potential market through messages, combinations of symbols, verbal and nonverbal. These messages take the form of brand names, salesmen's presentations, sales aids such as catalogs and brochures, direct mail pieces, print advertisements and broadcast commercials, packages and point-of-purchase displays, and other devices for reaching the market. To be effective, the message must attract and hold the attention of the receiver and it must convey the meaning intended by the communicator.

The message is the content of the communication; it is the WHAT in the definition of communication as "who says WHAT to whom with what result," the stimulus factors which impinge on the sensory receptors of the individual. Most communication research has used either written or spoken words as stimuli. Evidence on the impact of pictures and other visual stimuli is almost completely lacking in communication research, although studies of perception can be of some help here. This chapter will begin by considering some of the most important findings from communication research on the effectiveness of various aspects of the message, defined primarily in terms of the verbal content. Later sections will consider the perceptual impact of visual elements, including pictures, color, and layout, and the ways in which music conveys meaning.

With respect to verbal content, it will be found that the effectiveness of various types of messages is often dependent upon the characteristics of the audience. More so than in previous discussions, it will be necessary to qualify generalizations to take into account the characteristics of the audience, including both ability and motive factors and, most importantly, predispositions toward the subject of the message. These findings from the behavioral sciences do not provide a series of specific suggestions for the marketing communication strategist but they do suggest the conditions under which messages of various kinds are likely to be more or less effective.

AN OVERVIEW OF MESSAGE EFFECTIVENESS

Schramm has summarized four major requirements for an effective message. First, the message must attract and hold the attention of the intended receiver. It must employ such devices and have such content as necessary to get past the perceptual barriers of the receiver. Second, the message must employ symbols which refer to experiences common to both parties to the communication. As pointed out regarding the basic model of the communication process in Chapter 3, the symbols must have referents in the "mutually shared field of experience" of both communicator and receiver. Third, the message must arouse basic needs within the receiver and suggest a way of satisfying those needs. In other words, the message must motivate the receiver, or provide some incentive for him to respond. Fourth, the manner of meeting those needs that is suggested by the communication must be acceptable in the receiver's social situation.[1]

This set of considerations provides the necessary criteria for thinking about the determinants of message effectiveness. The message must establish contact with the receiver in a way which arouses the desire of the receiver to attend to and respond to the message. Predispositions provide both motivators (unsatisfied needs are potential motivators) and the perceptual filters through which messages must pass in gaining attention, being interpreted, and being retained. Chiefly for this reason, the discussion of predispositions and their influence, as well as methods for their identification and analysis, was developed before consideration of message effects. Likewise, social influences are important in defining the situation within which the receiver must respond to the message, and their impact must also be assessed prior to consideration of message strategies. A message has its effect according to the influence of predispositions and social pressures.

NEED AROUSAL

The ability of a message to attract and hold the attention of the receiver, and to convey the intended meaning to him, is a function of its

[1]Wilbur Schramm, "How Communication Works," *The Process and Effects of Mass Communication* (Urbana Ill.: University of Illinois Press, 1955), pp. 3–26.

ability to arouse relevant needs in the receiver. Unsatisfied needs are motivators of behavior. In this sense, need is synonymous with such other terms as "motive," or "drive," or "desire," all of which involve the concept of activating and energizing behavior.[2] Needs may be categorized in several ways: (1) physiological, psychological, and social; (2) primary and secondary; (3) congenital and acquired; and so on. One advertising practitioner has developed a list of eight "most basic wants": (1) food and drink; (2) comfort; (3) to attract the opposite sex; (4) welfare of loved ones; (5) freedom from fear and danger; (6) to be superior; (7) social approval; and (8) to live longer.[3] The validity of this list of basic needs can be tested by scanning any general appeal magazine. It will be found that most of the advertisements will use appeals in one (or more) of these basic categories.

Noticeably lacking in this list, however, are such higher-order needs as the desire for achievement and the need for beauty and aesthetic experience. Maslow[4] has suggested a hierarchy of needs as follows:

1. *Physiological*—for food, water, sleep, sex, and physical activity, among others.
2. *Safety*—for protection and security, for the familiar and the comfortable.
3. *Love*—for affection, belongingness, and acceptance by those one respects and loves.
4. *Esteem*—for self-respect and the respect of others, in the form of reputation, recognition, and prestige.
5. *Self-actualization*—for accomplishment and unique personal achievement.

This hierarchy of needs is more than a list, for it also includes some assertions about the relationships of these needs and how they influence human behavior. First, needs at a lower level must be satisfied before the higher level needs become effective motivators. "For the man who is extremely and dangerously hungry, no other interests exist but food. . . . Man lives by bread alone—when there is no bread."[5] Once a need is completely satisfied, it is no longer a motivator of behavior. However, as needs at one level are more or less satisfied, higher-order needs can come to have an influence. One result of this is that several needs may all operate, in varying degrees, to influence a particular behavior. Needs at one level need not be one hundred percent satisfied before the next level needs come into the sphere of influence.

[2]Bernard Berelson and Gary A. Steiner, *Human Behavior: An Inventory of Scientific Findings* (New York: Harcourt, Brace, Jovanovich, Inc., 1964) pp. 239–40.

[3]Melvin S. Hattwick, *How to Use Psychology for Better Advertising* (Englewood Cliffs, N.J.: Prentice-Hall, Inc., 1950), p. 139.

[4]A. H. Maslow, *Motivation and Personality* (New York: Harper & Row, 1954), pp. 80–106.

[5]*Ibid.*, pp. 82–83.

No person is ever free from needs at any level. Persons with highly developed self-actualization needs and the opportunities for satisfying those needs with above-average frequency still will be motivated by needs at the most basic physiological and safety levels. On the other hand, persons whose lives are a constant battle for food and basic physical comforts, or for respect and self-esteem, will be uninfluenced by appeals to self-actualization needs.

These concepts can be applied to groups and societies and cultures as well as to individuals. America in the twentieth century has been described as an "achieving society," and it is clear that the level of demand for goods and services necessary for the satisfaction of higher-order needs is increasing. The 1960's have seen a tremendous increase in the number of educational institutions as well as in the development of an interest in hobbies that permit satisfaction of individual needs for self-actualization. There has been increased popular interest in literature, art, and drama. There is a complex interplay between the needs of society and the needs of the individual, both of which lead to demand for goods and services and determine the effectiveness of various appeals.

These broad categories of needs may help the communicator to think about the task he is facing, but he will also need more specific information about the specific needs that will motivate his prospective customers. An advertisement cannot appeal to "physiological needs" in general; it must refer to such needs as those for specific vitamins and minerals and then show how the product can provide those requirements. An encyclopedia salesman cannot promise to satisfy "self-actualization needs" in general, but must demonstrate how owning and using his product will satisfy a desire for specific information needed as well as the general seeking motivated by curiosity. (He may also appeal to esteem needs and social striving from one's neighbors, and the love needs of the prospect as they relate to his children.)

The requirement for information on specific needs of the potential market-audience suggests the value of research on predispositions, as stated in the last chapter. It also suggests, in the case of personal communication, that the communicator should be trained to listen carefully and to stimulate the prospect's revealing of his needs by appropriate questions. Having listened and identified the specific needs that could motivate the prospect, the salesman has maximum opportunity to use the greater efficiency features of personal communication (especially the availability of feedback) to generate precisely tailored messages with the highest probability of a favorable response from the prospect.

Communication research has repeatedly found that communication which arouses needs first and then shows how the course of action advocated by the communicator will fulfill those needs is more effective.[6] It was suggested that this result was due to the fact that the receiver can more clearly perceive the instrumental value of the solution offered by the communicator if he has first been made aware of those needs.[7] This basic principle was probably known and used by successful salesmen long before the research results were produced.

TYPES OF APPEALS

As indicated above, appeals can be categorized according to the human needs which they fulfill. Clearly, then, the appeal will be effective only with those persons wo have unsatisfied needs of the kind being appealed to. Furthermore, the individual must be aware of those needs; they must be aroused before they can be appealed to. The needs appealed to will also, of course, reflect the nature of the product or service being sold. When there are several alternative needs which may be appealed to (as in the case of the encyclopedia, which can satisfy love, esteem, and self-actualization needs), the selection of the appeals should be based on a consideration of the best means of obtaining unique competitive advantage (product differentiation) as well as analysis of the importance of the various needs to potential customers. Again, this assessment would require some reasonably complete information obtained from research on predispositions among persons in the potential market.

In addition to categorizing appeals on the basis of needs, there are several other ways of looking at appeals that lend insight into the effectiveness of various kinds of messages. There is a distinction to be made between "rational" and "emotional" appeals, for example. Other kinds of appeals include threat and fear appeals, bandwagon appeals, and humorous appeals. Each of these categories is considered next.

Emotional vs. Rational Appeals

Most needs can be appealed to in two ways—through emotional appeals or through rational, "reason why" appeals. Which is likely to be most effective? A major problem in answering this question is to draw an unambiguous distinction between rational and emotional appeals. Rational appeals may elicit an emotional response, for example. In general, emotional appeals may be thought of as those relying primarily upon the use of sentimental and highly charged language, while rational

[6]Carl I. Hovland (ed.) *The Order of Presentation in Persuasion* (New Haven: Yale University Press, 1957), p. 135.

[7]Arthur Cohen, "Need for Cognition and Order of Communication as Determinants of Opinion Change," in Hovland, *op. cit.*, pp. 79–97, at p. 94.

appeals build strong arguments based on logic and supporting evidence for claims made. An emotional appeal in advertising is illustrated by the headline "Bring new excitment into your life" while a rational appeal is illustrated by "Get sharper pictures."

Furthermore, response to communication is the result of three different kinds of behavior: attention, comprehension, and acceptance. Emotional appeals may have greater attention value and may provide greater incentive to read through a communication to the end. Emotional appeals may also heighten the individual's interest in the message in a way which results in closer reading, more involvement and, as a result, greater comprehension. On the other hand, rational arguments may result in a higher level of acceptance of the message.[8]

One study involving the use of leaflets in a political campaign showed that emotional appeals are more effective than rational appeals.[9] The relative influence of each of the three elements of response was not identified, however.

Our earlier discussion of individual differences associated with persuasibility (in Chapter 7) suggested that arguments which rely upon logical argumentation are more effective with persons of higher intelligence, while those of lower intellectual ability are less influenced by such arguments.

To summarize, it appears that emotional appeals will be effective in attracting attention to the message and in providing incentive to read through the message while rational appeals may be more effective in obtaining acceptance of the assertions. Rational arguments are likely to have differential effectiveness depending upon the intellectual ability of the receiver. Some products such as office equipment obviously require rational appeals while others such as cosmetics require emotional appeals.

Threat Appeals

Threat appeals are the most extensively studied form of emotional appeals. A study of response to threat appeals might permit some generalizations about emotional appeals. Discussion of the influence of threat appeals will be easier if we first develop a basic model to explain the way individuals respond to such appeals. Threat appeals can be defined as those which suggest unfavorable consequences that will occur if the

[8]Carl I. Hovland, Irving L. Janis, and Harold H. Kelley, *Communication and Persuasion* (New Haven: Yale University Press, 1953), pp. 57–60.

[9]G. W. Hartmann, "A Field Experiment on the Comparative Effectiveness of 'Emotional' and 'Rational' Political Leaflets in Determining Election Results," *Journal of Abnormal and Social Psychology*, 31 (1936), pp. 99–141.

receiver does not follow the course of action recommended by the communicator. The "unfavorableness" of the consequences can range over a wide continuum from mild displeasure to major discomfort and even dire consequences such as physical injury or death.

In the model, neutral content cues (C) are followed by statements which evoke certain dangers and make them specific to the receiver. This "self-reference" is necessary if the threat is to be salient for the individual. This anticipation of possible danger results in an increase in the emotional tension (E). While in this state of emotional arousal, the individual is exposed to a recommendation (R) which suggests how to reduce the potential danger and the level of threat. This "reassuring recommendation" must then also be "personalized" by the receiver, and as he mentally rehearses the consequences of accepting this recommendation, the level of tension declines. This reduction of emotional tension serves to reinforce the recommendation, and learning takes place so that this mental process of accepting the recommendation will tend to occur when the individual is once again exposed to the same cues which arouse the original emotional tension. This chain of responses can be symbolized as follows:

Content cues (C) → Emotional reaction (E)

→ Reassuring recommendation (R)

This sequence tends to become habitual as long as acceptance of the recommendation results in a reduction in the level of emotional tension.

The $C → E → R$ model suggests several major considerations in the response to threat appeals. The appeal will be effective in reducing the amount of tension only if it contains a reassuring recommendation that can be personally accepted by the individual. Likewise, the content cues must be perceived as personally threatening by the individual. There are several ways in which emotional appeals can "miss the mark" and not have the desired effect on the receiver.[10] First, the threat may be regarded as improbable ("it probably won't happen") or as remote ("it might happen sometime, but there's no need to worry about it now"). Second, it may be discounted as not very significant ("if it happens, it won't make much difference"). Finally, the individual may simply see it as unimportant to him ("it may happen, but it won't happen to me"). There is good evidence that people tend to ignore potential threats as long as possible. It apparently takes convincing evidence before people take threats seriously. There is a basic psychological tendency to regard oneself as being personally exempt from potential danger.[11]

[10]Hovland, Janis, and Kelley, *op. cit.*, p. 64.
[11]*Ibid.*, p. 67.

The best-known experiment on the effectiveness of fear-arousing communication was reported by Janis and Feshback.[12] Subjects were
exposed to one of three communications on the desirability of dental
hygiene. These three messages differed according to the seriousness of
the consequences described as resulting from inadequate dental care.
The "minimal appeal" referred primarily to "cavities" and "decayed
teeth," while the "strong appeal" referred to pain from toothaches;
cancer, paralysis, blindness, and other secondary diseases; the pain associated with having teeth pulled and drilled; and mouth infections
including sore, swollen, and inflamed gums. Furthermore, the strong
appeal made such references in personal terms implying very strongly
that "this could happen to you," while the other appeals were presented
in more impersonal terms. A "moderate" appeal described the dangers in
a milder and more factual manner. All appeals stressed the importance of
good dental hygiene and advocated certain practices and habits. The
subjects of the experiment were high school students.

It was found that the strong fear appeal was most successful in causing receivers *to worry about* their dental health. More interesting, however, was the finding that the strong appeal was *least* effective in *producing conformity to the recommendations* of the communicator. They
reported the smallest change in dental hygiene practices when interviewed one week after the communication. The minimal appeal was
most effective in producing actual behavioral change, although the
moderate appeal was also more effective than the strong appeal. (It was
also found that the minimal appeal was most successful in producing
resistance to subsequent counterarguments. We shall return to this
point.) It is instructive to explore further the reasons why the strong
threat appeal may have been least successful in producing permanent
changes in attitudes and behavior.

There were no measurable differences in the amount of information
communicated by each of these communications. Strong fear appeals did
not seem to interfere in any way with the receiver's attention to the
communication. However, subsequent analysis showed that selective
recall tendencies had some influence. Persons exposed to strong threat
appeals were more likely to remember the negative *consequences* of the
threat, while the minimal threat group was more likely to recall the
causes of the threat. For the strong appeal group, the tendency to
remember the negative consequences made it less likely that they would
remember the causes. The result, then, was a lessened tendency to
accept the recommendations of the communicator with respect to how to
reduce the causes of the threat.

[12]I. L. Janis and S. Feshback, "Effects of Fear-Arousing Communications," *Journal
of Abnormal and Social Psychology,* 48 (1953), pp. 78–92.

The strong threat appeal apparently left the audience in a state of heightened emotional tension without the relief of the reassuring recommendation. The information from the experiment is consistent with the *defensive avoidance* hypothesis: "When fear is strongly aroused but is not adequately relieved by the reassurances contained in a persuasive communication, the audience will become motivated to ignore or to minimize the importance of the threat."[13]

From this research, it can be concluded that the use of threat appeals may be effective to the extent that they heighten attention to the communication and create need arousal consistent with the recommendations to be made by the communicator. There is a definite danger, however, that the threat appeal will go too far, creating an excessive level of perceived threat resulting in a reaction of defensive avoidance. If there is not acceptance of reassuring recommendations either because of excessive fear arousal or because they are not adequately conveyed by the communication, the result will be a learned tendency to subsequently avoid the cues which resulted in emotional arousal. In general, it appears that moderate threat appeals will be more effective than strong ones. Subsequent research has given additional support to the notion that when a communication results in a relatively high level of fear, the receiver will develop psychological resistances to the arguments, conclusions, and recommendations of the communicator.[14]

Bandwagon Appeals

A commonly used form of appeal is the so-called "bandwagon" appeal which says, in effect, "Everybody else is doing it, why don't you?" This is a special appeal to the influence of group pressure, and stresses the drive to conformity in the face of the opinions of relevant other persons. It is a well-known fact that the influence of social pressure may even go so far as to cause an individual to adopt an opinon or belief which is counter to the objective evidence at his disposal.

A very strong indication of the importance of "bandwagon" appeals was provided by the study of the 1940 Presidential election campaign by Berelson, Lazarsfeld, and Gaudet. They reported finding people who based their voting decision solely on the notion that it seemed clear that Roosevelt was going to win the election, and they wanted to vote for the winner.[15]

[13]Hovland, Janis, and Kelley, *op. cit.*, p. 88.

[14]I. L. Janis and R. F. Terwilliger, "An Experimental Study of Psychological Resistances to Fear-Arousing Communications," *Journal of Abnormal and Social Psychology,* 65 (1962), pp. 403–10.

[15]Paul F. Lazarsfeld, Bernard Berelson, and Hazel Gaudet, *The People's Choice* (New York: Columbia University Press, 1948), p. 108.

Bandwagon appeals call attention to a community consensus and thus appeal to the individual's desire for social approval. Our earlier discussions have suggested that compliance with the point of view advocated by a communication is often motivated by a desire for the approval of either the communicator or of other persons. Bandwagon appeals are a special instance of this influence and suggest the value of heightening the salience of group membership in communications if the norms and values of that group are consistent with acceptance of the point of view or course of action being advocated in the communication.

Humor

The user of humor in marketing communication was on the increase in the early 1970's and there was no evidence that this trend was about to change direction. Humor can increase the effectiveness and marketing communication if it helps the message to gain attention and if the use of humor is consistent with the basic selling message. Humor when creatively used may also permit a tasteful approach to advertising and selling messages for products which cannot be discussed in a straightforward fashion such as products dealing with body hygiene or home sanitation, to cite two examples.

There are no published reports, to our knowledge, of the influence of humor in persuasive communications, and there are only limited reports of studies to identify the major dimensions of humor. The evidence suggests that there are wide differences in individual preferences for humor and there do tend to be fashions in humor.[16]

The general guidelines for the use of humor in marketing communication would seem to be that the humor should not violate group norms, especially standards of propriety, and should be consistent with the basic selling appeal. It should draw attention to the selling message and not conflict or compete with other elements of the message. If humor makes the message more enjoyable, it is more likely to be remembered and to result in favorable attitudes.

MESSAGE STRUCTURE

The meaning conveyed by a message is a function of the way the message is put together, as well as the appeals and arguments which are the elements of the message. The relationships among these elements, or the message structure, can influence response to the communication in several ways.

[16]Mervin D. Lynch and Richard C. Hartman, "Dimensions of Humor in Advertising," *Journal of Advertising Research*, 8 (December 1968), pp. 39–45.

One-Sided vs. Two-Sided Arguments

Should the message include arguments both for and against the positions advocated by the communicator, or should it concentrate on the favorable points? Logic alone cannot resolve this question, since it is possible to give reasons why either message strategy is likely to be more effective. For instance, one-sided arguments can be more effective if the result of considering the negative points is simply to confuse the receiver. Two-sided arguments could be more effective if they resulted in a perception of greater fairness and thorough analysis on the part of the communicator. On the other hand, it might be that those initially opposed to the communicator's position would be reinforced in their opinions if they had the opportunity to rehearse their own point of view if it was presented by the communicator.

In one of the first reported experiments to scrutinize this problem, Hovland, Lumsdaine, and Sheffield examined the impact of orientation messages (in the form of radio transcriptions) for Army recruits.[17] The general conclusion from this research was that the effectiveness of one-sided and two-sided arguments depended upon the predispositions of the audience.

Influence of Intellectual Ability and Predisposition. Specifically, intellectual ability and whether the receiver was initially opposed to the stand taken by the communicator were found to influence response. One-sided arguments were more effective with those who were initially in favor of the point of view expressed by the communicator, while two-sided arguments were found to be more effective with those who were initially opposed. Better-educated men were found to be more influenced by two-sided messages, while less well educated men were more influenced by the one-sided argument. This research also found that omitting an important and relevant argument in presenting the negative side of the argument could, however, cause the two-sided message strategy to boomerang, because of the perception of intended trickery.[18] It should be noted that a true two-sided argument may be less effective in bringing about opinion change if it does in fact present both sides of the argument clearly and logically—a truly balanced presentation will tend to be without effect.[19]

Inoculation for Counterpropaganda. An interesting aspect of this controversy is the effectiveness of the two kinds of arguments in "inoculat-

---

[17]C. I. Hovland, A. A. Lumsdaine, and F. D. Sheffield, *Experiments in Mass Communication* (Princeton, N.J.: Princeton University Press, 1949), pp. 201–27.

[18]*Ibid.*, pp. 224–25.

[19]Joseph T. Klapper, *The Effects of Mass Communication* (New York: Free Press of Glencoe, 1960), p. 113.

ing" the receiver against subsequent messages. What happens when receivers are subsequently exposed to counterpropaganda? Again, it depends. Two-sided arguments, in general, seem to be more effective in inoculating receivers against subsequent messages which take the opposite stand. It seems that having been exposed to the counter-arguments and having heard them refuted, the receiver is better able to withstand the counter-communication. On the other hand, if the receiver is asked to publicly commit himself after being exposed to a one-sided argument, it appears that the one-sided argument can also be an effective inoculator. In this case, the fact of making some kind of public commitment (as in having to state one's feelings in front of other members of the audience, or to the researcher) probably explains most of the "inoculating" effect, rather than the structure of the message itself. However, there has been no systematic attempt to determine whether a two-sided message without public commitment is more effective than a one-sided argument with commitment.[20]

There is an interesting strategic implication in these research findings. If a new product or service is being introduced to the market (or a new practice such as wearing automobile seat belts), the market is almost completely "opposed" in the sense that the communicator is advocating some change in behavior. Two-sided messages will be more effective. Over time, as people adopt the innovation, more and more people become favorably predisposed and one-sided arguments will be more effective in reinforcing their behavior and encouraging repeat purchase. The suggestion is clear that message strategy should change at some point, approximately where half of the audience has become favorably predisposed. Some adjustment would also be required for the education factor, especially as this is correlated with time of adoption. Simulation may be a useful research technique for tracing the interactions among these factors and drawing strategic recommendations.[21]

These findings on the relative effectiveness of one-sided and two-sided arguments are a very good example of the generalization made at the beginning of this chapter that the effectiveness of messages is usually a function of the characteristics of the audience.

Conclusion Drawing

Another interesting question is whether the message should explicitly draw a conclusion or leave it to the receiver. One could argue that drawing a conclusion is likely to offend some receivers who object to having the "obvious" pointed out to them. On the other hand, not draw-

[20]*Ibid.*, pp. 115–16.

[21]Raymond A. Bauer and Robert D. Buzzell, "Mating Behavioral Science and Simulation," *Harvard Business Review*, 42 (September–October 1964), pp. 116–24.

ing the conclusion may cause some receivers "to miss the point" by either coming to the wrong conclusion or simply not pushing ahead to a conclusion of any kind.

One of the reasons for ineffectiveness in persuasive communication, and especially in marketing communication, may be that the receiver gets the information transmitted by the message but does not change his opinions or personalize the message in a way which has action implications for him. There is usually some requirement for the receiver to go beyond the explicit information contained in the communication to an implicit response of attitude change.

Usually Aids Persuasion. Hovland and Mandell conducted an experiment in which college students were exposed to arguments concerning the devaluation of currency. One group heard a message which presented several facts on this issue including the conditions which make devaluation more or less desirable. Another group heard the same message except that the communicator drew the conclusion. In the case of explicit conclusion drawing there was a significant increase in the number of students who changed their opinions in the direction advocated by the communicator.[22] Katz and Lazarsfeld similarly concluded that specific action recommendations were more likely to result in attitude and behavior change by the recipient of personal influence.[23]

Effect Depends on Audience. The general conclusion that it is better to draw explicit conclusions and recommendations should be cautiously applied with specific audiences, however. When the communicator is trying to persuade a receiver who is more expert than the communicator, conclusion drawing may be offensive to the receiver. This would be the case with a drug company detailman explaining a new drug to a physician or a textbook firm's field representative telling a college professor about a new book. Furthermore, with a more intelligent audience, it may be less necessary for the communicator to draw explicit conclusions, since the ability of the audience to draw conclusions is likely to be greater. There is less danger of missing the point or of false interpretation.[24]

. . . and on Issue. Finally, the kind of issue being discussed probably has some significance, although there is little research evidence on this question. It seems reasonable to expect that issues (or products) which are personal and ego-involving require less explicit conclusion-drawing. It may even be inappropriate for the communicator to draw conclusions in

[22]Hovland, Janis, and Kelley, op. cit., pp. 100–2.

[23]Elihu Katz and Paul F. Lazarsfeld, Personal Influence (New York: Free Press of Glencoe, 1955), p. 214.

[24]Hovland, Janis, and Kelley, op. cit., p. 103.

this case. There may be an above average possibility that the communicator's recommendations for action will miss the point or be perceived as not personally relevant by the receiver. The complexity of the issue is another factor to consider. Reason suggests that the more complex the issue, the greater is the likelihood that the audience will miss the point and, therefore, the more effective will be messages which draw explicit conclusions.[25]

One author has summarized all of these conclusions as follows: "Persuasive communications which present a complicated and unfamiliar series of arguments on impersonal topics to less intelligent people are more effective when the conclusion is stated explicitly than when the audience is left to draw its own conclusions."[26]

Active Participation

One of the distinguishing features of personal communication is that there is active participation by the receiver in the communication process. He functions as a communicator as well as a receiver and provides direct feedback to the other person in the communication setting. Mass audiences may also participate actively in the communication process. A speaker before a group of people may solicit their comments and reactions; audience members may be asked to discuss among themselves the issues being presented by the communicator. In yet another form of active participation, the individual receiver of a mass communication message such as a magazine advertisement or a television commercial may be given an implicit role in completing the message. Recent examples of this approach in advertising include the Kellogg's Cereal ads in which the last g was omitted from the name and the broadcast commercials for Salem cigarettes in which the jingle line "You can take Salem out of the country but . . ." is followed by a pause in which the receiver who has repeatedly been exposed to the commercial is encouraged to complete ". . . you can't take the country out of Salem." Effectiveness is likely to be enhanced by the more active involvement of the receiver.

Communication research provides ample evidence to support the notion that active participation is likely to lead to more opinion change in response to a persuasive communication. Experiments have elicited active participation in various forms: requiring receivers to read aloud the message, rather than silently; role playing; asking people to improvise messages in favor of a particular viewpoint; and so on.

Hovland, Lumsdaine, and Sheffield found that requiring the audience to make overt verbal responses in a training session significantly

[25]*Ibid.*, pp. 104–5.
[26]Arthur Cohen, *Attitude Change and Social Influence* (New York: Basic Books, Inc., 1964), pp. 7–8.

increased the rate of learning of the Army's phonetic alphabet.[27] Less intelligent groups profited most from the increased audience participation.[28] Whether active participation also increases the amount of opinion change, as opposed to the rate of learning, was not answered by this research. A study by Janis and King found that active participation induced by role playing augmented the effectiveness of persuasive communication.[29] Subsequent experimentation by King and Janis found that improvisation was more effective than oral reading in producing opinion change. The results of this latter experiment were confusing, however, in that oral reading produced less opinion change than silent reading, although this difference was not statistically significant.[30]

In reviewing these findings, Hovland, Janis, and Kelley argued that the evidence from these particular experiments did support a conclusion that active participation per se leads to more opinion change. Some of the possible reasons for this included greater attention when there is active participation and the fact that improvisation may increase the degree of comprehension of the content. It was also suggested that active participation may increase verbal learning which may, in turn, lead to greater retention.[31]

Early Commitment

Personal communication has the advantage of allowing the communicator to ask the receiver to make a commitment to agreement with successive points made in the communication. This is a technique frequently used by salesmen who will get initial agreement to a series of minor points or minor decisions before proceeding to the next and more significant part of his presentation. For example, an encyclopedia salesman will often get early agreement to such questions as "Don't you agree that this is a handsome-looking set?" and "Don't you agree that education is the most important thing we can provide for our children?" Likewise, the automobile salesman may ask the prospective buyer to make a series of initial noncommittal decisions as to color, basic model, type of transmission, and so on, before proceeding to the more basic issue of whether to buy an automobile.

These tactical maneuvers create a "climate of agreement" and are consistent with findings from communication research which show that early commitment leads to greater opinion change. In our discussion of one-sided vs. two-sided arguments, it was noted that one-sided argu-

---

[27]Hovland, Lumsdaine, and Sheffield, *op. cit.*, pp. 228–46.
[28]*Ibid.*, p. 240.
[29]Hovland, Janis, and Kelley, *op. cit.*, p. 220.
[30]*Ibid.*, p. 225.
[31]*Ibid.*, pp. 228–37.

ments which were followed by public commitment had the effect of insulating or inoculating the receiver against subsequent countercommunications.

There are two effects from early commitment. One is that getting early public (i.e., "open" or verbal) commitment after exposure to only one side of the argument insulates the receiver against subsequent countercommunication even when presented by the same communicator. This is a kind of "primacy effect" which favors the side of the argument presented first, although this is contingent on initial position. The second effect of early commitment is to create the "climate of agreement," as mentioned above.

The first effect was identified in an experiment conducted by Hovland, Campbell, and Brock.[32] After being exposed to one side of the argument (whether the voting age should be lowered), the student subjects were asked to write a paragraph expressing their opinions on the issue for publication in a magazine to be read by their peers. It was found that this group was much less likely to modify its opinions when exposed to the other side of the argument than were those who had only indicated their opinions on a questionnaire. Public expression of opinion appeared to "freeze" the subjects' views and to make them resistant to the other side of the argument.[33] These research findings are not unexpected when one considers the basic desire for consistency in one's behavior and the well-known tendency for people to stick to a position when it has been taken.

Order of Presentation

There are several issues involved in the general question of which arguments should be presented first in the communication. First and most basically, there is the question of whether it makes any difference. Is there a tendency for material presented first to be more or less effective than material presented later? Second, should positive or negative arguments be presented first? And third, how do predispositions influence the effects of order of presentation? Hovland, Janis, and Kelley suggested that it was necessary to distinguish between one-sided and two-sided arguments before one could analyze the influence of order of presentation.

In One-Sided Arguments: Climax vs. Anticlimax Order. They reported two conflicting research studies on the issue of whether the

---

[32]Carl I. Hovland, Enid H. Campbell, and Timothy Brock, "The Effects of 'Commitment' on Opinion Change Following Communication," in Carl I. Hovland (ed.), *The Order of Presentation in Persuasion* (New Haven: Yale University Press, 1957), pp. 23–32.

[33]Hovland, *Ibid.*, pp. 131–32.

strongest or the weakest points should be presented first in a one-sided message. The "climax" order consists of using the weaker points in one's argument first while saving the strongest for last; the reverse message strategy is called the "anticlimax" order of presentation. It was suggested that the contradictory findings on the relative effectiveness of these two strategies of presentation could be explained by analyzing the influence of three sets of factors: those relating to motivation to learn; those having to do with sequence effects in learning ("associative"); and those influencing acceptance of the message.

If the receiver is initially uninterested in the topic of the communication, use of the strongest arguments first may attract his attention and provide *motivation* for listening. This set of considerations would favor the anticlimax order of presentation. If order of presentation influences the way in which material is *remembered*, this could favor climax or anticlimax order. Here there is no general rule, however. Material at the beginning or at the end of a list of items is more easily remembered than material in the middle of the list, and there is no marked tendency for the items presented last to be better remembered, as argued for the "recency" effect. According to these observations, then, both climax and anticlimax would be more effective than a presentation which put the strongest points in the middle of the communication.

A consideration of "acceptance" factors suggests that the climax order will be preferable assuming that stronger arguments have more incentive value. Presenting the strongest arguments first would mean that subsequent weaker arguments would "let down" the receiver, causing him to lose interest, while the climax order would meet and exceed expectations created at the beginning of the communication. Thus, a review of several possible factors is inconclusive in favoring either climax or anticlimax order of presentation in one sided arguments.[34]

Once again we have a situation where the initial predispositions of the audience appear to make a difference. The attention value of an anticlimax order would seem to be preferred where the receiver is initially disinterested and needs motivation to listen. The acceptance value of the climax order would be preferred when there is some initial interest, for this is more likely to maintain interest and create final acceptance.

In Two-Sided Arguments: Primary vs. Recency Effects. Where a two-sided argument is used, analysis of attention, learning, and acceptance factors suggests a different set of considerations. Instead of the issue of climax vs. anticlimax order of presentation which applies to one-sided arguments, the two-sided argument problem involves so-called primacy and recency effects. Is the side of the argument presented first most

[34]Hovland, Janis, and Kelley, *op. cit.*, pp. 112–20.

effective (primary effect) or the side presented last (recency effect)? The attention value of positive arguments would seem to favor a primacy effect where the side presented first arouses interest in the topic and satiates that interest before the second side is presented. Learning effects suggest that the side presented last is likely to be better remembered immediately after the communication (both sides presented), thus entailing a recency effect, but that, over time, primacy effect would become important because the learning of the material presented first would interfere with the learning of the (contradictory) material presented last.

Analysis of acceptance factors becomes more complex in the case of two-sided arguments. First, attitudes toward the communicator will influence acceptance. When the communicator states first one position and then another, the audience is likely to become suspicious and distrustful. This would seem to favor a primacy effect. Secondly, the desire for self-consistency, as noted earlier, would favor a primacy effect. Having been persuaded by the first argument and adopted a modified viewpoint, it would be inconsistent to then change that position again. The first argument may inoculate the receiver against the second. Finally, the initial position of the audience would seem to make a difference. Those initially opposed to the position advocated by the communicator would probably be impressed with his ability to see their side (the negative side) of the argument. Similarly, those initially in favor of his viewpoint would be better motivated if first exposed to the positive sides of the argument. Conversely, positive arguments presented first would cause the defenses of those initially opposed to rise, while negative arguments would have the same effect with those who initially support the communicator's position. Thus, analysis of acceptance factors suggests that whether there is a primacy or a recency effect would depend upon both the initial position of the communicator and whether positive or negative arguments were presented first.[35]

Dependence on Initial Predispositions. Just as there can be no flat assertion about the relative effectiveness of climax and anticlimax orders of presentation, so there can be no unqualified assertion about primacy and recency effects. The influence of order of presentation for both one-sided and two-sided arguments is contingent upon the initial position of the audience.

Subsequent research reported by Hovland made the nature of this dependence more specific. The earlier suggestion that when two sides of an argument are presented by the same communicator, there may be a primacy effect because of the influence of decreased credibility, was confirmed in an experiment by Luchins, although he also noted marked dif-

[35]*Ibid.*, pp. 120–29.

ferences among individuals.[36] McGuire found that presenting information desirable to the receiver first was more effective in causing opinion change than the reverse order.[37] On balance, it seems that to present first positive arguments (those in favor of the communicator's position) has several advantages, including gaining attention, facilitating learning, and motivating acceptance, provided that the audience is initially in favor of the communicator's position. Where the objective is to change opinions and attitudes, however, the more effective strategy may be to rehearse the arguments against the communicator's assertions, increasing his credibility and minimizing the defensive reaction of the respondent. It should be remembered, however, that the findings here are incomplete in many aspects and any attempt to derive specific principles for "engineering" messages to be used in persuasive communications must use extreme caution.

The general conclusion that one may draw, however, is that the order of presentation does indeed have an influence upon the effect of the message. This influence depends primarily upon the initial predispositions of the receiver and his intellectual ability as well as the elements of the message itself. A distinction must be made about the influence of one-sided and two-sided messages, as well as the differences attributable to the order with which these arguments are presented. Active participation and early commitment can result in more attitude change, as can conclusion drawing, except where this is likely to be offensive to the receiver.

FREQUENCY AND REPETITION

Repetition, especially repetition with some variation in the method of presentation, has been found to improve the effectiveness of communication. It is interesting, however, that studies of cumulative exposure—a concept very similar to repetition—have not consistently found a relationship between amount of attitude change and cumulative exposure on an issue.[38] (Cumulative exposure as a concept includes exposure to a variety of sources and messages concerning an issue; repetition means exposure to the same basic message.)

Repetition and Retention

Hovland, Janis, and Kelley reviewed the results of early research on the effects of repetition and concluded that repetition increases the

[36]Abraham C. Luchins, "Primacy-Recency in Impression Formation," in Hovland, op. cit., pp. 33–61.

[37]William J. McGuire, "Order of Presentation as a Factor in 'Conditioning' Persuasiveness," in Hovland, op. cit., pp. 98–114.

[38]Klapper, op. cit., p. 131.

degree of retention up to a point. Beyond three or four repetitions the additional retention effects are insignificant.

Too frequent repetition, moreover, "without any reward, leads to loss of attention, boredom, and disregard of the communication. . . . Variation in form, style, and expression, together with repetition of the major points, is . . . a particularly effective solution to this problem."[39]

The effects of repetition have received considerable study from the advertising field. Politz has argued that advertising "represents a special case within the general law that learning progresses with repetition."[40] Given that forgetting will occur, repetition may be required to keep product and brand awareness and attitude levels at or beyond some minimum level. Otherwise, when the buying action finally occurs, the residual effects of previous advertising exposures may well be below the level required for any noticeable influence on behavior. This suggests that careful consideration must also be given to the frequency and timing of messages, as well as whether repetition is desirable or not. This issue involves the media strategy problem and its discussion is therefore postponed until Chapter 19.

Personal selling strategy, especially in industrial marketing, also involves some issues of repetition. Because of the complexity of industrial buying decisions and the fact that many people become involved in the buying organization, repeated sales calls become necessary. This leads to some complex issues of call strategy to be discussed in Chapter 17 on the allocation of sales effort.

Lucas and Britt report research done by Alfred Politz for *The Saturday Evening Post* which showed that a second exposure of the same ad to the same individuals resulted in both improved product knowledge and increased willingness to buy the product.[41] In addition, there is evidence that the effect of repetition in advertising is to reinforce the original response to the message.[42] The result is a reinstatement of source effect and the prevention (or diminution) of sleeper effect.

In a study of the effects of repetitive advertising in newspapers, Stewart found that repetition resulted in increased awareness and that it was economical to have up to fifteen exposures, whereas four exposures had some buying effects and eight exposures doubled the results.[43] Likewise,

---

[39]Hovland, Janis, and Kelley, *op. cit.*, p. 247.

[40]Alfred Politz, "What Is Essential To Know from Magazine Media Research?" *Media/scope*, 3 (April 1959), pp. 3–8, at p. 5.

[41]Darrell B. Lucas and Steuart H. Britt, *Measuring Advertising Effectiveness* (New York: McGraw-Hill Book, Inc., 1963), p. 218.

[42]Martin Weinberger, "Does the 'Sleeper Effect' Apply to Advertising," *Journal of Marketing*, 25 (October 1961), pp. 65–67.

[43]John B. Stewart, *Repetitive Advertising in Newspapers* (Boston: Division of Research, Graduate School of Business Administration, Harvard University, 1964).

a study by Zielske found that there is greater immediate recall of advertising (in this case, direct mail advertising) when several exposures occur in rapid sequence rather than being spaced out over a longer time period, but when recall is measured over a longer time period, exposure over a longer period of time is more effective.[44]

Influence of Message Quality

The effects of repetition depend at least in part upon the quality of the message itself. Repetition can have a negative or boomerang effect if the message is weak or offensive. If the message is basically believable and strong, repetition, especially with variation, can increase the level of attitude change and the achievement of communication objectives.[45] Humor probably loses its impact more quickly than other appeals under repetition.

To summarize, repetition can increase the amount of retained awareness and opinion change, especially if repetition occurs over a reasonably short interval. On the other hand, spreading the messages over a longer time period may result in a loss of continuity with subsequent forgetting and a decrease in message effectiveness.

PERCEPTION OF VISUAL STIMULI

In addition to words, the marketing communicator often uses visual symbols and devices to attract attention and to convey meaning. These include illustrations, color, typography, headlines, and the overall format of the message. These visual stimuli can influence the effectiveness of the marketing communication in several ways. Rather than attempt to review and illustrate the many ways in which visual elements are used in marketing communication strategy, we shall briefly review a few of the most basic behavioral principles involved. These principles can then be applied in several specific communication approaches.

Perception is the process by which symbols and cues are assigned meaning through reference to a set of categories of meaning based on previous experience. In addition to the categories of meaning, or predispositions, other influences on perception are the characteristics of the sensory receptors, the nature of the stimulus, and the relationship of the stimulus to its background. While the chapter focusses on the message or stimulus factors, the very nature of perception requires that these must be considered in interaction with the sensory receptors and back-

[44]Hubert A. Zielske, "The Remembering and Forgetting of Advertising," *Journal of Marketing*, 23 (January 1959), pp. 239–43.
[45]James F. Engel, Hugh G. Wales, and Martin R. Warshaw, *Promotional Strategy* (Homewood, Ill.: Richard D. Irwin, Inc., 1967), p. 222.

ground factors. These relationships are studied by the science of psychophysics.

Sensation

Visual stimuli are sensed through the eyes and are judged in terms of shape, size, color, lightness and darkness, and so on. As in other sensation, visual stimuli must exceed some minimum threshold intensity before they can be detected by the human sensory organs. There is a minimum in size, light intensity, and time of exposure prerequisite to seeing an object. Furthermore, *changes* in stimulus intensity must exceed a certain minimum fraction of stimulus intensity before they are detectable. These relationships are expressed by Weber's Law:

$$\frac{\Delta I}{I} = K$$

where I is the initial stimulus intensity, ΔI is the smallest change in stimulus intensity that can be detected by the sensor, and K is a constant that has a different value for each of the senses. This relationship may also be expressed in terms of the "just noticeable difference" (abbreviated "j.n.d.") that the senses can perceive. The notion of a j.n.d or threshold is illustrated by the concept of subliminal advertising, involving the use (with questionable success) of visual stimuli in the form of flashes on a movie screen that were supposedly just below the level of conscious awareness. (*Limen* is the Latin word for "threshold," and *sub-liminal* means "just below the threshold of the senses.")

Weber's Law expresses a fundamental fact about perception: the stronger the intensity of the original stimulus (I), the greater the intensity of the change (ΔI) required to produce a j.n.d. Perception is a relative thing. For example, the difference between the intensity of a 15- and a 25-watt light bulb is probably more noticeable to most persons than the difference between a 60- and a 75-watt bulb. Likewise, a price reduction from ten dollars to nine is more noticeable than a reduction from fifty dollars to forty-nine.

One application of Weber's Law is to the perception of a figure against its background. Color contrasts between figure and background, or size contrasts, or difference in light intensity can increase the impact of the stimulus. As an example, a ten-foot-wide outdoor billboard is much more discernible against the serene background of a New Hampshire roadside than a sign twice as large against the suburban and commercial hustle and bustle along the freeways into San Francisco.

Use of contrast is a common technique in marketing communication to secure attention and gain visual impact. Use of bright colors, use of white space as background for print advertising, use of large displays are all examples of an attempt to cope with the basic truths of Weber's Law relating to sensation.

Organization

We do not respond to cues in a piecemeal fashion but rather we organize our visual experiences into integrated wholes. These nine dots

. . .

. . .

. . .

are perceived in relation to one another. Viewers generally perceive this as a square or as three lines. (As a test of your ability to avoid the basic constraints of your learned perceptual organization tendencies, see if you can connect all nine dots with four connected straight lines.) There are several basic principles of perceptual organization including figure-and-ground, grouping, and closure. These principles have been developed by the Gestalt psychologists (*Gestalt* is the German word for "form," "shape," or "figure"). The Gestalt is the perceptual *whole* developed by the perceiver.

One of the basic organizational tendencies is that of defining *figure* and *ground*. The perceiver focusses on some aspect of the total visual stimulus; this becomes the figure and the rest of the stimulus becomes ground. These tendencies do not depend on the characteristics of the stimulus, as illustrated by reversible figure-ground patterns such as this one:

Continuous viewing of this figure will result in an alternating perception of either a goblet or two profiles as the figure, illustrating that the organization tendency lies with the perceiver and is not solely determined by the nature of the stimulus.

Another basic organization tendency is that of *grouping* of visual material, as was illustrated above with the example of the nine dots which are usually perceived as a box. Visual elements will tend to be grouped together according to similarity, proximity, and continuity. Again, the drive is toward organization, toward the formation of a Gestalt that finds consistent meaning in the chaos of the visual stimuli.

The final organization tendency to be discussed here is *closure*, the drive to find an organized, whole, continuous figure. In the figure below, the perceiver will fill in the missing pieces to form a closed figure.[46] He will see a dog, not twenty discrete blotches:

Judgment and Interpretation

The more ambiguous the visual stimuli, the more freedom does the individual have to develop such organizations as have greatest meaning for him and are most consistent with his predispositions. As the opportunities to exercise judgment increase, the influence of the individual's motives and expectations will increase. The characteristics attributed to the stimulus by the individual will reflect his needs, previous experience, and expectations.

Previous experience and resulting expectations lead to what have been called *perceptual constancies*. These include lightness and color constancy, shape constancy, and size constancy. Familiar objects tend to be perceived as maintaining their characteristics even if the physical stimuli have changed. For example, coal looks black and paper looks white even under tremendous ranges of light exposure because these are

[46]Bernard Berelson & Gary Steiner, *Human Behavior: An Inventory of Scientific Findings* (New York: Harcourt, Brace, Jovanovich, Inc., 1964), pp. 104–10. The figure is on p. 107. The original source is Roy F. Street, *A Gestalt Completion Test: A Study of a Cross Section of Intellect* (New York: Teachers College, 1931), p. 41.

the "memory colors" for these objects, the color we remember them to be. Objects also have familiar sizes and shapes and our perceptions will reflect what we are familiar with and therefore expecting when the physical attributes of the object actually change.[47] These are a special case of selective perception.

Use of Visual Elements

These aspects of the processes by which an individual responds to visual stimuli suggest opportunities for creative use of visual elements in marketing communication. Anything which leads to significant contrast, for example, is likely to create attention and therefore lead to more effective communication. Use of large advertisements and of large illustrations, or dramatic use of white space, or striking colors are all ways of attracting attention to the advertising and securing greater interest and readership.[48] Illustrations may be used to demonstrate product features in personal selling, where there is danger that certain verbal concepts may be misinterpreted.

Unique and bold type faces are often used to attract and hold attenton. Deeper contrast makes the advertising easier to read. Large advertisements are likely to attract more attention than small ones within a given magazine or other vehicle, with readership tending to increase in proportion to the square root of the space.[49] There are also different effects due to the position of an advertisement within the advertising vehicle although there are no striking regularities in this relationship. Nearby editorial matter, position on page, and distance from front and back cover seem to have some influence, for example. All of these are significant factors to keep in mind in analyzing the effectiveness of marketing communication.[50]

MUSIC AS COMMUNICATION

Music has long played an important role in marketing communication. Radio commercials frequently use musical jingles, often sung as well as played, which are highly memorable and occasionally annoying. With the advent of television it was to be expected that creative execution would focus on visual elements, and the result was a decrease in

[47]Julian E. Hochberg, *Perception* (Englewood Cliffs, N.J.: Prentice-Hall, Inc., 1964), pp. 45–61.

[48]*Advertising Age*, August 26, 1963, p. 4.

[49]Roger Barton, *Advertising Media* (New York: McGraw-Hill Book Co., Inc., 1964), p. 109.

[50]For a good discussion of the many details to be considered in designing an effective advertising program see Hugh G. Wales, Dwight Gentry, and Max Wales, *Advertising Copy, Layout and Typography* (New York: Ronald Press Company, 1958).

the use of music relative to radio. As we approach the Seventies, however, there is a marked increase in the use of music in television commercials, as well as its continued popularity in radio advertising.

Whether music can legitimately be considered a form of communication is an interesting question. If we phrase the question simply as "Does music convey meaning?" then the answer is affirmative: music does have meaning for individuals. Also, music has some interesting similarities to written and spoken languages, including grammar and syntax, in the form of melodic and harmonic rules. Music falls short of a formal definition of language, however, because the experiences which it evokes in listeners tend to be highly individual whereas a true language must convey detailed messages which are understood similarly by large groups of listeners.[51]

Response: Highly Emotional and Personal

Music can produce the deepest and strongest emotional response of any of the physical stimuli. Response to music does seem to be governed by the same basic perceptual processes as previously discussed for visual stimuli. The listener selectively perceives certain elements in the total complex structure of the music he is exposed to and these elements are highlighted and dominate the perceptual field while others are subordinated.[52] The responses produced by music lie in the "affective" or emotional realm rather than in the cognitive sphere, which is to say that they are very subjective. The images and feelings that are created are specific to the individual and are not widely shared. It is hard to get any kind of agreement from a group of experimental subjects on the "meaning" of a particular piece of music, for example, although they will all agree that it has meaning.

This fact of the subjective nature of the perception of musical stimuli means that the planned use of music in marketing communication is much more art than science. "The composer feels his way towards the satisfactory organizing of his material and the performer feels his way toward a satisfactory interpretation."[53] The richness of the emotional responses created by music makes it virtually impossible to predict the effect of a given piece of music upon a given individual. Of the various elements of music which convey meaning, it appears that *tempo* plays the largest role. Next in importance is *modality*—whether the music is in a major or minor key. *Pitch* is also significant in its emotional impact.

[51]Paul R. Farnsworth, *The Social Psychology of Music* (New York: Dryden Press, 1958), pp. 84–112.

[52]James L. Mursell, *The Psychology of Music* (New York: W. W. Norton & Co., Inc., 1937), p. 201.

[53]*Ibid.*, p. 14.

Harmony and *rhythm* seem to be of far less importance. [54] Also of significance in determining the individual's response to music are "the listener's personality structure, the mood held just preceding the listening period, the word-meanings of the libretto if there is one, and the attitudes built up in the listener toward music in general and toward the piece in question."[55] One early study discovered that the laws of primacy, recency, and emphasis which had been found to influence learning of verbal materials also applied to the learning of melodies.[56]

Despite the subjectivity of response to music, it can be used very creatively and effectively by the skilled person with musical training who has responsibility for developing marketing communications. While it is not possible to develop a set of principles of response, we can examine the influence of two major aspects of musical stimuli—tone and structure. An understanding of how these two elements influence response may suggest some opportunities for the use of music, as well as some limitations on its use in the creative execution of marketing communications.

Tone

Tones are physically distinct from noises in their structure. A tone consists of a fundamental together with its overtones, constituting the harmonic series.[57] Tones are the most subjective of all highly organized sensations. Tones are more subjective than noises and all sounds are more subjective than sight.[58] Tonal stimuli have been found to produce physiological changes in both humans and lower animals including an increase in blood pressure, pulse rate, respiration rate, metabolism, and the psychogalvanic reflex (skin resistance to electric current). These physiological reactions are the same ones which accompany emotion. Thus, music tends to produce the same physiological reactions as take place during emotion and these changes are produced by tone independent of the influence of rhythm or other elements of structure.[59]

Tonal stimulation has some other interesting effects, including the lowering of the threshold values for response to other stimuli. Odors, colors, and tastes too faint to be perceived have been found to come into conscious perception when accompanied by listening to tone. Visual acuity is also sharpened when listening to music.[60]

[54]Farnsworth, *op. cit.*, p. 99.
[55]*Ibid.*, p. 95.
[56]O. Ortmann, "On the Melodic Relativity of Tones," *Psychological Monographs*, 35, No. 1 (1926), pp. 1–47.
[57]Mursell, *op. cit.*, p. 21.
[58]*Ibid.*, p. 25.
[59]*Ibid.*, pp. 26–31.
[60]*Ibid.*, pp. 28–29.

Structure

Tone can be thought of as producing a more or less "pure" emotional response, one that is basically physiological. The structural components of music give it meaning, although it should be emphasized again that these meanings are highly subjective to the specific listener. Another way of saying this is that there are affective meanings to music that do not depend on convention or association, as do such other symbol systems as language.

There appears to be a basic relationship between tonal-rhythmic patterns and body movement. Most people cannot resist the urge to sway, or keep the beat, or otherwise make some kind of physical response to music, often at a nearly subconscious level. Music presents a moving perceptual pattern rather than the static pattern of many visual stimuli and there is, therefore, a relatively long latency of emotional response to music.[61] We talk about the "welling up" of feeling in response to music, implying this kind of delayed reaction.

Perceptually, we tend to organize the stimuli of music by reference to its source and through the noting of such qualities as tonal volume (which is distinct from intensity or loudness), timbre (tonal quality), pitch, rhythm, and the intervals among tones. We notice melodies which are sequences of tones that we perceive in a unified and organized fashion, following the basic principles of Gestalt psychology as noted earlier, rather than distinct separate pieces of the composition. Our selective perception of these aspects of music structure, when compared with categories of meaning stored in memory, determine our response to music as communication.

As a tool of marketing communication, music demands a high degree of creative insight. Because of the individualistic and subjective nature of response, it is virtually impossible to use music alone as a message tool for conveying meaning. The effective use of music requires carefully coordinated relationships with verbal and visual stimuli such as the motion of actors in a television commercial or the words used in a radio commercial. The total response to a television commercial, for example, will reflect the meaning that is conveyed by words in connection with music and in relationship to the visual movement of the commercial including both actors' movements and the way in which the film is cut and organized. Of all the tools of stimulation available to the communicator, music has the potential to produce the deepest emotional responses.

[61]*Ibid.*, p. 41.

SUMMARY

This chapter has explored knowledge and concepts from the behavioral sciences that help us understand the ways in which messages have an effect upon receivers. It was stressed that the physical characteristics of the messages used, including verbal, visual, and musical stimuli, are significant only in their interaction with the sensory and perceptual mechanisms of the receiver. Most of the generalizations offered about the effects of message content, for example, were couched in terms of the intellectual ability and predispositions of the receiver.

The most basic characteristics of effective messages are that they attract and hold the attention of the receiver. That is, the message must have the ability to gain his attention and it must motivate him to continue to devote his attention to it. Stated yet differently, the effective message is one which impinges on the senses with sufficient impact to become noticeable, which arouses needs in a way that motivates continued interest, and which promises to satisfy one or more needs motivating the individual.

Experimental evidence suggests several characteristics of verbal messages, whether spoken or in print, which can improve the likelihood of success. Various appeals and message structures will be more or less effective depending upon the initial state of the audience and the intensity of emotional arousal. Visual and musical stimuli can heighten the impact of verbal messages, although the impact of music is very subjective and difficult to predict and control.

These concepts from behavioral science are useful background for the marketing communicator as he begins to develop a message strategy. There are many other economic and strategic considerations involved in the development of effective messages, however. These are explored in the next chapter.

12

Developing Communication Objectives

Before the marketing communication strategist can turn to the specific task of developing effective messages, he needs a statement of the objectives that have been established for the communication program. Appraisal of the opportunity to communicate has resulted in the identification of the need for attention to specific market segments and specific sets of predispositions within those markets. Market measurement has provided quantitative estimates of the opportunity available in the market and the extent to which desirable response can be achieved from specific marketing actions.

The following discussion assumes that the marketing communication program is to be developed in the context of a well-defined marketing strategy. It will be assumed that basic marketing objectives have been established, including a definition of the market segments to which marketing effort is to be directed. The assumption is that final product characteristics have been determined and sufficient research has been conducted to indicate that the product is acceptable to consumers. The definition of the total marketing program will have resulted in a specification of the role of marketing communication in the accomplishment of marketing objectives. Some basic guidelines will have been drawn for the relative emphasis to be placed upon personal and mass communications in the accomplishment of communication objectives. Relationships among marketing channel and pricing considerations and the amount of funds available for the promotion of the product will have been determined. In other words, marketing strategy has been defined in terms of "push" and "pull" emphasis. Finally, it is assumed that there is sufficient knowledge of existing predispositions within the market and on patterns of influence operating within the market segments to be targeted. The company is assumed to have some minimum level of knowledge about attitudes toward its products, about company image, and about attitudes toward the products of competitors. This discussion of setting communication objectives will suggest in greater detail ways of looking at this information.

To the extent that the above assumptions do not fit a particular situation, that company is not ready to develop specific communication objectives. As repeatedly stressed, knowledge of markets, and especially knowledge of predispositions and social influence, is the basic building block for effective marketing communication strategy. Furthermore, communication activities can be judged only in the context of overall marketing strategy. Communication objectives are instrumental to the accomplishment of marketing objectives.

FUNCTIONS OF OBJECTIVES

Communication objectives perform several functions which result in a more effective marketing communication program. The setting of objectives is the first step in planning a communication strategy, facilitating the accomplishment of all subsequent steps, including control and evaluation. Because it comes first in the logical sequence of the planning process and because of its influence on all subsequent planning activities, the setting of objectives is probably the most important step in strategic planning.

For the moment, it will be useful to identify two categories of communication objectives: objectives for the *meaning to be conveyed* to the target audience and objectives for the *number of receivers* to be reached. The first set of objectives has major value in defining the message strategy to be employed while the second set of objectives relates more to the media strategy including the use of both personal and nonpersonal communication tools. The special case of setting objectives for the dollar level of communication effort including establishment of budgets will be postponed for discussion until Chapter 16. The present chapter concentrates on the specification of objectives to be used to guide the development of message strategy. Objectives for the level of effort are necessary inputs to the design of the media strategy. Recognizing that this is an artificial distinction among kinds of objectives for purposes of analysis, we shall try to suggest the relationships among the two kinds of objectives wherever appropriate in this chapter.

Defining Desired Results

Objectives define the results to be achieved. Communication objectives therefore must specify *who* is to be reached with the message, and this definition should be provided by the basic segmentation strategy adopted by marketing management. Communication objectives must also specify the *meaning to be conveyed*, as noted above. The problem here is to identify what it is the firm wishes to say about its product or service. A related set of objectives may specify the *response desired*, whether that be simple awareness, a change in predispositions, or actual buying action. These are complex questions to be discussed in the following pages.

Coordination

It is necessary to have a statement of the results desired from the communication program because this provides a set of criteria against which to evaluate alternative courses of action and subsequent accomplishments. Objectives establish expectations and help to organize and direct the resources of the organization toward a common purpose. Objectives help to insure coordination of the several elements of the communication program and the coordination of communication with other marketing activities. For this reason, communication objectives must be consistent with (derived from) objectives for total marketing effort and must be based upon a careful appraisal of the role of communication in the total marketing program. The results of this appraisal result in a definition of the relative importance of push and pull strategic emphasis, as noted earlier.

Evaluation

One of the key questions in the development of communication objectives relates to the subsequent evaluation of communication effort. Objectives provide the criteria for evaluation, the standards against which accomplishment is to be judged. This use of objectives suggests that one criterion against which to judge the objectives themselves, therefore, is the extent to which they permit precise measurement for purposes of evaluation. For example, it makes no sense to state objectives in terms of levels of awareness if there is no measurement of awareness. Likewise, it does not make sense to state objectives in terms of sales volume if it will subsequently be impossible to determine the contribution of communication to a given sales result.

To summarize briefly, communication objectives serve the purpose of organizing and coordinating organization resources toward common goals. They define the audience to be reached, the meaning to be conveyed, and the response to be obtained from the audience. These objectives may be useful in determining how the market audience is to be reached with a message strategy and a media strategy, broadly defined to include both personal and mass communications.

BUYER DECISION MAKING

The question "How should we communicate to the market?" must be answered in terms of how the receiver will use the information to be communicated. This use, in turn, is determined by the nature of the buyer's decision-making process. The complexity of the buying decision process will be reflected in such dimensions as the time required, the amount of information gathered, and the number of individuals involved in the decision. The specification of communication objectives must be based upon a careful appraisal of all of these elements.

The discussion in Chapter 7 emphasized the importance of individual differences, especially in terms of the amount of perceived risk in both the product performance and psychosocial consequences of buying and using the product. That discussion is directly relevant to the setting of communication objectives for it defines the role of marketer-provided information in the buyer's decision-making process. It is important to note that the amount of information seeking is likely to increase as the amount of perceived risk increases. Perceived risk is a function of the relative newness of the product, the familiarity of the brand name, purchase price, and the extent to which purchase and use of the product is socially conspicuous.

Planned Purchases

It is useful to distinguish between two broad categories of purchases: those which are the result of a careful appraisal of alternatives and consequences and those which seem to be spur-of-the-moment. Planned purchases are more common for higher-priced products such as automobiles, major appliances, furniture, major clothing items, and so on. Individual consuming units will demonstrate marked differences in the extent to which purchases are planned, depending upon the level of income and the availability of savings and credit to finance major purchases. A man earning $50,000 annually can easily afford to buy a pair of shoes costing $40 which he happens to see in a store window. (This would not necessarily be an "impulse" purchase; he may have been thinking about his need for a pair of shoes for several weeks.) A man earning $7,000 per year may have to carefully save and plan the purchase several weeks in advance. Or, the laborer also may buy the shoes on sight, arranging to pay for them over an extended time period. Other things being equal, however, higher-priced items are more likely to be the result of a carefully planned purchase.

Financial and Preference Planning. Planned purchases have two dimensions. First, the potential buyer must plan the commitment of his financial resources in such a way as to be able to afford the purchase, often through some kind of savings plan. Second, the potential buyer may carefully gather information necessary to appraise alternative courses of action. While he is "saving up" for a color television set, he may also be systematically evaluating several brands and dealers, through talking with people and reading advertisements. He may decide to buy a television set long before he decides on the model.

When the marketer is selling a product or service that is likely to be bought as the result of a planned buying decision, communication has a particular role to play. The objective of the communication program must be to provide potential buyers with sufficient information to evaluate the product according to whatever criteria are likely to be used by that buyer. (The marketers' communication program may suggest which criteria are most important.) The communication must stress the product qualities which distinguish this brand from competing brands. Most importantly, the communication must lead the potential buyer through the stages of the buying decision process from awareness through favorable attitude development to ultimate buying action.

The planned purchase will almost certainly require several message exposures over an extended time period. The frequency and timing of exposure therefore becomes important, as does the content of the communication. Because the potential market may contain prospective customers at all stages of the buying decision process, any single communication may have to provide information which arouses needs, suggests why this product is best suited to satisfy those needs, tells where and how the product can be purchased, and provides some incentive for buying action. On the other hand, different elements in the total communication program may be assigned specific responsibilities depending upon the stage of the buying decision process. Advertising may be used to generate an awareness of the availability of a new pharmaceutical among doctors, for example, with the detailman assigned responsibility for developing favorable attitudes, and mailed literature and samples designed to stimulate action.

Unplanned or "Impulse" Purchases

The word "impulse" has been placed in quotation marks because what may appear to be an unplanned or impulse purchase may actually be the result of a careful and systematic appraisal of alternative buying actions. In the example given above, the purchase of the $40 pair of shoes may appear to be "on impulse" as a man walks from one appointment to another past the shop window. On the other hand, he may have spent months looking for just that style before finding it in this particular shop. The housewife who grabs a package of toothpaste without even slowing down as she pushes her shopping cart past the display may appear to be purchasing "on impulse" although this brand may be one she recently decided to buy as the result of a careful conversation with her dentist. This is an important point; marketing people have probably significantly overestimated the amount of purchasing based solely upon "emotional" factors and "impulse." It is too easy to assume that because there is no observable problem-solving behavior, none has preceded the actual purchase.

Conditions Favoring Impulse Purchasing. Impulse purchasing does occur, however. It usually results from a "reminder" provided by some cues in the environment (point of purchase display, a short radio message, seeing somebody else with the product, etc.). Often, the cue may trigger a response not intended by the communicator. For example, hearing a radio commercial for Winston cigarettes may remind the housewife to buy a carton of Kents (her favorite brand) while she is in the supermarket

This kind of impulse purchasing characterizes frequently purchased, low-priced convenience goods of the kind sold in food and drug stores. The shopper does not make a conscious decision about which brands and sizes of each of the fifty to one hundred items she expects to buy in the weekly trip to the supermarket. Many purchases fall into one of two categories—those where she will buy a favorite brand (loyalty) and those where she will buy whichever brand is being offered at the best price this week. Only on a relatively infrequent basis will the shopper take the time to examine all of the products available to her and to evaluate systematically the relative importance of price and product features in her decision process. The amount of true decision making will vary depending upon the buyer's satisfaction with her present brand, her perception about the potential gain possible, the likelihood of unsatisfactory performance from other brands, and the perceived costs involved in gathering and evaluating additional information. Chapter 7 developed these considerations in much greater detail and they do not need further elaboration here.

Loyalty May Create Illusion of Impulse Buying. For products which are characterized by a relatively high degree of brand loyalty (which may reflect indifference as much as true preference), the objective of marketing communication is often to maintain what has been called "top-of-mind" awareness, that is, to provide constant reminders to potential customers so that they will think of this brand the next time they buy a product in that category. The implicit assumption appears to be that the probability of purchasing Brand X is closely related to the buyer's exposure to advertising messages for Brand X in proportion to his exposure to all messages for products in this category. When the objective is to maintain awareness, frequency of exposures and repetition become important communication objectives and shorter, more memorable messages become preferable. In addition, point-of-purchase promotion and display become significant marketing communication tools for impulse items.

New-Product Advertising May Be "Unbelievable." The marketer of a new product in this kind of marketing situation is faced with a slightly different problem. Not only must he obtain initial awareness, but he must also provide some reason for changing brand preferences to the consumer, as well as provide for sufficient recall of the brand name at time of purchase. Maloney has suggested that in such cases the new product's messages will not be "believed," although they may lead to buying action. He argued that a single message can do no more than nudge the prospect along the path from unawareness through to actual purchase of the product. By definition, an advertisement for a new product is saying, "Our new product is better than the one you are using." This message is likely not to be believed by the person who is quite satisfied with his present brand. The receiver may become *curious* about the new product, however, while not quite believing its claims. Thus, it may be possible to challenge the buyer to try the new product while maintaining his belief that his present brand is the best. In such a case, behavior change may precede attitude change.[1] Stated differently, the problem for the marketer of a new product in a category characterized by high loyalty may be to change impulse purchases to planned purchases, in that he must arouse the buyer's curiosity and interest enough to break the old habit. Special promotional deals can be particularly effective in inducing trial, that is, in getting behavior change (purchase of the new brand) before attitude change (preference for the new brand).

Brand Image

In certain product categories, brand "image" is a significant determinant of the consumer's buying decision. Whereas previous comments on planned and impulse purchases have concentrated on what we called "the problem-solving game" in Chapter 7, brand image considerations

[1]John C. Maloney, "Is Advertising Believability Really Important?," *Journal of Marketing*, 27 (October 1963), pp. 1–8.

are developed in the context of the "psychosocial game." It is first necessary to consider the conditions under which psychosocial variables are likely to be important. Then the discussion will turn to implications for the setting of marketing communication objectives.

Brand image can be thought of as the constellation of meanings surrounding a brand. It is the personality of the brand in the eyes of the consumer. Thinking of brand image as analogous to personality suggests the possibility of predicting product use on the basis of the extent to which a given brand image is perceived by the consumer as being consistent with his self concept. Before making the relationship to self-concept explicit, however, it is first necessary to look more closely at the concept of brand image itself.

Organizes Perception of Product. White pointed out that a basic function performed by marketing communication, and especially advertising, is "to help to organize and modify the *basic perceptual processes* of the consumer, so that he is guided toward *seeing* and *feeling* a product in a given predictable way."[2] According to this view, one of the major functions of marketing communication is to define a set of values and needs which are inherent in the role of the product and to supply the terms in which the product is to be evaluated. Advertising especially can create an image for a product, consisting of a set of values and needs which are identified with the product. It has been suggested that advertising can be made most effective if the characteristics consumers desire in a new product are first identified, then the product is developed to have those characteristics and advertising can be defined to communicate them.[3] Consumer research can suggest which characteristics are relevant—those constellations of meaning which consumers expect and assign to products in a given category.

Product categories vary significantly in the extent to which it is possible for marketing communication to define the values inherent in the product. In other words, image becomes important only if certain conditions exist. There are two sets of conditions under which brand image is likely to be especially significant. One is where the consumer is unable to discriminate among the brands of the product on any objective basis. The other is where the product has status and life-style connotations and is usually consumed in a socially conspicuous way.

Ability to Discriminate. For some products, the typical consumer is unable to discriminate between differences among brands on the basis of any sensory information. Taste, smell, feel, or whatever may be an inad-

[2]Irving S. White, "The Functions of Advertising in Our Culture," *Journal of Marketing*, 23 (May 1959), pp. 8–14, at p. 8.

[3]Norman L. Barnett, "Developing Effective Advertising for New Products," *Journal of Advertising Research*, 8 (December 1968), pp. 13–18.

equate basis for differentiating one brand from another. Beer and cigarettes are two examples of products where most consumers are unable to distinguish among most popular brands when such identifying information as packages and labels is removed and they are asked to identify their favorite brands or to discriminate among several brands.[4] In the absence of ability to make sensory discriminations, the kinds of cues provided by marketing communication become an important basis for distinguishing one brand from another.

Sensory discrimination is only one basis on which people may or may not be able to distinguish among brands. There are many products where brand identification and differences among brands are quite obvious but where certain knowledge and expertise is required to determine product quality and value. Skis provide a good example of a product where the inexperienced purchaser has virtually no basis for determining quality differences between one brand selling for $30 and another selling for $200. Even after using the product, it may take an expert to identify differences in product quality and performance. Musical instruments are another good example of a product where most persons cannot distinguish among brands with a wide range of product quality. Opportunities for marketing communication to add value to the product by associating it with a particular set of values and needs are greatest in these situations.

Conspicuous Consumption. Brand image also becomes more important when the product is consumed in the presence of others and takes on special meanings in a social context. The basic consumption motive may vary considerably, from wanting to show that one has arrived at a new level on the social ladder to wanting to show respect for friends. Cadillac and Lincoln automobiles have for years carried the connotation of high status, created in part through advertising, and in part by a high standard of engineering achievement and product quality. A housewife may take pride in serving her friends a more expensive brand of coffee because it shows one's good taste and desire to please friends. Even if the average consumer has trouble identifying brands of whiskey, the careful host may wish to serve only highly regarded, more expensive brands for fear of appearing chintzy to his friends.

Relationship to Self Concept. Products which are used in a socially visible way and which have strong brand images are one of the more important ways in which the consumer can express his self concept. A college professor may hesitate to buy a sporty car because it is not consistent with his self concept and the way he wants others to view

[4]James H. Myers and William H. Reynolds, *Consumer Behavior and Marketing Management* (Boston: Houghton Mifflin Co., 1967), pp. 15–20.

him. When a retail clerk in a men's clothing store sells a new suit, he will often assure the purchaser that the suit is consistent with the self image he wishes to convey to others: "It looks very good on you, Mr. Jones" is not so much a judgment of fit as of the appropriateness of the style and cut for this particular customer. Many housewives have strong preference for styles of furniture and appliances because these perform an important symbolic function in defining the life style they wish to express to other people.

Even in industrial marketing, brand images may be an important determinant of the purchase of certain products. Some companies may hope to give their salesmen a little more prestige by providing them with medium-priced cars, rather than the low-priced compacts used by competitors' salesmen. Some chief executives have probably approved the choice of a jet aircraft for use by the corporation partly because of its economic value in saving time and travel expense and partly because owning a jet seemed consistent with the corporate image and the way in which the chief executive viewed himself. When computers were put on the market, it is certain that some companies bought them because of their prestige value as well as their ability to solve complex problems and to speed up routine calculation and paperwork.

Some industrial companies pride themselves on having the latest production equipment and up-to-date technology. These companies are often the best targets for any product which indicates their forward-looking viewpoint. Similarly, many consumers find it important to be among the first persons to own a new product, whether it is next year's model of an automobile, the latest gadget in stereophonic equipment, or the newest laundry detergent.

For frequently purchased products, a strong relationship between the buyer's self concept and brand image will result in a high degree of brand loyalty. Beer and cigarettes are, once again, examples of products where people are quick to name "my brand" and to see this as quite distinct from all the other brands. Automobiles also incur a strong brand loyalty among a large segment of the population and this loyalty reflects in part the close connection between self concept and brand image.

Perceived Risk

Each of the above elements—inability to discriminate, high social visibility, strong relationship to self concept—may significantly increase the amount of perceived risk in a given purchase. The last two factors especially will increase the variability expected in psychosocial consequences. Other factors relating to the amount of perceived risk, it will be remembered from our discussion in Chapter 7, include the amount of previous experience with the product, the extent to which the product is known to vary in performance, and the amount of investment of time, effort, and money required for the purchase.

As the amount of perceived risk increases, the consumer will either avoid a decision (by lowering his goals or by relying on habitual purchasing behavior) or he will seek out additional information with which to assess the consequences of alternative courses of action. The message strategy should be based upon consideration of the amount of perceived risk involved in the purchase and should respond to the buyer's need for information according to the criteria the consumer will be using in his purchase. Sales presentations should be developed, and salesmen trained, for example, to provide the necessary technical information and comparisons with other products, if that is known to be important to prospective customers. If the psychosocial consequences are significant, the message should provide the necessary assurances concerning the social acceptability of the purchase.

In this section on buyer decision making, we have tried to show the many ways in which the nature of the buyer's decision process will be influenced by the nature of the product and the way in which the decision process creates a need for particular kinds of marketing communication. The buyer's need for information—both factual information about product performance and messages which develop a strong brand image—should be carefully appraised because it provides a major input to the setting of communication objectives. Without that information, the development of objectives for the marketing communication strategy to achieve is going to be a hit-or-miss proposition.

The notion of a buyer decision process is a central part of this argument. It is time to look more closely at the nature of the buying decision process, to make the steps involved explicit, and to relate that process to the development of marketing communicaton objectives.

THE HIERARCHY OF EFFECTS

At several stages in this text, we have used the notion of a continuum of response to marketing communication. In Chapter 2, it was stated that the purposes of marketing communication include developing awareness, helping potential customers evaluate the product, encouraging trial use of the product, and encouraging repeat purchase. In Chapter 3, the so-called adoption process was introduced and seen to be represented by five stages in the customer's decision process—attention, interest, evaluation, trial, and adoption. Chapter 9 considered the ways in which the buyer's information requirements and reliance on particular information sources vary according to the stage of the adoption process.

Alternative Views

A different way of viewing this process, also introduced in Chapter 3, is that proposed by Lavidge and Steiner.[5] They define a sequence of mental states through which the individual buyer passes as the result of exposure to advertising. This model applies equally well to any form of marketing communication, however. According to their model, the individual moves through the following stages: awareness, knowledge, liking, preference, conviction, and purchase. The first two stages fall into the *cognitive* dimension of behavior—that dealing with thoughts and conscious perception of sensory stimuli. The next two stages, liking and preference, involve the *affective* realm of behavior, that concerning emotions, attitudes, and feelings. The last two stages, conviction and purchase, are defined as being in the *conative* realm, which is the realm of motives and the stimulation and direction of desires.

Does Attitude Change Precede Behavior Change?

As discussed earlier in this chapter, there is reason to question whether this so-called hierarchy of effects is actually a good description of buying behavior. It was noted that there may be circumstances in which marketing communication results in a change in behavior (purchase) before there is significant change in attitudes (liking, preference, and conviction). One marketing scholar has examined the relevant literature on this issue and concluded that previous studies had not established a causal relationship between attitudes and behavior.[6] He asserted that, in the absence of better evidence on the relationship between changes in the prospective buyer's mental state and sales results, advertising could only be legitimately evaluated in terms of changes in sales volume. (This conclusion begs the equally serious question of how to establish an unambiguous cause-and-effect relationship between sales results and advertising effort, as we shall see in the following pages.)

A later study has, in fact, established a more direct relationship between changes in attitudes and changes in behavior. It was found that time series data on changes in awareness and attitudes were able to predict changes in market share for certain classes of products. Specifically, changes in awareness and attitudes were found to provide better predictions of market share for brands of instant coffee and analgesics than a simple extrapolation model. This was not true for deodorants.

[5]Robert J. Lavidge and Gary A. Steiner, "A Model for Predictive Measurements of Advertising Effectiveness," *Journal of Marketing*, 25 (October 1961), pp. 59–62.

[6]Kristian S. Palda, "The Hypothesis of a Hierarchy of Effects: A Partial Evaluation," *Journal of Marketing Research*, 3 (February 1966), pp. 13–24.

The authors of this study concluded that the affective dimension (attitudes, emotions, and feelings) did influence actual purchase behavior and argued that their data supported the hierarchy-of-effects hypothesis.[7] It should be noted, however, that these conclusions were based upon data on consumer behavior in the *aggregate*; it is not certain whether these generalizations are valid statements about the dimensions of individual behavior.

Direction of Causation May Vary

Perhaps the best way to deal with this controversy is to question the basic assumption that there is one direction of causation that applies to all buyers and all products. It may very well be that under certain circumstances it is possible to obtain behavior change without a prior change in attitudes. If the behavior change is to be permanent in those cases, however, there must be attitude change after the behavior change. In other cases, attitude change may be a necessary precondition of behavior change. The theory of cognitive dissonance suggests how information is gathered and evaluated following behavior change to bring attitudes and beliefs into agreement with the behavior that has already occurred.

Furthermore, just as needs at one level do not need to be one hundred percent satisfied before needs at the next level become motivators, so it seems reasonable to assume that attitudes need not be completely changed in favor of a course of action before that course of action is followed. For each product, however, there is likely to be some minimum level of attitude (measured as preference for the product, for example) that must be met before actual purchase behavior will occur. Furthermore, attitude change must probably reach some higher level before the change in behavior becomes relatively permanent.

Function of Perceived Risk

For products involving little perceived risk (insignificant performance and/or psychosocial consequences, little required investment, little uncertainty about consequences), the probability is higher that behavior change can precede attitude change. A coupon for 25¢ off on a pound of margarine is likely to encourage trial of the product even if the consumer has not made a careful mental evaluation. A decision to buy a new piano, however, is likely to be made only after careful evaluation and consideration of several alternatives. Because of the higher perceived risk and the significance of the decision, attitude change will be a more

[7]Henry Assael and George S. Day, "Attitudes and Awareness as Predictors of Market Share," *Journal of Advertising Research*, 8 (December 1968), pp. 3–10.

necessary predecessor of behavior change in this purchase. As an aid to developing favorable attitudes, and as a way to reduce the amount of perceived risk, most piano dealers allow free home trial, for the obvious reason that most potential purchasers want actual experience with the product before purchasing it, given the size of the investment required.

This line of reasoning leads to a familiar conclusion—that careful analysis of the product (in terms of consumer benefits) and the way it is bought should precede the development of marketing communication objectives. Awareness is a necessary condition for the purchase of a product and any communication program has to have awareness as its first objective. Attitude change is probably neither a necessary condition nor a sufficient condition for purchase to occur in a large number of buying situations. Where attitude change is not necessary for behavior change, it becomes possible to develop communication objectives dealing with direct purchase action, typically trial.

Eventually, Attitudes and Behavior Must Agree

The ultimate objective of a satisfied customer who is likely to repurchase the product requires careful attention to accomplishment of all stages of the decision process. If attitude change has not been accomplished before trial was encouraged, then it must be accomplished after. Repeat purchase (the "adoption" stage in the adoption process model) will result only if attitudes have been made consistent with behavior. If attitude change is to follow trial purchase, the product itself must meet the customer's expectations. Marketing communication can influence the nature and level of those expectations and can provide the customer with the criteria against which to evaluate the product. Marketing communication can also provide specific information with which to accomplish the postpurchase evaluation—even if it consists only of advertising messages which the purchaser can transmit to his friends and obtain the positive reinforcement of having them agree.

Whether the objectives of communication are stated as

Awareness → Attitude change → Trial → Adoption

or

Awareness → Trial → Attitude change → Adoption

these objectives *must* be stated. Otherwise, there will be no way of telling whether the marketing communication is being successful.

OBJECTIVES AND EVALUATION

One of the major functions of objectives is to guide subsequent evaluation; they provide standards against which to judge accomplishments.

In evaluation, objectives become criteria. If they are to serve that function well, their original definition must be responsive to the planned evaluation. It makes little sense to state objectives in such a way that future evaluation will be impossible. Likewise, it will do no good to state objectives in terms implying the use of measurements which will not be available at a later stage. These comments introduce two central issues in the evaluation of marketing communication: (1) the difficulties in establishing a causal relationship between a given sales result and communication effort, and (2) whether communication objectives should be stated in terms of changes in buyers' mental states or in terms of changes in sales volume and profits. Each of these issues will be discussed next.

Establishing Causal Relationships

When Mrs. Jones buys her first jar of Maxim coffee, it is impossible to determine whether that purchase was the result of the prominent display which her grocer had set up in the front of his store, the coupon she received in the mail, the many television commercials which she saw for the product, the fact that her neighbor served it to her on a recent visit, the advertisement which appeared in last week's magazine, or the unique shape of the package which happened to catch her eye. When the Boeing Company plant in Kansas City finally decides to buy a Hewlett-Packard oscilloscope, is this the result of the monthly sales calls made by the Hewlett-Packard salesman over the past two years? Were some more important than others? Did the company's advertising have any influence on this purchase? Should the salesman in Kansas City get credit for the sale if the purchase order was actually issued by the central purchasing office in Seattle? In that case, should the Seattle salesman get credit for the sale?

These two examples suggest the immense difficulty in trying to evaluate marketing communication effort on the basis of sales results. When a sale occurs it may be the result of a complex combination of marketing efforts exerted on the buyer over an extended period of time. The convincing information may actually have come from a noncommercial source—the next-door neighbor or an engineer in another company. Lags in the response to marketing effort result from the fact that buying decisions take time. Industrial buying decisions often involve many individuals (users, influencers, deciders, and buyers) who must follow complex and time-consuming procedures reflecting the hierarchical assignment of authority and responsibility within the formal organization.[8] A

[8]Patrick Robinson, Charles Faris, and Yoram Wind, *Industrial Buying and Creative Marketing* (Boston: Allyn & Bacon, Inc., 1967).

long time may likewise elapse between first awareness and final purchase action by the household consuming unit, as the process of evaluation extends over time and the household makes necessary financial arrangements for the purchase.

An attempt to evaluate any one component of the total communication mix may be frustrated by the complex interaction among the various elements of the communication mix and between communication and other marketing variables. The salesman cannot be held responsible for a decrease in sales volume in his territory, for example, if the company increased its prices to the point where customers could no longer afford the product. Or perhaps a change in trade margins resulted in a significant decrease in the number of dealers. Or a new advertising campaign, or point-of-purchase displays which gain dealer acceptance, may likewise result in sales increases that are beyond the control of the salesman, although his compensation may be determined by the extent to which he achieves a stated sales volume quota.

Another complex set of interactions are those between the advertising message and advertising media. If the company launches a new campaign involving a new creative approach and at the same time significantly revises its media schedule, it becomes virtually impossible to evaluate either component separately. Any time more than one variable is changing, it becomes necessary to use carefully controlled experimental designs to trace cause-and-effect relationships. Seldom can the marketer control all of the variables influencing sales volume sufficiently to develop unambiguous data on the causal relationship.

DAGMAR

In 1961, the Association of National Advertisers published a study edited by Russell H. Colley, entitled *Defining Advertising Goals for Measured Advertising Results*. The title has been replaced by the acronym DAGMAR in most subsequent discussions. The basic thesis of the DAGMAR study was that advertising goals should be stated in terms permitting precise measurement. Given the difficulty of establishing a causal relationship between advertising effort and sales results, as we have just discussed, the DAGMAR study proposed that the objectives of advertising should be stated as *communication* objectives—changes in levels of awareness and attitudes among well-defined target segments of the market. Obviously, this would require both a before- and an after-measure of whatever dimensions of awareness and attitudes were defined by the statement of objectives.

The basic assumption of the DAGMAR study was that there *was* a hierarchy of effects and that changes in levels of awareness and attitudes led to changes in sales volume. As previously discussed, this basic assumption can be challenged and there is no clear-cut answer to the problem of how attitude change is related to behavior change. The DAGMAR study saw the steps in the process as awareness, comprehension, conviction, and action.

Critics Insist That Only Sales Matter. The DAGMAR study has been criticized on several grounds. One author argues that its approach divorces advertising objectives from marketing objectives.[9] He points out that it is possible to be successful in achieving communication objectives but unsuccessful in achieving marketing objectives and cites the example of the manufacturer who spent several millions of dollars to (successfully) increase awareness of his product but realized almost no increase in dollar sales volume. Others have pointed to the expense and difficulty involved in obtaining reliable before and after measurements of changes in awareness and attitudes. This appears to be a special problem in industrial markets, where attitude measurement is not used as frequently as in consumer goods marketing.[10] Another study reported that industrial marketers had found the DAGMAR concept useful, however, and that a major reason for its contribution was the very fact that it stimulated attention to the basic need for measurement. This author continued to argue for going further in measurement of the true effects of marketing communication on sales volume.[11]

There is no easy way to resolve this dilemma. On the one hand, it is impossible to trace changes in sales volume to changes in the level and quality of marketing communication effort, whether that is in the form of advertising, personal selling, or other communication tools. On the other hand, there is something unsatisfactory to many managers about stopping evaluation at the stage of changes in attitudes when the relationship between attitudes and sales volume is so cloudy and the overall marketing objective *is* to increase profitable sales. Furthermore, it may prove to be just as difficult to attribute changes in *attitudes* to a given communication activity as it is to attribute changes in sales volume. Techniques of attitude measurement involve many sources of potential error and involve dynamic interactions among both formal and informal communications.

Objectives Must Be Specific. The only solution must be a pragmatic one: objectives should be stated in a manner that is most responsive to

---

[9]Seymour Smith, "DAGMAR—What's Wrong With Her Measurements?," in Frederick E. Webster, Jr. (ed.), *New Directions in Marketing* (Chicago: American Marketing Association, 1965), pp. 333–39.

[10]Robert L. Hartford, "DAGMAR in Work Clothes," in Webster, *op. cit.*, pp. 340–48.

[11]Sim Kolliner, "Measuring the Effects of Communication," in Webster, *op. cit.*, pp. 354–58.

the needs of management and the opportunities for measurement. Attention *should* be given to defining objectives in a way that permits measurement and one of the advantages of stating objectives in terms of changes in predispositions may be that it permits measurement where none was possible before. Since no one criterion is likely to have complete validity, management may insist upon several measures of effectiveness and objectives must therefore be stated at several levels. Over the longer run, marketing communication effectiveness should be consistently reflected in several measures of accomplishment including levels of awareness, attitudes, rate of trial, repeat purchase rate, and total sales volume.

Successful Communication May Not Mean Sales. There may in fact be situations where marketing communication effectiveness does not lead to marketing success. There are many examples to illustrate this circumstance, such as the new beer which was extensively advertised with a very effective campaign which won advertising awards and was known to generate high levels of consumer awareness and product trial. Unfortunately, this was one of the few instances where many consumers *could* distinguish significant difference in the taste of the beer and there was a low rate of repurchase. In fact, the effectiveness of the advertising probably hastened the demise of the product by the very fact that it achieved such a high rate of trial. In other cases, the problem has been less dramatic. The basic point is that communication may be successful while the total marketing program is ineffective due to weaknesses in the product, in pricing strategy, or in distribution.

In these conditions, it is good to have some idea of the effectiveness of the communication itself, independent of other marketing variables. For this reason, some measures of the accomplishment of communication objectives (changes in predispositions) are probably always desirable. The value of the DAGMAR concept is that it provides a partial answer to the problem of determining cause and effect relationships among the several criterion variables (awareness, attitudes, trial, repeat buying) and the several marketing communication variables. While marketing communication objectives must be consistent with overall corporate and marketing objectives, communication should not be held solely responsible for the accomplishment of marketing results.

FACTORS TO ANALYZE IN SETTING OBJECTIVES

Communication objectives are instrumental to the accomplishment of marketing objectives and marketing objectives are instrumental to the accomplishment of the basic objectives of the firm. Earlier chapters, especially Chapter 2 and Chapter 3, presented an analysis of several factors determining the direction of a company's marketing strategy. It was seen that the segmentation strategy should reflect a careful appraisal of the resource constraints within which the firm must operate, a definition of where in the market there are the best opportunities resulting from competitors' weaknesses, and identification of the opportunity for the firm to achieve unique competitive advantage. The market segmentation strategy defines the target audience for market communication effort in terms of the characteristics and the location of consuming units. A statement of objectives defines the responses desired from the market while a statement of segmentation strategy defines the intended receivers of communication.

Company

There are four aspects of the company that should be carefully appraised in setting communication objectives. First, overall company objectives and strategy should be carefully noted. These define the basic purpose the business is striving to achieve and all other aspects of strategic planning within the firm should be responsive to that purpose. If the firm's first objective is to contribute solutions to problems in a particular area of human endeavor, for example, this may provide a strong appeal and corporate identity theme within the advertising campaign.

Second, a careful assessment of basic company strengths and weaknesses should be one input into the setting of marketing communication objectives. If the company's sales force is poorly trained and has only modest educational background, it may be dangerous to develop a marketing communication strategy which defines top executives as a target to receive special sales attention. The advertising copy developed for a campaign may commit organization personnel to provide a level of service which they are actually incapable of providing. (This seems to be a problem with several domestic and international airlines' advertising campaigns.) Another organizational resource that must be carefully appraised is the reseller structure. Distributors may not be able to transmit accurately to their customers technical information about the product.

Each of these examples suggests a factor which may be a constraint on marketing communication activity in the short run. Over the longer run, each of these constraints can be removed by committing additional company resources to improvements in these areas. The sales force can be trained, the distributor structure can be strengthened, and the ability of the organization to provide customer service can be improved. In each case, the development of human resources is a necessary ingredient in the success of the marketing communication program.

Third, corporate image must be taken into account. The first step here may be a survey to determine the way in which the company is regarded by relevant audiences—customers, distributors, suppliers, and so forth. In the short run, the corporate image becomes a constraint. Over the long run, resources can be committed to the task of changing the corporate image. Even a strong, sharp corporate image can be a significant constraint on the firm. Potential customers may have such strong images of certain companies that entry into a new business will conflict with that image. In these cases, marketing communication must be specifically designed to attempt to bring about the necessary change in image and attitudes toward the company. A company long known primarily as a supplier of automobile and truck tires may have to devote large amounts of communication resources to changing its image as a necessary prelude to entering a broad variety of consumer markets, for example.

Finally, the establishment of marketing communication objectives must, as just noted, take into consideration the availability of the funds required to achieve a given objective. While all of Chapter 16 will be devoted to the problem of determining the level of effort, it should be recognized that all promotional activity must be treated as a current expense. Even if the benefits of a communication program can be clearly projected over a long series of years, thus justifying a major investment in introductory promotion, the financial requirements of the firm including capital budgeting and profit and dividend requirements may make a large current expenditure infeasible.

Product Benefits

A creative definition of the benefits available to the buyer from using the product should be a major ingredient in the development of marketing communication objectives. Earlier in the chapter, it was seen that customer needs, ability to discriminate product quality, the social visibility of product use, and the amount of perceived risk were significantly related to the nature of the product.

Small-group discussions with samples of people representing the target market segment can often identify significant dimensions to the product which are not readily seen by the marketer. One manufacturer of electronic equipment has a traveling display of his latest products that have either just reached or are about to reach the final stages of development and commercialization. This display is taken around the country (in a large van) and potential buyers are shown the products and asked for their comments and reactions. These comments are useful in deciding upon the final design of certain products and in determining whether the product is marketable, as well as in designing promotional literature, sales presentations, and advertising to sell the products. In the consumer field, interviews with consumers revealed that the Coca Cola

Company's new soft drink Fresca was described by people not in terms of its taste but rather in terms of the "experience" of drinking it. This became the basic theme of the advertising for the product.[12]

Market-Product Positioning

Careful analysis of the potential market in terms of basic needs, the extent to which existing products fill those needs, and the gaps in current product offerings by competitors can reveal opportunity for unique competitive advantage. This opportunity leads to a "positioning" of the company's product in the market. Product positioning consists of a definition of the basic meaning which it is intended that the market ascribe to the product. It provides the basic direction for message strategy—the so-called copy platform.

In advertising, product positioning is expressed in the "purchase proposition" defining the specific want-satisfying properties of the product that are to be stressed in advertising copy.[13] One advertising executive has referred to this as the Unique Selling Proposition (or simply USP) which provides the basic appeal and reason-for-buying for the product.[14]

Having defined a basic product positioning strategy, the marketing communication strategist can turn his problems over to those with the creative responsibility for developing communication tactics. Advertising copy must be written and commercials developed and produced. Sales presentations must be developed, either verbatim or in outline form, with appropriate sales aids. Point-of-purchase displays, packages, shelf talkers, flyers, and so on must be developed for communicating with the market. Creative people need the direction provided by a clear statement of communication objectives and a specific product positioning statement. In the next chapter, we shall examine the nature of the creative process.

SUMMARY

There are two kinds of marketing communication objectives: those for the meaning to be conveyed about the product, or objectives pertaining to message strategy; and those defining the number of messages to be delivered to specific audiences, or those relevant for media strategy. This

---

[12]Richard W. Bowman, "The Blizzard of '67," paper presented at the Eastern Regional Conference of the American Association of Advertising Agencies, October 22–23, 1968.

[13]Nugent Wedding and Richard S. Lessler, *Advertising Management* (New York: Ronald Press Company, 1962), p. 200.

[14]Rosser Reeves, *Reality in Advertising* (New York: Alfred A. Knopf, Inc., 1961).

chapter has focussed on the former, although there are significant inter-dependencies between the two types of objectives.

Objectives serve several useful purposes in directing marketing communication effort. First, they help to coordinate the various elements of the marketing communication program with each other and with overall corporate and marketing objectives and strategy. Second, they help to guide the creation of message and media strategy. Third, they provide standards against which to evaluate subsequent accomplishment. The function of evaluation is one of the most important and the most complex in the management of marketing communication programs.

In setting communication objectives, company, product, and market factors need to be carefully appraised to define the basic strategy for positioning the product in the market. In the typical case where consumers will be unable to differentiate clearly among brands of the product on solely physical and technical grounds, marketing communication can help to assign meanings and values to the product that will enhance its ability to satisfy certain needs. The value-enhancing role of marketing communication is greatest where the product has social visibility, status connotations, and significant product performance and psychosocial consequences. The objectives of marketing communication should be stated in terms that reflect the opportunity for changing basic predispositions within the market and adding value to the product itself. Objectives for changes in predispositions as well as objectives for sales volume should be clearly stated to guide management effort and to evaluate the contribution of communication within the total marketing mix.

13

The Creative Process

Creativity is a characteristic of an individual which permits him to develop new ideas and new approaches to problems. It is *not* synonymous with such descriptors as "far-out," wild, or impractical, as popular jargon sometimes has it. One of the most important aspects of creativity is its discipline and the fact that it relates directly to the solution of particular problems, rather than to the development of concepts, ideas, or objects which are unique but have no obvious value. Creativity is defined by one author as "ability to make new combinations of social worth,"[1] a definition which stresses the usefulness of creative output as well as its newness and uniqueness.

Creativity plays a central part in the development of marketing communication strategy. Most visible is the role played by the creative staffs of advertising agencies, including artists, copywriters, and others concerned with developing advertising campaigns. But this is certainly not the only way in which creativity becomes important in marketing communication. As the following paragraphs will show, creativity is a necessary ingredient in virtually all aspects of analysis and problem-solving in marketing. Furthermore, creativity is particularly significant in marketing because competitive effectiveness demands a continuous stream of ideas not only in the development of marketing communications, but in the development of new definitions of market segments, in the identification of opportunities for product innovation, in designing new distribution strategies, and in the development and implementation of pricing strategy. One of the major reasons for the central importance of creativity and innovation in marketing is that new strategies and tactics are often

[1]John W. Haefele, *Creativity and Innovation* (New York: Reinhold Publishing Corp., 1962), p. xi.

visible to competitors and easily copied. It therefore follows that a new marketing strategy, and especially a new marketing communication strategy, will give the firm only a relatively short-term competitive advantage, thus creating the need for yet another new approach.

CREATIVITY AS A PROCESS

In this chapter, we shall consider the nature of the creative process and problems involved in managing creative effort in marketing. Techniques for stimulating creativity will be reviewed and economic dimensions of creative effort will be discussed. The characteristics of creative persons will be examined, but only in the context of the larger problem of directing and supervising creative effort. The basic assertion of this chapter is that creativity requires direction and coordination, that it requires clearly specified objectives and discipline, and that creativity should never be confused with lack of direction and purpose.

Creativity Is Problem Solving

It follows that it is important to concentrate upon the *process* by which new solutions are generated rather than the characteristics of persons whom we call "creative." In other words, the development of new ideas is the result of a disciplined search for problem solutions rather than the more-or-less spontaneous output of a person with some unique ability or trait. The act of *creation* is best viewed as a response to an environmental stimulus by the creative person, rather than as the expression of an inner state of that person.

Bisociation

The basic element of all creativity is the identification of new relationships, "the ability to formulate new combinations from two or more concepts already in the mind."[2] Creativity can be thought of as the ability to identify such combinations while the creative process is the method by which they are identified. Arthur Koestler calls this process "bisociation"—the combination of one fact with another to develop a new insight.[3]

Most students of the creative process agree with the general notion that creative work involves a series of stages that occur over time, beginning with the identification of a problem to be solved and the collection of relevant information, followed by a period of relative inactivity in

[2]*Ibid.*, p. 5.

[3]Arthur Koestler, *The Act of Creation* (London: Hutchinson & Co., Ltd., 1964), p. 35.

which the material is dealt with at an "unconscious" or semiconscious level. This is followed by a rather abrupt insight or some major "illumination" of the problem, which must then be verified by a more systematic evaluation of the evidence.[4] While these stages have been given different names by different authors, there is agreement that the creative process consists of several distinct stages, that both interpersonal and intrapersonal forces are at work in the creative process, and that the stages need not always follow in the same order. For our purpose, the stages of the creative process will be labeled preparation, incubation, insight, and verification.

There is no clear-cut distinction between routine and creative problem solving. The distinction is one of degree, not kind, but it is an important distinction nonetheless. Routine problem solving can be reduced to a series of logical steps and computations and, theoretically, delegated to a computer. Creativity, on the other hand, is a uniquely human and personalistic process. Newell, Shaw, and Simon have said that problem solving is creative to the extent that one or more of the following conditions are found:

1. The product of the thinking has novelty and value (either for the thinker or for his culture).
2. The thinking is unconventional, in the sense that it requires modification or rejection of previously accepted ideas.
3. The thinking requires high motivation and persistence, taking place either over a considerable span of time (continuously or intermittently) or at high intensity.
4. The problem as initially posed was vague and undefined, so that part of the task was to formulate the problem itself.[5]

This last condition emphasizes the importance of preparation and problem definition, the first stage in the creative process.

STAGES IN THE CREATIVE PROCESS

Preparation

Creativity does not occur in a vacuum. It occurs only in the presence of facts about the environment and the problems to be solved. If creativity is defined as the ability to find new associations, new relationships among facts, it follows that the facts themselves must first be available.

Gathering the Facts. Preparation is probably the most important stage in the creative process in that nothing can happen without adequate

[4]Morris I. Stein and Shirley J. Heinze, *Creativity and the Individual* (Chicago: Graduate School of Business, University of Chicago, 1960), pp. 13–14.

[5]A. Newell, J. C. Shaw, and H. A. Simon, "The Processes of Creative Thinking," in H. E. Gruber, G. Terrell, and M. Wertheimer (eds.), *Contemporary Approaches to Creative Thinking* (New York: Atherton Press, 1962), pp. 65–66.

preparation. The ground must be laid for the subsequent application of energy, for incubation, and for the development of insights. Central to the concept of creativity is the notion of *going beyond* existing understanding, of developing *new* solutions, or finding innovative and unique frameworks within which to structure the facts. All of these views of creativity emphasize the importance of first having the facts at hand and of becoming familiar with them.

In developing marketing communications, application of creativity to message strategy requires a thorough familiarity with the nature of the market and the nature of the product. Equally important, as we saw in the last chapter, is a very clear statement of communication objectives defining the meaning to be conveyed about the product and the purpose toward which creative effort should be directed.

It is unfortunate that creativity is often seen as the opposite of fact finding; some observers seem to think that facts only hinder the creative process. Nothing could be further from the truth. Students of creativity in science, in art, and in business will agree on at least one basic point: facts are the basis for creative effort. Darwin's development of the theory of evolution was the result of dedicated and painstaking collection of information about all forms of animal life. Michelangelo studied anatomy and assiduously prepared himself for his creative endeavors. From the field of advertising, one expert has noted:

Creative people laugh themselves sick over their Hollywood image, of course. For they're the first to point out the springboard for their creativity is facts. Creative people are problem solvers. Give them the problems, the facts, the figures, and they'll come up with the creative solutions.[6]

Restructuring the Problem Statement. A key part of the creative process is the restructuring of the problem statement. Seldom is the first definition of the problem adequate for creative effort. Application of creative effort is required to modify and redefine the problem statement. Until the facts are in hand and have been "chewed on," creativity cannot be exercised, so it follows that creative problem definition can only come after there has been some reworking of the facts themselves.

The process of restructuring the problem can be thought of in Gestalt terms. It will be recalled from Chapter 11 that Gestalt psychologists emphasize the search for order and structure, which combines with the perception of physical stimuli to produce meaning. In the preparation stage, the person is searching for new wholes, new structurings of the facts available, new ways of viewing the evidence, and new associations among the facts.

[6]Bob Stone, "Facts: Straightjacket or Creative Springboard?," *Advertising Age*, February 10, 1969, p. 60.

Creativity and Analysis. There is clearly an overlap between "creativity" as we traditionally think of the word—the development of new solutions—and what we call "analysis." The good analyst is the one who derives the most useful insights from the facts at this disposal. It requires as much creativity to analyze a set of facts as it does to develop a new sales presentation. In business problem solving, the distinction between creativity and analysis is usually misleading; good analysis is creative and good creative effort is based on careful analysis. Analysis is a major part of the preparation stage as the creative person searches for a definition of the problem that stimulates the new insights required for creative problem solution.

Incubation

Truly creative work is difficult and time consuming. Seldom does the solution to the problem spring in mature form from the first wrestling with the facts and problem definition. Most observers of the creative process agree that there is the need to remove the problem from the conscious level of analysis, to "put it on the shelf," and to go about some other task, in order to let the creative process slowly work its way to a solution of the problem. There does seem to be some important role played by the unconscious in the creative process.[7] This is the incubation stage of the creative process.

Incubation can be thought of as a time of waiting when no solution has appeared after the work of preparation has been completed.[8] In the vernacular, we talk about "sleeping on it" in order to let the facts sort themselves out and to gain some perspective on a problem. Of course, this could be nothing more than procrastination or even laziness, were it not for the fact that eventually things do seem to work themselves out and the solution does, indeed, have a way of appearing rather suddenly at the end of the incubation stage. In other words, insight—the next stage of the creative process—is the best evidence of incubation.[9]

Implications for Managing Creative Effort. For those concerned with the management of creative people, it is important to realize that incubation is a necessary stage in the creative process. This has significant ramifications for the way creative work is organized and supervised, and these will be developed in a moment.

During incubation, the "solution" must be introduced into the problem definition. In other words, given the set of facts defining the problem, new facts or relationships must be identified before the problem can

---

[7]Stein and Heinze, *op. cit.*, pp. 13–14.
[8]Haefele, *op. cit.*, p. 66.
[9]*Ibid.*

be solved. Preparation sets the stage for the insights which can occur only through the slow process of incubation.

One of the most obvious examples of incubation is the way in which a person can awaken from a sound night's sleep only to find shortly after awakening that several new ideas come to mind. Many men find that some of their best ideas occur in the morning shower or when shaving. Others find that the relaxation of a fishing trip or some other form of recreation can result in the generation of such new ideas.

As a Reaction to Frustration. It is useful to think about incubation as synonymous with repression, although these are quite different mental phenomena. In repression, unfavorable experiences and emotional conflicts are pushed into the subconscious. Likewise, incubation may be a reaction to the frustration of being unable to solve a difficult problem. Just as emotional conflicts may be worked out in the subconscious, problems that initially seem unsolvable may be pushed into the subconscious where the mind continues to work on the facts gathered during the preparation stage.[10] Even though the problem is pushed below the level of direct consciousness, the tension still exists and the individual is still motivated to find a solution to the problem. The problem may actually reappear in the consciousness several times, more facts may be gathered or certain new structurings developed, only to find once again that the solution still does not suggest itself. As a result, the problem is once again pushed into the subconscious where incubation continues.

Insight

All creative work is characterized by insight, the rather sudden dawning of a solution to the problem, of a new way of describing the relationship among elements of the environment. Insight is a kind of mental breakthrough, and its validity is at once obvious to the creative person. This is the "eureka" phenomenon, although this may vary in intensity from a mild "That's it" to an explosive "That's It!" Incubation and insight serve to differentiate true creativity from the more routine kind of problem solving which occurs when well-known principles are applied to familiar problem definitions.

The literature of art and science is full of examples of the insight phenomenon. Beveridge has pointed out that truly important discoveries in science because of their revolutionary nature cannot be foreseen; rather they must appear suddenly and in a manner inconsistent with current beliefs.[11] The insight must be new, brief, and sudden.

[10]*Ibid.*, p. 75.
[11]W. I. B. Beveridge, *The Art of Scientific Investigation* (New York: Vintage Books, 1961), p. 43.

Some creative persons have reported awakening in the middle of the night from a sound sleep with fresh insights which were complete enough to be put immediately on paper. In fact, some of these people report the practice of always keeping writing materials beside the bed because such insights appear frequently and with sufficient regularity to warrant being prepared to record them. However, insight can occur at any time, with or without any obvious stimulus to produce it. But when it does appear, it has the characteristics mentioned earlier—it is new, brief, and sudden. "Insight is the distilled essence of much mental activity. It reaches directly to the heart of the matter and expresses it in a nutshell."[12]

Verification

Verification involves the elaboration of the basic idea produced in insight and its testing against available evidence. Verification usually involves some modification and revision of the basic idea developed through insight. Of course, verification may also prove that the insight was not valid—perhaps because some of the information gathered during the preparation stage was ignored or because subsequent information proves that the insight was inadequate. Verification of a basic insight may require the development of several new insights on minor problems relating to the major problem solved. Or, verification of one insight may lead to the development of insights into much more basic and fundamental problems that could not even be clearly defined until the first, relatively minor, insights had been developed and verified.

Requires Measurement, Time, and Effort. Verification is often a slow and painstaking process compared to the sudden and subconscious aspects of earlier stages of the creative process. It may take months of careful laboratory work to verify a basic insight. Many problems in physics have had this characteristic: important insights developed by creative minds working on a problem have required years of laboratory investigation to verify their existence. The existence of many subatomic particles had been postulated long before the evidence of their existence was developed, such verification often requiring the development of elaborate measurement devices and procedures.

In the workaday world of marketing communication, verification is the essential ingredient captured in such hackneyed phrases as "Let's run it up the flagpole" and "Throw it against the wall and see what sticks." To actually determine whether a creative approach will solve the problem as defined often requires the use of various tests of effectiveness such as field interviews, laboratory tests, and market tests. These devices will be discussed thoroughly in Chapter 15.

[12]Haefele, *op. cit.*, p. 91.

To summarize: the creative process consists of the stages of preparation, incubation, insight, and verification. Fact finding and problem definition, when they do not yield an immediate solution, result in moving the problem to an unconscious level where the mind continues to work on it until insight is produced which must then be verified by more careful procedures. Having defined and elaborated the stages of the creative process, the discussion now turns to the issue of managing this process.

MANAGING CREATIVE EFFORT

Creativity is an essential ingredient in the development of effective marketing communication strategy. Old ideas and old approaches to the problems of communicating with the market will not capture the attention and imagination of prospective customers, especially in the light of intelligent, creative competition of the kind which characterizes most markets. Marketing management can therefore benefit from thinking explicitly about the process by which creative effort can be directed and controlled to produce the most useful results.

Part of the problem of managing creative effort is the creative person himself. The creative person requires a certain environment. While it is dangerous to work with a stereotype of the creative person as a kind of "weirdo" who delights in being different and offending those who are most comforted by the little conventions of society, it is nonetheless true that creative persons are *to a degree* different from their less-creative fellow men. Attempts to manage creative persons must be sensitive to the ways in which creative persons are different and require a slightly different environment.

The Creative Person

A creative person can be defined simply as a person with above average ability to generate unique and useful solutions to problems in a given line of endeavor. The available evidence on the characteristics of creative persons is rather interesting.

First, intelligence is never a sufficient condition for creativity although it may be necessary in certain fields (such as the physical sciences) and unnecessary in others (such as graphic arts).[13] Creative persons do have a preference for situations that are less well structured, that require some resolution, and that are characterized by complexity and novelty.[14] They are also less dogmatic and tend to view authority as relative rather than absolute; they tend to make fewer black-and-

[13]Bernard Berelson and Gary A. Steiner, *Human Behavior: An Inventory of Scientific Findings* (New York: Harcourt, Brace, Jovanovich, Inc., 1964), pp. 227–28.
[14]*Ibid.*, p. 229.

white distinctions; they show less conventional and conformist behavior and more independence of judgment, both social and intellectual. They tend to have a better-developed sense of humor and are more willing to express whims and "irrational" impulses; "in short, to be somewhat freer and less rigidly controlled."[15]

Another author lists the creative traits as including flexibility of mind, tolerance of ambiguity, perseverance, discernment, and self-confidence.[16]

These characteristics of creative persons argue in favor of a relatively unstructured environment which permits a reasonable degree of individual freedom and flexibility. Given a clear statement of objectives and expectations to direct effort, the work situation should permit considerable latitude in relatively minor matters such as hours of work, reporting procedures, authority relationships, and other aspects of formal organization which can hinder the kind of activity consistent with creative preparation and problem definition and the expression of insight.

Need for Direction

Creative people are motivated by the knowledge that their creative output will be useful and valued. They have a deeply felt need to know that standards by which their efforts will be judged and the conditions under which they will be regarded as successful. A clear statement of purpose and objectives can be an immensely effective motivator of creative effort.

As noted earlier in our discussion of the importance of the preparation stage, creative people think of themselves as problem-solvers. Creative personnel in advertising agencies find it valuable to have contact with the client or, at least, a minimum amount of filtering and interference by other agency personnel. In research and engineering departments in industrial firms, scientific personnel greatly appreciate information from the marketplace indicating the need for product refinements and developments and defining customer problems to be solved by the advancement of technology.

In developing marketing communication strategies, it is irresponsible for the strategist to turn his problems over to a creative organization such as a firm specializing in producing sales aids, or an advertising agency, or a package design consultant, and to say "see what you can come up with." While occasionally the creative organization may be enticed by the idea of "having a free hand," the initial enthusiasm is likely to turn into frustration. Without adequate direction, the probability that the ideas generated will be acceptable to the client is significantly re-

[15]*Ibid.*, p. 230.
[16]Haefele, *op. cit.*, p. 79.

duced. It becomes a guessing game to figure out what the client will really find acceptable.

Group Processes

Group processes can be a significant aid to creativity, especially if interpersonal interaction is productive of stimulating ideas. Each individual can stimulate the other by adding facts, refining the problem definition, contributing an important insight, or otherwise stimulating the imagination of group members. Increasingly, advertising agencies, for example, are forming "creative groups" within the organization. These groups are assigned to a few accounts which become "theirs," giving some pride of authorship and a sense of responsibility that has motivational value. In addition, the talents of several people are focused on a common set of problems permitting the kind of stimulation mentioned above.

Brainstorming. Several techniques for stimulating group creativity have been developed and reported. Probably the best known is Osborn's "brainstorming" technique. Brainstorming is believed to work best with groups of six to ten people, a size that is often recommended by students of group creativity. There are several guiding principles to brainstorming techniques, including the following:[18]

1. "Free-wheeling" is welcomed; "wild" ideas are preferred.
2. Criticism and judgment are ruled out.
3. Quantity is wanted; the more the ideas to choose from, the greater the chances of finding a good one.
4. Combination, refinement, and elaboration are desired; group members are encouraged to work with ideas already presented, to try to improve them.

Working with these guidelines, the group is given a problem to be solved. Often, they are given the problem and some relevant information a day or two before the brainstorming session is actually to be held, thus permitting a limited amount of preparation and incubation. Once the brainstorming session is under way, it is common practice to force each group member's participation by going around the room in some systematic fashion requiring each member to offer a new idea—without initial concern with quality. Remember that the emphasis in the brainstorming session is upon the quantity of ideas, not the quality. Evaluation and selection of the "best" ideas occurs later, after the ideas have been generated. In other words, actual solution of the problem will not come in the brainstorming session but must wait until ideas developed in the brain-

[17]Alex F. Osborn, *Applied Imagination* (New York: Charles Scribner's Sons, 1953).
[18]*Ibid.*, pp. 300–301.

storming session can be evaluated and elaborated, and the best approaches selected.

There are many variations possible on the basic brainstorming technique, including such modifications as brainstorming each subset of the problem, either *ad hoc* or regularly scheduled sessions, or *not* disclosing the problem before the group meets. Advocates of the latter approach argue that disclosing the problem before the session starts will result in each participant's preliminary rejection of several ideas that might have potential value. One author has even suggested that brainstorming can be done on a "solo" basis, helping the individual problem solver to develop his individual creative ability.[19]

Synectics. While brainstorming is the most popular and most often used technique for stimulating group creativity, there are several others. Probably second in popularity is the "synectics" approach developed by William J. J. Gordon. Synectics is "an operational theory for the conscious use of the preconscious psychological mechanisms present in man's creative activity."[20] Application of the synectics approach requires formal training and specific steps for integrating trained personnel into the working environment must be planned.[21]

The basic purpose of the synectics approach is to permit the group to identify new ways of structuring problems and new insights into their solution. Gordon says that the two basic mechanisms of synectics are "making the strange familiar" and "making the familiar strange." To accomplish the former, traditional problem-solving approaches can be used, because most problem solving progresses by using familiar concepts to structure and analyze the facts at hand; the structure brings order to the problem and "makes the strange familiar."

Gordon points out that making the strange familiar is likely to produce rather superficial, not novel, solutions. Making the familiar strange is said to be a more difficult process, however, because each individual is held prisoner by his predispositions and habitual approaches to structuring and analyzing problems. To overcome these barriers to creativity, synectics relies on four mechanisms for making the familiar strange, each metaphorical in character: (1) personal analogy, (2) direct analogy, (3) symbolic analogy, and (4) fantasy analogy.[22] It is this process which gives *synectics* its name, since the word means "the joining of apparently unrelated elements." The synectics approach depends heavily upon allowing group members to "play" with apparent irrelevancies in

[19]Charles S. Whiting, *Creative Thinking* (New York: Reinhold Publishing Corp. 1958), pp. 89–90.

[20]William J. J. Gordon, *Synectics* (New York: Harper & Row, 1961), p. 3.

[21]*Ibid.*, pp. 6–7.

[22]*Ibid.*, pp. 22–56.

order to evoke new viewpoints and to generate energy to be directed toward problem solution. Individuals are encouraged to play with words, with total systems, and with relationships among elements in the total system of the problem. Gordon argues that play serves the function of "freeing preconscious fantasy levels of the mind," as well as other purposes.[23]

Brainstorming, synectics, and other group creative processes all have the basic purpose of using interaction to stimulate the individual's thought processes, and to help him break down old barriers and routine ways of viewing problems. Another function performed by the group is to provide motivational support for the creative person. In all cases, however, the group functions to stimulate and support individual creativity, not as a substitute for it.

The Creative Organization

Some organizations are more conducive to the maximization of the value of creative talent than others. The characteristics of the "creative organization" reflect the uniqueness of the creative person. Earlier, it was noted that he tends to be less deferential and obedient to authority, more mobile and less loyal, and so on. Gary Steiner noted also that the creative person was more likely to be attracted by opportunity than security and was at the same time harder to control, less predictable, and, in general, more difficult to manage. He described the creative organization as one which rewards creativity, has open channels of communication, has paths for the advancement of creative talent, and provides freedom in the choice of problems and the methods of pursuing those problems to be employed by the creative person.[24]

One of the most important characteristics of the creative organization is that it permits risk taking. Obviously, creativity involves sticking one's neck out, and this cannot be done with guaranteed success. Failure must be expected in the creative organization, not punished, and the organization must have enough "slack" to permit the absorption of errors and the correction of false starts. In the traditional form of organization, the most common philosophy of management seems to be "do the job or lose the job" while in the creative organization the better approach would seem to be to ask the creative person "What would you like to accomplish that is consistent with the purpose of the organization and how can we help?" In the creative organization, there must be some sense of freedom, an opportunity for the individual to follow up his hunches and in-

[23]*Ibid.*, pp. 119–43.
[24]Gary A. Steiner, "The Creative Organization," in Harper W. Boyd, Jr., and Joseph W. Newman (eds.), *Advertising Management* (Homewood, Ill.: Richard D. Irwin, Inc., 1965), pp. 312–18.

terests, and ample opportunity for creative individuals to interact, to stimulate each other, and to enjoy themselves. Gordon's synectics emphasized the importance of play in the creative process, and the creative organization must provide an opportunity for employees to have fun.

Notice that none of these requirements conflicts with the basic need for direction and for clearly specified objectives. Creative individuals want to know which results will be most useful to the organization and what is to be rewarded. While the individual may want some freedom to choose the problems he will work on, he wants to know that these problems are important to the organization and that solutions will be valued and rewarded.

Difficulty of Evaluation

One of the major problems in managing creative effort is the evaluation of the results of creative effort. Because truly creative problem solutions are unique, and because there is always the need for verification, evaluation is a very difficult process. The major pitfall in evaluating creative output is to apply one's own personal standards and biases when these may not be relevant to the problem to be solved. This is the key issue in the evaluation of advertising, in particular.

The basic purpose of marketing communication is to achieve the communication and sales objectives established for it during the planning phase. When the advertising department or the advertising agency, for example, presents a new campaign to top marketing management for its approval, management must *judge* whether the campaign will be successful, in the absence of good data. These judgments may be based upon past experience and intuition or plain, old "gutsy feel." There is no way to avoid the application of subjective judgment in such decision making, but there is the need to make sure that the criteria applied are consistent with the purpose of the advertising and are not based upon purely subjective, personal standards of liking and disliking.

Most laymen respond to marketing communication in personal terms. The untrained observer may say "I don't like that television commercial," a perfectly acceptable statement as long as it is not intended to mean "that advertising will not be effective in achieving its objective." Seldom does the layman have any basis for making the latter judgment. Likewise, it is easy for the businessman to confuse his personal aesthetic standards and his business judgments. While the responsible executive may reject certain creative approaches to marketing communication on personal rather than business grounds, especially when they violate standards of decency and truthfulness, he should always make clear which criteria he is using.

Previous chapters have repeatedly stressed the complexity of the process by which individuals singly and in the aggregate respond to marketing communication effort. Hopefully, that discussion has provided convincing evidence for the notion that purely subjective evaluation of marketing communication is likely to be full of error. The importance of the verification stage becomes obvious when this complexity is considered. Here we have a strong argument in favor of the careful testing of alternative marketing communication strategies.

CREATIVE SERVICE ORGANIZATIONS

The unique requirements of creative talent and the need for special organizational environments are two of the major reasons why the field of marketing communication is characterized by the existence of many creative service organizations, including advertising agencies, public relations firms, package design firms, management consulting firms specializing in sales strategy development, and so on. The specialization possible in such organizations makes it possible for them to attract, manage, and reward creative talent more effectively than an organization engaged in manufacturing or distribution or some other major function where purely creative effort would necessarily be a secondary concern. Likewise, such agencies offer to their clients a pool of talent that specializes in working with problems in a particular area where there is combined experience and expertise available in the creative organization. The creative people are stimulated by a continual stream of new challenges and this, by itself, is very rewarding to them.

The advertising agency is the most common form of creative service organization. Although advertising agencies were first established as brokers of newspaper space and created advertising messages only as an ancillary service, today the function of creating advertising messages and complete advertising campaigns is much more important. Most of the larger agencies also offer to their clients a wide variety of supporting services, including copy research, market research, marketing strategy consulting services, product design and testing, and development of point-of-purchase displays and aids for the sales force. For many of the larger, full-service agencies, "advertising agency" is a misnomer; they should be called "communication consultants" or some other name more descriptive of their total service offerings. For its basic services of developing advertising and placing it in advertising media, the agency is usually compensated by means of a 15-percent commission on the value of the advertising space or time. The agency will bill the client for the full amount and will be billed by the advertising media at full amount less the 15-percent discount. Other services are often charged for on a fee basis. The compensation issue has been a center of controversy for many years. That controversy will be reviewed in a moment.

Earlier comments about the unique attributes of the creative person and the requirements of the creative organization suggest certain guidelines for the marketing communication manager in dealing with creative service organizations.

Selection

The selection of a creative service organization is a step of critical importance in the development of the marketing communication program. This step can be performed well only if it is carefully planned and if there are clear criteria for evaluating those agencies that show an interest in the business. It is necessary to have, at the minimum, a clear definition of the requirements to be placed upon the creative organization, the services that will be required of it, and the tasks to be assigned to it.

Size is a key dimension to evaluate in the selection of a creative service organization. The smaller the agency, the more important will the client's business be to that organization and the more likely that agency principals will be working directly with client management. This has several advantages to the client, including the availability of experienced, senior talent and a minimum of communication problems in trying to establish contact with top management of the agency. On the other hand, the larger creative service organization can offer a broader variety of services and a larger (if not more experienced) pool of talent. Larger organizations also may be able to draw upon a wider variety of services from outside vendors (such as printing and television production, for example) and will have a broader range of experience to draw upon in solving a particular client's problems. There is also more security in dealing with a larger agency because the life of the agency is less dependent upon the health and welfare of a few major accounts and a few management principals.

Another dimension of major importance is the previous experience and track record of the organization. The ability of a creative service organization to solve a client's problems is going to be, in part, a function of its previous successful experience in dealing with similar problems. Examples of the previous work of the agency should be carefully evaluated as the basis for the selection decision.

Perhaps most important of all, however, is the talent and the operating philosophy represented by the organization. Both management talent and the talent of the creative staff (and these may be the same) must be assessed carefully by management of the client organization. Ability to generate ideas may not be as important as ability to establish a mutually rewarding and enjoyable working relationship. If there are going to be obvious difficulties in working with personnel in the service organization, or if the operating philosophy directing that agency seems to clash with that of the client company, the client should look elsewhere for creative help. The potential client should ask the agency to identify the specific individuals who would be assigned to his account and should evaluate them carefully.

A formal presentation by the creative service organization may be a desirable step in the selection procedure. Because these "new business presentations" require considerable investment of time and energy (and therefore dollars) on the part of the agency, a formal presentation should only be requested of serious contenders. During the presentation, the potential client should ask for examples of previous work, brief background information about the agency, its management, and other key personnel, and some suggestions on how the agency would approach the problems to be assigned to it.

Working Relationships

Good relationships between a client and a creative service organization do not just happen. They are the result of a carefully planned approach to the problems which they are trying to solve together and of specific attention to the maintenance of the relationship in a way which maximizes its value for both parties. First and foremost in the establishment of sound working relationships is a clear statement of objectives to tell the creative service organization what is expected of it.

In the particular case of the advertising agency, where the relationship is a continuous one and goes on for several years, the agency needs to have complete and up-to-date information about the company's marketing program, objectives, and plans, and information on the level of current performance against those plans. This relationship is quite different from that of a product and package design consultant, for example, who tends to work on a project basis for relatively brief periods.

Many of the requirements for an effective working relationship between an advertising agency and its clients stem directly from the nature of the creative process. These requirements play a central role in the guidelines for working with an advertising agency presented in Figure 13-1.

Compensation

A central issue in the maintenance of sound working relationships between a client and an organization providing creative services is the method of compensating the agency for those services. It is most common as a general rule (except in the case of advertising agencies) to pay for such services on a fee basis. The development of a new sales promotion, or the development of a publicity campaign, or the design of

1. I would remember that creative judgment is a very subjective thing.
2. I would remind myself daily that it requires special skills to recognize a great piece of creative work straight off.
3. I would bear in mind that the creative person is apt to see things somewhat differently than most of us.
4. I would ask for great advertising.
5. I would make certain my agency believed in my product.
6. I would inundate my agency with information.
7. I would act as though creativity is important.
8. I would never specify that I wanted a particular style of advertisment or commercial.
9. I would ask my agency to make an annual new business presentation.
10. I would make certain the creative people meet the top people in my organization.
11. I would pour on the praise.
12. I would make certain my agency understood exactly what I meant by creativity.
13. I would get to know the creative people who work on my account.
14. I would try to do something creative myself.
15. I would select a good advertising manager and pay him well.
16. I would avoid the "big presentation."
17. I'd make certain the agency had confidence in my research techniques.
18. I'd accept the probability that my agency may come up with a real turkey from time to time.
19. I'd ask my agency how I could be a better client.
20. I'd share advertising results with the agency, both the good and the bad.
21. I'd insist that the people who create advertising for my products also use them.
22. I'd radiate confidence in my agency.

Fig. 13–1. Forty ways to get creativity from an agency. (Source: James R. Heekin, Jr., "How I Would Get More Creativity from My Agency," *Advertising*

a new package, would be contracted and paid for on a fee basis. Obviously, an understanding about the basis for compensation should be developed prior to the beginning of work on the project.

The important exception here is the commission method of compensating advertising agencies. As noted earlier, it is common for the advertising agency to be compensated by the advertising vehicle whose space has been sold to the agency's client. The agency simply keeps 15 percent of the amount charged for time or space by the advertising vehicle. There are several strong arguments both for and against this method of compensation.

Reasons for a Commission System. Proponents of the commission system argue that it saves the problems of negotiating a fee for every service performed by the agency and permits the agency to offer a broader range of services. It eliminates price cutting and price competition in an industry where profit margins are very thin. The commission method is simple and it has been in use for years. It has been argued also that the commission method provides a tremendous incentive for

23. I'd do my best not to judge creative people on the basis of their personalities.
24. I would make certain my agency was making a profit.
25. I'd try to produce an atmosphere in which ferment and original thinking would flourish.
26. I'd investigate ways of directly rewarding the person responsible for a good creative job.
27. I'd ask for an account executive who had demonstrated a special talent for working with creative people.
28. I would pay for copy research.
29. I'd make sure the creative people were in on things—directly, personally.
30. I'd expect the account men to contribute directly to the creative task.
31. I'd be realistic about the potency of "ice box" campaigns.
32. I'd keep the advertising approval process simple.
33. I'd insist that the head of my company take a personal interest in the advertising.
34. I'd ask for my agency to concentrate its creative energies on:
    a. Positioning my product.
    b. Developing its personality.
35. I'd hold creative meetings at the agency's offices.
36. I'd practice saying "no." (In order to learn how to do this tactfully when rejecting an idea presented by creative people.)
37. I would never expose the agency, especially creative people, to my senior management unless their proposals had my backing 100%.
38. I would try to create an atmosphere in which "I pass" is acceptable. Sometimes the best creative people simply don't have an idea.
39. Keep yourself up-to-date on current trends in the world of communications and culture.
40. Turn the daily routine of living into a source of ideas.

Age, December 23, 1968, pp. 21–23. Courtesy of James R. Heekin, Jr.)

the advertising agency because successful advertising will result in the client's spending more for advertising, thus increasing the agency's income. While these arguments all support the commission method of compensation, it is probably fair to say that the major reason for the existence of the system is that it made sense when the agencies were primarily brokers of advertising space (with creativity only a secondary function, necessary to sell the space) and that industry practice changes slowly.

Problems With the Commission System. On the other side of the coin are several strong arguments against the commission method. It can be argued that the commission method provides an undesirable incentive for the agency to spend more of the client's money rather than to develop the most effective advertising. The way the agency maximizes its income is to convince its clients to spend more. Also, there is no compensation for generating new campaigns, so there is an incentive for the agency to run the same advertising over long periods. There is no necessary and direct relationship between the level of compensation and the level of service rendered, nor between the level of compensation and the costs incurred by the agency.

Use of Fees. Because of the difficulties inherent in the commission method, most advertising agencies today rely upon a combination of commissions and fees for their income. The nature of the compensation arrangements will also vary depending upon the contractual relationship negotiated with the client. The fee method brings compensation more in line with the services provided by the agency and with the costs incurred in providing that service. It permits the client a broader range of flexibility in the services it requests from the agency. Furthermore, it has tended to improve agency profits (which are not excessive by most reasonable standards) and has probably stimulated competition within the advertising industry. The fee method is especially helpful on industrial accounts, where media charges tend to be much less than in the case of consumer media, and it recognizes that commissions on most industrial media are simply inadequate to compensate the agency. A fee basis of compensation can also have the major value of making the agency more careful in the management and control of the time which agency personnel spend on the account.

Against these advantages, the fee method has several disadvantages, especially the time and difficulty involved in arriving at a satisfactory fee. There can be continual negotiation and argument concerning both the "general" fee and the fee for specific services. As a result, the relationship between agency and client can be seriously weakened. It may also lead to some price cutting. Another possible danger is that the client, who now has more control over the services to be rendered on his account, may not spend enough for such supporting functions such as copy research, thus jeopardizing the success of his total communication program.[25]

At the present time, there is no clear-cut trend either toward or away from the fee method of compensation. The balance between these two elements of compensation must be carefully arrived at in each individual situation. The agency should be allowed a reasonable profit while the client obtains all of the services he requires, and no more, with both agency and client personnel involved in the determination of courses of action on the account.

Evaluation

The output of the agency will be continuously evaluated in both pre-testing and in the full-scale marketing effort. From time to time, how-

[25]A. W. Frey and J. C. Halterman, *Advertising*, 4th ed. (New York: Ronald Press Company, Inc., 1970), pp. 116–19.

ever, it is also necessary to evaluate the entire relationship between the client and the service organization, to find possible weaknesses and to identify opportunities for improving and strengthening the relationship. The regularly scheduled performance review can significantly reduce the probability of a crisis which results in a severing of the relationship.

One of the most troublesome aspects of the advertising business is the frequency with which some accounts move from one agency to another. It is probably true that such moves are often made in ignorance; when sales are disappointing and the reason is not obvious, one of the easiest things to change is the advertising agency. Likewise, a change in the top marketing management of the client company can often result in a change of advertising agencies, as the new management tries to demonstrate its independence and determination to change things. A regular review of performance and documentation of accomplishments can help to minimize the amount of whim in the management of the agency-client relationship.

Evaluation of agency performance will employ many of the same factors used in the initial selection decision and the objectives which were established at that time. In evaluation, the client also has better evidence of the agency's response to his particular problems. Examples of creative output can be carefully scrutinized, perhaps using the results of carefully conducted laboratory and field research. Statistical analyses of relationships between communication effort and sales results can also be examined as one of several criteria for evaluating performance. Periodic review of the state of agency personnel and accounting procedures may also be useful as may a systematic examination of specific interpersonal relationships between agency and client representatives.

ECONOMICS OF CREATIVITY

The creative process must be carefully managed because it involves considerable expenditure of economic resources in the development of marketing communication strategy and because the quality of messages is a major determinant of the success of the strategy. It is therefore necessary to look specifically at the economic issues involved in the management of the creative process. The importance of dollar-and-cents considerations, when combined with the major measurement problems presented by marketing communication, make these among the most complex issues facing the marketing communication strategist.

The Value of an Idea

A good place to begin examination of the economic issue is to note the difficulty of placing a value on a creative idea. There is simply no good way of estimating the value of an idea until that idea has been implemented, used, and systematically evaluated—and even then the many problems of measurement are likely to leave the analyst without a good handle on the problem. A new sales approach, or a new package design, or a new advertising theme can have tremendous impact upon the marketing success of the firm. What was the value of the advertising theme "I'd walk a mile for a Camel" to the Reynolds Tobacco Company or the value of the "We're only number 2, so we try harder" campaign theme to Avis Rent-A-Car? How important to the success of Prell Shampoo was its unbreakable package? How valuable is great advertising for a mediocre product?

While experts may disagree on the magnitude, most would agree with the statement that the quality of the ideas used in the "message" part of marketing communication strategy is a major determinant of its success. At the minimum, it is probably true that an outstanding campaign is at least twice as valuable as an average campaign and the value may go much higher. Politz cites an example of two headlines, one of which pulled six times more inquiries than the other, and says "If a change only in a headline can produce differences of this order of magnitude, imagine how these differences might be compounded by changes in the whole copy treatment."[26] Likewise, one company estimated that its best salesmen were at least twice as productive as its average salesmen while the poorest salesmen were only half as effective as the average. While these are all crude estimates, they are attempts to put a quantitative estimate on what every marketing communication expert feels: that differences in the content of marketing communication have major differences in their effect on market response.

Gross' Proposal

Recognizing the basic fact that good ideas are at least twice as effective as poor ones, Irwin Gross has developed a model to explore the ramifications of this fact. From analysis of his model, Gross recommends that the typical advertiser should spend much more on creating advertising campaigns than he presently spends. It will be instructive to consider Gross' proposal in a little more detail.[27]

Generate More Alternatives. If the advertiser could generate a large number of independent (i.e., not produced by the same creative persons

[26]Alfred Politz, "The Dilemma of Creative Advertising," *Journal of Marketing*, 25 (October 1961), pp. 1–6, at p. 2.

[27]Irwin Gross, "An Analytical Approach to the Creative Aspects of Advertising Operations," unpublished doctoral dissertation, Case Institute of Technology, November 1967. A brief version of the argument is contained in Irwin Gross, "Should the Advertiser Spend More on Creative Advertising?", Proceedings of the 13th Annual Conference, Advertising Research Foundation, November 14, 1967.

and not using the same campaign themes) advertising campaigns, there is reason to assume that the effectiveness of these campaigns would be approximately normally distributed, as shown in Figure 13-2. Using the "average campaign" as having *relative* effectiveness equal to zero, this figure illustrates the basic assumption upon which the following argument is built. Gross sees the process of generating advertising campaigns as equivalent to taking a random sample from the distribution of relative effectiveness. The process of selecting an advertising campaign can be thought of as taking a sample of size n from the distribution and picking that alternative which has the highest expected value, E_n. Finally, the cost of generating an alternative is c, and cn is the cost of generating n alternatives.

Gross estimated that the average advertiser spends between 3 and 5 percent of his total media budget on creating the campaign. The usual practice is to ask the advertising agency to generate a campaign and that campaign is submitted for approval. Gross' model and analysis lead to the conclusion that several agencies should be asked to generate several campaigns, and these should then be screened by means of a scientific testing procedure. The campaign which scores best should then be placed in advertising media by the company's "agency of record." This procedure assumes that there are agencies that specialize in creating advertising campaigns (rather than providing an elaborate array of services) and that these agencies would be willing to submit campaigns for a fee, in competition with other agencies. Each of these assumptions will be examined more carefully in a moment.

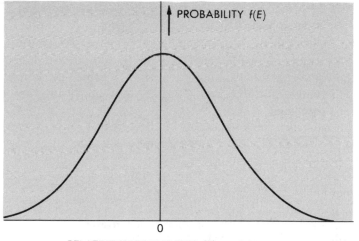

Fig. 13–2. Distribution of relative profitability of independently generated advertising campaigns.

Using some rather conservative assumptions about such factors as the reliability and validity of the screening technique and the relative value of "good" as compared with "average" campaigns, Gross concluded that the optimum expenditure level would be 15 percent of the media budget, a figure from three to five times greater than advertisers are spending at the moment, in his estimate.

Conflicts with Current Philosophy. These ideas are relatively new, and they have generated considerable controversy within the advertising industry. Industry observers argue against Gross' recommendations because they violate the basic premises of the advertiser-agency working relationship. These observers also maintain that most agencies do, in fact, generate several campaigns before they finally pick one to submit to the client for approval and that the basic trust of the traditional "one-to-one" advertiser-agency relationship is a necessary framework for the creative person to be effective. The importance of the preparation stage in the creative process has been stressed, and these critics point out that familiarity with the client's problems and the confidence that one's solutions will be used by the client are both necessary for the creative organization to function effectively.

Implementation of the recommendations of the Gross study would of necessity require that compensation be on a fee basis. Gross sees the commission system as one reason why the advertising industry is likely to resist his recommendations and feels that it is responsible for the relatively low rate of expenditure on creativity. Also, his proposal would require that agencies either set up completely independent creative groups and assign several to work on a given account, or else it would require the existence of many small creative agencies.

Gross has also pointed out that his basic assumption is that creativity is essentially a random process. Our knowledge of the creative process and its motivation is inadequate to permit us to direct it. Therefore, given the value of the outstanding campaign, it makes sense to generate several alternatives in the hopes of significantly improving the effectiveness of the campaign.

At the moment, implementation of these recommendations by many agencies seems unlikely. Most agencies are going to resist because of the additional expense involved and because they feel that the present arrangement does, in fact, generate several alternatives for every campaign that finally gets presented to client management and put into production. It is worth noting, however, that the editor of *Marketing Communications* has expressed the opinion that Gross' proposal points to the way of the future. He said, "The force of logic and the thrust of today's undercurrents augur in favor of the idea."[28]

[28]Walter Joyce, "Editor's Note: The Big Idea," *Marketing Communications*, 296 (September 1968), p. 86.

SUMMARY

The process of creativity is of central importance in marketing communication strategy. The stages of the creative process were analyzed to illustrate the importance of fact finding and analysis as the basis for the application of creative energy. The creative person was seen to require a certain kind of organizational environment in order to function effectively. Marketing communication as a field is characterized by the availability of several independent creative service organizations. The working relationship between the creative organization and the client is a major factor in determining the value of the ideas generated by the agency.

At several points in this chapter, evaluation has been discussed as a central problem in the management of creativity. A special point was made of the poor validity of subjective judgment in evaluating creative output. Gross' proposals stress the need for an effective screening technique. Problems of measurement and evaluation of creative effort have been reserved to Chapter 15.

This chapter has concentrated on the content of mass communication —advertising and public relations, packages, and similar devices—where it is possible to rely upon a creative service organization to generate ideas and where the resulting message will be used thousands of times. For most firms, however, personal selling is a more important element of the marketing communication program. In the case of personal selling, it is only rarely that an outside creative organization can provide help in developing the content of the communication. The very essence of personal selling, with its unique capability as a form of interpersonal interaction in which there is direct feedback and the opportunity to tailor messages to precisely fit the situation, argues against developing *the* message to be presented by the communicator. Rather, the need is to train the salesman to be an effective communicator, to develop effective messages as required by the specific communication situation. The next chapter will look at the requirements for developing effective salesmen and sales messages.

14

Developing Effective Salesmen

For most companies, the salesman is the critical variable in the marketing communication program. Personal selling is the characteristic form of communication as a push strategy, and push strategies are used by most industrial goods sellers and by many consumer goods firms as well. Many companies do not have the financial resources required to implement a large-scale pull strategy, with its heavy reliance on advertising expenditures in mass media. Even in pull strategies, the salesman's role can be of vital importance—in obtaining the cooperation of the retail trade, in setting up displays which provide good point-of-purchase tie-in with media advertising, and in assuring that the product is on the shelf to satisfy demand generated by advertising and sales promotion.

In planning the marketing communication strategy, care must be taken to specify clearly the role assigned to the salesman. As part of the problem of coordinating all elements of the communication mix, and defining the tasks to be accomplished by each element with specific target audiences, the work of the salesman must be specified. This work specification can provide objectives to guide his efforts and standards by which to judge his subsequent performance.

Simply specifying what is expected of the salesman is not enough, however, to insure that the job will be accomplished. While this is an absolutely necessary step, it is not sufficient. Of equal importance is the need to make sure that the salesmen are capable of accepting the responsibility assigned to them. Are they able to complete the communication task? Do they have the necessary knowledge and skills to do the job effectively? Is the quality of field supervision and other aspects of the field sales management program adequate for the demands to be made of the salesmen?

In this chapter, we shall consider the combination of salesman abilities and management policies necessary to insure successful execution of the personal selling strategy within the total marketing communication mix. Beginning with an analysis of the salesman as a communicator and the determinants of salesman effectiveness, the discussion will next consider recruitment, selection, and training procedures for developing effective salesmen. Consideration will also be given to the concept of a total manpower development program for salesmen, including the concept of a career path and management by objectives.

Although the comments in this chapter will focus upon the seller's own sales force, it should be recognized that these comments apply, with only occasional modification, to resellers' salesmen as well. The major difference is that the marketing communication strategist has little or no control over the resellers' salemen and the policies directing their effort. If a critical role is assigned to resellers' salesmen by the communication strategy, then they must also be prepared to accept this responsibility. One of the major assignments for the seller's salesmen may, in fact, be to work closely with resellers' salesmen to give them the necessary product knowledge and technical support, or to assure that they call on key customers, or otherwise to insure their effectiveness. In Chapter 8, we noted that a well-executed national marketing communication program may deteriorate at the local level when resellers' sales personnel, because of poor knowledge and little motivation, are unable to follow through to create a satisfied customer.

SALESMEN AS COMMUNICATORS

There are several ways of describing salesmen and their activities. For example, they can be thought of as storehouses of product knowledge, or as consultants on customer problems, or entities moving within an assigned geographic area and calling on customers with a specified frequency. These are not conflicting viewpoints, but they do highlight different aspects of the salesman's activities and responsibilities. For purposes of the following discussion, it is useful to recall briefly some earlier parts of this text which emphasized the role of the salesman as a communicator. Our evaluation of the problems of developing effective salesmen will define "effectiveness" in terms of changes in customer attitudes and behavior and will consider what the salesman needs to be effective toward that end. The analysis of salesmen as communicators permits the incorporation of all aspects of the salesman's role that influence his ability to develop effective messages.

Dyadic Interaction

In Chapter 6, the concept of dyadic interaction was introduced. The major elements of that concept are the notion that both parties in the dyad are functioning both as senders and receivers, as encoders and decoders, and the notion that the perception of the other person is a major part of the communication process. It was noted that persons are perceived as having both intentions towards the perceiver and certain representations of their environment through which they filter communication. In interaction, each person "sizes up" the other. A message developed by one party to the interaction is feedback to the other, permitting him to modify his perceptions of that person and the messages he sends.

In Chapter 9, personal communication was described as more efficient communication because instant feedback permits the communicator to adjust and tailor his message to the specific requirements of the situation. Whereas an advertising message may be delivered millions of times to an audience with a wide range of characteristics and as a result with a wide range of effectiveness, the salesman delivers his message once to the prospect for whom it was designed. Another individual receives a different message that is intended to be uniquely responsive to his predispositions. Furthermore, the salesman can deliver many messages, not just one, to a prospective customer and is better able to counter resistance from the prospect as he identifies it in the feedback he receives. While mass messages must be developed for a "typical" customer, personal messages can be designed for *this* customer. The overall objective in developing salesmen, therefore, must be to prepare them to develop effective messages for their customers and prospects. Above all, the salesman must be prepared for his role as a communicator.

"Systems Selling"

The effective salesman is a problem solver, a consultant to his customers. He must listen carefully to the feedback he receives and he must carefully phrase questions designed to identify customer needs—problems he can help them solve. The concept of the salesman as a problem solver is at the heart of the "systems selling" concept.

A system is defined simply as a collection of entities, a whole consisting of many parts. The basic contribution of systems analysis is that it focuses attention on higher-order problems and on interactions among system elements. For most forms of selling, the salesman must point out how his product or service can improve system performance. An example will help to clarify these statements.

A good example of systems selling is provided by the air freight salesman. In order to sell air freight service, the salesman must position his transportation service within the customer's total distribution system, including the other major system elements of inventories, warehousing, communication, and materials handling. He must show how use of air freight can result in better system performance despite the higher cost of transportation. Air freight may improve the customer's level of service or it may reduce his total distribution cost, by permitting a reduction in inventories or the damage incurred in-transit handling, for example.

Systems selling can be found in many (if not most) industries today. In the grocery business, for example, the manufacturer's salesman must demonstrate how the value of shelf space, turnover, margin, and national advertising support his argument that the retailer should stock his product. In the container industry, metal can manufacturers have successfully competed against lower-cost glass containers by showing how cans permit a reduction in *total* packaging cost by allowing faster production lines and in other areas.

Assumptions in Systems Analysis. System analysis is based on four assumptions. First, the objective is to maximize *system* performance, not the performance of any individual component. Second, any element of the system need not have optimal design; in fact sub-optimization may prevent total system optimization (as when buying the least expensive machine subsequently creates bottlenecks in a production line). Third, it is assumed that there is some interdependency or trade-off among system elements. Finally, the key assumption of systems analysis is that there are "synergistic" effects: the whole is greater than the sum of its parts. The elements of the system operating together produce a result that is different from what is possible with each element operating independently.

Criteria for Salesman Effectiveness. The reason for devoting this much attention to the systems concept is that increasingly competitive markets and more knowledgeable buyers demand the systems selling approach. They are looking for more complete problem solutions and demand a more complete response from their suppliers. The result is a significant increase in the demands placed on the salesman. First, he must be much more knowledgeable about his products and his company, especially those aspects of the company relating to its ability to provide customer service including technical service, distribution, and production scheduling. Second, he must be much more knowledgeable about his customers. He must know industry conditions, the customer's business operations, and where to look to obtain the detailed information required for the systems selling approach.

Like any problem solver, the salesman can effectively apply his creativity only when he is adequately prepared. The salesman needs to assure the customer that the course of action he recommends will solve that specific customer's problems and that his recommendations are based on a thorough analysis and understanding of that problem. It will be an important objective of any good sales training program to equip salesmen with the tools and concepts required to conduct such analyses.

Credibility

In Chapter 8, communicator credibility was analyzed in depth. The salesman as a communicator, it will be recalled, will be evaluated by the prospect in terms of a stereotype, at least until the prospect learns that this salesman is different from the stereotype. The salesman's role involves the goal of persuading people, and this intent to persuade is a cause of low credibility. Credibility is a function of both trustworthiness and expertise; a salesman with sufficient product knowledge and expertise can overcome the effects of perceived intent to persuade, or "bias."

The discussion of credibility also reviewed the selling situation as a special case of dyadic interaction. Salesmen are more effective with prospects who are like themselves, possibly because a salesman who is seen to be "like me" is also perceived as being more trustworthy. The individual characteristics of the salesman may not be important *per se* but only in relationship to the characteristics of the prospect. These findings about the effectiveness of buyer-salesman dyads are consistent with the general conclusion from research on personal influence that people are more likely to seek advice and opinions from persons who are like themselves.

The salesman stereotype is one source of the prospect's role expectations for a salesman. Another source of role expectations is the reputation of the selling company. Source (company) credibility influences communicator (salesman) credibility. The image of the company will create certain expectations about that company's salesmen in the buyer's mind. It is interesting to consider that the better the company's reputation, the greater are the expectations of buyers for that company's salesman in terms of his knowledge, sales ability, appearance, and overall approach. Rather than reducing the need to spend money on developing effective salesmen, expenditures for advertising and image-building activities can actually increase the need by creating higher expectations that the salesman must meet.

DETERMINANTS OF SALESMAN EFFECTIVENESS

There has been an evolution of thinking on the issue of whether there are certain characteristics that differentiate effective salesmen from the ineffective. If we phrase the question as "What makes an effective salesman?," we can briefly trace that evolution.

Personal Characteristics

Earliest attempts to answer the question considered those individual attributes of personality, appearance, background, education, experience, etc. which seemed correlated with sales ability. There is a close relationship to the stereotype of the salesman which sees him as aggressive, talkative, outgoing, and so forth. One result of this viewpoint was the development of rather elaborate selection devices, especially psychological tests and application blanks, designed to measure the extent to which applicants possess characteristics that have been found to differentiate between good and bad salesmen. There is a key assumption in this viewpoint that most of the control in buyer-salesman relationships is on the side of the salesman: given the right characteristics, the salesman can make the prospect buy. This viewpoint conflicts directly with the basic argument of this text that effective marketing communication requires a tailoring of effort to the desires and predispositions of the audience. In other words, the "salesman's traits" approach looks at only half of the dyad—the half with least control over the interaction.

A related viewpoint emphasized the salesman's actions rather than his traits. This viewpoint is seen in such concepts of salesmanship as AIDA (attention, interest, desire, action) and the "steps-in-the-sale" (approach, presentation, handling objections, close) formulation. This approach also included the stimulus-response formulations which saw the salesman as rather mechanically applying certain stimuli to the prospect in order to produce the desired buyer response. Obviously, this viewpoint also assigned most of the power in the dyadic relationship to the salesman.

Finally, there was need-satisfaction theory, which had the great virtue of shifting attention to the prospect. According to this view, the salesman must first identify the prospect's needs and then show how his products can fill those needs. This was consistent with a basic tenet of communication theory, as discussed in Chapter 11, that need arousal followed by argument is a more effective order of presentation than demonstration followed by need-arousal. Need-satisfaction views of salesmanship are really variants of stimulus-response views and assign a passive role to the prospect. These three views have, until recently, been among the most popular ways of looking at personal selling.[1] Interaction theory is a more recent development but is receiving widespread acceptance.[2]

[1]Harold C. Cash and W. J. E. Crissy, "Ways of Looking at Selling," in William Lazer and Eugene J. Kelley (eds.), *Managerial Marketing: Perspectives and Viewpoints*, 2nd ed. (Homewood, Ill.: Richard D. Irwin, Inc., 1962), pp. 554–59.

[2]Frederick E. Webster, Jr., "Interpersonal Communication and Salesman Effectiveness," *Journal of Marketing*, 32 (July 1968), pp. 7–13.

Empathy

As the importance of the salesman's ability to obtain and react to feedback in the dyadic interaction gained recognition, it was also recognized that some salesmen were more capable than others of performing these functions. This ability, called *empahty*, is a kind of social sensitivity involving the ability to sense the reactions one produces in others, to place oneself in the other fellow's shoes.[3] Mayer and Greenberg argue that empathy, along with a trait they call "ego-drive," is the most important characteristic of the effective salesman.[4] They also argue that it is possible to measure the extent to which a potential salesman has this ability, using a psychological test which they have devised. It is well to remember, however, that psychologists have for many years actively debated the concept of empathy and the extent to which it can be differentiated from such related concepts as "projection" and "identification." The literature of social psychology also suggests that tests designed to measure empathy and these related characteristics have suffered from low validity and reliability.[5]

While caution is warranted, the basic concept of empathy is nonetheless valid in analyzing the requirements for the effective salesman. Even if empathy is difficult to measure accurately, there is still need to assure that salesmen have the ability to sense the reaction their presentations generate in the prospect. Furthermore, this ability may not be an inborn trait but a characteristic that can be learned and acquired through practice. Role playing and related training techniques may significantly improve a salesman's empathic ability.

Knowledge

Basic to his ability to solve customer problems is the salesman's knowledge. The preceding comments on systems selling have suggested three major categories of salesman knowledge: knowledge of customers, products, and company. In addition, the salesman also needs some basic conceptual knowledge about the communication process and buyer behavior and about the selling process and its techniques.

Conceptual Knowledge of Buyer Behavior. It is useful to draw a parallel between the marketing communication strategist who develops a

---

[3]Gardner Lindzey and Edgar F. Borgotta, "Sociometric Measurement," in Gardner Lindzey (ed.), *Handbook of Social Psychology* (Reading, Mass.: Addison-Wesley, Inc., 1954), 1, pp. 405–48, at p. 427.

[4]David Mayer and Herbert M. Greenberg, "What Makes a Good Salesman," *Harvard Business Review*, 42 (July-August 1964), pp. 119–25.

[5]Albert H. Hastorf and Irving E. Bender, "A Caution Respecting the Measurement of Empathic Ability," *Journal of Abnormal and Social Psychology*, 47 (April 1952), pp. 574–76.

strategy for the market, or for specific market segments, and the salesmen who must develop a strategy with each prospective customer account he calls on. Account strategy, if it is to be effective, must meet the same criteria and be based upon the same kinds of knowledge and understanding as market strategy. Effective marketing communication strategies are based upon a careful understanding of the nature of the market, the product benefits, the nature of the communication process, and patterns of influence in the market or organization being sold to. Analysis of these factors requires conceptual knowledge about market behavior.

Likewise, a salesman needs conceptual knowledge in order to look objectively at the interaction as a form of communication and to understand clearly his role and its limitations. He must be able to analyze the "data" that will be generated by feedback. He needs to know how to ask questions to get the information he needs to understand that customer and his needs, as the basis for messages with a high probability of accomplishing his goals. To be objective about his work, the salesman needs some conceptual knowledge about communication which will help him understand and organize the experience he will have in the sales interaction.

Knowledge of the Customer's Buying Process. In addition to conceptual knowledge about communication and buyer behavior, the salesman also needs specific information about the nature of the buying process in the consuming unit. The insurance salesman must take time to determine the relative importance of the husband and wife in a family buying situation. The industrial and institutional salesman faces the complex task of identifying the locus of buying responsibility in the customer organization, and the various buying roles (influencer, user, decider, and buyer).

Knowledge of Products and Company. As repeatedly stated, the salesman also needs thorough understanding of his products and his company. He must be able to answer the question customers are going to raise, and if he does not have the information himself he must know how to quickly obtain it from his company. He must know who can provide that information and how to use them as a resource in his selling.

Knowledge of Selling. If the preceding comments have been critical of traditional approaches to the study of salesmanship, it is because other kinds of knowledge have been underemphasized in traditional approaches, not because salesmanship itself is unimportant. The salesman absolutely needs to have the basic skills of salesmanship in full command. He needs to know how to *apply* the concepts of communication and buyer behavior, the knowledge of specific customers, and the knowledge of his products and company, to get buying action. There is a body of knowledge about salesmanship that can be studied and learned, although it is often a big leap from what the textbooks say to actual field experience. A salesman may learn a "rule" of selling (for example "ABC," "Always Be Closing") long before he learns how to apply that rule. Stated differently, there is a distinction to be drawn between knowledge of selling and selling skills. While the former may be a necessary basis for the latter, the two are quite distinct and the salesman to be effective needs training in both.

Communication Skills

Given the distinction between knowledge and skills, it is necessary to comment briefly on the importance of the skills themselves. There are two broad sets of skills required of the salesman—the skills of the sender and the skills of the receiver. It is now obvious that listening skills are a prior condition for developing effective messages. Therefore, the skills of the receiver must be developed before the skills of the sender. The salesman must be taught how to listen to and analyze the prospect's comments, in order to identify buying needs, goals, and constraints, before he can be taught how to develop an effective sales presentation, because the requirements for message effectiveness are defined by the specific buying situation.

Skills are differentiated from knowledge and other forms of ability by the notion of "doing." A skill is the ability to do something competently. The development of communication skills, in contrast to knowledge of the communication process, requires the active participation of the learner and the use of real-world kinds of data and experiences. Since the required skills for the salesman involve listening and responding to prospects' feedback, it follows that the development of effective salesmen requires exposing the salesman to such feedback. Furthermore, it will be helpful if that feedback is in response to his own messages, not someone else's.

Despite the value of using real prospects and actual buying situations as part of the training program, it may be prohibitively risky to practice on real live prospects. In our discussion of training activities, we shall consider such techniques as tape-recorded sales calls, role playing, and the use of videotape to simulate the buying situation.

Supervision

The quality of field supervision is a major determinant of the success of the salesman. Many studies have provided convincing evidence that the local field sales manager is a key ingredient in helping the salesman to set goals for his own performance and in providing him with a continuous form of training and an environment conducive to a high level of performance.[6] It is nonsensical to assume that the salesman who has completed the training program has no further need for or interest in learning. Nothing could be farther from the truth. The new salesman is almost certain to be more highly motivated to learn once he is in the field and is confronted with evidence of his need for further knowledge and training and the frustrations of unsuccessful selling effort. The general "tone" of the environment and the morale of the sales force will also have significant impact on the individual's performance.

Supervisor vs. Supersalesman. At the same time, there can be little doubt that field sales managers are among the most poorly prepared for their responsibilities of any position in the modern marketing organization. They have one of the most demanding and complex jobs in marketing but they are seldom selected and trained according to the requirements of that job. More often than not, the field manager is a supersalesman, promoted to the job of manager because of superior selling skills and certain other motivations for change, such as the fact that he reached the top of the pay scale for salesmen, or the company wanted to concentrate his efforts on a few major accounts. As a result, the company loses an effective salesman and gains an ineffective sales manager, a man who can sell but who does not know how to manage and develop the skills of his salesmen [7]

In many companies, the economics of sales territory organization require that the sales manager handle certain major accounts, primarily because a full-time, nonselling manager represents an unjustifiable expense. There is a tendency in such situations, however, for the selling responsibilities to take precedence over the managing functions and the result is that the salesmen are less effective than would be the case if they had the benefits of full-time supervision.

Role in Manpower Development. Supervision can be defined as "the process by which the manager tries to improve the performance of his men by sharpening their skills and by providing an environment conducive to a high level of performance."[8] The field sales manager plays a critical role in developing standards of performance for his men (with their active participation in the goal-setting process), in helping them to develop their abilities in order to meet these standards, and in providing

[6]Rensis Likert, "A Further Interpretation of the Study Results," in D. Bowers (ed.), *Applying Modern Management Principles to Sales Organization* (Ann Arbor, Mich.: Foundation for Research on Human Behavior, 1963), pp. 41–45.

[7]Robert T. Davis, *Performance and Development of Field Sales Managers* (Boston: Division of Research, Graduate School of Business Administration, Harvard University, 1957).

[8]Kenneth R. Davis and Frederick E. Webster, Jr., *Sales Force Management* (New York: Ronald Press Company, 1968), p. 559.

necessary back-up and support when a situation goes beyond the control of the salesman.

Viewed in this light, the field sales manager's contribution to the organization should come from the way he develops his salesmen, not from his selling performance. He should concentrate on long-term goals and multiply his efforts through his salesmen, not concentrate on his short-term sales accomplishment. The organization of sales effort, and the procedures used to evaluate, control, and reward performance in the organization, must be consistent with the long-term objectives. If the sales manager is evaluated according to his own personal sales quota, and if he is compensated on that basis, he will behave like a salesman rather than a supervisor. The long-run costs to the organization are great. Too often, an ineffective salesman is the reflection of an ineffective sales manager rather than of his own lack of ability and interest. The quality of field sales supervision is an absolutely essential determinant of the salesman's effectiveness.

Motivation and Compensation

Programs for motivating and compensating salesmen have an important effect on individual performance, although the nature of the effect may be hard to identify and quite different from that intended by management. Compensation methods, for example, may be inconsistent with certain selling objectives, as when the objective of developing new accounts conflicts with the compensation of salesmen on the basis of current sales.

Motives and Incentives. In a strict sense, the manager does not "motivate" his salesmen; rather, he provides incentives which appeal to the individual salesman's motives. The effective sales manager is one who takes the time required to understand his men as individuals, to understand what "makes them tick." He then develops his methods of supervision, including the incentives he provides, to fit the peculiar needs of each individual.

Part of the stereotype of the salesman sees him as a truly "economic" man who is motivated primarily by the desire for financial gain. While there may be some truth to this element of the stereotype in that the opportunity for significant earnings is often a major attraction of a selling job, it is by no means true that money is the only effective way to motivate salesmen. More than one sales manager has been baffled by a situation in which the salesman begins to slack off bcause he is satisfied with his level of earning from the job and there are no other incentives for hard work in the situation.

Salesmen are no more or less complex in their motivations than other people. In Chapter 11, Maslow's need hierarchy was reviewed and five levels of needs were identified: physiological, safety, love, esteem, and self-actualization. Financial rewards may help to satisfy needs at several levels, including physiological, safety, esteem, and self-actualization. Monetary payoffs are a good way of keeping score on one's attainment. On the other hand, there are many needs which money cannot fulfill and which are nonetheless important for job satisfaction, including safety, love, esteem, and self-actualization needs.

Nonfinancial Rewards. The fact that the salesman works alone most of the time is a significant influence on the needs for particular kinds of incentives and rewards for salesmen. Because of the high probability that the average sales call will be unproductive, the salesman needs to be able to rebound from this disappointment in order to approach the next situation in good spirits and with confidence. His morale must be high and he must be secure in knowing that he will be evaluated fairly, according to criteria that he understands, and that his continued hard work, often without obvious results for the company in the short run, is known and appreciated. Even the most experienced experts on personal selling are continually amazed at the appreciation which salesmen can show for a seemingly insignificant nonfinancial reward such as a brief letter of thanks from the marketing manager or the president of the company. Perhaps the salesman has a bigger but more fragile ego than the average person so that recognition and praise have special significance for him.

Criteria Must Be Consistent With Objectives. In developing programs for rewarding salesman performance the first step is to specify the criteria by which the salesmen will be evaluated. These criteria should be directly related to the objectives of selling effort within the total communication strategy. The evaluation and compensation plan should reward behavior and achievement that is consistent with those basic objectives.

Analysis of the reasons why companies do not achieve communication objectives often reveals that the company's sales compensation plan is in conflict with those objectives. This is most often the case when the compensation plan is either a straight commission plan or a straight salary plan. When salesmen are paid straight commission on sales volume they are most likely to concentrate their efforts where the potential for current sales volume is the highest. As a result, they will overlook smaller accounts or accounts where some development work must be done (including completely new accounts) and they will tend to concentrate their efforts on those items in the product line which are easiest to sell.

They will also avoid customer service activities that do not yield measurable sales results. Straight salary plans give the company more control over the salesman's activities, in that the company can tell him to spend more time on customer service, for example, without having him object that this will reduce his income. Salary plans often do not provide sufficient incentive for increased effort, however, and tend to reward the salesman for a minimally acceptable level of performance. Salary plans provide no particular incentive for developing new accounts, or full-line selling, or market expansion activities unless changes in the level of salary are clearly related to specific evaluation criteria and measurement procedures.

Relative Contributions of Supervision and Compensation. The manner in which the organization provides incentive and rewards performance is a key determinant of salesman effectiveness. On the other hand, it is easy to overburden a compensation plan with objectives which are more appropriately assigned to another management tool. It is wrong, for example, to expect the compensation plan all by itself to provide the necessary incentive for superior performance. That is equally a task for supervision. Likewise, inadequate attention to certain items in the product line may require a more careful training procedure and in-the-field supervision of sales effort on those lines, not a revision of the commission rates on those products.

Characteristics of Good Compensation Plans. In order to achieve the objectives set for them, compensation plans must be understandable by the salesmen, and they must establish a clear relationship between effort and reward. The salesman must know how he will be paid if the plan is to influence his behavior in the way intended by management. The plan must be fair and consistent in the way it treats salesmen of equal ability, experience, and performance. It should be easy to administer so that there is little possibility of error and there are no delays in paying salesmen the money they have earned.

The level of pay provided by a compensation plan must be sufficient to attract and hold salesmen of the ability and competence required by the role of personal selling in the marketing communication strategy. The method of pay must assure that the salesmen are motivated to behave in the way required to implement that strategy. These are a difficult and complex set of requirements against which to evaluate a compensation plan, but a careful assessment of the relationship between compensation and the communication strategy is a necessary step in careful planning. Salesmen will perform in a manner that is most consistent with their self-interests. The compensation plan must be designed to assure that the salesmen are in fact rewarded for effort which is effective according to the objectives of the communication strategy. Through the compensation plan the salesman's self-interest can be directed toward company objectives.

Technical and Service Support

Except for the door-to-door peddler who carries his inventory with him and obtains payment on the spot, the salesman depends upon other people in the organization to fulfill promises which he makes to the customer. The trend toward systems selling, noted earlier, highlights the salesman's dependence upon other parts of the business for his effectiveness. The salesman for a manufacturer of machine tools must rely heavily upon the design engineering and production scheduling departments of his company to fulfill his commitments to his customer. There may be many times in his discussions with potential customers that he has to obtain the technical support of an applications engineering group in responding to a customer's problems.

Selling Team. In many kinds of selling, the salesman becomes the leader of a selling team consisting of people such as production specialists, packaging and logistics experts, and applications engineers in working with a customer to solve his problems. For example, a salesman selling fiberglass cord to a tire manufacturer may put together a team consisting of a research chemist, a production specialist, and an expert on testing procedures, all of whom meet with a team from the customer organization to discuss how use of this particular cord material can result in a better tire for that customer. The computer salesman, to pick another example, may be assisted by a "systems" specialist who has better technical knowledge of computing hardware, or a specialist in operations research and applications.

Customer Service. The salesman selling to retail outlets, whether his product is furniture, food, or something else, depends upon his back-up support for providing delivery when promised (which may involve resellers) and for the necessary tie-in promotions. When a grocery salesman sells a particular promotion to a retailer, he must also promise that the product will be available at the stated time and that the national, regional, and local media advertising will run as scheduled. This presents some complex problems of coordination.

Salesmen can be made ineffective by a lack of reliability in the backup services and support on which they depend to solve customer problems. Industrial purchasing people will report many instances in which they would prefer to deal with a salesman from one company because of his ability and knowledge, but that they must buy from another because the first company is unable to back up its salesman with service. The shame of this situation is that the salesman too often gets the blame for poor performance when he has little control over the factors determining his effectiveness with customers.

Marketing Mix and Market Potential

The foregoing comments on technical and service support can be generalized to include all elements of the marketing mix. A salesman's effectiveness, measured by the amount of sales output for a given level of effort, reflects much more than the salesman's ability. It also reflects the basic soundness of the company's product and service offering, its pricing policies, and its distribution channels, as well as the other elements of the marketing communication program.

Performance Reflects Potential. The salesman's performance also reflects the potential of the territory and accounts to which he is assigned. It is appropriate to remember how important these other factors are in appraising the salesman's efforts or the sales organization as a whole. One of the problems in evaluating salesmen by comparing their performances one with the other is that the existing measures of market potential may be inaccurate indicators of major differences among sales territories.

The reason for discussing marketing mix and market potential together is that there may be significant interactions among the two sets of factors. Distribution strategies clearly have a local market flavor, and the company's product and pricing strategies may be more or less effective, depending upon the preferences of customers as these vary from region to region, and on the extent of local competition. All of these factors determine the effectiveness of the salesman in the territory assigned to him.

To summarize, the salesman's effectiveness depends upon many factors in addition to his personal characteristics. His empathic ability may be of special significance but this ability may reflect his more general knowledge of buyer behavior and communication processes, and it can probably be developed through training. He needs specific knowledge about his customers, his products, and his company, and he should know how to depend upon the organization for support when the customer's problems exceed his own ability to solve them. The field sales management program will be a major determinant of salesman effectiveness with special emphasis upon the quality of supervision and programs for providing incentive and rewarding performance. Finally, the salesman's performance will also be significantly influenced by the other elements of the marketing mix, including product, pricing, and distribution channel arrangements, as well as the other elements of the marketing communication strategy. Development of an effective field sales organization requires programs for identifying qualified people and attracting them to the organization and a program for providing them with the necessary knowledge and skills to be effective communicators.

We have defined an "ideal" salesman with a particular bundle of communication skills and product and company knowledge. This model provides goals or a set of criteria for the company's sales manpower development program—recruiting, selection, training, and evaluation activities intended to field a sales force of optimum effectiveness. Next, we consider how these activities can contribute to the accomplishment of communication objectives.

RECRUITMENT AND SELECTION

Recruiting is the set of activities designed to identify persons who might be interested in, and qualified for, selling positions within the company. Selection is the related process by which information about the individual is gathered and analyzed to determine whether that person could be successful in the job for which he has applied. Because these processes provide the input of human resources into the sales organization, they are vital to its ultimate success.

Salesmen Are Made, Not Born

There has been a long-standing controversy on the issue whether good salesmen are "born" or "made." Some argue that the basic require ments for an effective salesman are acquired early in life and that by the time an individual applies for a sales job he either has what it takes to be successful or he does not. This, in brief, is the "salesmen are born" school. On the other side of the argument are those who feel that effective salesmen can be developed through the appropriate training procedures and that there is no particular mystique which the successful salesman has in his blood and bones. Earlier discussion of the "personal characteristics" views of selling provided argument and evidence that effective salesmen are "made" through the appropriate sales manpower development program.

Obviously, there are individuals who, in certain aspects, have a personality, interests, or an outlook that makes selling an unwise career choice for them. This is not to say that they could not be trained for selling jobs but that the process would likely be painful for both the trainer and the trainee. At the other extreme are individuals who do have the interests and personality that make a selling job particularly exciting and rewarding for them. In this case, the training job would be easier and the work would be more enjoyable for the individual. The assertion being offered here is simply that there is no magic set of personal characteristics and charm which guarantee success any more than there are certain characteristics which guarantee failure. Furthermore, and perhaps more importantly, the most important skills and abilities for effective selling are skills that can be learned—communication skills and concepts about buyer behavior, and product, company, and customer knowledge.

Given this viewpoint, selection procedures take on a different aspect. Effort can be concentrated on looking at the extent to which the man's interests and background prepare him for the requirements of the job. Those who subscribe to the "salesmen are born" school concentrate their attention and resources on the question of how to identify individuals with the necessary characteristics. Our viewpoint is that resources committed to training are likely to yield better returns than resources committed to a search for those characteristics which reliably distinguish good salesmen from bad salesmen and to development of psychological tests to measure those characteristics.

Job Description

The starting point for any manpower development program must be a carefully developed description of the salesman's job. This job description should derive from an analysis of the role of the salesman in the company's marketing communication strategy. What work is the salesman supposed to perform? The answer to this straightforward question should be simple, realistic, and to the point. Job descriptions often become unreasonable and require much more of the salesman than is necessary or than the company has any intention of paying for.

Closely related to the job description is the specification of the requirements for individuals who will fill that job. The latter set of requirements is usually called job specifications or *man specifications*. Given the work to be performed by the salesman, certain characteristics of the individual may be required such as health and physical fitness, age range, formal education, previous job experience, and communication ability (often stated as "speaking ability," which overlooks the equally important "listening ability"). Obviously, such character traits as honesty and integrity are also a must.

Sources

Salesmen are obtained from a wide variety of sources. Among the most popular are other companies (especially competitors), other departments within the company, institutions of higher learning, and employment agencies. The procedures followed in tapping these sources can vary widely, from relying upon the existing salesmen to identify such prospective job applicants whenever they can to the use of mass media to attract interested applicants.

In order to avoid crises caused by the sudden departure of a salesman, the company should have a planned program of manpower development including a continuous program of recruiting. Waiting until the vacancy exists can be a costly and ineffective recruiting strategy with significantly lower probability of finding the "right" man for the job.

Use of newspaper advertisements for attracting sales job applicants can be effective but it can also present significant problems. The copy used in recruiting ads is a key determinant of response. If the copy describes the man specifications in terms of a superman, the response is going to be relatively low. On the other hand, it is important to have an adequate and reasonable description of the requirements for the job in order to discourage habitual job-seekers and others who are not qualified. Screening interviews are expensive and the objective of recruiting advertising should be to attract those with the necessary qualifications to pass the screening interview.

Application Blank

The application blank is a low-cost tool that can be the single most important step in the selection process. The application blank should be carefully designed to obtain all of the information necessary relating to the ability of the job applicant to do the job—and no more information than is required. Most application blanks ask for personal data (date of birth, address, military status, etc.), educational background, previous experience, references, and some statement of the reasons why the individual is interested in this job and considers himself qualified to take it.

The application blank should be a direct reflection of the man specifications and these should relate to the job description and the role of the salesman in the communication strategy, as noted earlier. This selection tool can also reveal certain other important characteristics of the job applicant such as simple ability to follow instructions and willingness to provide information requested in sufficient detail. A sloppy, half-completed application is good evidence of low interest in the job or poor ability for it. More importantly, a carefully articulated statement of interests and reasons for applying for the job can supply significant insights into the extent to which the applicant matches the requirements for effectiveness on the job.

Let us stress again that training will be a significant determinant of salesman effectiveness. It is not to be implied that the selection process can ever be so effective as to preclude the necessity for training. One of the criteria for a selection procedure, however, is that it provide candidates with the necessary interests and aptitudes to complete the training program successfully. Application blanks can be used to reveal those aptitudes and to provide estimates of the probability of a successful training experience. The application blank can be especially helpful in revealing background factors that indicate a high risk of failure either in the training program or on the job itself.

Because of its importance, and its ability to provide necessary information at relatively little cost to the job applicant and to the company, the application blank should be carefully developed and tested. Care should be taken to make sure that information is not requested that is unnecessary or the asking for which is likely to offend the applicant. On the other hand, certain items that are not essential to the selection decision (e.g., wife's name, social security number, etc.) may be requested because the application blank becomes part of the employee's permanent record if he is hired.

Psychological Tests

Many selection procedures for selling positions require the applicant to submit to tests of one or more psychological characteristics. The major categories of psychological tests are tests of mental ability, tests of aptitude, tests of interest, and tests of personality. Familiar examples of each of these types are these four: (1) Otis Self-Administering Test of Mental Ability (intelligence); (2) Canfield test, "How Perfect is Your Sales Sense?" (aptitude); (3) Strong Vocational Interest Test (interest); and (4) Edwards Personal Preference Schedule (personality).

These various forms of psychological tests have significant variation in their validity and reliability. Intelligence tests probably have the highest reliability and validity while personality tests have the least. Our earlier discussion of the personal characteristics approach to the analysis of personal selling has also suggested some reasons why such psychological tests may be inadequate predictors of success on the sales job.

Measuring a Test's Contribution. In order to develop an effective psychological testing procedure, the user would have to conduct a carefully controlled experiment. He would have to submit a sufficiently large sample of job applicants to each of a large series of tests which he was considering using in his final selection procedure. He would next have to hire *all* of the applicants and carefully record their performance over time. After he had sufficient data (which would probably require several years) he could then statistically analyze the data to find which measures on which tests had the highest correlation with success on the job. Unfortunately, by this time so many other factors would have come into play to influence individual performance—including variations in sales territory, quality of supervision, and so on—that the relationship between sales success and whatever it was that the tests measured would be almost hopelessly confused.

Limitations. Performance on most psychological tests tends to be correlated with level of education. The simple ability to take paper-and-pencil tests (an ability which can be learned—in formal education) may be a major determinant of performance on these tests. These tests also permit a high degree of faking, especially by individuals who have frequently been exposed to such testing procedures. It is often rather obvious how the questions should be answered. For example, if a test asks an applicant for a sales job:

> When entering a cocktail party, are you most likely to—
> (1) wait in an inconspicuous place until the host identifies you?
> (2) get a drink, then sit down and see who will come to talk to you?
> (3) strike up conversations with persons you have not previously met?
> (4) seek out old friends?

it takes no great acumen to realize that certain answers (e.g., items 1 and 2) describe behavior which is probably inappropriate for successful salesman.

Personality tests are likely to have the least validity and reliability because the things they are designed to measure (personality characteristics such as dominance, self-sufficiency, creativity, and needs for autonomy and affiliation) are least well defined and have the least clear influence on selling performance. One author has concluded that the record of personality tests is "dismal" and "has not proved to be useful."[9]

Appropriate Uses. Psychological tests do have a role to play in salesman selection, however, if they are used carefully and appropriately with a clear understanding of their limitations. There are a few simple guidelines that can be helpful in making the appropriate use of psychological tests. First, psychological tests should always be treated as a rejection device, never as a selection device. Stated differently, an individual's performance on the test should be compared against some minimum acceptable standard of performance. The wrong use of psychological tests is to have all applicants submit to the test and then to pick the one or two applicants who score highest. Seldom if ever can one test permit good prediction of future job success. The test may be more useful, however, in identifying a basic lack of ability or interest which will pro-

---

[9] R. S. Barrett, "Guide to Using Psychological Tests," *Harvard Business Review*, 41 (September-October 1963), pp. 138–46, at p. 139.

hibit successful job performance. A low score on an intelligence test, for example, or a clear indication that an individual's interests are not consistent with those of a selling career, should be used to reject the individual from further consideration for that job.

Second, psychological test results. should be evaluated in connection with evidence from other sources, including the application blank and the personal interview. These tests can measure only one set of characteristics but there are many other factors to be evaluated in judging the probability that a salesman will be effective. Tests do have the one major advantage of being objective while other steps in the selection process are much more subjective. At the same time, the "objectivity" of the psychological test is perhaps misleading because of the large amount of judgment required to carefully interpret test results.

Third, the tests should be administered and judged by persons who are specifically trained and qualified in their use and interpretation. A lot of psychological testing procedures still resemble art more than science. At a minimum, the potential user of a psychological testing service should attempt to discuss the test with others who have been using it successfully. It is important to know whether the results claimed by those selling the test have actually been achieved and to obtain such evidence as may be available on the validity and reliability of that specific testing device.

Selection Interviews

The final stages of the selection process usually involve one or more personal interviews with the job applicant. It is typical for the selection process to consist of an initial screening interview (as when the sales manager visits the college campus to recruit) and then a series of interviews with both personnel department specialists and sales department personnel.

It is obviously helpful for the potential job applicant also to talk to the people he will be working with, if possible, for they will be a major determinant of his success and happiness on the job. One of the objectives of the selection interview is to convince the attractive candidate that this job would be one which meets his objectives.

Value of Multiple Interviews. The most desirable procedure is probably to have the applicant interviewed by several people independently who can then meet to compare their impressions. This avoids the tendency for one individual's standards and preferences to exert overriding influence on the selection process. Too often, "I liked him" becomes a substitute for "I think he would be effective in the selling job" in evaluating job applicants. The group interview (with more than one interviewer) also has its advantages but it may be unnecessarily frightening for the job applicant as he tries to answer several unrelated questions simultaneously. Such group interviews often turn into dialogues between people in the company or sessions in which each interviewer tries to impress the others with his toughness.

Artificial Pressure Is Undesirable. Nothing can discourage a job applicant quicker than an interviewer who tries to be "tough" or "cute" or otherwise show his ability to control and frighten the applicant. Such techniques have no place in the responsible selection interview. There are other, more effective ways of determining an individual's ability to respond under pressure. The interview itself puts the average applicant under enough pressure to be a reasonable simulation of the selling situation. If the objective of the selection interview is to determine the applicant's poise, knowledge, reasoning ability, personal appearance, and communication ability, it makes sense to treat that interview as a normal social interaction with a certain amount of formality and pressure, but without trying to destroy the applicant.

Exchange of Information. The selection interview should not duplicate the search for information contained in the application blank, but it may provide an opportunity to probe for such information. For example, it will always be useful to know the extent to which the individual enjoyed and was successful in previous employment and the reasons why he changed jobs. His interests and personal career objectives can be carefully developed and explored in the interviews.

The selection interview is the only situation in which the individual can really gain information about the nature of the job for which he is applying. Those who conduct the interview must be willing to tell the salesman about the company, the conditions under which he would be working, and any questions relating to the kind of work he would be doing. Our understanding of the determinants of successful salesmen is still at the level where the careful evaluation of a sales job applicant by an experienced sales manager can be the most valuable predictor of that applicant's future job success. Steps must be taken to assure that the interviewers are using the right criteria in their evaluations and that there is full communication among all those persons involved in interviews and in the selection decision. Interview guides and evaluation forms may be useful in this connection.

Well-planned procedures for evaluating and selecting sales talent for the organization pay big dividends into the future. These programs are the basic building blocks for an effective sales organization. The output of the recruitment and selection program becomes the input for the training program.

TRAINING

The sales training program provides the salesmen with the necessary knowledge, skills, and habits to perform their job effectively. In the absence of a formal training experience, the salesmen will "make do," relying on their existing knowledge and developing their own work habits, good and bad, in an attempt to survive on the job. Investment in training is investment in the future of the company and insures that personal communication resources will be available to execute the marketing communication strategy. Failure to carefully plan the sales training program or to commit the necessary resources and talent to its implementation will place expensive constraints on the communication alternatives available to the firm in the future.

Objectives

The objective of a sales training program should be to develop salesmen with the necessary knowledge, skills, and work habits to solve customer problems. In today's markets, there must be a significant element of creativity in the salesman—with an emphasis upon the necessary preparation and the ability to find unique and innovative solutions to the problems which define the buying situation for the customer. One element of this ability is the skill of the salesman as a communicator, his ability to create effective messages in the sales interview that will develop favorable attitudes toward the company and its products and will move the buyer toward purchase behavior. We should not lose sight of the fact that the ultimate objective of selling (and therefore of sales training) is to generate the maximum level of profitable sales for the company. Stated somewhat differently, the ultimate objective of the training program is to create a satisfied customer.

Program Content

Earlier analysis in this chapter has identified the two major components of *knowledge* and *skills* in the effective salesman. In addition, the salesman needs a set of attitudes toward the job and *work habits* that will help sustain and organize his effort in the field in the absence of direct supervision.

Knowledge. The major components of knowledge have been identified as communication, company, product, market, and customer knowledge. These do not require further elaboration now, but there are three observations to be made about the relative importance of each kind of knowledge. First, there is a tendency for sales training programs to over-emphasize product knowledge. Many training programs require the trainee to spend several months or even years learning about the company's products including how they are designed and manufactured, how customer orders are filled from inventory, and so on. In those cases where the salesman is also a product-service- and repair-man as well, there may be some justification for this emphasis. In most cases, however, there is lopsided attention to product knowledge, and inadequate attention to the basic knowledge of communication. This is the second observation: that companies tend to underemphasize the importance of communication knowledge.

Knowledge of communication involves the concepts that have been developed in this text. The salesman needs to understand the basic nature of the communication process so that he can understand his own work and interpret the facts of his experience. This conceptual knowledge will also help him to analyze customer behavior, to identify needs and buying influences, and to develop an understanding of the requirements for an effective selling approach. This knowledge is also a valuable base for the development of the specific knowledge and skills of salesmanship. More and more, textbooks and training manuals on salesmanship are building upon the basic concepts of communication theory.[10]

Third, the area of "company knowledge" often stresses policies and procedures that constrain the salesman's behavior rather than those aspects of the company that represent resources to be used by the salesman in his work. To be more specific, there is a tendency for company knowledge to concentrate on such areas as expense account management, handling of company-confidential records, use of company property, personnel policies relating to vacations, compensation, fringe benefits, and so on. There is often inadequate time devoted to understanding how the salesman can make maximum use of the company's personnel and physical resources in finding solutions to customer problems. Simply knowing whom to call to obtain particular kinds of information and how to handle such customer requests as for laboratory evaluation or production assistance can be extremely valuable to the new salesman.

While these comments focus upon the unique training requirements of new recruits, there are similar problems with programs for experienced salesmen as well. As the company changes and its resources change, the sales force needs to be brought up to date on the company's capability for solving customer problems.

Work Habits and Attitudes. The area of work habits and attitudes also should receive attention in the training program. Salesmen need guide-

[10]For an example of a book on salesmanship that builds on basic concepts of communication theory, see Joseph W. Thompson, *Selling: A Behavioral Science Approach* (New York: McGraw-Hill Book Co., Inc., 1966).

lines on how to plan their time and allocate it among various parts of the job including customer contact, sales planning, sales reporting, and so on. They also need guidelines on how to allocate their time among new and old accounts according to potential, nature of the problems, and so on. Some companies go very far in this direction, actually routing their salesmen from one customer to the next and specifying the length of time to spend with an account.

In this part of the training program, the focus should probably be upon general concepts such as the importance of time management and the need for planning account strategy, with less emphasis upon the details of how much time to spend with each customer, how to fill out reports, and so on. The effective salesman will be looking for ways to improve his use of his time and his planning, but he will resist attempts to tell him exactly what to do because he knows that each situation is going to be different and require specific planning.

Training Techniques

In a formal training program, several techniques can be used to provide the salesmen with the necessary knowledge and skills. Traditional methods of training are giving way to some exciting new techniques for developing effective salesmen.

Use of Printed Materials. The basic building blocks of any formal training program are printed materials which give the salesman the knowledge he needs about the company, its products, and its markets. Printed material has several advantages including the fact that the trainee can progress through the material at his own pace, that he can use his spare time to absorb the material, and that it does not represent a major cost item. There are also advantages to standardization of these materials, assuring that all trainees have a basic block of knowledge.

Lectures. Lectures are a common device in formal training programs because they permit the presentation of complex material and the use of audiovisual aids to further understanding. Lectures can be used for such diverse topics as product knowledge and knowledge of the communication process. The most effective lectures permit some participation by the trainees, allowing them to ask questions for clarification and elaboration and otherwise involving them in the learning process.

Group Discussions and Case Studies. Group discussions are a valuable learning device where the objective is to develop understanding and sophistication in analysis, as opposed to the straightforward acquisition of factual materials. When the sales training program turns to such topics as development of sales strategy and the analysis of buying situations, the analysis of case studies and similar tools for group discussion can have several advantages. In addition to the obvious advantage of heightening the participant's interest through participation, case discussion can simulate the real world in which the salesman will be operating. Case analysis can provide a motivational stimulus for further learning and the application of conceptual materials that have been developed in the lectures and printed material that he has been exposed to. Case studies have the advantage of being relatively unstructured, the same as the selling situations he will eventually face, and permit the sharpening of analytical skills.

Tape Recordings. Related to the use of case studies is the use of tape-recorded sales interviews. There are several possibilities here, including (1) a buyer talking to a salesman about his problems, (2) a salesman making his presentation, and (3) a buyer and a salesman interacting. Tape recordings have the merit of presenting aural (verbal) stimuli in the manner of an actual sales situation, while case studies are abstracted data which are assimilated through reading and in this sense do not simulate the real-world situation as well. One of the best uses of tape-recorded interviews is in connection with conceptual materials relating to the analysis of buyers' comments. This is an excellent way to develop the salesman's listening ability. For example, one company[11] gives its salesmen conceptual materials concerning the analysis of customer needs. Having been told that a presentation cannot be made until three sets of needs have been identified (personal, organizational, and product needs, in this example), the sales trainee is then asked to analyze tape-recorded sales interviews. He listens to the tape recording while following some printed guidelines. At key points in the interview, the trainee stops the tape recording and answers questions such as: Which needs have been presented by the prospect? What mistakes has the salesman made? What additional information does the salesman need before he can make his presentation? The printed guide book also contains answers to these questions to help the salesman learn while he is listening to the interview.

Role Playing. Role playing is now an accepted technique in many sales training programs. In the typical use of role playing, the trainee will interact with another person who assumes the role of buyer and tries to imitate the behavior of a typical buyer. Obviously, the objective of role playing is to simulate the interaction situation which the salesman will be facing with prospects. Role playing is most effective where the person playing the buyer's role is experienced and trained for this

[11]See the "Emery Air Freight Corporation" case in Davis and Webster, *op cit.*, pp. 507–18.

function. Otherwise, the role playing can become a kind of game and deteriorate into a play session rather than a training session.

Another valuable use for role playing is to ask the salesman to play the role of buyer. This sitting-on-the-other-side-of-the-desk can help to develop an understanding of the dyadic interaction and may be one way to develop empathic ability. It is well known that understanding of the position of the "other" person in any situation can be enhanced by asking the actor to play the other person's role. This technique has been used in such diverse situations as psychiatric counseling and the training of labor negotiators.

Videotape Recordings. One of the more recent devices developed for use in sales training is the videotape recorder. Many companies are currently experimenting with this technology; there is evidence of eventual widespread use. Videotape permits the use of television equipment to capture both the words and the actions of the actor. It can be used to record an individual's presentation (similar to practicing in front of a mirror) or to record role-playing sessions, or to provide an example of an interaction which the trainees are to analyze.

The impact of viewing oneself on a television screen is great. Most people have heard their own voices on a tape recording and remember how different they sounded from what they had expected. The image of oneself on television is even more dramatic and has the major benefit (sometimes a bit disturbing) of permitting an objective look at one's actions and mannerisms. It is hard to capture in words the impact of this experience, but it does seem to have real value in a sales training program. Because the salesman's actions will be effective or ineffective depending upon their impact upon the prospect, it makes sense that some knowledge of how he comes across can be valuable to the salesman as a learning experience.

A more straightforward use of videotape recordings is to show examples of sales interviews involving professional trainers who play the roles of buyers and salesmen. These interviews can be analyzed by the trainees as examples of good and bad selling techniques. In this use, the videotape is being used like a moving picture film, but it can be made with considerably less expense and fewer production problems.

Programmed Instruction. Another relatively recent development in sales training techniques is the use of programmed instruction. A "program" is defined as a carefully prepared sequence of items (called "steps" or "frames") presented to the trainee, each containing new information or a modified presentation of old information. After each frame, the trainee is required to make a response and he is told whether his response is right or wrong before proceeding to the next step. If the answer is wrong, the student is exposed to the information again (in a modified form, perhaps) and is then asked another question. The answer must be right before the trainee proceeds to new information.

The major advantages of programmed instruction are that it permits immediate feedback to reinforce learning and that it is flexible and can be geared to the ability and speed of learning of that particular trainee. There are several forms of programmed instruction, some of which require special equipment ("teaching machines") and some of which use simple printed materials in book form.

Programmed instruction's value is obviously limited to the teaching of factual and conceptual knowledge, although this may be an important building block in the development of communication skills. The program using the tape recordings, mentioned above, also involved the use of programmed instruction that the company had developed specifically for training its own salesmen. (It is possible to buy standard programs and to hire companies to develop programmed instruction materials for a specific company's problems.) These materials are expensive, but they can be reasonably economical in programs involving large numbers of trainees. Their greater effectiveness in many cases has more than justified their additional expense.

Field Experience

Before the sales trainee is "turned loose" on his own customers, he may spend several days or weeks in the field with an experienced sales man or sales manager. The key element in this part of the training program is the "joint call" in which both trainer and trainee are present in the sales interview. Either the trainee watches the experienced salesman or the trainer watches the trainee and provides a subsequent evaluation of his performance.

The joint call is often misused as a training device because of three difficulties. First, the experienced salesman often relies upon the "watch me, learn what I do, and do like I do" approach. There are several fallacies in this approach, including the basic fact that the salesman himself is not sure of what he is doing and is unable to define it. (There is an analogy to the difficulty of trying to explain how to ride a bicycle.) Another fallacy is that what works for one salesman is unlikely to work for another, given differences in their abilities, characteristics, strengths and weaknesses, and experiences. Second, this approach is often misused by the experienced man "taking over" the sales interview whenever it appears that the trainee is having difficulty. This significantly reduces the opportunity for the trainee to learn from the experience because the experience is no longer his, since he is not sure what the salesman is doing; and there is always the moot question whether the trainee might not have done better than the trainer. The third difficulty in using this approach is that it is often impossible for the trainee to be objective in evaluating his performance. He will be hard pressed to describe exactly what happens in that sales interview unless he has been prepared with the necessary conceptual knowledge to be objective about the experience and to organize the data at his disposal.

Supervisor's Role in Training

The preceding discussion of supervision emphasized the "continuous training" aspects of the field sales manager's supervisory responsibility. Field experience is not just a formal part of the training program that ends when the salesman is assigned his own accounts and leaves the formal training program. Rather, continual learning on the job should be the basic objective of the supervisor's relationships with his men, especially on those days when he travels with them. The emphasis should be upon continued learning, not upon criticism and evaluation, although the latter definitely has its place.

If the sales supervisor is to have an active role, either in the final stages of the training program or in the sense of continual training, he needs to be prepared for that responsibility. Certainly a successful selling career is not enough. There is a tremendous difference between the ability to do something and the ability to teach it. The skills of the teacher-trainer involve the ability to be objective about and to analyze the skills required for effective selling, and the ability to communicate that understanding to the trainee.

Because training requires unique skills and is a major responsibility, most companies centralize training program activity at the corporate or divisional level, with a staff of trained specialists assigned to it. This approach can be justified in companies with more than occasional training needs. If training is left at the local sales office level, some other responsibility—such as supervision or planning or key account strategy —must be sacrificed by the sales manager and there are major costs in this solution to the training problem. At later stages, however, it may be necessary to move the trainee into the field for the final steps in formal training, to get him "out where the action is" and begin to immerse him in the real-world, daily problems of the selling organization.

In considering the role of the field supervisor in training, it is well to make sure that the trainer himself has been trained for his responsibilities. If the supervisor is an ineffective trainer, chances are he has not been prepared for his training role.

Continuing Formal Training

In most companies, there is a continuing need for formal training. This function is often combined with sales meetings, either on an annual or semi-annual basis, to update the knowledge and skills of the salesmen as required. New products are the most common reason for a formal training session for the experienced salesman. Changes in forecasting methods, quota-setting procedures, sales reporting, or other policy and procedural matters can also create a need for formal training sessions. Changes in market and competitive conditions are also a common reason for a formal session.

Most good salesmen value highly the opportunity to learn, to develop their analytical skills, and to take time from the job for intellectual refreshment. A group of experienced salesmen can gain valuable insight into their daily activities as the result of discussing a sales strategy case. It gives them the chance to think objectively about the things they are doing on a day-to-day basis largely by force of habit. It can provide them with new concepts to help analyze the situations they are confronting. And formal training can give a significant boost to the morale of the field sales organization.

In these few pages, it has not been possible to do more than highlight some of the major issues and concepts in sales training. There is a very broad literature on the subject of sales training that should be consulted if there is need for more detailed information.[12]

MANPOWER DEVELOPMENT PROGRAM

Recruitment, selection, and training are three major steps forward in a manpower development program. But assigning trained salesmen to the field and preparing field sales managers for their developmental responsibilities do not complete the task of developing effective salesmen. The manpower in the field must be cultivated and refined and kept challenged and growing. Without challenge and continued personal development, the best salesmen will eventually leave the organization. Effective salesmen can be made more effective; there is a need to continue to develop the ability of the organization to cope with change and accept new responsibilities; and provision must be made for a stream of sales management talent to grow out of the sales force.

[12]Suggested references on sales training include Sections 10 and 11 of *Marketing Handbook* (New York: Ronald Press Company, 1965); Chap. 9 of Davis and Webster, *op cit.*; Part 6 of Albert Newgarden (ed.), *The Field Sales Manager* (New York: American Management Association, 1960); and W. J. Stanton and R. H. Buskirk, *Management of the Sales Force* (3rd ed.; Homewood, Ill.: Richard D. Irwin, Inc., 1969).

Concept of Career Path

The concept of a "career path" is a planned series of steps for professional advancement and growth within the organization. Along with these steps, or organization positions, there must be a set of policies and criteria for evaluating performance and moving individuals along the path from one position to the next. Basic to planning the career path is an audit of the existing manpower and problems in present policies and organization.[13]

Benefits. The career path concept involves three basic elements that can avoid several common problems in developing effective sales manpower. First, it provides for continuous review of an individual's performance and advancement when certain criteria are met. Thus, the dangers of outstanding people being frustrated by lack of advancement are reduced and the result should be less turnover, especially among qualified people. At the same time, unqualified persons are identified earlier, enabling management to take steps to minimize damage to the company and the individual. Second, it assures the planned availability of manpower as necessary, given the company's marketing and marketing communication plans. Third, it introduces the notion of a "dual path" into the sales organization.

Dual Paths. The "dual path" involves two career paths—one for professional sales talent and one for managerial talent. The traditional sales organization has management responsibility as a reward for a successful selling career. As noted earlier, the two responsibilities require different interests and motivations and one of the major reasons for the poor quality of field sales managers can be traced to this traditional assumption. There is no reason why a management position must be the only available organizational reward for superior selling performance. Why not create a professional track for the professional salesman, with appropriate financial payoffs and organizational status? Several companies have adopted this strategy and more are following.

Figure 14-1 shows one company's strategy for implementing the concept of the dual career path. In this new organization, it became possible to reward the successful salesman whose aptitudes were more in the selling area than in management with the position of Account Manager, which involved responsibility for a few major retail accounts and working at management levels of the customer organization where planning and strategy are important issues. Within each job title, the levels (I and II) did not represent differences in job responsibility but in the compensa-

[13]Andrall E. Pearson, "Sales Power Through Planned Careers," *Harvard Business Review*, 44 (January–February, 1966), pp. 105–16.

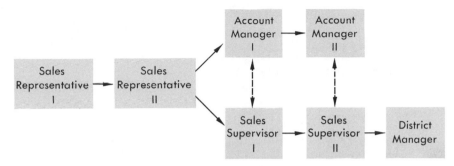

Fig. 14–1. An example of a dual career path.

tion and recognition which each level entailed. Furthermore, it was possible for a man to shift from one career path onto the other if he decided that he preferred, for example, to return to professional selling rather than to continue along the field management career path. The creation of Sales Supervisor positions in this organization also permitted men with management potential to gain initial supervisory experience earlier. In the old sales organization, Account Manager had been the only step between Sales Representative and District Manager.

Up or Out. A key element of the career path concept is an "up or out" policy at the early levels of selling responsibility. Either a man is qualified for higher-level sales responsibilities or for management position or he is not allowed to continue in the organization. (This policy, it should be emphasized, applies only to the sales representative positions.) This policy prohibits bottlenecks from developing in the career path and guarantees that the qualified individual will be identified and rewarded early.

Management by Objectives

The concept of "management by objectives" is not peculiar to sales force management, but it does have applicability here. The major notion of this concept is that the person being managed is consulted about his own desires and objectives and these become an integral part of the company's planning and objective-setting activities. On an annual or semi-annual basis, each supervisor would sit down with his subordinate and ask him what he hoped to accomplish in the coming period. This might be as specific as the number of new accounts to be developed, an increase in sales volume, or improvements in relationships and results with specific customers. It might also involve the individual's plans for self-development, such as attending a course at a nearby college or completing a phase in the company's training program.

The supervisor's role in the objective-setting process is not a passive one, however. He must assume responsibility for integrating the individual's goals with the company's objectives for the coming period, as established by management. He must also help the salesman to set realistic objectives for himself, objectives that represent sufficient challenge but that have a high probability of accomplishment. He must "tune" the salesman to the needs of the company and to his own abilities. Thus, the sales manager might suggest to the salesman that he should raise his sights slightly, showing confidence in the ability of the man to accomplish a higher goal and at the same time moving individual aspirations toward a level consistent with the firm's objectives.

It is essential that the salesman accept the objectives which are established in this procedure, however, and the supervisor must be careful not to set goals which the salesman no longer regards as his own. These objectives become the standards against which the individual will be evaluated and it is therefore essential that he accept them as reasonable criteria. Otherwise, the objectives lose their incentive value and, at the end of the period, the salesman will feel that he has been treated unfairly.

Performance Appraisal

Management by objectives is one approach to the problem of performance appraisal. In sales organizations, the salesman can be assured of some feedback on his sales performance. He will know how much he has sold and how that compares with various sales volume objectives that were established (probably in the form of quotas) at the beginning of the period. In this sense, the salesman's position is characterized by better feedback on performance than many other white-collar jobs. However, seldom is feedback on sales volume sufficient information for the salesman to evaluate his accomplishment.

There are many standards for evaluating the salesman other than the simple one of sales volume. It has often been noted that the salesman may actually have relatively little control over the amount of sales volume generated in a specific operating period. Personal development objectives may be equally or more important, both for the salesman himself and for the organization. Work habits and job attitudes should be periodically assessed. The salesman's responsibility for generating market information should be a part of the evaluation procedure as should the nature of his relationships with specific key customers, with his manager, and with other salesmen.

Every individual has a need for periodic feedback on his performance, to assess his own professional development, to provide recognition of past accomplishments, and to help him determine the extent to which he is achieving his personal objectives and fulfilling his aspirations. Every company has a major responsibility to its employees in this respect and, despite the availability of sales results, salesmen are no exception. The job description plays a key role in the evaluation process for it provides the standards against which the salesman should be evaluated. It should be remembered, however, that the salesman's performance will be a reflection not only of his effort and ability but also of the quality of his supervision, his territory, and the extent to which his efforts have been supported by the company's service and marketing program.

To prepare himself for the interview with the salesman, the sales manager should have available not only a record of the salesman's sales volume but such other records as provided by the sales reports and call reports required of the salesman. In setting objectives for the coming period, the manager reviews the salesman's accomplishments in the current period with him, using specific data wherever possible. This emphasis upon accurate and factual information is important, for it minimizes the possibility of argument about what was accomplished and what was expected. Care should be taken in planning the manpower development program to insure that sufficient data will be generated through the salesman's own reporting and through analysis of sales results, as well as in the documentaton of the objective-setting session, to insure the availability of adequate information for the manager.

Training for Management

Every complete manpower development program must make specific provision for the development of potential management talent within the organization. Like salesmen, managers are made, not born. Good management does not just happen in an organization, either. Specific programs must be developed to identify and nurture management potential. This can begin with the recruiting program in which some evidence of management potential may be one of the "man specifications" for the job. In setting objectives with his salesmen, the manager should help them to carefully evaluate their interest in, and potential for, managerial responsibility.

Persons identified as having management potential should be given maximum opportunity to test and develop that ability. One of the best ways to begin this process is for the local manager to ask the salesmen with potential to help him tackle certain significant management problems such as planning key account strategy, or developing the marketing plan for the coming period, or reviewing the company's customer service program. These assignments can help measure such abilities as analysis and planning. Another set of managerial abilities, those involving human relations, can likewise be tested by observing the salesman in his relationships with other salesmen, especially new salesmen whom he may be asked to help.

Some companies whet the appetite of their salesmen for possible managerial responsibilities by exposing them to formal training sessions in which problems of supervision and management are among the topics covered. This can help the men to better understand their manager's problems, to understand the requirements for effective management, and to assess their own ability and interest in such a position. It can also provide the beginnings of the body of knowledge the man will need if and when he is promoted to a position of management responsibility.

When a salesman is finally promoted to a managerial position, the worst thing that can happen to him or the company is to put him into the new position without formal training for that responsibility. Under those circumstances he is almost certain to continue to behave like a salesman and to suffer from the frustration of recognizing many new problems but having virtually no idea of how to cope with them. Management must realize that the requirements for effective field sales management are fundamentally different from those for effective selling. Steps must be taken to make sure that the sales manager has the necessary knowledge, skills, and attitudes for his job. The major job of the field sales manager is not selling; it is to develop effective salesmen.

SUMMARY

The salesmen are the key resource in most companies' marketing communication programs. The salesman is a problem solver and he must be trained with the right knowledge, skills, and attitudes to develop effective communication with his customers. The key skills of the salesman are the ability to listen and to analyze the data obtained through feedback in his interactions with customers to help them identify and solve their problems.

There are significant payoffs for the company that takes the time and effort to plan a manpower development program that begins with a description of the role of the salesman in the marketing communication strategy and follows through with programs for recruiting, selecting, training, supervising, and evaluating salesmen. The career path is a central concept in the manpower development program because it stresses the need for careful attention to the human resources of the organization and it points toward the critical distinction between the profession of selling and the profession of management.

The major task of field sales management is to develop effective salesmen, not to sell. The field sales manager is charged with responsibility for developing human resources for the future and for implementing the marketing communication strategy by assuring that the organization is able to deliver effective messages to the target audience in coordination with all other elements of the marketing communication program. The marketing staff can plan the strategy but it is line management in the field that has to get the job done through people—the salesmen.

15

Message Testing

In this chapter, emphasis is once more on the development of messages for mass communication, especially advertising. Because the message or messages chosen will be delivered thousands or even millions of times, small differences in message effectiveness can result in major differences in the achievement of marketing communication objectives. Funds spent wisely to test alternative message strategies can account for significant improvement in return on communication investment. Although comments in this chapter will concentrate on testing advertising messages, it should be recognized that many of the techniques to be described and evaluated may be applied, usually with some modifications, to testing other parts of the marketing communication strategy, including package designs, sales promotional devices, and public relations campaign themes. They may also help to evaluate alternative personal selling strategies, especially where the issue is selection of a standardized ("canned") sales presentation to be used by the sales force.

WHEN TO TEST

Message testing can take several forms and can come at several stages in campaign development. Certain elements of copy such as illustrations or headlines may be tested early in the creative process. Semifinished advertisements may be tested in rough form to determine the extent to which basic appeals are communicated by the message and believed by the audience. The advertisements may actually be placed in media, but on a limited basis, and subsequent data collected to evaluate the impact of the message. Or the messages may be evaluated after they have been used on a full-scale basis. In each of these situations, the reasons for testing the message are likely to be somewhat different but the overall aim is to determine the effectiveness of the message strategy. This objective is distinct from the more general one of evaluating a complete communication program.

This discussion of message testing will concentrate on what is probably the most common form of testing, the comparative testing of two or more message strategies that have been generated by the creative process prior to full-scale implementation. Figure 15–1 shows two advertisements that were tested for relative effectiveness. This form of testing is usually called "pretesting," as opposed to "post-testing," which occurs after the messages have been run in a purchased media schedule. Post-testing of messages must be done in conjunction with measurement of the effectiveness of the media strategy and other campaign elements and is therefore discussed in a later chapter on campaign evaluation.

Message testing may involve the use of comparative measurement of one message against another or the use of absolute measures which rate the message against a preset standard. In the following comments, it is assumed that the creative process has produced at least one execution of the basic message strategy—and more likely two or three alternatives that are responsive to management's objectives and do not have obvious problems that preclude their use. The task facing management is to determine which of these approaches will have the best chance of realizing the objectives established for the marketing communication program.

NEED FOR OBJECTIVES

A clearly defined message strategy and a specific statement of campaign objectives is obviously the first and most important input to a program of message testing and evaluation. The objectives established for the overall marketing communication program will have yielded a basic statement of copy strategy concentrating on the meanings to be conveyed about the product (or service) to be advertised, as noted in Chapter 12. One of the three major functions performed by the statement of objectives, it will be recalled, is to provide standards against which to evaluate accomplishments, as well as to guide the message creation process and to coordinate the elements of the marketing communication program.

The basic question in message testing is whether the message will result in the achievement of communication objectives and, if several messages are being compared, which message has the highest probability of achieving the best response from the market. How "response" is to be defined is a complex question, as we have seen in earlier discussions of the hierarchy-of-effects hypothesis. The basic logic of the hierarchy-

**Brand new formula reduces cavities.
Kids still like the stripes.**

Now you can take the fun toothpaste seriously.

"New Super STRIPE has been shown to be an effective
decay-preventive dentifrice that can be of significant
value when used in a conscientiously applied program
of oral hygiene and regular professional care."

The Council on Dental Therapeutics · American Dental Association

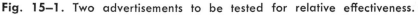

Make Super Stripe a part of your anti-cavity program · Regular dental checkups · Watch between-meal treats · Brush after meals

Fig. 15–1. Two advertisements to be tested for relative effectiveness.

(Courtesy of Lever Brothers Company; Ogilvy and Mather, Inc.)

of-effects hypothesis sees the consumer as progressing from awareness through attitude change to behavior change in response to exposure to communication. In Chapter 12, the arguments for and against this view of response to marketing communication were reviewed. The issue can be simply stated as whether the objectives of the communication program should be stated in terms of "sales" or "communication" (i.e., attitude change) objectives. This question is directly related to the measurement problem.

Sales or Communication Objectives?

Both sides of the argument can be defended. Those who prefer objectives stated in sales terms argue that the basic purpose of the firm's marketing activity is to generate the maximum level of profitable sales and that it is irresponsible to stop short of that objective in determining the criteria against which to evaluate marketing communication. Those who argue for communication objectives point out that present theory concerning how communication works and present measurement technology do not permit a precise assignment of sales results to specific communication actions. They also argue that the purpose of advertising is *not* to generate sales (which come from the combined influence of products, prices, distribution channels, and communications) but to create awareness and favorable attitudes, that is, to change predispositions, toward the company and its products.

The "Correlates-of-Effects" Hypothesis. A study by the Marketing Science Institute argued that the *ideal* measure of advertising effectiveness (in message testing) would be "the discounted present value of the difference in long-term profits which would be produced via the choice of one advertising alternative over another."[1] The authors of the report were quick to point out, however, that this ideal was unattainable with present levels of understanding and technique. They also suggested that the hierarchy-of-effects hypothesis should be replaced with what they called the "correlates-of-effects hypothesis." Because it is a moot question whether changes in attitudes *cause* or *precede* changes in behavior, they suggest that it would be sufficient to assume that changes in attitude were correlated with changes in behavior. This assumption would be sufficient to validate the use of measures of communication effects in message testing although it avoids the basic question of how communication works.[2]

[1]Homer M. Dalbey, Irwin Gross, and Yoram Wind, *Advertising Measurement and Decision Making* (Boston: Allyn & Bacon, Inc., 1968), p. 20.
[2]*Ibid.*, p. 24.

While this conclusion is less than satisfying to those who are concerned with the basic theoretical question, it does provide a pragmatic basis for proceeding with the measurement problem. A similar conclusion seems to have been reached by those who are responsible for conducting such evaluations. In a study sponsored by the American Association of Advertising Agencies (4A's), involving a survey of the research directors of the 50 advertising agencies with the highest levels of annual billings, respondents were evenly divided in their preferences for sales or communication measures. Fifty percent of the respondents agreed that sales results should be the chief criterion and 50 percent disagreed. (The question was phrased in terms of campaign results.) One respondent observed that "communications criteria beg the basic issue." The authors of this study noted that "there appears to be no universally accepted theory of how advertising works," and concluded that *"behavioral* and *attitude and opinion* measures, as predictors of future sales behavior, are the *best* measures of the *sales effectiveness* of an individual advertisement. Whether they are actually predictors of sales is a moot point."[3] [Italics in original.]

Message and Media Objectives

A distinction must be drawn between objectives established for message strategy and objectives relating to media strategy. Message strategy must be stated in terms of desired changes in individual behavior and response. Media objectives relate to the number of times the message is to be delivered (frequency and number of receivers) and the characteristics of the audience to be reached. Message objectives relate to the effectiveness of a single message delivered to a single receiver. The relevant measures of message effectiveness then are those relating to changes in the individual's mental state or behavior pattern. Thus, probability of purchase would be a meaningful measure of individual response to message exposure, but total sales volume would not be, because it would reflect the influence of both media and message strategies.

There are some important interactions between message strategy and media strategy. Reaction to a message is a function of the context in which it is delivered. Some media present unique problems of message design and execution and some messages require specific media for their execution. The mechanical features of the media present particular requirements for the message strategy. A given message will be more or

[3]Lee Adler, Allan Greenberg, and D. B. Lucas, "What Big Agency Men Think of Copy Testing Methods," *Journal of Marketing Research,* 2 (November 1965), pp. 339–45.

less effective depending upon the specific media vehicle that is used to deliver it. Advertising copy designed for *The New Yorker* magazine would probably be less effective in *Life* magazine, and vice versa, because of the mood of the magazine as well as differences in the characteristics of the audiences of the two magazines.

Nonetheless, it is possible to isolate message effects and media effects and care must be taken in the development of measurement techniques not to confuse the two sets of objectives or the two effects.

A MODEL FOR MESSAGE TESTING

Conceptualization of the measurement problem must begin by considering the factors or stages by which a message can have an "effect." Since techniques for message testing will measure one or more elements of effects of, or response to, the message being tested, it is necessary to be as explicit about those effects as possible in planning the measurement. The question to consider is: "How does an advertisement have an effect?"

Requirements for Message Effect

The basic model of the communication process developed in earlier chapters suggests one way of answering this question. If a message is to have an effect on an individual, he must: (1) be exposed to the message; (2) pay attention to the message; (3) perceive its contents (i.e., assign meaning to it); (4) remember it until it can be acted upon; and (5) act upon the message—i.e., respond to it in some overt way. These stages may be labeled *exposure, attention, perception, retention,* and *response.*

Exposure is independent of the content of the message but is instead a function of the media strategy. Exposure to a specific message requires that the medium be distributed to the individual, that the individual be exposed to the media vehicle in which the message appears—the issue of the magazine, for example—and that he be exposed to the message itself—e.g., the specific page on which the advertisement appears. Thus, exposure to the media vehicle and to the message itself are necessary preconditions to attention. On the other hand, attention is *not* assured even if there is exposure. In some kinds of message testing, one of the first problems is to determine whether the individual has been exposed to the media vehicle in which the message being tested appeared. This presents a major problem of measurement because of the high probability of false reporting (both by those who did see the media vehicle and those who did not).

Alternative Models. There are several alternative ways of viewing the hierarchy of effects necessary for advertising to have an influence. The Advertising Research Foundation's Audience Concepts Committee suggested a seven-step hierarchy:[4]

1. Media distribution
2. Exposure to the advertising medium or vehicle
3. Exposure to the particular advertisment
4. Perception of the advertisement
5. Recall of the advertisement
6. Communication
7. Persuasion.

Others have suggested a five-step sequence:

1. Media distribution
2. Exposure to the advertising vehicle
3. Exposure to the particular advertisement
4. Perception of the advertisement
5. Advertising influence.

Those who proposed this five-state model argued that "the fifth category, advertising influence, is a broad one which cannot be subdivided into smaller stages until more is known about the process of influence."[5] Our earlier review of the communication process has suggested that enough is, in fact, known about the process to divide it into attention, perception, retention, and response as suggested above.

What to Measure? Techniques for the evaluation of message effectiveness can focus upon one or more of the basic steps in the sequence, from attention through to response. The technique may measure the extent to which the message gains attention, how it is perceived, its memorability, or the actual response it produces. Response can be measured at several levels from the physiological or autonomic level of behavior through changes in verbal behavior (opinions) and changes in attitudes to changes in overt purchasing behavior. A message that is effective at one level, say attention, may be very ineffective at another level such as overt behavior change. Because measurement techniques do tend to measure only one level of effect, care must be taken to assure that the effects obtained are consistent with the objectives of the communication program. To find that an advertisement does attract a large amount of attention, for example, may not help much in evaluation of the message's ability to increase sales volume.

[4]Advertising Research Foundation, *Toward Better Media Comparisons* (New York: The Foundation, 1961).

[5]Edwin B. Parker, Stewart A. Smith, and John Scott Davenport, "Advertising Theory and Measures of Perception," *Journal of Advertising Research,* 3 (December 1963), pp. 40–43.

The Ideal Measurement Procedure

The Marketing Science Institute study referred to earlier put forth an "idealized measurement procedure" (IMP) which, although an unattainable ideal, does provide a set of criteria against which to evaluate any operational procedure. The seven basic categories in which measurement criteria were stated are these:

1. Scope of the advertising being measured
2. Responses measured
3. Conditions of exposure
4. Condition of measurements
5. Sampling procedure
6. Type of comparison
7. Data handling

According to their analysis, in these categories the IMP would have the following attributes. First, it would evaluate many insertions of the messages being tested in all relevant media for the planned campaign. Second, it would use actual purchase behavior, over time, as the criterion response. Third, respondents would be exposed to the message in a natural environment (such as the home) and in a natural advertising context (such as a regular issue of a magazine or a television program). Fourth, measurements would be obtained by a data collection procedure that was least likely to have an influence upon the response being measured, such as the unobtrusive observation of purchasing behavior or an audit of changes in the pantry stock in the respondent's home. Fifth, the sample would be selected on a probability basis with no restrictions, would be drawn from a universe of all individual purchase units (individuals or families in the potential market), and would be large enough to be representative and meet statistical standards of reliability. Sixth, it would compare alternative advertisements or campaigns against one another on a relative basis rather than against some arbitrary absolute standard. Finally, there would be no weighting of the data to correct for problems in data collection or analysis procedures.[6] Figure 15-2 reproduces a chart from the Marketing Science Institute study and compares several syndicated and nonsyndicated research techniques against these ideal criteria of the IMP.

The concept of the idealized measurement procedure does provide a good set of criteria against which to evaluate specific measurement techniques. It also is useful for identifying the specific aspects of a measurement technique that should receive attention in any attempt to analyze and evaluate alternative measurement procedures. Finally, the IMP concept provides a framework within which it is possible to define several basic issues in the measurement of message effects.

[6]Dalbey et al., op. cit., pp. 38–45.

CENTRAL ISSUES IN MESSAGE TESTING

There are several key issues in message testing. It will be most efficient to discuss them before turning to an evaluation of specific measurement techniques. Each of these issues is involved in the evaluation of each of the techniques and some redundancy can be avoided by considering the issues independently of the techniques.

The issues to be discussed are specific to message testing as opposed to more general issues of research. Referring back to IMP, it will be seen that the fifth and seventh attributes (sampling and data handling) are problems in any form of survey research and are therefore not discussed further at this time.

Natural vs. Forced Exposure

Some message-testing techniques expose the individual to the message under natural conditions, as when the test commercial is sent into a home along with regular television programming. Other techniques use artificial exposure conditions and force all members in the audience to pay attention, as when television commercials are tested in a theatre. There are several ways to distinguish between conditions of natural and forced exposure. The one used here defines forced exposure as any situation in which the respondent is aware that he is part of the test. Both methods have advantages and disadvantages.

Natural exposure has the obvious advantage of duplicating more closely the conditions under which the message must eventually be effective. In particular, natural exposure permits a testing of the ability of the message to attract attention whereas forced exposure requires the individual to pay attention. Conditions of forced exposure are typically also characterized by the opportunity for other people (either the interviewer or other respondents) to influence the individual's response to the message, as when the respondent is shown an ad and then asked to answer several questions about it.

Forced exposure situations, especially those that are conducted in a laboratory, permit greater control over exposure, and this has several advantages. As noted earlier, field methods with natural exposure require that the fact of exposure be established before the consequences of the message can be assessed. Natural exposure means that both media and message effects must be assessed. The possibilities for error under such conditions are great. Forced exposure can also yield more efficient research procedures because all of those in the sample can provide data on response to the message. Under natural exposure conditions, only a small minority of those contacted may actually qualify as having seen the ad and be able to answer questions about it.

SEVEN BASIC ATTRIBUTES OF A MEASUREMENT TECHNIQUE	IDEALIZED MEASUREMENT PROCEDURE (IMP)	SYNDICATE			
		Audience Studies Inc. (ASI)	Gallup & Robinson Magazine Impact Service (Aided Recall)	Gallup & Robinson, Inc. Total Prime Time (TPT)	Marder Ad Evaluation Program
1. Scope of the advertising being measured:					
a. Insertions	Many	One	One	One	One
b. Media	All relevant media for planned campaign	TV	Magazine	TV	Magazine
2. Response(s) measured	Natural purchase (over time)	Simulated purchase	Advertisement recall[1]	Advertisement recall[1]	Brand Awareness and Attitude
3. Conditions of exposure:					
a. Exposure environment	Natural	Theater	Natural	Natural	Natural
b. Advertising context	Natural	TV pilot programs out of context[1]	Natural	Natural	Natural
4. Condition of measurements:					
a. Method of data collection	Unobserved audit	Subject Questionnaire mechanical	Personal interview	Telephone interview	Telephone interview
b. Measurement environment	Natural	Awareness of test	Awareness of advertisement test	Awareness of advertisement test	Awareness of test
5. Sampling procedure:					
a. Sample element	Individual purchase unit	Individual	Individual	Individual	Individual
b. Restrictions	None	Geographic[2] Participation[3] Other[1]	Participation[2]	Geographic[2] Media[3] Participation[1]	Geographic[1] Media[2] Participation[3]
c. Method	Probability	Nonprobability[5] Quota	Nonprobability[3]	Probability	Probability
d. Size	Optional[1]	Batch (250)	Standard (400)	Standard (2,800)	Standard (4,800)
6. Type of comparison	Alternative advertisement or campaign	Norm or alternative advertisement	Norm or alternative advertisement	Norm or alternative advertisement	Alternative advertisement or campaign, and control
7. Data Handling	Unweighted	Unweighted	Weighted	Unweighted	Unweighted
	[1]Large enough so that similar results would be obtained if test were repeated	[1]In context for spot commercials seen between programs [2]Los Angeles area [3]Not all who are approached participate [4]People in high traffic centers, such as shopping centers [5]Controlled demographically	[1]Also idea recall and buying attitude [2]Not all who are contacted participate [3]Selected on a systematic basis	[1]Also idea recall and buying attitude [2]Philadelphia area [3]Viewers of program in which advertisement is placed [4]Not all who are contacted participate	[1]Subscribers in New York, Chicago, Philadelphia [2]*Saturday Evening Post* subscribers [3]Not all who are contacted participate

Fig. 15–2. Comparisons of idealized measurement procedure with various advertising measurement techniques. (Source: Homer M. Dalbey, Irwin Gross, and Yoram Wind, *Advertising Management and Decision Making*, pp. 37–38.

EXAMPLES OF MEASUREMENT TECHNIQUES

Milwaukee Advertising Laboratory	Schwerin Standard TV Testing Service	Starch Readership Service	NONSYNDICATED			
			Market Test	On-air TV Test	Psychogalvanometer Test	Split Run Test
any	One	One	One	One	One	Usually one
V, newspaper, unday upplement	TV	Magazine	All relevant for planned campaign	TV	All relevant for planned campaign	Newspaper or Magazine or Sunday supplement
laimed urchase over time)	Simulated purchase	Advertisement recall	Usually purchase related (over time)	Brand Preference	Physiological response[1]	Choice of several types—sales, inquiries, awareness, etc.
Natural	Theater	Natural	Natural	Natural	Laboratory	Natural
Natural	TV pilot programs	Natural	Natural	Natural	Often out of context	Natural
Subject diary	Subject Questionnaire	Personal interview	Audit or diary	Telephone interview	Mechanical recording	Personal interview or subject response
Awareness of test	Awareness of test	Awareness of advertisement test	Natural	Awareness of test	Laboratory	Awareness of test
Family	Individual	Individual	Reselling Organization (store)	Individual	Individual	Individual or family
Geographic[1] Media[2] Participation[?]	Geographic Participation[2]	Media[1] Participation[2]	Geographic[1] Participation[2]	Geographic[1] Media[2] Participation[3]	Participation[2]	Media[1] Participation[2]
Nonprobability[1]	Probability	Nonprobability[3]	Probability	Probability	Nonprobability[3]	Probability
Standard (1,500)[3]	Batch (300 to 700)[3]	Standard (200-300)	Optional	Optional	Optional	Optional
Alternative advertisement or campaign, and control	Norm or alternative advertisement	Norm or alternative advertisement	Goal	Norm	Alternative advertisement	Alternative advertisement or control
Unweighted	Weighted	Unweighted	Unweighted	Unweighted	Unweighted	Unweighted
Milwaukee; [2]Milwaukee Journal subscribers; Limited percent agree to join panel; Panel controlled demographically; Another 750 family panel is available	[1]Usually New York or Chicago, occasionally other cities; [2]Not all who are contacted participate; [3]Average audience in N.Y.C. is 300; in Chicago, 600 to 700	[1]Readers of vehicle in which advertisement is run; [2]Not all who are contacted participate; [3]Selection based on a quota	[1]Generally limited to relatively few markets; [2]Stores willing to participate usually limited	[1]Generally limited to relatively few markets; [2]Viewers of the show in which advertisement is placed; [3]Not all who are contacted participate	[1]Galvanic skin response; [2]Generally done in a laboratory which often deters participants; [3]Usually	[1]Readers of vehicle in which split is run; [2]Not all who are contacted participate

In the 4A's study of research directors' opinions, 21 of the 40 respondents favored natural exposure methods. Ten favored forced exposure, because it provided more data from a smaller sample at a lower cost with a better ability to control exposure. Nine of the respondents stated no preference.[7]

Influence of Context

Related to the issue of forced and natural exposure conditions is the influence of the context within which the message is presented.

While most natural exposure situations occur in the context of the home or the office, forced exposure can occur either in a laboratory or in a more natural setting. It is for this reason that a distinction has been made between the influence of context and the influence of exposure conditions.

There can be no doubt that context does influence response. In Chapter 8, research findings relating to the influence of attitudes toward communicators were reviewed and the influence of source credibility was identified as one of the basic determinants of response to communication. The ways in which qualitative media values can enhance the advertising message will be considered in Chapter 18.

In addition to influencing the credibility of the communication, media can also influence the ability and the willingness of the individual to pay attention to and to perceive the message. One author reported finding that "clear and significant differences were observed in preferences for identical advertisements when, by the experimental design, the only source of these differences was the medium environment in which the advertisements were exposed . . ."[8] The respondent may be influenced by the extent to which the message seems to "fit in" with other elements, both advertising and editorial, of the media vehicle. Reading and viewing habits may be quite different for different magazines or for daytime vs. nighttime television, for example. The respondent may be much more likely to report seeing an advertisement in a particular magazine (independent of the actual exposure) because of preference and respect for that magazine. An objective look at your own behavior is likely to reveal that you read some magazines very carefully, both advertisements and editorial content, while others are only scanned.

In laboratory tests—such as theatre tests of television commercials or trailers in supermarket parking lots or small group discussions—the respondent is going to be influenced by the context in which he or she

[7]Adler *et al.*, *op. cit.*

[8]Richard H. Ostheimer, "Comparing the Influence of Media Context on Advertising," in *1965 Proceedings*, Business and Economic Statistics Section, American Statistical Association, pp. 236–42 at p. 242.

views the ads. Seeing television commercials on a large movie screen or looking at enlarged versions of print advertisements on hardboard backings is quite different from viewing them in one's home. Reactions under these conditions are likely to be quite different from response in the natural context of the home.

Time Between Exposure and Measurement

Another dimension to the measurement problem is the time lag between exposure to the message and the measurement of response. In the situation of forced exposure, it is common for the measurement to occur immediately after exposure, although there may also be a carefully planned time lapse between exposure and measurement or between subsequent measurements. When exposure occurs under natural conditions, there is likely to be a wider range of possible lags between exposure and measurement.

Measurement immediately after exposure has the major advantage of ruling out the subsequent interference of competing messages over which the researcher may have little or no control. It also permits specific reactions to the messages being tested and a more detailed commentary on message elements by the respondent. However, the reaction immediately after exposure is likely to be different from the reaction after the typical lag between a consumer's exposure to the message and action in response to that message.

If a "reasonable" time lag is allowed to occur between message exposure and measurement of effect, then the situation more closely parallels the "typical" conditions under which advertising must be effective. This consideration may be important in that some ads will be more effective over time and will be better retained than others. As the time between exposure and measurement increases, however, the probability increases that the measurements will be contaminated by the influence of other messages.

Conditions of natural exposure heighten the problem because under natural exposure the respondents are likely to have been exposed to the message at different points in time. Assume that two test messages are inserted in a test edition of a magazine (a "split run" test) which is mailed on a Thursday. Some respondents may have received the magazine on Friday while others had to wait until Saturday or even Monday because of differences in mail service within the test area. Once the magazine was received by the household, it may have been read immediately or it may have lain on the coffee table for several days before anyone in the family looked at it. Variability in conditions of exposure may combine with normal sampling error to swamp any differences attributable to the messages.

The question of time between exposure and measurement is most serious for recall measures, those which ask the respondent to recall the advertisement and its specific elements with or without clues provided by the researcher. It is also an issue in measures of attitude change and in measures of purchase behavior. With purchase behavior, the customary planning period surrounding the purchase must also be considered. The longer the planning period and the longer the lag between exposure to messages and actual purchase behavior, the more difficult it will be to use purchase behavior as a measure of message effectiveness. For this reason, purchase measures of message effects are most useful with frequently purchased, relatively low-value consumer products. For consumer durables and industrial products, measures of changes in levels of awareness and attitudes may be preferred.

Kind of Behavior

In one sense, all measures of message effectiveness depend upon some kind of respondent behavior, even if it is only verbal behavior in the form of expressing opinions in response to the interviewer's questions. The distinction between opinions and attitudes becomes important in understanding this issue. If the respondent perceives that the interviewer is an agent for the advertiser and if he is motivated by a desire to be pleasant and helpful, then he may express opinions which are exaggerations of his actual attitudes toward the company and its products. Attitudes are (true) tendencies to act toward specific objects. Attitudes cannot be measured directly but must be inferred from opinions or overt behavior.

Differences between opinions and attitudes may be greatest in those situations where purchase motivation is complex (as in the case of cosmetics or automobiles) or where social norms and values are important in the purchase and use of the product (liquor or hygiene products). There are many situations in which the respondent is simply unable to be articulate about his basic attitudes.

Because of the difficulty of inferring attitudes from opinions, and due to the fact that attitude measurement typically depends upon the expression of opinions, researchers may attempt to measure actual behavior rather than verbal behavior. Here there are two classes of alternatives: the researcher may try to measure overt, physical behavior relating to purchase or he may try to measure physiological responses to messages.

Physiological measures offer the major advantage that the respondent is unable to control them. These are what the psychologist calls "autonomic" responses, responses that occur independent of the volition of the respondent. These include the galvanic skin response (GSR, which

measures changes in the electrical conductivity of the skin), pupil dilation, and salivation. Because of their involuntary nature, these measures
are "unbiased" responses to visual and aural stimuli. Unfortunately, there
is no theory upon which to draw inferences about the relationship
between these physiological responses and the ultimate objectives of
influencing predispositions and purchase behavior. Stated differently,
physiological responses are not valid measures of marketing communication effectiveness in the *strict* sense of "validity"—the extent to which a
test measures what it purports to measure. Despite this theoretical weakness, however, such measures are occasionally used and will be
described in the following section.

In addition to verbal behavior and physiological responses, there is
also overt or actual behavior that can be measured. The most common
form of overt behavior measurement in message testing is purchase
behavior, although one can also think of other forms of behavior that
would be of interest such as communication behavior (word-of-mouth)
and consumption behavior. Number of units purchased, time and frequency of purchase, and changes in buyer's inventory level can all be
classified as measures of overt behavior. These measures can be obtained
by observing consumer behavior in the retail store (and then questioning about message exposure), by tracking changes in consumer panel
data, and by actual auditing of the household's pantry shelf inventory.
Notice that these are all classified as *behavioral* measures and are distinguished from sales measures such as provided by retail store sales data,
shipments, or data on resellers' inventory changes, which are all aggregate measures and do not permit inferences about changes in individual
behavior in response to messages.

Attitudes Toward Ads or Products

Message-testing techniques can be classified according to whether
they measure the individual's response to the advertising as advertising
or whether they measure changes in the individual's attitudes toward the
advertiser and the advertised products. This distinction is often overlooked, although it seems to be a fairly obvious one and is definitely
important in determining the ability of the measurement technique to
predict sales responses to advertising. Ultimately, the objective of message testing is to predict the ability of the message to generate the highest level of profitable sales. Whether the respondent *likes* the advertisement or *thinks it would persuade him to buy* may have very little to do
with the actual ability of the ad to influence sales.

Some techniques of message testing put the respondent in the position of being an expert on advertising. That is nonsensical. It may pro-

duce interesting results, but they will be of little value to management. It is important that the measurement technique attempt to determine the extent to which the message attracts attention, conveys meaning about the product, influences predispositions, is remembered, and induces buying behavior. In a focussed group interview, for example, it would be legitimate to ask the respondents to compare alternative advertisements in terms of what each said to them about the product and its use. It would not be meaningful to ask them to comment on differences in headlines or illustrations or to answer questions about which ad is "best" except in terms of what it says about the product. The consumer simply is not a good judge of the effect that an advertisement will have upon him or upon others. It is for this reason that such techniques were regarded as the least effective among all evaluation procedures by the sample of research directors in the 4A's study referred to earlier.[9]

Relationship Between Creative Process and Research Techniques

The measurement techniques used and the way in which the results of such tests are interpreted can have a subtle but significant influence on the creative process and the nature of the message alternatives generated for management's evaluation. Analysis of the creative process has stressed the importance of the preparation stage, and it has been argued that the creative person is heavily dependent upon facts and upon a clear statement of objectives. At the same time, information provided by research *can* interfere with creativity. There is thus some validity to the point of view expressed by some creative people that research is antithetical to sound creative work.

If a client insists upon a certain evaluation procedure the result over the long run can be a great deal of sameness in the advertising he gets. Perhaps the best illustration of this is the so-called "slice-of-life" television commercial. In this creative approach, a problem is presented in the form of a conversational episode, usually involving two people. Early in the conversation a problem is revealed—"Tom didn't invite me to the dance." This is followed by a tentative diagnosis of the difficulty by the "friend." "Do you suppose it's because you've got . . . bad breath!?" The friend next proposes a solution—"Here, try my (brand of mouthwash)." The next vignette shows that the problem has been solved, as in this example when the girl who formerly had the problem is now seen happily dancing with her boyfriend, and there is usually an exchange of knowing smiles or a brief remark to show that both girls understand how the advertised product solved the problem. This slice-of-life technique has several attributes which make such commercials very memora-

[9]Adler *et al., op. cit.*

ble, especially the coherency of the story and the fact that an individual exposed to the commercial is likely to be able to reconstruct most of the commercial almost verbatim. As a result, slice-of-life commercials are likely to score very high on measures of retention. Similarly, use of retention measures is likely to favor the use of slice-of-life commercials or other approaches that are inherently memorable.

At the other extreme, advertising which attempts to build imagery around the product and uses rather artistic and ambiguous stimuli is likely to score very low on such retention measures, and respondents will find it very hard to articulate the contents of the advertising even if they have been exposed to it. This does not mean that imagery advertising is less effective than factual advertising, or that slice-of-life commercials are the most effective. It simply means that research techniques must be tailored to fit the objectives of the communicator and the message strategy that has been decided upon. One agency executive has argued that measures of retention (which he calls "memorability") should be used when the advertising takes an objective or factual approach to the sale of the brand and that measures of attitude change should be used when imagery objectives are predominant and the brand is being sold on a "subjective" basis.[10]

Another way to make advertising memorable is to use gimmicks and devices which shock the reader and attract his attention. These gimmicks can create high retention scores. Respondents will remember seeing the advertisement and will be able to recall its significant components. At the same time, the advertising may not be at all effective in selling the product. Such gimmicks may lower the efficiency of advertising in terms of its marketing impact. Alfred Politz has called this "the dilemma of creative advertising."[11] The effect of feedback from evaluation procedures on the creative process must not be overlooked.

Research Methodology

As a form of research, techniques for message testing must also be evaluated in terms of their basic soundness as research. In Chapter 10 there was a discussion of the basic elements of survey research. The criteria developed there for the evaluation of survey research, including sample selection, development of the data collection instrument, and the selection, training, and supervision of interviewers, should be reviewed, for they apply with equal validity to message testing.

[10]Frank Stanton, "A State of the Art Appraisal of Advertising Research Measurements," a talk presented at the Association of National Advertisers' Fifth Advanced Advertising Management Seminar, Princeton, N.J., September 15, 1966.

[11]Alfred Politz, "The Dilemma of Creative Advertising," *Journal of Marketing*, 25 (October, 1960), pp. 1–6.

In Chapter 10, three other techniques for gathering data were also discussed—group interviews, market tests, and experimentation. These are not independent research methodologies and may be used together, as when a market test is based upon a careful experimental design for the assignment of treatments to test cities and stores.

Experimental designs are often used in message testing to control for the influence of other variables or to permit the testing of other variables as well as messages in the same research program. Each of several messages being tested could be used in two or more test cities and differences in effectiveness observed at the end of a specified period. Use of experimentation is the only way in which clear cause and effect relationships can be established and this is true whether sales or communication measures of effectiveness are used.

Small groups can be a very effective research device for message testing, especially where the objective of the test is to gain some indication about how alternative messages will be perceived and the meanings which people will ascribe to products based upon various elements of the message. While small-group interviews do not permit any statistical projection of test results, they do permit the comparison of several alternative creative approaches against a set of qualitative criteria.

These group interviews are often called "focussed" group interviews in that carefully trained interviewers work with the group to keep them focussed on specific issues of importance for the research objectives. One variation of this technique allows the advertising managers and creative people to view the group discussion through one-way mirrors. The interviewer plays a relatively inactive role in the discussion but he does have a small earphone through which he can receive questions from those who are observing the group discussion. At the right time, he can raise the question for the group's attention. Persons who have used this technique report that it is very useful in identifying possible interpretations (and misinterpretations) of advertisements and provides real and important insights into the effectiveness of the ads. Such techniques permit the use of small samples of respondents, as when only two or three groups of twelve to fifteen each are used to evaluate alternative messages.

MEASUREMENT TECHNIQUES

In the following pages, several classes of measurement techniques will be described and evaluated. One or more specific techniques within each class will be discussed in detail. The specific techniques to be discussed are in no sense a complete or balanced list and the comments to be made about a specific technique should not be interpreted as a recommendation for or against its use. The desirability of using a specific technique is very much a function of the particular measurement problem and situation. Comments of an evaluative nature about specific techniques are intended only to illustrate the kinds of conditions under which each technique or class of techniques is likely to be more or less effective.

Content Analysis and Checklists

One of the most simple methods of evaluating an advertisement is to examine its physical characteristics and to compare its attributes with a checklist of objective considerations in evaluating an advertisement. Several techniques for content analysis have been developed over the years. They are intended to measure the "readability" of the copy of the advertising and involve a tabulation of such objective characteristics as number of words, sentence length, complexity of words, and sentence construction. The Flesch Method is probably the most common form of content analysis; it evaluates a piece of copy for reading difficulty according to a formula which evaluates number of words per sentence and number of syllables per word, as well as the frequency of personal references which, it is assumed, increase reader motivation.[12]

Checklists have also been employed in content analyses as aids to an assessment of the objective characteristics of the advertisement. Such features as the relationship between illustration and copy, length of headline, number of words in copy, and basic appeals may be checked against predetermined criteria. These criteria may be specifically related to the objectives established for this particular campaign, or they may relate to more general message characteristics such as appeals, understandability, or clarity.

Content analysis has been an important tool of the communication researcher. Studies of message effects, for example, have required a very careful assessment of the emotional and rational content of messages. A scholarly approach to the objective characteristics of messages is an important scientific tool.[13]

For the marketing communication strategist attempting to test alternative messages, however, content analysis has limited value. Most significantly, the objective characteristics of the message may have little to do with the ability of the message to persuade and to generate sales volume. True content analysis is a complex procedure requiring careful training and can be useful in evaluating emotional appeals and social variables in the message. Casual content analysis, on the other hand, is

[12]Rudolf Flesch, "A New Readability Yardstick," *Journal of Applied Psychology*, 32 (June 1948), pp. 221–33.

[13]Bernard Berelson, *Content Analysis in Communications Research* (New York: Free Press of Glencoe, 1952).

likely to produce rather trivial results. Checklists can help to systematize judgment and to insure that all important considerations are examined in appraising messages but they tend more to be restrictive than to stimulate creative effort. They tend to substitute routine for sophisticated judgment and the search for unique problem solutions. They do not measure the effects of communication at any level of response as suggested by the model for message testing developed at the beginning of the chapter.

Recognition Measures

Recognition measures assess both attention and retention effects and are one of the most common forms of message testing. Basically, recognition techniques involve showing the respondent a series of magazine advertisements and asking him if he remembers seeing that ad (under natural exposure conditions). Further questioning may probe the extent to which such message elements as headline, copy, and illustrations were noted and read.

Starch Readership Service. The best-known recognition method is the Starch Readership Service. This service conducts interviews with samples of size 200 to 400 on each issue of the magazines being evaluated. The first step in the interview is to make sure that the respondent has read the magazine issue. The interviewer then goes through the magazine page by page with the respondent, asking him (or her) whether and to what extent he read each advertisement that is half-page size or larger.[14]

Figure 15-3 illustrates a sample page from a Starch-rated magazine. It will be seen that the complete advertisement has been rated on three dimensions:

1. *Noted*—the percentage of readers who reported seeing the advertisement.
2. *Seen-associated*—those who not only saw the advertisement but associated it either with the product or with the company being advertised.
3. *Read most*—the percentage of respondents who said that they read more than half of the written material in the ad.

Separate scores are recorded for headlines, copy, illustration, and company name. It will also be noted that scores are typically recorded for both men and women. Because our example was taken from *Business Week* magazine, scores in the illustration are reported for men only. Figure 15-4 shows a listing of the Starch ratings for some of the advertisements in this issue of *Business Week*. Starch also supplies compara-

[14]D. B. Lucas and S. H. Britt, *Measuring Advertising Effectiveness* (New York: McGraw-Hill Book Co., Inc., 1963), p. 51.

tive data on cost and effectiveness measures based on averages for a product category.

Problems with Recognition Measures. There is much disagreement in the advertising industry about the value of recognition measures of message effectiveness. There are three major issues involved: (1) the amount of misreporting; (2) the extent to which retention is correlated with sales effectiveness; and (3) use of bogus ads as a means of checking on respondent reliability.

One line of questioning of recognition methods was sparked by a finding in a study conducted by the Advertising Research Foundation's Printed Advertising Rating Methods (PARM) committee.[15] This study found that recognition did *not* deteriorate with the passage of time. This finding had two possible explanations, either of which raised serious doubts about the validity and reliability of recognition measures. First, it had always been assumed that recognition scores were a good measure of the memorability of an advertisement and that recognition was a measure of memory. However, this finding suggested that the two might not be related, since forgetting would result in lower recognition scores over time. Second, it could be that recognition of an advertisement depended upon factors other than exposure to the advertisement.

Another study was very critical of recognition measures. It found that "noted scores after exposure were predictable prior to exposure with a correlation of .72" and that noting was a function of "respondent set."[16] Noting scores were predictable on the basis of interest in the product category, buying intentions or recent purchase, and magazine readership. On this last point, persons who read more magazines were more likely to report having seen an ad—to have a greater predisposition toward reporting noting. This was referred to as "noting set." Furthermore, two recognition measures were compared and it was found that they produced markedly different scores, which suggested that the measurement technique had a major influence on the results obtained, especially the extent to which the technique provided some incentive to the respondent to report having seen the ad. All of these factors—product interest, buying intentions, readership, motivation—can lead to significant misreporting in the recognition method.

Factors Influencing Memorability. Mechanical differences among advertisements can significantly influence their memorability, as noted earlier. Larger advertisements are more memorable, as are those which

[15]Darrell B. Lucas, "The ABC's of ARF's PARM," *Journal of Marketing*, 25 (July 1960), pp. 9–20.

[16]Valentine Appel and Milton L. Blum, "Ad Recognition and Repondent Set," *Journal of Advertising Research*, 1 (June 1961), pp. 13–21, at p. 18.

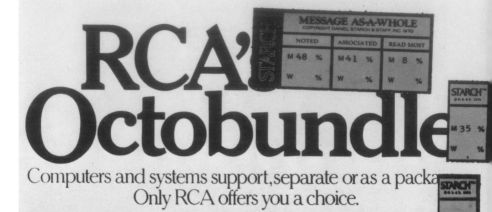

RCA's Octobundle

Computers and systems support, separate or as a package. Only RCA offers you a choice.

Bundling is getting your computer and support as a package. Unbundling is getting them separately. Traditionally, support came with the cost of a computer. Some computer makers still sell their machines that way. But only that way.

Others only offer support at a separate price. And in many cases, the customer is paying more than ever. RCA is the only major computer maker that gives you a choice. Whatever is better for you. On all our newer computers. Those being installed now, and in the future.
If what's better is a bundled contract, that's what you get. It includes support.

If unbundling is better for do it at a discount and p only for the support you Either way, it's RCA supp And that's some of the be the business. Just ask our customers.
The Octoputers are the ea computers to use. Now yc have easier ways to get th At RCA, doing business is easy—for you.

RC/I
COMPUTERS

61

Fig. 15–3. A Starch-rated advertisement from *Business Week* magazine. (Courtesy of Daniel Starch & Staff, Inc.)

STARCH
MESSAGE REPORT

66 ADS
BUSINESS WEEK   JUNE 6 1970

READERS

EXECUTIVE SUMMARY

PAGE 1

PAGE	SIZE & COLOR	ADVERTISER	RANK IN ISSUE BY NUMBER OF READERS	RANK IN ISSUE BY COST PER READER	PERCENTAGES NOTED	PERCENTAGES ASSOCIATED	PERCENTAGES READ MOST	COST RATIOS NOTED	COST RATIOS ASSOCIATED	COST RATIOS READ MOST
		PROFESSIONAL SERVICES								
15	1P	O H OVERMYER WAREHOUSING SER	54	44	17	15	1	75	85	33
56	1P4	BURNS SECURITY SERVICES	54	60	17	15	2	48	54	44
		COMMUNICATION/PUBLIC UTILITY								
35	1P	EDISON ELECTRIC INSTITUTE	58	47	20	14	1	88	80	33
		BANKING/FINANCE								
7	1P	FRANKLIN NATIONAL BANK	28	3	34	29	4	151	165	133
33	1P	CANADIAN IMPERIAL BANK COMM	37	11	32	25	2	142	143	67
40	X 1S4B	BANK OF AMERICA	4	27	69	52	7	109	104	89
91	1P	M.LYNCH/PIERCE/FENNER/SMITH	37	11	28	25	11	125	143	378
108	1S	NEW YORK STOCK EXCHANGE	17	29	42	36	17	93	102	289
120	1P B	U S TRUST CO OF NEW YORK	37	16	26	25	5	100	124	144
129	1P4	IRVING TRUST CO	37	41	33	25	6	93	89	133
		LIFE/GROUP/MEDICAL INSURANCE								
3	1P4B	CNA EMPLOYEE GROUP INSURANCE	21	29	59	33	8	143	102	144
21	1P	EQUITABLE ANNUITY PLAN	26	1	34	30	9	151	170	311
		FIRE/CASUALTY INSURANCE								
8	1P	ALLSTATE BUSINESS INSURANCE	47	21	19	19	5	84	107	167
		OFFICE MACHINES/EQUIPMENT								
2C	1P4	STEELCASE OFFICE FURNITURE	17	14	53	36	2	148	128	44
9	1P4B	TELETYPE MACHINES	44	51	36	25	3	87	72	89
61	1P4	RCA COMPUTERS	10	10	48	41	8	135	146	167
66	1S	IBM COMPUTER SERVICES	23	40	35	32	9	78	91	156
97	1P B	CMC KEYPROCESSING SYSTEM	45	20	35	22	10	135	109	300
127	1P B	3M MAGNETIC COMPUTER PRODUCT	43	17	20	24	5	107	119	144
		STATIONERY/MISC. PAPER GOODS								
113	1P	CROWN PRINTING PAPERS	52	36	20	17	1	88	96	33
86	1S4B	ANACONDA CO GENERAL PRO	7	51	58	46	10	71	72	89
90	1P4B	POTLATCH FORESTS INC GEN PRO	19	25	41	34	9	100	106	167
94	1S4B	DOW CHEMICAL CO GENERAL PROM	9	54	55	42	10	67	65	89
100	X 1S4B	CONTAINER CRP OF AMERICA G P	35	63	39	26	4	61	52	44
138	2/3P	AMERICAN SMELTG & REF CO G P	60	25	18	13	3□	114	106	144
		INDUSTRIAL MACHINERY/INSTR.								
13	1P	TRANS UNION CORP GENERAL PRO	28	3	42	29	6	187	165	200
36	1P	TORRINGTON BEARINGS	46	17	26	21	3	118	119	100
46	1S4B	COMBUSTION ENGINEERING I G P	19	60	47	34	5	57	54	44
50	1S	FMC CORP GENERAL PROMOTION	31	47	47	28	5	104	80	89

Symbols used with percentages: * / less than ½ of one percent ** / not applicable ⌐ / ads with fewer than 50 words.

Symbols used with size and color: A / center spread B / bleed C / cover D / digest approximate (island or corner) E / one page insert and one page r.o.p. G / gatefold H / horizontal I / island J / junior K / special position L / agate lines approximate N / inches approximate P / page S / spread W / pony spread ‡ / approximate # / insert & / one page plus the fraction shown. Numeral following unit of space shows number of colors. Numeral preceding unit of space shows

amount of space. **Symbols used to describe color on second page of spread:** x / black & white y / 2-color z / 3-color.

Readership costs are based on one-time card rates.

Rank in issue is included when 10 or more large space ads are reported. For trade publications special position charges are used if the premium exceeds 15% and the 2-page black & white rate is used for 1-page inserts.

Fig. 15–4. Portion of a Starch report for an issue of *Business Week* magazine. The advertisement shown in Fig. 15–3 ran in this issue. (Courtesy of Daniel Starch & Staff, Inc.)

use more pictures relative to words. Color is more memorable than black-and-white. One study reported that 60 percent of the variation in newspaper readership scores was explained by ad size (40 percent) and product advertised (20 percent).[17] Such attention-getting devices as the use of nude models or striking headlines, or illustrations of dramatic events such as fires and catastrophes, or the use of children as models, can all serve to increase the recognition scores of the advertisement.

Confusion. Recognition scores may also reflect confusion on the part of the respondent. If the advertisement is similar to other advertisements he has seen—especially advertisements for this same product—then the probability of misreporting is heightened. The use of familiar objects in the advertisement is likely to generate such confusion—as when illustrations or headlines or layout follow a familiar format.

To correct for confusion, it is common to use one of three methods to obtain a measure of misreporting. One is to use both a test group and a control group, with the latter not being exposed to the advertisement but subsequently interviewed concurrently with the test group, to obtain a measure of differences in attitudes and of misreporting.

The second technique involves the use of only one group of respondents, but the inclusion of advertisements that have not been previously run. Respondents may or may not be warned that there are fake advertisements among those they will see or hear. One study found that respondents' ability to distinguish between true and false ads is low, although an increase in the number of false ads used may increase the reliability of the measure of respondent credibility. In general, however, this study concluded that simple recognition measures have low validity as measures of readership of advertisements.[18] A similar study using radio commercials also found that claimed recognition of bogus commercials was high and that there were "campaign effects," the tendency to confuse one insertion in a campaign with another.[19]

The inclusion of bogus advertisements as a means of measuring respondent credibility and determining the extent of misreporting is not without problems. It may be that the inclusion of bogus ads is in itself a major source of confusion and encourages misreporting more than if such devices were not used. Defendants of recognition measures object to data on the extent of misreporting and argue that use of fake

[17]Verling C. Trodahl and Robert L. Jones, "Predictors of Newspaper Advertisement Readership," *Journal of Advertising Research,* 5 (March 1965), pp. 23–27.

[18]John Scott Davenport, Edwin B. Parker, and Steward A. Smith, "Measuring Readership of Newspaper Advertisements," *Journal of Advertising Research,* 2 (December 1962), pp. 2–9.

[19]Lawrence G. Corey and Richard M. Doub, "Awareness of Radio Commercials," *Journal of Advertising Research,* 3 (September 1963), pp. 17–20.

ads in an inappropriate method of establishing the incidence of false reporting.[20]

Adjusted Audience. The third method of correcting for confusion involves exposing a sample of respondents to a portfolio of test ads *before* they have been run in media. Some percentage, A, will state that they recognize a test ad—i.e., have seen it before—even though it has *not* been placed in media. This measure is called the "confusion factor." Then the ad can be run in a magazine (still on a test basis) and a follow-up survey conducted. This time, some percentage, B, will report having seen the ad and this percentage will include some false reporting. The extent of false reporting can be estimated by the pre-examination score, but the pre-examination score must be corrected because some of those who initially falsely reported recognition would in fact have been exposed to the ad when it was run. The formula for making these adjustments is as follows:

$$\text{Adjusted audience} = \frac{(\text{Postexamination score}) - (\text{preexamination score})}{100 - (\text{preexamination score})}$$

$$= \frac{B - A}{100 - A}$$

The numerator subtracts the confusion factor from the raw recognition score and the denominator is corrected to reflect the fact that some of those originally "confused" would in fact have seen the advertisement.[21]

Recognition vs. Recall Measures. Recognition measures have a major advantage over recall measures (to be discussed next) in that they depend less heavily upon the respondent's memory. In a recognition test, the respondent does not have to recall elements of the ad or otherwise prove that he has seen the ad by reconstructing its elements. For this reason, recognition measures may be more accurate than recall measures.[22] The reliability of recognition scores is also enhanced by their stability over time. However, the 4A's study found that recognition measures were among the least liked by agency research directors. The principal reasons cited were the fact that recognition is influenced by noncontrollable factors such as previous ad exposure and product experi-

[20]D. Morgan Neu, "Measuring Advertisement Recognition," *Journal of Advertising Research,* 1 (December 1961), pp. 17–22.

[21]Albert W. Frey (ed.), *Marketing Handbook* (rev. ed.; New York: Ronald Press Company, 1965), Section 17, "Advertising-Measuring Results," a section written by Joseph C. Seibert, pp. 19–20.

[22]Edwin B. Parker, Steward A. Smith, and John Scott Davenport, "Advertising Theory and Measures of Perception," *Journal of Advertising Research,* 3 (December 1963), pp. 40–43.

ence and that recognition does not assess the impact of the ad impression.[23]

Recognition May Measure Interest, Not Memory. While attention to and retention of the advertising message are necessary conditions for that message to be effective in achieving strategy objectives, they are certainly not sufficient. One line of reasoning suggests that "memorability" is not the problem with recognition measures after all. It can be argued that recognition is not a measure of *memory* but of *interest* in the advertisement and in the product being advertised. The evidence reviewed above suggests that this may well be the case. Wells has phrased this argument very well: ". . . recognition scores are not recognition scores at all. If advertisers stop thinking about recognition scores as measures of memory, recognition test results will be more useful because they will be easier to understand."[24] He further suggests that this is the reason that recognition scores do not deteriorate over time as they would if they *were* measures of memory. "Recognition scores have little if anything to do with memory. Instead they represent the respondent's subjective estimate of the probability that he looked at the ad when he went through the issue before."[25]

To summarize these comments on recognition measures of message effectiveness, such measures can be useful in assessing the ability of the ads to gain the reader's attention and interest under conditions of natural exposure. They can be used for both print and broadcast messages. Whether recognition measures "memory" or "interest" is an unresolved issue, but the result in the buyer's mind may be approximately the same in either case—a sense of familiarity and liking for the advertising which is probably correlated with attitudes toward the product. There is no evidence on the possible causal relationship between recognition measures and subsequent behavior, but the "correlates-of-effects" hypothesis suggests that they would tend to occur together. For certain limited purposes therefore recognition measures provide a valid measure of the effectiveness of a message, especially in terms of attention and retention effects.

Recall Measures

Recall measures are in many respects similar to recognition measures in that both involve surveys with persons previously exposed to the message, usually under natural conditions. Recall measures can be useful in

---

[23]Adler *et al., op. cit.*

[24]William D. Wells, "Recognition, Recall, and Rating Scales," *Journal of Advertising Research*, 4 (September 1964), pp. 2–8, at p. 3.

[25]*Ibid.*, p. 8.

assessing the attention and retention values of the message, as well as giving some indication of how the message was perceived. Many of the issues in the use of recognition measures apply equally to the use of recall measures.

One of the major problems with recognition is that it is "too easy" in that respondents may think they were exposed to the message when they in fact were not. As a result, recognition measures may overstate the true retention of the message. By the same token, recall measures may be "too difficult" in that respondents must give convincing evidence of having seen the message and of retaining many of its salient points, and must be able to articulate the content of the message in a reasonably thorough and convincing manner.

Gallup and Robinson Magazine Impact Service. Probably the best-known and most frequently used recall measurement technique is the Gallup and Robinson Magazine Impact Service. This is an "aided-recall" technique in that the interviewer provides certain clues which help the respondent recall elements of the message, although these are kept to a minimum. To collect the data, the interviewer will first show respondents a cover of the magazine issue being tested. In order to qualify for the interview, the respondent must accurately describe at least one picture story or article within the magazine; the interviewer may use the table of contents as a clue. Qualified respondents are then shown a list which contains all of the brand names or company names advertised in this issue and are also told that there are some names on the list which are not in the magazine. The respondent indicates which ads he thinks he saw and the interviewer then asks a series of questions designed to measure the extent to which the basic ideas in the ad were communicated and to make sure that the respondent did in fact see the advertisement. For each issue tested, a total of 200 men and 200 women are interviewed and their responses are recorded verbatim by the interviewer.

As a result, three measures are calculated:

1. *Proved name registration* (PNR) is a weighted measure of the percentage of respondents who accurately recalled message elements to the extent required to prove that they saw the ad.
2. *Idea registration* is an index of the extent to which specific copy points are recalled by respondents.
3. *Favorable buying attitude* is a measure of the extent to which those who recall the ad attribute it with developing favorable attitudes toward the company and the products advertised.[26]

[26]This description is based upon Dalbey *et al., op. cit.,* pp. 28–29, and Lucas and Britt, *op. cit.,* pp. 74–76.

Gallup and Robinson also provide data for comparing test scores with norms by class of product.

Carefully trained personnel are a must in the interviewing and in the editing process, because the measures are based upon coding of responses that have been recorded verbatim. There is a delicate balance between standards which are too high—permitting only a very small minority to prove recall—and standards which are too low—permitting guessing to substitute for accurate recall measurement. The interviewer and the editor both have a major influence in establishing and implementing those standards.

Desirable Features. Recall measures virtually eliminate one of the major problems in recognition measures, namely, confusion. Recall measures place much more stringent criteria on the respondent and, if anything, understate rather than overstate the effectiveness of the advertisement being tested. PNR scores are typically less than 5 percent.

Recall measures have several other desirable features. While some forgetting does occur causing recall to diminish with time, recall measures are reasonably stable over the length of time required for the test. This is especially true of aided-recall measures. One study found that TV viewing claims obtained by carefully controlled aided-recall measures were stable over periods ranging up to seven days.[27] It has been found that the visual components of televised messages are likely to predominate verbal elements in a recall test by a ratio of three to one. Ability to recall elements of a message seemed to be ordered as follows: pictures, print, voice, and sound (music). Longer messages did not result in proportionately more recall. Attention-getting elements were recalled more often than basic message elements.[28]

Recall of magazine advertisements has been shown to be independent of the position of the advertisement within the magazine. Differences in recall can be caused by a wide variety of factors dealing with the basic creative execution including use of color, product interest, previous advertising history, and differences in the copy. This same study found that it made no significant difference whether recalled material was positioned near editorial content or other advertising, but it did report that respondents are much more likely to recall advertisements which are oriented toward their own sex.[29] Another study likewise found that highly

[27]A. S. C. Ehrenberg, "How Reliable Is Aided Recall of TV Viewing?," *Journal of Advertising Research*, 1 (June 1961), pp. 29–31.

[28]Leland L. Beik, "Immediate Recall of TV Commercial Elements," *Journal of Advertising Research*, 2 (September 1962), pp. 13–18.

[29]Lester R. Frankel and Bernard M. Solov, "Does Recall of an Advertisement Depend on Its Position in the Magazine?," *Journal of Advertising Research*, 2 (December 1962), pp. 28–32.

visual magazine articles attracted more attention, resulted in more learning, and gave higher levels of recall.[30]

Problems in Use. There are several problems in the use of recall measures, however. As in the case of recognition measures, there is the fundamental question of the nature of the relationship between recall and the extent to which that message influences behavior. One critic of recall measures has said: "Learning and recall of factual information from mass communications does occur. However, recall and retention measures seem, at best, irrelevant to the ultimate effects desired, the changing of attitudes and behavior."[31] This same author reports a series of studies to determine the relationship between measures of recall and other measures of message effectiveness. He concluded that ". . . all 13 studies had this in common: they showed no relationship between what a person learned, knew, or recalled on the one hand, and what he did or how he felt on the other. The teaching and learning of factual information was not related to attitudes or behavior."[32]

Selective Retention and Perception Influence Recall. Selective retention may result in the inability of a respondent to "qualify" for an interview, although that respondent did in fact read the advertisement and modify attitudes based upon it. As a result, recall measures may understate the effectiveness of the advertisement. Predispositions have a significant influence on what is seen and remembered in an advertisement. It has been shown that people who read all or most of an advertisement do not necessarily remember the headline or the illustration of the ad, for example, but may instead remember only those elements which were of particular interest and value to them. The points remembered may be given only minor mention in the advertisement, although they take on special significance for the receiver, and the result may be that the respondent does not qualify as having seen the ad.[33]

Another study found that even when recall measurement immediately followed exposure there was significant misreporting. There seemed to be a tendency for respondents to embellish and add to the stimuli they had seen and to project their own values and interests into the message. These authors concluded that ". . . numbers generated by aided reports of exposure to ad elements may be of some interest and value as projective data, [but] they are substantially useless as factual reports of prior

[30]Allan Greenberg and Norton Garfinkle, "Visual Material and Recall of Magazine Articles," *Journal of Advertising Research*, 3 (June 1963), pp. 30–34.

[31]Jack B. Haskins, "Factual Recall as a Measure of Advertising Effectiveness," *Journal of Advertising Research*, 4 (March 1964), pp. 2–8, at p. 7.

[32]*Ibid.*, p. 6.

[33]Ronald Vickers, "A Pre-Test for Four Australian Print Ads," *Journal of Advertising Research*, 1 (December 1961), pp. 26–32.

exposure."[34] This criticism seems to be aimed particularly at the "aided" aspect of aided-recall measurements and the extent to which probing and stimulation of respondents can result in misreporting.

Media Influence. The medium in which the advertisement is viewed can exert a distorting influence on recall measures. As in the case of recognition measures, the "respondent set" toward the medium can significantly influence response. The individual's receptivity to a medium may be even more critical as a predictor of recall scores than product interest. This has been shown for both television and magazines, but it was found that product interest significantly affected recall of magazine ads but not recall of television commercials. Also, respondent set was a more critical predictor of magazine recall than of television recall.[35]

It does seem then that, as in the case of recognition measures, recall measures can be contaminated by many variables other than the message itself. Some factors such as product interest or the respondent's set toward a particular advertising medium can be controlled for as long as the objective of the test is to compare different advertisements for the same product to appear in the same medium. On the other hand, the basic issue of the relationship between measures of recall and the more important effects of changes in attitudes and behavior has not been resolved.

Recall Measures Are Preferred. In general, however, recall measures represent an improvement over recognition scores because they are more objective and more reliable measures of actual retention of the advertising messages. Recall measures can specifically indicate the extent to which the advertisement has registered the sponsor's name with the potential buyer and say something about the ability of the ad to deliver a meaningful and memorable message.[36] For these reasons, research directors rate recall measures very high in usefulness, preferring only measures of "comprehension" more than straight recall measures.[37]

Recall measures do provide a measure of the ability of the message to communicate and help to assess the effects of the message on perception as well as on attention and retention. The verbatim data collected as part of recall measurement can provide a rich storehouse of information on the nuances of meaning which are conveyed by the message to potential customers. The basic weaknesses of recall tests is their dependence on memory and the fact that memory measures are likely to be

---

[34]Eric Marder and Mort David, "Recognition of Ad Elements: Recall or Projection?," *Journal of Advertising Research*, 1 (December 1961), pp. 23–25, at p. 25.

[35]Dodds I. Buchanan, "How Interest in the Product Affects Recall: Print Ads vs. Commercials," *Journal of Advertising Research*, 4 (March 1964), pp. 9–14.

[36]Wells, *op cit.*, p. 8.

[37]Adler *et al.*, *op. cit.*

contaminated by many influences in addition to the message being tested. As noted earlier, recall measures may also favor advertising which is factual and relatively weak in terms of imagery and they may foster an undesirable sameness in a company's advertising. Also, recall measures become less sensitive and dependable for advertising which follows a basic theme over a long period of time. In this situation, the problem of confusion can become as significant in recall measures as it is in recognition tests.[38]

Opinion and Attitude Measures

The phrase "opinion and attitude measures" covers a wide variety of measurement approaches that are brought together for ease of discussion. The several techniques to be described under this heading typically involve forced exposure and ask the respondent to evaluate the advertising in terms of its ability to persuade him to buy or to influence his attitudes. They ask the respondent to attempt to be more or less objective about his or her preferences and responses to messages. At times, more direct measures of attitude change than opinion measurement are attempted, as when respondents are asked to make forced choices among brands to be received as prizes.

Conditions and Techniques of Measurement. In the typical test, respondents are shown one or more test advertisements and are then asked a series of questions relating to these advertisements. Tests are typically conducted in a group situation and respondents may or may not interact with one another as part of the test. Information solicited from respondents may be an attempt to measure any or all of several dimensions of response to the advertisements including believability, comprehension, persuasion, and liking or disliking for the advertising. In all of these situations where the respondent is aware that he is part of a test there is the danger that he will attempt to respond as an "expert" on advertising rather than in terms of his own personal reaction.

Methods of data collection for attitude and opinion measurement vary widely. Scaling techniques such as Guttman scaling, the semantic differential, and Likert scaling can be used for obtaining measurements. Simpler methods such as rank-ordering of alternatives and forced choices between pairs of advertisements may also be used. Interviewers may take verbatim notes on questions relating to content or persuasibility, or they may use a carefully developed coding procedure. Measurement often involves a before-and-after design in which attitude measurements are obtained both before and after exposure to the test messages

---

[38]Lucas and Britt, *op cit.*, p. 101.

and resulting differences carefully evaluated. There is a virtually limitless range of alternative data collection procedures and each has a certain logic to it, depending upon the specific purposes of the test.

Schwerin Service. One of the most widely used opinion- and attitude-measuring techniques is the Schwerin Standard TV Testing Service. These tests are conducted in theaters in New York and Chicago with samples drawn from telephone directories. Respondents are invited to preview a television program. Audience size is approximately 300 in New York and 600 to 700 in Chicago, although approximately four times as many invitations have to be extended to obtain this audience size. Before viewing the program, respondents are asked to select the brand of each of three product categories they would prefer to receive if they win a prize in a drawing to be conducted later. They then see a television program in which there are three commercials, one for each of the three product categories. After viewing the film, respondents are once again asked to indicate their brand preference for the drawing. The measure of message effectiveness is the percentage of respondents who change their brand preference after exposure to the commercial. These percentages can also be compared against average percentage changes for products in this category derived by the Schwerin Corporation from previous research.[39]

Variations on the basic Schwerin technique are possible, such as having respondents actually select a package of product when entering the theater and another when leaving, rather than indicating preference for brand choice contingent upon winning a lottery. These methods of measuring attitude change avoid some of the problems of asking for opinions. On the negative side, however, this measurement method can be criticized on the basis that it requests an immediate response to the commercial rather than allowing the normal lag to occur between message exposure and buying action.[40] The prechoice may also influence subsequent response to the commercials.

Telpex. The Telpex method of testing television commercials, developed in Great Britain, uses videotaped rough versions of commercials which are shown to relatively small groups of respondents (50 or so). These respondents are interviewed by carefully trained personnel and are asked such questions as whether they liked the ad, whether they believe that it is more likely to make them buy, and whether they prefer the advertised product.

[39]Robert D. Buzzell, "Predicting Short-Term Changes in Market Share as a Function of Advertising Strategy," *Journal of Marketing Research,* 1 (August 1964), pp. 27–31, and Dalbey *et al., op. cit.,* pp. 32–33.

[40]Lucas and Britt, *op. cit.,* p. 119.

The Telpex technique has several advantages, including relatively low cost of production, due to the use of videotape rather than moving picture film and the fact that commercials can be revised quickly and retested. The typical session involves the comparison of two or more alternatives. Questions used by the interviewers are flexible and designed to meet the particular needs of the client.[41] Further research on the Telpex method has shown that responses to the videotaped rough commercials do not differ from responses to finished commercials and that the results of the method are reliable. Telpex also offers the advantage of permitting diagnostic data on the advertisements that can be used to revise them as necessary. This method produces qualitative data that can be useful for modifying commercials that are still in developmental stages.[42]

In this latter respect, the Telpex method is similar to the use of focussed group interviews, a technique already discussed. Focussed group interviews produce qualitative information on consumer response to particular advertisements and can lead to modifications in semifinished ads.

Uses and Trends. Measures of attitude can be combined with techniques for generating measures of recognition and recall. It would be possible, for example, to interview two matched sample panels, one of which has been exposed to the ad and one not exposed. It would likewise be possible to expose each panel to one of two test ads. Then a series of questions on brand familiarity, belief in brand quality, and buying interest could be asked and differences observed could be attributed to differences in ad exposure.[43]

There does seem to be a trend toward heavier reliance upon attitude measures in evaluation of messages. Although such measures are often qualitative in nature and do not permit a precise, quantitative assessment of differences among alternative messages, they can provide rather clear indications of relative message effectiveness. As the function of marketing communication is more frequently defined in terms of changes in predispositions rather than changes in sales volume, attitude measurement becomes a more desirable form of copy testing.

The 4A's survey of advertising agency research directors showed that they best liked measures of "comprehension" which are simply measures of the extent to which the advertising is understood by, and has mean-

[41]John M. Caffyn, "Telpex Testing of TV Commercials," *Journal of Advertising Research*, 5 (June 1965), pp. 29–37.

[42]Nigel A. Brown and Ronald Gatty, "Rough vs. Finished TV Commercials in Telpex Tests," *Journal of Advertising Research*, 7 (June 1967), pp. 21–24.

[43]Jerome D. Greene and J. Stevens Stock, "Brand Attitudes as Measures of Advertising Effects," *Journal of Advertising Research*, 6 (June 1966), pp. 14–22.

ing for, receivers. Next in preference (tied for second place) came recall measures and measures of attitudes towards brands, companies, and users of the product (not attitudes toward the ads themselves). The agency men felt that comprehension is basic if the advertisement is to communicate what is intended and that measures of comprehension can be a valuable diagnostic tool. Comprehension measures are not frequently used it seems but they are regarded as of very high value when they are used. Similar reasons were given for preferring attitude measures—they respond to the specific purpose of the ad and are useful in diagnosis.[44]

Practitioners appear to be content with an assumption that attitude change is related to behavior change, even if the evidence of a causal relationship is unavailable. As predictors of buying behavior, changes in attitude do appear to have some usefulness. Measures of comprehension, believability, attitude change, and so on do relate more directly to the basic notion that advertising should be evaluated as a form of communication, a view that is increasingly gaining favor.

Attitude measures still have the basic weakness that they tend to be artificially derived in a situation different from the actual purchase context. Individuals are not always good judges of their own behavior or of the behavior of others but most measures of attitude ask them to make such judgments. (There are exceptions such as the brand choice technique used by Schwerin.) For many purposes, actual measures of behavior change would still be preferable as indicators of message effectiveness.

Purchase Behavior Measures

For the advertiser who insists upon measures of the impact of alternative messages upon actual purchase behavior, syndicated services are now available to provide such measures. These are fairly recent developments. One set of techniques involves the use of cable television in reaching two matched panels of test households. The other uses a house trailer set up in a supermarket parking lot.

Cable TV Labs. Community antenna television (CATV), generally spoken of as cable television, was first explored as a message-testing device in the so-called Milwaukee Ad Lab, sponsored by the Advertising Research Foundation. At least two commercial ventures were started as a result of this experiment. Adtel, Ltd., began selling its services in 1968 with a CATV installation in a medium-sized city in the southeastern United States.[45] The Split-Cable service was reported in the *Journal*

---

[44]Adler *et al., op. cit.*

[45]"Announcing an Exclusive Opportunity to Test the Effectiveness of Your Television Advertising," Adtel, Ltd., New York, undated.

Advertising Research in 1967.[46] In a CATV advertising laboratory, homes in the test city (which is assumed to be representative of the total United States population) are wired with CATV and designated as members of A and B panels. One panel can serve as a test unit and the other as a control unit.

Equipment at the broadcasting station, the cable head, permits the blocking of regularly scheduled network commercials and the insertion of test commercials in a manner which makes the household unaware of any difference in the transmission. This technical feature makes possible the controlled exposure of identified units of the population to the commercial under completely natural exposure conditions. (Or, the screen can be left blank for the duration of the commercial.)

Obtaining Measures of Effect. Given the fact of exposure, there are several alternative ways of measuring the effectiveness of the message. First, it is possible to conduct survey interviews in an attempt to measure changes in attitude. Second, members of each panel can be asked to keep a purchase diary, with the usual problems of providing incentive and control over the quality of the information. Third, it is possible to obtain several measures of purchase behavior.

The most direct method of measuring differences in purchase behavior is to conduct an audit of pantry shelves in homes in the two panels. Since all other conditions within the market and at the retail level are assumed to have an equal impact on both panels, any differences in purchasing can be attributed to differences in message effectiveness. Another behavioral measure can be obtained by mailing coded coupons to members of the panel and recording differences in redemption rates as a function of message exposure.

The CATV services are sophisticated and represent a substantial investment. As a result, the cost of the services is relatively high, although the information obtained may be a real value. Many forms of advertising research in addition to message testing are possible. Adtel was quoting a price of $75,000 per product category per year in 1968, with the provision that each product category would be sold to only one advertiser.

Trailer Labs. The trailer-in-the-supermarket-parking-lot technique also obtains measures of changes in purchase behavior as a function of message exposure: shoppers are interviewed, exposed to several commercials, and given a packet of coded coupons for price reductions on the advertised products which they can redeem on their shopping trip. The trailer can be moved from one location to another: shoppers don't expect to see the trailer when they arrive to do their shopping. Because it can

[46]Edward Wallerstein, "Measuring Commercials on CATV," *Journal of Advertising Research,* 7 (June 1967), pp. 15–19.

be completed quite quickly, the research technique does not represent a significant imposition on the respondents. Differences in coupon redemption rates are analyzed and related to differences in exposure. In this manner it is possible to simultaneously test two or more commercials for each of several product categories.

The advantages cited for the trailer technique are that the shopper actually spends her own money and that the research is conducted in the marketplace. The result is a reasonably representative buying situation and an opportunity to measure actual purchase behavior. The researchers can obtain a large sample relatively quickly and the technique can be used with children.[47] A possible disadvantage is the forced, unnatural exposure conditions.

As with other sales measures, the trailer technique has the disadvantage of not permitting control of certain important variables within the store, such as allocation of shelf space and the possibility of stock-outs. On the other hand, because purchase behavior occurs so soon after exposure and because researchers can be on the scene to check on the conditions in the store, these problems are minimized. Again, relative comparisons are more appropriate than absolute comparisons and the trailer technique does not permit the projection of quantitative results on sales volume obtained.

Other Measures of Purchase Behavior. There are many other ways of obtaining purchase behavior measures. Surveys of households can attempt to measure exposure to and recall of the advertisements and then attempt to measure subsequent changes in purchase behavior. Controlled exposure methods can be employed to handle that part of the problem with measurement concentrating on subsequent change in behavior. Consumer panel data may also be used to track purchase behavior.

In any measure of purchase behavior, there is the problem of controlling for the influence of other variables such as display and pricing, or changes in the competitive situation. No technique known can completely solve this problem, but the CATV and trailer techniques do make a big step toward reducing these difficulties.[48]

Physiological Measures

Interest in physiological measures of message effectiveness has been stimulated in recent years by the development of techniques and knowl-

[47]Ward J. Jenssen, "Sales Effects of TV, Radio, and Print Advertising," *Journal of Advertising Research,* 6 (June 1966), pp. 2–7.

[48]For a much more complete discussion of measures of sales response see Lucas and Britt, *op. cit.,* ch. 8, "Inquiries and Sales Measures," pp. 172–96.

edge for measuring pupil dilation. Such physiological responses have the major advantage that the respondent has no control over them. They are therefore "objective" measures of the impact of stimuli such as the verbal and visual content of advertising messages.

When exposed to stimuli which impinge on the senses of taste, touch, smell, sight, and hearing, the body responds with physiological as well as mental changes. Devices have been developed for measuring the magnitude of many of these changes. Three that have been used for evaluation of advertising messages are the galvanic skin response (GSR), salivation, and changes in pupil size. Pupil measurement is the most recently developed of these techniques and it is currently the only technique receiving significant attention, although some academic research has recently been reported on the galvanic skin response.[49]

Pupillometrics. In 1960, Hess and Polt reported their research finding that there was a relationship between pupil size and the interest value of visual stimuli.[50] By measuring the percentage of change in mean pupil diameter (which can be as much as 25 percent) in response to various pictures, the respondent's interest in the picture could be determined more objectively and precisely than through reliance on verbal reports. This technique was thought to have value where the visual stimuli had significant emotional content or involved important social norms.

Interest in *pupillometrics,* as it is called, developed rapidly in the advertising industry. In 1964, Krugman reported that Marplan, part of the Interpublic Group of advertising and marketing agencies, had completed over 70 studies using this technique. Examples cited included the selection of greeting card designs and sterling silver patterns. He said differences in pupil response had been small but real and called pupillometrics "a powerful new tool" for marketing communication.[51] Another researcher has reported applications in testing alternative package designs. This later study was especially interesting because it showed that exposure to reading material about the packages between exposures to slide pictures of the alternative packages significantly altered response to the packages.[52] Hess reported use of the technique to evaluate potential ads, current ads, and competitors' ads and suggested it has a diag

[49]Xavier Kohan, "A Physiological Measure of Commercial Effectiveness," *Journal of Advertising Research,* 8 (December 1968), pp. 46–48.

[50]Eckhard H. Hess and James M. Polt, "Pupil Size as Related to Interest Value of Visual Stimuli," *Science,* 132 (August 1960), pp. 349–50.

[51]Herbert E. Krugman, "Some Applications of Pupil Measurement," *Journal of Marketing Research,* 1 (November 1964), pp. 15–19.

[52]Richard S. Halpern, "Application of Pupil Response to Before-and-After Experiments," *Journal of Marketing Research,* 4 (August 1967), pp. 320–31.

nostic value in determining which elements of the ad are of greatest interest to the viewer.[53]

Questionable Relationship to Buying Behavior. While such techniques as pupillometrics have a basic appeal in their objective, scientific nature, they are of only limited value in message testing. They are expensive, require complex instruments, and are inflexible. Conditions of testing are very far removed from those of the marketplace and it is not clear if there is any relationship between autonomic behavior and actual change in predispositions or buying behavior.

USE OF MULTIPLE MEASURES

The preceding analysis has suggested that no one technique for testing message effectiveness is going to answer all of the questions management wants answered. Each technique has its strengths and its weaknesses. A logical conclusion from this is that the evaluation program should use more than one method to assess the potential contribution of alternative messages to the achievement of marketing communication strategy objectives.

It was brought out early in this chapter that there are several distinct mental stages through which the message works to ultimately influence behavior. Given that he is exposed to the message, the receiver must pass through the mental stages of attention, perception, retention, and response. Each of the measurement techniques discussed is more effective at some of these stages than at others. The best technique or set of techniques to use in message testing is a function of the objectives of the message strategy and the use of the data intended. Diagnostic data with which to modify rough advertisements are best provided by attitude and opinion measures while the attention-getting ability of the ad can be better measured by recognition and recall techniques, for example.

If there are multiple objectives for the communication program or if the testing program is to serve more than one purpose, then it is quite likely that more than one evaluation technique should be used. Depending upon the amount of planned expenditures for marketing communication effort, the expense of using multiple evaluation techniques may be easily justified.[54]

[53]Eckhard H. Hess, "Pupillometrics," in Frank M. Bass, Charles W. King, and Edgar A. Pessemier (eds.), *Applications of the Sciences in Marketing* (New York: John Wiley & Sons, Inc., 1968), pp. 431–38.

[54]For a report of the message testing practices of more than one hundred advertisers in the United States and Canada, see H. D. Wolfe, J. K. Brown, S. H. Greenberg, and G. C. Thompson, *Pretesting Advertising*, Business Policy Study No. 109 (New York: National Industrial Conference Board, 1963).

SUMMARY

In this chapter several classes of techniques for determining the effectiveness of alternative messages have been described and evaluated. While the list of classes of measurements and of specific evaluation techniques is very far from complete, it does contain examples of most of the important message testing approaches in use today.

At the same time, the critical issues in message testing have been identified and discussed in sufficient detail to provide some basis for the subsequent appraisal of techniques which have been eliminated from this discussion. Message testing must be evaluated just as any piece of research would be evaluated—in terms of its objectivity, validity and reliability, representativeness, and the ability to generalize from it. Care must be taken in sample selection and in the procedures by which data are collected and analyzed. But beyond that there are several issues peculiar to message testing, including conditions of message exposure, time lags between exposure and measurement, and the kind of behavior to be measured.

Underlying many of the difficulties in message testing is the basic lack of knowledge about how communication works to produce an effect in the receiver. Analysis has suggested that attention, perception, and retention are all necessary conditions, but not sufficient, for response to occur. Increasingly, marketers are phrasing the objectives of their advertising in communication terms. As a result, there is some shift toward measures of perception and attitude change as criteria of message effectiveness. Although the resulting data are hard to quantify, they do make a strong qualitative contribution to the diagnosis and understanding of how a particular message will influence receivers.

Cable television and the trailer technique also represent important steps forward in obtaining more objective (and quantifiable) measures of market response to alternative messages. They permit exposure and measurement of subsequent behavior change (as well as measurement of attitude change) under reasonably carefully controlled experimental conditions. While they are not ideal, as defined by the Marketing Science Institute's "idealized measurement procedure," they can make a significant contribution to the development of an effective marketing communication strategy.

The theoretical issue of "how communication works" is intertwined with the pragmatic issue of how to test the effectiveness of messages. Progress in either area will make a contribution to the other.

IV

Planning Communication Effort

Up to this point, emphasis has been on behavioral aspects of marketing communication. It is now time to introduce economic and financial considerations into the analysis.

The marketing communication strategist makes his contribution to the long run profitability of the firm by developing methods for delivering the maximum number of effective messages to prospective customers within the constraints of available resources. The first problem for the planner is to determine the level of communication effort. Appraisal of market opportunity must be combined with a consideration of the financial resources available to the firm and criteria for the rate of return on investments. Separate budgets must be set for each of the alternative uses of promotional funds.

Closely related to the determination of the level of effort is the requirement for a strategy to guide the allocation of limited funds among alternative modes of communication, products, markets, and specific customers. The analytical logic of economics and mathematics, combined in an approach often dubbed "operations research," can be a significant tool for analyzing both budget level and allocation problems. These tools of rigorous analysis, when combined with behavioral models of communication processes (especially models of response to communication effort), can significantly improve our understanding of the interactions among factors determining optimal spending strategies.

Allocation problems are among the most complex in developing the communication strategy. Because rigorous approaches must necessarily simplify the problem in order to cope with it, implementation of analytical solutions should also depend heavily upon the careful reasoning and judgment of experienced management. Another important implementation problem is the difficulty of measuring some of the key variables in determining optimum budgets and allocations. Statistical analysis, experimentation, and simulation can help to develop such estimates.

Two of the principal allocation problems in marketing communication strategy are the assignment of salesmen to territories and accounts, and the development of the advertising media plan. The basic elements of allocations are illustrated in Chapter 17 with a heavy emphasis on examples from personal selling problems.

Before tackling the problem of developing the advertising media plan and the media selection process, some qualitative considerations about media will be introduced in Chapter 18. Media effects on response to communication will be identified and media will be considered as a distinct element in communication strategy. Against this background, the discussion will then return, in Chapter 19, to allocation problems in the selection of media. Chapter 20 will review methods for evaluating, *post facto*, the contribution of advertising media to the accomplishment of communication objectives.

16

Determining Level of Effort

A class of decisions not previously discussed involves determining the level of effort to be expended in the marketing communication program. These are budget decisions, decisions about how much to spend. These decisions define a set of quantitative, financial objectives for the marketing communication program and establish yet another set of standards against which to evaluate campaign performance.

At several points, we have discussed objectives in one form or another. In Chapter 12, devoted to "developing communication objectives," a distinction was made between qualitative communication objectives dealing with the *meaning* to be conveyed about the product and quantitative objectives defining the *level* of communication effort. These qualitative objectives were an important input to the development of message strategy. The quantitative objectives to be discussed in this chapter become an input to the media strategy decision and other allocation decisions.

Another way of thinking about this important distinction is to define a difference between communication objectives and spending objectives. Communication objectives, it has been said, define *who* is to be reached by the communication strategy, the *meaning* to be conveyed about the product, and the *response* (change in predispositions or behavior) desired from the audience. Decisions about the level of spending attempt to apply economic and financial criteria to the development of marketing communication strategy to the end that the maximum contribution to the firm's financial objectives may be made. Determination of the level of effort defines *how much* to spend and requires consideration of criteria for the financial *return* desired on marketing communication investment.

While traditional accounting practice requires that marketing communication expenditures are usually treated as current operating expenses on the income statement rather than capitalized asset values on the balance sheet, much of the analysis that follows treats such expenditures as investments rather than current expenses. Because the benefits of many marketing communication expenditures (such as those for new product introductions, major packaging changes, and corporate advertising campaigns) are realized over several years, it makes sense—at least for management analysis and decision making, if not for corporate accounting—to treat these expenditures as if they were capital investments.[1]

Obviously, there must be coordination and consistency between communication objectives and spending objectives. Objectives for the desired market response (e.g., an increase from X percent to Y percent in the number of potential buyers who are aware of our products) have direct implications for the level of spending effort required. Conversely, limitations on the amount of funds available for marketing communication must be taken into account in setting communication objectives. There are valid reasons for making the distinction between communication and spending objectives, however. First, the problems themselves are quite different and can be most clearly understood if treated separately. Second, the analytical concepts required to cope with the two sets of objectives are somewhat different. Third, organizational responsibility for the two kinds of decisions tends to be distinct. Top management, financial management, and the highest level of the marketing organization are involved in the decision about spending level, based upon programs recommended by marketing operating personnel. Advertising and sales managers, product managers, and agency personnel tend to be more involved in the development of communication objectives and strategies.

USES OF BUDGETS

Decisions about the level of effort typically are expressed in the form of a budget. Budgets have two kinds of uses. First, they serve to make explicit the plan that is to *guide operating decisions* during the period of time covered by the plan. Second, they serve to *define the criteria against which to evaluate* cost, revenue, and profit performance at the end of the period.

[1]For one discussion of this issue, see Joel Dean, "Does Advertising Belong in the Capital Budget?," *Journal of Marketing*, 30, No. 4 (October 1966), pp. 15–21.

Relationship to Forecast

The sales forecast is an estimate of the revenue to be realized during the operating period. It is the top line of the pro-forma profit and loss statement. The sales forecast represents management's best judgment about the extent to which the potential market will respond to planned marketing effort. The sales forecast thus *results* from the analysis of market potential, planned marketing effort, and market response characteristics. The sales forecast, especially as it is derived from estimates of market potential, must also *influence* the determination of the level of marketing effort. Thus, the forecast and the planning of marketing effort are interdependent; one does not cause the other. Both must be considered and refined at the same time.

Determining the level of effort, that is, setting the budget, requires use of estimates of market potential, market response characteristics, and the preliminary sales forecast. The sales forecast must then be refined to reflect final decisions about budget level. On the other hand, there are several considerations, other than the preliminary sales forecast, in determining the level of effort.

Planning

The budget is an aid to planning. It is the manner in which planning becomes explicit, the results of planning get translated into specific operating criteria, and planning decisions get communicated to operating personnel. It makes management judgment explicit and translates this judgment into financial terms as required for purposes of direction and control.

A review of company practice in planning advertising effort found that budgeting was seen by managers as having four basic advantages:[2]

1. Forcing people to plan.
2. Enabling various levels of management to communicate with each other concerning proposed courses of action.
3. Coordinating the expenditures of funds and their allocation to projects.
4. Providing standards for measuring performance.

These advantages are advantages from planning as much as advantages from the specific activity of budgeting. The budget is essentially an instrument of communication and control to facilitate the planning process. And it does this in terms of dollars and cents.

[2]Richard J. Kelly, *The Advertising Budget* (New York: Association of National Advertisers, 1967), p. 4.

Planning and Control Unit

The organizational unit for planning and control purposes may be a single brand, a group of products, a sales territory or region, or some other grouping of activities, depending upon the purpose of the plan. The budget defines both a total level of effort and the allocation of effort among those control units. Allocation problems have an analytical logic of their own; we shall postpone discussion of them until the next chapter.

Product Management Responsibility. In most companies, planning of marketing communication effort takes place on an individual product or brand basis. One manager may be responsible for several products where volume is not sufficient to warrant full-time attention to individual products. The product manager will submit his recommendations to top marketing or corporate management for review and approval. While members of top management may exercise some initiative in defining how the marketing communication budget on that product is to be spent, they are typically more concerned with the total promotional effort and the aggregate dollars involved. It is usually the product manager's responsibility to determine how best to spend that money. On the other hand, they may assess the reasonableness of his budget request based upon a review of how he plans to spend that money.

It is typical for the product manager *not* to have control over the sales force activity on his products. Rather, he will share the sales force with several other product managers, each of whom competes for the time of the sales force through the use of effective promotions, sales displays, special incentive programs, and so on. The product manager may or may not be charged with the cost of selling effort on his product. If such charges are made, they are allocated typically as a fixed percentage of budgeted sales volume. The product manager's decision making will be limited to allocation of the budget between media advertising and sales promotion activities including consumer deals, reseller incentives, and perhaps sales force contests.

While there are sound organizational reasons for this division of authority and responsibility, it should be recognized that separation of personal selling and mass communication in this organizational form has some costs. The product manager first of all cannot precisely coordinate advertising, sales promotion, and personal selling effort on his brand because he has no responsibility or control over the sales force. Second, he cannot make any careful assessment of opportunities for optimum allocation of funds between advertising and personal selling. As a result, his tendency will be to attempt to obtain as much money as possible for advertising and sales promotion, given that these are the only revenue-generating tools at his disposal. Third, there will be poor coordination and control of selling effort vis-à-vis products and brands. Because sales activity is typically organized on a geographic basis, the control system of the firm will gather data on personal selling on a geographic basis. Rarely is it possible to determine exactly how much time the sales force spends on each product or class of products except by a very laborious and expensive special project to collect such data.[3]

Field Sales Management. In contrast to responsibility for mass communication, responsibility for personal selling tends to be organized on a geographic basis. A national sales manager may have reporting to him three to five regional sales managers in the typical field sales organization. There will then be one or more levels of field sales managers reporting to the regional managers. This first level of field sales manager typically carries the title of district (or area) sales manager, although there are many variations.

Directing and Controlling Sales Effort

Budgets can be established for each organizational level. These budgets will direct the efforts of the organizational unit during the planning period. The sales revenue objective becomes a *quota* and some part of the compensation of the salesmen (and, in some cases, the sales manager) will depend upon the degree to which that quota is obtained. As noted in Chapter 10, quota-setting and forecasting activities are very closely related. In addition, the sales budget is used to control the expenses incurred by the sales organization as it attempts to realize the forecasted revenue.

Setting the level of sales effort for the field sales organization requires an assessment of the availability of sales manpower during the period. If the manpower is not available, then plans must be laid for developing it through programs for recruiting, selecting, and training salesmen as noted in Chapter 14. This is in contrast to changes in the level of advertising and other forms of mass communication where adjustments can be made much more quickly, assuming the necessary funds are available. In adjusting the level of personal selling effort, there will be longer lags in the planning process. First, the funds must be available; then the

---

[3]For a good discussion of the organizational and control problems in the product manager system, see any of the following: David Luck and Theodore Nowak, "Product Management—Vision Unfulfilled," *Harvard Business Review*, 43 (May–June 1965), pp. 143–54; National Industrial Conference Board, *The Product Manager System*, Experiences in Marketing Management No. 8 (New York: The Board, 1965); Gordon H. Evans, *The Product Manager's Job*, AMA Research Study 69 (New York: American Management Association, 1964).

manpower must be obtained; next it must be trained; only then can the level of field selling effort be increased.

Sales quotas have both a motivational and a control value. When the forecast has been allocated to organizational units, it becomes a quota which is both a goal for the individual salesman to strive for and a standard against which to evaluate his performance. Quotas may be established for individual salesmen and sales territories, for districts, for regions, and for the entire national sales organization. At the national level, the quota is the company's sales forecast.[4]

Determining the Level of Advertising Effort

Advertising budgets state how much spending is planned during the coming period and may also state how that money is to be allocated among various advertising media and products. It may also show some allocation among geographic units, either sales organizational units or distribution regions, for example. Separate budgets may be established for each product or group of products, or divisions of the company.

An important issue in determining the level of advertising effort is to determine at which level of the organization such decisions should be made. As in the case of developing sales quotas, there are two classes of approaches. In the "top-down" approach, the decisions are made at the highest level of the organization and budgets and quotas are then broken down among organizational units. In the "build-up" approach, each independent organizational unit sets its own budgets and quotas and these are aggregated to produce a total company budget.

Advantages of a Build-up Approach. Each approach has advantages and disadvantages. Proponents of the build-up approach have two arguments in their favor. First, it has motivational value in that those who are going to be judged by these standards take responsibility for their determination. Second, it capitalizes on the information and expertise available at organizational levels closer to the marketplace. These arguments are especially important in situations of decentralized profit responsibility and organization. Each profit center must have responsibility and authority over those variables which significantly influence the profitability of that part of the business. (This is one of the major issues in the product management concept.)

Top-Down Planning Prevents Suboptimization. The major argument in favor of the top-down approach is that it prevents suboptimization. Suboptimization occurs when a subunit of the organization attempts to

---

[4]Kenneth R. Davis and Frederick E. Webster, Jr., *Sales Force Management* (New York: Ronald Press Company, 1968), pp. 289–95.

realize its own specific objectives and, in so doing, prevents either other parts of the organization or the total organization from realizing the highest level of goal accomplishment possible. An example of suboptimization would be spending excessively to promote one product when shifting funds to another would provide a better rate of return.

Making decisions about the advertising budget at the highest levels of the organization has several other advantages. It allows an explicit consideration of the financial aspects of such spending, including alternative uses for the money and the cost of capital to the firm. While it is quite understandable that each product manager will try to maximize performance (profitability or sales) of his brand, his so doing may prevent other product managers with greater opportunities from achieving the best results. There may be special considerations such as the need to spend heavily (and perhaps unprofitably) in the short term on new products.

Another important set of considerations involved in coordinating budget setting at the highest levels of the organization relates to the purchase of media time and space. Media costs can be reduced by taking advantage of the quantity discounts offered by most advertising media. These can be a significant factor (up to 50 percent reduction from list prices is possible) and they have the same effect as increasing the amount of money being spent if these decisions had been made independently.

Coordinating Personal and Mass Communication. Because of the organizational difficulties in coordinating personal selling and advertising, these problems must be handled by top marketing management. Individual product managers do not have the information or the authority required to make judgments about the relative importance of mass communication given alternative levels of personal selling effort. Only at the highest levels of marketing responsibility can these judgments be made when advertising responsibilities are organized on a product basis and personal selling is organized on a geographic basis.

A final reason for viewing advertising budget decisions from a total organization viewpoint is the need to regard such investments in the context of the firm's total capital budgeting problem. In this context, advertising is seen as one among many alternative uses of the company's financial resources. Decisions such as whether to spend to develop a new product, whether to build a new plant, and whether to open a new sales office must be compared against the same rigorous financial criteria for the simple reason that, given scarce resources, spending for one may preclude the opportunity for investing in one or more of the others during the planning period. In other words, capital budgeting explicitly recognizes the opportunity costs involved in decision making.

For these reasons, it will be assumed in the following discussion that decisions about how much to spend on the marketing communication program are being made at the highest level of the marketing organization. The analysis will use the logic of the capital budgeting decision and will assume that decisions are being made about the total product line. In the next chapter, the analysis will concern the allocation of the budget among alternative products, regions, and other organizational units.

TRADITIONAL APPROACHES TO BUDGET SETTING

It is only recently that management approaches to the determination of communication budgets have shown definite signs of evolving toward a rigorous, scientific consideration of the available information on market conditions, response characteristics, and financial constraints. Traditionally, budget setting has been largely guesswork and based mainly upon management intuition. While the traditional approaches to budget setting could be defended (to top management and to stockholders, for example) on some logical basis, they were far from optimal.

Percentage of Sales

Probably the most commonly used method of determining the marketing communication budget has been to forecast sales and to then take some fixed percentage of the forecasted revenue as the amount to spend for communication activities. There are several variations on this approach. One is to forecast sales, take a fixed percentage of sales for total communication effort, and subtract the committed expense of the sales organization with the residual being available for advertising and sales promotion. Another variant involves adjusting the percentage on some basis, typically either to reflect stage in the product life cycle (spend a larger percentage on new products) or to reflect expected changes in economic and competitive conditions.

Sales Cause Communication Effort. There are two obvious criticisms of the percentage-of-sales method. First, it puts the cart before the horse. Under this method, expected sales "cause" communication expenditures. It would be more logically sound to set first the level of marketing communication effort to be expended and then to set the sales forecast on the basis of the expected effect of that effort. Second, the setting of the percentage figure is purely arbitrary and is not related to the purposes of the marketing communication effort. Furthermore, there is no basis for assuming that the same percentage is always optimal. A commonly used guideline here, especially by retail stores for their advertising, is the percentage of sales being spent by similar firms, as reported by trade association studies.

A First Step in Planning. The percentage-of-sales method is not without its advantages, however. If nothing more, it brings some orderliness into spending for marketing communication, even if it is on an arbitrary basis. In industries where the important competitors all follow this kind of reasoning, it can result in a more stable competitive environment. Defenders of this method also point out that the relationship between promotional effort and sales results is usually not known and that percentage-of-sales methods do provide a basis for relating expenditures and results. This can be especially helpful in making sure that money to pay for the planned effort is available from expected revenues.[5] When the percentage ratio is modified to take into account particular operating problems and expected changes in the environment, this method is not without some rational basis, albeit rather thin.

Competitive Parity

Another intuitive basis for setting the level of communication effort is to try to determine what competitors are doing and to gear effort to that level. This particular rule of thumb is often used in determining the level of personal selling effort. When competitors add salesmen in a given area, the company may assume that it must do likewise in order to maintain competitive equilibrium. This is clearly not the necessary conclusion. The competitor may be planning to add a line of noncompetitive products, for example, or his present salesmen may be performing at a level significantly below ours.

Competitive parity is often found in setting advertising budgets as well. The rationale here seems to be that market share is proportional to advertising share and that the probability that a prospective buyer will purchase the product is a function of the number of messages he receives about each product advertised.

While the competitive parity approach does have the merit of taking competitive activity into account and making explicit recognition of the strategic aspects of marketing communication effort, it is based upon what is usually a faulty assumption. That assumption is that competitors somehow know better than we do how to determine budget levels. There is no reason to assume that what competitors are doing is optimal or correct in any sense.

As Much as Possible

As strange as this may seem as a criterion for spending, there have been several marketing success stories built upon the strategy of spend-

[5]Albert W. Frey, "Approcahes to Determining the Advertising Appropriation," in George L. Baker (ed.), *Effective Marketing Coordination* (Chicago: American Marketing Association, 1961), pp. 326–39.

ing as much as possible for marketing communication activities. Several cases involving consumer packaged goods have achieved prominence and success because the aggressive all-or-nothing methods of management provided sustained effort and resulted in establishing new products in the marketplace.

Especially for New Products. The as-much-as-possible method of setting marketing communication budgets is typically used in introducing new products in regional markets. Funds generated in one market will then be used to introduce the new product into another market. Saturation of local media is a typical objective in such a strategy, with the assumption that exceedingly high rates of advertising activity will have several desirable consequences including thorough distribution in retail outlets, very high levels of awareness, high consumer trial rates, and an overwhelming of competitors' "normal" efforts.

There may or may not be a provision for profit in such spending plans. The object may be to maximize sales volume by spending as much as possible in the short run, foregoing any profit taking in order to firmly establish a share of market that will result in long-term profit maximization. There is a necessary assumption that all marketing communication effort results in *some* increase in sales volume, although this may be less than the amount spent on advertising or selling effort.

Over the long run, this policy must be adjusted if the firm is to survive. There comes a time when such aggressive spending does not make sense and provision must be made for profit and for recovering the funds invested in market development.

Objective and Task

A more orderly procedure for determining the amount of money to spend on marketing communication effort is first to specify clearly the objectives to be accomplished by the communication program. Then, the specific communication tasks necessary to accomplish those objectives are defined. Then the costs of those activities are estimated and aggregated. This becomes the total communication budget.

The objective-and-task method can become quite scientific, as when survey findings, statistical analysis of historical data, and experimentation are used to provide information with which to specify objectives, and to determine the expense required to generate a given result. For this reason, this approach is sometimes called the "research-objective" approach. It still requires a large amount of executive judgment, although it analyzes available information in a rigorous framework.

Proponents of the objective-and-task method argue that, although it may not be ideal, it is a definite step away from guesswork and toward an objective and rational procedure for setting the communication objective. As Albert Frey so aptly put it, "One of the obstacles to doing a better job than we have done in deciding the right dollar expenditure for advertising is our too common attitude that there must be one best way to do so, equally applicable to all situations, and that until somebody—somebody else—comes up with that one best way, the prevailing degree of hunch, guesswork, and intuition involved in this decision must be accepted as inevitable."[6] A similar viewpoint was expressed by Schaffer and Orr, who argued for striking a compromise between elegant, logical (and unsupported) mathematical models and unscientific management practice. They advocated application of scientific methods through rigorous statistical analysis of historical sales data and curve-fitting procedures to estimate response functions.[7] The objective-and-task method is one step forward. As Frey points out, however, it may assume that more information is available than is actually the case. That is, there may in actual practice be no way of determining very precisely the tasks required to achieve a given objective.

The Media Schedule Approach. As an example of the objective-and-task approach, Frey recommended what he called the "media-schedule" approach (in the context of setting the advertising budget). The essential steps in that process were the following:

1. Set the dollar sales goal for the period ahead.
2. Define the potential market and its segments.
3. Determine present levels of awareness, attitudes, and purchasing in the relevant segments.
4. Calculate the increase in awareness and attitudes necessary to achieve the required increases in sales.
5. Determine the number of conscious message impressions required to produce the necessary changes in attitudes and awareness.
6. Determine the *total* number of actual messages that must be delivered in order to yield the necessary (net) conscious message impressions.
7. Determine the number of potential messages that must be delivered in order to generate the required number of actual messages.
8. Determine which media (and which schedules for using those media) will produce the desired number of potential messages at the lowest cost.

This last figure becomes the required advertising appropriation.[8] The distinction made here among the three kinds of messages—conscious

[6]*Ibid.*, p. 327.

[7]Kurt H. Schaffer and Earle W. Orr, Jr., "The Determination of Advertising Budgets for Brands," *Journal of Advertising Research,* 3 (March 1963), pp. 7–11.

[8]Frey, *op. cit.*

impressions, actually delivered messages, and potential messages—is the distinction made in the previous chapter among attention, exposure, and circulation.

While Frey's proposal is valid, it makes some critical assumptions that are probably not warranted. Those assumptions are that management knows, or can determine rather precisely, the relationships between pre-dispositions and sales results and between changes in predispositions and level of marketing communication effort. While such relationships might fruitfully be explored in carefully designed research studies, implementing the results of those studies in the kind of step-by-step procedure recommended is likely to be a very difficult task.

Fixed and Variable Components. Cyril Freeman, Manager of Advertising and Sales Promotion for the Worthington Corporation, has also developed a method for implementing the objective-and-task approach. This method assumes that "normal" advertising and selling activities are fixed commitments; it then concentrates on budget decisions about the "variable" advertising component. Given a sales forecast and a total marketing budget, management must establish communication goals, based on market analyses, and determine advertising's contribution to the accomplishment of each goal. While this method can be criticized because it concentrates on only one component of total communication effort, it can be extended to incorporate other variables and provides an orderly approach to budget determination.[9]

The logic of the objective-and-task method is appealing and is quite consistent with a view of the function of marketing communication as bringing about changes in predispositions as well as changes in sales. Because it is difficult to establish a direct causal relationship between level of communication effort and predispositions, however, implementation requires better information, at least about the extent to which these changes tend to occur together. In other words, the "correlates-of-effects" hypothesis developed in the last chapter may provide a way around this conceptual difficulty. Before examining these possibilities, however, it will be instructive to examine more closely the theoretical nature of the budgeting problem. From that analysis it will be possible to derive some guidelines for the kind of information needed by management to implement a more rigorous and rational approach to the determination of the communication budget.

THE BUDGETING PROBLEM

An important distinction can be made between the *conceptual* nature of the budgeting problem and the *measurement* problem. The concep-

[9]Cyril Freeman, "How to Evaluate Advertising's Contribution," *Harvard Business Review*, 40 (July–August 1962), pp. 133–45, 148.

tual problem is to define the conditions under which a given level of expenditure is optimum in some sense. Having defined those conditions it is next necessary to trace the logical consequences of certain courses of action and to relate these back to the optimizing conditions.

The measurement problem is one of empirically determining relationships among the variables defined as influencing the optimum. Previous discussion has suggested some of the important variables and relationships that must be measured in determining the optimum level of communication effort. Three of the most significant variables are market potential, the response function, and the cost of capital to the firm. The following discussion of the conceptual problem will examine other variables and the relationships among them. It will also consider different models for dealing with the budgeting problem.

The rest of this chapter will examine these two parts of the budgeting problem separately. First, we shall define the conditions for optimization of the communication budget and then examine methods of estimating the important variables and relationships.

THE CONCEPTUAL PROBLEM

At the heart of the problem of determining the level of marketing communication effort is the need to define the "optimum" budget. According to the criterion we have assumed throughout this discussion, the basic objective of the firm, and the one guiding its management in all decision making, is to maximize profits over the long run. Profit is defined in dollar terms or in terms of return on stockholders' equity, not as a percentage of sales. The resolution of this conceptual problem is important for management and has practical implications.

Marginal Productivity Criterion

Assuming that the objective of the firm is to maximize profit, the question now becomes: "Under what conditions will profit be maximized?" The answer is provided by the criterion of marginal productivity. Profits are maximized when the marginal return from a dollar invested in a given project (say an advertising campaign or the development of a new product) is equal for all projects and is equal to the cost of capital to the firm. This can be expressed as

$$r_1 = r_2 = \cdots = r_n = c$$

where r_i = rate of return on the ith project, for $i = 1$ to n
$\quad n$ = total number of projects
$\quad c$ = cost of capital to the firm

The marginal productivity criterion states that funds should be shifted from project X to project Y if the rate of return to project Y is higher. There are several important but quite reasonable assumptions embedded in this analysis. First, it is assumed that there are decreasing returns on each project, that is, each additional dollar invested accomplishes somewhat less than the previous dollar. Second, it is assumed that the decision maker knows (or can estimate) what the returns are from each investment. Third, it assumes that the firm knows its cost of capital, defined as the interest rate it would have to pay to obtain additional funds from an external source.

Note that the marginal productivity criterion implies that the firm should continue to raise capital until it has sufficient funds to spend to bring the rate of return on all projects down to the cost of capital. If the firm is able to earn 10 percent on its investment in a given project, and the cost of additional capital is 8 percent, then it should raise the money and make the investment.

But let us assume that, although the firm can make 10 percent return on investment, additional funds are not available. The equal marginal productivity criterion still applies. Investment should be shifted from one project to another until the last dollar invested in each project yields the same return. This will improve the average rate of return on the combined projects.

Problems of Implementation. There are several practical problems in implementing this criterion in planning marketing communication strategy. For one thing, the amount of investment in personal selling is very difficult to determine. If the objective is phrased as maximizing the return on stockholders' investment, it is almost impossible to determine how much of that investment is represented by a given sales district, for example, consisting of human and physical resources—offices, automobiles, other physical assets, and salesmen and their customers.

As noted earlier, a further restriction on use of this criterion is represented by traditionally accepted accounting practices which require that all expenditures for marketing communication be treated as current expenses. It is possible for purposes of the investment decision, however, to treat advertising and selling expenses as if they were relatively long-term investments. While annual profits usually cannot be calculated on this basis and reported to stockholders, internal decision making may be aided by considering promotional expenditures, especially for new products, as investments with payoffs coming for several years.

Assumption: Response Function Is Known. The critical assumption in this view of the problem is that the relationship between investment and result is known. In other words, it is assumed that the response function is known. Such an assumption is rarely warranted in the case of marketing communication. It is more likely to be known in planning a production facility or some other fixed investment.

The response function defines the rate at which the market will respond to changes in the level of marketing communication effort. It defines the annual return to be expected from a given level of communication investment. For this reason, estimation of the response function is a critical part of the budget determination problem.

Part of the conceptual problem is to specify the *shape* of the response function. At the conceptual level, the problem is which of several alternative "models" represents the best way of thinking about the relationship between effort and response. This is distinct from the measurement problem which involves estimating the parameter values in the model. So next we must consider alternative models for defining the response function as a way of estimating the marginal productivity of dollars invested in marketing communication effort.

Relationship Between Budget Level and Allocation. Before leaving the concept of marginal productivity, however, it will be helpful to note that the "budget" problem becomes an "allocation" problem depending upon how "projects" are defined. If the total marketing communication problem is defined as one project, then the problem of defining the optimum communication budget is one part of an overall allocation problem involving the firm's total resources. If personal selling, advertising, publicity, sales promotion, package design, and other elements of the communication program are defined as projects, then the objective of budgeting is to assure that the rate of return of each activity is equal to all the others. This is the problem of allocating the total communication budget among activities.

Simple Models

The simplest quantitative models of marketing communication treat sales as a continuous function of communication effort. These models take the form

$$S = f(E, Q, P, I)$$

where S = sales volume
  E — the level of communication effort
  Q = the level of product quality
  P = price
  I = uncontrollable economic factors ("income")

The notation "$= f(\quad)$" may be read simply as "is some function of"; and the nature of the functional relationship is not specified. For purposes of determining the optimum level of advertising effort, it would be assumed that all other factors had been determined (price, quality, and income) and that any changes in sales response would be a function of changes in the level of communication effort.

In such models, it is typical to assume that the functional relationship is continuous and differentiable, that is that the model can be analyzed using the tools of simple calculus. Figure 16–1 illustrates the typically assumed relationship between communication effort and sales response.

In order to complete the analysis, some cost function must also be assumed for communication effort. The objective of profit maximization is achieved when the difference between revenue and total cost is maximized, and this occurs where marginal cost equals marginal revenue (again assuming that the firm is operating in the range of decreasing returns to effort, that is, past the inflection point, P, on the S-curve in Figure 16–1). This problem can be rephrased to define revenue in terms of gross margin contribution after subtracting costs of production and distribution, leaving promotion as the only variable cost. It is typical in the simple model to assume a linear cost function for promotion—that is, each increment in effort costs a fixed amount. Given these assumptions, the optimum is defined by that point where marginal cost of promotion equals marginal profit contribution, which is the point at which the slope of the response function is the same as the slope of the cost function (which is constant). This is shown graphically in Figure 16–2, where E_1 and E_2 would both represent optimum budget levels according to the marginal cost equals marginal revenue criterion. This is not a sufficient criterion, however, as it can be seen that the level of spending, C, at E_1 is greater than the level of profit contribution margin. It clearly makes no sense to operate at that point since the company is spending more than it is getting back. E_2 represents an optimum budget level and profit is represented by the distance between the profit contribution (Y) and cost (C) curves at that point.

Mathematically, the conditions for optimization are given by the following equations (assuming that advertising is the only undetermined decision variable):

$$\Pi = f(E,Q,P,I) - C(E)$$
$$\Pi = Y(E) - C(E)$$

where Π = net profit
$Y(E)$ = profit contribution as a function of effort
$C(E)$ = promotional cost as a function of level of effort

$$\frac{d\Pi}{dE} = \frac{dY}{dE} - \frac{dC}{dE}$$

$$\frac{d\Pi}{dE} = 0$$

$$\frac{dY}{dE} = \frac{dC}{dE}$$

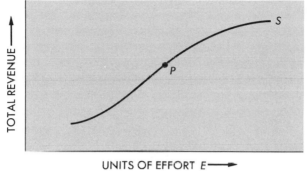

UNITS OF EFFORT E ⟶

Fig. 16–1. Assumed response function in a simple model.

To insure that the firm is operating at a point where there are decreasing returns (past the inflection point) and that profit contribution is greater than promotional cost:

$$\frac{d^2\Pi}{dE^2} < 0$$

and

$$Y(E) > C(E)$$

The first condition specifies that the slope of the contribution curve must be decreasing at the optimum point. The second condition simply states that profit must be positive, and that contribution must be greater than the cost of communication effort. Thus, both conditions rule out E_1 as an optimum in Figure 16–2.

This simple model is useful for seeing the essential logic of marginal analysis. But it also has several weaknesses. The major weakness of this formulation is that it is a one-period model. It assumes that promotion influences market response only in the period in which it is expended. Our knowledge of the communication process tells us that this is not a reasonable assumption. To incorporate interperiod effects, the formulation must be made "dynamic." Dynamic models attempt to examine the behavior of a relationship over time and from one period to the next.

Dynamic Models

Let us assume that we wish to make a decision about how much to spend for this period only. That is, we are not concerned about how much to spend in future periods. We are concerned, however, with the impact of this period's spending on response in future periods and the amount to spend in this period will also be influenced by the amount

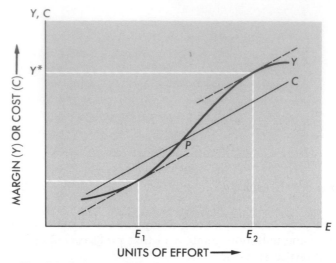

Fig. 16–2. Optimum budget level in the simple model.

that has been spent in past periods. A simple model to analyze this kind of decision situation has been developed by Julian Simon.[10]

This model incorporates four variables: (1) sales in the previous period; (2) a measure of the response to advertising in the current period; (3) the rate at which sales decline in the absence of advertising; and (4) the cost of capital to the firm. The model is formulated as follows:

Let

T = advertising period ($T = 1, 2, \ldots, m$)

t = revenue period ($t = 1, 2, \ldots, n$)

$T = t$

$R_{T,t}$ = net revenue caused by advertising in period T, realized in period t. ("Net revenue" equals "gross margin contribution," that is, revenue after subtracting production and distribution costs.)

$V_{T,t}$ = present value net revenue

A_T = advertising expenditure in period T

P_T = profit from advertising in period T

b = retention rate = 1 minus the decay rate of customer purchases from period to period in the absence of further advertising

ρ = discount rate; cost of capital to the firm

[10]Julian L. Simon, "A Simple Model for Determining Advertising Appropriations," *Journal of Marketing Research,* 2 (August 1965), pp. 285–92.

$$\sum_{T=1}^{t} R_{T,t} = \text{sum of sales in period } t \text{ caused by all prior advertising in periods } 1, 2, \ldots, t$$

This last term defines sales in period t *not* caused by advertising in period t, but caused by advertising in *all prior periods*. The central notion of this model can be thought of as a stock of "goodwill" which decays by a process analogous to forgetting as a constant percentage of the value of the stock at the beginning of the period. This stock is replenished or increased by "advertising" (in Simon's model, or, more generally "communication effort") in the current period. Simon shows that

$$P_T = \sum_{t}^{\infty} V_{T=t} - A_{T=t}$$

where

$$\sum_{t}^{\infty} V_{T=t,t} = \frac{1}{1-b\rho} \left(\sum_{T=1}^{t} R_{T,t} - b \sum_{T=1}^{t-1} R_{T,t-1} \right)$$

Although this expression is complex, the basic ideas are quite simple. The first equation states that profit from advertising in the present period is equal to the discounted, present value of net revenue minus the cost of this period's advertising. The second equation says that the present value of revenue in this period is the difference, discounted by the cost of capital, between net revenue caused by this period's advertising and the retained effects on revenue in this period from all advertising in previous periods. These relationships are expressed in the following definitions:

$$\sum_{T=1}^{t} R_{T,t} = \sum_{T=1}^{t-1} R_{T,t} + R_{T=t,t}$$

and

$$\sum_{T=1}^{t-1} R_{T,t} = b \sum_{T=1}^{t-1} R_{T,t-1}$$

In words, this last equation says that sales in the present period caused by advertising in prior periods is equal to sales in the past period multiplied by the retention rate. The prior equation is definitional and simply says that total sales in the present period are equal to sales caused by prior advertising and sales caused by current advertising.

The equation for profit, P_T, can be differentiated to determine the simple profit-maximizing rule

$$dA_{T=t} = d\sum_{t}^{\infty} V_{T=t,t}$$

which says that the firm should continue to advertise until the incremental advertising expense is equal to the (discounted) net revenue. This observation is completely consistent with the equal marginal productivity criterion for all projects, $r_1 = r_2 = \cdots = r_n = c$. If the last dollar spent on advertising brings in just \$1 of present value net revenue, the marginal return of any project, r_i, will equal c, and if all other projects are similarly considered, then $r_1 = r_2 = \cdots = r_n = c$.

Simon showed how to estimate the important parameters, retention rate and response to advertising in the current period, by analysis of historical data and traced through the ramifications of this view for budgeting policy in several different competitive situations. While the logic of the model is sound, it should be realized that the estimation problem is a very difficult one.

Other investigators have also considered the influence of communication in terms of changes in a stock of "goodwill" and the existence of a decay constant. Nerlove and Arrow have shown that optimum advertising level is a function of retention rate, response rate, and cost of capital, as well as price elasticity, in the following relationship:[11]

$$\frac{A^*}{pq} = \frac{\beta}{\eta(\alpha + \delta)}$$

where $A^* =$ optimum advertising expenditure
$p =$ unit price
$q =$ quantity sold
$\beta =$ elasticity of demand with respect to goodwill
$\eta =$ price elasticity
$\alpha =$ rate of interest (cost of capital)
$\delta =$ decay rate

Nerlove and Arrow view the function of promotional effort as to keep the stock of goodwill at an optimum level and current expenditures, which are view as an investment in goodwill, are a function of the decay rate. Palda's distributed-lags model also treats advertising as an investment with effects distributed over time.[12]

An Unexpected Result. The Nerlove and Arrow model has one particularly interesting sidelight. Under a certain set of conditions—a demand function that is linear in its logarithm, a linear cost function, and an "environment" (exogenous demand determinants such as consumer

[11]Marc Nerlove and Kenneth J. Arrow, "Optimal Advertising Policy under Dynamic Conditions," *Economica*, 29 (May 1962), pp. 129–42. This description of the Nerlove-Arrow theorem is taken from Kristian S. Palda, *Economic Analysis for Marketing Decisions* (Englewood Cliffs, N.J.: Prentice-Hall, Inc., 1969), pp. 177–81.

[12]Kristian S. Palda, *The Measurement of Cumulative Advertising Effects* (Englewood Cliffs, N.J.: Prentice-Hall, Inc., 1964), pp. 11–18.

income) that is changing at a constant rate (which may be zero)—Nerlove and Arrow showed that a constant percentage-of-sales criterion is optimum! The criterion that was accused of putting the cart before the horse may in fact be an optimum policy under these special (but not rare or unreasonable) conditions. There is still the difficult problem of determining *which* percentage figure is optimum.

Vidale and Wolfe have reported studies of actual market conditions which also considered dynamic effects.[13] Their model took the form

$$\frac{dS}{dt} = \frac{[rA(t)](M-S)}{M} - \lambda S$$

where S = sales rate at time t
  r = sales response constant
  $A(t)$ = rate of advertising at time t
  M = the saturation level (analogous to market potential)
  λ = the decay rate

The sales response constant was defined as the addition to sales per dollar of advertising when $S = 0$:

$$R = \frac{r(M-S)}{M}$$

or

$$r = \frac{M}{(M-S)}R$$

Their studies found that, when advertising was stopped at the end of several periods, having been maintained for time T, sales decreased exponentially according to the equation:

$$S(t) = S(T) e^{-\lambda(t-T)}$$

Sales response was highest in the initial phases of a campaign but the response rate was reduced as the saturation level was reached. These response characteristics are shown in Figure 16–3. Vidale and Wolfe examined the implications of their model in several situations including the case of a short, intense campaign, and examined the requirements for optimization under several different sets of conditions. Their studies provided evidence of the feasibility of conducting advertising experiments and obtaining results that were both reliable and reproducible. They found that response rates and sales decay constants varied signifi

---

[13]M. L. Vidale and H. B. Wolfe, "An Operations Research Study of Sales Response to Advertising," *Operations Research*, 5 (June 1957), pp. 370–81. This is one of several interesting and important models of response to advertising reprinted and commented upon in Frank M. Bass *et al.*, (eds.), *Mathematical Models and Methods in Marketing* (Homewood, Ill.: Richard D. Irwin, Inc., 1961), pp. 357–77.

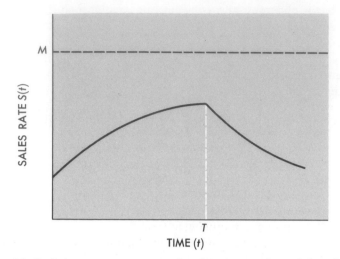

Fig. 16–3. Sales response to an advertising campaign of duration *T*.

cantly among products but that these two parameters, plus the saturation level, were important determinants of sales response in all cases studied.

Decision Making Under Uncertainty

All of the previous models have one important weakness: they do not consider competitive response except as it may be included in the sales response constant. Models based on game theory and decision theory have the advantage of permitting an explicit consideration of how the optimality of a given level of effort is contingent upon competitors' response to the firm's effort, as well as customer response.

The simplest case to explore with a game-theoretic formulation is the case of a constant-sum game, which may be defined as saying that total industry demand is not influenced by firms' marketing efforts. Only market share changes as competitors' spending changes. This model can also be phrased as a two-person game which assumes that the market is divided between the firm and "all other competitors."

Montgomery and Urban summarize well the essentials of a game-theoretic approach to models that consider competitive activity in determining the level of promotional effort. Their review provides the framework for the following remarks.[14] In the simplest model it is assumed that

[14]David B. Montgomery and Glen L. Urban, *Management Science in Marketing*, (Englewood Cliffs, N.J.: Prentice Hall, Inc., 1969), pp. 121–31. Their discussion of decision rules follows closely that of another excellent source: William J. Baumol, *Economic Theory and Operations Analysis*, 2nd ed. (Englewood Cliffs, N.J.: Prentice-Hall, Inc., 1965), pp. 552–58.

market share for firm j is proportional to its share of promotional expenditures

$$MS_j = \frac{A_j}{\sum\limits_{j=1}^{N} A_j}$$

where MS_j = market share of firm j, $j=1, 2, 3, \ldots, N$
A_j = promotional expenditures of firm j
N = number of firms in industry

The simple model can be modified to reflect the differences in the effectiveness of each firm's promotional effort:

$$MS_j = \frac{e_j A_j}{\sum\limits_{j=1}^{N} e_j A_j}$$

The coefficient e_j is a measure of sensitivity similar to that of elasticity.

In this model a firm's market share is a function of three variables: (1) the level of its promotional effort in the planned period; (2) the level of competitors' effort; and (3) the firm's promotional effectiveness (as determined by message strategy, quality of selling effort, etc.) compared to competition. The problem of setting the level of communication effort is now complicated by uncertainty concerning competitors' actions and payoff to the firm from its marketing communication effort will be contingent upon competitive behavior. This is illustrated in Table 16-1, which shows different possible payoffs from each of three budget levels contingent upon competitive effort.

Maximin Criterion. Under these conditions, there are several decision rules which the marketing communication planner could follow. A pessimist would use the *maximin* criterion. He would consider the worst possible outcome from each course of action, as follows:

Budget	Worst Outcome
$1,000,000	$100,000
1,500,000	300,000
2,000,000	500,000

Then he would choose that course of action which assured him of the best payoff under the worst possible circumstances. In this example, this would be the highest budget, $2 million, which would guarantee him a payoff of $500,000. (Notice that the best he can do with this budget is only $600,000.) The decision maker using the maximin criterion tries to maximize the minimum payoff, and is in this sense a pessimist and places high value on relative security, picking that situation that gives

Table 16–1. Payoff (in Profit Contribution) to the Firm's Promotional Effort as a Function of Competitor's Effort

(in thousands of dollars)

Firm's Promotional Effort	Level of Competitive Effort		
	1,000	2,000	3,000
1,000	800	400	100
1,500	700	500	300
2,000	600	550	500

him the best outcome if the worst comes to pass, as when competitors spend $3 million.

Maximax Criterion. The optimist or gambler is at the opposite extreme. He would use the *maximax* criterion and would try to maximize the maximum possible payoff. He would array the maximum payoffs from each budget level:

Budget	Best Outcome
$1,000,000	$800,000
1,500,000	700,000
2,000,000	600,000

He would choose a budget level of $1 million because this has the highest possible payoff associated with it. Thus, the maximax criterion yields different results from those with the maximin criterion. Which rule is used depends upon the decision maker's risk preference.

Hurwicz α Criterion. Both criteria can be criticized on the same basis —they consider extreme cases and do not take into consideration possible middle ground. A compromise is represented by the *Hurwicz α criterion*, which is a weighted combination of the maximin and maximax criteria. This is defined as

Criterion for strategy $i =$

$$(1 - \alpha) \text{ (best payoff to strategy } i) + (\alpha) \text{ (worst payoff to strategy } i)$$

where $0 \leq \alpha \leq 1$

$\alpha =$ an index of the pessimism of the decision maker

$1 - \alpha =$ an index of the optimism of the decision maker

Use of this criterion requires the calculation of the α value for each strategy and then selection of that strategy which has the highest α value. If we assume a slightly optimistic decision maker with α equal to .4 (which is used to weight the worst outcomes) and $(1 - \alpha)$ equal to .6 (which weights the best outcomes), then the following calculations would be made:

Budget		α Criterion Value
$1,000	(.4)($100,000) + (.6)($800,000) =	$520,000
1,500	(.4)(300,000) + (.6)(700,000) =	540,000
2,000	(.4)(500,000) + (.6)(600,000) =	560,000

In this example, the $2 million budget would be chosen, just as under the maximin criterion. The Hurwicz α criterion could just as well have favored the lower-level spending, as it would have if α had been set equal to .3 (representing a slightly more pessimistic decision maker) which would have resulted in selecting the $1 million budget.

Laplace Criterion. The Hurwicz α criterion considers only the extremes, but it does so with flexible weighting depending upon the α value chosen. The *Laplace* criterion (also called the Bayes criterion) considers all possible outcomes and weights them all equally on the assumption that the decision maker has no *a priori* basis for assessing competitors' possible strategies. This can be thought of as a "maximum ignorance" criterion. Under the Laplace criterion, our decision maker would make the following calculations.

Budget		Laplace Expected Payoff
1,000	⅓(800) + ⅓(400) + ⅓(100) =	433
1,500	⅓(700) + ⅓(500) + ⅓(300) =	500
2,000	⅓(600) + ⅓(550) + ⅓(500) =	550

This criterion uses an expected value calculation with expectations being represented by the equal likelihood assumption, thus weighting each possible outcome equally. Using the Laplace criterion, our decision maker would set his budget at $2 million.

Minimax Criterion. The final criterion to be considered is the *minimax* or *minimax regret* criterion. The decision maker who uses this criterion can be thought of as being motivated by a desire to reduce dissonance or postdecision doubt. He wishes to minimize his "regret" when all decisions (his and his competitors') have been made, where *regret* is defined as the difference between the maximum payoff possible if competitors spend at level j and the payoff which actually occurs if a nonoptimal decision was made. The regret matrix has elements R_{ij}, defined by

$$R_{ij} = \max_j P_{ij} - P_{ij}$$

Such a matrix is demonstrated in Table 16–2, which is based on the data in the original payoff matrix in Table 16–1. Notice that, for each possible competitive action, one budget level is optimal for the firm. This is max P_{ij}. The decision rule is to choose that course of action (budget level) which has the minimum value for the maximum regret. This is calculated as follows:

Budget	Maximum Regret
$1,000,000	$400,000
1,500,000	200,000
2,000,000	200,000

In this case, the decision maker would be indifferent between the last two budget levels and would have to use another criterion to choose between a budget of $1,500,000 and one of $2 million.

The preceding discussion has not considered game theory per se but has only considered possible criteria for choosing among alternative strategies. Game theory models explicitly consider how a competitor is likely to respond to a given course of action by the firm. A central notion in any game-theoretic model is the concept of an "equilibrium." An *equilibrium* is said to exist when none of the competitors can improve his position by changing his strategy unless one of the other competitors also changes his strategy.

Table 16–2. Regret Matrix for Promotional Effort
(in thousands of dollars)

	Level of Competitive Effort		
Firm's Promotional Effort	1,000	2,000	3,000
1,000	0	150	400
1,500	100	50	200
2,000	200	0	0

Game-Theoretic Models

The first game-theoretic models for promotional budget decisions were developed by Lawrence Friedman.[15] In the simplest form, a simple market model is set up, in which each firm's share of the total sales influenced by promotional effort is as follows:

$$S_A = \sum_{i=1}^{n} \frac{X_i}{X_i + Y_i} S_i \qquad \text{for firm A}$$

$$S_B = \sum_{i=1}^{n} \frac{Y_i}{X_i + Y_i} S_i \qquad \text{for firm B}$$

where S_i = total potential sales influenced by promotion in area i
X_i = company A's promotional expenditures in area i
Y_i — company B's promotional expenditures in area i

Several features of this simple model require comment. First, it sees sales as having two components—those sales influenced by promotional effort and those sales that are not, e.g., sales made solely on the basis of preference for product features and brand loyalty. Second, the model deals with promotional expenditure by area, and is concerned with the optimum geographic allocation of promotional effort in the face of intelligent competition. One of the several analytical insights which comes from this model is the set of conditions defining the optimum budget for firm A.

Friedman defined total costs of producing and selling an amount of sales, N, exclusive of advertising costs, A, as

$$\text{Total costs} = C_1 + C_2 N$$

where C_1 is the fixed costs and C_2 is variable cost per unit. C_3 is defined as gross return per unit sale. Friedman's analysis supported the conclusion that

$$\text{Profit} = C_3 \left[\frac{A}{(A+B)} \right] S - \left\{ C_1 + C_2 \left[\frac{A}{(A+B)} \right] S \right\} - A$$

where A = firm A's advertising budget
B = firm B's advertising budget
S = total potential sales

[15]Lawrence Friedman, "Game-Theory Models in the Allocation of Advertising Expenditures," *Operations Research*, 6 (September–October 1958), pp. 699–709, reprinted in Bass *et al., op. cit.,* pp. 230–241.

Using the classical maximizing conditions reveals that the optimum advertising budget for firm A is given by

$$A^* = \sqrt{(C_3 - C_2)SB} - B$$

In words, the firm's optimum advertising budget is the square root of the difference between profit contribution and variable cost per unit times the sales potential multiplied by the competitor's advertising budget, minus that advertising budget. Although Friedman phrased his approach in terms of advertising only, it can be easily reformulated in the general case of total promotional effort with an appropriate redefinition of costs.

Decision Theory (Decision Making Under Risk)

Statistical decision theory provides another important way of evaluating the influence of competitive activity under conditions of risk. (Montgomery and Urban make a distinction between decision making under *risk*—where it is possible to make subjective probability assessments of competitors' possible actions—and decision making under *uncertainty*, where such probability assessments are impossible.[16]) In the decision-theoretic approach, it is assumed that the expected value to be derived from a given course of action, such as a particular level of promotional effort, is a function of the "conditional" value of the possible outcomes (i.e., assuming each one occurs) multiplied by the probability of their occurrence. Three rules govern application of this *expected value criterion*. First, the possible outcomes must be mutually exclusive; that is, they must not overlap. Second, they must be collectively exhaustive; that is, they must include *all* possible outcomes. Third, the probabilities must sum to unity.

Subjective Probability. The key input to a decision theory formulation is the decision maker's subjective assessment of the probability of each of the outcomes possible from a given course of action. In the problem we have been using as an example, originally formulated in Table 16-1, the decision maker must subjectively estimate the likelihood of competitive spending at each of the three possible levels. Let us assume he makes the following judgments:

Level of Competitive Effort	Probability
$1,000,000	.25
2,000,000	.50
3,000,000	.25

[16]*Op. cit.,* p. 122.

He would then calculate expected value as follows:

Budget	Probability $\times$ Conditional Value	=	Expected Value
$1,000,000	.25($800,000) + .50($400,000) + .25($100,000)	=	$425,000
1,500,000	.25(700,000) + .50(500,000) + .25(300,000)	=	500,000
2,000,000	.25(600,000) + .50(550,000) + .25(500,000)	=	550,000

Given that the objective is to maximize expected value, the decision maker would choose budget level $2 million because this has the highest expected value. Although it turns out in this example that the expected value of the strategy is the same as the conditional value *if* competitors spend at a level of $2 million, no such correspondence between expected value and conditional value is necessary. It might have been that expected value from the chosen strategy was some number such as $625,000, which is different from any of the conditional values listed. In other words, if our decision maker chooses the third strategy, his actual payoff may be $600,000 or $550,000 or $500,000 contingent upon what competitors do.

This approach to setting the promotional budget has no particular magic to it, but it does have the advantage of providing a way in which the decision maker can make explicit his judgment about the likelihood that competitors will spend at a given level, and it permits a calculation of the influence of competitors' spending on the firms' budget decision. It is also possible to revise these subjective probabilities using data derived from market research studies, but that will not be demonstrated here.[17]

Before leaving this discussion of game-theoretic and decision-theoretic models, it is important to note that they implicitly assume that the response function is known. Furthermore, they tend to be single period models and do not consider the influence of promotional expenditures in this period upon sales response (or competitors' efforts) in subsequent periods. The problem of specifying conditional payoffs is a problem in specifying response. It is possible to structure the problem more flexibly using the decision-theoretic approach. In the previous examples, the objective was to consider possible competitive behavior, and it was assumed that the payoff to a given firm-competitors' strategy pair was known. Instead of specifying a single payoff, however, it would be possi-

[17]For an illustration of uses of decision theory in promotional planning see Paul E. Green, "Bayesian Decision Theory in Advertising," *Journal of Advertising Research*, 2 (December 1962), pp. 33–42. For an excellent exposition of the incorporation of research data into the revision of probability estimates, see Frank Bass, "Marketing Research Expenditures—A Decision Model," *Journal of Business*, 36 (January 1963), pp. 77–90.

ble to state an array of possible payoffs, and a probability (subjective or otherwise) for each payoff. There is much more flexibility in the decision-theoretic approach than we have indicated with the examples used here.

Stochastic Models

Stochastic models focus once more upon the problem of estimating response rates. They do so in terms of changes in the probability of purchase for each of the brands under consideration and in terms of so-called transition probabilities, the probability that a brand will be purchased in period t contingent upon the consumer's brand choice in one or more previous periods. These concepts were developed in Chapter 10.

A Linear Learning Model for Budgeting. The application of stochastic modeling to the development of budgets for promotional effort has been best developed by Kuehn.[18] Kuehn's model is a linear learning model in which it is assumed that all previous brand choices have some influence on this period's choice and that choice of brand A increases the probability that it will be purchased in the future. The mathematics of the Kuehn model are quite complex and will not be developed here. The model does yield a solution for the optimum level of advertising effort which is shown to be influenced by industry growth rate, sales response rate, the rate of decay of brand loyalty, cost of capital, and the relative effectiveness of the firm's advertising compared to competitors'. Kuehn distinguishes three kinds of sales: (1) those influenced only by loyalty (habit); (2) those influenced only by product characteristics; and (3) those influenced by advertising (interacting with product characteristics). Only the last are assumed to be influenced by advertising.

Kuehn's model has several attractive features, including the fact that it is dynamic and considers interperiod effects. It introduces discounting of investment in promotion as a financial consideration. Also, the view of consumer behavior as a learning process is intuitively appealing.

Although several pages have been devoted to the topic of the conceptual nature of the budgeting problem, it has failed to produce a general model for solving the budgeting problem. As yet, no general model has been developed. Each of the models reviewed has certain advantages, and introduces a particular point of view into the problem. None is complete, however.

In order to be useful, each and any of these models requires the estimation of the key parameters contained. One basis for choosing among alternative formulations of the budgeting problem may be according to

---

[18]Alfred A. Kuehn, "A Model for Budgeting Advertising," in Bass *et al., op. cit.,* pp. 315–48.

the data requirements of the model and the extent to which required data are available and appropriate estimation procedures known.

THE MEASUREMENT PROBLEM

Preceding comments have suggested several variables that tend to be important in most of the models discussed. These include the sales response rate, the sales decay rate, and market potential. Specific models create the need for additional estimates as well, but these three seem to be the most commonly identified (along with the discount factors). In static (i.e. nondynamic) models, there is no need to estimate the sales decay rate.

The following paragraphs will briefly review three classes of approaches for estimating these important parameters, as part of the problem of setting the communication budget. The three classes of measurement techniques to be discussed are statistical analysis, experimentation, and simulation.

Statistical Analysis

For most firms faced with the problem of setting the level of promotional effort, the first step is often to apply some form of analysis to available data on past sales and past promotional effort and to attempt to identify some relationship between the two. In Chapter 10, regression analysis and time series analysis were described briefly as two of the most frequently used methods of analyzing available statistical information. Here we shall consider the usefulness of such statistical techniques for estimating the important parameters in the budgeting decision—the sales response constant and the sales decay constant.

Correlation and Regression Analyses. The typical analysis would look at the time series of historical data on sales levels and some measure of promotional effort (advertising expense, number of salesmen, dollars spent on sales promotion, etc.), and attempt to measure the extent of correlation between these two sets of variables. The resulting analysis would reveal an equation of the form

$$Y = a + b_1x_1 + b_2x_2 + \cdots + b_nx_n$$

where the x_i's are measures of variables that influence sales volume, such as total advertising dollars, number of salesmen, or whatever measures seem appropriate. This equation could then be used to estimate sales volume from alternative levels of promotional effort in future periods. This would yield an expected revenue function which could be combined with a cost function and profit-maximizing budget levels could be determined by using straightforward optimization techniques. In this formulation the b_i's are estimates of sales response rates for each of the independent variables.

The analysis could be made dynamic by looking at the strength of the relationships between the level of sales in one period and the amount of promotional effort in each of several previous periods, with the number of periods used in the analysis determined by the strength of the relationships. This analysis would yield equations of the form

$$Y_t = a + b_{1,t}x_{1,t} + b_{1,t-1}x_{1,t-1}, + \cdots + b_{1,t-n}x_{1,tn} +$$
$$\cdots + b_{2,t}x_{2,t} + b_{2,t-1}x_{2,t-1} + \cdots$$

Refinements on the model can also be attempted in the search for stronger relationships, such as transforming the data into nonlinear form (logarithmic, exponential, etc.) or by a creative definition of certain variables such as "ratio of salesmen to retail outlets" or other non-obvious parameters.

Similar analysis can be conducted on a cross-sectional basis, that is, by comparing data on the basis of sales territories or states or major regions of the country, for example, rather than by time periods. This can be useful in isolating the effects of different levels of effort and it can also help to define important differences in response characteristics for the separate areas.

Palda analyzed the data on sales, advertising, and market conditions for the drug firm, Lydia Pinkham, over a 53-year period, and found that the demand equation had the following form:

$$S_t = k + \lambda S_{t-1} + \alpha \log A_t + \beta D + \gamma T + \delta Y_t + u_t - \lambda u_{t-1}$$

where S = sales
k = a constant (the Y-intercept)
A = advertising expenditure
D = a dummy variable that simulates the influence of advertising copy
T = a trend variable going from 1 to 53 for the years 1908–1960
Y = disposable personal income
$u_t - \lambda u_{t-1}$ = a "disturbance" or random error term

and λ, α, β, γ, and δ are constants expressing the influence of their respective independent variables on the level of sales in period t.[19]

The computer has today made it feasible, economically and otherwise, to explore a huge number of possible relationships and to analyze much larger blocks of data than previously. As a result, statistical analy-

[19]Palda, *Economic Analysis for Marketing Decisions*, p. 192.

sis has become a more accessible management tool. Along with this opportunity has grown increased opportunity for *its misuse*.

Some Pitfalls. Quandt raises some serious questions about the use of statistical methods for measuring the influence of advertising on sales results and in determining sales response functions. Among the more serious problems he identifies are the possibility of specifying the wrong direction of causality (as when point-of-purchase display is seen as a cause of sales when it may very well be a result), contaminated data, inappropriate models that fail to recognize important interactions among key variables, lack of sufficient detail in the data, and failure by the technician to assure that the data meet the assumptions necessary for proper use of the statistical tools. Quandt illustrates these problems by considering attempts to estimate relationships using various economic models incorporating both geographic markets and time periods.[20]

Experimentation

Although it may be somewhat expensive as a data-collection procedure, experimentation can be a tool of immense value to the marketing communication strategist in estimating important parameters and in determining the optimum level of promotional effort. The number of reported examples of the successful use of intelligent and large scale experimentation in the determination of promotional budgets and spending strategies is increasing and practitioners are becoming more aware of this important decision-making aid.

Experimentation can be designed to serve several distinct purposes and to estimate several important parameters simultaneously. Jessen described an early experiment to determine sales response to advertising which took account of the delayed effects of advertising in determining the optimum budget level.[21] He provided a detailed exposition of his experimental design that could have been very helpful to any manager wishing to plan similar studies. His study tested the influence of three budget levels in six markets over three time periods. Each budget level was tested in each area during the experimental period in order to eliminate area differences from the comparisons, and specific consideration was given to the *order* in which each budget level was used in each market area. These conditions were implemented by using two 3 × 3 Latin squares (three periods, three budget levels, and a total of six

[20]Richard E. Quandt, "Estimating the Effectiveness of Advertising: Some Pitfalls in Econometric Methods," *Journal of Marketing Research*, 1 (May 1964), pp. 51–60.

[21]Raymond J. Jessen, "A Switch-Over Experimental Design to Measure Advertising Effect," *Journal of Advertising Research*, 1 (March 1961), pp. 15–22.

market areas), or a "double changeover" design. With this design it was possible to estimate the sales response to each level of advertising and to select that level that was most profitable.

Adaptive Models and Continuous Experiments. In a more elaborate use suggested by John D. C. Little, experimentation is conducted on a continuous basis and the results are analyzed to set the budget level in each period.[22] Little's method is to develop a model of sales response to advertising based upon some preliminary estimates of the relevant parameters, and from this model the optimum level of advertising, x^*, is determined. The response function is assumed to be quadratic and there are diminishing returns to advertising. Little's approach is based on an assumption that competitive activity and changing customer preference and other market conditions will result in the important parameters changing over time.

To estimate the nature of these changes, Little suggests a continuous experiment in which a specified number of markets receive $\Delta/2$ less than the optimal rate, x^*, and the same number of markets receives $\Delta/2$ more than the optimum, where Δ is a parameter specified as part of the experimental design. These parameters are chosen in such a way that both the costs of poor information and the opportunity costs of operating (willfully) in a market on a nonoptimal basis (something other than x^*) are explicitly taken into account. The budget level is continually adjusted to consider the latest information on the parameter estimates and has the objective of maximizing expected profit.

A Successful Experiment. Newell reports the successful use of experimentation by the Anheuser-Busch Company to determine the optimum level of advertising effort for Budweiser beer.[23] These experiments attempted to determine the influence of advertising by comparing sales results from different levels of advertising in several markets over a six-year period. Experimentation was a necessary approach in order to isolate the effect of advertising from other important demand determinants including weather, economic conditions, competitive activity, product policy, pricing, distribution, and technological change.

Newell calls the response function "the Holy Grail of advertising" and says that their experiments did not find it, but they did find something of major importance. A random sample of 27 market areas was taken from the total of over 200 Anheuser-Busch marketing areas. These were

[22]John D. C. Little, "A Model for Adaptive Control of Promotional Spending," *Operations Research*, 14 (November–December 1966), pp. 175–97.

[23]Thomas M. Newell, *What is the Right Amount to Spend for Advertising?*, a paper presented at the A.A.A.A. Western Regional Annual Meeting, Palm Springs, California, October 6–9, 1968.

broken into three matched groups of nine each. (The actual figures were disguised in the Newell presentation, so his disguised figures are used to illustrate the method and the results obtained.) Each group received a different level of advertising: normal, half normal, and twice normal. (In actual practice, the range of spending varied from −100 percent to +300 percent, with the sample sizes much smaller in some instances.) The tests ran for a period between one and two years. The "normal" level of advertising was set according to the best judgment of the advertising department and advertising effects were measured in terms of changes in sales volume.

To determine the effect of advertising level, it was first necessary to forecast expected sales. This forecasting was done by a simple projection technique using a five-year, seasonally adjusted sales trend line. The results of the experiments showed that departures from the expected sales volume were very small and did not seem to be influenced by the amount of promotional effort. Anheuser-Busch management interpreted this finding to mean that the market was "saturated" with advertising effort (that is, the firm was operating out on the flat part of the S-shaped sales response curve) and that advertising expenses could be profitably reduced. The company did in fact cut back on its promotional spending and sales volume continued to increase.

Simulation

Simulation is a method for conducting experiments on the computer (or, less likely, with paper and pencil and desk calculator) rather than in the marketplace. The basic ingredients of simulation are a valid model of the process that management is trying to optimize and the capability of running through many decision periods, using the model, to determine the outcomes to alternative courses of actions and contingencies.

A simulation model of use in determining the level of promotional effort would have to contain a reliable response function describing how sales (or gross profit contribution) responded to changes in the decision variables) such as total advertising budget, number of salesmen, amount spent on dealer allowances, and so on. Other important variables such as consumer income and economic conditions, and competitive activity would have to be considered. These latter variables could be estimated using an essentially random procedure, as provided by the Monte Carlo method, for example.

Using the simulation model, the marketing communication strategist could calculate the probable outcomes from various levels of spending and select that one which was most profitable, given his assumptions about market conditions. Although there are as yet no reported instances of the successful use of simulation for determining the level of promotional effort in an actual management situation, there can be no doubt that such methods are being developed and will eventually come into widespread use among those marketers who spend enough money on promotional effort to warrant the expense of developing and maintaining the basic simulation model required for this approach.[24]

SUMMARY

Determining the level of effort in a marketing communication program is a very complex problem requiring sophisticated analysis and careful attention to both conceptual and measurement difficulties. Setting the budget is a major step in planning the communication program and decisions about the level of spending are the major input into the development of advertising media strategy and the staffing of the sales organization, as well as the planning of sales promotion, publicity, reseller support and related activities.

Although management has traditionally relied upon some rather intuitive and subjective approaches to the determination of the level of effort, there are signs that the procedure is becoming more scientific and more analytical. Developments in the modeling of marketing processes have provided some useful conceptual insights which, although incomplete, can help to organize the problem and to identify the important variables and relationships in the budgeting problem. This analysis can reveal the need for specific kinds of information in order to improve the accuracy of the budget-setting procedure. Important developments in measurement techniques are also making a contribution and these are coming from both improved understanding of powerful statistical techniques and their proper use and the increased use of experimental design in market research. Both of these classes of methods require the analysis of large amounts of data and the computer has therefore been an important part of this revolution.

In the final analysis, however, management judgment must be applied because the problem is much more complex and sophisticated than available analytical techniques. But well-informed management judgment is preferable to pure guess and the analytical techniques that were reviewed in this chapter suggest ways of structuring the budget decision problem that will reveal the need for specific pieces of information and

[24]A very promising start is reported by Jerome Herniter, Victor Cook, and Bernard Norek, "Microsimulation Evaluation of Advertising Budget Strategies," a paper presented to the International Meeting of The Institute of Management Sciences, New York City, March 27, 1969.

estimates of specific parameters. The most important parameter of all is the sales response constant, the rate at which the market responds to promotional effort.

While estimation of the response function requires rigorous quantitative analytical techniques, the underlying model must be based upon sound knowledge of behavioral processes. Before the statistical fishing expedition begins, it is useful to have a behavioral model that suggests what variables are likely to be determinants of demand and of response to communication effort. Behavioral models can also suggest the nature of the cause-effect relationship and the shape of the response function. Saturation effects and lags in response are examples of measurement considerations based on behavioral hypotheses.

It is unlikely that there ever can be a general model for determining the optimum level of promotional effort for all kinds of companies, products, and markets. The problem is simply too complex. Substantial strides have been made, however, in the development of models to aid and refine managerial judgment. Intelligent use of available decision-making tools can result in better informed and more intelligent solutions to the problem of determining the optimum level of communication effort.

17

Allocating
Communication Effort

Allocation problems are characterized by three elements: an objective, a budget constraint, and several projects. The allocation task is to assign the limited budget to the several projects in such a way that the objective is attained to the maximum possible degree. The previous chapter explored the analytical and measurement problems involved in setting the communication budget. In this chapter, the problem of allocating that budget will be the focus of attention. Several models dealing with the allocation of promotional effort will be described and evaluated. These models help us to understand the nature of allocation problems, and they illustrate the potential for attacking these problems in rigorous fashion.

LEVELS OF ALLOCATION PROBLEMS

There are several kinds of allocation problems in developing the marketing communication strategy. At one level are problems of allocating the total communication budget among the modes of communication: personal selling, advertising, public relations and publicity, sales promotion, and packaging. Alternatively, one can consider allocation of the total communication budget among the basic control units of the business: products (or brands); sales territories, districts and regions; or specific customers or customer categories, such as categories based on size. It is difficult to specify any general rules for which level of problem should be attacked first—i.e., whether one should first allocate among modes and then within each mode allocate effort among control units, or whether funds should first be allocated to control units and then divided among alternative communication modes. Figure 17–1 suggests some of the dimensions along which allocation decisions must be made.

Our strategy for dealing with the allocation problem will be as follows: First, we shall review the basic analytical framework for allocation problems from economics and management science. Next, in a review of material developed in earlier chapters, we shall deal briefly with the problem of allocation among modes. Then we will discuss, in primarily qualitative terms, the four principal kinds of allocation problems in communication: allocation among products, customers, and territories, and over time. Finally, treating mass communication and personal communication as separate allocation problems, we will consider the problem of assigning selling effort. Here the discussion will review those analytical approaches from management science that have been developed sufficiently to permit an increase in our understanding of such problems even if they fall short of providing specific solutions to management problems.

The problem of allocating the advertising budget among media will be dealt with in a separate chapter. There are two reasons for this separate treatment. First, before we can consider the media allocation problem we need to develop a better understanding of the nature of advertising media and the contribution which they can make to the effectiveness of the marketing communication strategy. Second, there is a

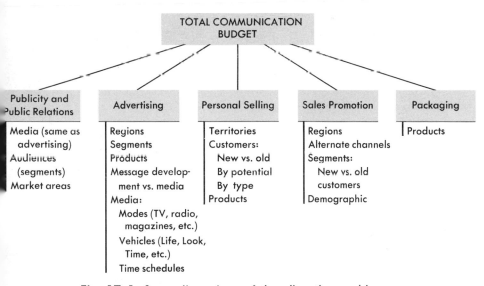

Fig. 17–1. Some dimensions of the allocation problem.

quite well developed body of knowledge pertaining specifically to the advertising media selection process that can be most efficiently presented in a separate chapter.

The relationship between budget-level decisions and allocation decisions should not be forgotten. Allocation and budget decisions are logically ordered in a hierarchy. Allocation decisions at one level set budgets for the next level, which must then be reallocated, and so on.

ANALYTICAL FRAMEWORK FOR ALLOCATION

When the similarity between the budgeting problem and the allocation problem is recognized, it comes as no surprise to learn that the analytical tools and concepts for coping with these two sets of problems are likewise similar. The logic of allocation analysis requires examination of four sets of considerations: objectives, budget constraints, the marginal productivity criterion, and response functions (including both response to effort and decay over time).

Objectives

The objectives of communication effort can be phrased in several ways, as we have seen. The three major classes of alternatives are profit, sales, or communication objectives. The objective, however classified, is to be maximized by the allocation decision—i.e., achieve the highest profit or the highest sales or deliver the maximum number of messages to potential customers or obtain the maximum amount of attitude change. It is assumed that the degree of objective attainment is a function of the amount of effort expended, with amount of effort defined either in terms of total communication or, more likely, in terms of amount spent for advertising, number of sales calls, or some other specific decision variable.

Budget Constraints

If there were no budget constraint there would be no allocation problem—or at least the allocation problem would be greatly simplified. The budget constraints consist of the limitations on the resources available for marketing communication strategy. There is a limited number of salesmen available in the short run and a limited amount of money for media advertising and for sales promotion. The problem is to develop a strategy for using these scarce resources which maximizes the value of the criterion variable (profit, sales, effective messages) specified by the statement of objectives.

There may be several budget constraints operating in a single allocation problem, as where there is a limited number of salesmen, operating on limited expense budgets, who can make only five calls each day. As the number of constraints increases, the allocation problem can quickly exceed the intuitive abilities of the strategist to follow through on all interactions possible and computations required without losing track of the possibility of violation of constraints. The complexity of the allocation problem has made it a prime candidate for computer-based operations research studies.

The Marginal Productivity Criterion

As we have seen, profits are maximized when the ratio of marginal revenue to marginal cost is equal for every project to which effort has been allocated, subject to the budget constraint. (To determine the optimum level of effort, additional funds are obtained until the marginal return–marginal cost ratios are all equal to the cost of capital to the firm.) This condition, as also noted earlier, assumes that the firm is operating in the range of decreasing marginal returns on each project (past the inflection point on an S-shaped response curve), that the functions are continuous and differentiable, and that cost functions are similarly well behaved.

To review briefly, the marginal productivity criterion simply states that the incremental returns to be derived from investing an additional unit of effort in each project should be equal. If the return from project B is greater than the return from project A, then it is necessary to shift resources from A to B to increase the overall level of goal attainment. A simple example of the application of this criterion can be seen in the case of allocation of advertising funds among modes where the cost-per-thousand-prospective-customers-reached should be equal for each mode. Otherwise, it pays to shift funds to the mode with lower cost-per-thousand and to keep transferring funds until, as higher-cost media vehicles are added each time within the mode, the cost-per thousand increases to the point where it is equal to that of the other modes. An analogous situation exists when the salesman must decide how to allocate his effort among new and old customers. He should shift effort from established customers to potential customers until the expected returns from potential customers are equal to those from established customers.

Response Functions

At the heart of the problem, once again, is the need to determine how the criterion variable (sales volume, attitude, market share, and so on) responds to changes in the decision variable. There are several ways of determining response functions, as we have seen. It is common to assume a shape for the response function (e.g., linear, exponential, S-shaped [logistic], or some other functional form) and to then attempt to estimated the important parameters in an equation describing that function. Our discussion in the last chapter considered two key parameters that must be estimated: a response constant for describing this period's response to promotional effort, and a decay constant which serves to make the model dynamic by describing how sales in this period are influenced by communication effort in previous periods. A third variable that may be important in describing the response function is the market potential (or saturation level, as defined by Vidale and Wolfe[1]), which becomes an asymptotic value for the response function as effort becomes very large in an S-shaped response function.

The Plausibility of the S-Curve. The S-shaped response function has a certain amount of intuitive appeal and plausibility. Zentler and Ryde[2] argued that this was a reasonable view of *individual* response to promotional effort and maintained that this opinion had been expressed by several experts with whom they had talked. This kind of curve, shown in Figure 17–2, is described by the following general algebraic expression:

$$R = M \frac{c_2 E^2 + c_3 E^3 + \cdots + C_n E^n}{1 + d_1 E + d_2 E^2 + d_3 E^3 + \cdots + d_n E^n}$$

where R is response, E is the amount of promotional effort, and M is the saturation level, the value that R approaches as E becomes infinitely large. n may have any value greater than or equal to 2 but the coefficients must obey the conditions

$$d_1 \geqq 0 \quad c_n = d_n \quad c_s \leqq d_s \qquad \text{for all } 2 < s < n$$

plus certain other complicated conditions to insure that R always increases as E increases. The coefficients determine the height and slope of the curve. The curve so described is consistent with a set of assumptions about response: Initial response to effort is small but the rate of response increases rapidly up to a point (I), beyond which each unit of effort produces slightly smaller (but positive) incremental returns. Point MA on the curve in Figure 17–2 is the point at which marginal response is equal to average response. One can think of a family of such curves (defined by different values of M, c, and d) for each of the geographic territories served by the company and among which promotional effort

[1]M. L. Vidale and H. B. Wolfe, "An Operations-Research Study of Sales Response to Advertising," *Operations Research*, 5 (June 1957), pp. 370–81, reprinted in F. M. Bass *et al.* (eds.), *Mathematical Models and Methods in Marketing* (Homewood, Ill.: Richard D. Irwin, Inc., 1961), pp. 363–74.

[2]A. P. Zentler and Dorothy Ryde, "An Optimum Geographical Distribution of Publicity Expenditure in a Private Organisation," *Management Science*, 2 (July 1956), pp. 337–52, reprinted in Bass *et al.*, *op. cit.*, pp. 410–27.

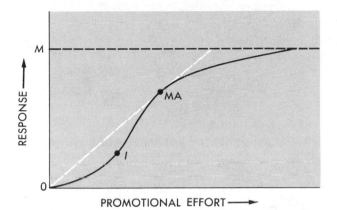

Fig. 17–2. An S-shaped response function. (Source: Zentler and Ryde, *op. cit.*, p. 339.)

is to be allocated. The portion of the curve between the origin and the inflection point is a region of *increasing* return to promotional effort, where each unit of effort produces a little more response than the previous unit. This assumes that a certain amount of effort is required to get the market going, so to speak, and to make some inroads against established competitive effort. An alternative is to assume decreasing returns from the outset with a curve that is always concave to the origin and has no inflection point. Because most analyses assume that the firm is operating beyond the inflection point, in the region of decreasing marginal returns, it does not make a great deal of difference which assumption is made.

Estimating Parameters in the Response Function. Estimation of response functions is the key measurement problem in allocation as well as in determining the level of effort. There is good reason to question whether, in fact, the response functions assumed in most normative models can be empirically estimated and verified. Such estimation problems may preclude determination of an optimum allocation scheme. Because our objective in this chapter is to understand the allocation problem and to explore alternative ways of structuring and solving such problems, we can play down the significance of the estimation problems. At the same time, we should note that such models as we discuss in this section may have little operational usefulness because of the difficulties of estimating the response functions underlying them.

One other comment about response functions is also in order. The typical approach is to assume the *shape* of the response function, to estimate the key parameters in that functional expression, and to then test the model against empirical data. Occasionally, several alternative shapes of models may be tried and compared against statistical criteria such as goodness-of-fit tests. The researcher must start by specifying a model of some kind, however. No optimization procedure will develop the model for him. In developing his response function, the researcher should operate from some of the basic notions of response to communication that have been developed in earlier parts of this text.

ALLOCATION AMONG MODES

Chapter 9 explored in considerable detail the issue of the relative effectiveness of mass and personal communication and their roles in a well-balanced marketing communication strategy. There are significant interdependencies between the two modes of communication, and the "optimal" communication strategy blends these two forms of communication in a way which maximizes the value of one to the other in a synergistic relationship.

Two important analytical concepts for thinking about the relative roles to be played by mass and personal communication are the diffusion process and the product life cycle. These two concepts describe the same phenomena from two different viewpoints. The common element is the attempt to describe the stages in growth, acceptance, and decline of a product. The diffusion process sees the problem in terms of changes in attitudes and adoption within the market, in other words, in terms of customer acceptance. The product-life-cycle concept describes the impact on the sales revenue and profitability of the firm.

The analysis in Chapter 9 suggested that mass communication was likely to be more effective in the earlier stages of the product's development, especially to the extent that such communication could be directed toward opinion leaders, who could generate word-of-mouth influence on their peers. Personal selling assumed a larger role as the product gained market acceptance and became a mature member of the company's product line. The reasons for changes in the relative effectiveness of mass and personal communication reflect differences in the characteristics of those persons who adopt products at various stages in the diffusion process and their characteristic ways of acquiring and acting upon information about new products.

Another relevant concept from Chapter 9 is the important distinction between push and pull strategies, the former relying primarily upon personal selling and the latter relying upon mass communication. The nature of the market, the availability of promotional funds, and the nature of the product were identified as major considerations in the push vs. pull decision.

Each mode of communication has certain strengths and weaknesses that must be carefully appraised as decisions are made about how best to reach the market and provide specific prospects with the information they need to reduce perceived risk and to progress through the stages of the buying decision. The mass media are typically best suited for the simple awareness function. They can announce a new product, remind potential prospects of the company name, keep the brand name in front of the customer, provide some limited amount of product information, and pave the way either for a sales call (in industrial markets) or for exposure to point-of-purchase personal selling or promotional materials (for consumer products). Product demonstration, specific application, and the careful development of need awareness and overcoming of objections may be required for complex, big-ticket items; this information is best provided by personal selling. Once initial awareness has been created, personal selling may be uniquely able to move the prospect through several stages in the buying decision and increasingly greater degrees of attitude change.

Problems relating to allocation among modes often involve some qualitative considerations about the relative effectiveness of mass vs. personal communication that can only be assessed by careful, subjective managerial judgments. It is better if these judgments can be based upon some reasonably sophisticated understanding of the communication process, and specific data about predispositions and characteristic buying decision processes, within the relevant market segments.

FOUR KINDS OF ALLOCATION PROBLEMS

It is useful to analyze separately four different kinds of allocation problems: allocation among products, allocation among specific customers, allocation among geographic areas, and allocation over time. These four kinds of problems are not mutually exclusive and they tend to occur together. The analytical framework for approaching each class of problems is somewhat the same, but the measurement problems tend to be quite different, as are the strategic implications of each.

Among Products

There are several ways of looking at differences among products and classes of products when decisions concerning allocation are being made. Products may be described in such terms as: stage in the product life cycle; whether new or established products; relative profit margin contribution; relationships to other elements in the product line; market share (or some other measure of market penetration); or percentage of total company sales volume. There are, of course, other ways of describing products.

A few common-sense observations about allocation among products are a good starting point for thinking about these kinds of allocation problems. New products must be treated as different from older products in that it does take time to establish new products in the market. Spending levels typically change over the product life cycle. Investment spending may occur at first to establish the product firmly in the market in the face of aggressive competition from old products. Eventually the new product can assume responsibility for carrying its own weight and making a contribution to profitability. Finally, it may be desirable to remove all promotional support from a product in the hope of maximizing the profit contribution on a product facing a distinct decline in sales revenue and consumer preference.

Other things being equal, it is always preferable to sell more-profitable products. For the multiproduct firm, there is a continual problem of adjusting promotional effort to stimulate the sales of more profitable products. This allocation problem is complicated by the fact that the most profitable products are not always the easiest to sell. For a variety of reasons, salesmen may avoid selling the more profitable items in the line—because they are relatively low-volume products and salesmen are paid on revenue, not profitability, or because the product requires knowledge which the salesman does not possess, or for any of several other reasons. Some products, despite their high profitability, may not be responsive to additional promotional effort. This is the case for repair parts for heavy industrial equipment, for example, which tend to carry profit margins well above those on original equipment but demand for which is not very responsive to sales effort.

Compensation Scheme To Obtain Balanced Sales Effort. Farley explored the conditions under which salesmen could be motivated to allocate their time among products in the line in a way which would maximize the profit contribution to the firm. He assumed that the firm wished to maximize profitability and that the salesman wished to maximize his own income. If the salesman has total time C available for allocation among products, the time devoted to each product, t_i, was shown to be optimal when the commission rate, as a percentage of the gross margin on each product, is the same for all products, as shown by the following conditions (assuming that quantity sold is a function of time spent on that product):

$$\frac{B_i M_i}{B_j M_j} = \frac{(1 - B_i) \, M_i}{(1 - B_j) \, M_j} \qquad \text{for all } i, j$$

and

$$\sum_{i=1}^{n} t_i = C$$

where B_i = commission rate, in percent, paid on product i
M_i = gross margin on product i
$i = 1, 2, 3, \ldots, n$
j = any i

The left-hand side of the equation describes the conditions under which the salesman maximizes his income, while the right-hand side describes the profit-maximizing conditions for the firm, according to the marginal productivity criterion. Farley points out that there may be sound reasons for not wanting to pay salesmen strictly on a commission basis, such as the need to use salesmen for non-sales-producing activities, but that if commissions are to be used, this plan should be optimal.[3]

One of the problems with implementing the recommendations to be derived from manipulation of this model is that it overlooks any differences in the ways in which the market responds to increases in sales effort. There may be reasons why salesmen should not allocate their effort among products on the basis of gross margin contribution. Such allocations overlook customer needs and say nothing about the level of demand. Furthermore, there are many factors other than demand or promotional elasticity which govern the profit contribution of a given product. The plan Farley recommends may fall short of optimally profitable results to the extent that sales are not a function of the amount of selling effort devoted to a product and to the extent that the response function is not similar for all products. The model is nonetheless interesting because it does attempt to relate allocation of sales effort to product profitability on a *ceteris paribus* basis.

A Model for Allocating Advertising. Vidale and Wolfe suggested that advertising funds could be allocated among products on the basis of responsiveness to advertising, profitability, and decay, according to

$$I_k = (R_{ok}/a_k)(1 - f_k) - \lambda_k$$

where I_k = return on capital invested in product k
R_{ok} = the "instantaneous" sales increase resulting from the campaign
a_k = total cost of advertising campaign for product k
f_k = the ratio of production and distribution costs to selling price

[3]John U. Farley, "An Optimal Plan for Salesmen's Compensation," *Journal of Marketing Research*, 1 (May 1964), pp. 39–43.

$\lambda_k =$ the exponential rate of sales decay of product k in the absence of promotion

With a budget constraint, the firm would array products according to I_k and continue to spend on successively less profitable products until the budget was used up. A similar procedure could be used to set the budget. Funds could be allocated to products until the rate of return decreased to the level of the cost of capital (or some other rate-of-return criterion established by management). The total funds allocated could then be summed to yield the total advertising budget.[4]

Products vary significantly in their promotional elasticity, the extent to which demand is responsive to changes in the level of effort. Therefore, estimation of the sales response constant is of prime importance in the decision to allocate effort among products or brands. Unfortunately, the problem of estimating response constants for each of several brands is very difficult and virtually impossible in the case of new products. Without some information concerning differences in responsiveness, it is hard to allocate funds rigorously on the basis of differences among brands.

Among Customers

As with products, so with customers—there are many different ways of describing them that have relevance for the allocation decision. Individual customers may be grouped by sales potential, as when A, B, C categories are drawn up to serve as the basis for determining number of sales calls to be made during the coming period. Customers may be classified on the basis of rate of usage, as when advertising strategies are developed to attempt to deliver more messages during the period to heavy users, based on some correlation between rate of usage and other characteristics which can serve as the basis for segmentation.

Customers may be described on the basis of any of several variables which are assumed to be related either to responsiveness to promotional effort or to their value as customers (such as usage rate). Industrial customers are often grouped on the basis of their industry affiliations (S.I.C. codes) or by size (number of employees, sales volume, number of offices, etc.). An important distinction may be drawn among direct and indirect accounts, or accounts at various levels in the distribution channel.

Direct vs. Wholesale Accounts. Buzzell described a study in which a specific company was faced with the problem of how to allocate effort between direct and wholesale accounts. The objective was to maximize

[4]Vidale and Wolfe, *op. cit.*

profit, subject to the constraint of a 10-percent return on sales. The response function was assumed to be of the form

$$Q_i = S(1 - e^{-a_i n_i})$$

where Q_i = quantity sold to customer type i
$\qquad S$ = saturation level of sales to either type of customer
$\qquad a_i$ = a constant describing the sensitivity of sales to changes in n_i
$\qquad n_i$ = number of salesmen serving customer type i
$\qquad i = D$ = direct customers
$\qquad\quad = W$ = wholesale customers

S, the saturation level (estimated at $12 million), is assumed to be the same for both classes of customers; it is the asymptotic value of the response function as the amount of sales effort increases. Response functions were based on empirical observations which resulted in estimating a_D at .01725 and a_W at .065. Assuming that the profit margin stays constant over all levels of sales volume (e.g., that there are no cost economies in production), the optimum allocation of sales effort to customers was defined as follows (in thousands of dollars):

$$\text{Profit} = .377[12,000(1 - e^{-.01725 n_D})] + .318[12,000(1 - e^{-.065 n_W})]$$
$$- 12(n_D + n_W) - 2,000$$

where .377 and .318 are the gross margins on direct and wholesale sales, respectively, $12,000 is the cost of one salesman's salary and expenses and $2,000,000 is the fixed cost of the sales organization. Differentiating the profit equation with respect to n_D and n_W and setting the results equal to zero:

$$78.039 e^{-.01725 n_D} = 12$$
$$n_D - 109.97$$
$$248.04 e^{-.065 n_W} = 12$$
$$n_W = 46.09$$

This solution says that the optimum number of salesmen would be 110 calling on direct accounts and 46 calling on wholesale accounts, for a total of 156 salesmen. If the total sales force size is restricted to N men, then the optimum allocation is found by differentiation to be

$$n_D = .79N - 14.07$$

and, since $n_W = N - n_D$,

$$n_W = .21N + 14.07$$

For an assumed restriction to 42 men, the optimum allocation was therefore 19 direct salesmen and 23 wholesale salesmen. The model was reformulated on a territory basis and produced results consistent with the first version.[5] This model illustrates the opportunities for allocating efforts among customer types where there are differences in the profitability and responsiveness of different classes of customers.

Similar analysis could be performed to yield optimum allocation of advertising effort among customer categories on the basis of the value of those customers to the firm. For example, customers would be put into categories of heavy, medium, and light users, and the value of each kind of customer estimated on the basis of amount and frequency of purchase. Next, it would be necessary to estimate differences in the responsiveness of each segment. The resulting data could provide the basis for a normative model for optimum allocation of advertising effort among the three market segments.

Among Territories

Several studies have examined the conditions under which promotional effort can be allocated optimally to various geographic areas within the total market. The Zentler and Ryde model described earlier in this chapter explored the conditions for optimum geographic assignment of promotional effort. Response functions of the form shown in Figure 17–2 were estimated for each geographic area. The conditions for optimum allocation were straightforward. Given n regions (Zentler and Ryde called them "countries"), with populations N_r and a total budget S, and given *per capita* response functions for each region defined by

$$R_r = \psi \left(\frac{P_r \theta_r x_r}{b} \right)$$

where P_r = promotional effectiveness per unit of expenditure in market r

θ_r = an index of brand preference in market r

x_r = promotional expenditure per capita in market r

b = a constant scale factor expressing the unit in which expenditure is measured

r = 1, 2, 3, ..., n

R_r = response, as previously

The objective is to maximize

$$\sum_{r=1}^{n} N_r R_r$$

subject to the constraint

$$\sum_{r=1}^{n} N_r x_r = S$$

[5]Robert D. Buzzell, *Mathematical Models and Marketing Management* (Boston: Division of Research, Graduate School of Business Administration, Harvard University, 1964), pp. 136–56.

Applying the marginal productivity criterion (expressed by the constant λ) and differentiating with respect to promotional effort defines the optimal allocation as

$$\frac{\partial R_r}{\partial x_r} = \lambda \qquad \text{for all } r$$

$$\frac{\partial^2 R_r}{\partial x_r^2} < 0 \qquad \text{for all } r$$

In other words, marginal responses are equal in all areas and to the right of the inflection point (I) on the response curve for each area. Because of the complexity of the algebraic expression for the response curve, a heuristic graphical solution to the problem was said to be necessary.

Despite these difficulties of solution, the Zentler and Ryde model is interesting because of its analytical logic. It demonstrates one view of the factors to consider in determining the optimum allocation of promotional effort among territories including consumer brand preference, response to promotional effort, and the relative expense of media in different market areas.

Because personal selling is typically organized on a geographic basis, problems of assigning effort to territories are much more common in personal selling allocation decisions than in mass communication. On the other hand, the proliferation of regional advertising media in recent years has made it possible more explicitly to consider important regional differences in the allocation of mass promotional effort.

Over Time

The allocation of promotional effort over time is very closely related to budgeting problems, as discussed in the previous chapter. The fact that sales in one period are influenced by promotional effort in previous periods and that sales in future periods will be influenced by promotional effort in this period must both be considered in setting this period's level of effort.

But the problem of allocating promotional effort *within* the budget period poses many problems of temporal allocation as well. In determining the advertising media schedule for a year, for example, there are several ways in which to space the determined number of insertions within a particular medium. Is it better to spread a budgeted six insertions in a magazine over the entire year on an every-other-month basis? two months in a row followed by two months out of the medium? six months in a row? or some other possibility?

There are similar problems in the assignment of selling effort to customers. For example, is it better to spend a longer amount of time on each of fewer sales calls or to make more short calls? A dynamic model for the assignment of salesmen's efforts to accounts will be explored in the next section of this chapter.

Sales promotions also pose some interesting problems of allocation over time. Occasional sales promotions to stimulate trial and to encourage repeat purchase by established customers can be very helpful and can produce benefits over a reasonably long time period. The coordination of such sales-stimulating sales promotions with reminder advertising in mass media poses some complex problems of allocation.

Analytically, it is not difficult to specify those factors which are likely to be significant determinants of the optimum allocation of promotional effort over time. These include the rate at which sales potential erodes in the absence of promotional effort, as expressed by the now-familiar decay constant, which is due to a combination of customer forgetting and the impact of competitors' promotional activity. The effect of a promotional expenditure in one period must be assessed in terms of the cumulative effects expected over several periods in the future, discounted by an appropriate factor to its equivalent present value.

These considerations will be examined more closely when the discussion in this chapter turns to dynamic models of allocation of sales effort, and in Chapter 19 when we consider the allocation of advertising budgets among media.

ASSIGNING PERSONAL SELLING EFFORT

The direction of sales force effort toward the most profitable market opportunities is a complex management task that lends itself to rigorous analysis only up to a point. It is easy to forget that the resources being allocated are human resources—salesmen who have feelings and attitudes toward their work which significantly influence their effectiveness. Salesmen cannot be arbitrarily moved around from one area to another, constantly shifting accounts and, perhaps, place of residence, to achieve some kind of "optimum" allocation during each planning period.

Although the response of the market to selling effort may be summarized mathematically, remember that the response itself results from the decisions of individual prospects to buy from individual salesmen with whom they have established a relationship of trust and confidence and perhaps even friendship. Customers are not indifferent to the salesmen with whom they deal. While customers may be a little short with their praise, they will be quick to complain about, and to stop buying from, a salesman they do not like and do not trust.

Implementing Results of Operations Research Studies

There are likewise many problems involved in implementing a rigorous analysis of the allocation of sales effort. Sales managers in the field, responsible for bringing about the changes recommended by such studies, may strongly resist such change, whether because they cannot understand the analysis or they disagree with its assumptions. For example, rigorous analysis of the allocation of sales effort usually begins with an assumption that all salesmen are of equal ability and that all salesmen are equally effective with all customers. Such assumptions, which may be quite valid as analytical bases upon which to consider the impact of alternative allocation strategies, fly in the face of the field sales manager's knowledge of his men and his profession. Implementation must take those important personal and qualitative considerations into account. Operations research studies are best treated as *guidelines* for management action.

Managers' Attitudes. The field sales manager, usually promoted to management responsibility on the basis of demonstrated selling ability, is often uncomfortable with generalization and rigorous analysis. He is more prone to concentrate his attention on the idiosyncrasies of each salesman-customer relationship and to pay attention to the details which tend to differentiate one situation from another, since these distinctions are the little differences to which his salesman's sense has attuned him, spelling the difference between success and failure in the selling situation.[6] These factors may be left out of the operations research study, but they must be evaluated and reincorporated in implementing the solutions of such studies.

Salesman and Market Characteristics. Decisions about the assignment of personal selling effort are expressed in such parameters as the average length of call, number of calls per day, number of accounts per salesman, number of calls per account by class of account, and number of sales territories. The principal factors considered in making such decisions are the potential business available from a specific account or territory (grouping of accounts), the number of calls the salesman is capable of making in a day (which is a function of the number of hours of selling time available and the location of customers), the average order size, profit margins, and the cost of maintaining a salesman in the field. Other considerations which may be of significance in a given situation

[6]David B. Montgomery and Frederick E. Webster, Jr., "Application of Operations Research to Personal Selling Strategy," *Journal of Marketing*, 32 (January 1968), pp. 50–57.

include the frequency with which competitors' salesmen call on customers, the extent to which primary demand is influenced by the total level of selling effort in the market, and customer order frequency.

Qualitative considerations of major importance in these decisions include the amount of non-selling effort expected of the salesman, such as customer servicing and reporting market information back to the company, and the amount of time required by specific products because of their technical complexity. The nature of the customer's buying decision process, and the frequency with which orders are placed, can also be major considerations.

The most common output from the sales force allocation decision is the statement of a sales territory, defined as the customers assigned to a particular salesman, usually but not always on a geographic basis. In simplest terms, the sales territory is determined by the total time available from the average salesman minus the time he spends on non-selling activities, divided by the product of average time per call and the required number of calls per customer per period:

Number of accounts per salesman =

$$\frac{\text{Total selling time available per salesman}}{(\text{Average time per call}) \times (\text{Required calls per account per period})}$$

This scheme overlooks any significant differences among salesmen in terms of abilities or selling responsibilities, and it likewise overlooks any significant differences among customers such as size and potential, and among territories such as travel distance between accounts and the distribution of customer sizes within a given territory.[7]

Allocating Sales Effort on the Basis of Potential

Let us consider first the most basic sales effort allocation problem, that of assigning effort to specific customers. At the minimum it would seem necessary to differentiate among customers in terms of their potential and the amount of business available from them. It would also seem to make a difference whether the firm is "in" or "out," that is, whether the customer is "old" or "new." Other things being equal, it would make sense to allocate more effort to those customers with the larger potential and to established customers, where the probability of obtaining a sale is higher.

A Stochastic Model. One of the first published studies of an operations research approach to marketing problems was John Magee's analy-

[7]For a discussion of the objectives of territorial design and the characteristics of an "ideal" sales territory, see Kenneth R. Davis and Frederick E. Webster, Jr., *Sales Force Management* (New York: Ronald Press Company, 1968), pp. 344–57.

sis of the allocation of sales effort to customers on the basis of expected sales volume.[8] This study added the sophistication of viewing customer response as a stochastic process rather than in deterministic fashion.

Magee's model defined c as the average number of cases of product ordered by a particular dealer in a given month. c can be estimated from sales records and becomes the best estimate of what that dealer would order in a future month, although his actual order may be different. Magee hypothesized that the distribution of the actual cases ordered could be approximated by the Poisson distribution,

$$E(n) = \frac{e^{-c}c^n}{n!}$$

where $E(n)$ is the probability that a dealer with an average order, c, will actually order n cases in a given month. This assumption was checked with available data and found to be reasonable.

Dealers can be arrayed according to the expected number of cases they will order and this distribution of dealers is defined by the probability density function $Y(c)$. Although this distribution would depend upon promotional effort, it is assumed at this stage of the analysis that all dealers receive "normal" promotion. Then the fraction of dealers who will order n cases in a specific month is given by

$$f(n) = \int_0^\infty \frac{e^{-c}c^n}{n!} Y(c)\, dc$$

$Y(c)$ was estimated from earlier experiments on response to promotion and found to be reasonably approximated by the simpler exponential equation

$$Y(c) = \frac{1}{s} e^{-c/s}$$

where s is the average number of cases ordered by the average dealer. Substitution in the earlier equation gives

$$f(n) = \frac{s^n}{(s+1)^{n+1}}$$

Effect of Reduced Effort. The firm that Magee studied had been following the promotional policy of allocating effort to the top 40 percent of dealers as defined by orders in the previous two months. Magee wished to appraise this policy. Several experiments were run to determine response to promotional effort and to assess the relative merits of other policies for the allocation of effort, including the assignment of promo-

[8]John F. Magee, "The Effect of Promotional Effort on Sales," *Journal of the Operations Research Society of America*, 1 (February 1953), pp. 64–74, reprinted in Bass *et al.*, *op. cit.*, pp. 444–55.

tional effort to all dealers. Results of these experiments showed that the expected value of the business to be derived from a dealer who did *not* receive promotional effort during a period was reduced by approximately 50 percent. This reduction occurred for two reasons. First, there was a probability of 0.3 that he would behave as if his characteristic order size, c, were zero. Second, if he did order (with probability 0.7), the expected value of this order was 0.71 what it would be if he *were* promoted. In other words, the probability of an order was reduced and the expected value of an order, conditional upon ordering, was also reduced. In this manner, it was possible to determine the effect of promotion.

Having isolated the effect of promotion on dealers, it was next possible to specify the level of sales resulting from any level of promotional effort. The number of cases to be ordered in a specified period will be

$$Q(a) = N \left\{ a \int_0^\infty c\,Y_p(c)\,dc + 0.5(1-a) \int_0^\infty c\,Y_{np}(c)\,dc \right\}$$

$$= \frac{Ns}{2} (1 + 2a - a^2)$$

where $Y_p(c)$ = the distribution of orders from dealers who receive promotional effort

$Y_{np}(c)$ = the distribution of orders from dealers who do not receive effort

N = the total number of dealers

a = the fraction selected to receive promotion

To determine the optimum, i.e., most profitable, level of promotional effort (defined as the fraction of dealers to receive effort), the analyst needs only to add price and cost terms as follows:

$$\pi = p \cdot Q(a) - TC(Q) - C(a) - FC$$

where π = profit

p = unit price

$TC(Q)$ = total costs (except for selling costs) of producing and distributing quantity Q

$C(a)$ = selling costs to promote to fraction a of all dealers

FC = fixed costs[9]

Substituting the earlier equation for $Q(a)$ into the profit equation makes it a single-variable equation which can be differentiated and solved to determine the optimum value of a—the proportion of dealers to receive

[9]This extension of the model is from David B. Montgomery and Glen L. Urban, *Management Science in Marketing*, (Englewood Cliffs, N.J.: Prentice-Hall, Inc., 1969), p. 264.

sales calls. Thus, this is one approach to the allocation of sales effort among customers as a function of expected sales and profits.

Magee's model suffers from the fact that it is a single-period model and does not consider lagged effects in response to promotional effort. Furthermore, it leaves unanswered the question of call frequency—how many times to call on a customer during a period—and instead assumes that allocation of effort to a given customer is on a simple either-or basis.

Influence of Potential: Old Accounts vs. New

Brown, Hulswit, and Kettelle developed a model for assigning effort to customers which considered the amount of sales effort to be devoted to a customer during the period as well as the effects of effort carried from one period to another.[10] The model also considered differences in the response characteristics of prospective customers and established customers. The firm actually studied was named (hypothetically) the Penstock Press.

A market survey revealed that Penstock's market potential was $30 million per year. The largest 520 customers out of a total of 13,000 were found to be responsible for half of Penstock's annual revenue, which was about $6 million. Further analysis showed that 3,900 customers were responsible for $26 million in annual revenue to all sellers in this market out of the total market of $30 million. This array of customers by potential is used later in the analysis to assign effort to accounts.

The next phase in the study of Penstock's operations was to conduct an experiment to determine responsiveness to sales effort. Eighteen company salesmen participated in the experiment and each salesman was assigned 36 customers to receive varying levels of sales effort. The three effort levels were "heavy" (16 hours per month), "medium" (4 hours per month), and "light" (one hour per month). Each of the salesmen had 4 "heavy" customers, 8 "medium" accounts, and 24 "light" accounts for a total of 36. Careful sales records were kept of changes in the volume of business done with each customer in the experiment, which took place over a four-month period. Analysis of the results revealed that there were significant lags in response to sales effort, although this tended to vary from one customer to the next. Approximately two thirds of the customers showed some response to increased effort by the third month of the experiment.

---

[10]Arthur A. Brown, Frank T. Hulswit, and John D. Kettelle, "A Study of Sales Operations," *Operations Research*, 4 (June 1956), pp. 296–308, reprinted in Bass *et al., op. cit.*, pp. 385–97, and in Kenneth R. Davis and Frederick E. Webster, Jr. (eds.), *Readings in Sales Force Management*, (New York: Ronald Press Company, 1968), pp. 326–38.

Results of the experiment were used to estimate two response functions:

$H(x)$ = the probability of holding a customer
            as a function of the level of selling effort (x)

and

$C(x)$ = the probability of converting a prospect
            as a function of the level of selling effort

The estimation procedures followed were essentially guess work concerning the shape of the response with estimates based on only a few data points. This analysis suggested that two hours per month gave a 95-percent probability of holding an established customer and ten hours per month gave a 20-percent probability of converting a prospect. These became the standards for allocating effort.

Sales effort was assigned to accounts on the following basis. Each salesman was assumed to have 110 hours per month of selling time available. (The experimental level of 120 hours was found to be a bit heavy.) If C is the number of prospective accounts assigned to the salesman and H is the number of established customers, then the recommended program would satisfy the relation

$$10C + 2H = 110$$

Equilibrium is defined as the point at which expected conversions of new customers equal expected losses of old customers. Using a target conversion rate of 20 percent and assuming management is willing to accept an .05 probability of losing an established customer,

$$.20C = .05H$$

Combining this with the previous equation yields $H = 25$ and $C = 6$, as the optimum assignment of accounts to salesmen under the stated assumptions.

The determining factors in this model are thus the probability of holding, the probability of conversion, and the amount of time available from a single salesman. These factors were also used to determine the optimum size of sales force.

Optimum Sales Force Size

If the following definitions are accepted:

T_C = expected time (months) required for conversion
T_H = expected holding time
x = cost of salesman, dollars per hour
and E = average sales expense per month per customer

then calling 10 hours per month on prospects and 2 hours per month on customers gives an average expense of

$$E = x(10T_C + 2T_H)/(T_C + T_H)$$

This expression for the average expense per customer can be combined with an estimate of average revenue per month from a customer:

$$R = aPT_H/ (T_C + T_H)$$

where P = total potential revenue from a customer
a = fraction of potential expected from a typical customer during the holding period

It is worthwhile to direct effort to a customer as long as expected net cost does not exceed expected revenue,

$$E = fR$$

where f = marginal sales expense. This expression can be combined with the two previous equations to obtain the potential of the smallest customer worth promoting:

$$P = \frac{x(10T_C + 2T_H)}{afT_H}$$

As a Function of Marginal Sales Expense. The parameters in this specific situation had the following values: $T_C = 5$ months; $T_H = 20$ months; $a = 0.5$; and $x = \$7.57$ per hour. Substituting these values yielded the solution,

$$P = \frac{68}{f} \text{ dollars per month}$$

This defines the optimum sales force size as a function of the marginal sales expense, f, which is the amount of additional revenue the firm is willing to spend on sales effort. If f equals 20 percent, for example, the smallest customer worth promoting has a potential of $340 per month. From the array of customers by potential developed as a first step in the study it is possible to determine that there are 1,820 customers with potential at least equal to $340 per month. Assuming that the average salesman can service 31 customers, as established earlier, then the optimum size sales force would be 59 men. Similar calculations are possible for any assumed marginal sales expense and corresponding level of minimum customer potential.

The Brown, Hulswit, and Kettelle model has several attractive features. First, it recognizes that the response of customers to sales effort is a stochastic process. In other words, there is some uncertainty about whether the firm can retain a customer, regardless of the level of sales effort (although chances improve with increased effort), and there is likewise uncertainty about the amount of effort required to get an order from a new account. Another attractive feature of this model is the way in which it explicitly considers these uncertainties and defines a trade-off between established and prospective customers and develops a call strategy which considers that trade-off and the cost of sales effort. On the other hand, there is a weakness in the model concerning the amount of time to spend with a specific customer. The assumption is made, based on a rather incomplete estimation of the response function, that two hours per month is the optimum time to spend on established customers and 10 hours per month for prospective customers. A more complete model would vary the amount of effort as a function of the amount of potential and the influence of past sales effort, for example.

The problem of how much effort to spend on prospective customers has been considered in other studies. Waid, Clark, and Ackoff conducted a study to determine the optimum level of sales effort taking into consideration differences in responsiveness between new accounts and old accounts.[11] One result of their analysis was a policy recommendation that the number of calls on a prospective customer should not exceed three. This rule can be a useful guideline, but there are obviously many situations in which the salesman is well advised to ignore it, as when the first call indicates no advantage to continuing to exert effort, while other accounts would warrant a much more persistent call policy.

A Dynamic Model

Each of the models reviewed so far has concentrated on a selected set of parameters and has left out certain others that were found to be important in other models. This review has suggested that the following factors would, ideally, be incorporated in a single model for the assignment of sales effort. First, it would recognize differences in potential. Second, it would recognize the lagged relationships between sales effort and response. Third, it would prescribe the number of calls to make upon specific accounts. Fourth, it would recognize the essentially stochastic nature of response to sales effort. Fifth, it would distinguish between prospects and established customers. In summary, it would prescribe number of calls as a function of a specific account's response characteristics, retention (or decay) of the effects of promotion, potential, and status.

[11]Clark Waid, Donald F. Clark, and Russell L. Ackoff, "Allocation of Sales Effort in the Lamp Division of the General Electric Company," *Operations Research, 4* (December 1956), pp. 629–47, reprinted in Davis and Webster, *Readings. . . ,* pp. 308–26.

Lodish, Montgomery, and Webster have formulated a model which has all of these features.[12] The model will be reviewed briefly because it does contain these essential features and is more complete than earlier models. As a practical device for assigning sales effort, however, the model has limited operational value. The model has not been tested sufficiently with actual data, and some of the parameters pose complex measurement problems.

Factors Influencing Sales. The model assumes that the optimum allocation of sales effort to a customer or a class of customers is a function of the prospect's potential, the profit contribution per unit of sales, past sales effort devoted to that customer, the history of sales to that customer, current effort to be devoted to that customer, the customer's response to sales effort, and the cost of each sales call. The central elements of the model are two probabilities: the probability that the customer will place an order with the seller during the period, and the probability that the order will be a given size conditional upon an order being placed at all. Customers are described by two rather complex characteristics—a smoothed sales history parameter and remembered sales effort. These are defined as follows:

$$H_t = \alpha \left(\frac{X_{t-1}}{\pi} \right) + (1-\alpha) H_{t-1}$$

where H_t — the smoothed history of sales to the customer entering period t

X_t = sales to the customer in period t

π = this customer's potential

α — smoothing constant $(0 < \alpha \leq 1)$

The current influence of past sales effort to a specific account is given by:

$$E_t - \gamma(E_{t-1} + S_{t-1})$$

where E_t = sales effort from past periods remembered at the beginning of period t

S_{t-1} = sales effort (number of calls) directed to the customer during period $t-1$

γ = a parameter representing the proportion of sales effort remembered from previous periods

Probability of Ordering. The probability, P_0, that an established customer will place an order during period t is said to be a function of smoothed sales history, remembered sales effort, and current sales effort:

[12]Leonard Lodish, David B. Montgomery, and Frederick E. Webster, Jr., "A Dynamic Sales Call Policy Model," a paper presented at the joint ORSA–TIMS meeting held in San Francisco, May 1–3, 1968.

$$P_0(H_t, E_t, S_t) = C(1 - e^{-GH_t} + (1-C)(1 - e^{-D(E_t + S_t)})$$

where C = constant defining the relative impact of history and remembered sales effort $(0 \leqq C \leqq 1)$

G,D = constants representing diminishing returns to sales history and remembered sales effort:[13] $(G \geqq 0)$; $(D \geqq 0)$

For a prospective customer, the probability of an order, P_{tn}, is a function
of remembered and current sales effort and certain other parameters. By
definition, prospects have no remembered sales history.

$$P_{tn} = P_{max}(n, E_t) \ [1 - e^{-Q(E_t + S_t)}]$$
$$= [e^{-knE_t}][1 - e^{-Q(E_t + S_t)}]$$

where n = number of previous periods in which the prospect has
received effort but has not ordered

P_{tn} = the probability that a prospect who has been called on
for n periods and has not ordered will order in period t:
$(t = n+1)$

$P_{max}(n, E_t)$ = the maximum order probability for a firm having a remembered sales effort E_t and having been called on for
n previous periods without buying: $(0 \leqq P_{max} \ (n, E_t) \leqq 1)$

k = a parameter expressing the reduction in P_{max} as n and/
or E_t increase

Q = a parameter reflecting diminishing returns to current and
remembered sales effort

The equation for P_{tn} can be thought of as describing the "aging" of
prospects over time. The last equation assumes that sales history and sales
effort can be partial substitutes for one another. It also suggests that the
probability that a prospect will buy *decreases* as the number of periods in
which no response occurred increases and as the amount of (previously
expended) effort increases. It is for these reasons that $P_{max} \ (n, E_t)$ is expressed as an exponentially declining function of n, E_t.

Amount Ordered. The conditional probability $P_{X_t}|_0$, that the customer
will order amount X_t at time t, if he orders, is assumed to be a random
variable having a Poisson distribution with mean sales rate λ_t:

$$\lambda_t(H_t, E_t, S_t) = \pi(1 - e^{-[AB(E_t + S_t) + (1-A) \ FH_t]})$$

where A = constant representing the relative importance of remembered sales effort and smoothed sales history $(0 \leqq A \leqq 1)$

B = constant representing diminishing returns to remembered sales effort $(B \geqq 0)$

F = constant representing diminishing returns to smoothed
sales history $(F \geqq 0)$

[13]The presentation here follows Montgomery and Urban (*op. cit.*, pp. 272–76),
which differs slightly from the original.

This is not the complete model, but it is sufficient to suggest the essential ideas around which the model is built. The model becomes increasingly complex and need not be fully presented here. The optimum sales effort to a customer during a period, S_t, can be determined by use of dynamic programming on a Markov process, as a function of smoothed history and remembered sales effort. Costs and profit margin are also considered. The Markov process considers the probability that a customer in history state i in period t, and having some remembered sales effort and receiving S_t sales calls during t, will be in history state i' in $t + 1$.

The major value of this model derives from its stochastic nature and its consideration of trade-offs among current sales effort, previous (remembered) sales effort, and previous sales results. The major difficulty in using the model, in addition to its complexity, is in estimating those parameters (C, G, D, A, B, and F) defining the trade-offs. These are likely to be different for each customer, but it may be possible to develop segments of classes of customers known to have similar response characteristics on the basis of easily measured factors correlated with these parameter values. The model is nonetheless valuable as a way of thinking about specific customer response to variations in sales effort.

Routing and Scheduling

The design of sales territories is often based upon a consideration of such variables as the amount of travel time and the optimum routing of a salesman among customers, in addition to considering the number of customers and the frequency with which they are to be called upon.

The so-called "traveling salesman problem" in operations research has received frequent attention in the literature, although the classic problem is not stated in realistic terms for the actual sales effort allocation problem. The classic traveling salesman problem is stated as: Define the shortest route to travel to visit all of the capital cities of the 48 states. Because there are $(n - 1)!$ or $47!$ possibilities, trial and error is out. There are algorithms for solving this kind of problem, which is essentially an allocation problem in which the objective is to minimize cost with the assumption that cost is a linear function of distance travelled. The problem can be made more realistic by considering different call frequencies as a function of differences in customer potential. Routing and scheduling must be modified to reflect the distribution of these characteristics within the territory. Solutions to the classic traveling salesman problem do not fit this more realistic problem.[14]

14*Ibid.*, p. 282.

Although a specific routing of salesmen has certain advantages in terms of obtaining control over salesmen's efforts and assuring adequate territory coverage, most firms do not follow the practice of actually routing their salesmen from one customer to the next. The salesman may not have the computational skills or the data to determine the least cost path to cover his territory as a function of required call frequencies for each customer; and this is an argument in favor of specific routing. On the other hand, most intelligent salesmen are likely to object to having management tell them exactly where to go. Furthermore, specific problems are likely to arise and conditions are likely to shift continuously, making flexibility in responding to customer needs a more important criterion than "least-cost" travel, which is likely to be a relatively small part of total selling costs especially when opportunity costs of not being able to respond when needed are considered.

The Assignment Problem

One of the major weaknesses of all of the models developed in this section was noted at the beginning—namely, that all of them assume that all salesmen are equally effective with all customers. In other words, salesmen have been assumed to be interchangeable. In actually assigning salesmen to territories, the sales manager would like to be able to take the individual salesman's strengths and weaknesses into account, especially as these may relate to specific characteristics of the territory.

These possibilities are provided by a special kind of linear programming; the problem itself has been given the specific name of "the assignment problem." The required input for the solution of this problem is a matrix of the profit resulting from assigning a particular salesman, i, to a particular territory, j. The estimation of these profit figures may not be easily done, but any less-rigorous assignment of sales effort would still require a similar kind of judgment, at least implicitly, and it is these differences in effectiveness with specific customers that the sales manager has in mind when he argues that salesmen are not interchangeable. Montgomery and Urban present a series of examples of solutions to the assignment problem.[15] Once the profit figures have been estimated, the assignment problem becomes one of routine computation.

SUMMARY

Allocation problems can be defined and analyzed rigorously, and this chapter has examined several attempts in this direction. While each

---

[15]*Ibid.*, pp. 287–90.

model examined had certain weaknesses, each provided a slightly different and instructive way of viewing the allocation problem.

Because most marketing communication programs are constrained by the availability of financial and human resources for promotional effort, care must be taken to insure that the available resources are directed to those uses which will return the greatest profit to the firm. While not all models considered all factors, it was seen that the optimum allocation is a function of market potential, response rate, retention (decay) rate, and lags in response to effort. The cost of additional units of effort and the profitability of products must also be considered. A preference has been shown in these comments for models that treat response as a stochastic process rather than in deterministic terms because the stochastic models seem to capture the inherent uncertainty in the problem.

As in the case of budgeting models, allocation models pose some very significant measurement problems which may, in many cases, preclude their use in a specific situation. The gain in managerial efficiency possible from using the model may be offset by the added cost of information required to implement the model.

Virtually every model that has been considered depends in some way upon the marginal productivity criterion. The fundamental rule of allocation is that the optimum exists when the ratio of marginal returns to marginal costs is equal for all projects, where "projects" may be sales territories, or customers, or products. While it is instructive to examine allocation problems using the tools of economic analysis and mathematics, it is necessary to remember that the allocation problem involves human behavior. Some understanding of the communication process is necessary for defining the shape of the response function, for example, and for suggesting how response to effort is likely to be distributed over time. On the other side of the coin, when the resources being allocated are salesmen and their time, shifting the strategy requires changing people. Implementation of the recommended personal selling strategy must be based upon a close understanding and appreciation for the needs and motives, strengths and weaknesses, of the salesmen and of the field sales managers.

18

Qualitative Values of Mass Media

Media carry messages and the mass media carry messages to the masses, large, non-interacting audiences. Mass communication is best distinguished from personal communication by the lack of interaction between sender and receiver and the lack of direct feedback. Messages to be delivered by mass media must be developed for the "average" or typical reader or listener delivered by that medium. The mass media include newspapers, magazines, radio, television, outdoor billboards, posters, car cards and transit advertising, films, and so on.

Advertising is mass communication. Many forms of sales promotion including cents-off coupons, contests, and merchandise offers typically also depend upon the mass media to create customer awareness and to solicit participation.

MEDIA OBJECTIVES

The objective of the marketing communication strategist in using mass media is *to deliver the maximum number of effective message exposures to prospective customers within the budget constraint*. There are four important parts of this statement of objectives, which is really a statement of media strategy as well.

Budget Constraints

First, notice that the last phrase refers to the budget constraint and does not say "at minimum cost." It is inconsistent to want both a maximum number of messages and the minimum cost. Rather, one must be taken as a "constraint" and the other as the optimization objective. Thus, we could have either the maximum number of messages subject to a budget constraint or the minimum cost for delivering a specified number of messages. The line of reasoning developed in previous chapters has argued for first setting the level of effort and then allocating that effort among alternative uses.

Prospective Customer Profile

The second important part of this definition is the phrase "prospective customers." Once a company has developed a marketing strategy, and has defined a target market segment, it is necessary to develop a method of delivering messages to persons in that segment. A segment may be defined by age and sex, as, for example, when prospects are defined as males, aged 18 to 60, with annual incomes over $7,000 per year. Messages delivered to persons with these characteristics have at least an opportunity to be effective. Messages delivered to other persons are more or less wasted.

Media Contribution to Message Effectiveness

The third aspect of this definition worth noting is the concept of *effective* messages. Earlier chapters have considered the characteristics of effective messages and have examined how creativity is a significant input to the success of the marketing communication strategy. The medium which carries the message can also influence the effectiveness of that message. In the following pages we will examine how the medium can make this contribution to message effectiveness. In general terms, however, the medium makes its contribution by the characteristics of the audience it delivers, by the addition of prestige or credibility to the message, by its mechanical characteristics (as when television permits the use of motion), and by the way in which the medium is used by its audience members (such as repeat exposures to a magazine's "pass-along" readership, and so on).

Concept of Effective Exposure

Finally, the definition of the objective of media usage emphasized the desire for the *maximum* number of effective message *exposures*. An "effective exposure" is one message delivered once to a prospective customer. Two exposures can be either the same message delivered twice to the same individual or one message delivered once to two different people. These are the dimensions of *frequency* (exposures per prospect) and *reach* (number of prospects), which play a critical part in the discussion of media strategy. Total exposures is the product of reach times frequency and part of the strategy decision is to determine the relative importance of reach and frequency. Given that decision, the problem then becomes one of purchasing media in such a way as to obtain the largest number of effective exposures for the available budget.

There are three distinct phases in developing the strategy for using advertising media. The first step is to determine the *kind* of media to be used—radio, newspapers, television, magazines, outdoor, or others. This decision requires an assessment of the unique requirements of the product or service being advertised and an assessment of the qualitative aspects of the alternative media possibilities. The second step is to select the specific media to be used—the specific magazines, newspapers, radio stations, and so on, in which time and space are to be purchased. The third step is the scheduling of media usage by week, day, hour, or whatever dimension fits the particular media selected. These last two decisions, selection and scheduling, define the media strategy and are to be discussed in Chapter 19. In the present chapter, we shall concentrate upon the decision about kinds of media and an assessment of the unique attributes and usage of each of the major classes of media.

DEFINITION OF QUALITATIVE VALUE

A good starting point for a discussion of the qualitative values of the mass media is to examine what we mean by the concept of qualitative value. The qualitative value of a medium can be defined as its audience composition, its editorial personality, or its contribution to advertising effectiveness. Weilbacher has examined the question of which definition is most useful.[1] Before stating his conclusions, each of these three alternative definitions of qualitative value must be briefly considered.

Audience Composition

When a marketing communication manager purchases time or space in an advertising medium he is buying the audience which that medium can bring to him. In addition to the obvious quantitative dimension to this decision—the number of exposures—there is the question of the *characteristics* of the audience delivered. The qualitative characteristics of audience members of interest to the communicator include level of education, income, number of children, and so on. One objective of media strategy is to find audiences with characteristics which fit most closely the definition of target market segments.

[1] W. M. Weilbacher, "The Qualitative Values of Advertising Media," *Journal of Advertising Research,* 1 (December 1960), pp. 12–17.

Weilbacher argued that there is no necessary connection between the characteristics of the audience and the extent to which that medium enhances the effectiveness of the advertising message. Effectiveness, as defined in Chapter 11 and elsewhere, is the ability of the message to change predispositions in a manner consistent with the objective of the communicator. Whether or not a medium contributes to an "effective" message may be independent of the characteristics of the audience it delivers. While this is not to deny that some media audiences are more valuable than others to an advertiser, this qualitative value is distinct from the ability of the medium to increase message effectiveness.

Image

Another definition of the qualitative value of an advertising medium is the image or personality of that medium, the way people use it and respond to it. In Weilbacher's words, "These qualitative values have to do with the role played by the medium or vehicle in the lives of the audience."[2] Another way of presenting this aspect of qualitative value is as a relationship between the audience member and the medium.

There are three problems with this concept of qualitative value. First, its dimensions are not clear and it is extremely hard to measure. Second, this qualitative assessment of the value of a medium is likely to vary significantly among individuals. Third, the extent to which this personality or image variable contributes to the effectiveness of an advertisement is specific to the product being sold. Thus, while there is probably a distinct image for each media vehicle, there is no obvious relationship between this characteristic and the effectiveness of a message with a specific market segment, and it would be very difficult to measure that influence.

Contribution to Message Effectiveness

The ability of an advertising medium to contribute to the effectiveness of an advertisement or an advertising campaign is an attribute that is distinct from either the characteristics of its audience or the personality of the medium. This definition of the qualitative value of an advertising medium does not contradict the previous two (audience composition and image), but it incorporates them and goes beyond them. This definition is also measurable. It is possible to insert the same message in two media and subsequently to test for differences in response among members of both audiences.

The major virtue of this definition of the qualitative value of a mass medium is that it recognizes that media are "effective" only in terms of a

2*Ibid.*, p. 13.

change in predispositions and that this is equally a function of the message. This definition of qualitative value says that the medium must be judged in terms of the contribution it makes to the effectiveness of the message. It is a logical corollary of this definition that statements about the effectiveness of a medium must be made specific to a particular message or class of messages.

This definition of the qualitative value of a mass medium also has an important weakness. Certainly, there are functions performed by a medium other than those enhancing the quality of the message. At the very least, the size and the quality of the audience delivered by that medium must also be considered.

There are, in fact, several ways in which a mass medium contributes to the accomplishment of marketing communication objectives.

STAGES OF MEDIA CONTRIBUTION

What is required for an advertising message to have an effect on the receiver? First, the medium must be circulated or distributed among an audience. Second, the receiver must be exposed to that particular medium vehicle (say, an issue of a magazine). Third, the receiver must be exposed to the message within the vehicle. Fourth, the receiver must pay attention to the message. Fifth, he must become interested in the message and read (or listen to) most or all of it. Sixth, he must retain that message until it can be acted upon, and he must "believe" the message to the extent of being willing to take action as a result of it. These six stages can be summarized as (1) circulation, (2) vehicle exposure, (3) message exposure, (4) attention, (5) perception, and (6) retention.[3] There is a clear relationship to the problems of measuring message effectiveness, as pointed out in Chapter 15.

The first three stages in determining message effectiveness are exclusively a function of the medium; the message itself has no bearing on circulation, vehicle exposure, and message exposure. Message exposure occurs, for example, when the reader of a magazine turns to the page in the magazine containing our advertisement or when the viewer watches television through the program interruptions. At this stage, the message also exerts an influence: whether the ad attracts attention is a function of such things as the headline, the illustration, use of color, and so on. These variables are also determined by the production characteristics of the medium. But the influence of the medium does not stop here, either. Both the message and the medium can influence perception and the

[3]This is a modification of a view presented by Seymour Banks, "The Role of Advertising Media in the Attainment of Advertising Objectives," in Henry Gomez (ed.), *Innovation—Key to Marketing Progress* (Chicago: American Marketing Association, 1963), pp. 248–53.

amount of retention, although perception would be mostly a function of the message itself. The amount or quality of retention, however, and the complete "meaning" conveyed by an advertisement is influenced by the medium as well as the message. For example, part of the meaning conveyed by an advertisement in *The New Yorker*, or *National Geographic*, or *Playboy* results from the very fact that the ad appeared in and is subsequently associated with that medium.

Each of the three possible definitions of qualitative value presented above therefore deals with a different aspect of the process by which media make a contribution to the accomplishment of communication objectives.

The difficulty in developing an *operational* definition of qualitative value is in developing measures of the extent to which the medium has contributed to message perception and retention. Seldom are such data available. Weilbacher's conclusion was that data which compare audience characteristics of alternative media are incomplete, but because such data are easiest to obtain they are the ones most readily available to the media planner. While the advertising media will make claims that their audiences have above-average "trust" and "confidence" in them, seldom are there reliable data available to support such assertions.

COMPARATIVE MEDIA EFFECTS

Communication researchers turned early to the question of which media provided the most value to a message and resulted in the most persuasion. The research question that received the greatest attention was which of two or more media was most effective in delivering a given message. The reason for stating the research question in this manner is obvious: an attempt to control for the effect of the message itself. This approach also creates a problem of interpreting the results, however. The fact is that the unique requirements and attributes of each medium mean that seldom if ever would the identical message be used in two media—say newspapers and radio.

To measure effectiveness, it was also necessary to control for such variables as exposure, length of exposure, and time since exposure. As a consequence, most of the studies were conducted in laboratory situations, and more specifically, with college students or with paid subjects. In either case, subjects were highly (artificially) motivated to pay attention to the message. The frequency and length of exposure were usually controlled. While this is a necessary step to provide a basis for inference about comparative effects, it is impossible to make statements about the relative abilities of the media to attract and hold attention for varying periods of time. These attributes would be important considerations in determining the value of a medium for an advertiser.

Recognizing these limitations on the research on comparative media effects, the results are still important and interesting for the marketing communication strategist. These studies did find that the very fact of media transmission acted, among other ways, to increase the potential of the message to persuade. There was evidence that the media are regarded with respect and that being associated with a particular medium could serve to enhance the prestige of persons, agencies, concepts, or products discussed or described in those media. The research also found that the several media do have differential persuasive power.[4]

Face-to-Face Communication Is Most Effective

These studies showed that face-to-face, personal communication was more effective than nonpersonal communication. Thus, a lecturer appearing in person was found to be more effective than a speech delivered through a wired loudspeaker.[5] In Chapter 9, the relative effectiveness of personal and nonpersonal communications was assessed and it was asserted that informal (personal, noncommercial) communication was the most effective of all. The significance of these laboratory studies is that the greater effectiveness of personal, face-to-face communication is found even in the absence of direct feedback. Studies of word-of mouth have consistently found that it is more effective than commercial sources and the reasons cited for that greater effectiveness have included the ability of the communicator to provide rewards for compliance, the presence of feedback, and the presence of social pressures to conform. While rewards for compliance and social pressure may be present to some extent in a lecture situation, feed-back is not.

The major reason for the greater effectiveness of the lecture format seems to be that the message impinges on both the aural and visual senses. The audience can see the lecturer as well as listen to him, and this seems to have some added impact. The lecturer is probably better able to keep the audience's attention and interest than would a wired speaker. This explanation is consistent with a finding, based on very limited evidence, that moving pictures result in better retention than print or broadcast media.

Aural Compared to Visual

Another general conclusion from these laboratory studies was that aural communication (radio or wired speaker) was more effective than visual (newspapers) and that this was especially true for audiences with

---

[4]Joseph T. Klapper, *The Effects of Mass Communication* (New York: Free Press of Glencoe, Inc., 1960), pp. 104–6.

[5]*Ibid.*, p. 106.

lower intelligence.[6] This advantage also seemed greater where the material was not too complex. For persons with exceptional intelligence or reading ability, and for more complex material, it was found that visual presentation resulted in better retention. All experiments also showed that concurrent aural and visual presentation was more effective than either aural or visual alone, but that aural is superior to print for most persons.[7]

Radio Audiences: "Suggestible"

Klapper generalized from these laboratory findings and other research to conclude that radio is likely to be more effective with the less-educated audience while print will be more effective with the above-average audience. The basic importance of reading ability should not be discounted as part of this explanation. Evidence from research on personal determinants of persuasibility, which we discussed in Chapter 7, supports a conclusion that persons of below average intelligence or education are likely to be more suggestible. Considering this fact along with the fact that radio audiences are likely to be drawn from lower cultural levels, Klapper concludes that "radio is the preferred medium of the more suggestible man."[8]

Klapper also refers to a study by Doob which showed that radio listeners "may envisage themselves as members of a gigantic group simultaneously engaged in listening to the same material and that this group feeling may increase the suggestibility of the audience."[9] Casual observation of the impact of radio on teenagers lends credibility to this observation, which is further supported by the success of radio fan clubs, especially in major metropolitan areas. There is evidence that radio listeners do value their affiliation with the radio station and think of themselves as part of a large group of listeners with whom they share this common interest and enthusiasm. Listening to the radio may give the listener more of a sense of personal involvement than reading a newspaper; listening is a more *active* experience in this sense.

Print Audience

On the other hand, print media offer several advantages to the communicator. In print media, the reader controls the length and frequency

---

[6]Joseph T. Klapper, "The Comparative Effects of the Various Media," from *The Effects of Mass Media: A Report to the Director of the Public Library Inquiry* (New York: Bureau of Applied Research, Columbia University, 1950), pp. 1–28; reprinted in Harper W. Boyd, Jr. and Joseph W. Newman (eds.), *Advertising Management: Selected Readings* (Homewood, Ill.: Richard D. Irwin, Inc., 1965), pp. 423–36, at p. 425.

[7]*Ibid.*, p. 427.

[8]*Ibid.*, p. 429.

[9]*Ibid.*, p. 433.

of exposure, and repeated exposure is possible. The format of a print medium is more flexible and treatment of an issue can be fuller. The reader can absorb the material at his own pace. Specialized appeal is more possible with print media, and there may be more "source effect" in print media than in broadcast. Print media probably have greater prestige, although there are no unequivocal research findings to support this contention.

Klapper quotes Lazarsfeld's observation that "in actual daily life, people on higher cultural levels prefer print to radio for the communication of comparable subject matter," and that this varies as a function of reading ability. He also quotes Lazarsfeld as saying that both those who prefer print and those who prefer radio give the same reasons for their preferences: "easier to understand," "more absorbing," and so on.[10] Given differences in interests and abilities, people use those media which are easiest for them to acquire, use, and comprehend and which are most "efficient" for them.

These early studies thus led to the general conclusion that personal communication was more effective than radio and that radio was more effective than print for the "average" person and for material of "average" complexity. Most of these studies were conducted before the days of television and leave out consideration of this important medium. An examination of these findings and the arguments which support them, however, will lead to the suggestion that television is less effective than personal communication but more effective than radio. Television, like face-to-face communication, presents both aural and visual stimuli. On the other hand, it does not require superior reading ability or education for comprehension of the message. There are no studies which prove this contention, however.

Television: Absorbing

Television would seem to be the most "real," or "lifelike," of all of the mass media. Common sense suggests that TV comes closest to the conditions of face-to-face contact and provides the most active sense of participation. The visual media, which include both television and films, are known to have a greater effect simply because they are visual and have been found at times to completely "absorb" their audiences, especially young children. Television, along with radio, derives an advantage from the fact that the audience can structure the situation and can participate creatively in the communication process.[11]

This overview of the comparative effects of the various media therefore can be summarized by a very general conclusion. In order of effec-

[10]*Ibid.*, p. 426.
[11]Klapper, *The Effects of Mass Communication*, pp. 111–112.

tiveness, other things being equal, the media are arrayed as (1) face-to-face, (2) television, (3) radio, and (4) print. It must be stressed, however, that there are four major weaknesses in this conclusion. First, not all results have been empirically determined. Second, all other things are never equal; the influence of the product or idea that provides the content for the message must be specifically considered in any strategic planning. Third, these results are by and large derived from laboratory conditions under unnatural conditions of exposure, attention, and motivation. Finally, there are no distinctions drawn between newspapers and magazines, or concerning the different types of magazines, both of which are important in developing media strategy.

Thus, these findings on the comparative effects of the media provide only a general background against which we can now consider more carefully the specific attributes of each of the several classes of media.

CHARACTERISTICS OF MASS MEDIA

As he appraises the value of the several classes of mass media, the marketing communication strategist applies several criteria.

Usage

Of central importance in determining the value of the medium is the manner in which it is used by potential customers. Obviously, the characteristics of prospective customers must first be decided upon before this assessment of media value can be made. The way people use an advertising medium varies for urban and rural residents, for example, and by level of education and income. The extent to which the medium is an integral part of the life style of the potential audience may also be significant.

Another dimension of usage is the characteristic advertising carried in that medium and the extent to which people came to expect such information. For example, certain magazines are regarded as a good source of information on fashions while newspapers are relied upon for learning about specials at local grocery stores.

Availability

A basic criterion of media value is whether that medium is actually available to and distributed among members of the potential market. This is a function both of the basis of segmentation and the actual availability of media. For example, segmenting the market on the basis of age requires that media be available to reach the specific age segments defined. Segmentation on the basis of such variables as personality raises the fundamental question of whether there are media available to reach a market defined on that basis.

There is no geographic area in the United States that is not reached by some form of media, but the amount and quality of media available do vary significantly on a regional basis. Likewise, various age groups and ethnic groups vary significantly in the availability of media which serve these particular segments of the population.

Availability is also limited by the number of broadcast hours on a TV or radio station and by other policies regarding product and copy acceptability. There is no guarantee that a given medium will actually have time or space for sale when requested.

Production Requirements

Mechanical and production requirements of the various media must also be considered in selecting among the classes of media. Use of television typically requires the use of filmed or video-taped commercials although it is possible to make do with less expensive executions of lower quality, such as live, spoken messages or still photography. Newspapers may likewise create the requirement for advertising mats to be distributed to all newspapers in the schedule. Magazines also have unique production requirements.

The unique requirements for effective advertising of a particular product may dictate the use of certain media, or at least give strong preference to a particular medium. Food products are most effectively advertised being served, rather than in the package, and can often be more effectively presented in color rather than black-and-white. Automobile advertising likewise benefits especially from the use of color, and motion as possible in television, although neither is an absolute requirement for automobile ads.

ADVERTISERS' MEDIA USAGE

Although advertising expenditures continue to increase year after year, there are no major shifts among the major media in their relative importance as advertising vehicles. All tend to share equally in the growth of advertising revenues, with some small variations from one year to the next. This fact is illustrated in the data presented in Table 18–1.

In examining Table 18–1, you will note that television is the only medium which has shown significant and consistent growth as a percentage of total since 1953, although all media have shown significant dollar revenue growth. The explanation is obvious. Television is the only truly

Table 18-1

Allocations of U.S. Advertising Budgets Among Media and Other Expenses, Selected Years

(dollars in millions; percentages of total)

Year	Total Advertising Expenditures	Newspapers	Magazines	Business Publications	Farm Publications	Television	Radio	Direct Mail	Outdoor	Point-of-Purchase Displays	Agency Income	Other Expenditures
1953	7,784	2,002	650	220	48	432	476	1,003	158	290	501	2,004
	(100)	(25.7)	(8.4)	(2.8)	(0.6)	(5.5)	(6.1)	(12.8)	(2.0)	(3.7)	(6.4)	(25.7)
1958	10,414	2,459	652	302	55	1,030	523	1,419	219	344	757	2,654
	(100)	(23.6)	(6.3)	(2.9)	(0.5)	(9.9)	(5.0)	(13.6)	(2.1)	(3.3)	(7.3)	(25.5)
1963	13,639	3,087	832	413	47	1,597	681	1,760	202	490	1,005	3,525
	(100)	(22.6)	(6.1)	(3.0)	(0.4)	(11.7)	(5.0)	(12.9)	(1.5)	(3.6)	(7.4)	(25.8)
1967	17,380	3,945	990	558	52	2,273	877	2,144	222	639	1,282	4,398
	(100)	(22.7)	(5.7)	(3.2)	(0.3)	(13.1)	(5.0)	(12.3)	(1.3)	(3.7)	(7.4)	(25.3)
1968a	18,350	4,182	1,020	582	52	2,500	956	2,232	246	677	1,346	4,557
	(100)	(22.8)	(5.6)	(3.2)	(0.3)	(13.6)	(5.2)	(12.2)	(1.3)	(3.7)	(7.3)	(24.8)

aPreliminary estimates.

Source: Seymour Banks, Ronald Reisman, and Charles Y. Yang, "Ad Volume Rises 5.6% to $18.3 Billion in 1968 as U.S. Economy Flourishes, Advertising Age's Yang Estimates Show," *Advertising Age*, March 3, 1969, pp. 45-46.

new medium in this list and did not gain widespread usage until the 1950's. More significantly, the growth of television does not appear to have diminished the revenues of any other media and changes in the "percentage of total advertising dollars" appear to have been equally distributed among all other media.

Industry Differences

Table 18-2 shows how the nation's leading advertisers in 1968 allocated their advertising dollars among media. These statistics are grouped by industry and show some interesting tendencies. Notice first that some industries show much more consistency than others. In automobiles, for example, all advertisers are heavy users of newspapers. In the food industry, by contrast, there is much more variability in the use of newspapers, and an equally large amount of variability in the use of spot and network TV. Notice that there is no beer or liquor advertising in farm publications.

Table 18–2

Media Expenditure by Top 125 U.S. Advertisers in 1968

Ad Rank	Company	Total	Percentage of Total Dollars								
			News-paper	General Maga-zines	Farm Publica-tions	Business Publica-tions	Spot TV	Net TV	Spot Radio	Net Radio	Out-door
	Cars										
1	General Motors Corp.	$199,701,016	30.6	22.6	0.4	2.5	5.2	19.8	12.5	2.8	3.7
5	Ford Motor Co.	106,149,810	22.6	19.7	1.3	2.0	3.6	26.2	18.9	2.2	3.5
10	Chrysler Corp.	72,508,258	20.1	21.0	0.3	0.8	2.2	32.3	19.4	2.8	1.1
71	Volkswagen of America	15,750,843	25.5	28.2	—	0.1	7.5	30.3	1.8	—	6.6
80	American Motors Corp.	13,976,685	20.8	20.7	—	0.4	10.7	41.1	3.1	2.3	0.8
	Food										
3	General Foods Corp.	109,856,147	5.1	4.2	0.1	0.3	47.2	39.9	2.1	0.4	0.7
15	National Dairy Products	52,021,316	25.1	18.1	0.2	4.0	24.6	26.5	0.5	0.5	0.5
16	General Mills Inc.	50,444,306	3.1	10.5	—	0.9	27.7	56.5	1.2	0.1	0.1
26	Kellogg Co.	36,534,972	7.1	4.3	—	0.5	36.3	49.0	0.1	2.7	—
28	Campbell Soup Co.	34,330,126	6.5	23.4	—	1.3	25.0	32.8	7.8	3.3	—
35	Norton Simon Inc.	27,481,841	9.7	18.9	—	2.0	37.2	20.9	5.7	1.1	4.5
36	Carnation Co.	27,166,872	4.3	8.2	0.2	2.1	23.0	60.4	1.7	—	—
38	Standard Brands Inc.	26,256,071	16.0	17.9	0.9	2.2	29.3	22.3	5.2	1.2	5.0
41	Corn Products Co.	23,445,614	8.9	23.6	2.0	1.1	44.1	14.8	1.5	—	4.0
45	Ralston Purina Co.	21,421,001	8.6	6.4	2.5	0.5	40.0	41.1	0.9	—	—
46	Armour & Co.	20,987,235	5.0	8.9	0.5	4.8	32.1	44.9	1.2	2.4	—
47	National Biscuit Co.	20,955,479	3.7	24.2	0.3	1.4	25.8	39.2	3.4	2.0	—
48	Quaker Oats Co.	20,821,381	2.5	7.2	0.1	0.5	40.5	48.0	1.1	—	0.1

Source: Advertising Age, August 25, 1969, p. 41. Reproduced with permission of Advertising Age.

Table 18-2 (Continued)

Ad Rank	Company	Total	News-paper	General Maga-zines	Farm Publica-tions	Business Publica-tions	Spot TV	Net TV	Spot Radio	Net Radio	Out-door
						Percentage of Total Dollars					
			Food (Continued)								
49	Pillsbury Co.	20,749,993	8.1	6.5	—	0.9	37.4	42.2	3.5	1.0	0.3
63	Borden Co.	16,932,136	17.0	10.8	0.9	1.0	43.5	20.2	3.8	2.8	—
66	Nestle Co.	16,129,969	4.9	5.4	0.1	—	46.2	31.9	11.4	—	0.1
78	Beatrice Foods Co.	14,217,596	8.1	4.7	0.5	0.1	28.9	49.8	6.3	—	1.6
95	H. J. Heinz Co.	11,579,596	3.5	3.7	—	3.5	55.6	33.7	—	—	—
104	Swift & Co.	9,958,709	21.9	11.4	0.1	5.2	19.7	36.5	3.1	—	2.0
109	Del Monte Corp.	9,162,704	8.6	39.5	0.1	—	26.2	13.0	4.8	7.0	0.7
118	Squibb-Beech-Nut Inc.	8,790,283	0.4	19.1	0.2	—	54.3	12.7	13.1	—	0.1
124	American Dairy Assn.	8,051,112	10.2	15.0	0.2	0.9	54.5	11.3	4.1	—	4.1
			Soaps, Cleansers (and Allied)								
2	Procter & Gamble Co.	198,742,093	1.0	6.8	0.1	0.4	40.7	50.8	0.2	—	—
6	Colgate-Palmolive	103,275,977	3.4	8.5	0.1	—	32.2	44.8	7.0	3.9	—
12	Lever Bros. Co.	63,565,703	3.2	6.8	—	0.1	39.0	48.3	2.5	—	—
32	S. C. Johnson & Son	30,243,847	0.4	1.4	—	0.3	13.5	84.3	0.2	—	—
113	Purex Corp.	8,970,223	35.1	37.8	0.4	3.2	12.3	6.5	0.7	4.0	—
			Tobacco								
8	R. J. Reynolds Tobacco Co.	77,039,215	1.5	11.1	0.4	0.3	14.0	60.1	8.9	3.7	—
9	American Tobacco Co.	72,955,289	7.2	17.4	—	0.2	31.2	41.0	1.7	0.6	0.7
19	Philip Morris Inc.	46,119,671	2.5	15.8	—	0.2	18.5	60.6	1.3	0.7	0.5
24	Brown & Williamson Tobacco	37,082,516	3.6	12.4	—	0.1	13.2	69.4	1.0	—	0.4
27	Liggett & Myers Tobacco Co.	36,240,962	7.8	24.8	—	0.8	8.9	45.2	8.4	2.4	1.8

Table 18–2 (Continued)

Ad Rank	Company	Total	Percentage of Total Dollars								
			News-paper	General Maga-zines	Farm Publica-tions	Business Publica-tions	Spot TV	Net TV	Spot Radio	Net Radio	Out-door
	Drugs and Cosmetics										
4	Bristol-Myers Co.	108,113,584	1.2	20.0	—	4.1	21.4	45.9	6.1	1.1	0.2
7	American Home Products	78,749,094	2.2	7.5	0.1	0.5	23.0	55.6	8.9	1.6	0.5
11	Sterling Drug Co.	60,767,053	5.5	13.5	0.3	0.8	15.8	56.3	3.8	4.0	—
14	Warner-Lambert Pharmaceutical	53,733,651	1.0	3.8	—	10.1	27.3	56.0	0.9	0.8	—
25	Miles Laboratories	36,593,042	0.7	5.5	—	1.9	27.0	63.8	0.4	0.7	—
40	Alberto-Culver	23,828,157	1.5	4.4	—	0.7	55.8	37.6	—	—	—
42	J. B. Williams Co.	23,347,960	0.3	7.2	0.1	0.4	1.4	88.4	2.1	—	—
44	Plough Inc.	22,078,396	4.6	10.4	—	1.0	15.6	50.7	6.0	10.4	1.3
50	Chas. Pfizer & Co.	20,628,910	—	12.3	2.9	5.5	14.5	55.9	7.2	1.6	0.1
51	Block Drug Co.	19,912,786	1.2	10.7	0.2	0.4	11.1	72.5	2.6	1.2	—
52	Johnson & Johnson	19,830,140	5.7	20.9	0.1	2.6	44.5	21.7	4.5	—	—
60	Norwich Pharmacal Co.	17,832,143	1.5	6.8	—	6.7	24.6	60.1	0.2	—	—
67	Carter-Wallace Inc.	15,867,206	0.4	0.3	—	0.8	47.4	43.3	7.0	—	0.8
72	Richardson-Merrell	15,709,131	0.3	4.7	0.7	6.0	29.2	57.2	1.8	—	—
81	Revlon Inc.	13,887,143	5.2	54.7	—	4.1	17.2	15.1	3.6	0.1	—
82	Smith Kline & French	13,672,563	—	14.2	0.9	8.0	10.8	51.2	11.9	1.3	1.7
83	Noxell Corp.	13,474,891	1.4	10.5	—	—	24.2	54.5	9.4	—	—
89	Chesebrough-Pond's Inc.	12,485,949	0.7	18.5	—	2.4	42.6	30.6	4.0	1.1	—
101	Merck & Co.	10,256,904	—	3.7	1.4	39.4	8.9	46.5	—	—	—
116	Beecham Group Ltd.	8,877,915	—	0.7	—	—	6.2	91.8	1.3	—	—
123	Avon Products	8,073,611	—	22.1	0.6	—	77.4	—	—	—	—

Table 13-2 (Continued)

Ad Rank	Company	Total	News-paper	General Maga-zines	Farm Publica-tions	Business Publica-tions	Spot TV	Net TV	Spot Radio	Net Radio	Out-doors
						Percentage of Total Dollars					
	Gum and Candy										
33	Wm. Wrigley Jr. Co.	28,168,020	9.5	2.6	—	—	73.8	—	11.5	2.6	—
91	Mars Inc.	12,286,899	1.8	2.8	—	—	51.3	44.0	0.1	—	—
	Metals										
100	American Can Co.	10,524,215	6.8	7.5	—	2.9	82.4	0.1	0.2	—	0.1
106	Reynolds Metals Co	9,389,358	9.0	10.9	0.5	10.2	14.0	54.2	—	—	1.2
125	Aluminum Co. of America	7,905,304	10.7	36.8	1.9	22.1	12.9	10.7	2.8	1.6	0.5
	Liquor										
18	Distillers Corp.-Seagrams Ltd.	46,353,367	27.2	54.1	—	1.8	2.2	—	—	—	14.6
57	Heublein Inc.	18,330,533	13.0	32.0	—	0.5	16.8	16.7	9.7	—	11.3
64	National Distillers & Chemical	16,504,682	26.3	51.6	—	6.2	0.3	—	—	—	15.6
77	Hiram Walker-Gooderham & Worts	14,536,530	40.3	46.7	—	1.7	—	—	—	—	11.3
119	Brown-Forman Distillers	8,781,093	42.5	47.8	—	—	—	—	—	—	9.6
	Beer										
61	Jos. Schlitz Brewing Co.	17,707,628	1.2	4.1	—	—	45.9	23.6	24.3	—	0.9
70	Anheuser-Busch Inc.	15,785,072	2.7	19.5	—	2.1	16.3	20.7	31.3	—	7.4
108	Falstaff Brewing Co.	9,287,061	4.0	13.6	—	—	49.7	1.0	22.9	—	8.8
111	Pabst Brewing Co.	9,070,908	0.6	—	—	—	62.7	20.8	9.9	—	6.0

Table 18–2 (Continued)

Ad Rank	Company	Total	News-paper	General Maga-zines	Farm Publica-tions	Business Publica-tions	Spot TV	Net TV	Spot Radio	Net Radio	Out-doors
							Oil				
37	Shell Oil Co.	26,281,538	6.4	11.2	2.6	1.6	42.6	26.1	8.8	0.2	0.5
55	Gulf Oil Corp.	19,267,311	10.0	5.4	0.9	3.5	4.9	70.4	1.2	2.1	1.6
62	Standard Oil of New Jersey	17,056,139	9.4	18.9	0.6	12.2	13.2	17.0	22.1	0.6	6.1
65	Standard Oil of Indiana	16,455,420	6.2	11.2	4.7	3.5	29.3	20.1	24.3	—	0.7
90	Mobile Oil Corp.	12,405,322	21.9	17.0	3.4	5.4	23.0	7.2	22.0	—	0.1
94	Texaco Inc.	11,779,736	11.7	10.3	1.9	6.9	8.1	42.6	17.3	—	1.2
107	Phillips Petroleum Corp.	9,325,182	0.6	7.7	0.2	6.2	12.1	62.8	6.0	1.3	3.0
112	Sun Oil Co.	9,008,980	3.8	8.8	0.9	4.1	21.6	22.9	36.9	—	1.0
120	Standard Oil of California	8,521,813	7.5	0.7	2.7	7.7	54.0	1.0	20.1	—	6.2
							Soft Drinks				
13	Coca-Cola Co.	55,992,564	4.7	6.3	—	1.0	53.4	14.9	17.3	—	2.4
23	PepsiCo Inc.	38,940,890	4.0	4.2	0.1	1.1	33.0	31.2	22.3	0.8	3.3
68	Seven-Up Co.	15,808,951	4.6	1.2	—	1.0	55.4	13.6	20.7	—	3.5
84	Royal Crown Cola Co.	12,988,426	1.9	0.2	—	0.4	45.5	16.2	31.3	—	4.6
							Tires				
43	Goodyear Tire & Rubber Co.	22,524,163	35.2	22.3	1.7	4.5	4.4	29.6	1.7	—	0.5
56	Firestone Tire & Rubber Co.	18,875,601	37.6	19.0	2.6	3.4	10.4	18.8	8.2	—	—
99	B. F. Goodrich Co.	10,608,280	20.6	5.7	2.1	12.0	5.9	45.5	4.7	3.4	0.1
115	Uniroyal Inc.	8,948,470	18.1	27.7	1.2	8.6	35.3	9.0	0.1	—	0.1

Percentage of Total Dollars

Table 16–2 (Continued)

Ad Rank	Company	Total	Percentage of Total Dollars								
			News-paper	General Maga-zines	Farm Publica-tions	Business Publica-tions	Spot TV	Net TV	Spot Radio	Net Radio	Out-doors
	Paper Products										
88	Scott Paper Co.	12,525,041	6.6	19.4	—	7.1	55.6	8.2	3.2	—	—
92	Kimberly-Clark Corp.	12,149,280	22.7	40.5	—	3.4	26.3	7.0	0.1	—	—
	Appliances, TV, Radio										
29	Radio Corp. of America	33,359,028	28.6	28.4	0.2	4.4	7.6	27.9	0.9	1.0	1.0
34	General Electric Co.	26,018,288	15.1	36.5	0.1	15.6	6.9	21.1	3.2	1.0	0.4
69	Westinghouse Electric Corp.	15,793,848	17.7	14.6	—	23.1	1.1	41.9	1.0	—	0.5
102	Zenith Radio Corp.	10,216,392	31.6	24.0	—	1.2	11.9	29.9	0.1	—	1.1
	Chemicals										
53	American Cyanamid Co.	19,793,455	2.1	15.8	3.6	22.4	11.8	40.6	2.2	1.4	0.1
58	Du Pont	18,145,755	3.2	23.3	2.6	25.4	3.7	27.8	4.9	8.2	0.9
73	Union Carbide Corp	15,571,804	4.8	7.9	0.2	19.9	3.7	59.6	2.5	1.4	—
110	Monsanto Co.	9,138,896	6.9	5.8	6.9	33.4	2.5	42.7	1.3	0.2	0.3
117	Dow Chemical Co.	8,870,317	3.1	19.5	3.5	21.4	17.7	33.8	0.4	—	0.5
	Airlines										
54	United Air Lines	19,598,383	18.2	11.2	—	1.7	25.9	32.7	8.5	—	1.7
59	Trans World Airlines	17,270,766	26.8	17.3	—	0.7	17.6	13.9	20.9	—	2.7
74	Pan American World Airways	15,529,593	20.7	14.1	—	2.4	15.9	21.7	23.9	—	1.2
76	American Airlines	14,707,972	21.6	10.9	—	2.2	20.4	21.3	18.0	—	5.6
79	Eastern Air Lines	14,036,286	38.7	5.3	—	2.9	24.9	7.5	20.3	—	0.4
	Photographic Equipment										
39	Eastman Kodak Co.	23,865,420	7.2	30.3	—	1.8	2.6	48.1	—	—	—
75	Polaroid Corp.	15,146,493	2.8	30.4	—	5.4	0.1	61.3	—	—	—

Table 18–2 (Continued)

Ad Rank	Company	Total	Percentage of Total Dollars								
			News-paper	General Maga-zines	Farm Publica-tions	Business Publica-tions	Spot TV	Net TV	Spot Radio	Net Radio	Out-doors
			Telephone Service, Equipment								
21	American Telephone & Telegraph	46,608,471	11.1	23.5	0.1	6.0	17.4	26.2	11.3	3.2	1.2
30	International Telephone & Telegraph	32,830,075	8.0	20.8	0.1	14.6	52.3	1.4	0.1	—	2.8
98	General Telephone & Electronics	10,983,532	3.7	19.6	—	16.9	24.3	31.2	2.0	—	2.2
			Others								
17	Gillette Co.	47,526,087	0.8	6.3	—	0.2	24.4	67.5	0.1	0.7	—
20	Sears, Roebuck & Co.	43,388,450	0.2	34.0	0.6	—	28.1	11.4	25.6	—	0.1
22	Loews Theatres Inc.	39,496,304	15.3	2.2	—	0.2	9.3	55.3	9.5	6.8	1.4
31	Rapid-American Corp.	30,952,229	8.8	22.3	—	3.1	1.2	51.3	0.7	—	12.6
85	Columbia Broadcasting System	12,819,522	20.0	67.8	—	2.0	3.0	—	5.6	0.6	1.0
86	W. R. Grace & Co.	12,643,638	4.0	13.8	5.2	6.9	19.1	39.4	7.7	2.0	2.0
87	Mattel Inc.	12,558,216	2.6	6.7	—	—	3.9	86.9	—	—	—
93	3M Co.	11,866,947	5.8	14.4	—	33.1	5.4	35.4	0.1	5.8	—
96	Ling-Temco-Vought Inc.	11,325,660	32.4	33.1	—	20.1	7.2	3.5	3.0	—	0.5
97	Textron Inc.	11,094,581	1.9	18.7	3.7	31.5	8.7	33.2	2.2	—	0.1
103	Sperry Rand Corp.	10,035,043	3.0	31.5	8.8	10.3	13.8	29.7	2.8	—	0.1
105	Armstrong Cork Co.	9,650,947	0.8	45.6	—	7.8	2.4	43.4	—	—	—
114	Singer Co.	8,962,052	3.0	21.2	0.2	9.9	1.6	60.4	3.5	0.2	0.4
121	Burlington Industries	8,485,888	8.1	24.8	—	15.0	10.7	35.6	5.3	—	0.4
122	Gulf & Western Industries	8,188,450	15.3	15.6	0.1	10.5	17.9	37.6	2.2	—	0.9

More importantly, however, there seems to be little agreement among industry members concerning the relative effectiveness of the advertising media. In virtually every industry represented by these 125 advertisers, there are markedly different emphases upon media by the several advertisers in that industry. There is no direct and obvious relationship between the nature of the product being advertised and the value of a particular advertising medium.

The cost of television limits its usage among smaller national advertisers. It should be noted that the figures given in Table 18–2 are for the largest advertisers, who are the principal users of television. Larger budgets are required for the effective use of television, due to the need for frequency and continuity and the costs of time, as well as the costs of producing effective commercials. An advertiser with many different products regularly advertised on television may find it economical to purchase a television show series and to become identified as the sponsor of that show. The expense of producing a television series is several hundred thousand dollars per week.

The discussion now turns to a brief examination of the attributes of the several major classes of advertising media: newspapers, radio, magazines, television, and outdoor billboards. We shall briefly consider the unique attributes of each class of media and any significant trends they have experienced or are expected to follow.

NEWSPAPERS

Newspapers are the oldest of the major advertising media. There are three classes of newspapers: dailies, weeklies, and Sunday papers. Dailies can be further distinguished according to whether they are published in the morning or the evening. In 1967, there were in the United States 1,729 daily newspapers with a total net paid circulation of 61,561,000. Of these, 327 were morning papers with a total net paid circulation of 25,282,000 while there were 1,438 evening papers with a total circulation of 36,279,000. Note that the average circulation of morning papers is over 77,000, which is about three times that of the evening papers with an average circulation of 25,000. There were also 573 Sunday newspapers with a total net paid circulation of 49,224,000, or an average of just under 86,000 circulation. Statistics on the number of weekly newspapers are not generally available because these vary widely in size and content, tend to be small, and are not reported in United States government census statistics. A rough estimate would be that there are about 9,000 weekly newspapers. The number of newspapers in the United States has been relatively stable for the past several years.[12]

[12]*Editor and Publisher Yearbook*, 1968.

Newspapers offer several distinct advantages to the advertisers. First and foremost is their "local" orientation and flavor. They offer timeliness in their editorial material and permit precise scheduling of advertising to meet specific communication objectives because of their publication frequency. In addition to time flexibility, newspapers also offer place flexibility, which can be a particular advantage in coordinating advertising with the pattern of distribution.

Circulation

Eighty-six percent of the homes in the United States receive at least one daily newspaper.[13] People come to depend upon newspapers for a record of the day's events and for local news as well as coverage of international, national, business, financial, and sports news. Morning newspapers (20 percent of daily papers) are more oriented toward a male audience while evening papers (80 percent) have more "entertainment" features, such as columns and feature sections which typically have greater appeal for women.[14] Sunday newspapers have wider and larger circulation than dailies and appeal to all members of the family. Weekly newspapers tend to cater to rural and suburban markets, and concentrate on local news and features rather than on national and international news.

Newspapers provide time and place flexibility to the advertiser and permit rather intense coverage of a given market area. They have a distinct advantage in that their circulation can be rather precisely determined in comparison to broadcast media. Newspapers permit a coordination of promotion with local distribution arrangements and permit the national advertiser to identify local distributors in local advertising. Cooperative advertising arrangements, in which the national marketer agrees to help pay the cost of the local distributors' advertising (the typical arrangement is for half of the expenses to be paid by each party), can be most easily implemented and controlled by use of local newspapers.

The timeliness of newspapers is also a disadvantage. There is limited opportunity for repeated exposure of the advertising because a given issue of a newspaper is relatively short-lived. Newspapers do not permit class selectivity or other forms of demographic segmentation, except for the fact that young people and teenagers probably do not read newspa-

[13]Robert Zacher, *Advertising Techniques and Management* (rev. ed.; Homewood, Ill.: Richard D. Irwin, Inc., 1967), p. 364.
[14]A. W. Frey and J. C. Halterman, *Advertising*, 4th ed. (New York: Ronald Press Company, Inc., 1970), p. 303.

pers to the same extent as older persons. A further problem in using newspapers in an advertising schedule is the difficult scheduling and contractual problems involved in using many, perhaps hundreds, of local newspapers.

Newspapers are represented by brokers and agents who can provide significant help in making the necessary contractual and scheduling arrangements with many local newspapers. Most advertising agencies have well-established relationships with such representatives to assist the national or regional advertiser who wishes to use newspapers as an important part of his media strategy.

RADIO

Over 98 percent of all United States homes owned radio receivers in 1968. Most homes had more than one radio, as indicated by the fact that there were over 192 million radios in the estimated 58.8 million homes in 1968. In addition, there were 65 million automobile radios, and another 10 million radios in public places. It has been estimated that in one day 75 percent of the total adult population (age 18 and over) listens to radio and that in seven days over 90 percent of the total United States adult population is in the cumulative radio audience. These statistics suggest that radio plays an important part in the lives of most Americans.[15]

Portability and "Background" Use

The portable radio has been an important factor in redefining the role of radio in the life styles of modern society. In the "good old days," the family would gather in the parlor around the radio console to listen to their favorite programs of humor, suspense, and situation comedy. The Great Gildersleeve, The Lone Ranger, The Shadow, and Lowell Thomas, Jr. are just a few of the programs which attracted faithful and regular audiences. Today, the functions of family entertainment seem to have passed to television and radio has taken a markedly different role. People now depend upon radio for immediate news coverage and to provide a kind of background to the normal routine of the day, whether indoors or outside. Driving monotony can be relieved by the car radio; the housewife, the student, and even the clerk can enjoy the background of radio music while devoting major attention to her, or his, work.

Radio may play a different function in the evening than in the daytime, although there have been no studies to show this. In the evening,

[15]*1968 Broadcasting Yearbook*, pp. 9 and 22.

more serious music and a different programming format may be in order. Persons who listen to the radio most heavily during the daytime may also be the most devoted watchers of TV during the evening.

Radio is available in virtually all parts of the United States although coverage may be a little thin and reception a little weak in some rural and wilderness areas. In 1968, there were 4,156 AM radio stations broadcasting on the air, 1,753 commercial FM stations and 325 noncommercial FM stations.[16] Frequency modulation (FM) radio broadcasting provides a clearer signal with less interference and therefore better quality reception is experienced by the listener. FM also permits the broadcasting of stereo. The disadvantage of FM is its limited range in distance, in comparison with AM (amplitude modulation) radio.

Selectivity

The advantages of radio are approximately the same as those of newspapers in that radio offers flexibility in geography and time. In addition, radio offers a substantial degree of audience selectivity in those market areas which are large enough to support several radio stations. Under those conditions, radio stations tend to develop programming formats to appeal to specific segments of the total market. As a result, audience profiles can vary significantly among radio stations, permitting a kind of class selectivity that approaches the kind of selectivity offered by magazines. Radio may be the only effective way of reaching the teen market in the medium-sized and large cities.

A trend of particular significance in recent years has been the development of radio stations appealing to specific ethnic groups within the population. Most significant has been the emergence of radio stations with a uniquely effective appeal for the Afro-American population. These developments have occurred mainly in the larger cities although certain areas with a heavy concentration of population from a given ethnic group may have radio stations which devote a segment of their programming to these specific audiences.

FM Radio

FM radio seems to have become differentiated from AM radio in recent years. In a 1967 study, it was estimated that 43 percent of all radio homes own at least one FM set. FM set ownership tends to concentrate in major metropolitan areas, reflecting the tendency for FM stations to concentrate in these areas; the greater selectivity of FM radio requires larger populations to provide a sufficiently large audience for

[16]*Ibid.*, p. 9.

profitable operations. FM radio stations are not as profitable as AM stations, because of greater selectivity, but the economic health of FM broadcasting is improving. While FM audiences are more selective and tend to be "up-scale," that is, above average in income and education, the FM listener profile is tending toward that of the AM listener. The greater selectivity of FM at the moment makes it a more efficient medium for reaching select markets, but this advantage may decrease as FM radio broadens its appeal and becomes more like AM radio. This 1967 study concluded that FM had reached the point where no distinction could be made between it and AM radio and recommended that AM and FM stations should be measured against the same criteria of audience, availability, costs, and efficiency in the media selection decision.[17]

Radio permits the advertiser to target specific geographic, age, and income market segments with a high degree of efficiency. At the same time, it is more difficult to estimate the audience provided by radio than it is in the case of print media such as newspapers. Radio, like television, does not permit repeat exposure. To obtain multiple exposures over a period of time, the advertiser must schedule his messages to achieve a repetition and continuity. Radio also provides the same local scheduling and contractual problems as local newspapers, although there are also sales representatives and brokers who can provide help in putting together a "package" or radio stations to fit the advertiser's needs. Radio has the further advantage of the availability of several national and many (50) regional networks of stations to permit precision in covering larger market areas than those covered by one radio station.

MAGAZINES

Magazines offer the advertiser the distinct advantage of selectivity. In recent years, the demise of the *Saturday Evening Post* and *Colliers* magazines after each of these general appeal magazines had enjoyed a very long history of successful contribution has underscored the trend for magazines to become increasingly specialized in their editorial appeal and in the audiences they serve. Some general-appeal magazines such as *Life* and *Look* are still available, but their editorial approach and format has changed to reflect the changing needs of their markets and the changing competitive situation in magazine publishing.

Classes of Magazines

There are many classes of magazines, and many different bases for classifying magazines. There is a distinction among weeklies, monthlies,

[17]Ogilvy & Mather, Inc., *A Review of FM Radio,* March, 1967.

and quarterlies, for example. There is a further distinction between magazines with controlled circulation (where subscribers must meet certain criteria such as occupation) and non-controlled, and between paid and non-paid circulation magazines. The most common basis for classifying magazines is the editorial content of the publication. A partial list of magazines with specific kinds of editorial content would be:

Professional	Gardening
News	Religious
Business	Fraternal and college
Home service ("shelter")	Fashion
Sports	Movie fan
Hunting and fishing	Literature

Many more categories could be offered. An important distinction can be drawn among magazines which appeal to either of the sexes and those which appeal to both.

Two important subclasses of magazines, often singled out for separate treatment in a discussion of advertising media, are business publications and farm publications. Some of these publications are in many respects more like newspapers than magazines. (*Advertising Age* is a notable example of a weekly business publication of particular interest and value to marketing communication strategists. *Advertising Age* refers to itself as "The National Newspaper of Marketing.") Business publications can have either general appeal (like *Business Week*) or a specific appeal (like *Traffic World*). Farm publications are directed toward farmers and may be either national or regional in their emphasis, and either specialized to specific crops or animals or with general appeal to all farmers.

Advantages and Disadvantages

Although there are literally thousands of magazines and many ways of classifying them, all magazines offer certain advantages to the advertiser. As noted earlier, the most significant advantage of magazines is probably their selectivity in providing an audience with a specific set of characteristics. In addition, magazines permit leisurely reading, have a longer life than newspapers, and permit repeated exposures to the advertising message. Repeated exposures may occur with the same individual, or with other individuals in the consuming unit (household or organization), or with individuals in another consuming unit. The latter two categories are referred to as "pass-along" readership and can be of major significance as a determinant of media value. The magazine may be kept as a reference and as a source of information about specific products. Magazines offer superior reproduction of advertising in comparison with newspapers, although this distinction has narrowed in recent years with the perfection of techniques for the color reproduction of newspaper advertisements.

Magazines have several disadvantages, including their infrequent appearance, their relatively "thin" penetration of the total population, geographical inflexibility, and the tendency for editorial matter to be somewhat dated by the time the magazine is distributed. This last "disadvantage" is not too serious, however. Magazines' editorial policies may minimize their dependence on news items that are likely to become dated quickly. Those magazines which *do* try to cover current developments, especially the weekly news magazines, have developed procedures and techniques for reporting news and printing and distributing the magazine with speed which is amazing.

Magazines have been found to lend their prestige to products advertised in them and some magazines have capitalized on this fact by offering their endorsement to products advertised in them. Such products are permitted to display a seal or some other symbol identifying them with the magazine, an identification which is assumed to have value because of the trust and confidence which readers place in the magazine. There is an interaction between the editorial content of the magazine and its advertisements which some have called "editorial preselling." The very fact of being advertised in a national magazine can lend prestige to a product.

Some of the more tangible benefits of magazines as advertising media include their ability to audit circulation quite accurately and to provide national coverage. At the same time, there has been a definite trend to regional editions in recent years and most of the general appeal media serving national markets permit advertisers the option of regional selectivity. The number of regional and demographic options can vary from three to over seventy for the major national magazines. This has several advantages for the advertiser such as coordination of magazine advertising with test marketing activity and with distribution arrangements. Regional editions have the obvious advantage of permitting regional marketers to use magazines without incurring the cost of waste circulation. Magazines further permit the advertiser to make use of creative, attention-getting devices such as pull-out gimmicks including coupons, gatefolds, accordion folds, and the like. Among the more common techniques to heighten attention value are the use of color, bleed page (no margin), use of white space, double-page spreads, white-on-black printing, and dramatic illustrations.

Another advantage of magazines worth noting is their ability to provide a split-run test of two or more alternative advertising creative executions. In a split-run test, every other copy of an issue would contain a given ad, for example. The regional edition feature of magazines can also be used to test alternative executions.

TELEVISION

Television is the newest of the major advertising media and has become a factor of major importance in modern society, both in terms of its impact on that society and the role it plays in people's lives. In 1968, it was estimated that television sets were in almost 95 percent of all homes in the United States and that on a given day over 65 percent of all adults watch television; over a seven-day period, the cumulative adult audience is estimated at 87 percent of the total population. The percentage of homes viewing television during the day varies from less than 25 percent during the 10 A.M. to 1 P.M. time period to over 60 percent in the 7:30 to 11 P.M. period. As of the end of 1968, it was estimated that about 23.9 percent of all U.S. households had color television. For households with over $15,000 in annual income, however, the figure was 49.0 percent.[18]

Television broadcasting has reached the point where it is possible for the citizenry to witness any major event taking place almost anywhere in the world at almost the instant that it happens. In recent years, American viewers have witnessed live broadcasts of such events as these: the assassination of Lee Harvey Oswald; the funerals of President John F. Kennedy and his brother Senator Robert Kennedy; the Winter Olympics from Grenoble, France; riots at the Democratic Party Convention in Chicago in 1968; the inauguration of President Richard M. Nixon; and the first steps of man on the moon. Television definitely provides a unique dimension to life in the last half of the twentieth century.

As an advertising medium, television has found a niche. Figures presented earlier in Table 18–1 showed that television is second only to newspapers as a use of advertising dollars, and for national advertisers it is certainly the most important medium, as shown by the data in Table 18–2. In 1968, there were 644 commercial TV stations (504 VHF and 140 UHF) and a total of 141 noncommercial (mostly "educational") TV stations. (VHF is an abbreviation for very high frequency and UHF for ultra high frequency.) There were three major national TV networks and 11 regional networks, and most viewing households had several stations among which to choose. The growth of community antenna TV systems was estimated to have reached 1,870 in 1968, thus improving the

[18]Fabian Linden, "Appliance Ownership," *The Conference Board Record,* 7 (June 1970), pp. 57–60.

quality of reception and the number of channels available for selection in the households served.[19]

Permits Active Participation by Audience

Television permits the viewer to actively participate in the communication and to structure the situation in such a way as to maximize its meaning for him. Through the effective use of the unique production features of television, many of which are shared with moving pictures, such as zoom shots, quick cuts, and close-ups, television can very effectively create a mood and a feeling which extends beyond the simple content of the photographed pictures and spoken words. Some observers feel that television commercials have made better use of these unique capabilities of television than have the providers of supposedly entertaining program fare. One explanation for this fact, if it is true, is that the advertiser is forced to do a complete communication job in sixty seconds or less and that this forces careful attention to techniques for conveying the intended meaning to the greatest possible extent.

Cost Is a Consideration

Television commercials have become more expensive (costs were up 72 percent in 1968 over 1963), partly due to the almost exclusive use of color (which adds about 25 percent to cost) and partly because of more sophisticated production. As one observer noted:

. . . today's taste and sophistication in execution demand more costly production values . . . . To stand out in today's TV clutter, you have to be different, not just colorful. To be different, today's creative groups demand more production values in the studio or on location. Today, you don't fake a villa in Italy . . . you go there.[20]

Several additional reasons for increased costs are cited including the cost of production personnel and the need for more careful attention to details which are intended to minimize the possibility of being charged with deceptive practices. For example, a detergent commercial showing a before/after washing situation must actually show illustrations of the same laundry before and after being washed with the sponsor's product. This requires that the entire production crew wait while the laundry is actually washed and dried during the filming of the commercial.

Television has several obvious advantages for the marketing communicator, including the opportunity to use both motion and color and geo-

---

[19]*Ibid.*, p. 9.

[20]Manning Rubin, *An Analysis of Television Commercial Costs: 1963 vs. 1968* (New York: American Association of Advertising Agencies, Committee on Broadcast Commercial Production, May, 1968), pp. 6–7.

graphic, time, and audience flexibility. The size of the audience is subject to major variation by time of day, and as a function of the programming content. Television dials are turned much more frequently than radio dials. The manner in which the commercial is executed is also important in determining the degree of message exposure. Techniques for measuring TV viewing and commercial effectiveness are very complex and are subject to rather large error.

Increasing Selectivity

The increased availability of multiple viewing channels, due to both community antenna systems and the proliferation of locally-oriented UHF stations, is expected to result in increased selectivity among TV stations serving a given market. Just as radio stations have tended to develop particular images with specialized appeals to particular segments of the market, so is television expected to move toward increased segmentation and "audience fragmentation." Another force tending to produce audience segmentation is multiple set ownership. As families acquire second and third TV sets (often of the portable variety) individual family members can become more selective in their viewing. Audiences can therefore be expected to become increasingly selective and to shrink for individual stations at a particular time of day. The medium will become increasingly personal and true portables will increase out-of-home viewing. Television will remain an important element of advertising media strategy, although the search for greater economic efficiency may result in a trend toward shorter-length commercials, 20- and 30-second rather than 60-second.[21]

OUTDOOR ADVERTISING

Outdoor advertising consists of both painted displays and billboards with large printed posters, as well as electric and painted spectaculars. The most common form is the poster billboard. There are over 300,000 standard billboards in the continental United States. These standard poster panels are 12 feet high and 25 feet long and take a 24-sheet poster that measures eight feet eight inches by 19 feet six inches.[22]

Billboards are typically located in high traffic areas in order to obtain maximum viewing opportunity. A common unit of measurement is the so-called "#100 showing," the usual buying unit, which means a sufficient number of billboards suitably located so that 93 percent of the

[21]Ogilvy & Mather, Inc., *Television in 1970: A Study of the Immediate Future of Commercial Television,* December 1967.
[22]Frey and Halterman, *op. cit.,* p. 312.

population in that market area will be exposed to the message an average of 21–22 times during a 30-day period. A "#50 showing" has a similar interpretation—exposure to 85 percent of the total population an average of 10–11 times in a 30-day period.[23]

Messages Must Be Short

The message content of a billboard tends to be very short, usually of a product identification nature. This reflects the fact that the driver of an automobile traveling down the turnpike at 60 miles per hour has time for only a quick glance at the message. Creative execution of outdoor messages requires special consideration of the basic problem of attracting attention—eye-catching illustrations, short but captivating and memorable headlines, and so on. For similar reasons, the location and positioning of billboards is a significant factor.

The circumstances of exposure make outdoor advertising differentially effective for products associated with driving such as gasoline and tires, and for retail advertising designed to generate traffic at the retail location (gas stations, furniture stores, ice cream stands, and so on). The most significant characteristics of outdoor advertising are its relatively low cost and its geographic flexibility. Although messages must be short, they can be placed in specific neighborhoods and traffic flows and can be delivered frequently. Outdoor advertising can be purchased either locally or on a national or regional basis. The value of a location is measured by an actual count of the traffic, by the Traffic Audit Bureau, a private research organization.[24]

Public Pressure for Change

Groups of concerned citizens have formed in recent years to oppose the use of outdoor advertising. Their criticisms are based upon aesthetic considerations and concern primarily the location of billboards along major arterial highways in a manner which obstructs the view of the countryside. There appears to be less concern about the use of outdoor advertising within urban areas. There are regulations governing the minimum distance away from the highway for all forms of advertising along major high-speed turnpikes in most states. The state of Vermont has taken steps to prohibit all advertising along major highways. Plans are being developed in Vermont to provide the highway traveler with the minimum information required for food, lodging, and service stations.

---

[23]Ogilvy & Mather, Inc., "O & M Pocket Guide to Media," 1969, p. 49.

[24]William M. Weilbacher, "Advertising-Media Strategy," Section 16 in Albert W. Frey (ed.), *Marketing Handbook*, 2nd ed. (New York: Ronald Press Company, Inc., 1965), pp. 11–12.

Whether other states will follow Vermont is uncertain, but it seems likely that the opponents of outdoor advertising will be vocal for many years to come.

OTHER MEDIA

There are many other media for carrying advertising messages. The two most important that have not yet been discussed are direct mail and point-of-purchase displays.

Direct Mail

Direct mail can be defined as any form of promotional material delivered to an address by the United States mail. The major advantages of direct mail are the possibility for any advertiser to launch a direct mail program and an unlimited amount of flexibility in designing both the content and the scope of a direct mail campaign.

There have been two significant developments in recent years to encourage use of direct mail. First has been the development of a capability for a high degree of personalization in the direct mail message. A combination of computer capability and high speed typewriters has made this possible. This kind of personalization is illustrated in Figure 18–1. A second development favoring direct mail has been the development of a capability and procedure for maintaining and selling mailing lists. Most companies that emphasize direct mail in their promotional mix depend upon sales of the names on their mailing lists for a substantial portion of their revenue. Most magazines also follow this practice and sell their subscriber lists.

Direct mail can be especially useful for reaching select markets and those which are difficult to reach through the mass media. Doctors and other professionals can often be reached most effectively in this manner.

A major disadvantage of direct mail is the difficulty of determining the value of a particular prospect list. Equally problematic is the large amount of waste circulation and the relatively small amount of reader interest. There is a good chance that the piece will never be opened (assuming it is delivered) and that, if opened, it will be quickly scanned and tossed in the wastepaper basket.

Point-of-Purchase Display

Point-of-purchase display fits the formal definition of mass media in that it is communication directed toward a large, undifferentiated audience. It is different from other mass media because it is located right at

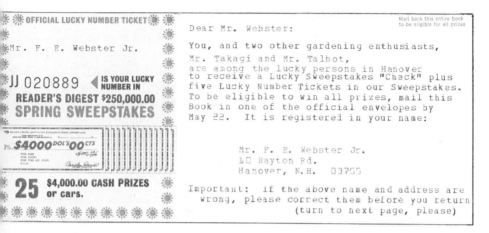

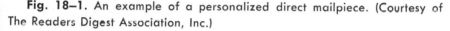

Fig. 18–1. An example of a personalized direct mailpiece. (Courtesy of The Readers Digest Association, Inc.)

the point of purchase, gets the prospect in a buying situation, and is integrated with product display and packaging considerations. Point-of-purchase displays are often designed to achieve a specific purpose such as to feature a special promotion or to encourage trial of a new product, usually with some special purchase incentive. For these reasons, further discussion of point-of-purchase display is postponed until we consider all forms of sales promotion in Chapter 22.

Special Media

The availability of advertising media is limited only by the imagination of potential advertisers. It will be remembered from Table 18–1 that "other expenditures" was a major category of advertising expense which includes these other media as well as internal advertising department operating expenses. Among the other kinds of mass media used for advertising are: matchbooks; sky-writing; programs for athletic events, concerts, and plays; small printed posters in store fronts and tacked on walls; bumper stickers, inserts in paperback books; calendars, pens and pencils, and other specialties; and clothing items with product identification symbols.

It is impossible to generalize about these media and the conditions under which their use will be effective. The closest to a generalization we can come is to observe that a specific communication objective may be best implemented by the use of one of these other, more specialized, media.

SUMMARY

The purpose of this chapter has been to explore some of the qualitative considerations involved in selection among alternative classes of media. The assessment of qualitative value is a preliminary step in the development of media strategy prior to the selection of specific media and the scheduling of advertisements in the selected media. Alternative and apparently conflicting definitions of media value were explored but the conflict was resolved by the realization that there are several stages through which the medium contributes to message effectiveness: (1) circulation or distribution, (2) vehicle exposure, (3) message exposure, (4) attention, (5) perception, and (6) retention. The first three stages were said to be largely the responsibility of the medium while the message and the medium interact to determine effectiveness in the last three stages.

A review of the comparative effects of media concluded that print media were more effective than broadcast for persons of above average intellectual ability and for complex issues. For the "average man," however, the order of effectiveness indicated was (1) face-to-face, (2) television, (3) radio, and (4) print. Media which involve both aural and visual stimuli and which permit some degree of active participation by the receiver seem to be most effective.

The rest of this chapter explored the current status and trends of each of the several media. All are growing as the economy and total advertising expenditures increase. The general trend seems to be toward more media specialization—limited appeal to selective market segments —for television as well as radio and magazines. More sophisticated audiences demand more sophisticated and efficient use of advertising media.

The key problem in developing an effective media strategy is to precisely match media characteristics with target market segment characteristics to obtain the maximum number of effective exposures with the budgeted level of expenditure. In the next chapter, we consider data on audience composition, the relative importance of reach and frequency, and techniques for selecting and scheduling media.

19

Media Strategy

Media strategy is reflected in the marketing communicator's plans for the purchase and use of media in the planning period. The selection and scheduling of media are the two principal sets of decisions required to develop a media strategy.

In Chapter 12, an important distinction was made between the "qualitative" and "quantitative" objectives of marketing communication. Qualitative objectives define the characteristics of the audience to be reached, the meaning to be conveyed to that audience, and the response desired from it. Quantitative objectives define the level of effort to be expended and the number of messages to be delivered. This chapter on media strategy is our last piece of unfinished business in developing communication objectives. Here we shall consider the problem of maximizing the number of messages to be delivered as a function of the number of receivers to be reached and the frequency with which the message is to be delivered to them.

The reasons for postponing this discussion of media strategy until other objectives had been dealt with are obvious. Media strategy cannot be defined until there is a clear statement of the marketing communication objectives including the characteristics of the target audience and a set of spending constraints provided by the budget. The media strategy has the objective of maximizing the number of messages delivered to prospective customers consistent with the budget constraint. The importance of the definition of the characteristics of the potential market will be elaborated upon in a moment.

Stated more precisely, the media strategy is a plan for achieving the objective of reaching the defined audience as frequently and effectively as permitted by the budget.

DEFINING THE TARGET AUDIENCE

The primary input to the media strategy is a careful definition of the characteristics of the prospective market. Media selection can be thought of as a process of matching the characteristics of the media audience to the characteristics of the target market segment, and doing so in a manner which maximizes the number of prospective customers reached and the frequency objectives that have been established. This leads to a definition of the concept of an *effective exposure* as a message delivered once to a prospective customer for the product or service being promoted. In order to select among alternative advertising media, the marketing communicator must have accurate information concerning the characteristics of the audience delivered by each medium. Problems with media audience data will be discussed in the next section.

The definition of the target audience should reflect several considerations including the benefits offered by the product, the spending power of the audience selected, and the opportunity to find a unique competitive niche. Market segmentation strategy leads directly to a specification of the characteristics of the audience.

Specific problems of media strategy should be considered in the market segmentation decision when it is initially made. Three sets of criteria must be considered in selecting a segmentation strategy; the *size* of the segment, the possibility of *measuring* the characteristics of segments as defined by the strategy, and the *accessability* of the segments so defined. Thus, it is difficult to use personality variables as the basis for market segmentation strategy because such variables are hard (some would say impossible) to measure and there are no media which efficiently deliver an audience with unique and definable personality characteristics. For all of these reasons, demographic variables such as age, income, occupation, number of children, education, race, and similar variables are the most common basis for defining the audience.

RATED EXPOSURE VALUE

As an aid to decision making, it is necessary to limit the definition of desired audience characteristics. Otherwise, the number of audience categories becomes unwieldy. For example, if there are three categories of income, three age groups, and three education categories, plus a distinction between male and female audience members, the analyst has defined 54 possible segments—too many for his analysis. For reasons that will become clearer in the following discussion, he would have to make separate assessments of the value of each segment in his marketing program and he would have to obtain data on each dimension for each of the media alternatives to be considered for inclusion in the schedule. To alleviate these difficulties, most analysts recommend that only a few variables be used to define the audience. These variables define demographic or economic characteristics that are associated with demand for the product.

Not all media audiences of equal size have equal value for the marketing communicator. Roughly speaking, the value of an audience is a function of the extent to which it matches the profile of the target consumer. Somehow, data on audience size must be adjusted to reflect the value of the audience. Kotler has suggested one straightforward method for making such adjustments to yield a measure of the *rated exposure value* for a medium.[1] The rated exposure value (or r.e.v.) becomes the effectiveness criterion for evaluating alternative media vehicles and the objective of the media strategy is to obtain the maximum r.e.v. for a given budget.

The r.e.v. of a particular advertisement, or "advertising unit," is a measure of four variables: (1) audience size and characteristics; (2) intermedia differences; (3) intramedia differences; and (4) advertising unit differences. Each of these variables will be explained briefly. The essential feature of the procedure is the development of an index (with average value 1.00) for each of these considerations that is used to adjust upward or downward the raw "audience" data.

Audience Size and Characteristics

The first step in making this adjustment is to define the target audience. Let us assume, for purposes of developing an example, that the marketer has defined three segments to which he wishes to direct his marketing effort. These segments are defined on the basis of age and are restricted to males. Let us further assume that the strategist wishes to compare two magazines with respect to their value in his marketing communication program, and that these magazines have audiences of equal size. The segments and the audience distribution of each magazine are as follows:

	Audience Size	
Segment	*Magazine A*	*Magazine B*
18–29	1,000,000	3,000,000
30–49	2,000,000	2,000,000
50+	3,000,000	1,000,000
Total	6,000,000	6,000,000

[1]Philip Kotler, "On Methods: Toward an Explicit Model for Media Selection," *Journal of Advertising Research*, 4 (March 1964), pp. 34–41.

The Penetration Ratio. Given the differences in audience composition, it is unlikely that the two magazines have equal value to the advertiser although they deliver the same total audience. Kotler suggests the following procedure for adjusting the value of the audience to reflect its characteristics. First, the strategist must determine the extent to which the product category and his specific brand appeal to each segment. Next, he must develop a "penetration ratio" for product and brand. Finally, these ratios are combined and used to adjust the audience size.

To illustrate this adjustment, assume the following figures:

Segment	Percentage of Adult Males in Population	Percentage of Product Sales	Percentage of Brand Sales
18–29	28	45	50
30–49	40	35	25
50+	32	20	25

Penetration ratios are calculated by dividing the "Percentage of Sales" figures by the "Percentage of Population" in each segment, and in this example they take on the following values:

Segment	Product Penetration Ratio	Brand Penetration Ratio	Average Penetration Ratio
18–29	1.61	1.79	1.70
30–49	0.88	0.63	0.75
50+	0.63	0.78	0.70

At this point, two aspects of this method become obvious. First, it is a rather arbitrary method. It is not *the* right way to determine the value of an audience, but simply one way of relating the audience characteristics to the segmentation strategy of the firm. Other methods could be developed for considering the importance of product and brand appeal, for example. Second, the "average penetration ratio" above simply divides the sum of the product and brand penetration ratios by two, thus giving them equal weight. There is no particular reason for this, other than convenience. If the strategist believed that his brand was underrepresented in the 30–49 age segment, he might want to reflect this by placing higher weightings on the product penetration ratios when they were combined with the brand penetration ratios.

The "average penetration ratio" as defined above gives an explicit quantitative assessment of the value of each segment to the communicator. The average penetration ratio is then used to adjust the audience data for each of the magazines under consideration as follows:

Segment	Average Penetration Ratio	Magazine A		Magazine B	
		Audience	Adjusted Audience	Audience	Adjusted Audience
18–29	1.70	1,000,000	1,700,000	3,000,000	5,100,000
30–49	0.75	2,000,000	1,500,000	2,000,000	1,500,000
50+	0.70	3,000,000	2,100,000	1,000,000	700,000
Total		6,000,000	5,300,000	6,000,000	7,300,000

Although both magazines had audiences of 6,000,000, they turn out to have quite different values in the communication strategy when appropriate adjustments are made for the characteristics of the audience. Because the youngest segment has greater product penetration and because this brand has particular appeal to the younger audience, Magazine B is a much more valuable medium for the simple reason that it has three times as many readers in the younger segment compared with Magazine A. On the basis of adjusted audience, Magazine B would be selected over Magazine A. (Notice that nothing has been said yet about other characteristics of the medium, or about the relative costs of the two alternatives.)

Scale Values. One last procedure is to consider how this assessment of the value of these alternatives, determined on the basis of age distribution of readership, can be combined with assessments of other variables such as income, regional distribution, etc. Similar calculations to those above for age could be made for these other variables. The problem is how to combine these multiple adjustments. The method suggested by Kotler is to calculate a "scale value" for each variable, which is derived by dividing the adjusted audience for that variable by the unadjusted audience. The age scale values for these two magazines would therefore be:

$$\text{Age scale value} = \frac{\text{Magazine A}}{\frac{5,300,000}{6,000,000}} = 0.88 \qquad \frac{\text{Magazine B}}{\frac{7,300,000}{6,000,000}} = 1.22$$

To determine the "total" adjusted audience value of a media alternative, the unadjusted audience would be multiplied by each of the scale values so calculated to arrive at a combined adjusted audience. There are two problems with such a procedure. One is to make sure that the variables are relatively independent. Thus, if age and income are used and these two variables are highly correlated, the result would be to exaggerate the effect of these two variables because of their interaction. The second problem is to determine the relative weights to be assigned to each scale value. While the typical procedure would be to give them equal weight, the scale values could be adjusted to reflect their greater importance. (Weights could be assigned which sum to one.)

This is only one method for adjusting audience data to reflect the importance of audience characteristics, but it suggests the approach which any method would follow. It makes explicit the criteria for matching audience profile with segments.

Intermedia Differences

Similar adjustments can be made to reflect the differential effectiveness of alternative advertising media. These differences in effectiveness reflect the "qualitative values of media" as described in the last chapter. The value of a particular medium for an advertiser was seen to be a reflection of the characteristics of the audience, as well as particular requirements for demonstrating the product and its benefits. For example, food illustrations typically benefit from the use of color, while camera advertising usually requires the use of pictures.

Such considerations can be quantified by use of an indexing procedure, and such quantification is necessary if judgments are to be reflected in adjustments of audience data. For example, assuming once again a "normal" value of 1.00, the media strategist might judge that for his products the value of radio is .95, television is 1.20, outdoor is .75, and magazines is 1.00. These index numbers would then be applied to adjusted audience figures to further reflect intermedia differences.

Intramedia Differences

Intramedia differences refer to qualitative differences among alternatives within a given class of media, such as the relative effectiveness of two television programs or the relative effectiveness of several magazines. These differences are a reflection of the editorial content and other factors influencing the credibility and the attention value of the media vehicles. Using a magazine example once again, *Glamour* magazine might be given a higher value by an advertiser of women's fashions than *Look* because its editorial content emphasizes matters of fashion, because the magazine is regarded as a trend-setter and an accurate source of information on style trends, and because it has been found that readers look at advertisements as closely as the editorial content in order to discern the latest fashion trends.

Once again, an indexing procedure could be used to reflect this judgment of the effectiveness of a particular media alternative. These judgments, while they can be aided by research studies, are not scientific reflections of carefully measured differences. The index numbers are simply a method for making judgment explicit and for combining it with data on audience size. Adjustments for intramedia differences would be applied to figures for adjusted audience, further scaled by indexes of intermedia differences.

Advertising Units

Finally, adjustments must be made for differences in the effectiveness of alternative treatments *within* a particular media vehicle. The term *advertising unit* is used here to refer specifically to a particular print advertisement, broadcast commercial, or outdoor billboard as defined by its size (space dimensions or time length), whether it uses color, and the time at which it appears. Thus, an example of an advertising unit would be a full-page, black-and-white advertisement in the December issue of *Boy's Life*.

The importance of these distinctions among advertising units is a function of the fact that the costs of media reflect such differences. There will be a different rate for each alternative size and for the use of color. Thus, these must be treated as separate advertising alternatives and it is therefore necessary to develop a measure of relative effectiveness against which to compare relative cost.

Previous comments apply to the problem of developing a measure of the relative effectiveness of advertising units. While these judgments may be based upon research (such as a study of the contribution of color to advertising effectiveness for a particular product class or brand), the measure of effectiveness will be an index reflecting management judgment.

To summarize, r.e.v. for a particular medium is a reflection of total audience size, adjusted to reflect audience characteristics, intermedia and intramedia differences, and the relative effectiveness of particular advertising units. Rated exposure value is therefore an adjusted audience figure and the objective of the media strategy is to maximize the value of r.e.v. within the budget constraint. While alternative procedures for making these judgments are available and may be preferred in a given situation, the r.e.v. method as presented by Kotler illustrates the important logical elements in considering each of these variables that determine the true value of a media schedule for the marketing communicator.

BASIC AUDIENCE MEASUREMENT CONCEPTS

The definition of the "audience" of a given media vehicle is not at all obvious. The basis for this assertion has been laid in earlier chapters where the contribution of media to the achievement of marketing communication objectives was described in terms of a model. This model, originally proposed by the Audience Concept Committee of the Advertising Research Foundation, defined the vehicle audience as consisting of prospects and nonprospects and said that there are six stages through which the vehicle contributes to the effectiveness of an advertising message:[2]

1. Vehicle distribution
2. Vehicle exposure
3. Advertising exposure
4. Advertising perception
5. Advertising communication
6. Sales response

Earlier chapters also suggested that the primary and distinctive contribution of advertising media was in the first three stages. Effects at the later stages are a result of the interaction of media and message to produce a hierarchy of possible communication effects.

Distribution

The most straightforward definition of audience for a media vehicle is the distribution of that vehicle. This statistic would be provided by the total subscribers of a magazine, for example, or the number of households with TV or radio sets able to receive a particular station. Notice that the concept of total physical distribution of media has more meaning for print media than for broadcast media.

A key consideration in the selection of media is the availability of accurate data on distribution of the media vehicle. Print media offer the most reliable statistics on circulation, provided by the Audit Bureau of Circulation for newspapers and magazines with at least 70 percent paid circulation. Measures of distribution for outdoor are provided by the Traffic Audit Bureau. The "distribution" of a television program would be the number of homes served by stations affiliated with the national network, without regard at this level of measurement for the question of whether these sets were tuned to that program.

Waste Coverage

Not all persons to whom the media vehicle is "distributed" will be prospects for the marketing communicator's product or service. In the example used earlier, since the product is assumed to be intended only for adult males, persons under 18 years of age and all females would represent "waste coverage" for the magazines described. While all media vehicles will have some waste coverage for any specific product or service, the problem is to keep this to a minimum in the advertising media schedule as a whole.

[2]Audience Concept Committee, *Toward Better Media Comparisons* (New York: Advertising Research Foundation, 1961).

Pass-Along Distribution

While waste coverage would reduce the value of a media vehicle, "pass-along distribution" would enhance it. Pass-along occurs in the obvious case where the subscriber to a magazine, for example, shares his copies with a nonsubscriber. A similar result occurs when there are multiple readers or viewers within the household. Thus, a television program may attract an average of four persons per household. A magazine may attract multiple readers within a subscriber family. The ability of the media vehicle to attract multiple viewers or readers is a function of both its editorial content and its basic media characteristics, such as the fact that monthly magazines are typically kept around for several weeks, thus enhancing the possibility of pass-along distribution. Newspapers are less likely to have pass-along distribution for the simple reason that their content loses value much more quickly. Studies of pass-along audiences have suggested that they are not influenced by advertising to the same extent as the "primary" audience.

Vehicle Exposure

The existence of pass-along distribution is the major reason why vehicle exposure may actually be greater than vehicle distribution. While some of those who qualify as "subscribers" may not actually receive the medium, the number gained through pass-along distribution is probably greater in almost all instances than the number lost from ineffective distribution. Vehicle exposure is often used as the measure of "audience," because it includes all persons who are actually exposed to the media vehicle, not just those to whom it was originally distributed. The media themselves obviously prefer this measure because it provides a more favorable basis for comparison.

Most media vehicles are able to provide information about vehicle exposure as well as distribution. National magazines typically conduct annual studies of their audiences using sample survey techniques. These studies provide reasonably accurate data on the demographic and socio-economic characteristics of the audience as well as measures of special interest to potential advertisers such as hobbies, inventory of particular products, and time usage patterns of subscribers. As an example of this kind of data, a magazine wishing to attract airline advertising might use these studies to determine subscribers' travel plans and intentions. In addition, measures of media usage are obtained including the number of persons who read an issue of the magazine and whether the magazine is passed along.

A variety of methods and devices are used to collect data on broadcast media. These methods and devices fall into three categories: (1)

recording devices attached to the set; (2) diary methods requiring self-reporting of viewing and listening habits; and (3) interview methods (telephone or personal interviews conducted during the broadcast or soon thereafter). The best-known method of measuring a television audience is the rating service offered by the A. C. Nielsen Company using an automatic recording device called an "audimeter" attached to the television set. Ratings are expressed as a percentage of all United States television homes. Data are available for the number of homes viewing for at least six minutes and those who stayed tuned for the duration of the program. This method does not provide information on the average number of persons watching a set. The A. C. Nielsen Company also maintains a panel of households who report their viewing in a diary.

Cost-per-Thousand

A frequently used measure of media efficiency for comparing media vehicles is the cost of reaching one thousand persons with that media vehicle. The crudest measure would simply divide the cost of the advertising unit by the vehicle distribution to obtain this figure, and all alternative media vehicles would be evaluated on this basis. There are obviously several shortcomings to this simple approach and it is desirable to adjust statistics on vehicle distribution to consider, among other things, audience characteristics, waste coverage, and pass-along distribution. For these reasons, it would make more sense to try to use adjusted audience figures and to further distinguish differences in vehicle exposure.

Duplication

Another important dimension to consider in building the media schedule is the existence of duplication among the audiences of several media vehicles. Imagine that the advertiser plans to use three magazines. The total audience delivered by these three vehicles can be divided into seven groups:

1. Those who see *only* Magazine A
2. Those who see *only* Magazine B
3. Those who see *only* Magazine C
4. Those who see A and B but not C
5. Those who see A and C but not B
6. Those who see B and C but not A
7. Those who see A, B, and C

Each of these seven groups is distinct; they must be combined to obtain a measure of the total unduplicated audience delivered by that media schedule. This number will be less than the sum of the three magazines' separate readership. These considerations are illustrated graphically in Figure 19–1.

A measure of the net unduplicated audience delivered by the combination of these three media would require that each of these seven categories be estimated separately. This would require data on the duplication between each pair of media as well as data on the three-way duplication and on the total audience of each medium. (Notice that the number who read *only* a given media vehicle would have to be calculated by substracting the pair duplications and the three-way duplication estimates from the total circulation for that media vehicle.) The *coverage* or *reach* of a given media schedule is defined as the net unduplicated audience delivered by that schedule. Reach or coverage is simply a measure of the total number of (unique) individuals in the combined audiences for all vehicles included in the media schedule.

Advertising Exposure

The measurement of advertising exposure is important because exposure is necessary, obviously, for the message to be effective. Even if the vehicle comes to the attention of the individual, the actual message may not. Media differ significantly in their ability to insure that vehicle exposure will lead to advertising exposure. The advertising medium can make a contribution to advertising effectiveness by increasing the probability of advertising exposure, as when a special appeal magazine is used

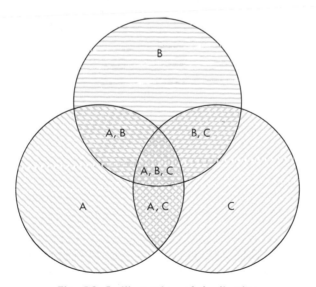

Fig. 19–1. Illustration of duplication.

because advertising is likely to be viewed more carefully by readers of special appeal magazines.

As indicated previously, advertising exposure is not just a function of the media vehicle. It is also importantly determined by the qualitative characteristics of the message itself, as well as the peculiar characteristics of the advertising unit such as size and color.

Advertising exposure is also a function of the positioning of the advertising within the vehicle. Thus, commercials placed within the middle parts of a television program are likely to deliver a larger audience than those placed between programs. Advertisements on the front and back covers of magazines, and those in the centerfold of the magazine, are likely to obtain somewhat more exposure than those messages distributed throughout the editorial pages.

Advertising exposure is therefore a function of the characteristics of the media vehicle, position within the media vehicle, creative execution, and characteristics of the advertising unit. The media vehicle does make a contribution of its own and concern with the measurement of advertising exposure is therefore legitimately considered as part of the media evaluation process.

The remaining stages of the effectiveness measurement process do not meet this criterion of being clearly and fundamentally related to the quality of the media vehicle. Advertising perception and communication, while they are undoubtedly influenced to some extent by the qualitative characteristics of the media vehicle including its prestige and credibility, are not primarily the result of the characteristics of the media. Rather, the communication effect of the advertising is a reflection of the characteristics of the message. Likewise, sales response is only vaguely related to the value of the media vehicle and should not be used as the criterion against which to evaluate media effectiveness.

To summarize, there are three levels at which the value of advertising media vehicles can be compared: vehicle distribution; vehicle exposure; and advertising exposure. Three other levels of communication effect—advertising perception, advertising communication, and sales response, while they are influenced to some extent by the choice of media vehicle, are not often used to compare media because many other factors influence these effects.

MEDIA AUDIENCE DATA

The previous sections of this chapter have suggested the basic importance of data on media audiences as the critical information base with which the media planner must operate. The selection of one class of media over another may be justified in part by the greater availability of data on that class. On this basis, most media experts would agree that the best media data are available on magazines. Television, on the other hand, provides only limited audience data.

There are four kinds of audience data of importance to the media planner. Data on distribution, audience characteristics, vehicle exposure, and advertising exposure would be most important, probably in this order. Measurements become less precise as one moves from distribution to advertising exposure.

Pressures for Improved Data

The increased reliance of marketing communication planners on computers and rigorous analytical methods has created major pressures upon the media to provide better audience data. At the same time, professional organizations such as the Advertising Research Foundation have encouraged the development of more accurate media data as well as better methods for analyzing those data. Perhaps the most important source of pressure for better media data, however, has been the basic shift toward segmented marketing strategies by the major advertisers. Increased marketing precision requires increasingly efficient use of advertising media which requires, in turn, accurate information about media audiences.

A review of the professional literature will reveal that advertising people do not hold media research in high regard. Because the ultimate objective of most media research is to convince potential advertisers that the particular media vehicle offers the most efficient solution to their communication problems, there is a basic problem of credibility. As one advertising agency official stated it:

The goal of most, if not all, media research is not to advance a general understanding of how media contribute to advertising effectiveness; rather, the goal is a bit more mundane: to attract advertising dollars. And all too often research findings are couched in the language of promotional trumpery; rarely do researchers concern themselves with the theoretical underpinnings necessary for properly evaluating existing media studies and designing new studies.[3]

This critic went on to suggest that measures of vehicle exposure were inadequate to the task of measuring media effectiveness. He stated a preference for measures of "impact," measures of the extent to which audience response to advertisements is affected by media. For reasons developed above, it seems unlikely that "clean" measures of media impact, so defined, can be developed.

Advertising practitioners continue to be strong in their desire to evaluate the contribution of media to total communication effectiveness,

[3]Stewart A. Smith, "Criteria for Media Comparisons: A Critique," *Journal of Marketing Research*, 2 (November 1965), pp. 360–69, at page 360.

however. Another advertising agency research executive expressed the opinion that

. . . as more and more attention is paid to the need for research on the attainment of advertising objectives, more and more effort will be devoted to evaluating the role of media in the communication process. . . . The growing use of sophisticated, experimental designs and evaluation procedures which run the gamut from communication criteria to sales data will provide us more and more information on the contributions of media to the attainment of advertising objectives.[4]

Up until the present time, at least, media planners have had to remain content with measures of vehicle exposure and audience characteristics as the basis for their media selection decisions. Occasionally, data on advertising exposure and measures of impact have been available from the print media. In most cases, however, and especially in the case of broadcast media, the media strategist is still trying to improve the quality of information on audience characteristics and vehicle exposure before moving on to the more complex problems of higher level measurements.

DIMENSIONS OF THE MEDIA PLAN

There are several separate decisions which must be made in constructing a media plan. The purpose of this section is to review the major dimensions of each class of decision and to suggest the major considerations involved in those decisions. It will be seen that there is a fundamental relationship between the media selection and scheduling decision and the basic marketing strategy of the firm, as well as a specific relationship between considerations of message strategy and those of media strategy.

Classes of Media

Assuming that there is a clear definition of the target market and of the audience to be reached, the first decision required in developing the media plan is to decide which of the several classes of media are to be considered in developing the media schedule. Although this text has considered questions of creativity and message strategy before those of media strategy, it is obvious that messages cannot be developed until the basic type of media to be used has been decided upon. It certainly makes a difference whether advertising is to be developed for magazines or television.

The media selection decision is typically made *within* a class of media. Thus, the first decision would be to use magazines, television,

---

[4]Seymour Banks, "The Role of Advertising Media in the Attainment of Advertising Objectives," in Henry Gomez (ed.), *Innovation—Key to Marketing Progress* (Chicago: American Marketing Association, 1963), pp. 248–53.

etc. Then, at the next level, the question would become which of the available media within each class to use.

Which class of media (or classes) to use should be a reflection of consideration of five important factors:

1. The audience to be reached
2. The product or service and its unique communication requirements
3. The nature of distribution channels used by the firm
4. The qualitative characteristics and availability of the mass media
5. Competitive considerations

Audience, Product, and Channel Factors. As discussed in the previous chapter, there are important differences in the use of media by different segments of the population. Young persons are reached more effectively by radio and magazines with special youth appeals than through other media. Older persons may be reached more effectively by television, as may very young children. Better educated persons are likely to rely more heavily upon print media. Such considerations suggest how the nature of the audience to be reached should influence the selection of media class.

The product or service being advertised may be able to derive particular advantage from use of a particular medium. High-fashion goods probably are presented most effectively in special-appeal print media. Automotive products may be advertised on the radio to certain advantage at those times when persons are most likely to have their car radios turned on, as they drive to and from work. To repeat an earlier example, food products are advertised to advantage in media which permit the showing of food in served portions and which permit the use of color.

The distribution channels used by the firm exert a fundamental influence on the marketing communication strategy in several respects. The whole range of influences will be discussed in Chapter 21. In the media choice decision, consideration must be given to the extent to which retailers expect or require promotional support at the local level. The availability of local and regional media is an important consideration where an objective is to support local distributors and/or to tailor the use of mass media to the pattern of regional distribution. The airlines pose an interesting variation of the "distribution channels" problem in that a good share of their advertising must be directed into those local markets where they have sales offices and scheduled service.

Qualitative, Availability, and Competitive Factors. The qualitative characteristics and the availability of the mass media, and specific requirements for their usage, must also be considered. These qualitative considerations can take many forms. It may be desirable, for instance, to obtain the endorsement of a magazine such as the *Good Housekeeping* seal of approval. A television special may provide unique opportunities for promotional tie-ins with dealers and for special sales promotions and contests. It would be advantageous for a manufacturer of phonograph records to sponsor a special musical program, for example, or for a leading men's clothing manufacturer to want to be represented in the advertising in a special men's clothing section of *Esquire*.

Availability is always an important consideration. A desire for maximum flexibility in responding to sales trends and local competitive considerations may influence a decision against the use of media which require closing times (the time at which advertising must be presented to the medium) significantly in advance of publication or broadcast dates. Certain classes of media may be "sold out" when the advertiser finally decides to use them. Television shows in the category required by an advertiser may be contracted for before the advertiser is able to indicate his final decision.

Competitive considerations may also influence the choice of a class of media in several ways. There may be a unique opportunity to appeal to a relatively large and overlooked segment of the potential market by searching out media that are ignored by others in the industry. On the other hand, advertising in a particular medium may be a necessary condition for competing effectively in some industry. Although there is no published evidence to support this assertion, a casual inspection of the *New York Times Magazine* (published only in the Sunday edition), suggests that manufacturers of synthetic textile fibers are expected by their customers to advertise in this particular vehicle. Likewise, it is hard to imagine an automobile manufacturer not making heavy use of television.

Concentrating media spending in one class of media can give an advertiser greater visibility within that medium, especially when competitors make little or no use of this medium. A major oil company followed this strategy several years ago and placed virtually all of its advertising in newspapers. One brand of liquor followed a similar strategy and used local newspapers to reach into a segment of the market—the rural and small-town market—that had been overlooked by other brands.

In passing, it should be noted that local newspapers are a difficult choice of advertising media for the national advertiser for two reasons. One reason is cost; advertising rates are substantially higher for national advertisers than for local advertisers. Because of this, national advertisers wishing to use local newspapers will often place their advertising money with the local dealer and ask him to spend it. The second reason for the difficulty in using local newspapers is the obvious complexity in purchasing, checking, and paying for the use of many—perhaps hundreds—of separate newspapers. This latter problem is minimized to some extent by the use of newspaper representatives and space brokers who are able to offer "package" deals which result in both lower cost and easier buying of many local newspapers.

The decision on class of media to use is a complex one requiring a high level of executive judgment concerning the fit of alternative modes of communication within the total marketing communication mix.

Reach

Reach was defined as the net unduplicated audience delivered by a media schedule. Reach is the best measure of media vehicle exposure and can be applied either to adjusted or unadjusted audience. For reasons developed early in this chapter, the concept of rated exposure value seems most helpful for each media alternative and the objective would be to maximize the rated exposure value delivered by a particular media schedule.

To say that we wish to maximize reach or to maximize rated exposure value is to say that we want to reach as many potential prospects for our product as possible. This may not be an effective criterion by itself, however, for three reasons. First, the advertiser may be spending so much that he could reach everybody at least once and still have a lot of money left over. Second, the problem of duplication makes it difficult to estimate the reach, or unduplicated audience, of a given schedule. Third, each insertion in a particular media vehicle results in additional coverage, further complicating the problem of defining reach. This last comment introduces the concept of "cumulative" audience.

Let us illustrate this by considering the case of a magazine with circulation of 5,000,000. One issue of that magazine will guarantee circulation of 5,000,000. When a second issue of that same magazine is purchased, the total coverage is not 10,000,000, for the obvious reason that many of the same persons who purchased the first issue will also purchase the second—including all those who are subscribers. However, some people who did not get the first issue will get the second issue, resulting in the fact that the total coverage of two insertions in this magazine is something greater than 5,000,000. This is the concept of cumulative audience—the more the insertions in a given medium, the greater the cumulative coverage, or reach, obtained. The problem of estimating the total audience delivered by successive issues of the same magazine is analogous to the problem of estimating the total audience for several magazines. The addition of one insertion or one more magazine will duplicate coverage of some audience members while it will also add new ones.

Audience Accumulation. Lucas and Britt reported two interesting studies of audience accumulation. One study of a weekly television program sponsored by the Ford Motor Company found that, over a four-week period, a total of 23,852,000 homes was reached once, while the average number of homes reached by a single week's program was 13,339,000. Of the total homes reached, 33.5 percent saw only one show; 29.2 percent saw two shows only; 20.4 percent saw three shows only; and 16.9 percent saw all four shows. Likewise, a study by *Life* magazine found that four consecutive weekly issues of the magazine were read by people 18 years of age and older in a total of 28,409,000 homes, while the average audience for a single issue was only 20,178,000 homes. This study found that 39 percent of the total four-week audience saw all four issues, while 20 percent looked into only one issue, 21 percent looked into only two issues, and 20 percent looked into only three issues.[5] These statistics show convincingly that the total reach or coverage of a media vehicle is a function of the number of insertions in that vehicle. Data for estimating the extent of audience accumulation must be obtained from the advertising media if this factor is to be assessed in the development of media strategy.

Duplication. The existence of duplication among media vehicle audiences poses a similar measurement problem. Some magazines provide estimates of the extent to which their subscribers are also reached by other media, but these data are not always available and often have questionable reliability. Furthermore, such data typically pertain to only a very small subset of all of the possible combinations that must be considered in estimating the total reach of a given media schedule.

In 1961, Agostini proposed that it was possible to estimate the amount of duplication in a media schedule with the formula:

$$\frac{C}{A} = \frac{1}{1 + KD/A}$$

where C = the net coverage of a set of m media
A = the sum of the readership of each medium included in the set
D = the sum of the duplicated readership of all pairs of media in the set
K = a constant = 1.125

This constant, which has come to be called "Agostini's constant," was estimated from a study of print media in France and was found to yield very accurate estimates of net coverage for hundreds of combinations of media.[6]

[5]D. B. Lucas and S. H. Britt, *Measuring Advertising Effectiveness* (New York: McGraw-Hill Book Co., Inc., 1963), p. 362.
[6]J. M. Agostini, "How To Estimate Unduplicated Audiences," *Journal of Advertising Research*, 1 (March 1961), pp. 11–14.

To estimate the net coverage of a media schedule with this formula, it is necessary only to have data on the readership of each medium and the duplication of each pair of media in the set, provided in the form of an $m \times m$ matrix where there are m media alternatives being considered. (Net coverage is the reach of a combination of *single* issues of two or more media, and is a measure distinct from either cumulative audience or reach which is not restricted to only one issue by definition.) Other authors have examined the Agostini formula and have concluded that although the value of the constant may vary slightly, it is a reasonable basis upon which to estimate net coverage.[7] A more complicated basis for estimating net coverage was proposed by Metheringham.[8] Metheringham makes some assumptions about the distribution over the population of the probability of exposure, and his method requires essentially the same information as the Agostini technique. The essence of both methods is to use data on pairwise duplication to determine the extent of duplication in the total media schedule.

Agostini has also proposed a method for estimating the cumulative audience obtained by using successive issues of the same media vehicle.[9] This method follows the same logic as the method for estimating duplication and requires data on the average audience for one issue of each media alternative and the accumulated audience for two successive issues.

The reach of a media schedule is therefore difficult but by no means impossible to estimate, given some preliminary data on duplication. One of the objectives of the media plan is to reach all potential prospects for the product being promoted and to do so in as efficient a manner as possible. Estimation of the reach of a media schedule requires consideration of the extent of duplication in the schedule, as well as the effects of audience accumulation from adding successive units of the same media vehicle.

Frequency and Repetition

When there is a budget constraint, and the objective is to maximize the r.e.v. of a media schedule, the media strategist has a choice to make between the relative importance of reach and frequency in his schedule. Two "exposures" can result from either two messages delivered to one prospect or one message delivered to two prospects.

[7]H. J. Claycamp and C. W. McClelland, "Estimating Reach and the Magic of K," *Journal of Advertising Research*, 8 (June 1968), pp. 44–51.

[8]Richard A. Metheringham, "Measuring the Net Cumulative Coverage of a Print Campaign," *Journal of Advertising Research*, 4 (December 1964), pp. 23–28.

[9]J. M. Agostini, "Analysis of Magazine Accumulative Audience," *Journal of Advertising Research*, 2 (December 1962), pp. 24–27.

There are many reasons why frequency and repetition may be desirable in the media schedule. Several messages delivered to a single receiver may be necessary to bring about the change in attitudes that must precede actual behavior change and result in purchase of the product. In a different sense, repetition may be a way of keeping the brand name in "top-of-mind awareness" so that it is most likely to be the brand chosen on the next shopping trip. This last consideration is important for frequently purchased consumer goods and where there is relatively little brand loyalty. In these situations, the ratio of brand advertising to total advertising in the product category is also an important consideration favoring repetition.

In a laboratory experiment evidence was gathered which supported a conclusion that probability of choice is proportional to frequency of exposure. This was found for both auditory and visual stimuli. Beyond a certain point the incremental effect of frequency of exposure was found to decrease, however. When a message was repeated too frequently (specifically when it was more than 50 percent of all messages), it seemed to form a background against which other messages stood out. This study also found that messages occurring nearer to the decision point in time were more effective.[10] All of these findings support the value of frequency and repeated message exposure.

In Chapter 11, we reviewed several findings on the uses of repetition in communication. The general conclusion of that discussion was that repetition can effectively increase the amount of retained awareness and opinion change, especially if repetition occurs over a reasonably short interval. However, spreading the messages over a longer time period may result in a loss of continuity with subsequent forgetting and a decrease in message effectiveness. Repetition is made more effective by variation on the basic theme, rather than repetition of exactly the same message which is likely to cause boredom or even active resistance.

In reviewing several studies of repetition in advertising, Lucas and Britt suggested that repetition of the same advertisement can increase both knowledge of the product and its claims and expressed willingness to buy the brand. They also cited evidence that both frequency (which refers to a time dimension between exposures) and repetition (which says nothing about time) may pay off at an increasing rate.[11]

An advertiser may for any of several reasons therefore decide that there is some minimum number of messages he wishes to deliver to each prospective customer during the coming period. The resulting frequency objective can be multiplied by the reach objective to determine the total

[10]L. A. Lo Sciuto, L. H. Strassmann, and W. D. Wells, "Advertising Weight and the Reward Value of the Brand," *Journal of Advertising Research*, 7 (June 1967), pp. 34–38.

[11]Lucas and Britt, *op. cit.*, p. 218.

number of exposures desired from the media schedule during the planned period. (Notice that this also provides, at least conceptually, a basis for determining the budget for the coming period assuming it is also possible to estimate the cost of an average exposure.) If there is a budget constraint that does not permit the accomplishment of both reach and frequency to the extent required, it is not obvious which dimension should be relaxed. While the logic of wanting to reach as many potential customers as possible suggests that it would be desirable to stick by the reach objective, it may also be that some minimum number of exposures is required for each prospect before he takes buying action and that delivering any fewer messages to the prospect means that all such messages are wasted.

Specific decisions are therefore required concerning desired frequency and its relative importance vis-a-vis reach as potentially conflicting communication objectives.

Continuity

Continuity is a concept related to frequency; it may be thought of as the time sequence of messages including the number of messages and the time lag between successive messages delivered to a prospect. One of the most widely accepted principles of advertising management is that continuity is necessary in order to derive maximum return from the advertising investment. The general line of reasoning in support of this position is that advertising builds a stock of goodwill which erodes over time, due to a process such as forgetting, and this stock must be continually replenished in order to protect the original investment. A corollary is that in each period a slightly greater expenditure is required to bring the stock back to a stated level if investments have not been made in prior periods.

In a competitive market environment the basic human process of forgetting is aided by the existence of competing messages which tend to drive out impressions created by earlier advertising. The extent of this effect could be estimated by use of experimental conditions to determine the rate at which sales decay in the absence of promotional support, although the opportunity costs of this research would obviously be significant. The value to planning of having a reliable estimate of the sales decay constant should not be underestimated, however.

Advertising Units

Decisions must be made about the size (amount of space or length of time) of the advertisements to used and whether color will be used in the advertising. These decisions must be made before advertising alternatives can be evaluated for the simple reason that cost (and therefore value) will be a function of the kind of advertising units employed.

The most popular options in radio and television are 10, 20, 30, and 60-second commercials, while magazines typically offer quarter-, half-, and full-page (and double-page) options. Newspaper space is usually purchased in number of column inches. In Chapter 11, it was shown that size and color are determinants of the attention-getting value of a message. In addition to attention value, there may be particular reasons why a given size of advertising unit is required—the amount of copy to be included in the advertisement, for example.

Costs of media typically do not increase percentagewise as fast as the amount of space purchased. For example, a 60-second time slot on network television does not cost twice as much as a 30-second slot, and a full-page ad in a magazine does not cost twice as much as a half-page. Likewise, advertising exposure appears to increase more slowly than the amount of space or time used. In some instances, it may even be that the shorter advertisement or commercial is *more* effective. As the costs of advertising media increase, advertisers tend to shift their preferences toward smaller advertising units within the media vehicle. In recent years, this has been especially the case in television where 30-second commercials have become increasingly popular while 60-second slots have decreased in importance.

Flighting

The concept of flighting refers to the bunching of advertising in a given media vehicle over a reasonably short time period. Flighting would result in a decrease in continuity. An example of flighting would be the concentration of all television advertising in a 6-week period during each 13-week quarter. The reasons for using flighting are the greater visibility and top-of-mind awareness which seems to result from concentrating advertising impressions within this narrow time period. A flighting strategy may be especially effective in highly competitive marketing situations where brand market share is very closely related to advertising share. The laboratory experiments mentioned earlier also found that flighting of messages was more effective than spreading them out over a longer time period in an evenly spaced sequence.[12]

MEDIA SELECTION DECISIONS

Having made the necessary decisions concerning classes of media, reach and frequency, continuity and flighting, and the kinds of advertising units to be used, the media strategist is in a position to begin the

[12]Lo Sciuto, Strassman, and Wells, *op. cit,* p. 35.

process of choosing specific media alternatives to be included in his media schedule. In order to make the media selection decision, the strategist needs four inputs.

Four Inputs to the Decision

First, he needs a clear and unambiguous statement of objectives which tell him the nature of the market to be reached and the relevant criteria against which to evaluate media alternatives. The concept of rated exposure value, defined at the beginning of the chapter, provides such a criterion. The objective would be to maximize the rated exposure value of the media schedule.

Second, the strategist needs a list of all of the media vehicle alternatives that he can consider and their costs. Earlier decisions about class of media and about advertising units will define such a list. An important dimension of this list is the necessary information about the audience characteristics as well as distribution and exposure. He also needs some estimate of the qualitative value of media alternatives to the advertiser, such as the weights used for intramedia differences in calculating r.e.v.

Third, the media strategist must know how much money he can spend. The budget constraint on the media schedule is derived from the complex decision making procedure for determining the level of marketing communication effort, and its allocation among communication modes, as reviewed in detail in Chapters 16 and 17.

Fourth, the strategist must consider a wide variety of constraints on his choice which derive from the nature of the media themselves and from management policies. As a simple illustration: it is not possible to have more than six insertions per year in a bimonthly magazine. Management may also impose restrictions such as requiring at least two insertions per year in a given magazine, or permitting no more than four in another, or having no more than six magazines in the total schedule.

These elements define the media selection decision as one of maximizing the objectives of the marketing communication strategy (stated in terms such as r.e.v.) subject to budget and other constraints. Before the advent of computers and operations research techniques, media selection required a very large staff of clerks to maintain the necessary data on available media and to work through the thousands of calculations required to make the media decision. The steps involved in the media selection decision were typically similar to the following.

Calculations Required

First, it was necessary to adjust audience data (usually data on vehicle distribution) in some way to reflect the value of the audience for that advertiser. A simple approach to this problem was to estimate the proportion of the audience that was actually prospects for the company's products and to deflate audience figures by the proportion of nonprospects. The next step was to put media costs on a comparable basis. This could be done by calculating a crude measure of cost per thousand, using the adjusted audience figures. Then the simplest way of choosing among media alternatives would be to select successively higher cost media as one moved down a list of rank-ordered media alternatives according to the adjusted cost-per-thousand data.

One of the major efficiencies offered by an advertising agency is its ability to keep a central file of current information on the tens of thousands of media alternatives available to the national advertiser and a staff of personnel necessary to maintain these data and perform the analysis required for obtaining an efficient media schedule. Even with the available data and manpower, however, it was never possible to assure that the very best schedule had been derived, for three primary reasons. First, it was virtually impossible to consider all possible combinations of media. Rather, rules of thumb and common sense had to be used to narrow the list of alternatives to be rigorously evaluated. Second, the available data were seldom adequate to determine precisely the value of an audience for a given advertiser. Such basic statistics as necessary to determine the proportion of prospects in the audience, for example, were seldom available. Third, the whole question of "impact" or the qualitative value of media vehicle alternatives had to be approached on the basis of untested management judgment. These judgments would be reflected in weights used to adjust audience data or in the decision as to which alternatives to include in the list from which the selection decision was made.

In the past decade there have appeared several more rigorous approaches to the media selection problem. These approaches reflect the availability of high-speed, large-memory computer systems as well as the development of analytical techniques for assessing the data available concerning media alternatives. The most commonly discussed methods are those which rely on the technique of linear programming for assessing alternatives.

Before reviewing these techniques, it is necessary to point out that only the first of the three reasons just cited for non-optimality in media schedules is improved by the computer, that is, the ability to calculate the values of many more combinations of media. The computer makes it possible to use more data and to perform the arithmetic much more quickly. As we shall see, however, the optimality of the media decision is still constrained by weaknesses in the available media data and the continuing need for frequent inputs of managerial judgment.

MATHEMATICAL MODELS FOR MEDIA SELECTION

Heuristic Models

Heuristics are rules of thumb. While heuristic models assure good solutions and assure that each new solution is slightly better than the previous one generated by the procedure, they do not guarantee optimal solutions. One of the earliest heuristic models reported was the Young and Rubicam advertising agency's "High Assay" model. This model requires data on the proportion of prospects in a given media vehicle audience and the cost of an insertion. The criterion for decision is to select that media vehicle which offers the lowest cost per prospect reached. This method is followed until a target exposure value is reached for that period (and not until a budget constraint is reached), and it delivers the schedule with the lowest possible cost, according to the assumptions of the model.[13]

Kuehn has proposed a heuristic model in which the media strategist selects insertions in the medium having the highest incremental consumer impact per dollar, a dimension which varies as a function of previous decisions.[14] Montgomery and Urban have reviewed several available heuristic models, including models developed by the British authors Lee and Burkart, and others, for both static and dynamic campaigns. The advantages cited for heuristic models are their flexibility and their ability to consider such factors as duplication, audience accumulation, decay, and nonlinear response characteristics.[15]

Linear Programming Models

Linear programming is a method for finding the optimal solution to an economic allocation problem in which all of the important relationships between variables are assumed to be linear. For example, it is assumed that the second insertion in a media vehicle is as effective as the first; it is assumed that costs are linear; and it is assumed that response is a linear function of the number of insertions.

Linear programming was one of the very first methods of operations research and, given its assumptions, this method does guarantee an opti-

[13]William T. Moran, "Practical Media Decisions and the Computer," *Journal of Marketing*, 27 (July 1963), pp. 26–30.

[14]Alfred A. Kuehn, "Models for Budgeting Advertising," in Peter Langhoff (ed.), *Models, Measurement, and Marketing* (Englewood Cliffs, N.J.: Prentice-Hall, Inc., 1965), pp. 135–37.

[15]David B. Montgomery and Glen L. Urban, *Management Science in Marketing* (Englewood Cliffs, N.J.: Prentice-Hall, Inc., 1969), pp. 140–43.

mal solution. A linear programming approach to the media selection problem would be formulated as follows:

Maximize

$$T = \sum_{i=1}^{n} \gamma_i x_i$$

where T = total exposures
γ_i = the rated exposure value of an insertion in medium i
x_i = the number of insertions in medium i
subject to

$$\sum_{i=1}^{n} c_i x_i \leq B$$

where c_i = the cost of one insertion in medium i
B = the media budget

This formulation simply states that the objective is to maximize total exposures subject to the budget constraint, given the cost of an insertion and the r.e.v. of the medium. Additional constraints may be included in the statement of the problem to recognize such things as the characteristics of the media themselves and management policies, as noted earlier. Management judgment provides weights that are used to adjust audience data to reflect the qualitative value of an exposure in a given medium and to adjust for different audience characteristics.

Linearity Assumption Is a Problem. The assumptions of linearity are the critical weaknesses in the linear programming models. Most analysts would agree that response is not a linear function of total exposures. The familiar S-shaped curve or a curve with a constantly decreasing slope is probably more reasonable as a description of response than a straight line. It is possible to approximate such curves by a series of straight lines, but this complicating factor does not solve the problem. Another, and more important, source of nonlinearity is the existence of quantity discounts for advertising media. Cost-per-insertion actually decreases as the number of insertions in a given medium increases. Third, multiple insertions in a given media vehicle are not equally effective. Thus, despite the fact that linear programming models yield optimal solutions given their assumptions, these solutions are not completely consistent with the "real world" and must be significantly modified using management judgment before they can be implemented.[16]

[16]For discussions of linear programming models for media selection, see any of the following: Ralph L. Day, "On Methods: Linear Programming in Media Selection," *Journal of Advertising Research*, 2 (June 1962), pp. 40–44; Frank M. Bass and Ronald T. Lonsdale, "An Exploration of Linear Programming in Media Selection," *Journal of Marketing Research*, 3 (May 1966), pp. 179–88; James F. Engel and Martin R. Warshaw, "Allocating Advertising Dollars by Linear Programming," *Journal of Advertising Research*, 4 (September 1964), pp. 42–48.

Furthermore, such methods are not devoid of the imperfections of intuitive judgment. It is necessary for the manager-user to estimate the weights to be applied to various segments of the audience and the assessments of the qualitiative impact of the media, just as it is in non-programming models. When judgment is applied in the form of constraints which are designed essentially to correct for the assumptions of linearity, the result is to introduce potential error of a different kind. On the other hand, the rigorous requirements of quantification can improve the quality and logical consistency of such judgments.

There are several other difficulties in using the linear programming model. One is the noninteger solutions permitted by such a model. Thus, the recommendation may be to purchase 3.6 insertions in medium Z, which is obviously impossible. The problem is that rounding this recommendation to 4.0 insertions is likely to be nonoptimal. Another problem is that these models cannot take into account the problems of duplication and audience accumulation (which is the same as saying that insertions do not have constant value).

Value Comes from Systematic Approach. Linear programming solutions are not without value to the media planner, however. Recognizing the fundamental fact that media selection problems are very complicated and that it is virtually impossible to trace through all possible combinations except through the use of computers and sophisticated analytical routines, linear programming probably offers some net gain in the media selection decision. The recommendations of such models must be used with caution, however, and not as a substitute for reasoned judgment. One benefit of the linear programming models has been that they have been a major source of pressure upon the advertising media to provide better data.

A wide variety of alternative programming methods has been proposed to correct for the deficiencies of linear programming. Integer programming is a method which guarantees optimal integer solutions, for example. Goal programming has been proposed as a method for permitting more careful consideration of several segments and for considering duplication. Each of these methods introduces additional computational problems and complexities of its own, however, and all fall considerably short of providing a panacea for the media selection problem.[17]

MEDIAC. One last model deserves our attention, however, because of its completeness and its "reasonableness" and because it has been designed to permit direct interaction with the model by the media strategist. This is the so-called MEDIAC model, developed by Little and

[17]See Montgomery and Urban, *op. cit.*, pp. 143–53, for a good review of these several methods of mathematical programming.

Lodish.[18] This model permits explicit consideration of market segmentation, market potential in individual segments, exposure efficiencies of different media in each segment, forgetting, diminishing returns at high exposure rates, differing media costs, and intermedia differences in the value of an exposure. In other words, it permits consideration of all the factors which have been identified in this chapter as being of importance in the media selection decision.

The MEDIAC model develops an estimate of the probability that an individual in a given segment will be exposed to a message as a function of characteristics of the advertising unit (color, size, etc.) and as a function of the medium used to deliver the message. The exposure is assumed to change predispositions to buy, but the extent of change is a function of the medium. There is forgetting as the level of predispositons changes over time, but it can be increased by exposure. There are diminishing returns to increased effort and response rate tapers off as the saturation level (market potential) is approached. The model is in an interactive mode permitting the user to communicate directly with the computer, using a teletype, on a real-time basis. Communication with the user is in English and asks him to supply the necessary information and gives him several options on the form of output. The user inserts the names of the media vehicles whose usage he wishes to evaluate. Another interesting feature of the MEDIAC model is that the objective is to maximize sales, not some measure of exposure. The major problems with the model appear to be its computation requirements which are very large due to the use of dynamic programming methods.

Simulation Models

The last class of mathematical models for media selection decisions to be discussed here is simulation models. As noted in discussions in previous chapters, simulation is a method for exploring the consequences of certain events on a system. Simulation permits the analyst to ask questions about "what will happen if . . ." using a model of the process that the manager is trying to control. Thus, simulation as an aid to media decisions would require a model of the market and the ways in which it responds to messages in various media.

Such a model is offered by the Simulmatics Corporation and involves a "microanalytic" simulation of 2,944 individual household units described by media habits and preferences as well as socioeconomic and

18John D. C. Little and Leonard M. Lodish, "A Media Selection Model and Its Optimization by Dynamic Programming," *Industrial Management Review,* 8 (Fall, 1966), pp. 15–24.

demographic characteristics.[19] The effects of a media schedule are measured in terms of coverage and frequency as well as total costs and audience profile. A similar model is offered by Amstutz.[20] The latter model has not been specifically used for the purpose of developing media strategy, however. Neither model is capable of determining the *best* media schedule. The purpose of simulation is rather to test the impact of different media schedules on criterion variables.

Schreiber has provided evidence of the difficulty of developing estimates of exposure probabilities to use in such simulations on the basis of actual distribution and exposure data.[21] He concluded that these technical problems were serious enough to restrict significantly the use of simulation as a tool for the analysis and selection of media schedules. Marc was more optimistic concerning the use of consumer panels to provide data on readership patterns for such simulation studies and described a method for using these data.[22]

Simulation offers a method for tracing through the impact of alternative media schedules and permits the comparison of many more options than would be possible using paper-and-pencil calculations. At the same time, its value to the media strategist is limited by the nonoptimality of its procedures and by the need to estimate exposure probabilities for units of the population, a task that poses some very difficult problems.

SUMMARY

Media strategy is an integral part of the total marketing communication strategy. Beginning with a definition of the target audience, or prospects, derived from the firm's segmentation strategy, the media selection and scheduling problem is to find that combination of media vehicles which maximizes the criterion variable (such as rated exposure value) subject to budget limitations and other constraints specified by management. This is a complex decision problem because of the almost limitless number of possible combinations of media that could be considered. It is further complicated by the need to consider the relative importance of reach (coverage) and frequency, continuity and flighting, and the need to adjust raw audience data to take audience characteristics into account.

[19]*Simulmatics Media-Mix: General Description and Technical Description* (New York: Simulmatics Corporation), 1962.

[20]Arnold E. Amstutz, *Computer Simulation of Competitive Market Response* (Cambridge, M.I.T. Press, 1967).

[21]Robert J. Schreiber, "Probability Assignments for the Simulation of Media Reach and Frequency," *Journal of Advertising Research*, 8 (June 1968), pp. 3–8.

[22]Marcel Marc, "Combining Simulation and Panel Data to Obtain Reach and Frequency," *Journal of Advertising Research*, 8 (June 1968), pp. 11–16.

The analysis of media problems requires a careful balance of quantitative and qualitative considerations relating to the value of a medium to an advertiser. Sophisticated analytical methods such as mathematical programming offer some limited assistance to the media strategist, but they fall short of being a panacea for media decisions.

Media audience data provide a fundamental problem of measurement in marketing communication. Ideally, one would like to be able to trace through differences in the effectiveness of alternative media vehicles to the ultimate accomplishment of sales response. This is the last stage in a model of media effects which begins with vehicle distribution and proceeds through vehicle exposure and advertising communication to actual sales response. Given qualitative differences among media in terms of impact, prestige, credibility, and similar dimensions, media analysis has to be more than a simple "numbers game." On the other hand, as one moves further along the hierarchy of effects, the influence of other variables such as the advertising copy and noncommunication factors become increasingly important. This basic measurement problem is explored in greater detail in the next chapter.

20

Evaluating Media Effectiveness

In the previous two chapters we have identified several important measurement problems. Having identified them, we typically passed on to consider the issue at hand, either the qualitative values of mass media or the selection and scheduling of media to achieve marketing communication objectives. In this chapter, we will deal with the measurement problem explicitly, although the discussion will for the most part be at the conceptual level rather than the technique level.

In the last chapter, a position was taken which said that measurement of media effect would have to be limited to the first three stages of the six-level process through which media advertising achieves its objectives. The argument was that later stages increasingly reflect the influence of the message and other factors to the point where media influence becomes the lesser of these two sets of considerations. This argument is valid but it does not remove from consideration the basic question of how to evaluate media effectiveness. While the media effects may be overshadowed by message effects in these later stages, it would still be helpful to have a measure of the extent to which media differed in their contribution to the effectiveness of the marketing communication program.

DEFINITION OF MEDIA EFFECTIVENESS

We have now established that the medium which carries the message can make its contribution to the accomplishment of marketing communication objectives in two ways: by delivering the message to an audience with the desired profile and by enhancing the meaning of the message itself. In algebraic form:

$$\text{Effectiveness} = \text{Audience} \times \text{Impact}$$

We have considered the question of impact largely as a qualitative factor: It was said that an assessment of qualitative differences among media should be reflected in the first stage of the media selection process—that of choosing classes of media to be used in the media strategy—and in subjective assessment of intramedia qualitative differences. Our discussion of media selection then concentrated on the choice among alternative media vehicles within each class using adjusted audience as the basis for comparison.

Previous discussion of the audience factor has proceeded by starting with a measure of vehicle distribution, then adjusting audience data for such considerations as duplication, pass-along coverage, accumulation, and so on, and finally applying subjective estimates of inter- and intra-media qualitative differences to yield an adjusted audience figure which was labeled "rated exposure value." The objective of the selection decision was to maximize the r.e.v. of the media schedule subject to the budget constraint. An alternative statement of the objective was to minimize the budget expenditure required to deliver the targeted r.e.v.

In those previous discussions, the application of qualitative judgments to adjust for impact was simply an attempt to transform data on "audience" to data on "effectiveness." Efficiency measures introduce the cost element into the assessment and permit comparisons of media on the basis of effectiveness per unit of cost. Thus, cost-per-thousand calculations using adjusted audience data are a measure of efficiency.

WHY MEASURE MEDIA EFFECTIVENESS?

Why should the marketing communication strategist have to concern himself with the measurement of media effectiveness? There are several reasons why it may be desirable to do so. First, the data provided by the media pertain to *all* products, and all advertisers, not to the particular value of that medium for this advertiser's product or service. Statements about audience characteristics such as age distribution, spending habits, and media preferences which are valid for the total audience may not be valid for the particular segment of the audience which represents the advertiser's market target and which will be attracted by his advertising.

Second, the advertiser can never know ahead of time the exact characteristics of the audience that will be attracted to his product through the particular messages he wishes to place in that particular medium.

This is a different point than the one above. It distinguishes the media audience question, discussed first, from the more complex problem of the extent to which that audience is attracted by the *interaction* of this advertiser's *message* with this particular *medium*. The specific question of "What kinds of customers will be attracted by our advertising in this medium?" can only be answered by carefully planned research after the advertising has been run.

Third, there is always the problem of the adequacy and reliability of the data presented by the media. While inadequacies in the data may not be the result of any intent to mislead potential advertisers, the fact of the matter is that most media audience data are collected using survey research procedures, with all the attendant sources of error. Furthermore, the interpretation of such data can often result in disagreement by intelligent and informed analysts. The media have the objective of attracting advertising revenue and the interpretation of the data will reflect that bias. Under certain circumstances, the advertiser may wish to obtain information in which he is willing to place more confidence for his particular purposes.

Fourth, the amount of money devoted to media usually is much more significant in the total communication budget than any category of expenditure other than personal selling. Message testing is usually seen as a legitimate investment of communication dollars, as a way of insuring the effectiveness of the investment in media. It makes every bit as much good business sense to likewise spend for research on media effectiveness as a method of obtaining information to improve the efficiency of media expenditures.

The kind of data collected by, and of most use to, the advertiser will more often supplement, rather than duplicate, the data provided by the media themselves. The marketing communicator is interested in information that can be used for several rounds of decision making, that can be used, for example, to provide adjustments for qualitative media values over several years of media selection. The information collected by the advertiser will be much more specific as to the interaction between media characteristics (both audience and editorial) and company-specific variables such as product, appeals, and messages. Also, the advertiser is in a better position to measure the last three stages of the six-level process: advertising perception; advertising communication; and consumer response.

WHAT TO MEASURE?

The advertising media cannot measure advertising perception, advertising communication, and consumer response in any meaningful way for the simple reason that each advertiser will have different products, different target markets, different appeals, and different messages. The variables over which the media have some control are coverage, exposure, and audience characteristics. Conversely, the advertiser has little control over coverage and exposure, although the qualitative characteristics of his message will influence the characteristics of the audience attracted to that particular *message*. It is virtually impossible for the advertiser to check on the data provided by the media with respect to coverage and vehicle exposure. The information requirements and collection abilities of the media and of advertisers are in this respect mutually supporting and relatively non-overlapping.

There are important differences in the interests of the media and the advertiser in the question of audience characteristics as well. The media typically provide some data on socioeconomic and demographic characteristics of *subscribers*. The advertiser wants to know the characteristics of *customers* attracted by that medium.

In determining what to measure in media research, in defining the objectives for such research and the variables to be defined and evaluated, many of the questions and techniques of message testing become relevant. The question of a hierarchy of effects appears in media research as well as in copy research, and the alternative measurement methods are similar to those encountered in message testing.

A Model for Evaluating Media

Discussion of the media measurement problem will be aided by the model proposed by the Advertising Research Foundation and shown in Figure 20–1.[1] Several features of this model require explanation. First, the horizontal line divides the audience into prospects (above) and non-prospects (below). Second, the small (open) bars represent the frequency distribution of people at each stage. In Stage II, for example, the solid bar represents those who were exposed to the vehicle at least once; the second bar is those who were exposed at least twice; and so on. What we have earlier referred to as the "hierarchy of effects" really begins in the fourth stage of this model with awareness occurring only when the advertisement is perceived by the receiver. (As pointed out in Chapter 15, some would include exposure—without awareness—as a first stage in the hierarchy.) Stage V of the present model, "advertising communication," would include all other stages of the hierarchy-of-effects model (knowledge, liking, preference, and conviction) short of actual purchase of the product. As used in this model, "consumer response"

[1]Paul E. J. Gerhold, "Better Media Planning: What Can We Do Now?," in *Better Measurements of Advertising Effectiveness: The Challenge of the 1960's*, Proceedings of the 5th Annual Conference of the Advertising Research Foundation (New York: Advertising Research Foundation, 1959), pp. 43–48.

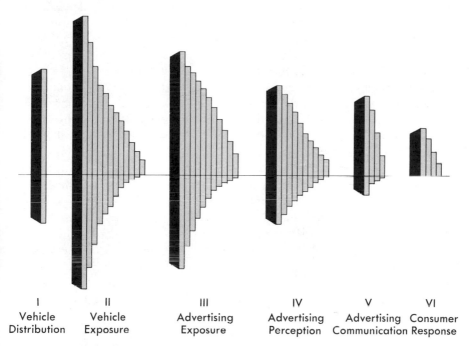

I	II	III	IV	V	VI
Vehicle Distribution	Vehicle Exposure	Advertising Exposure	Advertising Perception	Advertising Communication	Consumer Response

Fig. 20–1. A model for evaluating media effectiveness. (Source. Paul E. J. Gerhold, "Better Media Planning: What Can We Do Now?" in *Better Media Measurements of Advertising Effectiveness: The Challenge of the 1960's* [New York: Advertising Research Foundation, 1959], p. 44. Copyright © 1959 by Advertising Research Foundation.)

means actual behavior—purchase behavior. One could argue that attitude change was a form of consumer response, but that is not the usage proposed by the model.

Variables Measured at Each Stage. At each stage of this model, the variables to be measured are different. Vehicle distribution is measured by the number of copies of the magazine or newspaper or the number of radio or television sets within the reach of the signals broadcast. It is measured by total units of circulation. Distribution is a concept of very limited value for broadcast media vehicles. Media audience or vehicle exposure is the number of people actually exposed to the media vehicle. Measurements at Stages I and II are the same for all advertisers with messages in that media vehicle. Notice that the number of people exposed to an advertising vehicle may be much greater than the vehicle distribution measure. In the case of magazines, this might be a factor of three or more reflecting "pass along" distribution. In broadcast media, the exposure will probably be *less* than total distribution for the simple reason that not all sets within the range of the signal will actually be tuned to the station broadcasting the message. This is the reason why distribution measures have little value for broadcast media analysis. Multiple listeners or viewers for each set probably do not compensate for the large proportion of sets not tuned to that station.

Stage III, advertising exposure, can be measured by the number of persons physically exposed to the message, whether or not they were aware of that exposure. The distinction between awareness and exposure is a significant one, and whether we consider awareness as part of Stage III or Stage IV influences the way we talk about measurement possibilities at each stage. Assuming that awareness does not occur until Stage IV, measurements in Stage III must be limited to physical measures such as the number of persons who actually turned to that page or who were physically present when the message was broadcast into the home. Defined this way, measurement becomes difficult, although there are several possibilities such as coincident telephone interviewing for broadcast media ("What station is your radio tuned to?"). For print media, such techniques as using a small, unnoticeable amount of glue between pages of sample copies of the magazine may be used. Advertising exposure may not be the same for all advertisers in that media vehicle because position within the vehicle may make some difference. Since we have defined exposure as not including awareness, the qualitative characteristics of the message have no significant influence at the advertising exposure stage.

At Stage IV, measurement problems become significantly more complex because both the message and the media exert an influence. Advertising awareness could be measured by such techniques as recognition and recall measures, discussed in Chapter 15, but should also take into account the frequency of noting (and exposure). Advertising communication, Stage V, measurements must rely upon methods of attitude and preference measurement, and these will principally be statements of opinion obtained through interviewing procedures, although there are other possibilities such as projective tests and forced choice techniques.

Consumer response, Stage VI, is used here to mean an actual change in behavior. There are two methods of measuring change in purchase behavior—measures of changes in sales or changes in inquiries about the product. In actual practice, inquiry measures are probably more used than sales measures in media evaluation. Inquiry measures are easier to obtain and are more directly related to the combined effects of message and media and less likely to be contaminated by non-communication variables such as spottiness in product distribution. Response rates for coupon offers are the most obvious measure of media effectiveness.

A point made before but important enough to warrant repeating is that the first three stages are exclusively "media" effects while the last three are both media and "message" effects. The former are *audience* variables in the effectiveness equation, the latter are *impact* variables. The media themselves are in the best position to provide data at the first three stages, while the marketing communicator must take responsibility for generating data concerning the last three stages. The central measurement problem for the marketing communicator wishing to evaluate media is, therefore, to *isolate* media effects from message effects.

MEASURING AUDIENCE CHARACTERISTICS

The media user may be interested in going beyond a profile of the media audience to a more specific measurement of the characteristics of prospects for his particular product or service that are delivered by various media. The most straightforward method for such measurement is to conduct a survey of recent purchasers and to determine the influence of each of several media on them. This is not an easy task, however. Among the difficulties are those relating to multiple exposures, respondent confusion and forgetting, and the difficulty of getting an objective assessment of media influence from individuals. There may nonetheless be some value in asking recent purchasers questions relating to sources of information important to them at different stages in the buying decision process. Having established some measure of media use, and data on socioeconomic and demographic variables, the researcher could then use statistical techniques to measure the extent of differences among media in attracting customers with certain characteristics. Where there is controlled distribution of the product or service and where people have to come into a retail outlet to obtain that product or service, the opportunities for obtaining information on audience characteristics are much greater.

Follow-up on inquiries can also yield important information on audience characteristics. When these inquiries are turned over to a salesman for a personal sales call, it is possible for that salesman to obtain some information about respondent characteristics. Under these circumstances, it is also possible to determine the efficiency of various media in delivering audiences with characteristics relating to ability and willingness to buy. The "quality" of prospects generated by media advertising can be compared on such bases as percentage of inquiries resulting in sales or average dollar value obtained per inquiry. These may be highly correlated with audience characteristics.

While print media are often capable of providing good data on audience characteristics, broadcast media are seldom able to do so. Thus, the advertiser using television or radio may have to conduct research to determine the characteristics of the audiences being delivered by his media schedule. Local advertisers can especially benefit from such studies when they must choose among several competing local television and radio stations to carry their messages. A survey of customers may reveal rather dramatic differences in the value of local stations for this particular advertiser. Programming differences among local stations are likely to result in quite different audience profiles.

Lucas and Britt recommend that measures of media audience should be gathered in tests with specially designed advertising copy in order to minimize confusion with earlier advertising.[2] They suggest also that approved methods of measuring readership and recognition be used, especially with appropriate controls on recognition scores.

One of the most significant characteristics of an audience, and one that is least easily measured, is the extent to which members of that audience generate messages and extend the influence of that medium through word-of-mouth and opinion leadership processes. While some media audiences seem more preferable than others because they demonstrate the characteristics of opinion leaders (positions of responsibility in the community, above-average income and education, and so on) these characteristics can be misleading since we know that opinion leaders exist at several levels of society and in many specific areas where opinion leadership tends to be specialized. The unanswered question is to what extent a particular medium will be depended upon by those who are, in fact, opinion leaders within the community. While there is no obvious method for making this assessment, such research techniques as snowball interviewing could help to relate media influence and audience characteristics to the word-of-mouth phenomenon.

MEASURES OF IMPACT

Independent of the characteristics of the audiences they deliver, media contribute to marketing communication effectiveness by enhancing the extent to which advertising is paid attention to, believed, and remembered. This influence reflects the editorial content of the media vehicle and the extent to which that medium plays an important part in the lives of members of its audience. Media have "images" or "personalities" which reflect the experiences that people have and associate with these media over a period of years. The concept of source credibility applies with special significance to the question of media influence; it is an important dimension of media value and one of the hardest to measure.

Our model of media evaluation suggests three stages at which the differential impact of one medium over another can be assessed: advertising perception; advertising communication; and consumer response.

[2]D. B. Lucas and S. H. Britt, *Measuring Advertising Effectiveness* (New York: McGraw-Hill Book Co., Inc., 1963), p. 293.

Awareness and Perception

Measures of the contribution of media to advertising perception require a controlled experimental environment in which the same message is presented in two or more media and subsequent changes in the criterion variable (such as recognition and recall measures) can be used to assess the relative contribution of the media vehicle to advertising impact. There are two difficulties with this procedure. One is to control for the influence of such variables as exposure to other media vehicles and distribution of the test vehicles. The other problem concerns recognition and recall measures themselves. It will be recalled from the discussion in Chapter 15 that recognition measures reflect both attention and retention effects. Both media and messages may influence both attention and retention, and the interaction among these variables is likely to be complex. It was said that recognition measures have come in for heavy criticism from marketing communicators, partly because they do not diminish over time to the extent that one would expect if these were truly measures of memory. There is likely to be a large amount of confusion of several messages in respondents' reporting. Finally recognition should increase as a function of number of exposures, and it may be very difficult to determine differences in number of exposures among respondents.

Recognition and recall measures can be effectively used to compare results obtained by the same advertisement or commercials in two or more media to be evaluated. Used in this manner, commercial syndicated measurement services such as the Starch Readership Service can be a significant aid in comparing alternative media. If one believes that different media have different qualitative values and that the media and the message interact to take on particular value for a specific audience, then it is to be expected that the same advertisement placed in two or more different media vehicles will produce significantly different scores for noting, recognition, and reading. For this purpose, either recognition or recall measures would be appropriate since both sets of variables are going to influence the attention and retention of the advertising. Since the experimental design would hold messages constant in both media, the differences in either kind of measure would be attributable to the impact value of the media. The differences so identified could be used to determine whether certain media should be included in the list from which the media schedule is to be drawn. These differences could also be used to adjust audience data to yield rated exposure values for the media alternatives under consideration.

Recall measures are typically "conservative" and the percentage of respondents able to meet standards of proven recall may be quite small.

Relatively minor differences in media effectiveness may not appear in recall scores. Also, recall is probably influenced much more by message content than media context.

Attitude Measures

Attitude measures of two kinds are useful in evaluating media. The first kind is measures of attitudes toward alternative media and the second is measures of attitudes toward the company and its products as influenced by exposure to advertising in alternative media. Richard Christian has proposed the use of the "media attitude audit" as a method for determining the value of alternative media in the company's advertising program.[3] His suggestions pertain primarily to industrial advertising where they may have more applicability because of the ease of identifying prospects and obtaining their media attitudes and because of the importance of trade publications to industrial buyers. Figure 20–2 is an illustration of the rating form proposed by Christian for the media attitude audit. This device could be modified to be useful in assessing consumer media just as easily.

The concept of a media attitude audit can be criticized on the same grounds as any direct measurement of attitude. It relies upon statements of opinion which are made self-consciously by the respondent and which may or may not reflect true attitudes toward the media being evaluated or the true impact of those media vehicles. Persons may be poor judges of the extent to which they are influenced by a particular advertising medium. On the other hand, inspection of the form in Figure 20–2 will reveal that these kinds of questions have largely been avoided. Respondents are not asked to evaluate the impact that the magazines have on them; rather they are asked about their opinions toward specific aspects of the magazines such as editorial content.

The other kind of attitude measurement requires the assessment of the level of attitudes before and after exposure to advertising messages in each of the media being tested. Because media effectiveness is more appropriately stated in comparative terms rather than in absolute terms, this kind of measurement makes sense only when two or more media can be compared on the basis of differences in the effectiveness of a message delivered in each medium. To obtain such a measure, the investigator would interview a sample of respondents who had been exposed to the media being tested, under controlled conditions. Using attitude measures of various kinds, he would attempt to determine the extent to

[3]Richard C. Christian, "Evaluating Industrial Advertising—Realistically and Objectively," *Using Research in Advertising Decisions,* Proceedings of the Seventh Annual Conference, Advertising Research Foundation (New York: Advertising Research Foundation, 1961), pp. 73–79.

MAGAZINE RATING SURVEY

We would like to know how you rate several magazines on such points as EDITORIAL CONTENT, RELIABILITY, etc. Just circle the appropriate number under each of the magazines to indicate whether you feel it rates *very high, high, average, low,* or *very low,* for each of the points listed. PLEASE CIRCLE   ?   IF YOU FEEL YOU DON'T *KNOW* HOW THE MAGAZINE RATES ON ANY POINT.

PLEASE RATE ALL THREE MAGAZINES ON EACH POINT

1—Very High   4—Low
2—High   5—Very Low
3—Average   ?—Don't Know

	Magazine A Rating Scale High ⟶ Low						Magazine B Rating Scale High ⟶ Low						Magazine C Rating Scale High ⟶ Low					
LEADERSHIP... is it a leader in the industry... does it have stature in your field?	1	2	3	4	5	?	1	2	3	4	5	?	1	2	3	4	5	?
BUSINESS TRENDS... does it keep you up-to-date on legislation, market developments which may affect your business?	1	2	3	4	5	?	1	2	3	4	5	?	1	2	3	4	5	?
EDITORIAL CONTENT... is it well-written ... does it hold your interest... is it easy to follow?	1	2	3	4	5	?	1	2	3	4	5	?	1	2	3	4	5	?
VALUE OF THE MAGAZINE ... does it make a real contribution to your day-to-day efforts?	1	2	3	4	5	?	1	2	3	4	5	?	1	2	3	4	5	?
TECHNOLOGY... does the editorial content usually display expert knowledge of the subject and the industry?	1	2	3	4	5	?	1	2	3	4	5	?	1	2	3	4	5	?
RELIABILITY... are the articles or news stories believable, truthful, ... accurate, unbiased?	1	2	3	4	5	?	1	2	3	4	5	?	1	2	3	4	5	?
ILLUSTRATIONS... are they interesting ... do they help clarify the articles ... do they increase your interest in the articles?	1	2	3	4	5	?	1	2	3	4	5	?	1	2	3	4	5	?
Please check the magazine(s) you receive regularly	☐						☐						☐					

Thank you.

Fig. 20–2. Form used in media attitude audit. (Source: Richard C. Christian, *op. cit.,* p. 78. Copyright © 1961 by Advertising Research Foundation.)

which there were differences attributable to the impact of the media themselves. These measures would pertain to Stage V of the media evaluation model.

In practice, this kind of measure would be difficult to achieve, primarily because of the difficulty of controlling exposure to the media being tested and to other sources. Ideally, there should also be a before and after comparison, but the measurement of attitudes before exposure is very likely to influence attitudes after exposure.

Sales and Inquiry Measures

Arguments in favor of sales and inquiry measures will by now be familiar to the reader. It is felt by many that because the ultimate objective of marketing communication is to generate profitable sales, any measures which stop short of that level in the hierarchy of effects are not responsive to management's needs. Inquiry measures have the same rationale and they do measure a specific change in behavior clearly related to the generation of sales revenue and are thus measurements at the sixth and last stage of the media evaluation model-consumer response.

Inquiry measures are "clean" in that they cannot be influenced to any significant degree by other sources of information. When the respondent clips a coupon or mails an inquiry to a box number coded to reveal the media vehicle in which the ad was found, there is no problem of establishing the cause of that inquiry. Of course, some would argue that actually clipping a coupon or sending off for additional information may be only the last step in a sequence of effects resulting from exposure to a whole series of messages and media. While that may certainly be true, the fact remains that these effects would be similar for all media being tested. Furthermore, the actual inquiry does result from exposure to that message in that medium and that is what the analyst wishes to measure. Inquiry measures were among the very first methods of evaluating both messages and media.[4]

There is one great problem with inquiry measures, however. Not all inquiries are generated by prospects. There is a class of respondent that can be called compulsive coupon clippers who derive satisfaction from sending off for catalogues, samples, "additional information," and whatever else is offered in advertising in the mass media. Children, neurotics, lonely persons who enjoy getting mail—none of them true prospects—can significantly contaminate inquiry measures as the basis for comparisons of media. Again, media assessment on this basis would require the use of identical messages in the two or more media being tested, with response rates compared on a fair basis adjusted for differences in audience size (and perhaps for cost of the medium).

The measurement of sales results is not as "clean" as use of inquiry measures because of the problem of attributing a specific sale to a specific message carried in a specific medium. Carefully controlled experimental designs over long periods of time are required before true sales measures of differences in media effectiveness are possible.

A Test of Four Media. When he was Market Research Director for the Ford Motor Company, George Brown described the use of experimental designs by Ford to measure differences in media effectiveness.[5]

---

[4]For an intriguing view of early measurement attempts see Claude Hopkins, *Scientific Advertising* (New York: Lord & Thomas, 1923) republished (New York: Moore Publishing Co., Inc., 1952).

[5]George H. Brown, "Measuring the Sales Effectiveness of Alternative Media," in *Using Research in Advertising Decisions*, pp. 43–47.

Here, the objective was to evaluate the relative value of four *classes* of media—television, radio, newspapers, and outdoor. This necessitated sixteen different treatments in sixteen different market areas, as follows:

Treatment	Area Number
No media	1
TV only	2
Radio only	3
Newspaper only	5
Outdoor only	9
TV + radio	4
TV + newspaper	6
Newspaper + radio	7
Outdoor + TV	10
Outdoor + radio	11
Outdoor + newspaper	13
TV + radio + newspaper	8
Outdoor + radio + TV	12
Outdoor + TV + newspaper	14
Outdoor + radio + newspaper	15
Outdoor + TV + radio + newspaper	16

The experiments described by Dr. Brown required approximately three years for completion. The advertising treatment was run for a full model year, with a six-month "before" control period and an eighteen-month "after" control period. It is interesting that the preliminary experimental results reported by Dr. Brown showed a clear relationship between level of advertising and sales results but revealed no significant differences among the four classes of media with a particular set of copy approaches. Dr. Brown pointed out the possibility that with a different set of copy approaches, significant differences in effectiveness among the media would appear.

In the foregoing example, the differences analyzed were differences among market areas (where response was undoubtedly adjusted to reflect differences in market potential, but we are not told how.)

Other methods involve analyzing differences in individual consumers' purchase behavior as related to differences in media usage and exposure.

Separating Audience and Impact Effects. Landis has described a method for evaluating a television campaign which depends upon interviews to determine whether a person was exposed to advertising on television and to then determine whether or not the advertised product had been purchased during a specified time period.[6] In this example, it is very likely that viewers will be quite different from nonviewers and the major piece of evidence to support this is the simple fact that viewers

[6]Jack B. Landis, "Methods of Evaluating Television Advertising Effectiveness," *Using Research in Advertising Decisions*, pp. 49–54.

chose to watch this particular program while others did not. It is likely that these viewer-nonviewer differences will also influence product purchase. It is therefore hard to determine whether differences in purchase rates between viewers and nonviewers are due to differences in audience characteristics or differences due to the impact of exposure to the advertising message in this particular medium. (Notice that this example does *not* compare competing media alternatives.) The results obtained by Landis are shown in Figure 20–3 and indicate that viewers are significantly more likely to have bought the product than nonviewers.

From the data comparing viewers and nonviewers, it is hard to disentangle the two kinds of effects—those due to differences in audience characteristics and those due to the fact of viewing. To accomplish this distinction, a "matched group" of nonviewers is extracted from the sample of nonviewers to provide exactly the same age distribution as obtained for viewers. This is the last column in Figure 20–3, which can be compared to the first column (viewers). Multiple regression can also be used to separate the influence of viewing from the influence of other variables. If not only age but several other variables such as education, income, occupation, city size, and family size were also thought to be important, the interactions among these variables could only be separated by using a statistical technique such as regression. The simple tabular format used to isolate the effect of age in Figure 20–3 would no longer be sufficient.

Need for Experimental Design

In attempting to determine a causal relationship between differences in some criterion variable such as consumer response or attitudes and the decision variable of media choice, it is necessary to use an experimental design. The problem of isolating the effect of other variables can never be completely resolved but the use of experimental design permits the

	Viewers		Non-Viewers		Matched Group	
	Number	Buy	Number	Buy	Number	Buy
Young	270	85	540	130	270	65
Old	156	36	629	92	156	23
Total	426	121	1,169	222	426	88
Per Cent Buying	28.4%		19.0%		20.6%	

Fig. 20–3. Using sales differences to evaluate television program. (Source: Jack B. Landis, *op. cit.*, p. 51. Copyright © 1961 by Advertising Research Foundation.)

minimization of such interference and allows for a statistical estimate of its impact. One of the factors that can be controlled for with an experimental design is the use of copy (messages). To assess the impact of media, the message should be held constant. For intermedia comparisons, this is difficult to do since the symbols used are different.

Experiments have been used successfully to compare several media alternatives and to isolate such differences from differences in response attributable to differences in the markets in which the experiments were conducted.[7] Experimental designs usually use sales measures as the criterion variable, although other measures such as recognition and attitude scores could also be used. Differences in exposure and differences in purchase can be measured using panel and diary techniques, or through interviews and pantry audits.

It takes an understanding management with a long-term viewpoint to support experimental studies of media effectiveness. One of the treatments in an experiment often is the "no advertising" condition, with the result that the opportunity cost of lost sales is an explicit cost to consider in evaluating such experiments. Management must understand that the long-term benefits of better information on media effectiveness justify the short-term opportunity costs of lost sales and the out-of-pocket costs of the experiment.

USING EFFECTIVENESS MEASUREMENTS

Several uses of measures of media effectiveness have already been suggested and they need only be summarized here. Four kinds of effects have been identified: intermedia effects; intramedia effects; multimedia effects; and media-message effects. Information about each of these kinds of effects will have a somewhat different use in management decision making about media strategy.

The most common kind of media measurement problem involves intermedia effects—differences attributable to qualitative characteristics of the classes of media. Studies comparing magazines with television, for example, involve a measurement of intermedia effects. This was the kind of study reported by Dr. Brown for the Ford Motor Company. These studies provide information useful in decisions about which classes of media to include in the media schedule.

Intramedia effects result from the comparison of one media vehicle with another within the same class, as when magazine A is compared with magazine B and magazine C. These measures can be used to

[7]Stanley Canter, "The Evaluation of Media Through Empirical Experiments," *Proceedings* of the Eleventh Annual Conference, Advertising Research Foundation (New York: Advertising Research Foundation, 1965), pp. 39–44.

exclude certain media vehicles from the list of alternatives to be considered for the media schedule and they can be used to adjust the audience statistics of those media that are included. Such adjustments can be made to reflect both audience characteristics (such as the proportion of true prospects) and the impact value of a message delivered in that media vehicle.

Multimedia effects are much more difficult to measure but are an attempt to assess the "synergistic" effects of using two or more media simultaneously. The assumption would be that some media can contribute to the effectiveness of other media—as when newspaper advertising features information about the sponsor's television program, to take a simple example. The experiment described for Ford Motor Company would have permitted this kind of measurement, but no such effects were identified in that particular study, possibly because of the copy used in the test. The existence of multimedia effects could be used to build the media plan by suggesting how to combine classes of media to produce the best result. With such measurements available it would still be very difficult to measure precisely the increment in effectiveness attributable specifically to the interaction of the media.

Media-message effects result from the same kind of synergistic interaction between media and message. Their identification would require the careful, experimental assessment of both media and message effects separately and then the further assessment of their interaction. This is sophisticated research that could be used to suggest the appropriateness of certain kinds of appeals for certain media vehicles and vice versa. Information from such studies could be used to determine whether the expense of generating different creative approaches for different media vehicles was warranted. Should the same copy be used in *Playboy* and *Life*? Such measures could help to answer that question. It was the basic notion that such interactions do exist which provided the major rationale for looking at media effectiveness in the first place. Media cannot provide such information to the advertiser but must assess media influence independent of the message.

SUMMARY

The assessment of media effects is one of the most complex and least refined areas of marketing communication. Difficulties in measurement stem mainly from the problem of isolating the relative importance of media and message effects and from controlling for the influence of the many other variables that determine awareness, attitudes, and behavior.

The six-stage model of media contribution to advertising effectiveness is a useful device for thinking about the measurement problem. In the first three stages (vehicle distribution, vehicle exposure, and advertising exposure), the media vehicle itself makes the major contribution to advertising effectiveness. In the last three (advertising perception, advertising communication, and consumer response), the influence of the medium is probably not as significant as the influence of the message, although the medium still makes a definite contribution. Media contribute to advertising effectiveness by the audience they deliver and through adding to the meaning conveyed by the message. These two dimensions pose quite different measurement problems. In the first case, the advertiser must determine the characteristics of the prospects and customers obtained through the medium (and these may be quite different from the profile of the typical audience member for that medium). In the second case, the problem is to assess differences in the hierarchy of effects that are attributable to media.

The measurement problems and techniques for evaluating media effectiveness are similar to those for message testing. Experimentation offers the opportunity for assessing most clearly the existence of cause-and-effect relationships. Several variables can be used as criteria including recognition, recall, attitude, inquiry, and sales measures and each has certain advantages and disadvantages depending upon the measurement objective and situation.

The results of studies of media effectiveness can be used to evaluate the media schedule that has been used by the marketing communicator. More importantly, these studies can reveal the opportunity for significant shifts in media strategy—principally in the classes of media used. Furthermore, these studies can provide an empirical base for the important qualitative judgments that must be part of any intelligent media selection procedure. Thus, the result of evaluating media effectiveness should be a more effective and efficient media strategy.

V

Supplemental Communications

The principal ingredients of marketing communication strategy are personal selling and media advertising designed to stimulate demand for the firm's products and services. Personal selling and product advertising have been the focus of the previous twenty chapters dealing with the analysis of markets, messages, and media. That the effectiveness of the salesman and of product advertising may depend upon "other factors" such as resellers' efforts, sales promotion, deals, point-of-purchase display, packaging, corporate advertising, public relations, and publicity has been mentioned only incidentally. Attention now turns to these "other" forms of communication. While these parts of the marketing communication program are "supplemental" to the main tasks of personal and mass communication, they are no less important.

Effective supplemental communications are basic to a successful marketing communication strategy. If the marketing channel (resellers) cannot follow through on national advertising with local promotional support and product availability, these mass communications will not yield a sales result. If there are weaknesses in packaging and branding, mass and personal communications are under a real handicap. If corporate and brand images are weak, credibility and impact suffer at all stages of the communication strategy. A lack of effective consumer and trade incentives to stimulate trial, stocking, or usage of the product can stall communication at the awareness or preference stage. Without adequate attention to these supplemental communications, personal selling and media advertising efforts will reach only a fraction of their potential effectiveness.

Earlier chapters have prepared the way for analysis of the supplemental parts of the communication program. The same communication objectives of creating awareness, preference, and buying action are involved and the same behavioral processes are operating. There are problems of budgeting, allocation, and evaluation to be resolved. Familiar analytical concepts can be applied in a new context.

Chapter 21 develops the role of the retailer and other kinds of resellers in the marketing communication strategy. While analysis of marketing channels often concentrates on the flow of goods (and pricing) from producer to consumer, the viewpoint here emphasizes the management of the flow of influence through the reseller structure. Chapter 22 discusses the use of sales promotion, deals, and display to stimulate buying action by both resellers and consumers. Chapter 23 analyzes packaging and branding as part of the communication program. Finally, Chapter 24 considers mass communication where longer-run objectives are often more important than this year's sales results. Corporate advertising, public relations, and publicity are examined as activities that enhance the effectiveness of efforts to stimulate profitable sales, that produce benefits in areas of corporate activity other than marketing, and that draw upon the skills of the marketing communicator.

21

Channel Members' Roles in Strategy

The marketing channel consists of the resellers (distributors, wholesalers, retailers, and other kinds of middlemen) between the manufacturer and the ultimate consumer. It is that path along which the goods flow as they move from producer to consumer. A "direct" channel is one in which the only transaction is between the manufacturer (or the firm providing the service) and the ultimate consumer and is, in a strict sense, no channel at all. The most common channel arrangement for manufactured goods is probably the manufacturer-wholesaler-retailer-consumer channel, although there are of course many alternative arrangements possible.

It is common to think of channels as defined by the flow of *goods*. Resellers often take physical possession of the goods, keep them in inventory, and become the legal owners of the products they offer for sale. In this view, channels can be defined by the stocks and flows of goods between producer and consumer.

From the viewpoint of the marketing communication strategist, however, it is also necessary to recognize that there is a flow of *influence* from producer to consumer. This flow of influence may or may not follow the flow of goods along the marketing channel. Whatever provisions are made for the flow of influence, it must be coordinated with the flow of goods. Stated differently, it is necessary to define and plan the role of channel members in the marketing communication strategy as well as in the physical distribution strategy of the firm.

527

In many discussions of the functions of resellers, the phrase "channel of distribution" is often used. We prefer the phrase "marketing channel," for the reason that the word *distribution* emphasizes the physical flow of goods and tends to overlook the communication or influence function performed by resellers.

To undertand the opportunity for using marketing channels in the marketing communication strategy, it is necessary to analyze the functions performed by a marketing channel, the marketer's relationship with the resellers he is using, the nature of the market (especially the consumer's decision-making and shopping patterns), and the nature of the product being sold. The central question in this analysis is "What aspects of the total communication task can be performed most efficiently by resellers?" When the role of channel members in communication strategy has been defined, it is then necessary to design specific aspects of the marketing communication program to implement that role. Such problem areas as packaging, point-of-purchase display, consumer deals, and cooperative advertising must be approached with a very specific consideration of the role of channel members in the communication strategy.

PUSH VERSUS PULL STRATEGIES

From the point of view of the communication strategist, the channel decision has already been made. He must take the existing channel arrangements as given and attempt to take maximum advantage of the opportunity and the constraints provided as a result. The nature of the firm's marketing channel, and the importance assigned to the performance of channel functions, will reflect the company's basic marketing objectives and strategy. As pointed out in Chapter 2, the distribution mix, the goods and services mix, and the communication mix are the three central elements in marketing strategy. Thus, from the communication strategist's vantage point, the definition of basic marketing strategy at a higher level of the organization provides the channel arrangement that must be integrated with the communication mix.

Another way of seeing this relationship is to recall the distinction between push and pull strategies, developed in Chapter 9. A push strategy was defined as a marketing strategy that relied upon personal selling through the marketing channel from producer through resellers to consumers as the basic flow of influence. A pull strategy, on the other hand, relied heavily upon mass communication directed at the ultimate consumer. In order to encourage resellers to exert influence upon their customers as required to make a push strategy effective, the marketer must provide sufficient economic incentive in the form of high margins, as well as other support of resellers' activities. A push strategy assigns a major responsibility for marketing communication to resellers, as opposed to the pull strategy where the manufacturer assumes major responsibility for generating demand. Other hallmarks of a push strategy were said to include a product of high quality with important "hidden" benefits, and price per unit high enough to justify the expense of personal selling.

There are certain necessary relationships among the various elements of the total marketing mix in the sense that choices in one area constrain the choices available in another area. For example, a policy of selective distribution (a few resellers, carefully chosen, probably with exclusive territories) will typically require the use of relatively high margins. While these relationships do not always occur together by any means, they do represent a general tendency in marketing strategies. The nature of such relationships is suggested in Figure 21–1 where several continua are defined that tend to be correlated. In other words, a firm's marketing strategy is likely to find it operating toward one end or the other on each of these continua although there are certainly important exceptions.

The role of resellers in the marketing strategy is determined in part by requirements for "product adjustment," the modification or "tailoring" of product attributes to fit the needs of consumers. Cigarettes, for example, require no adjustment and therefore tend to be marketed with pull strategies in broad distribution. Men's suits are an obvious example of a product requiring adjustment; these tend to be sold in selective distribution arrangements with relatively short channels. A "long" marketing channel would be one in which there were several resellers between the producer and the ultimate consumer; short channels have few resellers, as when the manufacturer sells direct to retailers without going through distributors or wholesalers.

The nature of these relationships among elements of the total marketing mix has been pointed out in the formulation of "parallel systems

Mass (Pull)	◄——— Communication ———►	Personal (Push)
Low	◄——— Price ———►	High
Low	◄——— Margins ———►	High
Low	◄——— Amount of Product Adjustment ———►	High
Broad	◄——— Distribution ———►	Selective
Long	◄——— Channel Length ———►	Short

Fig. 21–1. Relationships among marketing mix elements. A firm's marketing strategy will tend to cluster within a narrow range on each of these continua. For example, pull strategies (relying on mass communication) tend to require low price, low margins, and so on.

theory" by Aspinwall.[1] The basic tenet of parallel systems theory is that there is a necessary relationship between communication systems and distribution systems in the marketing mix because both are constrained by the nature of the products being sold. Specifically, replacement rate and standardization (the opposite of adjustment) are the two most important attributes of products which determine both distribution and communication requirements. The amount of adjustment required is a direct determinant of the amount of personal communication required in that the seller must first determine the particular needs of the potential customer and then specifically point out how a particular version of the product or service being sold can satisfy those needs.

CHANNEL FUNCTIONS

In defining the role of channel members in the marketing communication strategy, it is important to begin by analyzing the functions performed by channel members within the total marketing strategy. Channel analysis is assisted by an understanding of the basic functions which must be performed either by channel members or by the manufacturer or by the consumer himself as the product moves from producer to consumer. In other words, there is a set of functions which must be performed if a successful transaction is to take place. Which of the three—marketer/manufacturer, resellers, or customer—actually accepts responsibility for that function may reflect several factors including customer preferences, availability of channel members to perform the function, etc. The advent of the discount house reflected a willingness on the part of consumers to assume responsibility for several of these functions (credit, delivery, and so on) in return for lower prices. It also reflected the fact that traditional high retail margins were no longer required because these functions could be performed more efficiently using modern methods. In designing channel strategies, the marketing manager must consider two principal sets of factors—the customer's preference for various services (how much he is willing to pay to have these services performed for him and their value to him) and the cost of having these functions performed by the several levels and types of resellers available to him.

The functions which must be performed in marketing a product or a service can be defined in several ways. A generally accepted list is: (1) buying, (2) selling, (3) transportation, (4) storage, (5) standardization and grading, (6) financing, (7) risk taking, and (8) market information.

[1]Leo V. Aspinwall, "Parallel Systems of Promotion and Distribution," originally in *Cost and Profit Outlook* (October 1956), reprinted in Ben M. Enis and Keith K. Cox, *Marketing Classics* (Boston: Allyn & Bacon, Inc., 1969), pp. 277–84.

This definition of functions was the basis for the so-called functional approach to the study of marketing (as opposed to the "commodity," the "institutional," and the "management" approaches). The functional approach to the study of marketing was based on the valid premise that each of these was necessary in the marketing of all products. The question was not which functions could be eliminated in the search for greater efficiency but which of the several institutions available for performing that function could do so most efficiently and effectively.

The first function in our list, *buying*, requires some explanation. It can be understood most readily by examining the retail level of a distribution system. One of the most critical managerial activities in a retail business is decision making concerning the assortment of merchandise to be bought, stocked, and offered for sale. (Some lists of marketing functions include *assorting*, meaning the provision of an assortment of merchandise. Others will also include *sorting*, which is a break-bulk function, as when a farmers' cooperative buys members' egg production and classifies the eggs according to size.) Every business firm has a buying function; marketing channel members buy for the specific purpose of resale, usually in virtually unaltered form, as opposed to manufacturers who buy components, sub-assemblies, and so on. Buying is therefore a critical function of channel members, especially as it enables them to provide a competitive assortment of merchandise to their potential customers. The assortment offered for sale is a major determinant of consumers' preferences for various retail establishments and of the retailer's competitive effectiveness.

The selling function is at first blush easily defined and quite straightforward. Some observers have lumped buying and selling together under the heading of the "contactual function," noting that buying and selling are activities which occur simultaneously and that one requires the other.[2] There are several ways to define selling, however. One is to look at the transfer of legal title to the goods and to say that a product is "sold" when the seller gives up his title of possession. Another is to define selling as the function of promoting the product—pointing out its benefits to a potential user and actually offering to give up title. Recognition of these two different definitions of selling raises some interesting questions. For example, does a retailer *sell* a box of Wheaties if he puts them on his shelf and subsequently takes the consumer's money? Strictly

[2] Edmund McGarry, "The Contactual Function in Marketing," *Journal of Business*, (April 1951), pp. 96–113. McGarry defines the contactual function as "all efforts in the marketing field the aim and purpose of which is to form a bond of mutual interest in the first instance between the marketer and his customers and, in a broader sense, between the producer and the consumer." He defines *propaganda* as a second function (persuasion). Our definition of selling would include elements of both contactual and propaganda functions as they were defined by McGarry.

speaking, he has sold the product because he first took legal title to the merchandise and subsequently relinquished title in exchange for a financial consideration. On the other hand, it can be argued that he did no *selling* because he did not communicate with the customer in any way other than by making the product available on his store shelf. While we do not propose to resolve this argument here, it is important to note that selling is actually a complex set of activities involving the offering for sale of a product or service.

Transportation is the physical movement of goods to create time and place utility for the potential customer. Time and place utility are important dimensions of the total product offering. Transportation is a unique marketing function in that it has resulted in the development of a major industry. Common carriers (railroads, trucking companies, arilines, and so forth) specialize in performing this one marketing function. Every marketer has the alternative of performing the transportation function completely by his own devices (owning his own trucks, for example) but the high investment required is prohibitive to most.

Storage is the creation of place utility by providing a stock of merchandise in good condition at a particular location. There are warehousing firms which specialize in this function, although it is more characteristically performed by resellers in connection with other functions. In addition to creating place utility, the storage function also maintains the product in marketable condition, as when frozen foods are maintained in special cold rooms, or where a dry environment is necessary to maintain product quality.

Standardization and grading are most obvious in the marketing of agricultural products. A dairy may perform both functions by testing the milk that it buys from farmers for butterfat content (with the price paid determined by the amount of butterfat) and then separating the cream and the skim milk which are subsequently recombined in the necessary proportions to produce a standardized and uniform butterfat content. Meat packing houses perform the grading function and this determines the price to be charged. In manufacturing operations, the product is typically a standardized product when it is produced by the manufacturer, and there is no necessity for grading.

Financing the transaction is often a critical step in completing the sale. Some classes of products, such as automobiles, are mostly bought on the basis of medium- to long-term financial contracts. Consumer credit companies and full-service banks specialize in the performance of this marketing function. The importance of the financing function is obviously related to the price of the product; more expensive products are more likely to require the reseller's performing the financing function

—extending credit terms to customers. If the financing function is typically performed by resellers then the ability of the reseller to perform this function would be an important criterion against which to evaluate alternative channel arrangements and specific resellers.

The function of risk taking can appear in several forms. One of the most obvious is the risk of product obsolescence which must be assumed by the owner of an inventory of style merchandise or products which change model frequently. Risk taking is an important function performed by the dress shop, for example, as well as by the camera retailer. Both are likely to have obsolete articles left in their inventory at the end of the selling season. Typically, the larger the amount of risk, the higher the margins required. Another way of compensating for high risk is for the manufacturer to offer to assist the retailer to sell obsolete merchandise (as when the manufacturer agrees to share some of the expense of markdowns, for example). Another form of risk taking is the result of the extension of credit with the possibility that customers will subsequently default in their payments.

The market information function can be critical to the marketer and can be the major consideration in choosing among alternative channel arrangements. For many firms, the resellers are their eyes and ears in the marketplace, the only source of information on changing customer preferences and competitive conditions available to the firm. Such information can be vitally important in designing the product line for example, or in modifying pricing policy or otherwise spotting market trends that will influence the effectiveness of the firm's marketing strategy.

In defining the role of channel members in the communication strategy, the important point to keep in mind is that the more important the channel member is in performing each of these functions, the more likely that the channel member must be given an important role in the marketing communication strategy. The more functions performed by the reseller, the more likely that the potential customer will look to that reseller as a source of product information. The more functions performed by the reseller, the more control that reseller will have over the total transaction and the stronger will be his relationship with potential customers.

FACTORS INFLUENCING RESELLERS' ROLES

The role assigned to various resellers in the firm's marketing strategy in general and its marketing communication strategy in particular will reflect several considerations. The most important of these are consumer buying patterns, the nature of the product, competitive practices, the availability of resellers, reseller credibility, and the amount of control desired by the marketer over the distribution of his product and the relationship with customers. Each set of factors is examined briefly.

Customer Buying Patterns

Perhaps the most important factor to consider in choosing a marketing channel is the nature of customer buying patterns. Other things being equal, it makes sense to try to make products available to customers where they expect to find them. An evaluation of customer buying patterns requires that the marketer first identify the nature of the customers he is selling to; next he must consider questions relating to *how* people buy his products (do they expect credit? how frequently do they purchase? and so forth); finally, he may ask *why* they buy his product. The answer to the "why" question is also related to the nature of the product and products can be classified according to the patronage motives which direct purchasing behavior.

Products (and retail outlets) can be classified into three categories: convenience goods, shopping goods, and specialty goods. Each represents a rather distinct set of buying motives and shopping patterns. Convenience goods are frequently purchased, low-dollar-value products that people are usually unwilling to spend significant time shopping for. While they may show high brand loyalty, consumers will be unwilling to go from one store to another in an extended search for their brand. Beer and cigarettes are in this category, as well as most food and household products. Convenience products are usually sold in broad distribution (so they are "conveniently available") and there is little or no personal selling involved. Convenience goods are characterized by pull strategies. Subclassifications within the convenience goods category define impulse, emergency, and staple goods.

Shopping goods are products that the buyer is willing to "shop" for. He will compare the alternatives available from several retail outlets and he is willing to invest time in identifying and comparing alternatives. Shopping goods tend to have higher dollar value and different brands may be distinguished from each other by marked differences in product quality (heterogeneous goods) or by important price or terms-of-sale differences among competing resellers in the absence of marked differences in quality (homogeneous goods.). Furniture is an example of a heterogeneous shopping good where there are very important differences in the quality of alternative product offerings and in the suitability of those alternatives for a particular customer. Price differences may be less important in this instance. Most consumers would probably regard major appliances and even automobiles (within a price range) as essentially similar in quality and would be more inclined to seek out important price differences in their shopping.

Specialty goods are such things as pharmaceuticals, pipe tobaccos, flowers, and books. The potential customer knows what he wants and will actively search out a retail outlet. When he finds the product he is looking for, he buys it with little or no comparison of alternatives. There is often a high degree of brand loyalty involved (in cigars and pipe tobaccos, for example). Specialty goods are often sold in specialty shops —retail outlets which specialize in a narrow range of products (such as florists, pharmacies, and bookstores)—and a given brand will be available in only a few outlets within a specified market area.

The two major dimensions along which these distinctions among classes of goods have been drawn are the buyer's willingness to shop and the extent of his brand preference. The opportunity for the reseller's activities to influence consumer decision making are obviously greatest where the potential customer has low brand preference and is most willing to shop. This would be the case with "heterogeneous" shopping goods. At the other extreme, most forms of convenience goods involve little willingness to shop, sometimes with a large amount of brand loyalty (although not to the extent of causing the consumer to search elsewhere when this brand is out of stock), and thus provide limited opportunity for resellers to influence the consumer's decision making. In order to define the range of alternatives available to him, the marketing communicator should examine existing information concerning both consumer motives and brand preferences in order to define the "class" of goods he is selling.

Knowing how and why people buy the product is obviously a basic piece of information upon which to develop both the distribution strategy and the communication strategy. The opportunity to exert selling influence at the retail level is a function of the consumer's buying patterns. The objective of marketing channel strategy can be thought of as that of maximizing the probability that the potential customer will find the product where he looks for it—that our brand will come to his attention when he is trying to satisfy his needs. It is also important not only to make the product physically available but also to make available such information as the consumer requires in his decision making and that will maximize the probability of the marketer's brand being chosen.

The Nature of the Product

It has not been feasible to discuss consumer buying patterns without also discussing the nature of the product, because buying patterns are a function of the product being sold. Earlier sections of this chapter also pointed to the importance of the amount of adjustment required in selling the product as a basic determinant of the role of channel members in marketing communication strategy. A related consideration is the amount of post-sale service and maintenance required for this kind of product. The ability of resellers to provide such service may be an important part of the potential customer's assessment of alternative resellers and should likewise be considered in the marketer's assessment of alternative channel strategies.

The relative importance of each of the marketing functions will be determined by the nature of the product, both in terms of its physical characteristics and in terms of the way it is purchased and used by consumers. In the industrial equipment field, for example, the manner in which the equipment is used and relied upon by customers may require the immediate availability of repair parts and of 24-hour service arrangements. Customers will be unwilling to have a piece of equipment costing thousands of dollars and critical to their continued operation out of service for any length of time.

Another important consideration relating to the nature of the product is the extent to which persons must be trained or educated to use the product properly and in a manner which insures the highest level of customer satisfaction. Office equipment manufacturers often maintain direct distribution channels in order to assure that customers are adequately trained to derive maximum benefit from using the product. Sewing machines are typically sold in connection with provision for assuring that customers have adequate opportunity to learn how to use them to maximum advantage. The manufacturers of Tupperware plastic kitchen and household wares found that traditional retail outlets did not have sales personnel capable of demonstrating and explaining how to use the products to maximum advantage and this was a major consideration in the strategic decision to rely upon direct, personal selling as the basic marketing communication element.

Competitive Practices

The channel strategies being followed by competing marketers in the same industry must also be analyzed carefully as the basis for defining the role of resellers in the marketing communication strategy. Whether competitive practices should be followed or avoided is a moot question.

On the one hand, it makes sense to follow the patterns developed by competitors because these industry practices will, over time, have resulted in a particular set of customer buying patterns and expectations. For example, one would not expect to find automobiles or cigarettes for sale in a department store and few shoppers would therefore seek out such products in these outlets. Traditional ways of doing business build up over time and significantly condition the behavior of potential customers in the marketplace.

On the other hand, the opportunity to derive significant competitive advantage through a unique segmentation strategy often revolves around finding a significantly different way to distribute the product to ultimate consumers. Probably the best known example of a successful deviation from industry channel practice is the Avon Products, Inc., strategy of selling cosmetics and related items direct to housewives using Avon salesladies who call at the customer's home. Virtually all other marketers of cosmetics follow the traditional practice of selling through department stores and drug stores.

Each company is going to face a slightly different set of conditions in appraising the constraints and opportunities presented to it by the marketplace and existing industry practice.

Reseller Availability and Characteristics

A practical question that must be answered in developing the channel strategy is whether resellers with the required characteristics are available in sufficient numbers and in sufficient market areas to permit their efficient and effective use. A firm entering a new line of business often finds that there are few resellers available to it because existing channels of distribution are rather completely controlled by existing competitors. On the other hand, one of the most important elements of a successful marketing strategy in a growth industry or in a new product category (such as the snowmobile industry in recent years) is the marketer's ability to secure the cooperation of the best available resellers to present his product to the market.

Of course, the characteristics of resellers must be carefully appraised as the basis for both the decision about which channels to use and about the selection of specific reseller companies within the selected channels. There are a host of detailed but very important questions which must be satisfactorily answered in defining the extent to which a given reseller or class of resellers is to be relied upon. Among the most important questions are the following:

Are channel members—

in contact with the class of customers we hope to reach with our marketing strategy?

financed well enough to provide the necessary services such as maintaining inventories of our products and parts and extending credit?

managed well enough to insure continuity of representation in the market area over time?

staffed well enough, and are staff members trained adequately, to provide the necessary selling support and customer service?

located advantageously to secure good coverage of our potential market and to meet the needs of local customers for ease of access, parking, etc.?

eager to sell our products because they see a major opportunity for their own business to grow and because they have a favorable set of attitudes toward our company and our products?

Positive answers to each of these sets of questions must be forthcoming if the relationship with resellers is going to be mutually productive and profitable. While these considerations seem obvious enough, it is true that many channel decisions are made without an adequate examination of each set of factors. The result is less than optimum market coverage, incomplete follow-through in marketing communication strategy, and less-than-satisfied customers.

Reseller Credibility

Customer buying patterns will reflect in part an assessment of reseller credibility, both by class of trade and for specific resellers. Credibility, it will be recalled, is a function of both trustworthiness and expertise. When a person decides whether to purchase a movie camera at a camera shop or a discount house he is making an assessment of the trade-offs between credibility and price. (This may be an unfair comparison for the discount house which has competent, trained sales and service personnel in its camera department.) Especially if the person feels somewhat lacking in this ability to judge movie cameras, he may rely upon the advice of the camera shop whose personnel he sees as being both more competent and more trustworthy than the discounter's.

Some classes of trade probably have higher credibility for certain classes of products than for others. For example, a jeweler is probably a more credible source of information about watches than a drug store, although watches are sold through both kinds of outlets. A distributor specializing in one kind of equipment may be perceived as more expert in that line of equipment than one selling a wide variety of equipment in several fields. In general, specialization implies expertise and this tends to be correlated with credibility. Specialty shops typically provide more "service" (i.e., perform more of the marketing functions) and therefore require slightly higher profit margins (and prices) than "mass merchandisers."

Individual resellers likewise have reputations in the local areas that they serve. Although such differences in local reputations among competing resellers may be hard to determine, they should be considered to the extent possible in the choice of local representatives. The credibility dimension is especially important where the reseller is given a major role and responsibility in the marketing communication strategy, and where his efforts make a major difference in the customer's final buying decision.

Such assessments are often inadequately made, with the result that major inefficiencies are introduced into the marketing communication strategy.

Amount of Control

In some markets, especially industrial markets, the manufacturer may wish to maintain effective control over the marketing channel and the relationship with the final customer. In other situations, the marketer may be quite willing to relinquish all responsibility and control to resellers. In industrial markets, such considerations as the need to protect and maintain product quality and to insure adequate technical applications assistance may dictate a direct relationship with ultimate users.

Where the relationship with ultimate customers is controlled by resellers, the manufacturer obviously becomes dependent upon the resellers and his welfare is a function of their effectiveness in accomplishing the marketing task. In the automobile industry, domestic manufacturers have a much larger degree of control over marketing channels and over the relationship with the ultimate customer than do foreign manufacturers who depend heavily upon a large number of relatively small, independent distributors.

Policies of exclusive distribution arrangements are often intended to insure that the dependence upon particular, independent resellers works to the manufacturer's advantage. The dealer who sells only one manufacturer's products is more likely to put his best effort forward for that manufacturer than if he handled several competing products. In order to secure that kind of cooperation, however, the manufacturer may have to agree to not make this product available to directly competing resellers in the area served. While we cannot explore the many legal considerations involved in such arrangements, the reader should be aware of the fact that such arrangements are likely to receive the careful scrutiny of government agencies interested in preserving competition.

There are differences among alternative channel arrangements in the extent to which they permit the manufacturer to maintain control over the channel and over the relationship with the customer. Brand loyalty may be difficult to maintain in certain channels where resellers consciously try to develop store loyalty and to replace the customer's reliance upon brands. It has been reported that retail furniture stores, for example, will remove the manufacturer's brand name from merchandise in order to prevent "shopping" and to break down the influence of the manufacturer with the customer.

An evaluation of each of the sets of factors described and discussed above is necessary to define the role of resellers in the marketing communication strategy and the extent to which resellers will be relied upon for communicating selling messages to potential customers. The first consideration, the nature of customer buying patterns, is the most important and is very intimately related to the nature of the product. The nature of customer decision making and shopping behavior is influenced by the nature of the product and is a major determinant of the opportunity to deliver effective selling messages through the marketing channel. The more the potential customer relies upon the reseller for information and assistance in the buying decision, the more important must be the role assigned to that reseller in the marketing communication strategy. The extent of the manufacturer's reliance upon resellers is a direct function of the extent of the customer's reliance upon those resellers. As the manufacturer becomes more dependent upon the reseller to complete the marketing task, the more important it becomes to develop methods for directing the reseller's efforts along those lines that will be most advantageous to the manufacturer and the more resources must be directed toward controlling and guiding the relationship with resellers.

ASSISTING CHANNEL MEMBERS

Channel members are typically firms owned and managed by independent businessmen who will be interested in maximizing their own welfare. They will be interested in maximizing the manufacturer's welfare only if they perceive that doing so is in their own best interest. In other words, the goals of the manufacturer and the goals of the reseller must be made "congruent" if there is to be a cooperative relationship that works to the advantage of both.

The ability of the manufacturer to control the relationship with resellers will thus be a reflection of the extent to which resellers perceive that cooperation is in their own best interests. The challenge facing the marketing communication strategist is therefore to develop programs and methods for dealing with resellers which help both achieve their goals simultaneously. Because of the dependent relationship it follows that it is in the marketing communication strategist's interest to take steps to maximize the effectiveness of the reseller, even if other manufacturers also benefit to some extent from this improved effectiveness.

Decisions about the amount of resources to commit to improving the effectiveness of channel members must be made according to the same criteria that guide other budgeting and allocation decisions. Investment in training resellers' salesmen, for example, should be made only if there will ultimately be a return on that investment that is greater than the return possible from investing those resources in other projects, such as increased national advertising or improved training for the firm's own salesmen. This logical basis for allocation decisions has been developed previously and need not be repeated here except to observe that the logic of marginal analysis applies with equal force in the area of reseller strategy.

There are several ways in which the marketing communicator can assist channel members in implementing the promotional responsibilities they have been assigned as their role in the communication strategy.

Salesman Training and Sales Aids

If the reseller is to be given responsibility for the selling function it is important that the necessary steps be taken to insure that the reseller's salesmen are adequately prepared for their responsibility. Most basic is the product knowledge possessed by the reseller's salesmen, although there are other important considerations. If the customer will expect information and assistance from the reseller's salesman—if the salesman is expected to perform as a problem solver rather than as an order taker —steps must be taken to make sure that the salesman can fulfill those expectations.

There are as many ways of training the reseller's salesmen as there are for training company salesmen. If reseller's salesmen will be spending a substantial part of their total time upon this manufacturer's products and if a well-trained salesman is critical in the success of the manufacturer's marketing communication strategy, it makes good sense not only to provide him with the necessary product knowledge but also to train him in all aspects of the selling job (product knowledge, salesmanship, market and customer analysis, and work habits) that will influence his on-the-job effectiveness. The manufacturer may, for example, conduct a sales training school for all resellers' salesmen or may have several field sales trainers working with resellers' personnel.

There are major opportunities in most industries and at most levels of the channel to significantly improve the effectiveness of sales personnel. Retail sales clerks are seldom adequately trained to provide the assistance which customers expect. Industrial distributors' salesmen in many industries are regarded as clearly inferior to the salesmen representing manufacturers on a direct basis. A well-trained salesman can be the important competitive difference in a buying situation where products are of uniformly high quality, are similarly priced, and so forth.

Training resellers' salesmen is not a one-shot affair, however. Most selling requires a continuous updating of salesmen's product knowledge and a continuous polishing of their selling skills. Furthermore, a steady stream of communications can serve an important motivational purpose with a decentralized sales organization. Product modifications occur frequently, product availabilities shift, prices and delivery schedules are modified, and so on. There are special deals, promotions, contests, and new selling ideas that must be communicated to the resellers' salesmen and that can keep the manufacturer's products in the front of the salesmen's awareness. Figure 21–2 provides an excellent example of a mailing to a distributor sales organization which serves several of these purposes. (The Elgin Leach Corporation markets the Elgin street sweeper line and the Leach line of refuse collection truck bodies through an organization of approximately 100 independent equipment distributors throughout the United States and Canada.) Keeping resellers' salesmen up to date with the knowledge and skills required to respond to customers' needs and to adjust to the seller's needs is an important way of assisting resellers in implementing the role they have been assigned in the company's communication strategy.

Missionary Selling

A "missionary salesman" is a salesman on the payroll of the manufacturer whose function is to assist resellers' salesmen. Any orders generated or written by the misionary salesman are turned over to the reseller for fulfillment and the reseller receives credit for such orders. The missionary salesman may accompany the resellers' salesmen on customer calls or he may call alone. In either case his objectives are to create goodwill for the manufacturer (and thus to maintain some control over the relationship with customers), to help solve customer problems requiring specific, expert product and technical knowledge that may not be possessed by the reseller's salesmen, and to assist the resellers in building strong relationships with their customer.

Among the more important functions performed by missionary salesmen in the grocery trade are setting up displays in retail outlets, refilling retail shelves, and otherwise obtaining sell-through at the retail level that will generate additional sales volume for the wholesaler. The "detailmen" employed by pharmaceutical firms are a form of missionary salesman whose job is to acquaint physicians with the latest new products and to assist the local pharmacist in generating volume for the manufacturer's products. In the industrial field, missionary salesmen are most likely to concentrate their efforts upon training and working with reseller's salesmen although they may also call on end-users or buying influentials.

Cooperative Advertising

Manufacturers selling frequently purchased consumer goods may rely heavily upon cooperative advertising allowances for retailers as a basic element in the marketing communication strategy. A typical cooperative advertising arrangement is for the manufacturer to pay 50 percent of the amount spent by the retailer for local advertising up to a certain maximum amount, provided that the retailer features the manufacturer's products in the advertising and provides evidence that the space was in fact purchased. One of the major benefits of cooperative advertising for the national marketer is that local advertisers can obtain space in newspapers at lower costs than can national advertisers due to discriminatory rates. A major problem with cooperative advertising allowances is in obtaining proof of performance which assures that the manufacturer actually gets the advertising exposure for his products that he is paying for.

Although the 50–50 arrangement is probably the most typical, there are many other common arrangements. One is for the manufacturer to pay all media costs incurred by the retailer up to some specified amount, usually some specified percentage of the reseller's total purchases of the manufacturers' products, such as 2 to 3 percent of total invoices. Successful implementation of cooperative advertising arrangements requires that there be a carefully drawn contract which specifies the duties and obligations of both parties including the kind of evidence to be submitted to prove fulfillment, the kinds of advertising which will be paid for, the type of media to be used, requirements for identifying the manufacturer's products prominently within the advertising, the extent of the manufacturer's financial cooperation, the way in which payment is to be made, etc.

When properly done, cooperative advertising offers several major benefits in the marketing communication strategy. First, it fulfills the basic purpose of all advertising of delivering persuasive messages to prospective customers. Second, it makes the manufacturer's product line more valuable and attractive to resellers and is likely to stimulate their attention to those products. Third, it provides information to potential customers on local availability.

There are, however, many problems in using cooperative advertising, most of them of an administrative nature involving the problems of proof of performance, and so on. Some manufacturers give up trying to enforce cooperative advertising contracts but continue to give allowance because competitors do it. In this circumstance, cooperative advertising allowances are nothing more than a price cut and an uneconomic use of marketing communication resources.

BULLETIN

No. 2272 – May 16, 1969

DEAR ELGINITE:

Several important items to report . . . . first an analysis and a run-down on the ELGIN-LEACH Product Line . . . . let's go to press . . .

THE LEACH LINE

Things are moving at Leach Company ... and whereas we cannot promise "immediate delivery," we are optimistic about our ability to narrow the production gap. As you know, the acceptance of LEACH Equipment ... at all levels ... has soared above and beyond everyone's best estimates. The preference for the LEACH 2-R PACKMASTER is increasing every day. Contractor users will not accept substitutes to it, and that's because it packs the best payloads ... holds up better than any other unit ... and is simply the all-around best value to them.

The trend to bigger units continues, yet our Standard PACKMASTER business increases. LEACH Container sales continue to grow ... and the outlook of LCC&DS is really UP ! ... (with a breakthrough of even greater proportions a definite possibility !)

LEACH is "ON-THE-MOVE" in all dimensions ... more production than ever before ... more acceptance than ever before and more possibilities for profit for you in the future.

* * * * * * * * * *

THE ELGIN LINE

The Star Performers of the ELGIN Line are "doubling in Spades" to those of the LEACH Line. Most prominent, of course, is the ELGIN PELICAN ! This great "bird" has spread its wings to cities ... villages and hamlets at a record pace all over the nation ... and you will be happy to know this outstanding fact:

ELGIN PELICANS ARE NOW OPERATING IN EVERY ONE OF OUR 50 UNITED STATES !

There will be a Special Bulletin published on this subject soon ... but the underlying significance of this accomplishment cannot be overestimated. This means the ELGIN PELICAN is now an established ... accepted ... way of street and highway cleaning. And, of course, it goes even beyond that ... because we are experiencing an important increase in PELICAN business in Industrial and Contract Sweeping ... in every segment of the sweeper business.

(FLASH ! . . . LOOK FOR THE "BOSTON PELICAN CONTRACTING STORY" IN THE NEXT SANITATION DIGEST.)

* * * * * * * * * *

(please turn page)

Fig. 21–2. A mailing (reproduced in part) to distributors for the Elgin Leach Corporation. (Courtesy of Elgin Leach Corporation.)

POWER BRAKES FOR ELGIN SWEEPERS

There are three possible combinations of power brakes on all WHITE WINGS and PELICANS as follows:

Description	Engine	Price
Hydrovac power brakes	Gasoline engine	Included in sweeper price as standard
Hydrovac power brakes	Diesel engine	$295.00 list
Wagner hydraulic power assist power brakes	Diesel engine	Included in sweeper price as standard

The hydroease power brake equipment formerly included as the standard diesel power brake is discontinued, effective immediately.

Please keep this in mind on future orders.

* * * * * * * * * *

NEW CHANGES ON PELICAN AND WHITE WING SPECIFICATION SHEETS

IMPORTANT .... Please see attached REVISED specification sheets for the ELGIN PELICAN and WHITE WING of particular importance.

* * * * * * * * * *

SPECIAL PRICE ON BROOM FILLING MACHINES

Elgin Sweeper Company has on hand three power driven broom filling machines and is willing to sell these to distributors (subject to prior sale) at a substantially reduced price.

The list price of this equipment is $640.00 or $512.00 net f.o.b. Elgin to distributors.

As a special close-out price, Elgin will offer these three at $350.00 each net f.o.b. Elgin.

Of the three units that are available, one is equipped with a 220/440 volt electric motor, and two with 115/230 motors.

Here's your chance to get a real bargain.

* * * * * * * * * *

ROTOGRAVURE SECTION ... SEE ATTACHED

Fig. 21–2. *Continued.*

SHIPPING SCHEDULES

    ELGIN —   All Standard Sweepers . . .   6 – 7 weeks

                    EDUCTORS —— Models "L" and "M" . . .   2 – 3 weeks

    LEACH —   Contact Chicago Office

NOTE: Above delivery schedules SUBJECT TO CHANGE WITHOUT NOTICE. All bids with penalty clauses MUST be cleared with Chicago Office before firm commitments may be made.

* * * * * * * * * *

Cordially,

Arch

Arch F. Gott
President and Sales Manager

AFG:bd
Enclosures

Fig. 21–2. *Concluded.*

Where-to-Buy Advertising

One of the most obviously useful ways in which the national marketer can assist local resellers is by running advertising which prominently features the names and addresses of local resellers. These advertisements direct interested prospective customers to the outlet and their use is based upon the premise that, just as sellers are seeking buyers, so are buyers seeking sellers. Figures 21–3 and 21–4 both illustrate "where-to-buy" advertising. Figure 21–3 lists a retail outlet and is aimed at the consumer who wishes to know where to buy. Figure 21–4 lists sales offices and is aimed at the industrial buyer. An interested potential customer could call the telephone number of the sales office nearest him.

"Where-to-buy" information is most important for specialty goods and for some kinds of shopping goods. Convenience goods in broad dis-

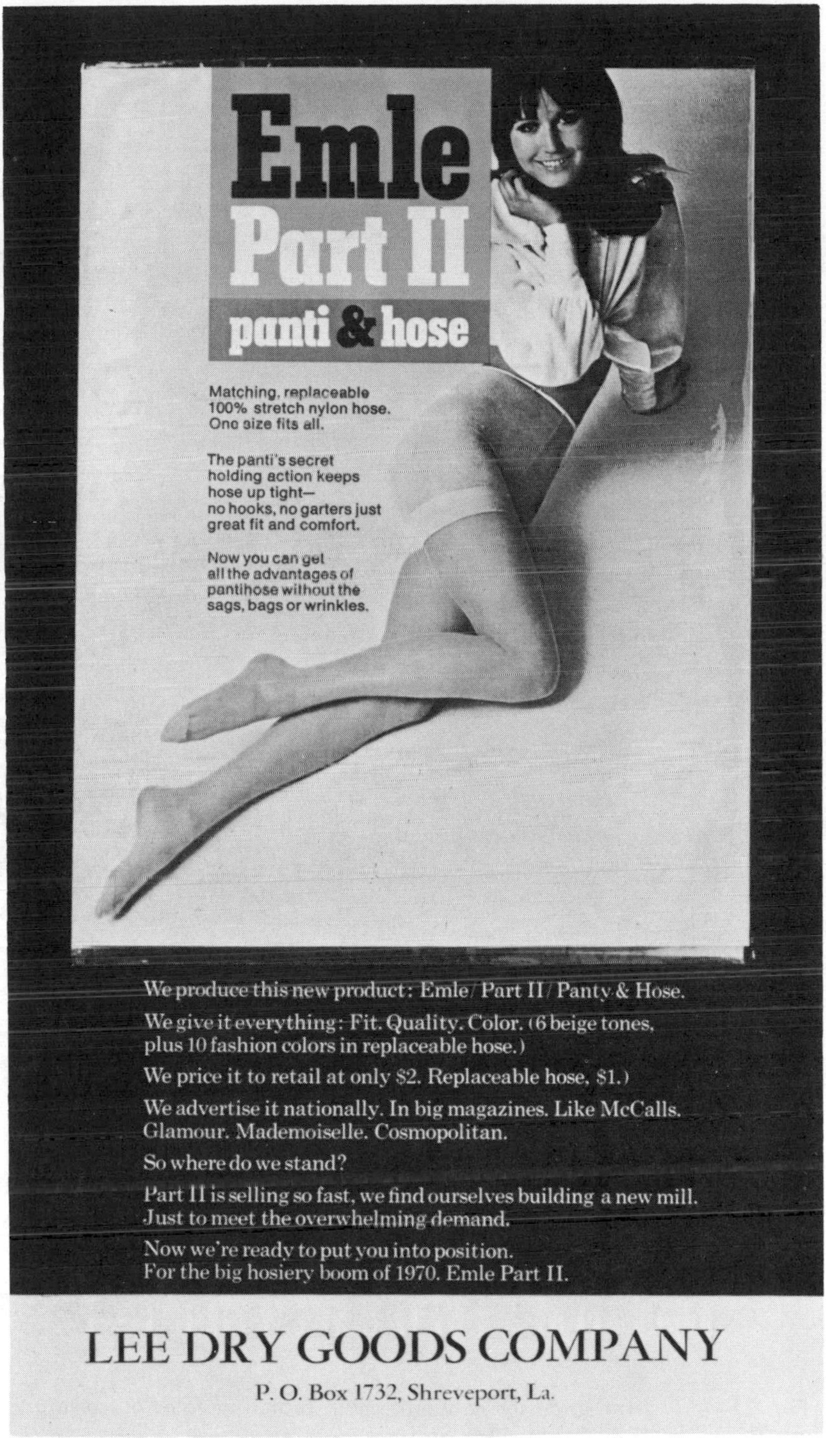

Fig. 21–3. A "where-to-buy" advertisement featuring retailer's name. (Courtesy of Emle Mills, Inc.; Nadler & Larimer, Inc.)

If you're in a business where you need answers in a hurry, Sony has a little box for you.

Inside, we've put all the answers we could think of: Answers to simple problems like finding 6.7% of $280,000. And complicated problems like $\sqrt{\frac{\Sigma x^2}{N} - \left(\frac{\Sigma x}{N}\right)^2}$.

The Sony Answer Box.

Answers that flash onto the display panel, without a sound, before your fingers even leave the keys.

Here's an example: to multiply 12.8 by 1.62, all you do is press

and, instantly, the display panel flashes

Simple? It's not much more difficult to figure

out everything from payroll and cost analysis to share-of-market.

The Sony Answer Box goes all the way to 99999999999999, runs on AC or a rechargeable battery pack, and it weighs just 14 pounds so you can take it anywhere.

Answer Boxes come in three sizes: the 400W with one memory bank ($925), the 500W with two memory banks and three registers ($1125) and the 600W which also gives you an automatic square root function ($1250).

For more information, or to see a Sony Answer Box in action, write us at any of our sales offices below. Or call (212) 361-8600 and ask for Mr. Fred Brockway.

He's our man with all the answers.

Sony Electronic Calculator.

Business Products Division, Sony Corp. of America.

New York—585 Fifth Avenue, New York, New York 10017 (212) 758-3933   Dallas—2600 Stemmons Freeway, Dallas, Texas (214) 638-5850
Los Angeles—401 Coral Circle, El Segundo, California (213) 678-3011   Chicago—37 South Wabash Avenue, Chicago, Illinois 60603 (312) 641-1690
Washington, D.C.—123. 25th Street, N.W., Washington, D.C. (202) 659-3290   San Francisco—54 Cypress Lane, Brisbane, California (415) 467-4900
Detroit—28545 Greenfield Road, Southfield, Michigan (313) 353-6866   Northern New Jersey—39 Hudson St., Hackensack, New Jersey (201) 488-2244
©1969 Sony Corp. of America, 47-47 Van Dam St., L.I.C., N.Y. 11101

Fig. 21–4. A "where-to-buy" advertisement featuring sales office information. (Courtesy of Sony Corporation of America.)

tribution do not need the support of "where-to-buy" advertising. This kind of advertising lessens the probability that a potential customer, who has become aware of the product and has developed favorable attitudes toward it as the result of effective media advertising, will not be able to find a local retail outlet permitting him to follow through with actual shopping and purchase behavior.

A variation on "where-to-buy" advertising that is becoming increasingly common with the spread of Wide Area Telephone Service (WATS) is the featuring of a telephone number to be called to find the name of the nearest retailer. Television and radio advertising may feature a local telephone number or one that can be called (collect) from anywhere in the United States to obtain this information.

Developing Copy

Another way in which the local reseller can be aided by the national marketer is through the provision of advertising copy to be used by the reseller. This is often done in connection with cooperative advertising arrangements where the national firm will provide newspaper mats that can be used by the local newspapers. In other cases, the national firm may provide copy to be used by the local radio station or it may simply provide a list of ideas for the retailer to use as he develops his own local promotional program.

Deals and Display

Especially significant in follow-through on the creation of awareness and interest by national media advertising is the development of consumer deals, trade deals, point-of-purchase displays, and other devices intended to stimulate trade stocking of the merchandise and consumer trial and purchase. These devices are vitally important in the success of many marketing communication strategies and deserve significant attention. They provide the subject matter of the next chapter and further discussion is postponed until then. It is important to recognize, however, that such devices are very closely related to the role of the reseller in the marketing communication strategy.

CONTROLLING RESELLERS' PERFORMANCE

In addition to making provision for assisting and motivating resellers' promotional efforts, marketers must make adequate provision for controlling the activities of resellers. Care must be taken to assure that resellers provide the services which the manufacturer expects and has contracted for and that the quality of the reseller's efforts remains at a high level.

Such provisions become more important when the manufacturer is heavily dependent upon relatively few resellers for market coverage in a given area and for follow through with other elements of the marketing communication strategy.

Margin and Inventory Policies

The major device that the manufacturer has for controlling resellers' performance is the plan by which he compensates them for their performance. The size of the margins offered at various stages of the marketing channel is a major determinant of the quality of the promotional effort received from channel members. In general, the higher the margins offered, the more services performed by resellers for the manufacturer and the better the quality of that service. This is by no means always true, however. It may be difficult or even impossible to significantly influence the quality and level of service provided by channel members by providing above average margins. This is illustrated by the case of the manufacturer who provided jobbers with a 10 percent margin while his competitors were providing only 5 percent margins. The manufacturer slowly came to realize that he was not receiving any better service than that received by his competitors. Jobbers did their job in the same way regardless and were unwilling to devote more time to the higher margin products. This reflected the fact that jobbers tended to react to the market rather than to attempt to influence it—they were order-takers more than sales promotion agents.

It is not uncommon for manufacturers to require resellers to maintain some minimum level of inventory in each of the major product lines which the manufacturer offers for sale. This is to minimize the probability that other elements of the communication program will be unsuccessful because the goods are not available to end users. Thus, as a necessary condition for being a distributor for a given product line, the reseller may have to agree to maintain at least so many dollars worth of inventory. These requirements may be stated in terms of some minimum purchase rate on a monthly, quarterly, or annual basis. In other cases, such as automobiles, the manufacturer may decide how many units will be shipped to each outlet—as a minimum—and the reseller is obligated by the terms of his contract to accept such goods when they are shipped to him.

Quotas and Bonuses

Like a company's own salesforce, it is possible to direct and reward resellers' performance through a carefully designed and administered system of quotas and bonuses. These quotas and bonuses may apply to reseller firms or to individual resellers' salesmen, or to both. Quotas may be based upon a reasonable estimate of market potential and related to past sales as well as estimates of future business.

To illustrate the operation of a system of quotas and bonuses for resellers, we can take a brief example from the industrial field. A machinery manufacturer pays his resellers a straight commission of 20 percent on all business shipped. The margin is represented by a discount from the list price paid by the ultimate customer. Each year, the manufacturer develops a sales forecast and, using trade association and industry information sources on the number and size of potential customers in each reseller's market area, allocates a percentage of the total national forecast to each market area on a percentage basis which places equal weight upon last year's sales and this year's forecast, as a percentage of total United States sales in that market area. For example, assume that the market area covered by reseller A produced 5 percent of last year's company sales and is estimated to have 7 percent of total United States market potential on the basis of the number and size of potential customers. This reseller's quota for the coming year would then be 6 percent of the total national forecast. Let us assume further that the forecast is for sales of one thousand units; this reseller's quota is then 60 units. Furthermore, the company arbitrarily decides that each reseller must produce at least 50 percent of his total quota in each of the company's two major product lines. Therefore, in order to successfully reach his quota objectives, this reseller must sell 30 units of product X and 30 units of product Y; 35 units of X and 25 units of Y is not good enough.

Subject to all these qualifications (which, in this case, are quite acceptable and agreeable to the resellers), the reseller who reaches quota receives a retroactive bonus of two percent on all business sold to date and on all business written through the end of the sales year. Thus, if the reseller sells 30 units of X and 30 units of Y his effective commission rate becomes 22 percent on all business written during the sales year, whether he sells only 60 or more than 60 units in total.

This brief example is probably not a "typical" example in any strict sense but it does illustrate the kinds of arrangements by which manufacturers can attempt to direct and control the selling activities of resellers. Notice that this system encourages full-line selling and that it provides continued economic incentive as the extent of market penetration increases and the selling job supposedly becomes tougher.

In the example we have been using, the manufacturer pays commissions (discounts from list price) to the principals of the reseller firm. The compensation of individual salesmen in the reseller company is left to the manager of that company. There are other situations in which manufacturers find it desirable to provide economic rewards to individual salesmen in resellers' firms, although these rewards are often in the form of merchandise and other non-cash incentives. Manufacturers often conduct sales contests for dealers' salesmen, for example.

Supervision and Evaluation

There is a useful analogy to be drawn between the individual reseller firm as a member of the marketing channel and the district sales office as a member of the sales force. Both can be directed and motivated by financial incentives and quota systems, and both require supervision and periodic evaluation. Compensation is never a substitute for supervision and evaluation, although both can work together toward the same objectives.

Quota systems and inventory policies can provide a set of standards against which to evaluate distributor performance. If a reseller consistently fails to reach quota and if he is frequently in violation of basic inventory policies, these are both strong signals that the reseller is unwilling or unable to fulfill the important responsibilities of his role in the marketing strategy. Market coverage, and sales volume, will be below levels which management has defined as reasonable and desirable. Marketing communication management will be unable to follow through with potential customers to obtain the ultimate objective of the marketing communication strategy—profitable sales.

Periodic assessments of reseller firms can spot such difficulties before they become damaging and while there is still opportunity to strengthen the reseller operation. A good tight control system can have real benefits for the manufacturer and for the reseller.

In addition to information and criteria on specific operating results, such as volume sold, the manufacturer can assist his resellers and provide a kind of consulting service to them by periodic examination of the basic management and financial structure of the reseller organization. Although the manufacturer may have little power to correct such difficulties when they are identified, the diagnostic assistance may be sufficient to bring about corrective action. Provision for managerial succession, identifying the need for short-term injections of additional capital, an opportunity to mechanize costly aspects of office or warehouse operations—these are examples of problems and opportunities which the large national firm may be able to help the local reseller identify and cope with.

The manufacturer's salesmen may be the critical link in this evaluation and control process. Their most important function may not be to generate orders but rather to build the reseller organization by training its salesmen and by consulting with reseller firm principals concerning problems that involve the long-run welfare of both firms. If the manufacturer's salesmen are to be given this important responsibility, they must certainly be trained, supervised, and rewarded in a manner which insures the effective performance of that function. Properly trained and armed with the right diagnostic aids, the manufacturer's salesmen can gather and submit necessary information to marketing management and staff analysts for perusal and for the taking of appropriate action. In addition to permitting the diagnosis of potential problems from the manufacturer's viewpoint, this information can also be analyzed, summarized, and reported back to the reseller so that it has maximum value to him as well. If this information is truly valuable to the reseller as he manages his own business, he will not only be more willing to provide it to the manufacturer but he will also have the opportunity to improve his effectiveness and his value as a member of the marketing channel.

SUMMARY

Marketing channel members are often charged with responsibility for carrying through in the final stages of the marketing communication strategy to achieve the specific results of customer buying action. The extent to which the reseller actually influences the potential customer's decision making is a function of the nature of the product being sold and the manner in which buyers shop for this product. The more functions performed by the reseller the more significant his influence upon the customer and the more dependent the manufacturer becomes upon resellers for successful completion of the marketing task.

Marketing communication strategies must be coordinated with other elements of the marketing mix as the flow of influence goes from producer to consumer. In a push strategy, the flow of influence tends to follow the flow of goods and the reseller has a critical role to play in the marketing communication strategy. In a pull strategy, the flow of influence is more or less direct from producer to consumer, although the resellers may still exert significant influence through the channel.

Having defined the role of the marketing channel members within the marketing communication strategy, the manager must take steps to assist the channel members in their performance of these functions and to control and direct their efforts along lines of mutual advantage. The manufacturer's salesmen may have special responsibilities for training, working with, and evaluating resellers and their sales personnel. While the traditional view of the manufacturer's salesman defines his principal function as writing orders and obtaining sales volume, an equally important responsibility may be to improve the effectiveness of those channel members whose efforts ultimately determine the extent of the market's response to promotional effort.

The development of marketing communication strategy must therefore specifically consider the role of channel members and the steps that are to be taken to obtain maximum returns from promotional dollars directed toward the marketing channel structure.

Sales promotions, deals, and point-of-purchase displays are among the most important devices for stimulating reseller's efforts and for communicating with ultimate consumers at the retail level. These devices are examined in the next chapter.

22

Sales Promotion, Deals, and Display

The ultimate objective of marketing communication strategy is to generate profitable sales volume. Obviously, this requires that customers actually purchase the product. In earlier discussions, we have seen that the objectives of creating awareness and generating favorable attitudes are quite consistent with this objective of sales volume, but having created awareness and favorable attitudes does not guarantee that the final step of actual buying behavior will result. Sales promotion, deals, and point-of-purchase displays have the specific objective of generating sales volume by encouraging customers to actually purchase the product.

Sales promotion, deals, and display are among the most flexible tools in the marketing communication strategist's kit. They can be implemented within a reasonably short time period, especially if they have been already planned for use in contingency situations, and they can be tailored to achieve very specific, short-term marketing objectives. They are very powerful but limited communication tools. They complement, but in no sense substitute for, mass communication (advertising) and personal selling. They must be carefully integrated and coordinated with other parts of the total communication program. This discussion of these short-term marketing tools will therefore frequently stress problems of coordinating sales promotion, deals, and point-of-purchase display with advertising and personal selling.

These tools are also frequently used in combination. Media advertising is typically used to acquaint potential customers with the availability of a special promotion—such as an offer of merchandise in return for a stated number of labels and some minimum amount of cash. The sales force must be provided with the necessary sales aids and incentive to explain the promotion to retailers. The salesman's objective may be to get additional shelf space in the retail store or to obtain permission to set up special displays featuring the merchandise offer along with a generous stock of the product. A special trade deal (for resellers), such as one free case with every five ordered at the regular price, may likewise be featured in the salesman's presentation as a means of getting adequate stocking. Thus, sales promotion, deals, and display all work closely together, and must be coordinated with advertising and personal selling to achieve the ultimate objective of increasing sales of the product.

These techniques are characteristic of pull strategies, especially as found in consumer packaged goods. Less elaborate forms are found with other product categories, and even in some industrial selling situations, but they are found less frequently. While they are most appropriately used to achieve specific marketing objectives, they can also have the "defensive" purpose of retaliation against competitors' activities in many situations. The "wheeling-and-dealing" phase of the competitive battle in the marketplace usually finds sales promotions, deals, and displays as the principal weapons. Meeting a specific competitive situation is one of the most common reasons for using one or more of these tools and this chapter will frequently stress the tactical and competitive aspects of marketing communication strategy.

With this brief overview by way of introduction, let us step back and define our terms more carefully as a first step in the analysis of this important aspect of marketing communication strategy. Next, we will take a broad look at the advantages and disadvantages, objectives and problems, associated with these tools. Then, each specific set of activities—sales promotion, deals, and point-of-purchase display—will be described and analyzed in greater detail. The chapter will conclude with a summary evaluation of the use of these tools in an integrated marketing communication strategy.

DEFINITIONS

Sales promotion, deals, and display can be defined under the general term of "short-term inducements to customer buying action." They share the characteristic of being action-oriented and typically have a specific purpose such as to increase dealer stocks or to increase the rate of trial. Such inducements to buyer behavior are a vitally necessary follow-through to the more general, long-term objectives of mass communication. This is especially the case in heavily advertised consumer packaged goods sold through supermarkets where there is no personal selling at the point of sale and where a special incentive or reminder is often needed to "trigger" the consumer's buying action.

Sales promotion is often used as a rather general term to describe all marketing actions that supplement advertising and personal selling, are conducted for a limited time period, and seek to induce buying action.[1] This general definition includes the concept of "deals." In this chapter, however, we will reserve "deals" for separate attention for reasons to be explained in a moment. The more common forms of sales promotion (excluding deals) include contests, merchandise offers, free samples, and special financial incentives for resellers' sales personnel. It is hard to define this term more precisely because by its very nature it is a "catch-all" phrase and the variety of possibilities within this area is limited only by the richness of the marketer's imagination.

There is a possible source of confusion in the fact that the phrases *promotion* and *sales promotion* have quite different meanings. The word "promotion" has been used synonymously with "communication" and refers to virtually all activities that we have defined as marketing communication strategy. "Sales promotion" has the much more limited definition given in the last paragraph with an emphasis upon three dimensions: (1) supplementary; (2) short-term—conducted for a limited time period to achieve specific objectives; and (3) intended to produce buying action.

Deals are defined more precisely in this discussion as temporary price reductions offered to consumers, resellers, or both. There are several forms of deals including coupons offering a stated reduction from shelf price; "label packs" with a price reduction clearly announced on the label; simple price reductions offered to resellers or to final customers; two-for-one offers; cash allowances (to either the trade or to the consumer); and trade buying allowances (such as one case free with five, to repeat an earlier example). Deals are probably the most common form of sales promotion, defined in the general sense.

Point-of-purchase display, or simply "display," includes all visual materials, other than the product itself and simple price information, installed at the point of purchase. Display has the usual objectives of reminding customers to buy, and more often than not features some deal or sales promotion offer to provide special buying incentives. Point-of-purchase displays include such familiar devices as window displays featuring particular products, store window posters, special floor displays and bins for carrying the product—often placed at the end of the aisle or "gondola" in a supermarket or in other high-traffic locations, and

---

[1]Kenneth R. Davis, *Marketing Management*, 2nd ed., (New York: Ronald Press Company, 1966), p. 708.

countertop cardboard signs, often simply copies of the company's national print media advertising.

Other writers have used different definitions of each of these phrases, especially the phrase "sales promotion" which, as already noted, usually includes deals as they have been defined here. The distinction here is better suited to our purposes, however, because it separated those activities which feature a reduction in the price of the product from those that do not alter the selling price.

AN OVERVIEW

This section considers the objectives of sales promotion, deals, and display, to the extent that these three forms of marketing communication activity have several objectives in common. More specific objectives and details will be considered in subsequent sections. This section also examines the role of resellers and of the sales force in connection with short-term buying inducements. Finally, the section will define some of the more important and more general problems in using these tools.

Objectives

There are two broad classes of objectives for short-term supplementary marketing communication activities: (1) to increase buying action by ultimate customers or (2) to increase selling effort by resellers and the sales organization. These objectives are definitely complementary and a given special program may have elements designed to achieve both kinds of objectives.

The objectives of sales promotion, deals, and display relate to buying action, either trial or repeat purchase. Objectives at earlier stages of the hierarchy of effects may be accomplished by the mass media and by personal selling. While the mass media, and more especially personal selling, may provide sufficient incentive to produce buying action, it is more likely that some kind of special incentive will be required to convince people to modify their buying behavior. The need for special incentive will be especially true for frequently purchased consumer goods.

More often than not, special buying incentives are aimed primarily at consumers who are *not* regular users of the brand, although there are exceptions to this statement. The objective in this case is to change behavior, to cause consumers to shift from existing brand preferences and purchasing. A special incentive (most likely, a deal—a short-term price reduction) is often used to provide the inducement to shift.

Another way of thinking about the objectives of these devices is to state that the purpose of most promotions and deals is to increase the rate of *product movement* and/or the *stock of merchandise* at all levels of the pipeline from producer to consumer. This definition emphasizes the importance of aiming promotional efforts at both resellers and consumers at the same time. If consumers are to be urged to try the product or to increase their rate of purchase (as when multiple unit pricing deals are used to increase the consumer's pantry stock), then it is also necessary to make sure that stocks at the retail level are increased sufficiently to fulfill the demand created by consumer incentives. Likewise, some special incentives may be required to get shelf-space, displays, and retail selling effort as necessary to move the product into the consumer's hands. The several possible levels of objectives for product stocking and movement, and possible incentives for achieving those objectives, are illustrated in Table 22–1.

There may be *defensive* reasons for offering special buying incentives. In terms of the model of stocks and flows, an objective may be to increase consumer stocks for the purpose of taking our regular customers "out of the market," and insulating them against promotional activity by competitors. (Some companies have also gone to giant-size packages for

Table 22–1. Short-Term Marketing Communication Objectives, Stated in Terms of Changes in Products Stocks and Flows.

Objective	Inventory Stocks and Flows	Possible Incentives
Company warehouse withdrawal	Company warehouse	Salesman's contest
Increased retailer ordering	Ordering	Special price discount
Increased retailer stocks	Store	Case buying allowances
Increased retailer displays	Shelf	Display allowances
Increased retailer selling	Selling	"Push money" for retail sales clerks
Increased consumer buying	Purchase	Coupon
Increased consumer stocks	Household	Multiple pricing
Increased consumer use	Use	Merchandise offer requiring labels to be sent in

☐ = Stocks   ⬭ = Flows

this reason.) If competitors' promotional activities (aimed at getting our customers to shift their buying habits and brand preferences) can be anticipated, then it may be possible to encourage our loyal customers to "stock up" sufficiently to significantly reduce the competitors' impact.

More generally speaking, the defensive objective may simply be to meet the competitor's special incentives with special incentives of our own, without any particular thought to the tactical maneuver of taking customers out of the market. In other words, if brand X offers a 5¢-off label to the market, then competitive brand Z may feel compelled to send out coupons simply to regain initiative with consumers. (Brand X may retaliate by offering a coupon as well as the special label pack, and the battle rages.)

To summarize, objectives may be stated in terms of salesmen and reseller selling activity or in terms of reseller and consumer buying activity. Objectives may be offensive or defensive. While it is more common to use special promotions to try to attract new triers and new customers, it is not uncommon to use sales promotions, deals, and display to provide better values and increased buying incentives for existing and loyal customers. Each of these kinds of objectives is included in a list of objectives for sales promotions, deals, and displays, identified in a study by the Marketing Science Institute:

1. Informing customers of a new brand;
2. Transforming consumer attitudes toward an established brand;
3. Calling attention to improvements on established products;
4. Increasing customers' warehouse and storeroom inventories at the expense of competitors—"trade loading";
5. Reducing the rate of erosion of an established product's position in the face of vigorous competition;
6. Holding optimum levels on production and factory inventories;
7. Securing additional shelf space;
8. Encouraging special displays;
9. Providing a talking point for salesmen;
10. Sampling new triers of the brand;
11. Resampling customers lost to competitors;
12. Holding "loyal" customers;
13. Persuading consumers to buy a large package size;
14. Stimulating increased usage by present users;
15. Improving market share; and
16. Confounding a competitor's market test.[2]

Role of Reseller

The reseller obviously has a central role in most programs featuring sales promotions, deals, and displays. In many cases, the consumer pur-

[2]Patrick J. Robinson et al., *Promotional Decisions Using Mathematical Models* (Boston: Allyn & Bacon, Inc., 1967), p. 10.

chase behavior that is intended by the strategy actually occurs in the retail store. The responsibility of the reseller may take several forms including: providing additional shelf space; permitting the setting up of special displays; redeeming coupons; lowering the shelf price; stocking the shelves with special label-pack merchandise; or simply carrying heavier-than-usual stocks of merchandise in anticipation of heavier-than-usual demand created by a special incentive. It is not uncommon for the reseller to have to perform several of these functions if the promotional program is to be successful. The responsibility of the reseller can be quite complex in these situations and his full cooperation is an absolute necessity. Under such circumstances, it is obviously important that the role of the reseller be carefully planned and that he be given adequate lead time to implement his role in the strategy.

The reseller's problem is frequently a different one from that of the manufacturer, and a moment's reflection on the nature of that difference produces some insights into one of the most important sources of difficulty with short-term buying inducements as a part of the marketing communication strategy. In a nutshell, the reseller may be taking from Peter to pay Paul. He may be giving additional shelf space and other special attention to Brand X at the expense of Brands Y and Z. Furthermore, if all he is doing is shifting consumers' purchases from one brand to another, and if the reason for shifting is a reduced price, then he may end up with less revenue and more work in shifting around shelf positions, and so on. If nothing else, the special buying incentives can be a nuisance. Regular-pack merchandise may have to be either sold out or held in storage in order to accommodate the special label-pack merchandise. The reseller may have to mark down all of the merchandise for the sale and then mark up all remaining merchandise when the special program is completed. As a result, the reseller may come to regard sales promotions, deals, and displays as nothing more nor less than a big nuisance, taking management and store personnel time, causing confusion, increasing his costs of operation and, perhaps, resulting in lower sales revenue than he would otherwise receive.

While this is only one side of the argument, it is enough to show that sales promotions, deals, and displays are not an unmixed blessing. It also suggests why it is very hard to obtain complete trade cooperation in the conduct of such special incentive programs. The reseller has a critical role to play and the advantages to him of cooperating are not always obvious.

The foregoing comments have been made in the context of retailers, although the word "reseller" was used to keep the discussion sufficiently general. While these difficulties may occur at all levels, they are obviously of special significance for the retailer—because he provides the shelf space, the display, and may actually bring both the special buying incentive and the product itself to the consumer's attention. Nonetheless, a similar problem in arousing trade enthusiasm may exist with jobbers and wholesalers and with distributors in an industrial market who demand a satisfactory answer to the question of "What's in it for me?" as a condition for their cooperation.

Role of Sales Force

We are thus led to the next set of considerations: it is usually the sales force's responsibility to obtain the cooperation of resellers by explaining the features of the special incentive and the reasons why their cooperation is both valued by the manufacturer and to their own selfish advantage. The salesman also needs to understand his role in this strategic move; he needs to be trained to fulfill the responsibility that the strategy assigns to him. Furthermore, he may require some special incentive to make it worth his while to promote one brand and one deal over another. This can be a special problem in the multi-product company.

In consumer packaged goods companies especially, where the sales force may sell as many as fifty or more separate brands, salesmen may be forced to choose among several brands to promote in a given period. One company has estimated that its sales force typically has about fifteen separate sales promotions, deals, and displays to feature in any given selling period. This figure does not compare favorably with another observation that the salesman can typically feature no more than five brands or deals on a given sales call; neither time nor the buyer's patience permit it. Under such conditions, the salesman has to make some choices. Where possible, he will certainly tend to make such choices in a manner which reflects his own self interest. He will try to judge the impact of his effort on his total sales volume, for example, or upon his commission income. He may perceive some incentives as more attractive and easier to sell than others.

Like the reseller, the salesman needs adequate lead time to plan his own selling activities. He needs adequate information and details to be able to present a complete story to his customers and to answer their questions about the details of administering the program ("How do I get reimbursed for coupon redemptions? When does the national advertising program run? Will case buying allowances be subtracted on the invoice or will additional merchandise be shipped?" and so on).

If the salesman has not been provided with adequate information, or if he finds it difficult to explain the terms of the deal and how it works, he will tend to ignore it in favor of other parts of his responsibility. The importance of planning the salesman's role in the special promotional program and of preparing him to assume that role cannot be overstated.

Problems

There are many problems in the conduct of a program involving sales promotions, deals, or displays. As the foregoing comments indicate, problems of coordination and control are at the head of the list. The "logistics" of such a program can be very complex and require careful planning and administration and involve both resellers and the company's own sales force. There are other problems as well. To help organize this discussion, we shall first consider problems relating to consumer reaction, then we shall turn to problems relating to resellers.

The trend is to more and more promotions and deals. It is instructive to simply stroll through a supermarket and notice the high percentage of brands that are currently being offered on a special incentive of one form or another. One result of this may be a large amount of consumer confusion, frustration, and even anger. Some customers may feel that they are being deceived by all of this activity. Consumers may legitimately ask whether there is such a thing as a standard price for a particular brand. They may also become disenchanted when initially created expectations are not fulfilled or when a form of promotion gains such prominence in a product category that it becomes abusive. The various "contests" that were featured by gasoline companies in the mid-1960's produced this reaction to the point of stimulating proposed legislation to outlaw such contests. Furthermore, there were abuses of the "lottery" method of promotion to the extent of actual fraud in some cases and this produced further resentment. Obviously, this reduces the effectiveness of such methods of promotion.

In another sense, consumer reaction even when it is favorable can be a problem. If consumers respond as desired by management and actually buy more, has the program been a success? Not necessarily. Customers may have bought ahead and put the product on the pantry shelf without actually increasing the rate of consumption. This is not necessarily bad (if the objective has been to forestall competitive activity, for example) but it can create some serious problems. A successful promotion may result in an out-of-stock position that subsequently discourages interest in the brand at both retail and wholesale levels. Furthermore, the company may respond by increasing production and increasing inventories at all levels with the realization coming slowly that customer buying actually dropped off sharply after the period of the promotion. Excessive inventory costs are the inevitable outcome.

Consumer response to sales promotion and deals can produce a "kinked" demand curve representing a short-term shift in demand with-

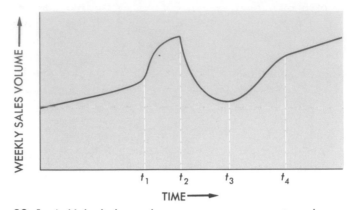

Fig. 22–1. A kinked demand curve as a response to sales promotional activity.

out any real long-term change in consumer buying habits. Figure 22–1 illustrates this form of response to promotions and deals. There it can be seen that the special incentive was introduced at time t_1 and was halted at t_2. Sales begin to drop significantly and finally begin to reverse direction at t_3. At time t_4 sales seem to be resuming their normal growth pattern as evidenced by the trend prior to t_1. While kinks due to promotional activity may be obscured by other sources of demand variability, they increase the difficulty of using sales volume data as the basis for strategic decision making. David Ogilvy has pointed out that such special incentives make it very difficult to evaluate the effectiveness of media advertising.[3] It is not necessary for the kink in the curve to actually "bottom out" below the trend line (as at t_3 in Figure 22–1) for there to be significant problems in using sales data for evaluating strategic effectiveness. Borrowed sales from future purchases can simply aggravate the seriousness of the kink and problems of interpretation.

Shifting our attention to the response of resellers to special incentives, there is also the problem of confusion and frustration. As indicated in the discussion of the role of the reseller, such confusion can be expensive in that it can raise his inventory and ordering costs. As a result, the frustrated reseller may simply refuse to cooperate.

The trend toward more promotions and deals may actually discourage retailer stocking, for example, rather then encourage it. A retailer who used to purchase in 50-case lots and never was out-of-stock may now buy no more than 10 cases at a time because he doesn't want to be "stuck" with regular-priced merchandise in his back room when he has

[3]David Ogilvy, *Confessions of an Advertising Man* (New York: Atheneum, 1963), p. 102.

label-packs (cents-off) on the shelf. One result may be more frequent stock-outs. As a protection against this problem of trade acceptance, some manufacturers have reportedly adopted the practice of sending retailers a check for merchandise on hand at the beginning of the deal period, and then billing them for the same amount when the deal is finished, to save them the cost of having money tied up in duplicate inventories.[4]

The reseller's ability to accept or reject a deal is a function of several things including the extent to which the deal is promoted in mass media and his contractual relationships with suppliers. The grocer may be free to accept or reject manufacturers' offers of special merchandise as far as any contractual obligation is concerned, but the consumer may demand that he stock it if she has been made aware of the deal by mass communication. On the other hand, the exclusive retail dealer for a line of watches or silverware or appliances may be required to feature special deals as part of his contract with the manufacturer.

Having reviewed briefly some of the general problems with sales promotions, deals, and point-of-purchase display from both the consumer's and the reseller's viewpoint, the discussion now considers each kind of promotional activity in somewhat greater detail.

SALES PROMOTION

Using the narrow definition of the term "sales promotion" as developed earlier in this chapter, a sales promotion can be thought of as *any special buying incentive which adds value to the product or service being offered while maintaining the list price.* Reductions from the regular price are specifically eliminated from this definition. A sales promotion increases the utility of the total product offering to the customer while maintaining the price. A sales promotion thus involves the notion that "something extra" is offered to the consumer. There are several categories of sales promotions, each of which is a slightly different method of offering the customer "something extra."

Premiums

A "premium" is an offer of merchandise at a significant value to the consumer. Examples of premiums include toys offered to children for sending in one or more boxtops and a small amount of money, special packages containing a small toy or other prize, products packaged in special reusable containers (such as packaging instant coffee in a carafe), and the offering of merchandise that has product identification

[4]Robinson, *op. cit.*, p. 15.

on it, such as windbreaker jackets with a motor oil additive label affixed on the breast. One of the most familiar kinds of premiums is the offering of coupons *with* the product (rather than mailing them to the household, or including them in advertising) that are redeemable for valuable merchandise. Certain brands of cigarettes use coupons that can be redeemed for premiums, and this device has also been used successfully by some food marketers that put a coupon good for so many "points" on each package of their branded products.

Premiums have been used successfully by many consumer goods marketers to build good will with loyal customers and they have also served to help many marketers significantly increase their share of the market. They may be used to attract new customers and to encourage them to try the product for the first time. Or they may be used to build loyal customers and to encourage repeat purchase as when a premium requires the collection and redemption of many coupons or labels from the products being promoted or when sets (such as dishes) are offered piece by piece. There are several problems in using premiums, however.

Selecting Attractive Premiums. The most significant problem in using premiums as a sales promotional strategy is to pick those which will have significant appeal for the consumer. Some of the factors to consider are the cost of the premium to the consumer, the extent to which the price at which it is offered represents a true value, and the uniqueness of the premium offered relative to what competitors can offer and the availability of the premium to the public at large. Products which are very expensive, are available at low cost to most consumers, or lack distinctiveness are not likely to attract significant numbers of new customers or to build a stronger relationship with existing customers.

Premiums which are *too* attractive or represent *too* significant a value can be ineffective as well. In this case, the purchaser may actually be buying the premium rather than the product and there will be no long-term benefit to the marketer. The costs of servicing a large amount of one-time demand may not be justified by the volume of repeat business.

It is common for merchandise premiums to be "self-liquidating," meaning that the amount of money required from the consumer is sufficient to pay for the cost of the product and the costs of shipping and handling. For merchandise which carries a large markup at retail, the result can still be significant savings for the consumer. Self-liquidating premiums that are distinctive may still represent a significant value to the consumer.

The most effective merchandise premiums are probably those which use merchandise which has some functional or logical relationship to the product being promoted. Thus, it makes sense for a marketer of baby foods to offer an engraved sterling silver baby spoon for $1.00 and a boxtop from one of its cereal products. A manufacturer of sugar-coated cereals may likewise offer a set of plastic bowls and cups featuring the animal character that has come to be identified with its television advertising. A brewer has offered clear goblets with the brand symbol on them. In each case, the consumer using the premium will be reminded of the product and has an additional small stimulus to become brand-loyal.

Merchandise premiums may also be used to provide a special *selling* incentive to the sales organization or to resellers. Some companies have effectively appealed to their salesmen's wives by offering trading stamps to the salesmen for achieving specific objectives, and mailing to the wives the merchandise catalogues describing the merchandise available for redemption. Other companies offer their salesmen specific merchandise prizes—such as shirts, golf clubs, and tickets to sporting events—for achieving specific objectives. The sales volume or new account objectives that provide the target for such efforts are usually short-term, rather easily achievable, and supplementary to the more general objectives that direct selling effort throughout the year.

Contests

Premium offers typically involve the offering of a specific product or relatively small payoff for a definitely stated action—such as sending in two boxtops to receive a toy doll. A contest involves an uncertain payoff and much larger possible rewards. A person who joins a credit card plan may be offered a chance to win a trip to Europe in such a contest. Or, the person who drives into a gas station may receive a metal token worth $5,000—if he happens to be one of several possible winners out of the several million who will receive tokens; otherwise, the token he receives may be good for nothing more than jingling around in a child's pocket.

Lotteries and Legal Considerations. There are legal reasons why it may be desirable to require no purchase as a necessary condition for entering the contest, which is really a lottery. A "lottery" is technically defined as a scheme for the allotment of prizes by chance. Several national and state governments rely upon lotteries as a major source of revenue; the number of persons paying the price of entry and the price of a single ticket in the lottery, when multiplied together, equal a sum much larger then the total of prizes to be awarded. Such is the basic logic of the lottery and of the contest as a promotional device. The price of entry into a lottery intended to provide a short-term buying incentive may be the purchase of the product or simply responding to an offer and entering the marketer's place of business or returning a mailed piece describing the contest.

One of the major criticisms of contests is that they may tend to deceive the customer. The supposed deceptive tendencies are based on the consumer's overestimation of the likelihood of actually winning. Here, the critics may have a valid point, especially when the media advertising describing such contests is carefully scrutinized. In many cases the prizes to be awarded and the chances of winning are subtly exaggerated by some carefully chosen words. There have likewise been cases where the "winners" were notified that what they had won was a chance to send in a "deposit" (of $25 in one case that comes to mind) that would permit them to be considered for the "grand prize" yet to be awarded. (In this case, the offer was suspected of being fraudulent and the Postmaster General of the United States became officially concerned.)

Contests for resellers are often an effective device for stimulating their interest and, more especially, for securing larger orders and more desirable shelf space from them. All retailers agreeing to set up a special display for a month, for example, may have their names entered in a drawing where the prize is travel or merchandise.

Salesmen's Contests. Contests for salesmen are very common. Among other benefits they help enliven the salesman's work and provide a specific, short-term objective to stimulate his day-to-day selling effort. In both resellers' contests and salesmen's contests the prizes offered must be valuable enough and desirable enough to provide real incentive. (There is an apocryphal story about the sales contest that no salesman wanted to win because the prize was a one-week trip to the home office with his wife.) When travel is offered as the prize, for example, it should involve a destination that is attractive, probably a destination that the salesman would not be able to visit on his own. It should also be possible for the salesman to avail himself of the prize when and if he wins it. It is irresponsible, for example, to offer a prize of a trip to Europe for two weeks without also allowing the salesman to take his wife along as part of the prize.

Salesmen's contests should not be used as a significant part of the salesman's compensation for the simple reason that prizes are awarded on a chance basis. The salesman should receive full compensation for the work he performs and contests should have a definitely supplementary role in the total company compensation program.

Sales contests, it should be noted, have the possibility of contributing significantly to the problem of the kinked demand curve. A contest may encourage the salesman to oversell and to overload dealers' inventories, only to have several "lean" weeks after the contest is over. In addition to the direct costs of the prizes in such a contest, there are other (perhaps more significant) indirect costs such as the cost of fluctuations in production rates and inventory levels and other perturbations of the physical distribution system. Sales contests are an effective supplementary incentive provided they are not intended to correct for basic weaknesses in the company's plan for motivating and supervising its sales force.

CONSUMER DEALS

As defined earlier, a deal is a *short-term reduction in the price* of the product or service being offered. For purposes of this discussion, a distinction is made between consumer deals (where price reductions are offered to ultimate consumers) and trade deals (where resellers receive price reductions). The more common forms of consumer deals include: simple reduction in the marked shelf price; a special "label pack" announcing the amount of the reduction (e.g., "5¢ Off Regular Price"); coupons inserted in magazines or mailed to the consumer; and two-for-one offers. (Trading stamps are a form of price reduction, but they are offered by the retail store rather than by the product manufacturer and they therefore do not fit our definition of "deals.")

An often-quoted study of consumer preferences found that, of all kinds of sales promotions, consumers most preferred cents-off offers. Sixty-one percent of the respondents reported this preference, compared with coupons, premiums, and contests.[5] These findings did not measure the extent to which women prefer sales promotions in general but only measured their preferences among types of promotions.

Objectives of Deals

Whereas sales promotions increase the value for the consumer by offering "something extra" in addition to the product, deals provide additional value by reducing the price paid. Both have the objective of providing additional buying incentive.

Deals are typically used in two situations—when the marketer wishes to increase the rate of trial among potential customers and when he wishes to retaliate against some specific competitive action. The housewife looking for ways to stretch her limited budget may be quite attracted by the possibility of saving a few important pennies on such frequently purchased products as frozen orange juice, cake mixes, coffee, and frozen vegetables. Where she perceives the differences among brands to be relatively insignificant, the offering of a coupon may provide an attractive reason for trying a new brand.

[5]Alfred Politz Research, Inc., "Women Shoppers' Opinions of Special Offers," survey conducted for Association of National Advertisers, Inc., 1963, quoted in Robinson, *op. cit.*, p. 16.

Consumers who try new brands often stay with them simply because the product proves satisfactory and the possible benefits from experimenting with other brands are perceived to be small relative to the degree of uncertainty and the possible negative consequences. In other words, the perceived risk of brand switching may be too high for behavior to change. A special price reduction may provide the necessary reason. Studies suggest that reducing the amount of investment required is one strategy for overcoming the perceived risk in a purchase situation.[6]

These facts suggest that deals may be a useful method for increasing the rate of trial and for increasing the number of loyal customers. (Remember that trial will generate loyal customers only if the product itself actually lives up to promises made for it in media advertising and to expectations that customers have generated about the product.) These facts also suggest that competitors who try to steal away customers may be successful in doing so and that it pays to try to combat competitive dealing activities. Retaliatory dealing is a frequent occurrence in the markets for consumer packaged goods.

Dealing has also been used to try to cloud the results that competitors obtain from test markets. Recognizing that this tactic raises some intriguing issues of business ethics, it should also be recognized that this is not an uncommon occurrence. In the hopes of discouraging a potential competitor from entering a market, an established marketer may identify that potential competitor's test markets and attempt to depress the market's level of response to the new product by offering a special deal.

Conditions Favoring Use

Deals are most effective for products which do not have a high degree of brand loyalty. The desired response from the market is obviously easiest to obtain where small differences in price will produce a significant consumer response. Where consumers have strong brand loyalty, the few cents in reduction from retail price possible may not be sufficient to justify switching. A related observation is that the stronger the degree of brand loyalty, the larger is the amount of price reduction necessary to encourage short-term switching.

Deals are also most effectively used in those markets where they are a relatively infrequently used competitive weapon. In product categories where dealing is the rule rather than the exception, it is hard for one brand to maintain any effective competitive advantage using deals and

[6]Donald F. Cox, *Risk Taking and Information Handling in Consumer Behavior* (Boston: Division of Research, Graduate School of Business Administration, Harvard University, 1967), pp. 1–19.

the more desirable strategic paths would be to search for another method of gaining the consumer's attention and favor. (On the other hand, the very fact that competitors rely so heavily upon dealing may narrow the range of the strategic alternatives.)

The "Deal-Prone" Consumer

One factor to consider in evaluating the contribution of consumer deals in the total marketing communication strategy is whether certain consumers are more likely to accept a product offered on a deal. In other words, is there a type of consumer who is more likely to buy a deal? A study designed to answer this question provided a tentative "yes." There are a few characteristics that tend to be weakly correlated with acceptance of a product offered on a deal basis.

The study of the deal-prone consumer found that there were four characteristics significantly related to the probability that the consumer would buy the product on a deal basis: (1) age of the housewife; (2) concentration of purchases on a favorite brand; (3) number of brands purchased; and (4) total amount purchased. These four variables explained about fifteen percent of the variability in the "deal-proneness" index, which was a measure of the extent to which the consumer purchased a brand on a deal basis adjusted to reflect the frequency with which the brand was offered for sale on a deal basis.

The most significant of these variables was the age of the housewife, with older housewives being more likely to buy the product on a deal basis. The possible explanation is that older housewives are more knowledgeable, have more buying experience, and know how to search out the "specials." It may also be that older housewives are more constrained by their budgets because they have larger families, but this explanation was not supported by an analysis of the data. It might also be suggested, conversely, that the younger housewife is likely to have lower income and therefore more likely to buy on a deal basis, but this was not the case.

Amount purchased was *negatively* correlated with deal proneness, a result different from what might be expected on an intuitive basis. It could be argued that the heavy user is more likely to search out deals, since expenditures in this product category are more significant for her. The data, however, suggested that heavier users were less likely to buy the product on a deal basis. This may reflect the fact that heavier consumers must buy more frequently and therefore are less likely to purchase the product on a deal basis. Analysis of the data did not reveal any relationship between deal-proneness and the frequency of purchasing, however. This finding raises some doubt about the ability of deals to fulfill the often-stated objective of attracting heavy users.

Finally, the study found that persons who were more likely to buy a brand on a deal basis were likely to purchase more brands within a product category and they devoted a small proportion of their total purchases to a favored brand. Both of these are dimensions of brand loyalty —number of brands purchased and concentration of purchases upon a favored brand. In both cases, there was, as expected, a negative relationship between brand loyalty and deal proneness. The data did not permit a determination of whether low brand loyalty "caused" or "resulted from" deal proneness. The data did indicate, however, that deal-prone consumers switch brands more frequently, thus raising some doubt about the ability of a deal to attract new consumers who will subsequently become loyal customers.

While this study suggested that the deal-prone consumer was somewhat older, less brand loyal, and a light user, it should be emphasized that it did not reveal that the "deal-prone" consumer is a distinct consumer type.[7]

TRADE DEALS

Trade deals are temporary price reductions offered to resellers of a product. A common practice is to use a trade deal to insure sufficient reseller stock of a consumer deal, although trade deals may be used independently of consumer deals. The objectives of a trade deal are always to obtain additional dealer stocking and display and, frequently, to follow through on consumer deals.

Trade deals may take several forms: a reduction in the case price; a temporary offer of cooperative advertising allowances contingent upon ordering some minimum number of cases, with the allowance stated as so much per case; special quantity discounts; buying allowances stated in terms of merchandise such as "buy five and get one case free"; and actual cash rebates, usually contingent upon performing some service such as setting up special displays of merchandise.

The previous chapter on the role of the reseller in the marketing communication strategy emphasized that resellers are independent profit-seeking businesses with their own objectives and constraints. The reseller's decision making about the deals that are offered to him by manufacturers reflects his own best assessment of the costs and benefits of stocking that deal. The reseller is, most significantly, relatively indifferent between selling one unit of Brand X at the usual price and one unit of Brand Z at the usual price. When Brand X is offered to him on the basis of a special buying incentive, it may provide sufficient justifica-

[7]Frederick E. Webster, Jr., "The 'Deal-Prone' Consumer," *Journal of Marketing Research*, 2 (May 1965), pp. 186–89.

tion for stocking more of Brand X relative to Brand Z because, assuming no change in retail price, the result will be a slightly higher profit on all units of Brand X sold and therefore a slightly higher total profitability in that product category. Thus, whereas consumer deals may decrease the profitability of the product category to the reseller, trade deals may increase it.

A key question in analysis of the reseller's role in short-term promotional strategy is the issue of control. Typically, the trade deal involves some obligation on the part of the reseller to perform a certain function —set up a special display, redeem consumer coupons and present them as evidence of having earned the special allowances, or place local advertising. While it certainly makes sense from the manufacturer's viewpoint to make sure that services paid for are in fact received, resellers may regard the necessary checking and control procedures as an imposition on their own business dealings or as an indication of lack of trust. This is not common, however, since most resellers have become accustomed to the "rules" of proof of performance where that is a condition for accepting a special deal.

The Marketing Science Institute study reported some sentiment among retailers in favor of more freedom in how they spend promotional allowances granted by manufacturers. Retailers argued that greater flexibility permitted to them would result in a more effective use of the manufacturer's promotional funds.[8] The same result is achieved when manufacturers stop asking for such proof of performance and simply grant promotional allowances on the assumption that they will be used most effectively by the trade. In other words, giving up on enforcement is the same thing as announcing a new, more flexible policy.

EVALUATION OF DEALS

Because they are so often used together, and because reseller cooperation is a major key to the success of consumer deals, this section will evaluate both consumer deals and trade deals. The purpose of this section is to summarize the conditions under which use of deals is likely to be an effective use of promotional dollars and to suggest how such funds can be used most efficiently.

An excellent study on the effective use of deals was reported by Hinkle. From his extensive survey of company practices and reseller attitudes, Hinkle reported the following conclusions:

1. The closer together the deals for a brand, the poorer the results.
2. Attempting to load the retailers so as to preclude their acceptance of an invading brand's offer is costly and largely futile.

[8]Robinson, *op. cit.*, pp. 13–15.

3. Dealing is more effective for newer brands than for established brands.
4. There are cases of luxury brands that seem to have been unscathed by price-deal competition. But to qualify for this immunity, the product must have no weaknesses of quality or distribution.
5. Deals are not substitutes for advertising, and . . . they are as much as two or three times more effective when a brand's advertising share level is sustained rather than reduced.[9]

These findings have been taken from various points within the Hinkle article, which, in general, concluded that manufacturers of consumer packaged goods were probably relying too heavily upon temporary price reductions as an element of marketing communication strategy. Hinkle also found frequently inadequate planning of the use of deals and failure to give the trade adequate lead time to plan for the deal when offered to consumers. Retailers were reported to be putting pressure on manufacturers to maintain inventories with the confusion of frequent price deals being a major reason why retailers were unwilling to assume the responsibility for inventories. Hinkle was critical of marketers for unimaginative use of deals:

The tendency is to grasp the transitory opportunity of sales by the most convenient means available, so long as it provides some short-term advantage over the competition . . . . Historically, there have been more similarities than differences in the methods used by competitors to implement temporary price reductions. It seems reasonable to conclude that such behavior may merely create a cancelling effect over time. . . .[10]

In other words, there is a tendency to rely upon short-term price reductions as a cure-all for declining sales volume, without adequate diagnosis of the basic causes of the decreasing competitive effectiveness. Problems of inadequate distribution, or poor product quality relative to new competitors, or a "tired" brand image, or inadequate media advertising cannot be solved, or even alleviated for very long, by reducing the price. Given the large amount of dollars involved in dealing, this area of the promotional strategy should not be left out of the careful analysis and planning which produce benefits in developing mass communication and personal selling strategy and tactics.

On a more positive note, the conditions most conducive to the effective use of deals are careful management analysis and planning, adequate planning and preparation of resellers' and sales force efforts, a relatively new product (that can still attract new users), no exceptionally strong brand loyalty to existing brands, and no significant weaknesses in product distribution and quality. Money spent on dealing is wasted when its expenditure is not adequately planned, when the trade is not

[9]Charles L. Hinkle, "The Strategy of Price Deals," *Harvard Business Review*, 43 (July–August 1965), pp. 75–85.
[10]*Ibid.*, p. 85.

approached in a manner which permits careful, positive evaluation and planning of necessary implementation stages, and when the product itself or the distribution system is not strong enough to support a heightened level of consumer interest in the brand.

Consumer panel data can provide an important basis for the analysis of dealing effectiveness. Rates of trial, brand switching, and the development of brand loyalty can be monitored by the analysis of panel data and changes in such measures of buying behavior as frequency of purchase, number of units purchased, length of brand runs (consecutive purchases of the same brand), and switching behavior. Analytical measure of major help in planning future use of competitive deals include calculations of the probabilities of purchasing various brands as a function of purchasing history.

As in other areas of marketing communication strategy, experimentation can provide significant information as the basis for future planning. Experimentation and specifically the ability to control the influence of several variables may be especially helpful in evaluating sales promotions and deals because of the problems created by the "kinked" demand curve, as mentioned earlier. The use of matched pairs of test cities (one to receive the deal and the other to serve as a control) may help resolve this important measurement problem.

POINT-OF-PURCHASE DISPLAY

Point-of-purchase display includes any special treatment at the point of purchase including special displays of the product itself, special display racks and devices, and visual materials designed to attract consumer attention and to stimulate buying action.

Objectives of Point-of-Purchase Display

Point-of-purchase display may be defined to include displays of the product in a store window, on merchandise shelves, at the end of a counter, in bins at high traffic locations within the store, or at the checkout counter or cash register. In short, display can be virtually any way of presenting the product itself (or visual reproductions of it) to the customer. "Point-of-purchase" can be defined as the store, the counter, or the cash register.

Special displays have repeatedly been shown to be an effective way to produce substantial increases in sales volume in the short-term. Increases of 200 to 300 percent are not uncommon from the use of displays to dispense the product when these displays (often cardboard bins or special stacking arrangements) are given preferred positions within the store. One source has suggested thirty different objectives for the use of display:

1. Build immediate sale of the product.
2. Demonstrate the product.
3. Promote the sale of related items.
4. Feature a new product.
5. Show the actual package or a reproduction.
6. Increase the unit of sale.
7. Sample the product.
8. Introduce a new product.
9. Feature uses.
10. Show price.
11. Give product seasonal appeal.
12. Create new interest in product.
13. Dispense the product.
14. Distribute coupons.
15. Dispense printed materials.
16. Feature a premium.
17. Stimulate interest in a contest.
18. Show a line.
19. Feature combination offers.
20. Promote sale of product as an ingredient.
21. Point out product's special features.
22. Get display for cumbersome product.
23. Make extra sales at the cash register.
24. Get attention by motion.
25. Get attention by light.
26. Promote impulse buying.
27. Protect a fragile product while displayed.
28. Advertise institutionally.
29. Sample materials.
30. Give a quality product a quality background.[11]

These uses are not mutually exclusive and one could argue that they are not all of equal stature as objectives, but the list does illustrate the diversity of purposes served by display.

There are two broad categories of objectives for point-of-purchase. One class of objectives relates to a tie-in with media advertising and sees displays as performing essentially a reminder function. The other class of objectives is to create consumer interest and stimulate buying action without earlier brand awareness or preference. The latter can be more legitimately called "impulse" buying, although there are several problems with the use of this term.

Reminder To Make Planned Purchase. In the first kind of use, it is assumed that potential buyers are already aware of the product and

[11]Albert Wesley Frey (ed.), *Marketing Handbook*, 2d. ed. (New York: The Ronald Press Company, 1965), Section 18, "Sales Promotion," by Alfred Gross, pp. 7–8.

have developed a set of attitudes toward it. When the shopper is in the store she may need a "reminder" to restore her awareness of the brand and to recall her attitudes toward it. In this view, the function of display is to "reactivate" the hierarchy of effects; it is assumed that triggering of awareness will cause the rest of the cycle to occur spontaneously and will lead to buying action. There is some evidence to support this view. One study has found that approximately one half of grocery purchases are "unplanned" in the sense that the consumer does not come into the store with a conscious decision in mind to purchase a specific product *and* a specific brand. Only one out of four purchases was specifically planned for both product and brand to be bought.[12] This can be explained partly by an observation that many women adopt a "wait-and see" attitude toward shopping, hoping to select those products which are being featured and which promise the best value. Display can thus be an important influence on the consumer's actual buying behavior. This "reminder" function of display can be most effective with brands which she knows and has previously purchased.

Suggestion To Try New Brand. Although it is a distinction of degree, not kind, the other category of objectives relates to brands with which the consumer is less familiar. In this case, a heavier burden is placed upon the display to perform all communication functions including both awareness and incentive to actual buying behavior. (It is doubtful that display can exert any significant influence on attitudes *per se*. Rather, display may stimulate behavior which will then be evaluated to bring about some small changes in attitudes *after* the purchase decision.) Displays of new products, or of products with a significant price reduction to encourage trial, are in this latter category. With new brands, display alone is probably not as effective as it is on established, well-known brands. New brands may require the additional incentive of a deal before a display can stimulate buying action.

The reminder function can be performed in a more subtle way, as well as by actually displaying the product itself in an attractive manner. It is common for some advertisers to have small reproductions of their media advertising mounted on a small cardboard stand for display on the retail counter. This device serves to remind the consumer that the product is nationally (or regionally) advertised, and this may be taken as a symbol of quality—a kind of source credibility. It associates both the product and the retailer with the high prestige of the mass media, especially when a phrase such as "As Advertised in *LIFE*" has been overprinted on the advertisement itself.

[12]David T. Kollat and Ronald P. Willett, "Customer Impulse Purchasing Behavior." *Journal of Marketing Research*, 4 (February 1967), pp. 21–31.

Impulse Buying

It is often stated that an objective of product display is to stimulate impulse buying. There is reason to question this statement in many cases because of the basic nature of impulse buying behavior. A definition is necessary: Impulse buying is any purchase that is not specifically planned. There is no implication here that the purchase is "irrational" or is not related to the satisfaction of a specific need or buying objective. While it may appear to be "spur-of-the-moment" in nature, it may actually be the result of careful prior decision making that resulted in a "wait-and-see-what-is-available" attitude.

Display may be a major cue, as noted earlier, to trigger actual behavior for such unplanned purchases and it therefore can be a powerful strategic weapon for products that are frequently purchased on an unplanned basis. An example of such a product might be candy bars and chewing gum, which are frequently displayed at the checkout counter to appeal to this kind of purchase. This is undoubtedly a major reason why it was possible for the Hershey Chocolate Company to compete effectively in the United States for many years without the use of consumer advertising (a policy that was changed in 1969). True unplanned purchasing is not uncommon, therefore, especially for products that have relatively low retail prices. In this case, display can contribute to significant sales increases because the amount of perceived risk involved in the purchase is very low and the consumer therefore needs little information as the basis for decision making.

It is important to recognize, however, that purchasing behavior which *appears* to be unplanned may actually be carefully planned but the result of a long and deliberate search. Assume that a gentleman has decided that he needs a summer-weight, dark blue suit that does not cost more than one hundred dollars. His first shopping trip to find such a suit may have been unsuccessful and he may have decided to keep looking, at a more relaxed pace, until he finds what he wants. If he is in another part of town one day, spots such a suit on display in a shop window, and runs in to make the purchase, the store owner may perceive this to be an unplanned purchase, although it has in fact been carefully planned. Often, an "impulse" purchase may be better described as the final discovery of a product that the consumer has been searching for.

Problems with Display

Display has a unique and an important role in the marketing of most consumer products and with a large proportion of industrial products (those sold through distributors) as well. The actual physical presentation of the product with a display device can be an effective substitute for personal selling at the retail level, and the display can provide an important tie-in with mass advertising. At the same time, display is expensive and may involve considerable waste of promotional resources.

The costs of display may represent several factors. If a special four-color printed cardboard bin is used, for example, the display piece itself may cost several dollars. A salesman may have to spend an hour or more setting up the display piece and stocking it with merchandise. It may be necessary to provide some financial incentive to the store manager to persuade him to allocate store space to this display. The sum of these costs may be as much as fifty or even one hundred dollars, although there is no meaningful statistic that can be quoted from research studies.

Such investment can be wasted if the display piece never leaves the back room of the store, or if it stays up for only a few days before being replaced by a competitive display. The probability of having displays left in the storeroom can be minimized by an effective program for obtaining the attention of the sales force in setting up such displays, and if the display is integrated with other sales promotional tactics to insure reseller cooperation. Another method of insuring that resellers make good use of expensive display materials provided by the manufacturer is to charge some small amount for such displays. A metal rack of solid construction intended for more-or-less permanent use in the store may be actually sold to retailers. Having paid for it, the retailer is more likely to value it, although the cost may have the undesired effect of discouraging the use of such displays. A compromise may be to require dealers to specifically request any such materials sent to them, rather than shipping displays routinely to all retailers.

SUMMARY

Sales promotion, deals, and display may be critical in assuring the success of the marketing communication strategy. They can provide specific incentive to buying action and have the unique ability to substitute for personal selling at the retail level. These tools may be used offensively or defensively and they may be used with new or established products, although the arguments examined seem to favor their use with new products and for offensive reasons.

In recent years, short-term buying incentives and especially temporary reductions in price, or "deals," have become much more common. From several quarters this has led to a suggestion that these devices have been overused and have produced waste in marketing communication strategy. One of the major reasons for such waste appears to be the relatively unplanned, hit-or-miss methods used to implement such tactics. Lack of planning is reflected in the inability of the reseller to respond to or accept these deals and displays and his tendency to shift responsibility for inventories back to the manufacturer. The specific objective of obtaining better stocking by the trade may not be achieved as a result.

Objectives for the use of sales promotions, deals, and display may be stated in terms of increasing sales force and reseller selling efforts or in terms of increasing reseller and customer buying action. The success of a short-term program using these tools is going to be greater to the extent that each of these objectives is given sufficient weight to insure that the movement of products through the marketing channel to the ultimate consumer proceeds without interruption. The stocks-and-flows model presented early in the chapter provides a visual statement of the need for careful planning, coordination, and control of several kinds of incentives to achieve the overall objective of profitable sales volume over the longer term.

23

Packaging and Branding as Communication

Packaging and branding play two important roles within the marketing communication strategy. They identify the product and they convey meaning about it. The design of a package, including its shape, material, color, and copy, can provide important cues about the nature of the product. The brand (a name or symbol), especially as that brand takes on meaning from mass communication, becomes a constellation of meanings and a symbol with a unique interpretation by customers and potential customers.

Creativity plays an important part in packaging and branding, for the design of packages, brands, trademarks, and corporate identification symbols ultimately requires execution by a skilled creative artist who can capture the essence of what the marketing communication strategist has defined as the objective. It is difficult to talk about packaging and branding without becoming involved in the nuances of creative design. The purpose of this chapter, however, is to suggest the role of packaging, branding, and other forms of product identification in the total marketing communication strategy, not to discuss the aesthetics of design. The factors to be discussed here, when carefully analyzed, provide the basis upon which a statement of objectives can be defined for the creative consultants who must ultimately execute these ideas.

There is an important relationship between packaging and branding as communications and the display of the product on the retail shelf. Also, packaging and premiums, as a form of sales promotion, are often very closely intertwined as problem areas for management decision making. Likewise, there are important relationships between the problems of packaging and branding and the development of corporate identity symbols. The problems of sales promotion and display were discussed in the previous chapter and served to introduce some of the tactical considerations concerning actual product display that will be further discussed in this chapter. In the next chapter we shall consider corporate advertising, public relations, and publicity as elements of the marketing communication strategy, and the specific question of *corporate* identity symbols will be discussed further.

In the present chapter, our concern is with packaging and branding (and product labeling) as *communications*. More specifically, our primary concern is with packages, labels, and brands as symbols that convey meaning about the product, as variables which produce a psychological response in potential customers. This is only one of many functions performed by packages and other forms of product identification. Before considering the specific problems of packaging, labeling, and branding as communication, therefore, it may be helpful to examine other functions performed by packages and to position communication functions within the complete set of functions.

FUNCTIONS OF PACKAGING

Packaging is one of the most important areas of management decision making within most companies, although responsibility for the function tends to be dispersed throughout the organization. As a result, precise estimates of the cost of packaging, as one indication of its importance, are very hard to determine. The packaging industry is said to be the third largest in the United States, and many companies have reported that packaging is one of the two or three most important items in their total purchases. For many consumer goods, the cost of the package may be considerably greater than the cost of the product ingredients. The economic importance of packaging reflects the many functions performed by the package and the extent to which these pervade the organization. At the minimum, packages are important in manufacturing, shipping, and marketing operations, and other functional areas of the organization may well be involved in decision making about packaging.

Containing

This function is so obvious that it may be overlooked in any listing of packaging functions. It is the most basic of all functions performed by the package—that of containing the product. Most grocery products must be placed in a container because they are not solid in form. Cereals, beer, flour, coffee, toothpaste, snack foods, and so on cannot be sold except in portioned packages that physically hold the product in a form that permits it to be transported, stored, and served in a convenient manner. Packaging is essential to mass marketing and efficient self-service retailing as we know it today.

Protecting

Many products deteriorate or become damaged unless they are protected from the atmosphere and from the abuses of physical handling. Most food products will decompose or otherwise become unpalatable unless they are protected from oxygen, moisture, and sunlight. Examples of products which deteriorate rapidly are breakfast cereals, baked goods, carbonated beverages, fruits and vegetables, and dairy products. Mass merchandising involving several levels of resellers and processors absolutely depends upon the protective ability of packaging. Were it not for advances in packaging technology such as high-barrier protective coatings and strong, inexpensive packaging materials, the consumer would still be purchasing many items directly from the farmer. Many modern food items such as instant coffee and cake mixes would not be feasible without adequate package protection.

Manufactured products other than foods require protection as well. Although a radio, for example, may not deteriorate when exposed to the atmosphere, it will be in bad shape by the time it reaches the consumer— stacked, tossed, and carted several times, each operation subjecting it to pressures that could damage it beyond use—unless it has been carefully protected by packaging.

Handling

A related packaging function is to facilitate physical handling of the product. It is almost impossible to physically handle light bulbs, for example, unless they have been placed in a package. Physical handling involves the manual operations of lifting, moving, stacking, and so on. These functions may be performed many times with the typical product as it moves from the factory to the consumer.

Packaging is therefore a key factor to consider in evaluating the total cost of physical distribution.[1] A high-cost solution to the packaging problem may be justified if this permits the reduction of other costs such as handling and product damage. On the other hand, the use of premium-priced transportation, such as air freight, may be justified by the

[1]For an excellent discussion of the concept of total distribution cost (which specifically considers the interaction among cost elements), see John F. Magee, *Physical Distribution Systems* (New York: McGraw-Hill Book Co., Inc., 1967).

more careful handling and the lower costs of product damage which, in turn, permit a lower-cost solution to the packaging problem.

Dispensing

When the product finally reaches the hands of the consumer the most important function performed by the package is to permit the easy use of the product. There is nothing more frustrating than the package that will not open or that results in injury to the user—such as metal staples that jab or edges that cut. Likewise, it can be annoying to find a package which requires hours of practice before it can be used without spilling. For some forms of packaging, an important consideration is the amount of the product dispensed at one time. (The all-or-nothing catsup bottle has become legendary in this respect.)

Many food and beverage products are sold in packages which serve as the container from which the product is physically consumed. Examples include individual portion ice cream products, beer in bottles and cans, and TV dinners. Other packages are intended to facilitate the cooking of the product, such as frozen vegetables to be boiled in a plastic bag (and permitting the addition of special sauces to the product) and pastry products that can be heated in their foil containers.

In all of these functions—containing, protecting, handling, and dispensing—the package is an extension of the product itself. These functions therefore do not relate directly to the communication dimension of the marketing strategy. They are more appropriately considered as part of the product policy and strategy (or of distribution strategy) because of their direct contribution to product form utility.

From another vantage point, packaging can in some instances be considered as part of the pricing strategy of the firm. When premiums are included in the package, or when coupons are printed on the package, or when multiple units are packaged together, or when extra-large package sizes are used, the company is really considering packaging as a pricing weapon by adjusting the relationship between quantity (or total unit value measured in some other terms) and price paid. While there is a definite relationship to marketing communication strategy, these two strategic considerations can be defined and analyzed separately.

Product Identification

In addition to all of the functions defined so far, the package (including the physical container, the label, and the brand name) serves to identify the product. This is a communication function. These visual elements serve to distinguish this product from other products and they convey to potential customers an impression of what the product is, what it does, and what it means. Such identification provides a basis for the development of consumer preference. It is these uses which we shall concentrate upon in this chapter—packaging, branding, and labeling as communication.[2]

SYMBOLISM IN PACKAGES AND BRANDS

In basic communication terms, packages and brands serve as *symbols*. It will be recalled from Chapter 3 that symbols are any objects in the environment used by the communicator to convey meaning—information, ideas, emotions, etc. Symbols are most commonly words and pictures, but they may also include physical objects (such as the package), gestures, and more subtle cultural variables. Symbols take on meaning through association, and the process by which such associations are formed in very complex and tends to be closely related to basic cultural influences. Shapes, textures, and other dimensions of packages have meanings that reflect basic attitudes of the society toward these dimensions. Another view of the symbolic meaning of packaging can be gained by considering how different cultures have different tastes in such related design areas as architecture, art, and the styling of household items such as furniture and pottery.

Design

Design is that complex combination of shapes, colors, textures, and the relationship among these elements as they define a given object. Professional designers have a well-developed ability to create designs to fulfill particular functions. Like other creative consultants, package designers are problem solvers. The selection of shapes, colors, materials, pictures, copy, and other variables to define a package to perform a stated communication function is a task requiring the highest order of creative ability.

In 1965, the United States Trade Center in London, England, was the site for a display of several product and package designs that were judged by a committee of professional designers to have exceptional merit. These designs were reproduced in a booklet entitled *Design USA*. The exhibit was sponsored by the United States Department of Commerce in cooperation with the Industrial Designers Society of America and the Package Designers Council. Figure 23–1 presents several examples of packages that were included in the selection.

---

[2]For an expanded discussion of all of the functions performed by packaging in the marketing mix, see Leonard M. Guss, *Packaging IS Marketing* (New York: American Management Association, 1967).

Courtesy of Donald Deskey Associates, Inc.

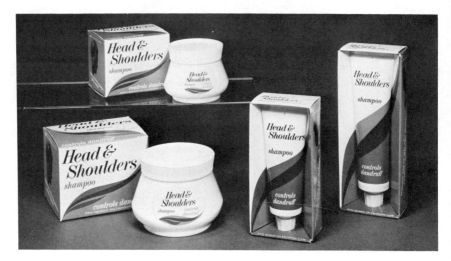

Courtesy of Walter Dorwin Teague Associates, Inc.

Fig. 23–1. Packages judged to have outstanding design.

Courtesy of Walter Landor & Associates, Inc.

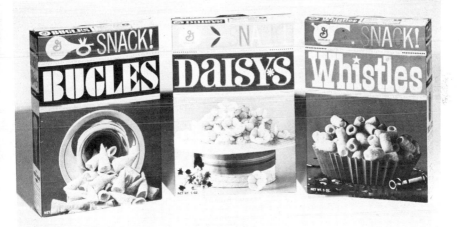

Courtesy of Ruder, Finn & Fujita, Inc.

Fig. 23–1. Continued.

587

These packages are distinctive and convey a constellation of meanings and feelings about the product. The General Mills snack food packages not only picture the product but also convey the idea that these products are associated with fun activities. They relate product shape to product name in a creative way and tell the potential customer what the product is. They also define the products as coming from General Mills, identified by the script *G* in the left-hand corner. The Head and Shoulders packages are interesting because they show both *primary* packaging (actually containing the product) and *secondary* packaging (to facilitate display and handling). The plastic tube (the primary package) is designed to permit safe use in the shower, and its design is effectively integrated with that of the cardboard box (the secondary package) in a distinctive way—by standing the tube on its head—to attract attention to the product. The shape of the Micrin bottle is reminiscent of old apothecary bottles and can be associated with the healthful purpose for which the product is intended while at the same time showing the distinctive blue color of the product itself. The Spice Islands wine vinegar bottles are highly pleasing, aesthetically, and convey a gourmet impression about the product, partly because of the similarity to an actual wine bottle and the interesting display of tarragon within the bottle itself. These examples are chosen only because they illustrate how various aspects of the package convey meaning about the product while at the same time representing a high level of creative accomplishment.

Design conveys meaning by its physical attributes. Through the subtle working of cultural influences, persons develop psychological associations with such physical dimensions of packages as color, shape, and materials. Color conveys meaning in several ways. White, for example, is associated with such attributes as purity, cleanliness, and coldness while red is warm, harsh, and exciting. Shapes also evoke a constellation of meanings. A spherical shape has connotations of softness and femininity while pyramids are more masculine, strong, and aggressive. Materials also arouse feelings, such as the association of metal with the attributes of strength, coldness, brittleness, and durability. Plastics might be associated with such feelings as newness, lightness, and cleanliness.[3]

Imagery

The physical attributes of a package, as defined by its design, convey meaning through the association of physical properties with particular feelings. Packages also convey meaning in another way, through the dimension of imagery. While "imagery" is difficult to define satisfacto-

[3]Burleigh B. Gardner, "The Package As A Communication," in M. S. Moyer and R. E. Vosburgh (eds.), *Marketing for Tomorrow . . . Today* (Chicago: American Marketing Association, 1967), pp. 117–8.

rily, it is used here to specifically mean the attribution of meaning to a package and a brand name through the use of mass and personal communications. While design is an important dimension of the physical package, imagery is an important psychological dimension more associated with the brand name than with the package itself. A name such as KODAK or YUBAN or COKE has no particular meaning until it is given that meaning by other communications and, over time, acquires a constellation of meanings that represent the individual's summary evaluation of all information he has received about that symbol.

Consumer research is usually necessary to determine the meanings which persons do, in fact, attribute to particular designs and brand names. Our understanding of these processes is not sufficiently developed to permit prediction of the meanings people will assign to packages and brands. Rather, the designs must be tested by asking people to state the associations which come to mind. These associations will change over time as people become exposed to more and different stimuli concerning the brand, and therefore it is desirable to run periodic checks on brand image.

COMMUNICATION FUNCTIONS OF PACKAGING

There are several specific functions performed by the package (and its label) as a method of communication. As with other forms of communication, the objective of packaging is to create awareness of the product, develop favorable attitudes, stimulate buying action, contribute to successful product use, and to create a satisfied customer. Packaging makes its contribution to the accomplishment of this objective in several distinct ways.

Attract Attention

For products sold through mass merchandising techniques and specifically for products sold in supermarkets and similar retail outlets, the package must perform the communication function in the store. It is a substitute for personal selling in this sense. With the typical supermarket stocking something like 10,000 separate items, the marketing communication strategist has the important assignment of making his product stand out in the crowd. Before any other communication functions can be achieved, the customer must be made aware of the product. The package (as part of a display on the shelf) must perform the essential function of attracting the customer's attention.

There are two aspects of this task of attracting attention. The first is simply the perceptual problem of obtaining sufficient impact upon the potential customer's senses to actually register an impression. Effective use of color, shape, and other design variables can contribute to the attention-getting ability of the package. The second aspect of attention is that of identifying the product by relating it to previous information. When the package comes into the consumer's perceptual field there is no guarantee that she will correctly identify it as Brand X and associate it with impressions and information gained from advertising and so on.

The problem of attracting attention is therefore one of making a perceptual impact and facilitating positive associations. Packages must be tested for their ability to perform these functions by actual in-store tests. A serious evaluation of the actual store conditions to be encountered in displaying the product should be an important part of the package design process.

Provide Distinctiveness

The sharpness and accuracy of the consumer's perception of the product are a function of the extent to which the package distinguishes the product from its competitors and from other items in the company's product line. The package can also provide distinctiveness by relating it to a specific company and its product line. These are all dimensions of the basic function of providing product identification.

An example of the factors considered in developing packages that provide distinctiveness for the product has been reported by the Merchandising and Sales Promotion Manager of Kitchens of Sara Lee. He defined the role of packaging in the introduction of a new line of frozen baked goods as including the following functions: (1) to convey a strong brand image; (2) to give a connotation of the finest quality; (3) to illustrate the product; (4) to provide appetite appeal; (5) to differentiate products in the line from each other; (6) to avoid confusion for both the consumer and the retail stock clerk who must maintain the display.[4] Each of these functions is a part of the general problem of providing product distinctiveness.

As pointed out in the previous two chapters, the competitive battle is ultimately decided in the retail store when the consumer encounters the range of alternatives on the store shelf. Some writers dramatize this fact by referring to "the moment of truth" when the housewife stops in front of the product display and reaches out to choose among the alternatives available to her. Even if she is aware of the brand and has favorable attitudes toward it, even if the reseller has carefully stocked it on the

---

[4]Charles R. Patton, "Design for Management or Marketing?" in Frederick E. Webster, Jr. (ed.), *New Directions in Marketing* (Chicago: American Marketing Association, 1965), pp. 221–27.

shelf, and even if the package actually announces a special buying incentive, she still may not buy it if she cannot find it or does not recognize it on the shelf.

Influence Attitudes

The package can contribute significantly to the consumer's attitudes toward the product. As indicated in the discussion of design, physical attributes of the package can be an important source of meaning assigned to the product itself. The package can evoke feelings that actually determine the purchase decision.

In addition to the physical design of the package, other elements such as the label, including the brand name or trademark, can likewise influence attitudes. The predispositions toward various brands which the consumer has upon entering the retail store may be altered when she actually inspects the products on the shelf. Sales promotions and deals announced on the label can influence predispositions, or they can stimulate buying action without any significant influence on attitudes in the short term. Information on the label concerning product ingredients, method of preparation, number of servings, suggested product uses, and so on can make a major contribution to the consumer's attitudes toward the brand.

Facilitate Display

Some packages are easier to display and more effectively displayed than others. It is important to remember that the consumer will not view the product in single units but will be exposed to multiple product facings on the shelf in close proximity to competitors' offerings. The consumer will not see one tube of Colgate toothpaste and judge it on that basis. Rather, she may see as many as ten or twelve facings, each consisting of a stack of five or ten tubes. The other brands of toothpaste will surround it on either side. A package viewed in isolation may take on quite different appearance from that same package when viewed in multiples of as many as 50 to 100. The pattern (or "Gestalt") formed by the total display is the important dimension to consider, not the individual package unit. Figure 23-2 illustrates a package that was judged to be of exceptional merit for display purposes.

Requirements for effective display may conflict with the objective of creating a unique, attention getting package. Distinctive designs are often not symmetrical and "boxlike" to the extent desired for purposes of stacking the product on the retail shelf. Odd shapes and sizes may create so many stocking difficulties that the retailer eventually takes the product off the shelf altogether.

Fig. 23–2. Package design that facilitates effective display. (Courtesy of Robert Zeidman Associates, Inc.)

Inform and Educate

The package may have an important function to perform in informing and educating persons about the nature of the product and its intended uses. These functions may be the matter of strict legal control by the Food and Drug Administration and several other governmental agencies. These are communication functions of major importance for pharmaceutical products, or proprietary drugs, for example. A prescription drug may be sold in a package which indicates very clearly the conditions under which the drug is to be used for treatment including the indications which it is designed to treat, the dosage, method of application, and conditions under which it should not be used. It may also indicate significant side effects that should be watched for and may prescribe antidotes for improper use.

For many products, instructing the consumer as to the proper use of the product is a significant communication problem for, if proper conditions are not followed, the result may be unsatisfactory product performance. Products which must be cooked, for example, or which must be mixed together, require a clear and precise statement of instructions.

Paint and varnish containers may provide instruction on the label as to proper methods of surface preparation, necessary atmospheric conditions, and methods of application. Marketers who fail to provide customers with the best information on how to obtain maximum benefit from use of the product are courting potential marketing disaster from improper usage and dissatisfied customers generating unfavorable word-of-mouth.

Ingredients of the product are in many cases required to be clearly stated on the label as a matter of law. To illustrate, the addition of artificial sweeteners must be clearly announced. Likewise, there are now strict regulations concerning the statement of the amount of product contained in the package. Information about ingredients can be especially important for persons who are allergic to specific ingredients such as eggs or wheat germ. Other persons may simply want to know such information as the basis for their buying decision because of the greater security they feel from having such information. A statement of ingredients can also help the customer to understand what the product is and how it will be used.

Each of these communication functions—attracting attention, providing distinctiveness, influencing attitudes, facilitating display, and informing and educating—must be carefully considered in designing a new package. A statement of the packaging requirements that emerge from an analysis of these functions should provide the set of directions to be given to the design consultant or other creative talent used in developing a new package.

BRANDS AND TRADEMARKS

So far, our attention has been concentrated on the package itself, the physical container that holds the product, as a communication device. The *brand* is a nonphysical entity, often with no inherent meaning, used to symbolize the product. More formally, a brand is "a word, mark, symbol, design, term, or a combination of these, both visual and oral, used for the purpose of identification of some product or service."[5] The function of a brand is to distinguish the product from competitors and to associate it with a company and its line of products. Examples of famous brands in the United States (and in other countries in most cases) include Marlboro cigarettes, Botany men's clothing, Scotch cellophane tape, Bayer aspirin, and Gillette razor blades. Figure 23–3 presents several brands that are symbols and designs rather than only words.

[5]Albert Wesley Frey (ed.), *Marketing Handbook,* 2nd ed. (New York: Ronald Press Company, 1965), Section 6 by Robert I. Goldberg, "Packaging," p. 36.

Fig. 23–3. Some well-known brand symbols.

Some brand names become so well known that they serve as generic names for a whole category of products. For example, "Kleenex" (a registered brand name of the Kimberly Clark Company) is often used as synonymous with facial tissues. In many countries, a "Gillette" (Gillette Safety Razor Company) is the word used for a razor blade. "Coke" (Coca Cola Company) is sometimes used to refer to any cola drink. In each case where this generic use occurs, the company owning the brand name may take steps to remove the brand from such generic use, since it has lost the distinguishing ability which is the basic purpose of branding. Examples of generic names that were once registered trademarks include cellophane, escalator, aspirin, and linoleum. Brand names that have been protected from threatened generic use include "Band Aid" (Johnson & Johnson) and "Orlon" (duPont).[6]

Strictly speaking, a trademark is distinct from a brand, although they are used in many cases to mean the same thing. "Trademark" is a *legal* term for symbols of product identification. A trademark is registered as the property of the company that uses the word or other symbol to identify its products and services. A trademark must have some distinctive characteristic such as a symbol or design or lettering that distinguishes it from a simple English word. For example, it would be impossible to register the word "auto" or "peanuts" as a trademark. Under the Lanham Act, trademarks are registered when the product is shipped in interstate or foreign commerce. It is usually advisable to formally register a trademark with the federal government. The term of such registration is for twenty years and is renewable every twenty years thereafter.[7]

Functions of Branding

The advantages of branding are relatively obvious. The brand permits product identification, differentiation, and distinctiveness. Branding takes the product out of pure competition and permits the development of loyal customers who will purchase on a repeat basis. The product is no longer a simple commodity but has an identity of its own, a distinctiveness which gives the marketer some degree of control over the product. Brands with established reputations can often obtain higher prices in the market place because of added customer trust and confidence.

But there are also disadvantages which are not always so obvious. The simple act of branding a product is of little significance unless the marketer is also willing to invest substantial amounts of promotional effort in creation of brand identity and image. Furthermore, the marketer is now held responsible for the product. If the product fails to meet the customer's expectations, the customer may communicate that fact to the marketer who is now clearly identified with the product. Wishing to protect his promotional investment in the brand name, he may feel it expeditious, if not necessary, to commit company resources to the pacification of the dissatisfied customer, whether the dissatisfaction is his "fault" or not.

There are several factors to consider in the selection of brand names. The most important is to make sure that the brand name has not been used by another product and is, in fact, legally available for use on the

[6]*Ibid.*, p. 40.
[7]*Ibid.*, p. 37.

new product. The brand should also have some relationship to the product and should be consistent with the "image" that is intended for the product. Characteristics of effective brand names include brevity, readability, memorability, and general appropriateness and connotations. These may at times be conflicting objectives; "Head & Shoulders" is not brief, but it has appropriate connotations for a dandruff-controlling shampoo, it is readable, and it is memorable.

Family Brands

Family brands are brand names (or trademarks) that are applied to several products to give a complete product line. Examples of family brands include Birdseye frozen foods, General Electric appliances, Kodak cameras, and Jantzen sportswear. There is assumed to be a prestige value in this broad product line identification.

Family brands permit several advantages including greater shelf impact, sometimes called the "billboard effect," from having many products displayed side by side. New products can be introduced without significant investment in developing brand name awareness. The brand "image" can be transferred reasonably quickly to the new product through its association with other items in the line.

A possible disadvantage of family branding is the lack of distinctiveness for the individual product. There is also the danger that certain new product entries may be perceived by the consumer as inconsistent with the rest of the brand. Most importantly, a major failure for a new product can badly tarnish the image of the family brand name. The prestige value of the family brand can be diminished considerably and consumer attitudes toward the whole line can be shifted significantly by bad experience with one product in the line.

Brand Image

Over time, the brand takes on a set of meanings that are distinct from the physical product, although the product itself is an important contributor to the brand image. Other sources of inputs to the consumer's perception of brand image include mass communications (both messages and the association with particular media), word-of-mouth about the brand, impressions of retail outlets, and impressions of the company that sells the brand.

There is obviously an important interaction between media advertising and brand image. Continuity of advertising over time can provide the necessary basis for the slow, reasoned development of a brand image according to a stated set of objectives. In contrast, constantly shifting advertising campaigns can result in an indistinct brand image. The sum total of shifting impressions received by the consumer can lead to a general lack of sharpness for the brand in the consumer's perceptions. For the development of a coherent brand image, it is necessary to consciously and carefully plan the communication strategy that will lead to the necessary associations of specific desired attributes with the product in the consumer's mind. The package is a major source of cues relating to the basic personality of the brand, as perceived by the consumer.

The relationship between the package, the brand, and the mass communication strategy of the firm is a direct one. To understand the development of brand image, it is helpful to consider the relationship between branding, packaging, and the mass communication.

RELATIONSHIP TO MASS COMMUNICATION

Without branding, it would be impossible to have mass communication in the firm's marketing strategy. If there were no brand name, no unique identification of the manufacturer's product and differentiation of it from competitor's products, then there would literally be nothing to talk about. (This statement is not true for industry promotional efforts; there is no need for an identifiable brand in order to promote such commodities as milk, cigars, or railroad services as generic product and service classes.) If the objective of marketing communication strategy is defined as the creation of preference for the company's products and services, then it is obvious that an identifiable brand name is the *sine qua non* of effective marketing communication strategy.

Advertisements Featuring the Package

For some products, the package itself is the most logical central element to show in any print advertising. Deodorants, motor oil, and sugar are examples of products that must be shown in their package to have any significant identification and meaning for the consumer. Other products depend upon packaging and the distinctiveness of the brand name to differentiate the product from that of competitors. Scotch whisky shown in a goblet does not give any cues as to the distinctive features of the brand. Rather, the package must be shown before the product can have any identity of its own. Figures 23–4 and 23–5 show two examples of advertising that features the package as the dominant item in the advertisement.

Advertisements To Aid Product Recognition

One task that can usefully be assigned to media advertising is to provide the potential buyer with sufficient information to permit identifica-

Whenever we start to show our age, we do a little face lifting. Isn't that just like a woman?

No salt salts like Morton Salt salts.

Fig. 23–4. An advertisement featuring a package change. (Courtesy of Morton Salt Company; a Division of Morton International, Inc.; Needham, Harper & Steers, Inc.)

Fig. 23–5. An advertisement featuring a gift package. (Courtesy of 21 Brands, Inc.; Cunningham & Walsh, Inc.)

tion of the product on the retail shelf. This can be an especially significant consideration for new products which the consumer has not previously seen or purchased. If the consumer is made aware of the product, develops some favorable attitudes toward it, and becomes interested in trying the product, she must of necessity know what to look for when she goes shopping. Figure 23–6 shows an advertisement that prominently features the package and would permit the consumer to identify it on the retail shelf. Notice that the package is distinctive in several respects, including typeface and the white-on-black printing technique, facilitating product identification and recognition.

Featuring Advertising on the Package

Just as it makes sense to show the package in the company's advertising, it may also make sense to use elements from the advertising campaign on the package itself. One packaging expert has expressed this argument as follows:

. . . a simple selling message or visual device taken from the advertising and integrated with the package design does not interfere with the universally recognized symbol of the product.

Advertisers spend vast sums to develop basic concepts and themes, yet all too infrequently do these concepts and themes appear on the package. Of course, a short-term advertising theme which is soon to be abandoned should *not* appear on the package. But a long-term concept in which millions of dollars are invested should, wherever possible, be made a feature of the package.[8]

Featuring the central advertising copy theme on the package would permit the clear transfer of advertising impact to the point-of-purchase situation. It would facilitate product identification as well as association of brand image with the actual product.

Advertising and Image Building

The brand image is the sum total of feelings, attitudes, and ideas which the consumer comes to associate with a brand name. These associations are formed through exposure to mass communication as well as through exposure to the product itself and to word-of-mouth communication about the product. Mass communication is the principal tool which the marketing strategist has for developing the image he wishes his product to have.

Every brand acquires an image. Whether that image is good or bad does not only reflect the basic attributes of the product and the package

[8]Eugene S. Mahany, "Advertising and Packaging—The Agency Role in the Relationship," in American Management Association, *Consumer-Oriented Packaging* (New York: Packaging Division, The Association, 1967), AMA Management Bulletin No. 106, pp. 5–13, at pp. 11–12.

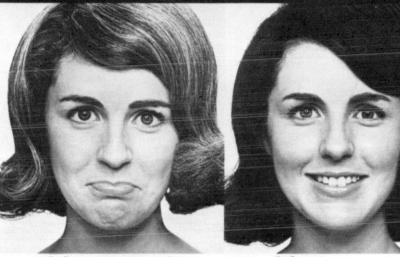

Tecnique just gave Bill Crossan a new improved wife.

(Bill Crossan's old gray-haired wife.)   (Bill Crossan's new brunette wife.)

Tecnique Shampoo-In covers twice the gray as the leading color lotion for gray.

Adds a gentle touch of color to all your hair.

Tecnique* covers twice the gray. And lets you go a little blonder, darker, or accent your own shade. Something the leading color lotion for gray simply cannot do!

Tecnique's 12 shampoo-in colors last longer too. Long after the leading color lotion has faded, Tecnique still gives radiant color and body. Just shampoo-in when your hair grows out.

Give your husband a new, improved wife with Tecnique. You may get a new, improved husband.

Fig. 23–6. An advertisement to aid recognition. (Courtesy of Shulton, Inc.; Compton Advertising, Inc.)

itself. The brand image also reflects the planning and execution of a mass communication strategy designed to convey the desired meanings for the brand. In this respect, a brand image is similar to word-of-mouth—every product has it. It may be positive or negative. Given that it is going to occur, it is necessary to take steps to insure that it develops to the greatest advantage to the marketer.

A concern with brand image development should be reflected at several stages in the development of advertising strategy including:

1. The selection of basic selling appeals to convey the subtle shadings of meaning that will give the brand the desired position in the consumer's perceptions.
2. The use of advertising techniques—color, illustration, typefaces, etc.—that contribute to the desired impression.
3. Avoiding the use of short-term buying incentives which convey meanings that conflict with the desired brand image. Frequent dealing is inconsistent with a desire to achieve a quality brand image, for example.
4. A striving for continuity in campaign elements to permit the development of a consistent and distinct brand image over time.
5. The selection of advertising media that enhance the qualities of the product that are thought to be most significant to potential buyers—quality or economy or youth, for example. This is the question of the qualitative values of advertising media.
6. The design of evaluation studies to measure shifts in brand image as well as other more direct measures of communication effectiveness.

When considerations of brand image are brought to the forefront, it can be seen that it is important to take a long-term view of the function of advertising. In addition to the purpose of creating awareness and reaching the maximum number of potential customers with effective messages, it is likewise important to think of an individual advertisement as "a contribution to the complex symbol which is the brand image—as part of the long-term investment in the reputation of the brand."[9]

SUMMARY

The package and the brand are elements of the marketing communication strategy (as well as elements of product strategy) because they identify the product and convey meanings about it. Packages convey meaning because of their design and physical properties while brands convey meaning through more subtle associations in the consumer's mind created over time by mass communication, word-of-mouth, experi-

[9]Burleigh B. Gardner and Sidney J. Levy, "The Product and the Brand," *Harvard Business Review*, 33 (March–April 1955), pp. 33–39, at p. 39.

ence with the product, and other sources of information about the brand.

The package and the brand are in one sense substitutes for the salesman at the retail level. When the consumer finally enters the retail store, the package (and related display variables) has several functions to perform including attracting attention, providing product distinctiveness, influencing attitudes, and informing the consumer as to appropriate use, product ingredients, and other information necessary to a wise purchase decision.

Branding is more "symbolic" in nature than packaging. The brand distinguishes the product from its competitors and removes the product from pure competition as a simple commodity. The brand itself has no meaning except as assigned to it by advertising and other sources of information about the product. Over time, there evolves a brand image that is the constellation of attitudes, feelings, and ideas that the brand evokes in the mind of the consumer. Brand images develop slowly and can to a significant extent be controlled by a careful planning of advertising activity to achieve the necessary position in the consumer's perceptions.

Just as products and brands have a unique identity or image, so do companies. In the next chapter, we shall examine the communication activities of corporate advertising, public relations, and publicity as contributors to corporate image. Included in our analysis will be the topic of corporate identity symbols, which are very similar to brands. We shall also consider the impact of corporate image upon other elements of the total marketing communication program.

24

Corporate Advertising, Public Relations, and Publicity

In addition to communication efforts designed to promote sales of products and services offered by the company, there is another set of communication activities that have a longer-term objective. This longer-term objective is to promote the identity and reputation of the company. Company identity and reputation, or "corporate image," objectives are not just ends in themselves, however. A strong corporate image has many benefits for the company including, but not limited to, the promotion of its products and services. Corporate advertising, public relations, and publicity activities cannot be evaluated by examining short-term changes in levels of awareness and attitudes toward products and brands. Over the long run, however, these activities contribute to the company's profit and revenue objectives.

CORPORATE IMAGE

The central concept in this area of the marketing communication program is that of the corporate image. Corporate image can be defined as the identity and reputation of the corporation (or, more generally, the company) in the minds of the various publics whose attitudes are important to the company—customers, employees, stockholders, suppliers, community officials, etc. The corporate image is only one of three images that may be important to the company. For strategic decisions about individual products and brands, product and brand image may also be important and each of these three kinds of "image" is distinct from the others.

The concept of the corporate image is not complex or difficult to understand. It can be thought of simply as the "personality" that the company has created in the minds of its various publics. Notice that it is a subjective concept, and that different publics may hold different images. Suppliers may view the company in a fundamentally different light than customers or investors, for example.

There are many aspects of corporate advertising, public relations, and publicity that are not directly related to marketing communication strategy. These will be defined more precisely in a moment, but here it can be noted that such objectives as attracting employees and capital are legitimate objectives for corporate advertising and public relations but they are not part of marketing communication, strictly speaking, which implies a more immediate concern with the generation of profitable revenue. Over the longer-run, however, these objectives also contribute to the generation of profitable revenue and to the definition of the corporate image. And the corporate image *is* important to marketing communication strategy in the sense that *all marketing communications both contribute to and are interpreted in the context of the corporate image.* The corporate image is therefore an important element to consider in the total marketing communication strategy.

Organizationally, the marketing department is usually responsible for corporate advertising and public relations activities. There are three major reasons. First, most of the tools and skills necessary for the successful planning and implementation of a corporate advertising and public relations program are within the expertise of the marketing department and, more specifically, the marketing communication strategist. Second, marketing objectives *are* an important part of the total corporate advertising and public relations activity. Third, normal marketing communication activities—media advertising, personal selling, reseller strategy, sales promotion, packaging, and branding—are a major contributor to the overall corporate image.

Sources of Corporate Image

Any object, person, activity, or piece of information relating to the corporation and the conduct of its affairs is a potential contributor to the individual's perceptions of the corporation. To take a specific example, the image of the Radio Corporation of America may reflect the following factors:

1. Exposure to RCA's advertising, including the media in which it has been placed, copy, and illustrations, including personalities used in the advertising.
2. An awareness of the fact that RCA is the parent of the National Broadcasting Company and subsequent evaluations of NBC radio and television programming that contribute to an evaluation of RCA in total.
3. Public statements of officers of RCA, including testimony before governmental agencies, announcements to the financial community, and so on.
4. Exposure to local RCA dealers, including their window displays, visits into the store, the local dealer's reputation for service and honesty, and the local dealer's advertising.
5. Word-of-mouth concerning RCA products from friends and neighbors who own them.
6. Actual experience with RCA products in the home and in public places such as hotels, both at home and abroad.
7. Association of RCA with the trade name Victrola and the famous brand symbol of the dog listening to "his master's voice."
8. Exposure to contests and premium offers by oil companies and other marketers featuring RCA appliances.
9. Acquaintance with persons who work for the Radio Corporation of America in various capacities—including salesmen, engineers, clerical personnel, etc.
10. Use of RCA computers and input-output devices.

This list is intended to be only illustrative of the kinds of information that can contribute to a person's image of a corporation. There are certainly other sources of information that could be added to this list. The point is that virtually *any* piece of information can contribute to the total impression of a company; each new impression creates some increment in the total impression.

The concept of corporate image is an important application of the principles of Gestalt psychology. It will be remembered from our discussion of the Gestaltist school of perception in Chapter 11 that there is a basic perceptual tendency to form a whole out of the various stimuli to which one is exposed. The perceiver will actually force structure and completeness upon a set of stimuli. It is this basic process which seems to be at work in the development of a corporate image.

The corporate image is shared by a large proportion of the total public. Said differently, although image is a subjective phenomenon, it is also a generalized phenomenon in that a sample of persons will show important similarities in their judgments of the total corporate personality. The image is not formed on the basis of facts per se but on the basis of subjective evaluations and impressions of facts about the company as they are received from these various sources.

Source Credibility

The concept of corporate image is very similar to that of source credibility in the specific case where the source is the company. As noted in Chapter 8, trustworthiness and expertise are the two major dimensions to credibility. In the specific case of selling companies, credibility may be thought of as a combination of technical capability and reputation for consistent quality. A corporation striving to become more "credible" is essentially trying to improve its image.

Source credibility is an important determinant of response to communication because it provides the *context* within which all marketing communications are interpreted. Consideration of the dimension of credibility suggests the importance of a sharp and favorable corporate image as the basic building block for an effective marketing communication strategy. In Gestalt terms, the corporate image is the background against which the potential customer evaluates informational cues received from advertising, sales personnel, the package, and other elements of the communication program. A strong, favorable image can improve the effectiveness of the company's selling and advertising efforts and can be an important source of strength for resellers. A poor, weak company image can retard and even destroy the effectiveness of the other elements of the marketing communication strategy.

Measurement

Corporate image can be measured and such measurements are a necessary informational input to the development of a corporate advertising and public relations strategy. Most standard methods of attitude measurement can be applied to the specific problem of assessing corporate image. Survey techniques are commonly used. A probability sample of respondents is drawn from the potential audience and any of several techniques may be used to collect the data required. Among the more common data-collection procedures are these: asking respondents to name and rank-order the companies they know in a particular industry; asking respondents to match a list of adjectives to a list of companies; sentence-completion and word-association measures; and various attitude-scaling techniques, such as the semantic differential and Likert scaling (which measures the strength of a respondent's agreement with a particular statement).

Many other techniques of attitude measurement can be applied to the problem of measuring corporate image.[1] One author has recommended that the tendency to ask respondents to indicate the "ideal" corporation as a point of comparison should be avoided because it can produce spurious results. The ideal company is too abstract a concept to be reliable and not all of the characteristics cited will be equally important. The trick is to find which of several characteristics of top-ranked companies differentiate them from companies with poor images. A technique for making this kind of comparison was suggested by Cohen.[2]

Such measurements can suggest the extent to which the corporate image is either helping or hurting the effectiveness of specific elements of the marketing communication program. They can suggest the need for additional investment in corporate advertising, public relations, and publicity, and they can suggest the specific tasks to be assigned to these communication activities. The dimensions that need strengthening, or the impressions in consumers' minds that need to be corrected or modified, or the need to sharpen a particular attribute can be suggested rather specifically by these data.

It is important to remember that oftentimes simply changing the communication is not enough. A poor image may reflect not only inadequate communication activity but also basic inadequacies in the products and services of the company. These basic weaknesses must be corrected before communication designed to improve the corporate image will be successful. For example, an airline that has a poor image and is characterized as having careless baggage handling, poor on-time flight performance, and inadequate in-flight service cannot change its image without first improving baggage handling, on-time performance, and in-flight service. Then communication to persuade potential customers that these defects have been corrected can be effective.

Corporate Identity Symbols

Recalling an earlier distinction between identity and reputation as the two dimensions of image, symbols and names are used to create a distinctive identity for the company. Identity is simply a recognition of the company as a distinct entity and differentiated from other companies whereas reputation includes all of the qualitative attributes associated with that entity. Corporate identity symbols are devices—words, pic-

[1]Charles Winick, "How To Find Out What Kind of Image You Have," in Lee H. Bristol, Jr. (ed.), *Developing the Corporate Image* (New York: Charles Scribner's Sons, 1960), pp. 23–37.

[2]Louis Cohen, "The Differentiation Ratio in Corporate Image Research," *Journal of Advertising Research*, 7 (September 1967), pp. 32–36.

tures, sounds, and so on—which uniquely identify the individual company.

Corporate identity symbols have several uses. They serve to identify all products marketed by the company, whether or not they are identified by the same brand name. Corporate symbols are used in advertising to clearly signify the sponsor of the advertising. Company trucks may carry the symbol, as may employee uniforms, stationery, and buildings. Figure 24–1 illustrates several well-known corporate identity symbols. Notice that some of these corporate symbols are also brands, but not all are.

Fig. 24–1. Well-known corporate identity symbols.

Like any other symbol, over time the corporate symbol acquires a constellation of meanings that are evoked whenever the symbol stimulus is perceived. The corporate symbol thus becomes a kind of shorthand for all of the impressions that the perceiver has about the company.

In recent years, there has been a flourish of activity in the development of new company names and symbols. A major reason for this has been the rash of mergers which has characterized American industry, as well as the diversification of companies into many new lines of business with the result that they have outgrown their old names and images. For example, The Rexall Drug and Chemical Company was for years identified more or less exclusively by its retail drugstore operations. With company expansion into increasingly diverse fields of endeavor, the old corporate name and old corporate identity become increasingly constraining. As a result, the name of the company was finally changed (Mr. Justin Dart was chief executive officer at the time) in 1969 to Dart Industries, as indicated in the advertisement in Figure 24–2. A similar

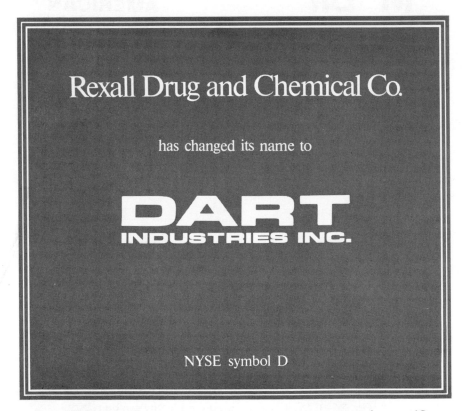

Fig. 24–2. An advertisement announcing company name change. (Courtesy of Dart Industries; Batten, Barton, Durstine & Osborn, Inc.)

step was taken by the Union Tank Car Company in changing its name to Trans Union Corporation, as announced in the ad in Figure 24–3, and in developing a new corporate symbol.

In Figures 24–4 and 24–5, advertisements announce the new corporate symbol without any change in name. These two advertisements are interesting in that they also indicate the reasons for the name and symbol changes.

Corporate identity symbols have no particular value unless they are actively promoted and are associated with specific attributes through company advertising and other activities designed to make the symbol familiar to the public. The symbol takes on meaning over time as people are exposed to information about the company and have either direct or indirect contact with the company, its products and services, and its dealings. Some corporate symbols become trademarks and are used to promote the products of the company. Two examples are the "Big G" for General Mills products and the GF identification mark used by General Foods on its products. The marketing communication contribution of the corporate identity symbol, and reasons for devoting specific planning

From now on Union Tank Car will be known as Trans Union Corporation.

It'll be easier for all of us.

Trans Union is the new parent company of Union Tank. And it has everything going for it that Union Tank Car has.

It will direct the expanding Union Tank Car business plus the dozen or so companies that have grown up around our 77 year old leasing corporation. Our new name and structure make us more flexible. And easier for us to be stronger in all our areas of service. To say nothing of the fact it's going to be easier for you to watch us grow.

TRANSUNION**CORPORATION**

Fig. 24–3. This advertisement also states a change in company name. (Courtesy of Trans Union Corporation and Earle Ludgin & Co.)

MANUFACTURERS HANOVER CORPORATION

A new corporate symbol:

Manufacturers Hanover Corporation is the one-bank holding company whose subsidiary is Manufacturers Hanover Trust Company. The new corporate structure places the Bank in the best possible position to be more useful in more ways to its present and potential customers.

A new symbol for investors:

The listing of Manufacturers Hanover Corporation on the New York Stock Exchange enables the public to share more easily in the future of a great financial organization by providing a broader market for its securities.

MANUFACTURERS HANOVER CORPORATION

MANUFACTURERS HANOVER TRUST COMPANY
Subsidiary

Fig. 24—4. A new corporate symbol is the burden of this advertisement. (Courtesy of Manufacturers Hanover Trust Co.; Young & Rubicam, Inc.)

effort to corporate identification, have been stated by a consultant in the field as follows:

. . . in the supermarket, in the drugstore, in the catalogs of industrial products, every brand and every company are struggling to gain the awareness and understanding of the consumer. They are struggling against the rising costs of communicating, against the increased density of communications in the market. In that struggle, companies look desperately for visual and verbal

This symbol has a great future behind it.

North American Rockwell

We're a 2.6 billion dollar company, America's 28th largest. With more than 100,000 shareowners. Of our 110,000 employees, more than 15,000 are scientists and technicians. We play a major role in 19 different industries. Our plants, in 28 states, manufacture over 100 different product lines —everything from Apollo space-craft and textile machinery to

Rockwell-Standard automotive components, Hatteras fiberglass yachts, Aero Commander® aircraft and Sabreliner business jets. Few companies possess the technological and scientific know-how of North American Rockwell. And by drawing on this vast technological reserve and applying it to our product lines, as well as to the development of new

products, we'll continue to manage change. Instead of just letting it happen. You'll be seeing a lot more of our new symbol in the future. Watch for it. It'll grow on you. To find out more about us, write for your copy of our 1968 Annual Report. North American Rockwell, P.O. Box 707, El Segundo, California 90245.

Fig. 24–5. An advertisement announcing a new corporate symbol. (Courtesy of North American Rockwell; Batten, Barton, Durstine & Osborn, Inc.)

shorthand methods of making themselves known. Symptomatic of that struggle is the fact that we are creating new symbols, new trademarks, new corporate names, and new brand names at a faster rate than legal organizations can realistically assimilate them.[3]

The corporate identification program is an attempt to gain quick and accurate recognition and to arouse favorable predispositions in the chaotic swirl of communication activity in the marketplace. This need is well exemplified by the McGraw-Hill advertisement in Figure 24–6.

Relationship to Branding

Product and corporate identification are very similar in their objectives and methods. Products are identified by brand names and symbols and companies are identified by company names and symbols. Both sets of identifiers may be registered as trademarks. Many times, product and company identification are the same; examples such as IBM, GE, and Ford come to mind immediately.

The relationship between brands and company identification becomes a significant issue in the multiple division and multiple product firm. Company practices vary tremendously on this score. Some companies such as the Procter and Gamble Company permit individual brands to identify themselves with the company only for very brief introductory periods. The motivation here is to make each brand independent and to promote healthy, vigorous competition among company brand entries in the same product category (such as Gleem and Crest toothpastes). Other companies, such as General Mills, identify all brands with the corporate identity symbol (the "Big G") with the expectation that this will contribute to favorable attitudes and evaluations of each individual brand. (These symbols often are *logotypes*—the use of distinctive typeface or lettering to express the company's name.)

The corporate name and symbol can serve as an umbrella under which to introduce new products to the market. In this respect, the function of the corporate name is similar to that of the family brand, as discussed in the previous chapter. It can create a much higher level of initial market acceptance for a new brand, especially when the product is perceived as high risk. Ford Motor Company put its whole corporate identity behind the introduction of the Maverick in 1969, and potential customers evaluated the new car in the light of their previous impressions of Ford automobiles and, probably most specifically, the Mustang introduced in 1965. At the same time, potential customers knew that the

---

[3]Joseph M. Murtha, "Corporate Identification—Who Needs It?," in American Management Association, *Packaging Considerations for the Marketing Man* (New York: The Association, Packaging Division, 1966), Management Bulletin No. 85, pp. 6–10, at p. 7.

Fig. 24–6. An advertisement stressing the need for corporate identification. (Courtesy of McGraw-Hill Publications, a division of McGraw-Hill, Inc.)

Ford dealer and service organization was behind the new automobile. This provided assurance of dependable and available service as well as associating the new brand with recent themes in Ford advertising such as "Ford has a better idea" and "the going thing." As a result, Maverick as a distinct brand took important dimensions to its meaning from the whole host of associations which the market had formed for the Ford Motor Company. Similar factors operated in the introduction of the Ford Pinto in 1970.

Corporate identification can make a new brand more credible and can improve the effectiveness of brand-oriented communications. It can significantly reduce the amount of perceived risk in purchasing a new brand. At the same time, the new brand needs a distinct identity of its own, to differentiate it from other brands in the company's line and from competition. Distinctive brand images are a key part of the company's market segmentation strategy.

CORPORATE ADVERTISING

Corporate advertising is the use of mass media to develop awareness of, and favorable attitudes toward, a corporation. The media time or space used for the corporate campaign are purchased in the same manner as for product advertising. The advertisement will feature information about the corporation and its functions, however, and, in many cases, not specific products with the intention of generating favorable demand for those products.

For corporate advertising more so than for product advertising, the objectives are to influence predispositions more than to generate specific action. Corporate campaigns are intended to generate awareness and favorable attitudes so that over the longer term, various publics will respond more favorably to the corporation—as a marketer, as a supplier, as an employer, as a member of the local community, and so on. In many respects corporate advertising is a form of public relations, but it is distinct from other forms of public relations in that it makes use of the mass media.

Objectives

Several conditions may give rise to a set of specific objectives for a corporate advertising program, which is typically designed to fulfill a particular communication need. Periodic audits of the predispositions of various publics of importance to the company can provide important evidence of the need for a corporate campaign. Conditions that might indicate the need for a corporate campaign include the following:[4]

1. A corporate name change.
2. Mergers and acquisitions.
3. A changed marketing strategy with greater emphasis upon "pull through."
4. Salesman inefficiency.
5. Adverse publicity.
6. Labor recruitment problems.
7. Plans for the introduction of several new products.
8. Planned diversification.
9. Threats in the environment such as governmental actions or the possibility of an attempted takeover by another corporation.
10. Common markets served by multiple product divisions.
11. Need to attract additional capital.
12. Plans to enter new markets.
13. Significant inroads by new competitors.

Corporate campaigns are the most complex and demanding of all advertising for the reason that they have a much broader scope, are designed to reach a broader variety of publics, involve all aspects of the company, and have objectives that are more general and difficult to articulate and evaluate. All sources of information about the company, both those that the company controls and those that it does not, must be assessed for their role in contributing to the desired end result of a favorable image.

The chief executive of the company may inject himself into the planning and execution of the campaign, further complicating the life of the marketing communication strategist. It is quite appropriate for the chief executive to take this active interest because of the essential importance of the campaign to the welfare of the corporation in total. Most importantly, the problem of defining the objectives for a corporate campaign must be resolved by the chief executive officer. The key question in formulating a corporate campaign is "What does the company want to be known for?". This question gets right to the heart of the basic objectives and purpose of the firm and only top management can resolve that question. This is certainly one of the most important of all of the functions of the chief executive—developing corporate objectives and operating philosophy. It is not surprising that many corporate campaigns are built around the words of the chief executive.

[4]Paul Funk and John Frost, "The Corporate Campaign: Final Exam for the Adman," *Industrial Marketing*, 53 (November 1968), pp. 48–55.

Types of Campaigns

Although any categorization of corporate advertising campaigns must be rather arbitrary, it is useful to look at several different approaches to the execution of the corporate advertising task. From an appraisal of the communication needs facing the corporation and of the environment in which it is operating, a specific statement of corporate communication objectives should be developed. These objectives might be as follows:

1. To create an awareness of the (new or old) company name and the nature of its activities.
2. To correct mistaken impressions about the company and its activities among specific segments of the public.
3. To generate interest in the company among members of the financial community.
4. To broaden the public's understanding of the technological activities and capabilities of the firm, with the long-term objective of improving sales volume.
5. To attract qualified personnel into company employment by stressing the challenges and pleasant working environment that the company offers.

The statement of objectives will focus upon a particular segment of the total public and will define a specific message to be conveyed to that segment. The tendency to settle for nebulous "better image" kinds of objectives should be avoided because these objectives do not provide adequate direction for the development of copy, for the selection of media, or for the subsequent evaluation of campaign effectiveness.

The approaches used in corporate advertising do tend to fall into certain categories. One somewhat light-hearted attempt to label these general approaches is as follows:[5]

1. The "People of . . ." approach, stressing the capabilities and interest of the company.
2. The "Issues confronting us" approach, emphasizing the role of the company as a responsible citizen interested in contributing to the solution of social problems.
3. The "Leading edge of technology" approach, explaining the company's research and development activities in a way which highlights both product quality and contribution to general public welfare.
4. The "We've changed our name" approach, with the specific objective of promoting the new corporate identity.
5. The "Don't overlook us as an investment" approach, designed to sell the company's stock.

[5]*Ibid.*, pp. 54–55.

6. The "Salute to . . ." approach that features some group, an occupation, or employees, often a group of persons who are potential customers for the company.
7. The "Market-by-market" approach that says to potential customers "we are capable of understanding your problems and finding solutions to them because we understand your particular industry."
8. The "Senators, are you listening?" approach, favored by companies in the defense industry and also used by those who are the target for proposed legislation to regulate industry activities.

Another very popular approach, not clearly identified in the above categories, can be called the "Did you know we are also in the ―― business?" approach. As more and more companies become diversified and significantly expand their product lines, one of the major corporate communication problems is to keep the company reputation and image growing with its activities. In this case, the objective may be much more closely related to marketing objectives: creating awareness and favorable attitudes toward the company and its products among direct and indirect potential customers. Figures 24–7 through 24–11 illustrate several different approaches to the corporate advertising task.

Implementation

The problems of implementing a corporate advertising campaign are in principle no different from those for any other mass communication effort. The definition of qualitative and quantitative objectives is a necessary first step, defining target audiences and desired changes in predispositions (based upon a prior audit of existing predispositions). Other implementation decisions required include selecting appeals, developing effective messages, setting the advertising budget, and allocating it among various media. The analytical schemes and techniques presented throughout this text apply to the specific case of corporate advertising as well as to development of marketing communication strategy for specific products.

As noted in the discussion of objectives, the major differences in corporate campaigns (compared to product advertising) stem from their complexity. There may be many (say eight or ten) distinct publics to be reached with the campaign. Because of the fact that it is a corporate campaign, there may be important decisions to make concerning budgetary responsibility for the campaign—how divisions should participate financially in the program. The development of a new corporate symbol may involve working with creative consultants on an intensive basis to coordinate a broad variety of considerations including those relating to marketing (packaging and branding, advertising, dealer requirements,

If he'd have leased his ships from us, he could have discovered America ten years earlier.

We'd have leased him everything he needed in the line of transportation and storage equipment from ships and barges to railroad cars to terminals the first time he asked for it.

We know a good idea when we hear one.

After all, we at GATX—you know us, the Tank Car people—have been making it easy for American business to move their products for the last seventy years.

Of course, we've learned a few things about transportation problems in our time.

We've learned it's easier and cheaper for you to lease your equipment instead of buying it.

When you sign the lease, selling the equipment when you're through with it isn't your problem, it's ours. And we can find a user a lot easier than you.

Also, we'll take care of your service and maintenance problems.

But, most important, when the lease runs out your responsibility runs

out with it. That way, as new products come along, you can lease new equipment to move and store them.

As you can see for yourself, leasing your equipment is a smart way to do business.

So call General American Transportation Corporation, Chicago.

It could even open up some new worlds for you. **GATX**

Fig. 24–7. A corporate advertisement featuring company activities. (Courtesy of General American Transportation Corporation; Edward H. Weiss & Co.)

The Great Unknown.

Brilliantly beating everyone to the punch, Keene creates an Interior Systems Division. Only to find that fame still eludes us.

Who knows what ideas lurk in the minds of Keene?

It's ironic. We sniff out a new market, invent a new division to exploit it, and all anyone can say is "What's an Interior System?" Even before they pose the inevitable "Who's Keene?"

The background is clear: many of our divisions turn out building products. Doors, lighting, movable walls, acoustical dingbats, and so on.

We pondered: why not combine all our products and sell entire systems? Where everything is designed to fit together before it has to be put together. Where we work out all the problems before we ship out the products.

Architects can go back to architecting, builders back to building. An architect, for example, asks us for a certain room noise level, instead of figuring it all out himself. And a builder won't spend half his time making things fit that weren't designed to fit in the first place.

In short, we take care of many steps that cost plenty when other people have to take them. And since we're responsible for the whole show, everything shows up when, where, and as it should. Time is saved all around. Money, too. And because Keene is the only company that makes, combines, and sells entire interiors as systems, new markets and growth areas are opened up, too.

So, now you know what an Interior System is. And you know what kind of ideas have made Keene what it is. (After all, we've taken less than 2 years to grow from $2 to $90 million.) Now, will you please try to remember our name?

KEENE
CORPORATION
299 Park Avenue, New York, N.Y. 10017

We've just begun to grow.

Fig. 24–8. A corporate advertisement featuring company name. (Courtesy of Keene Corporation; McManus, John & Adams, Inc.)

Should welfare just keep their bellies full, or help keep them from getting a bellyful of welfare?

Some of those who get welfare are happy enough with hand-outs. But others get fed up with just being fed, and want to learn ways to help feed themselves.

No doubt about it, hunger is a right-now thing. And many taxpayers feel that's what welfare should be all about — an emergency measure. To provide sufficient food, proper clothes, adequate housing. Right now. And that anything more is none of government's business.

Others believe welfare should go further. That government is obligated to help eliminate the causes of poverty and deprivation.

The point is, where do you stand? Your taxes support welfare. Your opinions, suggestions, ideas should support the people who legislate and administer it. So it's important that you write your public officials and tell them what you think on this vital issue, and others like it.

We hope you'll write your letters on Hammermill Bond — world's best-known letterhead paper. But whether you write on Hammermill Bond or not . . . write. A paper-thin voice is a powerful persuader. Hammermill Paper Co., Erie, Pa., maker of 33 fine printing and business papers.

Hammermill urges you to write your public officials.

Fig. 24–9. A corporate advertisement featuring social issues. (Courtesy of Hammermill Bond Paper Co., Inc.; Batten, Barton, Durstine & Osborn, Inc.)

etc.) and many not related to marketing (identification of buildings, painting transportation equipment, and so on).

Implementation may involve many communications that are not normally dealt with by the marketing manager. Annual reports to stockholders, technical papers in scientific journals, films for broad community use, and the company's house organ may all be altered to reflect the new corporate advertising campaign and must be coordinated with it. Finally, measurement problems may be particularly complex and yet particularly necessary in trying to rationalize so complex a strategic problem as developing the corporate advertising campaign.

These complexities of implementation lead to two important conclusions. First, careful planning and coordination are at least as important for a corporate advertising campaign as for any other element of the marketing communication strategy. It is dangerous to assume that the corporate campaign can be treated as a less important effort, something that the marketing communication strategist does in his "spare time" or as a residual part of his total responsibility. Second, it is necessary to assign specific responsibility for the planning and execution of the corporate advertising campaign. Because the objectives and the details of implementation are distinct from the day-to-day problems of managing the product communication effort, a manager of corporate advertising (or of public relations) should be assigned this specific responsibility if the budget is sufficiently large to support this degree of specialization. The perspectives and the problems of the corporate advertising campaign are fundamentally different and require their own careful attention.

The Egocentric Predicament

Before leaving the topic of corporate advertising and moving on to the more general topic of public relations, there is one aspect of corporate advertising that results in frequent criticism and, probably, extensive waste for these communication efforts. It is relevant to ask about much corporate advertising, "Who cares?" The question is intended to be a serious one and may reveal that nobody cares other than the top management of the company. A new president may feel a strong need to have his company better known. A better image may be a major source of "psychic income" to him as part of his compensation from the job, and he has it in his power to spend the company's money in this way.

A surprisingly strong piece of evidence on the nature of this "egocentric predicament" in corporate advertising is provided by the extensive use of the pronoun *we* in most corporate advertising. This usage indi-

Sallie Taylor would be the first to tell you.

TRW can be replaced.

Her car came from the factory with about 185 TRW parts in it. And she knows there are more in her future if she needs them; service departments everywhere are stocked with TRW engine and chassis replacement parts.

But the growing automotive replacement parts business is just one of the many ways TRW touches Sallie's life. And yours.

Your radio, your stereo and your color television depend on TRW electronic components. The jet planes you fly in have TRW fuel pumps and turbine blades, as well as bearings and radio components.

TRW systems and services are involved in everything from submarines and satellites to solutions of civil problems like traffic, urban renewal, crime, air and water pollution.

TRW has grown to be a billion-dollar company with over 80,000 people in more than 300 worldwide locations. And although we're proud to be a breakthrough kind of company, we have to admit that there are times when being replaced is a good way to get ahead.

TRW INC., Cleveland, Ohio—A Diversified Technology Company Specializing in Products, Systems, and Services for Commercial, Industrial and Government Markets.

Fig. 24–10. A corporate advertisement featuring company products. (Courtesy of TRW, Inc.; Fuller & Smith & Ross, Inc.)

cates the tendency for much corporate advertising to consist of blowing one's own horn and often reveals that the company is talking to itself more than to potential customers. When corporate advertising becomes self-conscious and emphasizes the cleverness and even the cuteness of the advertiser, it can become uninteresting, boring, and offensive. Many critics agree that this is the tendency for the majority of corporate advertising.

Previous analysis has suggested the important role played by corporate identity and by corporate advertising campaigns in contributing to the effectiveness of other elements of the marketing communication strategy. That analysis refutes the conclusion that all corporate advertising is wasteful. On the other hand, there *is* a great deal of corporate advertising that appears to have little purpose other than to make top management feel good. As one critic noted:

> In any event, the advertising that a company does to tell people that it exists and to describe the parts that make up its sum does not make the most engaging kind of reading.
>
> Readers don't care; they have no pressing incentive to read about a company's identification system or structure; still, it is no less legitimate for the company itself to try to get itself known for what it is.[6]

Once again, the answer to this problem may lie with creativity. Most corporate advertising cannot claim to appeal to a basic need of the consumer. A reaction of indifference is to be expected unless creativity can make the advertising itself so interesting that the reader is attracted to it. Nothing short of outstanding creative effort is going to gain the reader's attention and provide sufficient incentive to read about the unique attributes of this particular company. Lack of reader interest and incentive coupled with mediocre creative executions lead to much corporate advertising that is dull, boring, uninteresting, and therefore wasted.

PUBLIC RELATIONS

Corporate advertising is one form of public relations. In general, public relations is defined as "the activities of a corporation, union, government, or other organization in building and maintaining sound and productive relations with special publics such as customers, employees, or stockholders and with the public at large, so as to adapt itself to its environment and interpret itself to society." This is a general definition that emphasizes that customers are only one of several publics that the public relations program is designed to influence. Some prefer a definition which emphasizes the social responsibility aspects of public rela-

[6]"Industrial Ads in '68—Year of the Conglomerate," *Marketing Insights*, 3 (April 7, 1969), pp. 8–11, at p. 8.

Fig. 24–11. A corporate advertisement featuring company capability. (Courtesy of Libbey-Owens-Ford Co.; Fuller & Smith & Ross, Inc.)

tions, such as "the management function which evaluates public attitudes, identifies the policies and procedures of an individual or an
organization with the public interest, and executes a program of action
to earn public understanding and acceptance."[7]

Public relations is often identified with a kind of surreptitious influence peddling that takes place "behind the scenes" and results in decep-
tion and misleading information and impressions. This is an unfortunate
stereotype created by the questionable tactics of a small minority of the
early forerunners of the modern public relations manager, such as the
press agent and the lobbyist. (It should be emphasized that these are
also honorable professions.) It is also true that any person who identifies
himself as specifically seeking to influence public opinion comes in for a
certain amount of natural fear and criticism. In contrast to the stereotype, however, it can be said that the modern public relations expert is
in the vast majority of cases a true professional who draws upon the
best available knowledge and techniques of communication to solve the
problems of clients in a responsible manner.

Experts in public relations stress that the actual communications that
result from the public relations program are only the visible results of a
program that goes much deeper. One author emphasizes that there are
four parts to the public relations program:[8]

1. A social philosophy of management
2. An expression of this philosophy in policy decisions
3. Action resulting from policies
4. Communications which explain, reveal, defend, or promote these
   policies to the public to secure its understanding and goodwill

Scope

The discussion of the objectives of corporate advertising campaigns
stressed that corporate advertising is only one form of public relations,
although many of the statements made about the objectives of corporate
advertising apply to public relations in general. In addition to corporate
advertising, public relations involves such communication activities as
these:

Internal company publications
Financial reporting to stockholders
Participation in local community affairs

[7]Bertrand R. Canfield, *Public Relations,* 5th ed. (Homewood, Ill.: Richard D.
Irwin, Inc., 1968), p. 4.

[8]*Ibid.,* pp. 5–10.

Working with government agencies to further a program or purpose which the company believes has merit

Contributing financially and otherwise to charities and community activities

Permitting the use of company facilities or equipment for nonbusiness purposes.

Allowing employees to actively participate in political activities while still in the full-time employ of the company

Providing speakers or displays for educational institutions

The list could be extended considerably, but the point is merely to show that public relations involves a broad scope of activities beyond the confines of marketing communication strategy. The relationship with marketing strategy will be explored more carefully in a moment.

Important Publics. One way to express the scope of public relations is to identify the various important publics with whom the company (or other organization) is seeking favorable relationships. These include the following:

1. Customers
2. Employees
3. Supplies
4. Dealers and distributors
5. Stockholders
6. Governmental institutions
7. Educational institutions
8. Local community
9. Social welfare organizations
10. Press
11. Trade and professional associations
12. Financial community
13. Public at large

It is unnecessary to indicate in detail why each of these publics is potentially important to the corporation or to engage in discussion (which usually becomes argument) concerning whether an interest in public relations is motivated by the selfish drive for profit or by some more altruistic purpose such as promoting community welfare. The basic purpose of any program designed to promote better relationships with any public is to promote the mutual welfare of both the company and that public. Public relations inevitably involves a recognition of the interdependence of the company and the environment within which it operates, including specific individuals and institutions within that environment. The larger the corporation, and the more diverse its operations geographically and otherwise, the more complex and demanding become the requirements for effective public relations.

Public Relations Tools. All of the tools of the marketing communication strategist are available to help with the specific problems of public relations. These include advertising media, the dealer organization, the sales force, and publicity (to be discussed next). The public relations profession has also come to realize that the basic concepts of the behavioral sciences and of communication theory are as applicable to public relations as to other aspects of marketing communication. A recent textbook in the field has emphasized that effective public relations strategy and management requires theoretical and practical understanding of communication and of attitude and behavior change.[9]

Both formal and informal communication are important to the public relations activities of the firm. Word-of-mouth about a company as an employer, as a customer, or as a potential investment can be very important to the long-term health of the company. Companies can also generate their own communication media to serve particular purposes within the public relations program, such as a newspaper to keep company employees informed, periodic mailings to stockholders, and seminars to improve the management performance of supplier companies. Public relations involves a broad scope of communication activities, with a wide range of possibilities for the development of specific communication devices to solve particular needs.

Relationship to Marketing Communication

Public relations is intertwined with marketing communication strategy in two respects. First, many of the publics of importance to the welfare of the company are publics directly involved in the marketing communication process—customers, salesmen (employees), dealers and distributors, the media, and trade associations. Second, the company's marketing communication activities are an important source of information and impressions about the company to its various publics. As part of the "public-at-large," members of each of the several specific publics of importance to the company are exposed to its mass communication activities and other evidences of its marketing strategy.

Consumer Publics. Particular consumer groups may be of special importance to the company and may be best reached through a public relations program rather than as a part of the marketing strategy per se.

[9]Edward J. Robinson, *Communication and Public Relations* (Columbus, Ohio: Charles E. Merrill, Inc., 1966).

Students may be an important consumer group for a company to communicate with because of their future spending power. To illustrate, a winery in California may provide a tour of its facilities and host a wine-tasting party for college students who may one day be important consumers of its products. A public utility may invite grade-school and high-school students to visit its power-generating station for the joint purposes of contributing to their education and providing them with a generally favorable impression of the company as a supplier of services in the local community.

Social groups such as women's clubs, church associations, service organizations, and political parties may be effectively reached through public relations which have the purpose of stimulating members' interest in the company's products as potential customers. A local dairy may on this basis donate ice cream for a church supper or an automobile dealer may allow a service club to drive one of its new cars in a local parade. The ways of using good public relations activities to create favorable attitudes toward the company among potential customers are numerous indeed.

As in the case of corporate advertising, so in the case of public relations in general: these activities all contribute to the image of the company. This image provides the context or background against which specific marketing communication activities are evaluated and responded to. Public relations activities of all kinds both directly and indirectly influence the "credibility" of the company.

Customer Relations. Customer relations is often regarded as a part of public relations rather than marketing communication in the narrow sense. When customer complaints are received in the form of telephone calls or letters, or when defective merchandise is returned to the manufacturer, it is especially important that procedures be set up for attending to the problem in a courteous and efficient manner. Careless handling of a customer complaint can have serious consequences on the overall corporate image as the disgruntled customer tells friends and neighbors about his bad experience. This risk is heightened by the possibility that the customer is also an opinion leader or otherwise influential in the local community.

Viewing consumer relations as part of public relations has several possible consequences. The public relations manager may assume responsibility for training company personnel other than salesmen on the proper method of handling customers and customer complaints. Credit department personnel may need this kind of training, for example, as may customer service representatives or any other company employee who is not a salesman but who has frequent contact with customers. Nowhere can this need be more clearly seen than in an airline where the customer's total impression of the airline is a function of his interaction with telephone sales personnel, baggage porters, check-in counter personnel, stewardesses, flight crew members, and ground crews. Each of these can significantly influence the customer's attitude toward the airline and must be trained to fulfill that responsibility.

Resellers as Local Representatives. As representatives of the company in the local community, resellers are occasionally called upon to perform some special service in the local community—such as the donation of merchandise to a worthy cause or providing a representative for a meeting involving community affairs. The public relations manager may design a program for improving the ability of local resellers to assume such responsibilities. Programs for improving the effectiveness of the local reseller as a businessman in general (for example, help with office records, personnel practices, or data processing) may also be provided as part of the firm's public relations activities.

These are only a few of the many ways in which public relations and marketing communication activities overlap. Others include providing employees with samples of new products (to build morale and to create spokesmen), demonstrating new products to interested professional groups, and cooperation in industry trade association promotional activities that have the purpose of stimulating industry demand. These examples are sufficient to support the observation that public relations and marketing communication are mutually dependent functions within the firm. Public relations, because it depends upon the skills and tools of the professional communicator, may be appropriately considered as part of the total marketing communication strategy. Although it is not limited to the objective of promoting the sale of the company's goods and services, the ultimate objective of the business is to create a satisfied customer and public relations has a critical role to play in achieving that objective.

PUBLICITY

Publicity is a unique form of marketing communication in that it is information about the company and its products that is conveyed by the mass media *as part of their editorial content.* It is distinguished from advertising by the fact that it is *not paid for.* Publicity is *not* synonymous with public relations and it is not the same as promotion in general. Rather, the term is reserved for that set of marketing communication activities that includes the use of the mass media without charge.

Greater Credibility

Publicity has the major advantage of greater credibility because the source is perceived to be the medium carrying the message rather than the company selling the product or service. A news broadcaster or a newspaper column editor is a more credible communicator that a salesman or a public relations official. The advantages of credibility are much more important in the use of publicity than the fact that the media carry the message for no charge.

Economic Value

The economic value of the free publicity should not be understated, however. Stan Freberg, a famous entertainer who turned to a career as a professional creative consultant, once designed an advertisement for Pacific Airlines with the headline "Hey There! You with the Sweat in Your Palms!" This distinctive headline and the equally distinctive copy were quite effective in attracting attention to the airline and generating a large amount of publicity that significantly extended the impact of the airline's very limited $250,000 advertising budget.

Another example illustrates the possible relationship between media advertising and publicity. Figure 24–12 illustrates one of several print advertisements used in a campaign for Trans World Airlines, developed by the company's advertising agency, Wells, Rich, and Greene. A story concerning the effectiveness of the TWA campaign in bringing about the change in employees' attitudes toward customers subsequently appeared in *Time* magazine. That story is reproduced in Figure 24–13. It is quite possible that persons who read that story in *Time* magazine would be impressed by the news that employees were, in fact, changing their behavior as promised by the advertising. The result of the publicity is to make the advertising more believable. Certainly, the publicity has promotional value for TWA. This example also illustrates a point offered elsewhere in this text that company advertising has an important influence on the morale and effectiveness of company personnel. Furthermore, promises made in the advertising must be fulfilled by people who actually interact with the customer. Finally, the point should be made that this publicity did not just "happen." A manager of public relations or marketing activities for TWA or for Wells, Rich, and Greene almost certainly devoted a major effort to having this story appear in *Time*. In a sense, the effectiveness of the advertising campaign virtually depends upon the "credibility boost" that such publicity can provide.

Generating Publicity

How does a company go about generating favorable publicity for the company and its products? It makes a concerted and carefully planned effort to provide the press with information about the company, its products, and its activities which is *newsworthy*. Because the media are in

We put our money
where it does you the most good.

Airlines have been spending a fortune on silly gimmicks to get your business. Like crazy costumes and funny hats for hostesses.

Gimmicks that don't give you any of the creature comforts that make you happy.

We took a fling at it ourselves, then you told us what you really wanted.

On TWA, our gimmicks are limited to superb drinks, food cooked right on board, soul-satisfying stereo music, and good movies* to make the time pass more quickly.

And since people make people happier than anything else, we're giving our people a million dollar bonus to give you the exceptional service that will make you

happier than any other airline can make you. It's up to you to tell us whose pockets to put this money into.

Get the names of our people who live up to our promise. Put them on the ballots you'll receive on board, and drop those ballots into the bonus boxes you'll find at our terminals.

We think you'll like flying with us, because we're in the airline business.

Not show business.

**Our people make you happy.
We make them happy.**

*By Inflight Motion Pictures, Inc. on transcontinental non-stops.

Fig. 24–12. An advertisement for Trans World Airlines. (Courtesy of Trans World Airlines; Wells, Rich, Greene.)

That Million-Dollar Smile

Jaded by pastel planes and miniskirted stewardesses, bored with imitation-fur lap throws and delicatessen sandwiches, airline passengers are being enticed with a new frill. Since April, Trans World Airlines has been trying to attract business with an idea as cold as cash and as warm as a smile. It is offering employees a chance to exchange courtesy for $1,000,000.

As part of its "Happiness Campaign," TWA divided its employees into groups according to their job categories and the size of the cities in which they are based. The groups compete against each other to see which can best please the public. The judges are the customers; they mark ballots to cite those who give them the snappiest service. Employees in winning groups receive $100 each and a chance to draw for bigger prizes ranging up to a sports car or $2,700 in cash.

Jackpot. The campaign has had its effect on service. Reservation clerks, sporting straw skimmers with hatbands proclaiming "Happiness," give the weather report as they announce the gate number. While demonstrating oxygen masks, stewardesses tell passengers about the epicurean banquet that lies ahead. One Pittsburgh cargo handler helped his group win by carrying a big box out to a shipping customer's car, stowing it in the trunk, then walking around to open the car door—and bowing.

If nothing else, the campaign has lifted employee morale. In the first of four contests, 14 of the 125 competing city groups have won $256,100. According to the balloting among large cities, Chicago has the sweetest stewardesses, Kansas City the cheeriest flight officers, and Paris the nicest reservation clerks. In Paris, Reservation Clerk Denise Boivin picked up $1,000 and, for her victory statement, borrowed a slogan from another company: "Everyone is trying harder."

Earnings Up. The campaign was the idea of TWA's adwoman, Mary Wells Lawrence, who also started the battle of the frills in 1965 when she persuaded Braniff to paint its planes pastel and outfit the stewardesses in original Pucci culottes. After she married Braniff President Harding Lawrence, it became obvious that the family relationship was too cozy for business. The conflict was resolved last summer when she won the TWA account and Braniff dropped her. Last week she announced that earnings of her agency, Wells, Rich, Greene Inc., rose 63% to $801,000 during the first half of its fiscal year. The total was boosted in part by TWA's $30 million ad budget.

As for TWA, President F. C. Wiser says: "We are happy being happy." He has little else to take comfort in. Earnings dropped 47% last year as airport delays mounted, labor costs soared and the line added more planes than it could profitably fill. For the first four months of 1969, TWA suffered a deficit of $17 million. Its executives could obviously use a Happiness Campaign themselves.

TWA WINNER & SUPERVISOR IN ROME
Money really can bring happiness.

Fig. 24–13. Publicity generated by the TWA campaign. (Courtesy of Time, Inc., and Trans World Airlines.)

the business of informing their audiences, they demand that materials used as the basis for publicity should have inherent news value and be of interest to their audiences.

Publicity materials are always presented to the media with the understanding that they will be edited and adjusted to fit the needs of the audience and not to conform strictly to the wishes of the company. Thus, there is some risk involved in the use of publicity in that the company loses control over the communication. Virtually all of the mass media are candidates for use in the publicity program.

To obtain favorable publicity, the communication strategist must know the requirements for being effective. He must understand both the audience he wants to reach and the persons and procedures influencing the use of publicity. Personal contacts with the mass media may be especially important. The production and editorial requirements of the media must be thoroughly understood so that the information base for the publicity is made available to the right people, in the right form, at the right time.

When properly done—carefully planned and implemented with the necessary attention to the details required for effectiveness—publicity can be a powerful tool in the total marketing communication program.

SUMMARY

Corporate advertising, public relations, and publicity all have elements that go beyond the specific objectives of creating awareness, developing favorable attitudes, and stimulating sales of the company's products and services. On the other hand, these three areas of communication activity contribute directly to the effectiveness of the marketing program by their influence on company image. The image of the company becomes a context within which the effectiveness of all marketing communication activities is determined.

The analytical tools and the basic concepts of communication theory apply equally well to the development of these supplemental communications as they do to the development of the company's personal selling and advertising strategies. The need for careful planning is especially significant for corporate advertising and public relations because of the several publics that must be reached and the complexity of the communication task. The importance of creativity is likewise heightened in this area by the fact that the company talking about itself is not a topic of inherent interest for the individual. If the topic is of little interest, a special burden falls on the message to provide incentive to the reader or listener.

There is a two-way relationship between corporate advertising, public relations, and publicity and the more specific activities of marketing communication. Each contributes to the effectiveness of the other and the two are inextricably related in their impact on the consumer. A legitimate distinction can be made, however, between the relatively long-term objectives of corporate advertising, public relations, and publicity, and the more specific short-term objectives of advertising, personal selling, sales promotions, and similar marketing communication devices intended to produce profitable sales volume.

This chapter concludes our review of the many aspects of marketing communication strategy that supplement, extend, and support the basic communication variables of advertising and personal selling. We have considered the central role of resellers in the communication strategy; the problems of developing effective sales promotions, deals, and point-of-purchase displays; the contribution of packaging and branding to product identification and to buyer attitudes; and the overall contribution of corporate advertising, public relations, and publicity. In the following chapter we shall consider the problem of coordinating and integrating all of these tools into a coherent marketing communication strategy.

VI

Program Evaluation and Control

The development of a marketing communication strategy has been seen to require information about the size of the market and about existing predispositions, establishment of communication objectives and budgets, the creation and evaluation of advertising messages and an effective sales organization, evaluation and selection of mass media, and the careful planning of supplemental communications. When these steps have been completed, the total marketing communication strategy is *almost* ready to go. All that remains is for these elements to be coordinated as they are produced and implemented and for careful measures of campaign effectiveness to be developed. These steps are critical to the success of the marketing communication strategy.

If the total management process can be defined by the three stages of analysis, planning, and control, it is the *control* of marketing communication strategy that provides the focus for our last two chapters. In Chapter 25, criteria and techniques for the coordination of the several parts of the communication program are described and evaluated, including consideration of the formal organization for strategic decision making and its implementation. Chapter 26 develops an overall model for the evaluation of total communication campaign effects.

Strategic planning must be a continuous process. If measurement and evaluation are carefully planned, the results of this year's communication program can be systematically assessed as the basis for next year's strategy.

Without this careful planning of the evaluation process, management loses a major opportunity to learn from its own experience. With such evaluation, strategic planning becomes a continuous activity of increasing effectiveness and efficiency.

25

Coordinating Communication Elements

It has been the basic argument of this text that the several elements of the marketing communication program should be planned in an integrated context. Suboptimal decisions result to the extent that any one element of the communication strategy is planned without a considera tion of its interdependence with other communication elements. As individual modes of communication have been analyzed in earlier chapters, an attempt has been made to identify the major areas of overlap with other strategic elements. It was also suggested that the basic methods of analysis and planning (for both budget level and allocation problems) and the central model of communication effects were useful devices for decision making concerning each strategic element.

MARKETING COMMUNICATION: SYNERGISTIC EFFECTS

A marketing communication program is more than the sum of its parts. It is a "synergism"—a system of interrelated elements in which total system performance reflects not just individual element performance but also their interdependent contributions. One of the most significant challenges facing the marketing communication strategist is the design of programs which maximize these synergistic effects. In addition to his analysis and planning of advertising, personal selling, reseller effort, sales promotion, deals, display, packaging, branding, corporate advertising, public relations, and publicity, he must specifically analyze and plan for the interaction of system elements to maximize the effectiveness of total communication investment.

The coordination of communication elements is a complex problem of analysis and planning. Present tools and concepts of strategic planning do not permit a precise resolution of these complex interactions but they do permit the problem to be approached in a rigorous, logical fashion. Coordination issues also give rise to some complex questions of organization structure and functioning.

The problem of coordination will be approached in three ways. First, the problems associated with the functional interaction of system elements will be explored, against the basic framework of the communication process. Second, the temporal dimension of coordination will be examined—the problem of coordinating all communication elements and activities against a schedule involving deadlines of various kinds. Third, the problem of organizing for communication strategy will be explored and alternative organizational arrangements will be briefly reviewed.

FUNCTIONAL COORDINATION

The synergistic effects of communication are the most complex aspect of the problem of coordination. How can advertising be most helpful to the salesman? How can consumer deals be coordinated with advertising and with reseller strategies? How much of the total public relations effort should be devoted to consumers as a public, and to marketing-related functions? These are all questions of coordination of communication functions.

Model of Communication Effects

The framework for a consideration of these functional interdependencies is the familiar "hierarchy-of-effects" model. The hierarchy-of-effects model proposed by Lavidge and Steiner,[1] originally presented in Chapter 3, divided communication effects into three categories: (1) *cognitive* effects, including ideas and the conscious perception of stimuli; (2) *affective* effects, meaning those involving emotions, attitudes, and feelings; and (3) *conative* effects, those dealing with the motivation, stimulation, and direction of desires and behavior. These can be relabeled as (1) awareness, (2) attitude change, and (3) behavior change. Earlier discussion of message testing suggested that the "hierarchy-of-effects" model could be replaced with a "correlates-of-effects" model

[1]Robert Lavidge and Gary Steiner, "A Model for Predictive Measurements of Advertising Effectiveness," *Journal of Marketing*, 25 (October 1961), pp. 59–62.

that left open the question of whether attitude change would precede or follow behavior change. The argument was advanced that, over time, attitudes and behavior would have to be brought into balance. In the near term, however, it would be possible for many products to secure behavior change (such as product trial) before attitude change had been accomplished.

Using this simple three-stage model—awareness, attitude change, and behavior change—let us now consider the contribution of various communication modes to the accomplishment of communication objectives. The contribution of a given communication mode at each stage will reflect three considerations: (1) the "communication efficiency" of each mode, (2) the economic efficiency of each mode, and (3) buyers' preferences for information sources, as a function of stage in the decision process and stage in the diffusion process.

The general objective of the total communication program is to create awareness, develop favorable attitudes, and stimulate actual purchase of the product. The objective of any single element of the communication program should be more specific, however. In designing the marketing communication strategy, the planner must consider specifically which of several alternative communication modes to depend upon for accomplishing each of the three stages of communication effect, and he must consider how to blend these in the most effective manner.

Figure 25–1 suggests the major options available to the communication strategist to accomplish each of the three stages of communication

Communication Stage	Communication Mode
AWARENESS	Advertising (Reach)
	Personal Selling
	Direct Mail
	Reseller Effort
	Display (Including Packaging)
ATTITUDE	Personal Selling
	Advertising (Frequency)
	Public Relations (and Corporate Advertising)
	Branding and Packaging (Design)
BUYING ACTION	Sales Promotion
	Deals (Consumer and Trade)
	Display
	Reseller Effort
	Personal Selling
	Direct Mail

Fig. 25–1. Communication modes available at various stages of communication.

effect. While mass communication can create awareness and stimulate the development of favorable attitudes, it is not as likely to lead to specific buying action. Rather, reseller efforts and other activities at the point of purchase are necessary to stimulate buying action. Public relations and corporate advertising can influence attitudes toward the company and its brands, but are not generally thought of as tools for creating product awareness.

Let us consider more specifically the contribution that each of the major classes of communication tools can make to the effectiveness of *other* parts of the total communication mix. In this discussion, emphasis will not be upon the principal function of that mode of communication but rather upon its contribution to the effectiveness of other modes.

Personal Selling

Because it is a central communication element, it is hard to think about personal selling as contributing to the effectiveness of other, sometimes relatively minor, parts of the total communication mix. In those push strategies which use the salesman to accomplish all three levels of response (awareness, attitudes, and buying action), the salesman is seldom assisted significantly by other communication tools. He may depend upon leads generated by advertising, but he is likely to carry responsibility for all the levels of response.

This is not true in a pull strategy, where the salesman's job can be defined as one of obtaining reseller support and making sure that displays are set up on the schedule necessary to coordinate with media advertising. The salesman's role is critical here, nonetheless, because the pull strategy obviously breaks down if the product is not displayed and stocked adequately at the retail level. Furthermore, the salesman may have major responsibility for obtaining reseller support in the form of cooperative advertising or otherwise convincing resellers to assume responsibility for generating demand at the local level.

The salesman may also be a critical factor in implementing a sales promotion strategy such as a deal or a contest. In addition to setting up displays featuring the deal, he may also be responsible for such details of administration as arranging for dealers to be reimbursed for coupon redemptions, or coordination of relationships between wholesalers and retailers.

In the pull strategy, the salesman contributes to the effectiveness of advertising by making sure that consumers who have been made aware of the product and have developed favorable attitudes toward it can find the product when they go shopping. His key responsibilities are to obtain reseller support and to set up displays.

Advertising

Advertising can create awareness of a company and its products, and it can do this in an economically efficient manner due to the large audiences delivered by the mass media. It can also contribute to the development of favorable attitudes toward the company and its products, although this is likely to be a relatively slow process requiring multiple message exposures over a long time.

Advertising contributes to the effectiveness of the salesman in two ways. First, it can generate leads (as when advertisements contain coupons inviting the reader to write for additional information). Such leads can increase the salesman's productivity by cutting down on the number of cold calls he makes and by insuring that all new prospects contacted have at least some interest in the product. Second, advertising can improve the salesman's effectiveness by its contribution to credibility— by adding to the prestige of the company, making its name better known, and associating it with the mass media. At the same time, a better "image" can increase customers' expectations for the company's salesmen, creating the need for a higher level of salesman training and ability.

Today it is rare for a company not to advertise to some extent, at least to support its salesmen and its resellers. Even if corporate advertising is the only form of advertising used, it can improve the morale of the sales force and of resellers by associating their efforts with a "nationally advertised" firm and products. A major objective of a national advertising campaign may be to obtain the credibility of the mass media which can then be used as a selling point by the resellers. A men's shoe company may run a single ad in *Playboy* and then provide its retailers with countertop placards picturing the ad and saying "As Advertised in *Playboy*." This results in a particular set of connotations or "image" for that line of shoes.

Sales Promotions, Deals, and Displays

Our discussion of sales promotions and deals suggested that the major function of these devices is to stimulate a follow-through on consumer advertising, and these communications are therefore supplementary to the basic pull strategy. They provide an inducement to buying action, something that may not be provided by media advertising. They can help overcome the fact that there is little or no personal selling by clerks in the supermarket or drugstore.

Display may be used to create awareness as well as to stimulate buying action, but simply putting the product into stores is not likely to be effective over the long run. Awareness requires mass media as well as effective display. If a consumer has seen an advertisement for a new product, the probability is higher that she will actually purchase the product when she sees it on display in the store than if she has not seen the advertisement.

In the absence of such buying incentives, consumers must have favorable attitudes at or beyond some "threshold" level before they will engage in buying action. For attitude change to be at a level sufficiently high to produce behavior change, appeals must be very strong and the basic needs must be sufficiently important that a reasonable number of exposures to information about the product will arouse needs sufficiently to cause the person to engage in the desired behavior. For many products and services, this seems like an unreasonable burden to place upon mass communication. It may be more realistic and more efficient to say that attitude change is only going to occur as the result of favorable experience with the product and to then rely heavily upon short-term buying incentives to create buying action. In this sense, sales promotion, deals, and display contribute to the effectiveness of advertising by stimulating buying action that accomplishes the ultimate purpose of the advertising (to generate sales), but in a way that is not possible for advertising alone.

Resellers

Resellers contribute to the effectiveness of the total marketing communication program in two ways. First, they may assume some responsibility for the communication activity itself, as when (in a push strategy) resellers' sales clerks are expected to explain the product to potential customers, or when retailers advertise the product at the local level, or by providing display space to actively promote the product.

Second, they provide the physical facilities for making the product available to potential customers. The coordination of the distribution strategy with the communication strategy is clearly a managerial issue of major importance in marketing. Communication can be effective in generating satisfied customers only if the product is available at the time and place required by potential customers. Every person "reached" by the media strategy is an effective exposure only if the product is also available to that customer.

Resellers therefore contribute to advertising effectiveness, and extend personal selling effort as well, by pushing the product, by providing physical distribution, and by providing display of the product.

To summarize, an effective and efficient marketing communication strategy will result only if the right mix of communication elements has been pulled together to accomplish awareness, favorable attitudes, and buying action, with each communication element making its distinctive contribution in the most efficient manner and, at the same time, contributing to the effectiveness of other system elements and therefore to the system as a whole. Advertising decisions cannot be made without consideration of their impact on personal selling, reseller effort, and sales promotion effectiveness. The salesman is aided by advertising, as well as by sales promotion, in accomplishing his objectives. These objectives may be to actually generate sales revenue (a push strategy) or to get adequate distribution and display (a pull strategy). All communication elements must be evaluated for their contribution to total system performance, not just for their distinctive contributions.

THE DOLLAR CONTRIBUTION METHOD

Cyril Freeman, Manager of Advertising and Sales Promotion for the Worthington Corporation, has proposed a method for specifically evaluating the contribution of each communication task.[2] This method depends upon management judgment and is not an optimization technique in the management science sense. The dollar contribution method does provide a rigorous method, however, for considering the relative importance of each communication element in the total budget. We mentioned this technique briefly in Chapter 16 as one approach to the determination of advertising budgets. Here, we will look at the method in a little more detail because it provides a logical method for analyzing the problem of interdependence among communication elements.

Objectives; Marginal Contribution; Steps in the Sale

There are three central inputs to the dollar contribution method. First, there must be a statement of specific communication objectives such as "persuading x customers to visit y dealers over a three-month period," or "establishing product awareness among x percent of the total market within y months." Second, some estimate of the contribution of each communication mode (personal selling, advertising, sales promotion, etc.) to the total task is necessary. The marginal contribution of each communication mode can be used to evaluate trade-offs among system elements—such as comparing one salesman with $25,000 more media advertising. Assume, for example, that the choice to be considered is between either twelve salesmen and $50,000 media advertising or fourteen salesmen and no media advertising. The question then becomes

[2]Cyril Freeman, "How to Evaluate Advertising's Contribution," *Harvard Business Review*, 40 (July–August 1962), pp. 137–48.

one of evaluating advertising's contribution to the sales effectiveness of each of the salesmen.

The third input required is some reasonable description of the steps involved in making a sale and their relative importance. An example used by Freeman concerns an industrial company that saw the sales process as having six steps with the relative importance indicated by the percentage figures:

Making contact	10%
Arousing interest	15
Creating preference	25
Making specific proposals	15
Closing the sale	10
Keeping sold	25

(Notice the definite similarity to our simple three-stage model: awareness, attitudes, and buying action.) There is no ideal procedure for making this judgment, but a pooling of estimates by several managers might improve the validity of the procedure.

These three inputs—objectives, a measure of marginal contribution for each communication mode, and an estimate of the relative importance of steps in the sales task—can then be used to determine the relative importance of each communication element in the total communication task. Notice that the value of this approach is very much determined by the quality of management judgments concerning these basic inputs.

The dollar contribution method proceeds by looking at each mode of communication in terms of its contribution to the total task. Following an example developed by Freeman, a specific objective of increasing awareness from 38 percent (determined by a survey of potential buyers) to 50 percent was established for advertising, and an advertising budget of $100,000 was established. Next, management estimated that achieving this objective with advertising would contribute to the salesman's effectiveness as follows—

a 30% increase in salesman efficiency in making contact

a 33⅓% increase in interest-arousing effectiveness

an increase of 10% in preference-creating effectiveness

no measurable contribution to making proposals or closing orders

an estimated 10% increase in the salesman effectiveness in keeping prospects sold, to insure reorder business

These estimates were then combined to yield an estimate that advertising could contribute about 13 percent to the total communication task, as follows:

Selling Task	Weight $\times$	Estimated Contribution of Advertising to Selling Task	$=$	Total Advertising Contribution
Making contact	10%	30%		3%
Arousing interest	15	33⅓		5
Creating preference	25	10		2½
Making specific proposals	15	0		0
Closing the sale	10	0		0
Keeping sold	25	10		2½
Total	100%			13%

This percentage figure (13 percent) can then be applied to the total sales revenue to develop a dollar estimate of advertising's contribution to the total selling task.[3] This is a valuable method for developing an advertising budget, for example, but its major contribution is probably that it forces an explicit consideration of the relationships and interdependencies among communication modes. It provides a rigorous basis for thinking about the problems of functional coordination.

Comparing Alternative Communication Investments

This figure also provides a basis for comparing alternative communication investments. In the above example, if the total revenue of the firm (in this market segment) was $15,000,000, then advertising's contribution would be estimated at $1,950,000. The advertising budget of $100,000 could also have been used to support four additional salesmen at a cost of $25,000 each. If it was further assumed that each of the new salesmen would be an "average producer" and would generate $500,000 in revenue, their total contribution would be $2,000,000 *minus* 13 percent ($260,000) or $1,740,000, which is $210,000 less than the amount of revenue provided by investing the money in advertising. According to this comparison, then, advertising is a better marketing communication investment at this point in the company's marketing history than would be the hiring of additional salesmen. The decision about whether to invest in both forms of communication could be resolved using the return on investment criterion suggested in our chapter on budgeting.

[3]*Ibid.,* p. 142.

The dollar contribution method is a useful method for thinking about the interactions among communication elements in contributing to the accomplishment of specific communication objectives, and of evaluating the contribution of specific elements to the total marketing communication task.

COORDINATION OVER TIME

The foregoing discussion has considered the coordination of functional elements in the total communication program. An equally important set of planning problems involves the coordination of communication over time. This scheduling problem has two dimensions: planning the development of communication materials and coordinating the introduction of a new promotional campaign.

Developing Campaign Materials

The development of campaign materials is essentially a production problem. The production typically involves the creation of materials such as advertising copy and contest ideas and then the printing or filming of these materials. Examples of the kinds of production problems involved include the printing of display devices, coupons, and contest entry forms; developing newspaper mats to be sent to dealers; filming of commercials; and printing of billboard poster sheets.

In addition to the development of the actual advertising materials and sales aids, the necessary space must be purchased and scheduled carefully. Closing dates for magazine printing must be met with delivery of necessary materials to the publisher; taped and filmed television commercials must be made available to networks and local stations; salesmen must have the necessary catalogue sheets and samples in time to begin the introduction. These problems of coordination place major importance upon the ability of vendors of advertising materials to meet promised delivery dates, and upon the marketing communication manager's ability to follow through when schedules slip with careful attention to these important details.

Several different organizations and agencies may become involved in the development of a complete communication campaign. Advertising agencies usually have highly developed skills in working with vendors of creative services, talent, and materials, as well as in coordinating the placement of advertising in media. Agencies have well-established relationship with television commercial production companies, for example, and with the various specialized printers required to put together the packages, deals, displays, catalog sheets, mailing pieces, and so on necessary to implement a special promotion.

Implementing the Campaign

When the necessary materials are available, the next coordination problem is to get the materials to the right place at the right time. Dealers must receive announcement of special promotions in time to order the product through warehouses and into the store's inventories. Display devices must be available at the store in time to have product on display when advertising schedules for a special promotion "break" in the local market. Salesmen must complete the selling cycle with all of their accounts before the advertising breaks.

Problems of implementation are complicated by the many items that must be carefully coordinated and by the different lead times required to accomplish certain functions. Shipment of deal merchandise may only take two weeks from factory to retail outlet, but complete coverage of all accounts to obtain "sell-in" on the deal may require a one-month sales program. Dealers may require several weeks' notice if they are to cooperate in a special promotion, such as a label pack. Furthermore, these elements may require careful sequencing. For example, dealer contact may have to be completed before shipment can begin. It may take a month to contact all dealers. Lags in the order cycle must be anticipated at all levels. Changes in inventory levels and in the rate of flow among inventories must be carefully planned and coordinated at all levels of the distribution system.

A timetable of necessary activities and required completion times is a must for the satisfactory coordination of campaign elements during the implementation of the campaign. Adequate communication to the various parties involved—vendors, agencies, resellers, and salesmen—cannot be maintained without a careful timetable. The time required to complete each task and lags in the decision processes involved must also be considered, including variability in those time periods. It may usually take two weeks to get final client approval of copy prepared by the advertising agency, but this may vary from less than a week to a month or more depending upon the nature of the copy and other factors beyond the control or prediction of the advertising agency account executive.

Critical Path Analysis

Complex projects involving many interdependent activities and varying lead times can be more efficiently managed by using a set of management techniques that can be grouped under the general label of "critical path analysis." The most common methods are PERT (program evaluation and review technique) and CPM (critical path method), although there are many variations.

Critical path analysis was originally developed to manage weapon systems development projects. The Polaris weapon system, under the program management of the Lockheed Missile and Space Company, led to the development of PERT by the U.S. Navy's Special Projects Office in connection with Lockheed and the management consulting firm of Booz-Allen and Hamilton. The central analysis in developing a critical path network for a project is to identify the activities that must be completed and the events that must occur, in the necessary sequence, in order to produce the desired end result. Activities take time and lead to events. An activity would be "develop a display piece according to specifications" and the event would be the completion of the display piece. "Get client approval" would be an activity and the event would be the granting of approval (perhaps by signing a specific document).

Subjective Estimates of Completion Times. Activity completion times typically cannot be estimated with certainty, and possible variability can be considered in several ways. A typical procedure with PERT is to ask project managers to estimate the most optimistic, most likely, and most pessimistic times required to complete each activity. These estimates can be combined according to several formulas; the most commonly used weights the most likely time with a value of 4 while the most optimistic and most pessimistic times are given weight 1. The total is then divided by 6 to obtain the estimated activity completion time. Another method is to work with the mean and variance of a frequency distribution of an assumed form, such as the beta distribution.

Defining the Critical Path. Completion times for each activity required for the accomplishment of a given event can then be analyzed to determine the "critical path" through the network, which is the longest time required for task completion. All activities on the critical path are "critical activities." These concepts can be understood more clearly by reference to Figure 25–2. The lettered circles are events that must occur (A could stand for management approval to go ahead with the project) and the arrows represent activities required to produce an event. Times are indicated along with the arrows. The critical path is the longest time required to produce the final result and is determined in this case to be the path A-B-F-H, which will require 9.0 weeks to complete. The most important activity is B-F. Having identified the critical path through this network, management can now anticipate possible bottlenecks. The critical activity B-F can be given special attention and even special resources to insure that this activity has been completed as expeditiously as possible. Activity A-B is also on the critical path, as is activity F-H. Notice that activities C-F and E-F must also be completed before event F can occur.

Critical path analysis has been used by several companies to coordinate the activities associated with the introduction of a new product,

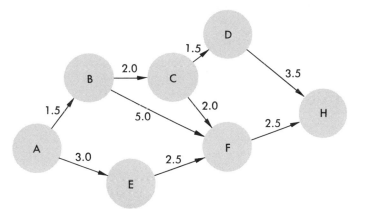

Fig. 25–2. A simple illustration of a critical path network.

including all aspects of market development and marketing communication.[4] Critical path analysis has several benefits including the fact that it permits the anticipation of bottlenecks, it identifies interrelationships among project elements, and it permits frequent checking of progress against a clearly stated schedule of activities and events. Complex projects require that the determination of critical paths and other calculations be performed on a computer. Critical path analysis can also provide a basis for simulating the effects of alternative resource allocations upon total project completion costs and times. With or without the help of the computer, critical path methods offer a logical and systematic approach to the complex problems of coordinating and implementing the many aspects of a total marketing communication strategy.

ORGANIZATION

Problems of coordination and control of marketing communication strategy are closely intertwined with the question of organization. The formal structure of an organization reflects its strategy for achieving the necessary coordination of organizational functions and for obtaining the advantages of specialization.

Traditional Structures

The most typical form of organization for marketing communication strategy involves a separation of responsibility for advertising and for personal selling. Public relations and sales promotion may be distinct functions or they may be considered part of the advertising manager's

[4]Yung Wong, "Critical Path Analysis for New Product Planning," *Journal of Marketing,* 28 (October 1964), pp. 53–59.

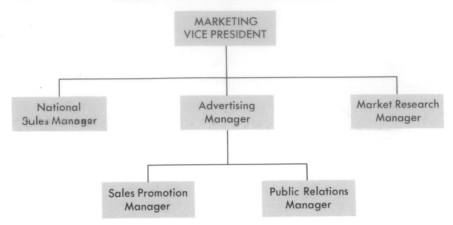

Fig. 25–3. A traditional organization with separate responsibility for mass and personal communications.

responsibility. The national sales manager is usually responsible for only the management of the company's field sales force. Reporting to him are usually several regional or district sales managers. A common form of the traditional organization structure is illustrated in Figure 25–3.

Problems of organization were discussed in Chapter 16 as part of the problem of establishing responsibility for the determination of budget levels for advertising and for other forms of communication effort. It was specifically noted that the product management form of organization, widely used by marketers of consumer packaged goods, separates responsibility for advertising and sales promotion from that for the field sales effort. This significantly reduces the opportunities for effective coordination of mass communication and personal selling. Determination of the optimum allocation of effort between these two modes of communication must be made at the highest level of the marketing organization and this raises the question of whether top marketing management can ever be well enough informed to make this determination as effectively as those who are more involved in day-to-day decision making and strategic competition.

In companies using the product manager form of organization, it is typical for the product manager to be responsible for all planning and strategic considerations relating to advertising and sales promotion on his brand. Details of implementation such as media placement, advertising production, and the mechanics of creative work, are handled by a separate advertising department.[5]

[5]David L. Hurwood and Earl L. Bailey, *Advertising, Sales Promotion, and Public Relations-Organizational Alternatives,* Experiences in Marketing Management, No. 16 (New York: National Industrial Conference Board, 1968), 38–39.

Table 25–1
Organizational Arrangements for Advertising, Sales Promotion, and Public Relations

Responsibility of Advertising Department	Where Advertising Is at Corporate Level	Where Advertising Is at Divisional Level
Advertising only	40	12
Advertising and sales promotion	72	44
Advertising and public relations	46	10
Advertising, sales promotion, and public relations	69	27
	227 [a]	93 [a]

[a] Total survey involved 267 companies. Fifty-three companies had advertising departments at both corporate and divisional levels. They are included in both columns above.

Source: National Industrial Conference Board, *Advertising, Sales Promotion, and Public Relations—Organizational Alternatives*, Experiences in Marketing Management, No. 16 (New York: The Board, 1968), adapted from Table 6, p. 43.

Public relations is a difficult organizational problem because it combines both marketing and non-marketing functions. Employee and community relations are quite distinct from demand stimulation activities and to combine them under the marketing department may not be the most satisfactory assignment of responsibility. Important nonmarketing functions are likely to receive less-than-desirable levels of attention under such an arrangement.

One study found that most companies assigned responsibility for sales promotion to the advertising department. Seldom was the advertising department responsible for advertising only. Most frequently, it had responsibility for sales promotion and, occasionally, for public relations. These findings are summarized in Table 25–1.

There are several considerations involved in the assignment of organizational responsibility for advertising and related functions. The basic elements of the product and the market are, as always, of major importance. There are important distinctions between industrial and consumer goods companies as well. Because of the relatively greater reliance upon personal selling in industrial marketing strategies, advertising is more often likely to have an emphasis on corporate image building rather than on specific products. It is common, therefore, for public relations and advertising to be organizationally combined in industrial goods firms. Advertising is also more frequently combined with sales promotion in industrial firms.[6]

[6] *Ibid.*, p. 46.

Corporate level advertising departments have several important contributions to make in a company that also has divisionalized advertising responsibility. The corporate department can handle such problems as financial control, coordination of media schedules for several brands, and implementation of corporate policies relating to promotion—such as the use of certain appeals, or the use of corporate logotypes. The corporate department may retain the right to adjust copy for advertising on specific brands, and it may also perform all legal functions. Among other benefits of coordination, there is also the possibility of achieving a certain company "look" in the advertising, a potential contributor to credibility and to advertising recognition.

The Marketing Communication Manager

Some companies have adopted what is called "the communications concept" involving centralized responsibility for all communication activities, usually with the exception of personal selling. The job title manager of marketing communication is most common, although vice-president—communication is also found. Companies adopting this form of organization cite as its advantages the opportunity for better coordination and control of all communication functions toward the efficient accomplishment of specific communication objectives. The communication job is said to encompass "all communications of a marketing nature, both to and from the company's customers, as well as to and from its salesmen. In addition to traditional advertising and sales promotion activities, these include sales meetings, sales training, catalogues, and communications research."[7] This was said by one marketing manager to insure that proper emphasis can be given to each communication element, based upon marketing objectives.

This possibility does not exist unless personal selling *is* included in the total communication mix. Simply to combine mass communication under one responsibility and to leave personal selling under separate jurisdiction is to overlook the major opportunity, in most companies, for obtaining better coordination of marketing communication functions.

The total integration of marketing communication strategy, as advocated by this book, can best be implemented by the kind of organization structure suggested in Figure 25–4. A manager of marketing communication is responsible for advertising, sales promotion, sales force management, and public relations. His responsibilities are made distinct from three other key marketing management functions: physical distribution, market information, and product development. (Strong arguments can be made for each of these three specialties, but that is beyond the

[7]*Ibid.*, pp. 46–49.

Fig. 25—4. A marketing organization with integrated responsibility for marketing communication strategy.

scope of this book.) The traditional marketing organization separates responsibility for mass and personal communication in a manner that is undesirable.

Recognizing Communication Expertise As a Specialty. It is possible to identify several potential problems with the manager of marketing communication position suggested in Figure 25—4. The most obvious argument is that this is too broad a range of activities and responsibilities for one man to handle except in a very general manner, such as required at the marketing vice-president level. The rebuttal to that argument is that the specialization occurs at the next level of the organization. The manager of marketing communication should concentrate his attention upon overall communication strategy and the optimum combination of communication elements, according to the guidelines suggested earlier in this chapter. His job is to minimize the amount of suboptimization in specific communication elements.

A second argument against the manager of marketing communication is that public relations responsibility should not be part of the marketing function. Here, there is no easy answer. The organizational assignment of public relations responsibility must reflect the relative importance of marketing vis-à-vis other functions in public relations. Other things being equal, centralization of public relations responsibility within the marketing function is justified on two bases. First, the manager of marketing communication should be the leading expert on communication of all kinds; his department should contain the specialized skills, knowledge, and resources necessary for effective communication. Second, all public relations activities have an impact on the company's image and this in turn has a definite impact on the total marketing communication program.

Communication Strategy and Field Sales Management. A final argument against this organizational arrangement that should be briefly considered is that sales force management requires a particular set of skills and a background of field sales experience. It may also require extensive travelling, taking the manager away from his desk where he should spend time on strategic planning. Again, this argument can be rebutted by observing that this specialization is available at the next level in the organization in the form of the sales force manager. It should be emphasized that the manager of marketing communication's major responsibilities are for coordination and integrated, strategic planning. In the traditional organization, this function was performed by the top marketing executive, to whom the advertising manager and the national sales manager reported. This new organization form has the advantage of permitting more specialized consideration of marketing communication in total.

A major argument for the manager of marketing communication is that he can possess a particular kind of expertise not available elsewhere in the organization—the conceptual knowledge of communication processes and of budgeting and allocation techniques—necessary for efficient communication strategy. The kind of knowledge developed in this text is a major requirement for true professionalism in marketing communication; it is generally not possessed by today's operating management such as the advertising and sales managers. These concepts inject a unique viewpoint into the consideration of marketing strategy, a viewpoint not likely to be found at the highest level of the marketing organization nor at the lower, more specialized levels. A manager who can think about marketing communication *as communication* can make a unique contribution to the effectiveness of the company's total marketing effort.

STRATEGIC PLANNING

The manager of marketing communication is less involved in day-to-day decision making and operations than are the four managers who report to him. On the other hand, he is more concerned with strategic planning, and can devote more time to strategic planning of communication as a coordinated function than is possible for the marketing vice president. He can bring to bear the conceptual knowledge of communication as a distinct expertise with the result of greater efficiency and heightened effectiveness for marketing communication investment.

Heightened effectiveness in the communication strategy can be the critical difference in markets and industries where product differences among competitors are minimal, where distribution efficiency has been achieved by all major competitors, and where standardized production technology leaves little opportunity for unique competitive advantage. In such conditions, marketing communication can provide the key to competitive advantage and above average profitability.

This text has been built around a framework of strategic planning. The various parts and chapters of the book have been designed to follow the logic of strategic planning. Briefly stated, strategic planning may be thought of as the process that provides answers to three questions:

Where are we?
Where do we want to be?
How do we get there? [8]

Strategic planning results in a pattern of resource commitments which tends to make the company unique in comparison with competition. It also permits a flexible response to the acts of intelligent opposition.

The appraisal of communication opportunity—the analysis of predispositions and their sources—was seen as a necessary first step in the development of marketing communication strategy. The definition of objectives was seen to require a careful analysis of company strengths and weaknesses and of market opportunity. Creative development of messages, of salesmen, and of media strategy were seen to be the critical difference in determining competitive effectiveness. Qualitative analysis of media and of messages, and the careful pretesting and rigorous evaluation of these strategic elements, were explored in detail because these are the critical decision areas of marketing communication.

Planning Requires Prediction of Market Response

These problems define the work of the manager of marketing communication as a strategic planner engaged in the search for relative advantage in the face of intelligent opposition. Strategic planning involves analysis and prediction of the operating environment; it is decision making with the best possible view of the future impact of those decisions. Every marketing communication decision involves a prediction of market response and the quality of those predictions depends upon the planner's knowledge of his markets and of the communication process. The particular expertise of the marketing communication specialist can significantly improve the quality of predictions of market response to communication and therefore is the basis upon which to build an effective marketing communication strategy.

[8]For this concept of strategic planning I am indebted to my colleague Professor James Brian Quinn of the Amos Tuck School of Business Administration at Dartmouth College.

Strategic planning integrates company activities toward clearly stated objectives and within the constraints provided by company policies. It allocates the company's limited resources in a manner consistent with threats and opportunities in the environment and in a manner reflecting the strengths and weaknesses of the company. It matches resources to opportunities and in anticipation of the acts of competition.

Finally, strategic planning integrates the activities of various components of the organization toward a consistent set of objectives. (This aspect of corporate planning is often called "mission planning" because it is concerned with the integration of the several "missions" of separate organizational units toward a common purpose.) It recognizes the interdependencies of multiple products, multiple divisions, and multiple company functions and attempts to deal with the synergistic effects of those interdependencies. We have argued in this chapter that the manager of marketing communication position within the organization, reporting directly to the marketing vice president, is the most effective way to achieve this kind of integration in strategic planning for marketing communication.

SUMMARY

Marketing communication strategy requires the coordination of the several functions—personal selling, advertising, branding and packaging, sales promotion, deals, display, corporate advertising, public relations, publicity, and reseller effort—to achieve the best level of performance, overall. The marketing communication strategy is a system of interdependent elements that yields a result greater than the sum of its parts. Careful consideration of these interactions is a necessary ingredient of strategic planning.

Coordination of communication elements over time, including both the development of campaign materials and the careful scheduling of implementation details, is a second aspect of the coordination problem. While new management techniques such as critical path analysis can assist in this function, major reliance must be placed upon a skilled manager who can set up a schedule for achieving necessary results and a system for monitoring the accomplishment of successive stages in implementation.

Traditional organizational arrangements for the management of marketing communication often combine two or more elements of mass communication such as advertising and public relations within the same department. Seldom, however, is there the necessary coordination of mass communication and personal selling except at the highest levels of the marketing organization. At this level, there is likely to be inadequate information about the conduct of communication activities, and a lack of the required professional expertise, necessary for the true integration of strategic elements.

Current practice provides only a small amount of evidence suggesting a new form of corporate structure—the Manager of Marketing Communication reporting to the Marketing Vice President. Companies have thus far approached such integration with appropriate caution but the logic of strategic planning combines with the central importance of marketing communication strategy to suggest that more and more companies will organize on the basis of the communication concept.

A critical step in the strategic planning process is the evaluation of the results of a given strategy and the tactical adoption of strategy in response to feedback on results. This evaluation process is the subject for our next and last chapter.

26

Campaign Evaluation and Feedback

Evaluation of campaign effects and feedback of the results of such evaluation are the final stages of strategic planning. As results are evaluated they will frequently suggest the value of altering the strategy and the process of planing marketing communication strategy begins anew. In this sense, strategic planning in marketing communication is a continuous process. Data on the results of this year's campaign become inputs to next year's campaign and the process becomes self-renewing.

In this chapter attention will focus on the evaluation of the marketing communication strategy in total, although specific evaluation of individual campaign elements cannot be completely avoided. The discussion will tend to favor pull strategies relying on mass communication more than push strategies relying on actual personal contact at all levels but it will not overlook the evaluation of selling effort. Concepts introduced earlier in consideration of message testing and media evaluation will be used but the discussion of these specific strategic variables will not be repeated. Results of total communication effort rather than individual strategic elements will be emphasized, but use of the results of evaluation will require that campaign effects be traced back to specific campaign elements.

EVALUATION MUST BE PLANNED

Evaluation really begins when objectives are established for the marketing communication program because these objectives will become the major criteria against which the strategy will be evaluated. There is often the need for a benchmark, some measure of where we stand, as a preliminary to subsequent evaluation. To establish such benchmarks, it is necessary to do a survey or otherwise develop an empirical data base. Because of the importance of such guidelines for evaluation and because studies both to set benchmarks and to measure results require planning and budgeting, evaluation must be carefully planned.

Planning for evaluation of marketing communication strategy is also important because of what happens in the absence of such planning. Without planning, evaluation becomes subjective (even emotional) and arbitrary. Personal judgments about the aesthetics of campaign elements, statements by the chief executive officer or the marketing manager to the effect that he "liked the advertising" or "heard good things about our salesmen," are likely to be given undue authority.

The development of campaign elements can be significantly helped if the evaluation process is planned simultaneously with the campaign itself. Strategic thinking can be sharpened by the early resolution of subtle ambiguities in campaign objectives. A vague statement about a goal of "strengthening attitudes" will be more clearly defined when the question is answered "What will we measure to determine relative success?"

Without carefully planned evaluation of the campaign, management has little basis for the adjustment of present strategy or for the development of more effective strategy in the future. The results of inadequate evaluation include the repetition of previous errors, a failure to make adequate response to market opportunity, and inefficiency in the expenditure of promotional resources. Without adequate planning for the evaluation of marketing communication strategy, management misses the opportunity to learn from its previous experience in an organized fashion.

ROLE OF OBJECTIVES IN EVALUATION

Evaluation is intimately related to the establishment of objectives. Objectives define where we want to be; evaluation is the process of determining how close we came to getting there. Objectives are the criteria against which performance is said to be good or bad. Objectives are the goals of the marketing communication strategy.

Earlier discussion of objectives suggested several classes of objectives including both qualitative and quantitative objectives, those concerning the meaning to be conveyed about the company and its products and those concerning levels of awareness, reach, frequency, and changes in attitudes, as well as measures of activity by salesmen and dealers, and measures of revenue and profit accomplishment. The purposes of marketing communication are many and varied. As stressed in the previous chapter on coordination, these purposes are interdependent. These interactions significantly complicate the evaluation problem. Evaluation must deal with both individual campaign elements and with the total communication program.

The interaction of campaign elements is a major reason for the frustration which researchers have experienced in attempting to develop methods for evaluating advertising specifically. One observer has commented that trying to evaluate advertising on the basis of sales results is like trying to evaluate Mickey Mantle on the basis of whether the Yankees win or lose.[1] Mickey Mantle may play his best game while the Yankees are losing. Advertising or any other single campaign element may be contributing at its maximum level of efficiency and effectiveness while sales volume is decreasing. Each campaign element is a contributing factor to the success of the total program; no single campaign element can insure success.

In order to come to grips with the measurement problem it is necessary, once again, to consider the basic process of how communication works. In earlier discussions, the hierarchy-of-effects model has been explored many times and has been looked at from many different angles. If any generalization can be drawn from those earlier discussions it is that communication is a complex process. A logical conclusion is that any simple measurement or single criterion variable is going to be an inadequate basis for campaign evaluation. It will measure only one of the many effects of the total communication program and will emphasize the effects of some campaign elements and obscure the effects of others.

The analytical structure developed in this text can be summarized in a model of how a *total* marketing communication strategy produces a series of results that move the firm toward the accomplishment of its objectives. This model serves as a brief summary of earlier chapters while providing a framework within which we can come to grips with the problem of evaluating campaign effects.

A MODEL OF CAMPAIGN EFFECTS[2]

A campaign takes shape as the marketing communication strategist sets objectives, develops guidelines for the relative importance of mass

[1]Gail Smith, "How GM Measures Ad Effectiveness," *Printer's Ink* (May 14, 1965), pp. 19–29.

[2]Several elements of this model are taken from Paul E. J. Gerhold, "How Advertising is Measured, and How It Probably Works," a paper presented at the 1969 International Marketing Congress of the American Marketing Association in Atlanta, Georgia, June 17, 1969. While the model presented here is different in many respects, Mr. Gerhold's paper stimulated its development.

(pull) vs. personal (push) communication, develops message and media strategies, and pretests various campaign elements. This stage precedes the actual communication process, but it initiates it. A sound campaign will be based on a careful assessment of current conditions and past accomplishments. The most important inputs to campaign development include measures of existing predispositions among relevant market segments, a reliable measure of market potential, and a sound conceptual model of the communication process.

Effects on Buyers

When the campaign is developed and the planning job is complete, messages are distributed to potential customers and resellers via sales force activity and the distribution of mass media. Vehicle exposure and message exposure are necessary preconditions for mass communication effectiveness. Only if there is message exposure can the communication actually influence a potential customer. Cognition then occurs, but it occurs in a manner which reflects the predispositions of the receiver and involves selective exposure to both media and messages, selective perception, and selective retention. The interaction of the receiver's predispositions and the creative execution of the campaign produces some gradual change, hopefully favorable and consistent with the objectives of the communicator, through the processes of learning, forgetting, and attitude formation. For a specific brand, the problem is both to increase favorable predispositions toward that brand and to reduce them toward other brands. Repetition of the message, and the relative frequency of exposure to messages concerning competing brands, are important determinants of changes in predispositions. Attitudes toward the selling company and attitudes toward the actual product are both important in determining consumer response.

As the buyer develops favorable attitudes this may (but will not necessarily) lead to the generation of word-of-mouth, informal communications among members of a social group such as a family or a neighborhood. Over time these messages will flow among groups and opinions about the product or service will spread through the social system. Opinion leaders are a significant variable in this process, especially to the extent that they may pass on the contents of mass media to persons not exposed to those media. Informal communication may be more effective than formal (marketer-dominated) sources in producing attitude change and in stimulating buying behavior.

Effects on Marketing Effort

Another set of effects are the increased selling effort, and the increased effectiveness of that effort, by both the company's own salesmen and by its resellers. Special incentives and contests may be developed to stimulate this increased effort but it can also result from the "pull" effects of mass communication as well as from the greater credibility created by mass communication. Of course, salesmen's efforts may be stimulated directly by innovations in supervision, training, compensation, and control procedures without any necessary inputs from mass communication strategy.

Increased selling effort will improve product availability. The increased selling effort may result in the opening of new accounts, making the product available in a broader geographic area or making it more broadly available within a given area. Existing resellers may improve their inventories and the possibility of out-of-stock problems is therefore reduced. Actual display of the product may also be improved, due in part to the direct selling activities of salesmen trying to set up display, partly because of the "pull" of mass communication, and partly due to the pressures of increased inventories. Increased display may also reflect the aesthetic appeal and creative approach of the display piece itself or it may reflect the attractiveness of a special premium, contest, or deal featured on the display.

Increased product availability is desirable only if there is simultaneously an increase in purchasing activities by end-users. Special promotions can increase purchasing activities. Assuming that product availability has been achieved, the result will be increased sales. Notice that in the absence of product availability, however, increased purchasing activity will not result in increased sales, and these should therefore be treated as separate effects of the campaign. Increased sales may be a misleading indicator of success, however, if there is not also increased product usage. Otherwise, inventories accumulate either in the retail outlet or on the consumer's shelf, and a subsequent slump in sales will erase earlier, transitory, favorable campaign effects.

Effects on Costs

The communication strategy—especially in its public relations and corporate advertising aspects—can also reduce the firm's total costs in several subtle ways. Among the possibilities for cost reduction are the easier availability of capital through improved corporate image; reduced costs of personnel hiring and turnover; and reduced transportation costs as the result of broader and more efficient distribution.

Marketing communication costs may also be lowered directly through such efforts as the attainment of quantity discounts from more concentrated media purchasing. The cost of obtaining a given level of revenue in one year will be lower, other things being equal, than in the previous year if the company has been spending wisely in previous years and can now derive benefits from the lagged effects of earlier efforts. Improved brand image and company image may also create a stronger consumer franchise and may save the costs of price concessions that would otherwise be necessary to remain competitive.[3]

The combination of increased sales and reduced costs can produce the ultimate result of improved profitability. The objective of marketing communication strategy is to generate *profitable* sales revenue and profitability is the ultimate objective of the firm.

Each Stage Permits Measurement

This view of the process of campaign effects is summarized in Figure 26–1. It is at the same time both a summary of this text and a view of the evaluation problem. With the exception of the stages of campaign development (and perhaps without that exception), *each of these effects can be measured in the evaluation of marketing communication strategy.* Techniques are available for measuring each of these variables and processes. At which levels should the campaign be evaluated? That depends upon the objectives that have been established for each of the several elements of the communication program and for the program as a whole. It also depends upon the particular measurement conditions facing that communicator and the degree of error he is willing to tolerate in measurement techniques. Finally, and most importantly, it depends upon the use that will be made of the measurement—the decisions that will be based upon it.

The point is that no one measurement can do the complete job of evaluation. There is no such thing as *the* campaign decision. There are many decisions—about messages, about sales call patterns, about media selection, about promotions and deals—and the information required for each decision that leads to a total campaign effect must be gathered separately.

But there is still the nagging problem of the interaction of campaign elements and the problem of evaluating the total campaign. As information is being gathered to evaluate the effects of individual elements of the campaign, information must also be gathered to evaluate the effects of the campaign as a whole.

The viewpoint of this text has argued for a *new* set of objectives and of decisions in the marketing strategy: *communication* objectives and decisions. These strategic elements lie between marketing strategy as a whole and the elements of marketing communication: advertising, personal selling, sales promotion, and reseller strategies. Conceptually, mar-

[3]*Ibid.*, p. 3.

A. CAMPAIGN DEVELOPMENT
    Setting Objectives
    Push vs. Pull
    Message Strategy
    Media Strategy
    Pre-testing

B. MESSAGE DISTRIBUTION
    Sales Force Activity
    Vehicle Distribution
    Vehicle Exposure
    Message Exposure

C. COGNITION
    Selective Exposure
    Selective Perception
    Selective Retention

D. GENERATION OF FAVORABLE PREDISPOSITIONS
    Learning (Repeated Exposure)
    Forgetting
    Attitude Formation
        Company Image
        Brand Image

E. GENERATION OF WORD-OF-MOUTH
    Within Groups
    Among Groups

F. INCREASED SELLING EFFORT AND EFFECTIVENESS
    Resellers
    Salesmen

G. INCREASED PRODUCT AVAILABILITY
    Distribution
    Inventory Levels
    Display

H. INCREASED PURCHASING ACTIVITY

I. INCREASED SALES

J. INCREASED PRODUCT USAGE

K. REDUCED COSTS

L. INCREASED PROFITS

Fig. 26–1. The process of campaign effects.

keting communication strategy as a new level of strategic decision making is presented graphically in Figure 26–2. With this new conceptual level in marketing strategy there is also a new measurement problem at this level: the measurement of campaign effects.

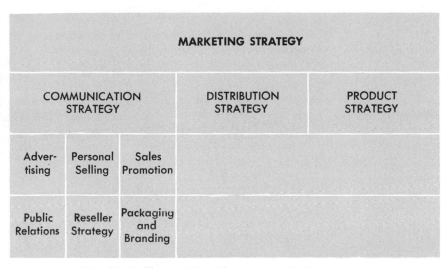

Fig. 26–2. The building blocks of marketing strategy.

CONCEPT OF A CONTROL SYSTEM

As we consider communication strategy as a system of interrelated elements, and as we consider the role of evaluation in providing feedback with which to keep the system "under control," it is helpful to consider specifically what we mean by the concept of a control system.

The control process involves four steps:

1. Setting objectives and standards against which to evaluate system performance
2. Obtaining information on actual performance from the operating environment
3. Comparison of performance against standards
4. Taking corrective action to bring the system more closely in line with objectives

Planning and control are obviously very similar processes. Both are part of strategy. Planning is forward-looking and involves the process by which objectives are developed and resources organized, and the allocation of these resources to specific tasks. Control involves the execution of the strategy including the monitoring of performance, comparison with standards, and adjustments of the system as necessary to more effectively achieve stated objectives. Diagrammatically, a control system is depicted in Figure 26–3.

This view of the communication process as a control system brings us back to the basic model of communication developed in Chapter 3. Feedback was discussed as the process by which the source determines

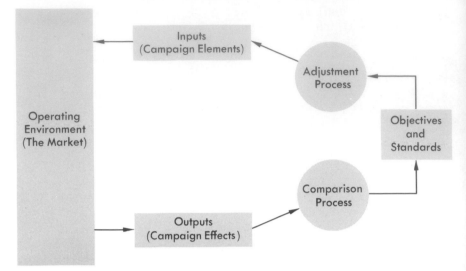

Fig. 26–3. Marketing communication as a control process.

whether or not his communication has been successful in producing the desired response, that which motivated him to communicate in the first place. In marketing communication strategy, objectives are stated in terms of desired responses from the market and the "feedback" stage consists of monitoring those responses, comparing them with objectives, and adjusting the strategy as indicated. Conceptually, therefore, both communication and the evaluation process can be thought of as control processes in which feedback is the critical element for monitoring and adjusting system performance.

METHODS OF EVALUATION

Within the framework of the campaign effects model presented in Figure 26–1, it is possible to assess the desirability and usefulness of various measures of campaign effects. The following discussion will concern only measures of campaign effects after the strategy has been implemented—that is, post-tests rather than pretests. Message testing, a form of pretesting, was discussed in Chapter 15 and evaluation of media as the basis for media strategy decisions was considered in Chapter 21. Several of the techniques discussed in those chapters also apply to the measurement of campaign effects.

Several methods of campaign evaluation will be considered and their uses will be related back to the specific decision variables and strategic elements for which such measurements are most useful. Which methods to use must be determined for each specific decision situation; there is no one best method or combination of methods that will be right for all companies.

Consideration of the process by which marketing communication strategies produce results is helpful in understanding the options available to the evaluator. If communication is thought of as a flow of influence from marketer through salesmen, media, resellers, and opinion leaders to ultimate consumers, with attitudes and product flows and inventories shifting to reflect the influence of communication, we begin to see the nature of the measurement problem. Because communication is a process involving flows of influences and of products, management must decide at which points it wishes to intercept the process and take one or more measurements. Among the classes of measurements possible are those relating to exposure, communication (cognition, attitude change, and word-of-mouth), selling activity, product availability, purchase and consumption behavior, sales, and profitability.

Measures of Exposure

Measures of exposure include the use of data on media distribution (vehicle exposure) and on recognition (message exposure). Each of these classes of measurement has been discussed earlier and has been found to be inadequate in at least one respect. Measures of media distribution stop short of any communication effect and do not get at the critical interaction between message and media vehicle in determining response to communication. Recognition measures were found to suffer from their tendency to overstate true exposure and from the impact of respondent confusion, especially for campaigns involving strong basic themes with only minor creative differences in execution of specific advertisements. For both reasons, measures of exposure are rather inadequate as measures of campaign effectiveness.

For decisions about media strategy, however, these measures have much greater value. It is sometimes useful to ask respondents where they remember seeing an advertisement or, more generally, where they first heard about the product. While there may be substantial differences between what people report about media exposure and their actual exposure, their responses may be useful in assessing the relative attractiveness (or credibility) of alternative media for them. Asking a sample of prospective customers about their exposure to, and preference for, alternative sources of market information may be a very revealing exercise and may suggest new media alternatives.

Surveys of media exposure can also be helpful in identifying the existence of word-of-mouth, the characteristics of opinion leaders, and the media habits of leaders and followers. While such research requires careful design and may necessitate the use of sophisticated interviewing techniques, it is by no means impossible. It may also be useful to match samples of users and non-users of the company's products in an attempt to spot differences in media habits.

Measures of exposure are therefore useful in media decisions but of limited usefulness in total campaign evaluation.

Measures of Communication

The term "communication" is used here to mean the three related processes of cognition, attitude formation, and generation of word-of-mouth in the model of campaign effects.

Measures of communication were advocated in the Association of National Advertisers' DAGMAR study.[4] It will be recalled that this study was the first to specifically argue the futility of using sales and profitability as measures of advertising effectiveness because these two variables are influenced by so many factors other than advertising. However, the strength of the DAGMAR argument depended upon the validity of the hierarchy-of-effects hypothesis that changes in levels of awareness and attitude (communication effects) led to changes in sales. This assumption can be challenged on both logical and empirical grounds.

The DAGMAR study made a valuable contribution to our understanding of the process by which advertising exerts an influence. It also contributed to the practice of marketing management by advocating both a clear statement of objectives and careful planning of evaluation as a central part of the development of advertising strategy. It did not go far enough, however. Although arguing for the basic value of stating advertising objectives as communication objectives, the DAGMAR study ignored the interaction of advertising with other marketing communication elements and, in general, stopped short of the total communication concept that has been evolving more recently. As such, the DAGMAR study proposes an incomplete solution to the problem of campaign evaluation.

At the same time, it must be recognized that many important firms have reported the successful use of DAGMAR-inspired measurements of campaign effects. No less an advertiser than General Motors has reported heavy reliance upon a DAGMAR-oriented approach.[5] General Motors adapted the approach to its own particular needs, developed a research procedure for its implementation, and extended the communication objectives to include an economic evaluation of the value of goal

[4]Russell H. Colley (ed.), *Defining Advertising Goals for Measured Advertising Results* (New York: Association of National Advertisers, Inc., 1961).

[5]Smith, *op. cit.*

accomplishment. The most important use for this approach, according to published reports, was in the evaluation of alternative media. The procedure that was developed permitted an estimate of the percentage of the target market reached by the various media being evaluated, both individually and in combination. Survey results are projected to the total target market segment and changes in awareness (as a percentage of total market segment) are estimated. A cost-per-thousand comparison is then developed for the various media. Note that awareness is the measure of communication. Successive waves of interviews are used, beginning with a benchmark study (a critical part of the DAGMAR approach) and followed by five more interviews, with some respondents carried from one interview cycle to the next depending upon their statement of buying intentions.

Changes in Awareness or Attitudes. Measures of communication effect require the measurement either of levels of awareness or of changes in attitudes. Recall measures may be useful here although they have the disadvantage of understating the effects attributable to the campaign. Levels of awareness may be indicative of the effectiveness of the media schedule but they may be inadequate measures of the ability of the campaign to influence attitudes and buying tendencies.

Attitude measurement in the evaluation of campaign effects has two distinct tasks to perform. One is to measure the extent to which the campaign has succeeded in convincing potential buyers that the benefits offered by the brand are in fact important. The second is to measure the effectiveness of the campaign in associating this brand with that particular benefit. To illustrate, advertising for Crest toothpaste must first convince people that it is a desirable thing to reduce dental cavities; it must next convince people that Crest is the most effective toothpaste in reducing cavities. Without the prior development of "benefit attitudes," association of the brand with that product benefit has no persuasive value.[6] Measures of attitude designed to aid in campaign evaluation should therefore attempt measurements at both levels of influence.

Relating Predisposition and Behavior Change. Where possible, it is helpful to go beyond measures of attitude and attempt to relate differences in attitude to differences in propensity to purchase, on a statistical basis. Likelihood of purchasing, or rate of purchase, or amount purchased can be correlated with attitudes on various dimensions. These studies may also reveal which sets of attitudes have the strongest impact on actual purchase behavior. In this manner, measures of attitude can be

[6]Norton Garfinkle, "New Developments in Tracking Advertising Effectiveness," paper presented at the 1969 International Marketing Congress of the American Marketing Association, Atlanta, Georgia, June 17, 1969.

useful guides to the development of communication strategy and most specifically in the development of message strategy.[7]

For the specific purposes of evaluating advertising, as opposed to total campaign effects, measures of attitude change have an advantage of being relatively "pure." Other variables in the communication program are not likely to have significant influence on attitudes in the short term. Further, none of these other communication elements is likely to have attitude change (among buyers) as a specific communication objective. For strategies which rely upon media advertising, the consumer is less likely to be directly exposed to personal selling or reseller effort. For all of these reasons, attitude measures may be good measures of advertising —especially of message strategy and of basic appeals—in the short term. To criticize measures of communication on the basis that attitude change does not have a necessary relationship to actual changes in sales volume is to hold advertising responsible for more than it is really capable of alone. As noted earlier, however, the advertiser may wish to push as far as possible to determine the influence of communication strategy on company sales and profitability. In this case, he must go beyond the evaluation of advertising to the broader evaluation of campaign effects.

Measures of brand and corporate image, a form of attitude measurement, fall into the categories of measures of communication. These studies are most useful to management in evaluating total campaign impact if they are conducted at regular intervals over a sufficiently long time period to detect basic trends in brand and corporate image.

Measures of communication also include attempts to determine the value of a campaign in generating word-of-mouth for the product or service. Asking people to state where they first heard about the brand is one crude method for determining the influence of informal sources of communication. Another possibility is to interview persons in market areas adjacent to but not included in test market areas and therefore (theoretically) not exposed to formal communications concerning the product. It can then be assumed that awareness is an indicator of exposure to word-of-mouth.

Finally, for the sake of completeness, it should also be mentioned that physiological measures of response—pupil dilation, GSR, and eye movement—are measures of communication in that they do attempt to measure psychological reactions by means of autonomic responses. As noted in Chapter 15, however, there is no evidence and little reason to believe that such responses have any relationship to actual behavior, either in the form of change in predisposition or change in buying behavior.

[7]James H. Myers, "Quantitative Contributions to Advertising Strategy," paper presented at the 1969 International Marketing Congress of the American Marketing Association, Atlanta, Georgia, June 17, 1969.

Measures of Selling Activity

In many situations, measures of the amount of selling activity generated during the period covered by the plan are the best that can be done to measure campaign effects. Measures of activity have special merit in many industrial situations and especially in marketing in the defense and aerospace industries where time lags become very long, multiple levels of buying influence among subcontractor tiers become very complex, and technological and cost situations are, in the last analysis, the most important determinants of competitive effectiveness. Under such conditions, to hold salesmen responsible for sales results is next to impossible and holding mass communication responsible for sales volume is clearly impossible.

Salesmen's Call Reports. Measures of selling activity by the company's sales force can be determined through careful provision for the reporting of sales call activity at regular intervals. Call report forms and reporting procedures should be reasonably brief and easy to use to minimize the likelihood that salesmen will ignore or falsify these reports. Salesmen object, and rightly so, to reporting procedures which take hours of their time, either away from their personal time or away from time that could be better spent in front of the customer.

Measures of sales force effort must be compared against previously determined standards. Quotas or bogeys on number of calls per day or per week may be established. It is also desirable to have special activity quotas to implement special objectives for the communication program such as the development of new accounts or expanding the geographic market coverage or establishing better contacts with key buying influentials in customer organizations. Each of these objectives can be translated into specific activity quotas.

Measuring Reseller Activity. Evaluation of resellers' selling activity is a harder task but by no means an impossible one. Company salesmen working in a missionary capacity may be able to develop quite reliable information concerning changes in the activities of resellers' salesmen as the result of particular programs implemented during the period. It may be possible to ask resellers' salesmen to file very brief reports (for example, on a postcard) after each call they make in which the manufacturer's product is discussed. While sales volume quotas may be established for resellers, activity quotas are much more difficult to implement because of the manufacturers' very limited degree of control.

Spot-checking and the use of unidentified "shoppers" are methods for measuring the amount of selling activity by retailers and their sales clerks. Prizes may be offered to any sales clerks who mention the manufacturer's product when the unidentified shopper comes into the store. This technique is at once a method for stimulating selling effort and for evaluating it.

In addition to these measures of the amount of selling activity, it is also important to have measures of the effectiveness of the selling activity. The objective of the communication program may not be to increase the number of sales calls made by salesmen or the amount of time spent by resellers' salesmen but to make them more effective in their selling. Sales supervisors can travel with the company's salesmen to assess changes in their effectiveness and company salesmen can call with resellers' salesmen for this purpose. Such subjective evaluation can be quite valid, especially as a measure of the results of training programs designed to develop effective selling activity.

Measures of Availability

One result of the marketing communication program may be improved product availability at the retail level and at prior levels of distribution. Syndicated research services are available to provide this information on stocks and flows of products throughout the distribution system. Such information can be used to evaluate sales force activity and reseller performance, and to make inferences about changes in the level of consumer demand as a measure of the effectiveness of advertising.

Store Audits. The A. C. Nielsen Company provides information to its clients on product movement and changes in retail inventories for products in the food, drug, cosmetic, confectionery, tobacco, and variety categories. This information is obtained by an actual physical count of inventories at the beginning and the end of the period and a careful checking of invoices to determine the flow of goods into the store. As a result, it is possible to calculate the flow of goods out of the store. These data are available for all brands in a given product category and permit the determination of changes in market share and other measures of competitive effectiveness.

Retail store audits can also be performed by the selling company itself and this is most efficiently done when the company sells through its own retail outlets. Company missionary salesmen can also perform some of this function with resellers as part of their call routine. Because the work is very time-consuming, however, it is not typically a function performed by the salesman.

Warehouse Withdrawals. Information on the withdrawal of products from the regional warehouses of chain grocers is gaining in importance as a measurement for the control of marketing strategy. Several large grocery store chains are offering these data to marketers for a fee. In addition, at least one commercial service is now available: Selling Areas–Marketing, Inc. (SAMI), a division of Time, Incorporated. SAMI provides data on approximately 85 to 90 percent of total grocery sales in the market areas reported on.

Warehouse withdrawal information has several advantages as a data source for the control of marketing communication strategy. It is more quickly available than store audit data and the total coverage offered by the sample may be better. Warehouse withdrawal data reflect the ordering activities of the retail outlets within the chain and therefore provide a measure of the effectiveness of the company's salesmen in getting product orders into retail outlets. This information is especially useful for evaluating the effectiveness of product displays, consumer deals, and trade deals, as well as in spotting problems in distribution coverage such as stock-outs. Information is available to clients for their own brands and for all other brands in the product categories for which data have been purchased.

Data on product availability are therefore especially helpful in evaluating short-term buying incentives and other elements of marketing communication strategy designed to achieve short-term results and to meet specific competitive situations. They provide only vague measures of the effectiveness of media advertising and of true changes in consumer preferences and predispositions.

Measures of Purchase and Consumption Behavior

The ultimate response desired from the market is a change in purchase and consumption behavior (which will be reflected in increased revenues and profits for the selling company). Assuming there is adequate product availability, the true effectiveness of the company's marketing communication strategy cannot be evaluated short of this stage in the process of campaign effects. Unless the strategy results in favorable changes in consumer behavior, it will not be effective in meeting its objectives.

There are several ways to determine changes in the level of purchasing activity. The simple counting of coupon redemptions and of inquiries generated in response to advertising are examples of straightforward measures of purchasing activity. (The latter may or may not also lead to the generation of sales revenue.) Purchasing activity, it should be remembered, may precede attitude change and other effects of "communication," as the term was used above. Measures of purchasing activity may be especially helpful as the basis for decisions concerning sales promotions, deals, and display as well as in the evaluation of advertising appeals, message strategy, and reseller strategy.

Consumer panel data are heavily relied upon by packaged goods manufacturers as sources of information on purchasing and consumption behavior. Households that are members of these panels report regularly on their purchases of products in many categories, by brand, amount, where purchased, and whether the product was purchased on a deal basis. These panel data can be carefully analyzed using sophisticated statistical techniques and models of buyer behavior to derive reasonably accurate estimates of such parameters as brand loyalty and switching, rate of usage, store loyalty, shopping patterns, and deal proneness. These measurements can be used to evaluate total campaign effects as well as to provide inputs to decisions about media strategy, message strategy, short-term buying incentives, and budget levels.[8]

Measures of Sales

Each of the preceding classes of measurements can be criticized on the ground that it does not place an economic value on the accomplishments of marketing communication and therefore falls short of the mark. That criticism is a sound one when one considers the large sums involved in marketing communication strategy and the need to devote careful economic reasoning to the analysis of communication strategy. None of the previous methods is helpful in determining advertising budget levels in any precise way, for example, and in comparing alternative expenditures against carefully stated economic criteria such as return on investment.

Sales data provide a basis for making such economic comparisons. The problem with using sales data is that a sales result reflects the interaction of many campaign elements: advertising messages, media, and budget levels; personal selling quantity and quality; reseller effectiveness and product availability; sales promotions, deals, and displays; and so on. Sales results summarize the effects of this campaign and previous campaigns. Sales data also reflect not only the seller's marketing communication strategy but his competitors' strategies and their relative effectiveness in a changing market environment. The president of a company manufacturing steel products recently remarked that, because his sales were ahead of last year by 38 percent, he thought they were having an excellent result until he determined that the industry was growing at the rate of 43 percent and he realized that his company was actually less effective than its competition.

Need To Compare with Potential. Sales measures can be used to determine campaign effects provided they are used in connection with

[8]For a thorough discussion of techniques of panel data analysis, see W. F. Massy, D. B. Montgomery, and D. G. Morrison, *Stochastic Models of Consumer Behavior* (Cambridge: MIT Press, 1970).

reasonable estimates of market potential and there are no significant changes in distribution strategy or in product mix that would explain the differences in sales volume. Data collected as part of the company's regular accounting and control procedures can be used to measure changes in sales volume, by product line, customer category, geographic area, or other unit of control.

Sales measures are the most common criterion for the evaluation of salesmen's performance. Sales volume accomplishment must be compared with measures of market potential before it can be a fair basis for the evaluation of salesmen. Most companies use measures of market potential in forecasting sales and in the setting of sales quotas as well as some measure of past sales accomplishment in the territory, and use the resulting quotas as the basis for evaluation of individual salesman performance and for compensation.

For sales force management decisions, therefore, sales measures are the most useful basis of evaluation. In addition to their use in supervision, compensation, evaluation, and control of salesman performance, sales volume information is also a major input to decisions about territory revision as well as changes in the level of sales effort.

Sales measures for the evaluation of selling effort are justified in part by the fact that the geographic area covered by a salesman is usually reasonably small and is completely under the control of the salesman. It is *his* territory and he is responsible for all customers in that territory. It can be reasonably assumed in such evaluations of selling effort that the effects of other elements of the communication program such as advertising are the same for all territories. Sales results are then used to evaluate the salesman as an individual performer; this is a reasonable basis for evaluation if, and only if, adequate adjustments are made to reflect differences in market potential, competitive conditions, and the experience, training, and supervision of the salesman himself.

As measures of the effectiveness of campaign elements other than personal selling, sales measures present some major difficulties. While it may be reasonable to assume that the influence of advertising is the same on all sales territories, it is *not* equally reasonable to assume that selling effort is equal in all areas when evaluating advertising. While advertising can produce communication effects, it cannot alone produce product availability, purchasing behavior, and sales results.

Sales measures of advertising also cannot, without necessary controls and adjustments, reflect the relative influence of message, media, and spending level. The separate evaluation of each of these contributors to campaign effectiveness is one of the key issues of campaign evaluation.

Experimentation Is Required To Measure Interactions. *Experimentation* is the only solution to the problem of sorting out the several effects of the total marketing communication program, as well as their interdependence. Use of experimentation to determine the effects of advertising was first reported by the U.S. Department of Agriculture. Hoofnagle reported that the Department's earlier attempts to use quantitative techniques such as time series and regression analysis were unsatisfactory measures of advertising effectiveness because they did not permit control and adjustment to account for differences in other factors such as changes in price and in product availability.[9] With the cooperation of resellers, controlled rotational experiments were designed using test cities and control cities to measure the impact of promotion and advertising upon sales volume. Statistical analysis of experimental results was then a more valid procedure because of the conditions under which the data had been generated and collected. In addition, survey interviews were conducted and a consumer panel was established, the former to measure changes in awareness and predispositions and the latter to track changes in purchasing behavior.

An earlier study in the Department of Agriculture was concerned with the more specific question of message testing.[10] This earlier work on the evaluation of alternative appeals provided the basic experience with experimental technique that was applied to the more general problem of campaign evaluation. This earlier study also used sales results as the criterion of effectiveness.

While a detailed discussion of experimentation as a research technique is beyond the scope of this text, a brief description of experimental design may be helpful.[11] Experimentation permits the comparison of alternatives—where each alternative is characterized by only one difference from another alternative with which it is to be compared. For example, if the marketing communication strategist wished to compare three levels of advertising effort, two media schedules, and two campaign themes, he would have a total of 12 (3 times 2 times 2) alternative "treatments" to compare in his experiment. The experiment would then proceed to systematically evaluate the effects of these three variables by comparing the effects of a change in each variable while all the others are "held constant" by the experimental design. In this example, the experimenter might also attempt to control for changes in the environment by simultaneously monitoring sales results in test areas where no experimentation is being conducted.

[9]William S. Hoofnagle, "The Effectiveness of Advertising for Farm Products," *Journal of Advertising Research*, 3 (December 1963), pp. 2–6.

[10]Peter L. Henderson, James F. Hind, and Sidney E. Brown, "Sales Effects of Two Campaign Themes," *Journal of Advertising Research*, 1 (December 1961), pp. 2–11.

[11]For a thorough discussion of experimentation as a research technique, see Seymour Banks, *Experimentation in Marketing* (New York: McGraw-Hill Book Co., Inc., 1965).

Experimental Designs. With experimental designs, sales measures become possible as measures of campaign effects. Through statistical analysis, especially regression analysis, the effect of each of the experimental variables on sales results can be estimated.

Latin square experimental designs involve the use of "balanced" treatments in that the design insures that each treatment appears at least once in each time period and in each sampling unit. The number of treatments in a Latin square design is equal to the number of time periods and sampling units. In a *factorial* design, the number of treatments equals the number of possible combinations of each of the test variables, as in the example above involving a total of twelve treatments. If the factors being evaluated are independent, the number of treatments can be reduced. Where there is interaction among the variables, the factorial design can permit the estimation of the effects of that interaction—as when budget level effects are a function of the media strategy. Factorial designs can therefore be especially useful in evaluating total campaigns. Experimental designs become complex very quickly, however, and experts advise that it is best to keep the design as simple as possible, to facilitate subsequent analysis.[12]

An important extension of the use of experimentation in marketing, and especially in monitoring the effects of the level of communication effort, has been proposed. It argues for the use of an *adaptive control process* in which continuous experimentation is used to measure differences in sales results attributable to differences in advertising budget level. This method was discussed briefly in Chapter 16 as an aid in the process of determining the level of effort. Now, we can view the same procedure as a method of *controlling* the marketing communication strategy and of providing feedback for the adjustment of campaign parameters. The method involves spending at an above average level in *n* markets, at below average level in another *n* markets, and normal advertising in the remainder (i.e., the majority) of markets served. Sales *changes* in the several markets are monitored over time and the results are used to estimate parameters of sales response in the basic budget-setting mode.[13]

The concept of adaptive control systems is especially attractive because it combines the sophistication of experimentation with the basic analytical logic of the control process as the last stage in strategic plan-

---

[12]For examples of the use of Latin square and factorial designs to evaluate alternative communication strategies, see William S. Hoofnagle, "Experimental Designs in Measuring the Effectiveness of Promotion," *Journal of Marketing Research*, 2 (May 1965), pp. 154–62.

[13]A non-mathematical description of this method is contained in John D. C. Little, "Adaptive Control Systems in Marketing," a paper presented at the 1968 International Marketing Congress of the American Marketing Association, Philadelphia, Pa., June 17–19, 1968.

ning. It provides a reliable source of information to perform the feedback function in updating the communication strategy. The feedback is used to update the basic model of the market response process which the manager is attempting to influence. While the expense and attention required to develop an adaptive control system would undoubtedly be high, it should have significant advantages for the firm wishing to develop a rigorous basis for the evaluation of campaign effects in general and of budget levels in particular.

The use of sales results to measure campaign effects therefore requires careful attention to the problem of determining cause and effect relationships. Only through experimentation can such effects be determined unambiguously.

Profit Measures

Marketing communication is a major contributor to the profitability of company operations. But it is certainly not alone in that responsibility. While it is useful to make careful estimates of the profit margin contribution of sales volume generated by communication, and to specifically account for the expense of the promotion activity required to generate that sales volume, it is impossible to say that communication *causes* profitability.

Careful cost accounting in marketing communication is a necessary basis upon which to build an estimate of the profitability of alternative marketing communication strategies. The marginal return from spending levels for various modes of communication should be periodically assessed as an aid in decision making concerning the relative importance of the various modes in the strategy as a whole. Planning of sales promotional activities can be aided especially if there is a reasonable estimate of profit contribution compared with the cost of specific promotional activities such as premium offers and deals. Allocation decisions are most dependent upon the comparison of costs and revenues associated with alternative expenditure patterns.

To relate company profitability to marketing communication strategy is a very difficult task. This difficulty can be expressed by repeating the analogy to a baseball team. A team's record of wins and losses reflects several factors. It reflects the contribution of each team member, in the position to which he has been assigned by the team manager. Some strengths and weaknesses may seem to be critical—such as pitching and hitting—but the total result is a reflection of all members working as a team. Furthermore, the team record reflects the resources, strategies, strengths, and weaknesses of each of the other teams in the league. The season record reflects the ability of the team to compete, game after game, throughout the season.

Company profitability is a sum total of performance reflecting the resources deployed in the pursuit of objectives and the managerial skill with which the strategy was planned and implemented. If the company meets its profit objectives, marketing communication certainly can be credited with only part of the contribution. If profitability is disappointing, marketing communication alone cannot be blamed. While every effort should be made to relate measures of communication effectiveness to estimates of profitability, profit alone is not an adequate measure of campaign results.

CONCEPTUAL KNOWLEDGE AND THE PROFESSIONAL MANAGER

There are many factors which distinguish the professional from the nonprofessional. One of the hallmarks of a profession is the expertise of those who occupy the profession. The practice of management has been evolving toward the status of a true profession for many years as a body of knowledge is developed which applies to the problems of managing complex profit-motivated or budget-constrained organizations.

It is the author's opinion that the body of knowledge summarized and discussed in this book will one day be a necessary part of the professional tool kit of the marketing manager. The problems of marketing communication can be attacked more effectively and more efficiently if the conceptual tools are applied to the collection, organization, and analysis of information relating to the market environment within which the firm is operating. At the present time, the marketing communication concept is in its infancy and only a minority of firms are using these concepts and tools in strategic planning. These firms are currently deriving a competitive advantage as a result. As these concepts are refined and as they "diffuse" through the practice of management, they will become necessary rather than merely advantageous. The result will be a more professional approach to the practice of marketing management.

The practice of a profession must rest on a systematic body of knowledge of substantial intellectual content and on the development of personal skill in the application of this knowledge to specific cases. The purpose of this book has been to help the reader develop his professional knowledge and skills as a manager.

SUMMARY

Evaluation of campaign effects and the feedback of that information to adjust the elements of strategy are the final stages of the strategic planning process. They both conclude the strategic planning process and renew it. The results of last year's program become the base from which this year's strategy is designed and the marketing communication effort moves forward toward the achievement of corporate goals.

Evaluation and objective-setting are intimately inter-related activities. Objectives provide the standards for evaluation and evaluation provides an important set of inputs for the setting of objectives. Both objective-setting and evaluation must take place within the context of a model of how the communication process works. A final model was presented in this chapter which showed an integrated view of how a marketing communication campaign produces a result that is consistent with the company's ultimate objective of profitability. The major stages in that process were campaign development, message distribution, cognition, generation of favorable predispositions, generation of word-of-mouth, increased selling effort and effectiveness, increased product availability, increased purchasing activity, increased sales, increased product usage, reduced costs of doing business, and increased profits. Theoretically, it is possible to evaluate communication strategy by taking measurements at any of these stages.

Measures taken at the earliest stages of message distribution typically have very limited usefulness because they are so far removed from the true objectives of marketing communication. On the other hand, measures at the later stages become increasingly contaminated by the effects of other elements of marketing strategy and of the overall corporate strategy for achieving its profit objectives. Depending upon the specific strategic decisions that will be required, a combination of measures of communication, effort, product availability, purchasing, and sales is probably necessary to develop a sound evaluation of total campaign effectiveness. Experimentation provides a method of evaluating the effects of several strategic elements in interaction and simultaneously, as well as for estimating the effects of each element independent of its interaction with over variables.

A view of marketing communication as a total system where the total effect achieved is greater than the sum of the effects of the independent elements requires measures of interaction. Experimentation provides the measurement and communication theory provides the conceptual framework within which to organize and analyze this information. This combination of a sound data base and the necessary conceptual knowledge for analysis is the hallmark of the professional marketing manager.

Name Index

Subject Index